RAIL VENTURES®

Rail Ventures Publishing
Ouray, Colorado

Editor: Jack Swanson
Authors: Jack Swanson, Jeff Karsh
Contributing Writers: Den Adler - Pere Marquette, Lake Cities and portions of
Cardinal, Empire Builder, Lake Shore Ltd. and
Algoma Central
Ted Scull - Portions of Northeast Corridor
Copy Editor: Doris Swanson
Cartography: Jim Swanson
Cover Design: Country Graphics
Cover Photo: Empire Builder at Cascade Tunnel, Washington -
by Doris Swanson

Published by Rail Ventures Publishing, P.O. Box 1877, Ouray, Colorado 81427
Manufactured in the United States of America

Sixth Edition, 1994

Special Thanks: To Patricia Kelly, National Railroad Passenger Corporation
and Claude St. Hillaire, VIA Rail Canada.

ISBN 1-879949-16-4

Additional copies may be ordered directly from Rail Ventures Publishing, Box
1877, Ouray, CO 81427. Add $2 to retail price for postage and handling.

Table of Contents

Passenger Train
Routes in the U.S.

VIA Routes
Other Rail Routes
Ferry Service
O **Cities**
(Due to space limitations,
not all stations appear
on this map.)

Passenger Train
Routes in Canada

7

444

Main Passenger Train Routes in Mexico

Dash 8-32 BWH locomotive
DON R. FLYNN

Welcome Aboard

Trains have always had a special mystique. Their sheer brute strength, the thunderous sounds of locomotion, iron against iron, steel against steel—all have contributed to the world's fascination with these mechanical wonders. To ride on a train has been the epitome of romantic adventure. Wonderful names such as *Empire Builder, Sunset Limited* and *California Zephyr* have added to the magic, and being immortalized in both song and legend has further assured a course bound for glory.

Today, in an age of high-tech everything, it is still these nostalgic intangibles that fuel the modern iron horse. And across the years, one aspect has remained particularly constant, an aspect which this guidebook is specifically designed to enhance—the freedom to savor the sights of our great continent without the concerns or distractions found in all other forms of travel.

A steady stream of panoramas is limited only by our attention. Most certainly there are the soaring monarchs of the Canadian Rockies, the white sand beaches of Southern California and the foliage of a New England autumn to thrill our senses. But also there are the scenes which convey a sense of casual acquaintanceship with so many people and places along one's journey—the fastidiously sculpted woodpile, the backyard heap of time-worn appliances, the elderly couple tending their garden. Then there are the sounds, from the labored growl of a determined ascent ("I think I can . . . "), to the heroic arrival at the station across the pass ("I knew I could . . . "). These are joys reserved solely for the train passenger. No other conveyance affords the opportunity to absorb so much in such a relaxed state of mind.

North America's passenger rail network is a remarkably extensive one, serving nearly every major metropolis in the United States, Canada and Mexico. One can board a train in Halifax, Nova Scotia and traverse the continent to San Diego, California without having to set foot outside a train station. Or, journey from the subarctic climes of Churchill, Manitoba to the southern tropics of Mexico, with only a short cab ride across the Mexican border interrupting the rail experience.

To be sure, trains will never whisk anyone from New York to San Francisco in a fraction of a day. They will and do, however, cradle the traveler on an overnight journey between Chicago and New Orleans and then bestow a relaxed and refreshed arrival in the very heart of the city. The ability to simply enjoy the aspect of getting there, the ease of movement in an uncrowded environment, the savoring of a meal while the countryside slips by—these are the experiences reserved exclusively for the rail traveler.

About This Guide

Traveling on a train can be an adventure filled with enjoyment and excitement. Yet as with most pursuits, those who know the ropes can more readily savor such an experience. *Rail Ventures* wants you to have the "inside track," and is designed to better acquaint you with the special nuances inherent in rail travel.

Finding Things in this Guide

The guide is divided into three major travel sections: United States Rail Service, Canadian Rail Service and Mexican Rail Service. Each of these sections begins with general information about train travel in that particular country. Following this general information, the sections for the U.S. and Canada contain very extensive descriptions of the rail routes and the trains that use them. The information for Mexico is more limited, giving brief descriptions of that nation's trains.

At the front of the book, national rail maps display all routes and major stops in each country. Routes on the maps are keyed to page numbers in the text where all the details for that route will be found. This is the quickest way to locate specific route information. There is also a detailed index at the back of the book for easy reference to any city, train or other subject in this guide. An appendix precedes the index and lists reservation and information phone numbers in the U.S. and Canada.

Getting There

Besides comprehensive route descriptions, information for each long-distance train includes: services and accommodations on board, distance and time it takes to complete the entire route, and approximate arrival and departure times for selected cities. Arrival and departure times are not precise, but are given in general terms, such as: "Early Morning," "Late Afternoon," etc. in condensed schedules.

Obviously, when planning a trip it is important to verify exact times. See the general information section of the appropriate country for how to obtain current schedule data.

Viewing Along the Route

For the U.S. and Canada, *Rail Ventures* provides a running description ("route log") of points of interest to be seen along each major route. The description of each point of interest begins with the approximate elapsed time in minutes since departing the last scheduled stop; i.e., 0:25 would be 25 minutes from the last scheduled stop while 1:25 would be one hour and 25 minutes. The name of each stop is shown in boldface and is preceded by a train stop symbol.

In most instances, route logs are presented from east to west or north to south. To use in reverse order, start at the end of the log and read the parenthetical times rather than the boldface. "Right" and "left" would be just the opposite and, of course, "depart" and "arrive" should be interchanged.

These logs are written in a succinct style to allow the reader to quickly determine what is being observed or what to watch for without distracting from the scene. These will not only help plan your next train trip but also be a great travel companion—rather like adding sound to a silent movie.

What to Do When You Arrive

Although all stops on logged routes are described, more than 70 major cities are covered in considerable detail. Included are some logical places to stay, some of the more interesting attractions (many within walking distance of the station), how to find other transportation (buses, cabs, rental cars, etc.), where you can obtain tourist information, where the stations are located and station services—redcaps, luggage carts, restaurants, etc. There are maps showing station and hotel locations and points of interest for many of these cities.

On-Board Accommodations

Since many readers have not traveled by train in recent years (if ever), an equipment chapter is included which describes the various types of passenger equipment (e.g. Amcoaches, Superliner Sleepers, etc.) giving an insight as to what to expect after boarding.

City Accommodations

The selection of hotels and motels in *Rail Ventures* is based on location, quality and reasonableness of rates—the latter, of course, being relative to each city. Large convention-oriented hotels have generally been omitted unless they are next to a station. Location is usually within a mile of the station, particularly in cities where connections are frequently made.

If no hotels are near the station, then accommodations are included near some of the major attractions, usually in the central business district. Some bed and breakfasts have been shown since their popularity is growing and there are an increasing number of downtown B&Bs offering reasonable alternatives to high-priced hotels.

Unless otherwise noted, the rate shown for each establishment is the rack (regular) rate for the least expensive (standard) room for two people based on weekday rates for late summer prior to this guide's publication date. Canadian accommodation rates are shown in Canadian dollars which should translate into lower U.S. dollars.

It is almost always possible to avoid paying a metropolitan hotel's rack rate. Discounts are commonly given for business travel (corporate rates), seniors, AARP members, weekends (in larger cities but not for B&Bs), special promotions, etc. As a hotel manager once stated: "The more questions you ask, the lower the rate." Bear in mind, however, that any discount must be obtained at check-in or earlier. There are also "consolidator" discounts, clubs, discount reservation services, etc. One reservation service called Quikbook offers discounts up to 40% and represents several hotels listed in *Rail Ventures*. Anyone can use their service free of charge. If a hotel is represented by Quikbook, a QB and the discount rate appears after the description of the hotel. You can make reservations through Quikbook by calling 1-800-221-3531 (in New York City, 212-473-4688, ext. 5). And Amtrak has its own package offerings that include discounted hotel rates for train travelers. To obtain a booklet describing Amtrak package travel, call 1-800-USA-RAIL.

Toll-free reservation numbers (within the continental U.S.) for the following "chains" are not shown in the text and are listed here to avoid repetition:

Best Western	800-528-1234
Choice Hotels	800-228-5151
Days Inn	800-325-2525
Hampton Inn	800-HAMPTON
Hilton Hotels	800-445-8667
Holiday Inns	800-HOLIDAY
Hyatt Corp.	800-228-9000
Howard Johnson's	800-654-2000
LaQuinta Motor Inns	800-531-5900
Radisson Hotels	800-333-3333
Ramada Inns	800-272-6232

Sheraton   800-325-3535
Travelodge   800-255-3050
(These numbers will get you a reservation clerk particularly skilled at selling an establishment's higher-priced rooms, so be persistent in asking for their lowest rate if that's what you want.)

About Mexico

Mexico is treated somewhat differently than the U.S. and Canada. Emphasis is placed on what to expect (or not to expect) while traveling by train through that country and how to make reservations and obtain tickets.

A detailed description of the famous Copper Canyon trip is also included.

Symbols

 A scheduled train stop.

 Train station services.

 Visitors information center.

 Other available transportation.

 Accommodations, usually within a mile of the train station.

 Some major attractions.

 Train enters a different time zone.

PLEASE NOTE

The train schedules, fares and routes shown in this guide, as well as accommodation information, are always subject to change at any time. City maps are designed to show locations of stations, hotels, attractions, etc. These maps are not always drawn to scale and major streets may be omitted for simplification.

United States Rail Service

After World War II, two events almost spelled the demise of rail service in the United States—the "taking off" of the airlines and the invention of the Interstate Highway. To thwart disaster, Congress in 1970 came up with a legislative solution known as Amtrak (The National Railroad Passenger Corporation). The idea was to relieve the nation's railroads from operating their unprofitable passenger trains and to turn these trains into a viable form of transportation.

After more than two decades of improvement, today's trains are modern, comfortable and attractive. Their timeliness record frequently excels that of the airlines, and on-board personnel are a far cry from those uniformed curmudgeons of postwar days. The food is quite good in full-service dining cars with meals, wake-up coffee and orange juice as well as newspapers included with bedroom fares. And there are even movies and bingo on many of the long-distance trains. Today, Amtrak operates more than 250 trains each day on 24,000 miles of track, serving more than 550 cities. The system carries 22 million passengers each year.

Reservations - Reservations can be made at any Amtrak ticket office, travel agent, or by calling Amtrak's toll-free reservation number, 800-USA-RAIL. (Local numbers may sometimes be used and are shown in the Appendix and in the station information for certain cities.) If reservations are made by phone sufficiently in advance, Amtrak will mail tickets and bill the customer. If time is short, usually three weeks or less, you will be given a specific time within which you must purchase your tickets, either from a ticket office or authorized travel agent. If tickets are not purchased by that date, your reservations will be cancelled. A computer-furnished reservations number is assigned when reservations are made, and it is important to retain this number for future reference in obtaining tickets or changing reservations. If your travel plans change, sleeping car reservations should be cancelled at least 48 hours before train time to avoid paying a "substantial penalty." Club Service seating should be cancelled at least one hour before departure.

Be sure to reserve sleeping-car accommodations early since these are frequently sold out months in advance, particularly on the more popular trains during the summer and holidays. Seating on trains with unreserved coach service is not guaranteed.

It is possible to upgrade accommodations once on board if such space is available. Passengers wishing to upgrade to sleeping accommodations, Club or Custom Class should see the conductor or the Chief of On Board Services.

Amtrak also offers "Thruway Buses" that make train/bus connections for many off-line cities. Amtrak makes reservations for these as well as some other selected bus routes.

Payment - Tickets may be purchased with the following credit cards: American Express, Carte Blanche, Diners Club, Discover, Japan Credit Bureau, MasterCard, Visa and Air Travel Card. These cards are also accepted in the dining car and for the purchase of tickets on board (except JCB). Payment may also be made by personal check, except in California where customers must be over age 62 to use this mode of payment. Purchases must be for at least $25 and some form of photo identification is required along with one of the credit cards listed above. For a $15 service charge, it is also possible to pay locally for tickets which are to be picked up at another Amtrak ticket office. This can be particularly helpful when a son or daughter calls from college and hasn't funds to get home for Christmas.

Travel Agents - Authorized travel agents will be glad to make train reservations and sell tickets, and since they are paid a commission by the carrier, there is no extra charge to the customer for this service. This certainly simplifies things. The only disadvantage—once the agent issues the tickets, there may be a penalty for changing or cancelling reservations.

Timetables - Amtrak publishes system-wide timetables semiannually, coinciding with the nation's changeover to or from daylight saving time. These schedules can be obtained free of charge from any Amtrak ticket office, authorized travel agency or by calling 800-USA-RAIL. Times shown for each stop are the prevailing local times. Bear in mind that if a train is running late, stops at stations may be shorter than those indicated in the timetable. There have been instances of passengers detraining under the mistaken assumption that the train will be at a particular stop 20 or 30 minutes, only to find the train (and their luggage) gone when they return to the station area.

Times and routes are always subject to change, and timetables may not necessarily reflect current schedules.

Fares - All coach travel is one class except for Club Service and Custom Class (available on some trains in the East and Southern California) which, because of the more luxurious seating and service, have a higher price tag. Also, certain service in the Northeast Corridor is designed as Metroliner service. These trains are scheduled for fewer stops and make better time, so a premium is charged for Metroliner tickets. And, quite logically, for sleeping cars you must pay an accommodation charge over and above the basic coach fare. In the heavy travel months, this additional charge ranges from as low as $59 a night for a single Slumbercoach berth to a range of $300 to $600 for a deluxe bedroom. An economy bedroom on a Superliner will run somewhere between $150 and $300. But there's a bonus. Meals are included with the price of sleeping car accommodations (except Slumbercoach).

Coach fares can range from about 9¢ to 13¢ per mile for long-distance runs, while shorter routes may be as high as 34¢. However, these figures are deceptively high since there are almost always special discounts available. Round-trip excursion fares offer savings and there are also family plans that allow not more than two children (per fare-paying adult), ages two through fifteen, to travel at half-fare if accompanied by a parent. Children under two travel free.

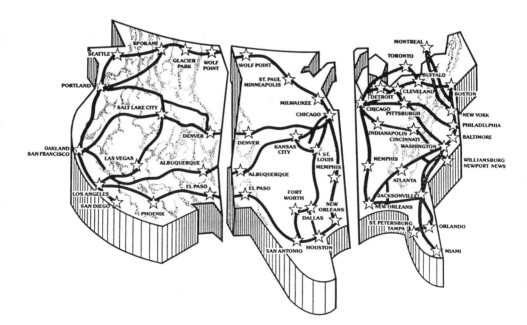

Amtrak's All Aboard America Fare is very attractive, particularly when a round trip is involved. This fare divides the country into three regions—Eastern, Central and Western. The Eastern extends from the Atlantic Seaboard west to Chicago and New Orleans. The Central is that region from those two cities west to a line from Wolf Point, Montana through Denver, Albuquerque and El Paso. The Western region extends from that line to the West Coast. These fares change with the seasons, but as an example, the summer fares prior to this publication allowed a round trip within any one of these regions for $199, within two adjoining regions for $279 and anywhere in the U.S. for $339. Rates are usually lower during the winter months. One stopover is allowed each direction as well as the destination point, and you should not be penalized if Amtrak's schedules require that you "overnight" in a city where you must make train connections. Perhaps the best feature is that the return can be on an entirely different route.

Amtrak sells USA Rail Passes which allow unlimited rail travel in the United States for a fixed fare and for a limited period of time. These can be used only by non-residents of the United States, and are only sold outside North America.

Those 62 and older may travel at 15% off the lowest available fare, except during certain holiday periods. Keep in mind that group rates are established from time to time with discounts determined by the size of the group. This may not seem important, but on occasions, as few as three adults have been considered a group.

Reduced or discounted fares do not normally apply to bedroom charges. Stopovers are permitted at no extra charge unless you are traveling on a special excursion rate.

Amtrak Travel Packages - Amtrak offers a bevy of travel packages that amount to a discounted hotel rate when booked with Amtrak travel. Twice a year, Amtrak publishes a *Travel Planner* that lists these bargains. Amtrak has also introduced some economical train/plane combination packages worth considering.

These package hotel rates apply only to bookings through Amtrak, and there is limited availability. If you must cancel, it should be done through Amtrak. It takes one to three working days for Amtrak to confirm hotel reservations while they check on availability.

For information, check with your travel agent or call Amtrak at 800-USA-RAIL, and ask for the tour desk.

Stations and Connections - Rail stations are frequently located in the heart of town, giving the rail traveler a city-center point of arrival or departure. It may not be advisable to attempt connections between trains having scheduled arrival and departure times within an hour of each other. Amtrak will, however, "guarantee" connections when scheduled arrival and departure times are an hour or more apart. This guarantee means that Amtrak will make other arrangements for you to reach your destination (usually on the next train) if a late train causes a missed connection. Amtrak may also provide overnight hotel accommodations if appropriate.

It is important to keep in mind that some cities have more than one rail station, such as Buffalo, NY. This will be a consideration when planning connections if the trains involved each use a different station.

Metropolitan Lounge - First-class passengers (Club and sleeping car passengers) can use the Metropolitan Lounges located in the stations of New York City, Philadelphia, Washington, DC and Chicago. These lounges are rather elegant rooms with a quiet and relaxed atmosphere, offering complimentary hot and cold drinks, newspapers and magazines, private conference rooms and other niceties.

Dining - Most long-distance trains carry full-service dining cars that provide complete menus for three meals a day. Lighter fare will be found on other trains in cafe-type or lounge cars. Cafe service includes tray meals, such as light breakfasts, microwave sandwiches and beverages, while sandwiches, beverages and other snacks are available in lounge cars. It is also quite acceptable to bring your own lunch on board, but food should not be taken to the train's dining areas.

To reduce the problem of waiting for a dinner table during peak travel periods, on some trains, reservations are now taken early in the day at your seat, and you can select any one of three or four seatings for dinner. Dinner prices range from about eight to thirteen dollars, luncheons five to six dollars and breakfast four to five dollars. A typical dinner menu might include a selection of baked chicken, seafood, roast beef, New York strip steak or lasagna. Lunches may include salads and sandwiches, while breakfast may offer bacon and eggs, pancakes, French toast and hot or dry cereal. Cafe and lounge cars serve simpler fare at lower prices.

Sleeping - As mentioned above, sleeping car accommodations are available for an additional charge. (See the Equipment chapter for a description of these accommodations.) Although a bed is by far more restful for most train travelers and certainly more private, a majority of overnight travelers will prefer the coach, most because of the lower cost, some because they will reach their destination early in the morning and want the convenience of sleeping until the last possible moment.

If you do decide to sleep in your coach seat, pick out a seat near the center of the car to avoid noisy door action that is guaranteed to occur all night at each end of the car. Although Amtrak provides pillows, it might also be a good idea to have a blanket or coat with you just in case the air conditioning becomes too efficient. If two are traveling together and only single seats are available, the conductor may ask someone to move so that the couple can sit together. If not, move to adjoining seats in your coach as soon as some become available, frequently at the next stop, taking the destination slips above your seats to your new location. Be sure to let the conductor know this since a seating chart is sometimes maintained so you can be notified of your stop.

If you should be in a bedroom, plan to pack so that everything you may need at night is handy. Many veteran train riders will take along an extra small suitcase or bag to hold only those items they will need in their bedroom. This is particularly advisable if two people are trying to use small quarters such as an economy bedroom on a Superliner.

Lounge and **Club Cars** - Some trains carry lounge cars where passengers can smoke and obtain beverages and light snacks. Superliner lounge cars offer excellent viewing of the passing scenery, with large windows wrapping up over the top of the car. Club cars are on a few Northeastern Corridor trains (between Boston and Washington, D.C.), and offer more luxurious reserved seats with snack and beverage service at your seat. Fares are higher, of course, for club seating. (See the Equipment chapter for examples of lounge and club cars.) Also, Custom Class, with reserved deluxe coach seating and complimentary coffee, tea or juice and newspaper, is available on many daytime trains.

Smoking - You can smoke cigarettes in certain designated cars or in designated sections of cars on trains that have more than four-and-a-half to six hours running times between end points. You can also smoke in your bedroom, except on the Washington-Chicago Capitol Ltd. and the Seattle-Los Angeles Coast Starlight.

Baggage - Stations at most larger cities handle checked baggage (baggage to be carried in the baggage car) permitting each passenger to check up to three pieces of baggage without charge, not exceeding 75 pounds each or 150 pounds total. Extra baggage may be checked, but it is subject to a surcharge. Bags should be checked at least 30 minutes prior to departure (even earlier during crowded holiday periods), and will be ready for claiming at your destination within 30 minutes after arrival. Generally, baggage can be checked through to your final destination even when making connections from one train to another at the same station. (But like the airlines, if the connection is tight, there is a risk your checked luggage may arrive the day after you do.)

Personal baggage can also be carried on board, but coach passengers are limited to two pieces of carry-on per passenger. These are stored either in overhead racks or in special storage areas of the car. Sleeping car passengers can carry on as much as can be accommodated in their rooms. But remember, some accommodations are fairly tight such as economy bedrooms on Superliners. Most travelers leave the bulk of their luggage stowed in the luggage bins available near the entrance of the Superliner sleepers (with the disadvantage of lack of security).Amtrak encourages you to check your larger bags.

There should be another luggage consideration when you plan short stopovers. If an overnight visit with a friend in a particular city along the route is planned, pack so the things you don't need for that night can be left in a locker or the baggage-check room at the station rather than hauling your entire wardrobe with you. Locker rental rates are for only 24 hours. Many stations have eliminated lockers and will hold luggage in the baggage room for a dollar an item.

Baggage should always have an I.D. tag with your name and address.

Bicycles - Bicycles must be checked and can only be handled between stations with checked baggage service. Arrive an hour early since you must box your bicycle before checking it, handlebars turned and pedals removed. There is a $5 charge and Amtrak will supply the box (but not the tools).

Pets - Except for guide dogs, pets are not permitted on trains.

Tipping - Tipping dining-car waiters is customary, and the same amount that one would tip in a restaurant would be appropriate. Also, many sleeping car passengers tip their car attendant for the extra services they frequently provide; $3 to $5 per night is appropriate—if the service has been good. Some even tip their car attendants in advance believing this will ensure the service they want throughout their trip.

Radios - Earphones must be used listening to radios, tape players, etc.

Redcaps - Assistance with baggage is furnished at many stations by uniformed redcaps. This service is free, although tipping is appropriate. It is not advisable to accept service from anyone not in a redcap uniform. Redcap service is generally available only in larger cities. The station services shown in this guide for larger cities indicate whether this service is available.

Boarding - If the ticket agent has not told you your car location, ask the gate attendant as you enter the train platform. This can save a walk in the wrong direction in a city like Denver where you have to make a choice—left or right—when reaching the train.

Traveling with the Kids - Small children (and their parents) can get more enjoyment out of a train trip if the kids have some diversions. Drawing paper and crayons can be helpful as well as picture books and games. Older children also enjoy drawing and reading, and also might enjoy postcards to their friends. The entire family can enjoy following the train routes using this guide as well as a road atlas.

Unaccompanied Children - Children ages eight through eleven may travel alone under certain conditions (check with Amtrak in advance) but must pay an adult fare.

Important - Train times shown in this section are given only in general terms (such as "Early Morning"), and are for use in planning before making reservations. Since times are not specific and schedules are always subject to change, actual times should be ascertained from the carrier or a travel agent before setting out on your trip. Fares and food prices are also subject to change. Also, routes, fares and stops can be altered without notice.

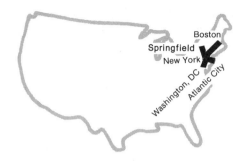

Northeast Corridor

Amtrak's 457-mile Northeast Corridor, running between Washington and Boston, carries fully half of the national corporation's 22 million annual riders.

The Northeast Corridor Improvement Project, a long-term commitment to provide reliable high-speed service on the existing roadbed, has resulted in additional sections rated for speeds up to 125 miles per hour. Between New York and Washington, regular-fare conventional trains now offer the fastest schedules ever, while the premium-fare Metroliner Service trains all have less than three-hour running times making them the fastest regularly scheduled trains in the Western Hemisphere. Such service has allowed Amtrak to become the number one carrier of passengers between these two cities.

On the 231-mile New York-Boston segment, the fastest trains equal the former New Haven's highest average speeds and match the running times, when the slightly longer Hell Gate Route to and from Penn Station is taken into account.

Nearly all corridor trains carry modern high-density (84 seats) Amfleet I cars. In addition, Boston-Washington trains usually have one roomier 60-seat legrest Amfleet coach. The majority of the New York-Philadelphia "Clockers" use high-density Heritage-Fleet coaches, mainly built in the 1950s and 1960s. (Historically, Clockers were hourly Pennsylvania Railroad trains between New York and Philadelphia.)

Boston-Washington through trains carry premium-service club cars with two-and-one seating, attendants and offer free meals, wine and snacks. Pre-boarding is another convenience. One overnight train provides sleeper service with free continental breakfast served in the compartment before arrival at terminal stations. (In New York City, Washington, D.C. passengers are permitted to board or detrain from a separate sleeper at convenient early-morning or late-evening times, even though New York arrivals and departures for this train are in the middle of the night.)

New York-Washington Metroliner service trains carry the rebuilt Amfleet I cars with 60-seat low-density coach seating and even roomier two-and-one club car seating. Smoking is not permitted on Metroliners. Amdinettes, cafe cars with table seating, provide food, drink and lounge service on all these trains and on selected Boston-Washington runs. Otherwise, all trains carry Amcafes with snack counter take-out service. No food is provided on the Philadelphia Clockers or on the coach-equipped mail trains.

Through Springfield-New York-Washington trains and the Inland Route trains (Boston-New Haven via Springfield) provide Amfleet I, Amcafe and sometimes club car service. Other Springfield-New Haven trains carry through cars to Washington, D.C. which are added to or taken off Boston-Washington trains at New Haven.

Several Northeast Corridor stations have recently received outstanding restorations, making them worth a special detour to explore. The most notable are Baltimore Penn Station, the Wilmington, Delaware station, Newark Penn Station, Washington Union Station and Philadelphia's venerable Thirtieth Street Station. The remodelled New Haven Station now serves as the city's intermodal transportation center.

New York's Penn Station, Amtrak's busiest, has undergone extensive rebuilding, and Boston's South Station has been in part restored and in part added to, creating an intermodal train, bus and subway station. Stamford and Boston's Back Bay have new stations and Providence's station has been relocated along a newly realigned track through downtown.

The finer points of several smaller stations are noted in the route guide.

The former New Haven's "Scenic Shoreline Route" is one of the finest corridor routes in the country. From spectacular views of the Manhattan skyline while crossing Hell Gate Bridge to mile after mile of New England coastal seascape, the Shore Line route to Boston is a veritable feast for the keenly interested sightseer. Also running in the Corridor are daily trains to and from Atlantic City via Philadelphia, one extending to Springfield, MA, the other to Richmond, VA. There is additional weekend service to and from Atlantic City.

The route log for the Corridor is divided into four sections: New York to Boston, New York to Washington, D.C., New Haven to Springfield and the newer Philadelphia to Atlantic City segment which branches off of the Corridor at Philadelphia.

Route Log

New York to Boston—For route from New York to Washington, D.C., see page 30; New Haven to Springfield, see page 41; Philadelphia to Atlantic City, see page 43.

To enjoy it all, be sure to sit on the right-hand side of the train when leaving New York, and on the left leaving Boston.

The log shows elapsed times for trains making those stops made by most trains.

NEW YORK CITY, NY - The first reported real estate transaction in the "Big Apple" was in 1624 when Peter Minuit, the Dutch colonial governor, supposedly purchased Manhattan Island from the Indians for $24 worth of goods. This set the pattern and tone for the city. Today, New York remains not only a world center for finance and trade, but also for transportation, fashion, the performing arts and many other industries.

To the uninitiated, it may seem the conventional wisdom about this city ("a nice place to visit but I wouldn't want to live here") is backwards. While the natives seem to have everything at their fingertips, the visitor often sees the Big Apple as more of a big hassle. The secret is knowing how to cope—or maybe better stated, how to get around safely and conveniently in a town with an intimidating subway system, plodding buses, and cabbies that can't speak English. The transportation section below offers some tips that should make your visit more enjoyable.

Although New York has more than its share of problems, the town can be an exhilarating experience. That may be why more tourists come here than any other city in America.

As of April 7, 1991, all of Amtrak's New York City trains use Pennsylvania Station, leaving Grand Central Terminal for commuters only. However, Metro North commuter trains operate between Grand Central and Amtrak stations at Yonkers, Croton-Harmon, New Rochelle, Stamford and New Haven.

Pennsylvania Station, bounded by Eighth and Seventh avenues at 31st and 33rd streets, is directly beneath Madison Square Garden.

The station is multi-leveled, with all trains arriving at the Platform Level. Immediately above that is Level A which houses the Long Island Rail Road (commuter) station and subway entrance; continuing upward, Level B is the Amtrak station with escalators to the other three levels; and Level C is at street level with entrances and taxis. All levels are handicapped accessible.

There are both video monitors and display boards with arrival and departure information. And besides a refurbished

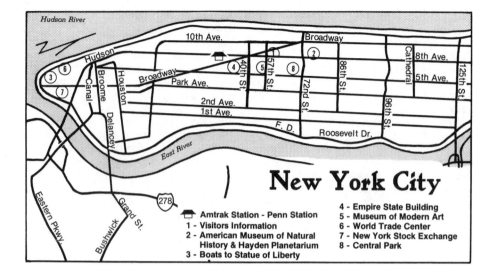

New York City

🚆 Amtrak Station - Penn Station
1 - Visitors Information
2 - American Museum of Natural History & Hayden Planetarium
3 - Boats to Statue of Liberty
4 - Empire State Building
5 - Museum of Modern Art
6 - World Trade Center
7 - New York Stock Exchange
8 - Central Park

waiting area, first-class ticket holders now have a separate waiting area called Metropolitan Lounge. This plush, club-like room has many niceties, including its own rest rooms, a self-service beverage counter, desks, fax machines, etc.

Redcap service is available and numerous retail outlets are here. For reservations and information, call (212) 582-6875.

The Island of Manhattan is rather compact and many of its attractions can be reached by walking. When walking is not appropriate, there are several options.

Cabs are what most visitors resort to, even though there is a comprehensive bus and subway system. If this is your choice, make sure the driver fully understands your destination before he starts out. There are two kinds of taxis: licensed (yellow medallion) taxis and unlicensed (gypsy) taxis. Use the licensed variety. Those that are available have their roof lights on, and some vigorous waving and shrill whistling should get their attention. Don't expect to catch one in the rush hour and never in the rain. Even evening theater time can be bad; consider taking a cab earlier to a restaurant that's near the theater so you can walk to the play during this busy period. New York cabbies uniformly expect a tip—generally 20% is

acceptable.

Buses are slow, even slower than the traffic, but they are more civilized than the subway, and you can see the sights as you go. Unfortunately, they tend to come in batches and, like everywhere else, ignore schedules. But they are easy to use, and route diagrams are posted at many of the stops. You must have the exact change or a token.

The **subway** is usually the fastest way to get around. Statistically, it is safer than the streets in spite of its reputation. Stick to the safer routes, sit toward the center of the train when it isn't full and travel when they're being well used. The daylight hours are the best. On the other hand, avoid the unpleasant rush hours.

Token booths are at each station. If you plan to use the subway more than once, buy enough tokens to avoid waiting in line again. Ten-packs are sold for convenience but at no discount. They may also be used on the city buses.

Commuter trains make New York City possible. Metro North has three lines that head north out of Grand Central: The Hudson Line that runs along that river to Poughkeepsie; the Harlem Line that goes farther east, through Scarsdale and north; and the New Haven Line that runs up the coast to that city, with three northerly branches to New Canaan, Danbury and

Waterbury. The Long Island Rail Road serves virtually all of Long Island from Penn Station. PATH (Port Authority Trans Hudson) offers excellent service to Hoboken, Jersey City and Newark, with connections to New Jersey Transit. PATH trains run south from 33rd Street along the Avenue of the Americas (Sixth Ave.) and also from the World Trade Center.

Intercity buses operate from the Port Authority Bus Terminal at 8th Ave. and 41st St. **John F. Kennedy International Airport** (JFK) is 15 miles east of midtown, **LaGuardia Airport** is eight miles northeast, and **Newark International Airport** is 15 miles southwest.

The automobile is not really useful in New York City, but if you must rent one, Avis, Budget, Hertz and National all have **rental car** locations in midtown.

New York Convention and Visitors Bureau, Two Columbus Circle (59th St. and Broadway), 10019; (212) 397-8222.

This is a town where a moderately priced room will run well over $100 for two people during the week. The hotels shown below are conveniently located near Penn Station or other attractions.

Weekend packages are common among New York hotels, and "deals" change frequently. Check with your travel agent for best weekend rates.

-Comfort Inn Murray Hill, 42 West 35th St., 10001; (212) 947-0200. Just across from the Empire State Building. Three blocks from Penn Station. $89.
-Ramada at Madison Square Garden, 401 Seventh Ave., 10001; (212) 736-5000 or 800-223-8585. Venerable, Stanford-White-designed hostelry, formerly the Statler. Its phone number (Pennsylvania 6-5000), made famous by Glenn Miller, is now longest in continuous use in the city. Expect a long wait at check in. Reserve through Quikbook, 800-221-3531, for discount. Directly across from Penn Station. $89.
-Herald Square, 19 West 31st St., 10001; (212) 279-4017 or 800-727-1888. Small, nicely refurbished budget hotel, in shabby neighborhood. Three blocks from Penn Station. $75.

-Southgate Tower Suite Hotel, 371 Seventh Ave., 10001; (212) 563-1800 or 800-637-8483. Just as convenient for train travelers but much less frantic than the Ramada. Diagonally across intersection (31st St. & 7th Ave.) from Penn Station. Reserve through Quikbook, 800-221-3531, for substantial discount. $145.
-Portland Square, 132 West 47th St., 10036; (212) 382-0600. Smallish rooms, but good value. Near Rockefeller Center, about a mile from Penn Station. $75.
-Salisbury, 123 W. 57th St., 10019; (212) 246-1300 or 800-223-0680. Pleasant atmosphere and staff. Across from Carnegie Hall, about two miles from Penn Station. Continental breakfast. $112.
-or try sleeping beneath Penn Station (but not with the homeless) if you are arriving from or departing for Washington, D.C. The Executive Sleeper, which is carried by the Night Owl, arrives in Penn Station from Washington about 3 am but is set off on a siding, and you may stay on board as late as 8 am. Southbound, the sleeper departs New York about 3:30 am, but you may board and occupy your room as early as 9:30 pm. Arrival in Washington is about 8 am. A complimentary continental breakfast is served in your room. The bedroom surcharge (for two) is a bargain $80.

An indispensable tool for enjoying New York City is the **Visitors Guide and Map,** available free from the New York Convention and Visitors Bureau. This is a handy, well-designed handout that packs a lot of information on a single sheet of paper.

Perhaps the best bargain in the city is **Circle Line Sightseeing Yacht** tours around Manhattan, which let you see both the city and harbors. For a bird's-eye view, of course, both the **Empire State Building** and the **World Trade Center** observation decks are magnificent vantage points on a clear day. The one and only **New York Stock Exchange,** at 20 Broad Street, is the focal point of the world of finance and can be seen from the visitors' gallery or by guided tour. And boats to the **Statue of Liberty** are boarded at the southern tip of Manhattan.

Museums are in abundance. The **Museum of Modern Art,** 11 W. 53rd St., and the **American Museum of Natural History,** 79th and Central Park West, are national treasures. **Lincoln Center for the Performing Arts,** Broadway and 64th, is renowned for its musical virtuosos. And, of course, **New York's theaters** offer something for every taste.

0:00 (0:29) Departing New York's Pennsylvania Station, travel eastward under Manhattan streets and East River rising to surface on Long Island in Sunnyside section of Queens.

0:08 (0:26) To left are extensive rail yards for Amtrak and New Jersey Transit trains. All passenger equipment is cleaned, stored, serviced and provisioned here before their next trip. Tracks dropping down to right pass through mechanical washers then loop under main line into Sunnyside Yards.

0:10 (0:19) At Harold Tower interlocking, our elevated Hell Gate Route separates from Long Island Rail Road line that continues on to Jamaica and points east.

The Hell Gate Route, once officially known as the New York Connecting Railroad and completed in 1917, joined the Pennsylvania Railroad with the New York, New Haven and Hartford, permitting for the first time, a direct, all-rail route between Washington, Philadelphia, New York, Providence and Boston.

Prior to the Hell Gate Route, the only through train, the Federal Express, used a transfer ferry to complete the missing rail link between terminals in the Bronx and the New Jersey side of the Hudson River.

The Hell Gate Route climbs through Astoria, a heavily Greek and Italian community, swinging back over the East River onto Wards and Randalls islands. On a clear day or night, the view of the Manhattan skyline is nothing less than magical, and it is worth moving temporarily to the city-side to take in the glorious spectacle.

0:18 (0:11) Down to left is Manhattan State Hospital, a grim-looking structure built just prior to World War II. To right, small vessels moored at river's edge are New York City sludge boats, popularly referred to as "honey barges." They haul treated waste out to sea for dumping about eight miles beyond Ambrose Channel light tower. Next to sanitation facility, City of New York maintains its Fire Department Training Academy. Four-story windowless brick tenement is used for simulation of real fires and can sometimes be seen erupting in flames for exercise purposes. Often a red fireboat is tied up nearby. Leaving Hell Gate Viaduct, train drops into a cut through South Bronx, a severely depressed area of New York City, then crosses Hutchinson River.

0:25 (0:04) Huge, stark Coop City apartment complex rises to left, as train crosses Pelham Bay drawbridge.

0:28 (0:01) At Shell Tower interlocking, Hell Gate Route joins Metro-North Commuter Railroad Line from Grand Central Terminal. Frequent New Haven Line trains from Grand Central operate the 72 miles to New Haven. Prior to and during early years of Amtrak operations, some Amtrak trains ran out of Grand Central to Boston in addition to those operating through Penn Station and south to Washington.

0:29 (0:00) Arrive New Rochelle.

NEW ROCHELLE, NY - This is the first high-level platform commuter station encountered northbound. High-level platforms, a phenomenon of the Northeast, allow for rapid boarding of trains without having to drop the train's steps. The 1848 station was modernized in 1991.

0:00 (0:17) Depart New Rochelle and gather speed on four-track electrified Shore Line Route. First tree-lined suburban streets appear in Connecticut, and brief glimpses of Long Island Sound begin after Greenwich and at Cos Cob.

0:17 (0:00) Arrive Stamford.

STAMFORD, CT - At Stamford, a burgeoning city boasts clusters of new corporate headquarters. Modern office buildings and hotels surround the new transportation center. Nearly all Amtrak trains stop here to serve local communities and to allow passengers to make convenient connections with Metro-North's New Haven Line trains. An eight-mile, single-track electrified branch line runs from Stamford north to New Canaan.

0:00 (0:25) Depart Stamford.

0:10 (0:15) At South Norwalk, Metro-North trains stop to allow transfers to the 24-mile Danbury Branch, operated outside of rush hours.

0:14 (0:11) At Westport, scenery improves substantially, and one of first wooden barn-style stations appears. Through trees, most houses seen are worth small fortunes—some even more. Tidal marshlands open up between Westport and Green's Farms.

0:19 (0:06) Southport, 49 miles from Grand Central, may be considered end of intensively used commuting stations, though some daily riders originate even farther east. Approaching Bridgeport, scenes become industrial and urban once again. On right, simple dock serves as landing for Bridgeport and Port Jefferson Steamboat Company's ferry Grand Republic, operating year-round service across Sound to Port Jefferson on Long Island's North Shore. Fanciful Moorish-style building to left houses P. T. Barnum's personal and circus memorabilia collection.

0:25 (0:00) Arrive Bridgeport.

BRIDGEPORT, CT - Passengers for the Metro-North's 32-mile Waterbury Branch change here for the line up the scenic and historic Housatonic and Naugatuck valleys.

0:00 (0:24) Departing Bridgeport, line crosses first Pequonnock then Housatonic rivers and runs through Milford, last Metro-North station stop, before skirting harbor on approach to New Haven.

0:24 (0:00) Arrive New Haven.

Seconds after coming to a stop in New Haven, the lights will go out and the air circulation will cease for about seven minutes, while the electric locomotive is traded for a diesel engine for the remainder of the trip to Boston. Trains to Hartford, Springfield and other Inland Route stations between here and Boston branch off to the north. Historic New Haven Station, which was closed for many years, is now a major transportation center for Amtrak and commuter trains as well as local and long distance buses.

NEW HAVEN, CT - This is the home of Yale University, where historic personages such as Noah Webster,

Nathan Hale and William Howard Taft studied. Black Rock Fort and Fort Nathan Hale, restored Revolutionary War forts, and the Peabody Museum of Natural History, containing the world's largest natural history painting, are of particular interest.

0:00 (0:31) Depart New Haven.

Finally, when out of reach of New Haven's urban influence, the landscape becomes genuinely rural for the first time. It is this 69-mile stretch, as far as Westerly, where the Scenic Shore Line earns its name. Rocky hillocks rise out of tidal marshes laced with meandering streams. Isolated houses loom large on the tiny offshore Thimble Islands. The broad sweep of Long Island Sound is visible for long intervals while the train races fast through the Connecticut resort towns of Guilford, Madison and Clinton.

0:31 (0:00) Arrive Old Saybrook.

OLD SAYBROOK, CT - Note the handsome wooden station dating from 1873, one that has changed little in more than 100 years. Passengers leave here for the Connecticut River town of Essex and excursions on the steam-hauled Valley Railroad, a few miles to the north. It is here that the Connecticut River flows into Long Island Sound.

0:00 (0:18) Depart Old Saybrook.

0:03 (0:15) Look both ways while rumbling across drawbridge spanning Connecticut River. Until 1931, nightly steamer service plied between New York and numerous landings on river as far north as Hartford.

Between Old Saybrook and New London, the Shore Line parallels the sandy beaches at Rocky Neck State Park and along Niantic Bay, at times less than 100 feet from the lapping salt water.

0:18 (0:00) Arrive New London where elegant red-brick 1887 H. H. Richardson railroad station also houses local restaurant.

NEW LONDON, CT - New London, located on the River Thames (rhymes with James), grew up with the whaling industry and other commercial maritime pursuits to become one of the most important ports on the New England coast. Today, the Coast Guard and its

Academy, the Navy and the shipyards keep the area humming to a similar salty tune. Nautilus, the world's first nuclear submarine, was launched in nearby Groton.

Virtually at the station's doorstep, three different ferry operators run boats to Fishers Island, Orient Point and Block Island (summer season only).

0:00 (0:14) Leaving New London, swing right to pass over Thames (and route of Montrealer) where a quick look upstream may reveal Coast Guard sail training ship Eagle. Scan both ways for nuclear submarines and other vessels downstream at General Dynamics shipyard.

0:12 (0:02) Approaching Mystic, water laps both sides of embankment. New drawbridge and track realignment are important improvements to Northeast Corridor, permitting higher speeds and more reliable service. Glance to either side for hundreds of moored sailing and motor yachts.

0:14 (0:00) Arrive Mystic.

MYSTIC, CT - The station built in 1905 has recently received a complete restoration. The two-tone wooden depot once served as a model for Lionel's Lionelville station. Amtrak and local community groups joined forces to reopen the building as a train information and local community center and gift shop.

Mystic is best known for its 19th-century Seaport Restoration housing a fine collection of private residences, an aquarium, a large fleet of ships and a working shipyard. In addition, Mystic offers many lived-in houses that formerly belonged to ship captains, a noted aquarium and several windjammer cruise operators.

0:00 (0:10) Depart Mystic.

0:05 (0:05) At Stonington, one of Connecticut coast's most attractive towns, look for large Victorian structure (a former hotel) next to water on right-hand side.

0:10 (0:00) Arrive Westerly.

WESTERLY, RI - This older Rhode Island city has an industrial background which provides several factory buildings facing Amtrak's brick and granite railroad station.

0:00 (0:14) Depart Westerly and head inland into extensive wooded areas of evergreen and deciduous trees. From here through Davisville train is permitted to run at 110 miles per hour, longest fast stretch of track between New York and Boston.

0:14 (0:00) Arrive Kingston.

KINGSTON, RI - The town's blue-gray Victorian-style wooden station is particularly attractive. An old New Haven baggage cart to one side appears to be holding up a large tree. The nearby University of Rhode Island, the resort towns of Newport, Narragansett and Jamestown are popular destinations for passengers leaving the train here.

0:00 (0:26) Depart Kingston.

0:12 (0:14) At East Greenwich, there are close-up views of Narragansett Bay and numerous yacht marinas. Some trains stop here.

Upon approaching Providence, the track has been realigned away from downtown and closer to the hillside state capitol building.

0:16 (0:10) Cemetery on right seems overgrown with bewildering array of tombstones.

0:24 (0:02) Campus of University of Rhode Island is now off to left.

0:26 (0:00) Arrive Providence where Capitol comes into view. Brown University buildings can be seen on hill above and to right.

PROVIDENCE, RI - Providence is the capital of the smallest state in the nation. Closely associated with the sea during its early years, it has become one of the important commercial and financial centers of the East. Old State House, where the Rhode Island General Assembly renounced allegiance to King George III on May 4, 1776, still stands at 150 Benefit St.

0:00 (0:25) Depart Providence and scenery becomes flat and dull as train runs fast through Attleboro and Canton.

0:25 (0:00) Arrive Route 128.

ROUTE 128, MA - This suburban stop is used mostly by passengers using the Beltway which circles Boston.

0:00 (0:18) Depart Route 128.

The final approach to Boston is slow,

Pulling into Boston
SCOTT HARTLEY

finally sinking below grade shortly before Back Bay Station.

0:15 (0:00) Arrive Boston's Back Bay Station.

BOSTON (BACK BAY), MA - This station, just three miles from South Station, serves the Back Bay area of Boston. Besides Amtrak, their station is also a stop for MBTA commuter trains and the Orange Line subway with direct service to Boston's North Station and the northern suburbs.

0:00 (0:05) Depart Back Bay Station, emerging slowly from below grade.

0:03 (0:02) On right, building signage modestly proclaims "Gillette World Shaving Headquarters." Coachyards appear on right.

0:05 (0:00) Boston's huge central post office facility appears on right upon train's arrival South station.

BOSTON, MA - First settled in 1630, Boston and the nation's history have always been closely intertwined. English Puritans endured early hardships here, including death from disease and cold, but held on through those difficult years. Its location on Boston Bay soon made it the most important port in America, with trading vessels sailing to and from all parts of the world. Its port, yet today, is one of the world's busiest.

The American Revolution had its roots in Boston when British troops fired on a gathering of citizens in 1770, killing several. The Boston Tea Party was held in 1773 and Paul Revere's historic ride started here. It was the early cultural center of the nation having such residents as Hawthorne, Emerson and Longfellow. Historically a leader in education, the city still enjoys the distinction of being a major focal point of scientific and medical research. There are a quarter of a million students attending 50 colleges and universities in the greater metropolitan area.

Boston is the largest city in New England with a metropolitan population of nearly three million. It is the capital of Massachusetts, and the city has an impressive collection of financial institutions. There is a unique blend of new and old architecture in its downtown district (the oldest part of the city) where there is a maze of twisting, narrow streets. This historic area is easily toured on foot, but a good map is a requisite.

South Station, Atlantic Ave. and Summer St., 12210. This glorious old station, constructed largely of pink marble just before the turn of the century, has undergone a massive rehabilitation project. Started in the 1980s, the result is a modern-day gem of a depot.

An enormous canopy encloses a spacious and airy waiting room that houses traditional (but quite modern) benches, some very inviting lunch stands, dining tables and slick arrival and departure boards, one for Amtrak and one for commuter trains. Around the perimeter are shops and services, including ticket windows (be sure to note the elegant ceiling over the separate ticket lobby), a bank, shoe repair, a newsstand and other retail operations. Redcap service is available.

A direct passageway leads to the adjoining MBTA station (Red Line).

Call (617) 482-3660 for reservations and other information.

As mentioned above Amtrak has a second convenient in-town facility, **Back Bay Station,** 145 Dartmouth St.

Cab stand is at the station; Checker, 536-7000 and Red & White, 742-9090. **Local buses** and **subway** are in front. Also, various **commuter trains** use this station. For bus, subway and commuter train information, call MBTA, 772-3200. Commuter trains also use the North Station, 150 Causeway Street. **Greyhound** and other intercity buses now operate out of South Station. **Rental cars** are not available at the station, but Budget will pay cab fare to their Long Wharf location, about a mile from the station. **Logan International Airport** is just across the harbor and can be reached by subway (Blue Line).

Boston Common Information Booth, Tremont Street at West Street. Also, **Boston National Historical Park Visitor Center,** 15 State Street at Devonshire St. Both of these centers are on the "Freedom Trail." Write or call Greater Boston Convention and Tourist Bureau, Prudential Tower, Box 490, 02199; (617) 536-4100. **Bostix Ticket Booth,** at Faneuil Hall, provides tickets and information for theaters and other events and attractions; (617) 723-5181.

Because of Boston's ubiquitous and easy-to-use "T" (rapid transit), numerous hotels may be considered "convenient" for travelers not minding a subway ride.

-**Chandler Inn,** 26 Chandler St., 02116; (617) 482-3450 or 800-842-3450. A small, popular hotel, operated as a bed & breakfast. A bit out of the way, but a reasonable walk to the "T" and only three blocks from Back Bay Station. Quiet neighborhood. Twelve blocks from South Station. $84.

-**57 Park Plaza Hotel** (Howard Johnson), 200 Stuart St., 02116; (617) 482-1800. High rise with spacious rooms, all with balconies; in the Theater District. Five blocks from Back Bay Station and ten blocks from South Station. Four blocks from the "T" (Boylston or Arlington on Green Line). $140.

-**Lenox Hotel,** 710 Boylston St. at Copley Pl., 02116; (617) 536-5300 or 800-225-7676. Recently redecorated small hotel in Back Bay. About three blocks from Back Bay Station and the "T," about two miles from South Station. $149.

-**The Eliot Hotel,** 370 Commonwealth Ave. (at Mass. Ave.), 02215; (617) 267-1607 or 800-44ELIOT. Small, European-style, mostly suite hotel in Back Bay, across from the "T" (Auditorium on Green Line). About a mile from Back Bay Station and three miles from South Station. $105.

-**Bed and Breakfast Associates Bay Colony, Ltd.,** P.O. Box 57166, 02157;

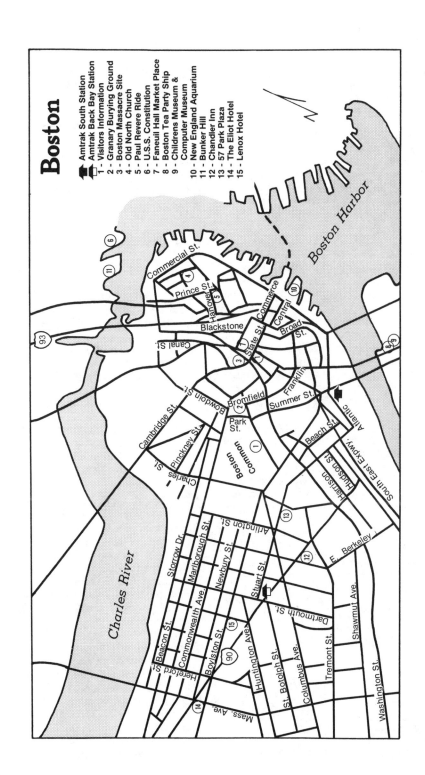

Boston

- Amtrak South Station
- Amtrak Back Bay Station
1 - Visitors Information
2 - Granary Burying Ground
3 - Boston Massacre Site
4 - Old North Church
5 - Paul Revere Ride
6 - U.S.S. Constitution
7 - Faneuil Hall Market Place
8 - Boston Tea Party Ship
9 - Childrens Museum &
    Computer Museum
10 - New England Aquarium
11 - Bunker Hill
12 - Chandler Inn
13 - 57 Park Plaza
14 - The Eliot Hotel
15 - Lenox Hotel

(617) 449-5302. Boston's oldest and largest B&B reservation service.

⭐ Three of Boston's attractions are within two blocks of the station on Congress Street. The **Boston Tea Party Ship and Museum,** on the Congress Street Bridge, is a replica of the original brig "Beaver" on which the famous act of protest took place in 1773. Just beyond is the **Children's Museum,** with "hands-on" exhibits; it's one of the best such institutions and is extremely popular. Adjacent, is **The Computer Museum,** the only one of its kind, with more "hands-on" exhibits that entertain the kids as well as the grown-ups.

Most of Boston's historic points of interest are along the **Freedom Trail,** a walking route through downtown Boston marked by a red stripe along the sidewalks. Maps of the route and descriptions of the things to visit along the way may be obtained from the visitors center. Highlights of this tour include: **Faneuil Hall** and **Quincy Market,** a very large, popular collection of produce stalls, delis, shops, bakeries and restaurants; **Boston Common,** originally used as a militia training ground and pasture for cattle; **Granary Burying Ground,** with gravesites of Paul Revere, John Hancock and Samuel Adams; **Old North Church,** which is the city's oldest church and the site of the signal by lantern notifying patriots across the river whether the British were arriving by land or by sea; **Paul Revere House,** the oldest structure in Boston; the **USS Constitution** ("Old Ironsides"), launched in Boston in 1797 and fought in more than 40 engagements; and **Bunker Hill Pavilion,** 200 yards from the USS Constitution, has a film and sound show recounting the history of the battle at Bunker Hill.

For a non-history break, visit the **New England Aquarium** on Central Wharf with a coral reef, sharks and sea turtles among 2,000 aquatic creatures on exhibit.

New York to Washington, D.C.

📷 **NEW YORK, NY** - See page 21.

0:00 (0:14) Depart New York's Penn Station and head westward beneath streets of Manhattan toward Hudson River. Twin tubes, technically known as North River Tunnels, each carry single sets of tracks beneath Hudson. Tunnels were first opened in 1910 when Penn Station was completed, allowing Pennsylvania Railroad to gain competitive presence in New York City. Until then Pennsylvania's passengers had to be ferried across Hudson from New Jersey terminal.

0:05 (0:09) Surface in North Bergen, New Jersey, some 2¾ miles from Penn Station, and curl southward toward wetlands known as Jersey Meadows.

0:08 (0:06) Off to left, familiar silhouettes of 110-story World Trade Center and legendary Empire State Building, world's second and third tallest buildings (only Chicago's 1,454-foot Sears Tower is taller), can be seen on left. These modern wonders are engineering masterpieces. Over 100,000 people populate World Trade Center's 110 stories on any given workday, a structure that can safely sway up to three feet in high winds.

0:09 (0:05) Cross Hackensack River while flood of vehicular traffic streams across same waterway on New Jersey Turnpike.

0:13 (0:01) Cross Passaic River and enter heavily industrialized outskirts of Newark. PATH's shops will be on left.

0:14 (0:00) Arrive Newark's Pennsylvania Station.

📷 **NEWARK, NJ** - Anchoring the northern end of New Jersey's industrialized core, Newark has the dubious distinction of being one of the world's most important manufacturing communities as well as the largest city in the state. Such stature has not come without serious urban problems, but Newark will undoubtedly survive and continue its role as a world producer.

The town has literally grown up in the shadow of New York City. Newark International Airport has become one of the nation's busiest because of this proximity. And Newark generates considerable business for Amtrak, with commuters transferring here to PATH trains for lower Manhattan.

0:00 (0:33) Upon departing Newark, travel on elevated track through more residential and industrial suburbs.

0:04 (0:29) Pass through Elizabeth, a manufacturing metropolis whose industrial roots date to pre-Revolutionary days—a time when Elizabeth was New Jersey's capital. Both Aaron Burr and Alexander Hamilton lived in this historic city.

0:06 (0:27) Large General Motors assembly plant spreads out on right.

0:08 (0:25) Glide into Rahway on elevated track where old brownstones line each side of right-of-way.

0:09 (0:24) Enter Metro Park, an impressive, modern business and industrial park on left.

From here to Trenton, there are large industrial complexes bearing familiar names such as Revlon, Delco, Johnson & Johnson, American Standard, Bayer Aspirin and Trans America, incongruously interspersed with farms and pastureland.

0:16 (0:17) Pass through New Brunswick, home of Rutgers University which was founded in 1776. Although a state university, it took its name from a generous donor in 1825. First intercollegiate football game was played here in 1869 with Rutgers winning over Princeton by a mighty score of 6 to 4.

0:17 (0:16) On right, beautifully landscaped Johnson & Johnson headquarters often has various waterfowl gallivanting on front lawn.

0:25 (0:08) On right, whimsical cow-shaped shrubbery makes appropriate landscaping for Walker Gordon Milk Farms.

0:26 (0:07) Pass through Princeton Junction where connections are made to trains of New Jersey Transit for Princeton University, just three miles west of here. Branch was originally built in 1865 by Camden & Amboy Rail Road Transportation Company, one of earliest railroads in America. School is nation's fifth oldest institution of higher learning.

0:33 (0:00) Arrive Trenton.

TRENTON, NJ - The capital of New Jersey is home to more than 400 industries. British and Hessian troops were housed here during the night General George Washington and his army made their famous Delaware River crossing. "The Old Barracks" have been reconstructed on their original South Willow

Street site where, ironically, man-made artifacts dating to 2000 B.C. have been recently uncovered.

0:00 (0:31) Depart Trenton and cross Delaware. It was on Christmas Eve, 1776, that Washington crossed its icy waters just eight miles northwest of here to attack Trenton's Hessian Garrison. Ensuing Battle of Trenton marked first victory by Washington over German mercenaries. Off to right, beyond bridge with sign "Trenton Makes – The World Takes," can be seen glistening gold dome of New Jersey's State Capitol, built in 1792 and second oldest continually used statehouse in U.S.

0:05 (0:26) On left, numerous small boats dot picturesque inlet of Delaware River.

0:12 (0:19) Campus of Holy Family College is on right.

0:18 (0:13) On left, note Sterling Paper Company's unique clock tower.

0:19 (0:12) Juniata Terminal Company, easily identified by sign at left, restores antique railroad cars for private car owners. Enormous shops (50,000 square feet) house various railroad artifacts such as Robert Kennedy's funeral car. Company usually has interesting array of rail cars parked outside in view of main line.

0:20 (0:11) North Philadelphia's newly remodeled station is at right.

0:26 (0:05) Cross Schuylkill River as it meanders through Fairmont Park.

0:27 (0:04) On left is skyline of downtown Philadelphia, while city's popular zoo is in foreground. Two-story brick structure at trackside is called Zoo Tower (Zoo for its closeness to Philadelphia's Fairmont Park). Tower oversees Corridor's most complex junction where train traffic is sifted through maze of tracks without a single crossing at grade.

0:28 (0:03) In distance to left is Philadelphia Museum of Art, known for not only fine art but its prominence in movie "Rocky." And in foreground, along far shore of river and immediately after zoo is Boat House Row, home to numerous racing scull clubs. Crews can frequently be seen practicing their rowing skills along this stretch of Schuylkill.

0:29 (0:02) To left, City Hall can be seen, topped by enduring statue of William Penn—a long-time informal height restriction for buildings in Philadelphia. Barrier was broken, however, with construction of One Liberty Place, now visible as tallest structure on skyline.

0:31 (0:00) Arrive Philadelphia beneath venerable 30th Street Station.

PHILADELPHIA, PA - William Penn's desire to form a colony for "religious minorities" and the fact the British Crown owed a debt to his father combined to give birth to Philadelphia. King Charles II gave a large parcel of land to Penn to enable him to create such a settlement in the New World, and in 1682 Penn founded the colony of Pennsylvania ("Penn's Woods") in memory of his father. He soon identified a peninsula between the Delaware and Schuylkill rivers as the site of Philadelphia, Greek for "City of Brotherly Love."

Penn's chief surveyor was asked to lay out the city in a grid pattern with five public squares to provide both sunlight and fresh air for the city's residents—the first recorded effort toward urban planning. These five public squares still exist. The city flourished both economically and culturally, becoming for awhile the second largest English-speaking city in the world.

The city's history is tightly interwoven with America's independence. The Second Continental Congress met in what is now called Independence Hall, and it was here the decision was made to prepare the Declaration of Independence. Philadelphia was the nation's capital until the year 1800.

Although the city showed signs of urban decay after World War II, the 1960s saw a great renewal effort. Today, Philadelphia is a distinctive city of nearly five million, with attractive office buildings, restored town houses and a collection of cobblestone streets illuminated by old-fashioned lampposts.

30th Street Station, on the edge of downtown at 30th and Market streets, is the main passenger train station serving Philadelphia. It is perhaps the best of the grand-style stations with everything done in excellent taste. A massive "rehabilitation" project was completed in 1991.

This is Amtrak's second busiest station in passengers served (New York's Penn Station is first). There are redcaps, restaurants, snack bars, newsstands, a bookstore and other shops. Pay-parking, behind the station at 30th and Arch streets, is open 24 hours. SEPTA commuter trains also operate from this station. A Metropolitan Lounge serves first-class passengers.

For reservations and other information, call (215) 824-1600.

Penn Center Station, 1617 John F. Kennedy Blvd. (also referred to as "Suburban Station") is located in the heart of downtown about a mile east of the 30th St. Station. It can be reached by commuter train in a few minutes from the 30th St. Station; no charge for those holding Amtrak tickets.

Cab stand is at the 30th Street entrance; Yellow Cab, 922-8400. Nearest **local bus** stop at 30th and Market streets just outside the station, 574-7800. **SEPTA commuter trains** serve both suburbs and downtown from this station's upper level and also provide service to Terminals B, C, D and E at the airport. A **subway** station is across the street at the same intersection. Hertz, Avis and American International have **car rentals** available at the station. National, Sears and Budget are located nearby. **Philadelphia International Airport** is approximately ten miles south of the city center.

Philadelphia Visitors Center, 16th St. and John F. Kennedy Blvd. (adjacent to Penn Center Station); (215) 636-1666 or 800-537-7676. Write Philadelphia Convention & Visitors Bureau, 1525 John F. Kennedy Blvd., 19102.

Holiday Inn Center City, 18th and Market streets, 19103; (215) 561-7500. Nine blocks to the 30th Street Station; three blocks from Penn Center Station. $88.

-**Society Hill Inn,** 301 Chestnut St., 19106; (215) 925-1394. A small, homey hostelry, convenient to Independence National Historic Park. Includes continental breakfast. $95.

-**Bed and Breakfast, Center City,** 1804 Pine, 19103; (215) 735-1137 or 800-354-8401. B&B that also acts as a reserva-

Philadelphia

Amtrak 30th St. Station
Penn Center Station
1 - Visitors Information
2 - Independence Nat'l. Historic
    Park
3 - Betsy Ross House

4 - Todd House
5 - Penn's Landing
6 - Holiday Inn Center City
7 - Society Hill Inn
8 - B & B Center City

tion service for other downtown B&Bs. Eight blocks from Penn Center Station. $40 to $80.

For other downtown bed and breakfast reservations, **All About Town Bed & Breakfast of Philadelphia,** P.O. Box 562, Valley Forge, PA 19481; (215) 783-7838.

Philadelphia's charm is in its history. Of greatest historic significance is **Independence National Historical Park** in the area of 5th and Chestnut streets. It can be reached by Transit bus; parking is at 2nd and Sansom Street. The Park includes: **Independence Hall,** originally built between 1732 and 1756 as the Pennsylvania State House, the Declaration of Independence was adopted and U.S. Constitution was written here; **Congress Hall,** adjacent to Independence Hall, was first built as a courthouse and later used by the U.S. Congress from 1790 to 1800 and is where Washington delivered his first message to Congress; **Liberty Bell Pavilion** is the location of America's most beloved symbol of freedom, the Liberty Bell; and the **City Tavern, First Bank of the United States, Car-**

penters Hall, and **Franklin Court,** all just east of Liberty Bell Pavilion. The Visitors Center, at Third Street between Chestnut and Walnut, has a film about the American Revolution which is shown every hour.

The **Betsy Ross Flag House,** 239 Arch St., was the home of Betsy Ross who is credited with making the first American flag. The **Todd House,** 4th and Walnut streets, built in 1775, was the home of Dolly Todd Madison. And **Penn's Landing,** waterfront area in the vicinity of Delaware Avenue and Chestnut Street, is where William Penn first stepped ashore. Old naval ships are anchored here, including a World War II submarine. Also, a trolley runs along the Delaware River.

0:00 (0:21) Depart Philadelphia.
0:01 (0:20) On right stands University of Pennsylvania's Franklin Field.
0:02 (0:19) Pass Philadelphia Convention Center complex, on right.

33

0:05 (0:16) Miniature railroad is amusing exhibit fronting large General Electric plant on left.

For the next few miles, depart the industrial congestion, and venture through some of the most handsome residential neighborhoods one is apt to encounter on any route.

0:08 (0:13) Tower at trackside named "Baldwin" identifies town of Eddystone where Baldwin Locomotive Works, producer of more than 1,500 locomotives, was once major industry. Former Eddystone facility still stands on left.

0:09 (0:12) Chester, with its ancient brownstones bordering tracks, could easily pass for oldest town in Pennsylvania, which it is.

0:13 (0:08) Leave Pennsylvania and enter Delaware. Unique state boundary was formed in 1681 as section of a circle with center at spire of Old Court House in New Castle, DE. Delaware River comes into view on left. Enormous vessels traverse its wide expanse while a burgeoning maze of machinery and apparatus awaits their arrival at dockside.

0:14 (0:07) Sprawling acreage of Phoenix Steel Corporation extends for miles on right.

0:18 (0:03) Cross Brandywine Creek which flows south to meet Christina River before emptying into Delaware.

0:19 (0:02) Christina River joins on left with drawbridges every mile or so. Immediately thereafter, enter grounds of Fort Christina Park at Wilmington. Here, in 1638, a Swedish expedition, under command of Peter Minuit, came ashore and established first European settlement in Delaware. On right, note "Old Swede's Church," erected in 1698. Maintaining services to this day, church is oldest in North America still standing as originally built. Adjacent log cabin is authentic 200-year-old structure.

0:21 (0:00) Arrive Wilmington. Attractive depot, accented by old brass weather vane atop spire, is an historic 1905 structure which underwent a 10.4-million-dollar restoration in 1984.

WILMINGTON, DE - Shortly preceding the Swedish settlement, Dutch, English, and American colonists all played integral roles in Wilmington's formative development. Yet, perhaps most important, the abundant water power of the Brandywine River Valley was soon harnessed to provide an extensive gristmill industry, enabling Wilmington to emerge as an active center for trade and marketing, with easy accessibility along the Delaware River.

In 1802, Eleuthere duPont established a black-powder mill upon the banks of Brandywine Creek. From these humble beginnings, the duPont Corporation has evolved into one of the largest producers of chemicals, plastics, synthetic cloth and dyes in the U.S. It is still, today, the foundation for Wilmington's claim as "Chemical Capital of the World."

0:00 (0:42) Depart Wilmington. For next several miles, beautiful farmhouses and lush agrarian settings alternate paradoxically with expansive industrial complexes.

0:09 (0:33) On left note large Chrysler Corporation plant.

0:11 (0:31) Once through Newark, DE, cross Delaware state line into Maryland at Mason and Dixon's line, surveyed by those two Englishmen in 1776 to resolve a boundary dispute between Pennsylvania and Maryland. Two small stone markers rest on boundary. Bear southwest through lushly wooded landscapes and quaint residential districts, where prominent influence of Colonial architecture and platting within these beautifully preserved communities imparts a real sense of living history throughout region.

0:16 (0:26) Northeast River appears on left. Northeast, Bush, Gunpowder, and Back rivers are all inlets of Chesapeake Bay.

0:19 (0:23) Pass through Perryville on eastern bank of Susquehanna River. Delightful old brick depot stands out on left.

0:20 (0:22) Cross Susquehanna River. Large steel bridges span river on right, while multitude of sailboats adorn marinas on both banks.

0:21 (0:21) Pass through Havre de Grace. Charming bayside community is home to last working light tower on upper Chesapeake Bay.

0:23 (0:20) Pass through Aberdeen where U.S. Army Ordnance Museum exhibits array of historical military hardware, uniforms, and the like.

0:26 (0:16) Cross Bush River.

0:28 (0:14) Pass through Edgewood. Just north is birthplace of William Paca, one of fifty colonists to sign Declaration of Independence.

0:30 (0:12) Cross Gunpowder River. It was here on January 4, 1987 that Amtrak's Colonial, just out of Baltimore and traveling in excess of 100 mph, slammed into three Conrail locomotives which, in spite of cautionary and stop signals, had just pulled onto main line. Tragedy resulted in 16 fatalities and 176 injuries.

0:33 (0:09) On left, border facilities of Maryland National Guard. Martin Marietta operation is immediately adjacent.

0:35 (0:07) Back River appears on left.

0:39 (0:03) Enter city limits of Baltimore atop elevated track bed. On right, clusters of high-density brownstones are huddled along hillsides, while on left, beautiful old church presides in foreground of downtown skyline.

0:42 (0:00) Arrive Baltimore. Depot, like many other Northeastern facilities, features a fascinating combination of architectural forms, stretching many stories skyward from cobblestone walkways below. Also of interest are numerous placards and billboards touting current cultural offerings of area.

BALTIMORE, MD - Started as a harbor town in 1729, Baltimore is now a city of varied nationalities and independent neighborhoods. It has long been one of the more important shipping, financial and industrial centers for the East. Although many of the older portions of the downtown have been razed and renewed, much of our nation's early history can still be virtually seen and felt amongst the city's retained landmarks.

During the War of 1812, Francis Scott Key penned the words to the *Star Spangled Banner* while witnessing the battle of Ft. McHenry from a ship in the harbor. For a brief period during the American Revolution, Baltimore served as the nation's capital. It is also the birthplace of baseball's Babe Ruth.

Pennsylvania Station, 1515 N. Charles Street, has been finely restored to its original grandeur. The station is about a mile north of downtown, but public buses and rubber-tired "trollies" provide easy access during the day.

The station has a snack bar, a newsstand and redcap service. A manned information counter is located in the center of the station with bus schedules and other information. There is a Citibank ATM center on the premises and a Travelers Aid counter. Arrival and departure information occurs on electronic display boards and public address announcements are unusually understandable. Closest parking is a half block away on St. Paul. Covered parking is about a block on Lanvale, between Charles and St. Paul.

Cab stand is at the station; Yellow Cab, 685-1212; and Sun Cab, 235-0300. There are direct phones to Avis and Hertz for **rental car** pick up at the station. Nearest **bus stop** for southbound buses (to downtown) is one block away on St. Paul Street. **"Trolley"** service to downtown is available on Charles Street in front of the station, from 11 am to 7 pm; fare is 25 cents. **Subway-Metrorail** information, call 539-5000. **MARC** commuter trains use Pennsylvania Station and travel south on the Northeast Corridor tracks to Washington, D.C., then west to Gaithersburg. MARC trains also use a separate line between the downtown Camden Station and Washington. Call 800-325-RAIL for MARC information. Certain Amtrak and MARC trains stop at **Baltimore-Washington International Airport,** the quickest (about 15 minutes) and cheapest way ($4 to $6) to get from Baltimore to this airport. Although the MARC fare is somewhat cheaper, the free shuttle bus between BWI station and the terminal theoretically is only for Amtrak passengers.

Baltimore Convention and Visitors Bureau, 300 W. Pratt St., 21201; (410) 837-4636 or 800-282-6632. A visitor information center is also located at the Inner Harbor. Some information is also available at the station.

Lodging shown below is located in two desirable areas, the beautifully reclaimed Inner Harbor area and historic Fell's Point. Fell's Point and the Inner

Harbor are connected by the rubber-tired trolleys, and the Inner Harbor and Penn Station are also linked by this pleasant form of transportation.

-Days Inn Baltimore Inner Harbor, 100 Hopkins Place, 21201; (410) 576-1000. Attractive high rise located downtown on the trolley route, about four blocks from the Inner Harbor and a mile from the station. $90.

-Admiral Fell Inn, 888 S. Broadway, 21231; (410) 522-7377 or 800-292-4667. Elegantly renovated inn on the waterfront in Fell's Point. On the trolley line. Excellent restaurant. Complimentary continental breakfast. Free shuttle service throughout the city; if not available, inn will pay for cab fare from the station. $120.

-Celies Waterfront Bed and Breakfast, 1714 Thames Street, 21231; (410) 522-2323 or 800-432-0184. B&B, overlooking the waterfront in Fell's Point. On the trolley line. $90 to $140.

The **Inner Harbor,** at Pratt and Light streets, is a waterfront showpiece in the heart of the city. Restaurants, shops, harbor tours and harbor activities are delightfully compatible in this urban setting. The **U.S. Frigate Constellation,** the world's oldest floating ship, is docked here and can be boarded.

The adjacent **U.S. Maritime Museum** is actually comprised of three vessels: the submarine U.S.S. Torsk, the Lightship Chesapeake and the U.S.C.G.C. Taney. And next door is the fine **National Aquarium in Baltimore** with aquatic exhibits, including a coral reef, sharks, eels, jellyfish, whales and a rain forest. Moving ramps carry visitors through much of this outstanding facility. For a view of the city, an **observation deck** is on the 27th floor of the World Trade Center, also at the Inner Harbor. **Maryland Science Center and Davis Planetarium,** 1601 Light Street, is at the southwest corner of the Inner Harbor. Displays range from Chesapeake Bay to outer space. It's also the Hubble Space Telescope visitor center.

Fell's Point, just a mile east of the Inner Harbor and easily reached by trolley (or water shuttle in the summer), is Baltimore's old waterfront neighborhood—it's one of the oldest waterfront communities in the country. Once a tough district known for its sailor-filled bars, Fell's Point has become a mixture of Georgetown and Greenwich Village. The shipyards where the renowned Baltimore Clippers were once built are gone, but this is still a working community, and tramp steamers and harbor tugs are common sights. About half of the row houses that line its Belgian-block paved streets have been restored. Unusual shops, a public market, some offbeat eateries, old inns and fashionable bed and breakfasts make this an enjoyable place to visit.

For an entirely different look at Baltimore, **Lexington Market,** in the downtown area at Lexington and Eutaw streets, is a zesty crush of market stalls, brimming with seafoods, meats, produce, ethnic foods—and humanity.

Fort McHenry National Monument, at the foot of E. Fort Ave., southeast of the city, is the site of Baltimore's successful battle against the British during the War of 1812, and inspired Francis Scott Key to write the words of the *Star Spangled Banner.* A water shuttle from the Inner Harbor is available during the summer months. And **Oriole Park** at Camden Yards (new home of the Baltimore Orioles) is next to Camden Station mentioned above.

And for those interested in trains and streetcars: The **Baltimore Streetcar Museum** is at 1901 Falls Road, where one can see the streetcar history of the city, as well as take a mile-long streetcar ride; and the **B. & O. Railroad Museum,** Pratt and Poppleton streets, is in a fine, old circular roundhouse, over 100 years old, with a world famous display of old locomotives and other rail artifacts.

0:00 (0:24) Depart Baltimore, noting old stone bridge on right. Proceed into eerily lit century-old B & P Tunnel—a dark, wet, 7,492-foot bottleneck. Emerge minutes later amidst another covey of old brownstones.

0:10 (0:14) Extensive cemetery lines route on right.

0:12 (0:12) On right pass distilleries of Calvert Whiskey.

Baltimore

Amtrak Station
1 - Visitors Information
2 - Inner Harbor
3 - Lexington Market
4 - National Aquarium
5 - Camden Station
6 - Days Inn
7 - Fells Point

Mt. Royal Ave.
Oliver St.
Mt. Royal Ave.
Preston St.
Biddle St.
Chase St.
Eager St.
Read St.
Madison St.
Monument St.
Mt. Vernon Pl.
Centre St.
Hamilton St.
Franklin St.
Mulberry St.
Pleasant St.
Saratoga St.
Saratoga St.
Lexington St.
Lexington St.
Fayette St.
Baltimore St.
Redwood St.
Water St.
Lombard St.
Pratt St.
Portland St.
Camden St.
Monument
Orleans Viaduct

Maryland Ave.
Charles St.
St. Paul St.
Jones Falls Expwy.
Greenmount Ave.
Guilford Ave.
Howard St.
Park Ave.
Cathedral St.
St. Paul Pl.
Hillen St.
Front St.
Orchard St.
St. Mary St.
Pearl St.
Liberty St.
Paca St.
Eutaw
Howard
Lexington St.
Greene St.
Hopkins Pl.
Hanover
Sharp St.
Charles St.
Calvert St.
South St.
Gay St.

45
40
40
40
83
40

0:18 (0:06) Baltimore-Washington International Airport is a stop for some trains where Amtrak passengers are shuttled directly to and from airport's terminal. Guidelights for end of runway are on left. Passing through Odenton, note interesting old hotel peeking through trees on right.
0:24 (0:00) Arrive New Carrollton.

NEW CARROLLTON, MD - This very modern station serves the northern suburbs of Washington, D.C. There is a Metro station here with subway and bus service to D.C., Virginia and Maryland.
0:00 (0:09) Depart New Carrollton and cross Maryland state line into District of Columbia.
0:04 (0:05) Cross Anacostia River. Black Entertainment TV Network facilities are on immediate right. Then watch for blue and gold dome of National Shrine of the Immaculate Conception off to right, largest Roman Catholic Church in U.S. and seventh largest church in world.
0:07 (0:02) Approaching Washington, silhouette of Washington Monument can be discerned in distance on right.
0:09 (0:00) Arrive Washington, D.C.

WASHINGTON, DC - The nation's first president played a guiding role in developing what would become the country's capital. Not only did he personally select the men to lay out and plan the city, Pierre Charles L'Enfant and Andrew Ellicott, he also chose the sites for both the White House and the Capitol Building.

The result of such presidential involvement is an unusually well laid-out city, with broad streets, many radiating from small parks and circles, lined by imposing marble edifices. It is handsome geometry—and one of the reasons Washington is among the most visited towns in the U.S.

The city is easy to see. Many of its attractions line the Mall—a lengthy, broad esplanade, stretching from the Capitol Building on the east to the Lincoln Memorial on the west. An extensive, modern and easy-to-use subway system makes it possible to do more venturesome exploring without a car, a real plus since heavy traffic is constant and parking is scarce.

Union Station, 50 Massachusetts Ave., NE, located on Capitol Hill, is undisputedly the nation's premier train station. Thanks to a heroic renovation effort, Union Station is no longer a national eyesore, but a gleaming showpiece of marble floors, mahogany woodwork and gold-leafed ceilings.

When Daniel Burnham's beaux-arts masterpiece was first opened in 1908, it lived up to his simple creed: "Make no little plans." It was large enough to hold the entire U.S. Army—then 50,000 in number. It reached its zenith of activity during World War II when no less than 5,000 employees worked here. Subsequently, rail travel declined and so did Union Station. Surviving a 1983 runaway train that crashed into its main concourse, a 1960 effort to demolish it, and finally the 1968 National Visitors Center fiasco, it has now undergone a triumphant resuscitation.

An electronic arrival and departure board over an information counter greets passengers entering the front doors. There are over 120 retail shops, restaurants and fast-food outlets; there is even a nine-screen theater.

The station is laid out on three levels. The street or main level contains Amtrak ticket offices, waiting areas and boarding gates as well as banks, rental cars, shops and cafes. The lower level is a huge food concourse and movie theater, while the upper level has a large collection of "destination" shops and boutiques.

New, European-style storage lockers issue a ticket to the customer with a code to be punched in to claim stored items. (Read instructions concerning rates carefully—the rates can be quite steep!) Luggage carts and redcaps are available. There is a special Metropolitan Lounge for first-class ticket holders. A large directory in the waiting area has phone lines to numerous inexpensive hotels. A 1,400-car garage guarantees space for Amtrak passengers. Enter on H Street or Massachusetts Ave. Elevators and escalators take patrons to the station.

For Amtrak reservations and other information, call (202) 484-7540.

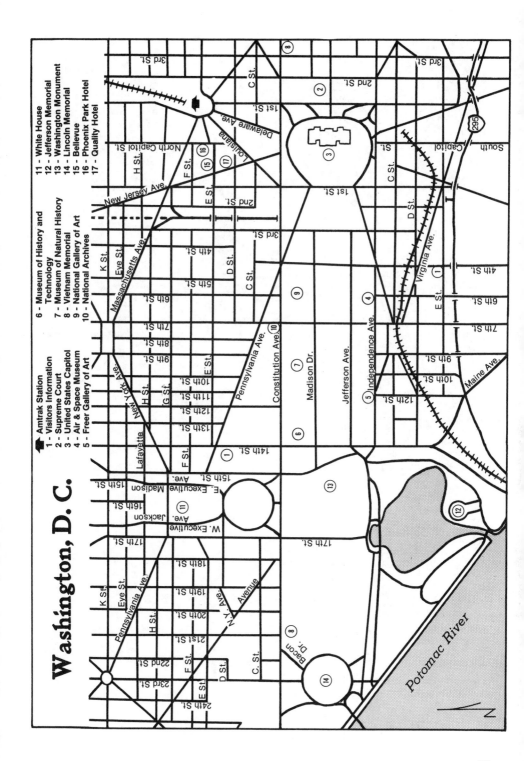

Washington, D.C.

- Amtrak Station
- 1 - Visitors Information
- 2 - Supreme Court
- 3 - United States Capitol
- 4 - Air & Space Museum
- 5 - Freer Gallery of Art
- 6 - Museum of History and Technology
- 7 - Museum of Natural History
- 8 - Vietnam Memorial
- 9 - National Gallery of Art
- 10 - National Archives
- 11 - White House
- 12 - Jefferson Memorial
- 13 - Washington Monument
- 14 - Lincoln Memorial
- 15 - Bellevue
- 16 - Phoenix Park Hotel
- 17 - Quality Hotel

Union Station - Washington, D.C.
JACK SWANSON

Cab stand is at the station; Diamond, 387-6200. Cab fares in D.C. are based on zones, rather than being metered, and rates are somewhat higher during the evening rush hour. A Metrorail **subway** stop (red line) is at the station, as well as the nearest **local bus** stop; call 637-7000 for information. **Tourmobiles,** a convenient way to see many of the sights, also stop at the station. Both Avis and National have **rental cars** available at the station. **Washington National Airport** is just across the Potomac in Virginia and can be reached by Metrorail. **Dulles International Airport** is much farther south, about 27 miles from the station. **Baltimore-Washington International Airport** is 31 miles northeast of the station and can be reached by some Amtrak trains. A shuttle is provided for Amtrak passengers between the BWI station and the airport terminal.

Washington Convention and Visitors Association, 1212 New York Ave., 20005; (202) 789-7000. **Visitors Information Center,** 1455 Pennsylvania Ave. (between the Willard and Washington hotels).

The hotels shown here are within easy walking distance from the station and are also convenient to the Capitol, the Mall and the Metro. All rates are summer rates which are often lower than rates for the rest of the year.

-**Bellevue Hotel,** 15 E Street, NW, 20001; (202) 638-9000 or 800-327-6667. Nicely remodeled older hotel. Two short blocks from the station. Special rates for Amtrak passengers. Buffet breakfast. $105.

-**Phoenix Park Hotel,** 520 North Capitol Street, NW, 20001; (202) 638-6900 or 800-824-5419. Smaller hostelry with deluxe accommodations, only a block from the station. Special rate for Amtrak passengers, $105.

-**Quality Hotel Capitol Hill,** 415 New Jersey Ave., NW, 20001; (202) 638-1616. Four blocks from the station. $98.

For a reasonable fare, the popular **Tourmobile** takes passengers on a narrated tour of 18 historic sites, including Arlington Cemetery, while another route goes to historic Alexandria and Mt. Vernon. Passengers are permitted to reboard throughout the day at no extra charge.

The attractions shown below are along or near the Mall, and a healthy walker (read hiker) theoretically could reach them all on foot from the station. The Metro or a taxi, however, might be considered for those points of interest near the east end of the Mall.

The **Smithsonian Museums** are mostly spread out along the Mall. Some of the more popular ones include: The **National Air and Space Museum,** with superb displays of aircraft, from the Wright Brothers' plane to modern-day space vehicles; the **Freer Gallery of Art** with fine displays of Oriental and other art; the **National Museum of American History,** displaying aspects of the nation's history and development; and the **National Museum of Natural History** with collections including the Hope Diamond.

Some other popular points of interest along or near the Mall include: the **United States Capitol,** at the east end of the Mall with chambers of both houses of Congress and guided tours available every 15 minutes; the **Supreme Court,** just east of the Capitol, with tours except when the court is in session; the **National Gallery of Art,** comprised of two buildings with a large collection of Western and American art; the **National Archives,** the resting place for the Constitution, the Declaration of Independence and the Bill of Rights; the **Washington Monument** with an elevator to the observation room at the top (waits can be long); and the **Lincoln Memorial** anchoring the west end of the Mall.

Not far from the Mall are the **White House** at 1600 Pennsylvania Avenue, NW, which has been the home and working office of each president since 1800, and the **Jefferson Memorial** on the south bank of the Tidal Basin.

New Haven to Springfield

0:00 (0:16) Departing New Haven, Inland Route trains swing northward away from shoreline route and angle across Connecticut, directly toward Hartford.

0:01 (0:15) Gaggle of Metro-North commuter train cars repose in rail yards at right.

0:08 (0:08) Incongruously colored (pink) tanks comprise Wyatt Fuel Company tank farm.

0:16 (0:00) Arrive Wallingford.

WALLINGFORD, CT - One of Connecticut's older cities, Wallingford is known for its silver manufacturing. Note classic old brick church with fine spire just after station on right.

0:00 (0:06) Depart Wallingford.

0:06 (0:00) Arrive Meriden.

MERIDEN, CT - This city of nearly 60,000 is home to the world's largest producer of silverware—International Silver Company. At its main plant visitors can see Heritage House, furnished to illustrate 18th-century life in America, while silversmiths and pewters demonstrate early methods of production.

0:00 (0:08) Depart Meriden.

0:02 (0:06) Former facilities of International Silver Company make forlorn scene at right.

0:03 (0:05) Idyllic Silver Lake stretches along tracks on right.

0:08 (0:00) Arrive Berlin.

BERLIN, CT - Here, first tinware in America was produced in early 1700s.

0:00 (0:11) Depart Berlin.

0:11 (0:00) Arriving Hartford, marble capitol building with its gold-leafed dome looms above train on right. One of Hartford's more unusual industries, gold-beating, provided the gild for this elegant structure. Some fine historical exhibits are housed within.

HARTFORD, CT - Referred to as the "Insurance Capital of the World," more insurance is underwritten in Hartford than in any other city in the United States. Other major employers include Colt Industries, makers of firearms (including the famed Colt "45") and Hueblein Industries of alcoholic beverage renown.

The town had its first permanent inhabitants in 1633 when a trading post was established by the Dutch. The nation's oldest statehouse is still preserved near the center of town.

During its development, Hartford fostered some of America's greatest intellectuals. In 1874, Mark Twain built a whimsical brick mansion (it looked more like a Mississippi riverboat), and penned Huck Finn and Tom Sawyer as well as many of his other beloved tales. Noah Webster was born in West Hartford, and although best known for creating the first comprehensive American dictionary in 1783 he authored the "Blue-Backed Speller" which was still in use during the early part of this century. Harriet Beecher Stowe ("Uncle Tom's Cabin") also lived here.

0:00 (0:12) Depart Hartford.

0:04 (0:08) First glimpse of Connecticut River, flowing southeastward toward its Atlantic mouth at Old Saybrook, is afforded on right.

0:07 (0:05) Windsor, CT, located in shade-grown tobacco country, is one of Connecticut's earliest settlements, having been founded by Plymouth colonists in 1663. This is a stop for some trains. Newly remodeled station serves buses as well as Amtrak.

0:08 (0:04) Farmington River is now crossed. This broad stream follows a 60-mile serpentine course from its Algonquin-State-Forest birthplace, only 20 miles straight west of us, to its Connecticut-River joinder just east of here.

0:12 (0:00) Arrive Windsor Locks.

WINDSOR LOCKS, CT - This New England manufacturing community also serves as the location for Hartford's airport (Bradley International Airport) which is just west of here, as well as the Bradley Air Museum which houses a collection of vintage military aircraft.

0:00 (0:19) Depart Windsor Locks and roll under Interstate 91, stretching from New Haven northward to Vermont-Quebec border.

0:01 (0:18) Across Windsor Locks Canal, on right, sign on factory reads "Dexter-Nonwovens Division."

Dexter Corp. is an American institution. It is the oldest corporation listed on the New York Stock Exchange and quite possibly the third oldest continually operated company in America. This particular plant manufactures long-fiber papers which Dexter then makes into tea bags (world's largest supplier), oil filters, surgical gowns and other paper products. Although the canal was constructed in the early 1800s to provide a shipping bypass needed to avoid a dam further upstream, it now provides fresh water (critical in paper production) to Dexter.

0:04 (0:15) Having tired of following west bank of Connecticut River, rails now cross to eastern shore.

0:06 (0:13) Rumble past Enfield, on right, where Jonathan Edwards, perhaps Colonial New England's most effective revivalist, delivered one of his greatest sermons—"Sinners in the Hands of an Angry God." Although his voice was weak, and he read from manuscripts held closely to his near-sighted eyes, his logic and power were extraordinary. Edwards eventually became president of College of New Jersey—now known as Princeton University.

0:11 (0:08) After passing through Thompsonville, leave Connecticut and enter Massachusetts.

0:15 (0:04) On right, orange and black building is home to Basketball Hall of Fame.

0:19 (0:00) Arrive Springfield.

SPRINGFIELD, MA - An important manufacturing city of the Northeast, Springfield had its start as a mere trading post in the 1630s. In 1794 the United States opened an important armory here, now the Springfield Armory Museum. Today, the Basketball Hall of Fame is located here.

For route between Boston and Springfield, see Lake Shore Ltd. log, page 66.

Philadelphia to Atlantic City
(Atlantic City Express)

With the meteoric rise of Atlantic City from a rather forlorn seaside resort to one of the nation's most visited cities, Amtrak has stepped in to share in the resulting transportation bonanza. Several trains now travel daily between the Boardwalk and Philadelphia where con-

nections are easily made to other points along the Northeast Corridor. There is also a through train that originates in Springfield, MA.

Service is provided on reserved Amfleet coaches, with sandwiches and beverages available on board. Club cars are also carried by each train. The one-way trip from Philadelphia takes about 1¼ hours.

0:00 (0:33) Depart Philadelphia's 30th Street Station northbound.

0:02 (0:31) Philadelphia Museum of Art is at right, then on far banks of Schuylkill River are handsome boat houses, home to several rowing organizations. Houses make a particularly delightful sight after dark, with each outlined by strings of lights.

0:03 (0:29) Philadelphia Zoo (America's first) slips past on right, easily identified by statuary of zoo's inhabitants.

0:04 (0:28) Cross Schuylkill River, a waterway often used by boating crews for practicing rowing skills.

0:07 (0:26) Almost every city has an area that can only be described as ugly, and tracks now pass through what must be Philadelphia's worst—depressing shells of commercial buildings and wretched-looking row houses paint a grim scene on both sides of right-of-way.

0:10 (0:23) Juniata Terminal Company, easily identified by sign at right, restores antique railroad cars for private car owners. Enormous shops (50,000 square feet) house various railroad artifacts such as Robert Kennedy's funeral car. Company usually has interesting array of rail cars parked outside in view of main line.

0:11 (0:22) Pass rail intersection known as Shore Interlocking and depart Northeast Corridor tracks that head north to New York City and Boston.

0:13 (0:20) Ornate clock tower highlights facilities of Sterling Paper Company off to right.

0:16 (0:17) Cross expansive waters of Delaware River, forming boundary between Pennsylvania and New Jersey. Delaire Bridge was originally built in 1895/6 as a swing span, but was retrofitted with a vertical lift section about 30 years ago during a widening of river's channel.

0:24 (0:09) Slicing through parking lot of Cherry Hill's Garden State Race Track, modern glass and brick betting facilities are seen just to left.

0:33 (0:00) Arriving Lindenwold, large assemblage of PATCO (Port Authority Transportation Corp.) commuter trains rest in PATCO's yards awaiting duty between here and Philadelphia.

LINDENWOLD, NJ - This city of 18,000 is the heart of Philadelphia's easternmost "suburbs." As well as Amtrak service, PATCO trains can be ridden into the heart of that Pennsylvanian metropolis, and New Jersey transit trains can be taken to Atlantic City.

0:00 (0:43) Depart Lindenwold.

0:08 (0:35) Having slipped from heavily populated sections of New Jersey, train now courses through bucolic New Jersey forests.

0:09 (0:34) Tree nursery spreads out on left.

0:26 (0:17) As train nears ocean, terrain and architecture take on a seacoast appearance. Soil becomes sandy, then marshy, while quaint three-story, white-with-green-trim Victorian home appears on right.

0:38 (0:05) High rises of "new" Atlantic City now rise dramatically, dead ahead.

0:41 (0:02) Cross channel known as Beach Thorofare, part of Intracoastal Waterway system (world's longest).

0:43 (0:00) Arrive Atlantic City's new train station. City's new convention center is to be constructed just beyond.

ATLANTIC CITY, NJ - Atlantic City is a place of memories rapidly being engulfed by the new order of legalized gambling. The fashionable piers are gone, replaced only by a three-layered shopping arcade called Ocean One, which now serves as a token of what once was an Atlantic City trademark.

The famous Boardwalk with its herringbone slats is still the main beat of the sightseer, angling along the white sand beach for nearly five miles. The honkeytonk shops and arcades that have long lined this thoroughfare continue to stand their ground but are overshadowed by the ostentatious gambling palaces that now share space along this hallowed shore. A thousand years from now, this will be a suitable subject for archaeological excava-tion and speculation.

There are three reasons to come to Atlantic City: to gamble, to take in the shows or just to look and relax in the midst of a unique bit of Americana.

Atlantic City Rail Terminal, One Atlantic City Expressway (at Kirkman Blvd.), is one of Amtrak's newest stations. The inside has an open glass-and-steel atmosphere—efficient, practical and attractive, adorned with black steel-mesh benches. (The outside, however, has all the appeal of an aircraft hangar.)

A large electronic display board registers arrival and departure information for both Amtrak and New Jersey Transit trains that also use the station. There is a snack bar and a visitor information counter in the lobby. Train platforms are both high-level and covered. Parking is adjacent to the station. The Boardwalk is within walking distance, just five long blocks to the east. The convention center, adjacent to the station, is home to the annual Miss America Pageant and the world's largest pipe organ.

Cab stand is at the station; Atlantic City Yellow Cab, 344-1221. **Jitney** service to the Boardwalk is also available for about a dollar. **Buses to all casinos** depart regularly from the station, $5 round trip. **Harrahs** has had free shuttle service for Amtrak passengers. **Municipal Bus Terminal** (the former railroad terminal) is two blocks from the station. **Bader Field Airport** is only a few minutes from the center of town.

Convention and Visitors Bureau, 2314 Pacific Avenue (at Mississippi), 08401; (609) 348-7100 or 7130. Conveniently located between the station and the Boardwalk (behind Trump Plaza).

Caesars Atlantic City Hotel Casino, Arkansas and Pacific avenues, 08401; (609) 348-4411 or 800-443-0104. On the Boardwalk and closest hotel casino to the station; five blocks. $115 (includes package).

-Quality Inn, S. Carolina and Pacific avenues, 08401; (609) 345-7070. A block from the Boardwalk and a mile from the station. $75.

Casino gambling and **big-name shows** are popular ways to pass the time in this seaside resort, but there are other things to see, which can easily be accomplished in a day. The **Boardwalk,** with its strolling hordes, is remarkable in and to itself. Along this planked walkway are the sights, sounds and smells that are uniquely Atlantic City. Visit **Ocean One's** three tiers of shops, restaurants and arcades suspended out over the Atlantic. Its upper balconies provide excellent panoramas of the city. Be sure to note the memorial plaque commemorating Charles Darrow, the inventor of the game of *Monopoly,* the game that borrows heavily from the city's street names, located appropriately at the corner of Park Place and Boardwalk. Walk through the **Trump Taj Mahal,** a vastly overstated version of the Indian architectural wonder. Try out the elevated, covered, **moving sidewalk** that sucks patrons from the Boardwalk area and takes them on a one-way journey to the Sands and Claridge. Its walls are a nostalgic photo gallery, while the sounds of performances from days past fill the air. Lastly, for some rare Atlantic City memorabilia, visit the **Atlantic City Art Center** and **Historical Museum** on Garden Pier, the northernmost spot on the Boardwalk.

Other Northeast Service

Besides Northeast Corridor trains, including those that run up the Connecticut Valley terminating at Springfield, MA, Amtrak offers Inland Service trains linking Boston and Washington, DC by way of Springfield.

During the summer months, there is weekend Cape Cod service between New York City and Hyannis, Massachusetts.

AEM7 - Metuchen, NJ
HOMER R. HILL

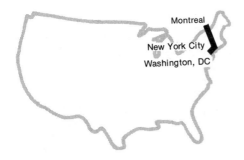

Montreal
New York City
Washington, DC

Montrealer

This is one of Amtrak's two trains to Montreal. Each is as different as night and day—literally. The Montrealer is an overnight expedition through Massachusetts, New Hampshire and Vermont with Washington, DC its southern terminus; while the Adirondack's more direct route up the Hudson and west shore of Lake Champlain is a daylight run, and with New York City its southern endpoint.

The Montrealer's out-of-the-way route (it is 114 miles longer than the Adirondack's path between New York and Montreal) provides winter access to some of New England's better ski areas, while in the summer, there is some wonderfully pastoral viewing of Vermont's maple syrup country in the early-morning hours. Covered bridges and forests interspersed with small dairy farms enhance the scene.

Northbound Schedule (Condensed)
Washington, DC - Late Afternoon Departure
New York, NY - Midevening
Amherst, MA - Middle of the Night
Montpelier, VT - Early Morning
Montreal, Que. - Midmorning Arrival

Southbound Schedule (Condensed)
Montreal, Que. - Late Afternoon Departure
Montpelier, VT - Late Evening
Amherst, MA - Middle of the Night
New York, NY - Early Morning
Washington, DC - Early Afternoon Arrival

Frequency - Daily.

Seating - Heritage Fleet coaches.
Dining - Tray meals, snacks, sandwiches and beverage service.
Sleeping - Bedrooms and roomettes.
Baggage - Checked baggage handled at some stations.
Reservations - All-reserved train except for local travel between Washington, DC and New York City.
Length of Trip - 731 miles in 18½ hours.

Route Log - Springfield, MA to Montreal

For route between Washington, DC and New London, CT, see that portion of Northeast Corridor log, pages 21 and 30.

0:00 (3:10) Depart New London's Union Station and immediately leave Amtrak's New York-Boston line, heading north on Canadian-owned Central Vermont (CV) tracks. This well maintained but less-than-busy line will carry us to Canadian border, traversing rural Connecticut, Massachusetts, New Hampshire and Vermont. Then under Gold Star Memorial Bridge carrying I-95 traffic over Thames River.

0:02 (3:08) Pass through small CV yards in East New London, containing abandoned roundhouse and turntable. Then, following west bank of Thames, slip past U.S. Coast Guard Academy.

0:30 (2:40) At Norwich, where America's first cut nails were produced, depart Thames River.

1:00 (2:10) Through Willimantic, where collection of antique rolling stock reposes north of Amtrak station.

1:40 (1:30) Trundle past Stafford Springs, noted for its mineral water springs. John Adams, nation's second president, came here to bathe after hearing about water's "curative powers."

1:55 (1:15) Leave Connecticut and enter Massachusetts.

3:10 (0:00) Arrive Amherst.

AMHERST, MA - Education and literature permeate this New England community. Amherst College, University of Massachusetts and Hampshire College are all located here, and three well-known American poets, Dickinson, Frost and Field, all resided here. Noah Webster also lived in Amherst.

Amherst also serves as a stop for nearby Northampton, just a few miles to the west. Northampton was the very heart of the religious revivalist movement during the first half of the 18th century and was home of Johnathan Edwards. Later, Northampton was home to "shy, silent" Calvin Coolidge, the country's 30th president. Smith College is now located there.

0:00 (0:50) Depart Amherst.

0:17 (0:33) Trestle carries CV over Boston & Maine's east-west main line, then cross Millers River.

0:32 (0:18) Another trestle and train crosses to west shore of Connecticut River.

1:10 (0:00) Arrive Brattleboro.

BRATTLEBORO, VT - Rudyard Kipling, whose stories and poetry gave heroic support to the British Empire, lived here for four years near the end of the 19th century. His wife was a Brattleboro girl. An old rail station houses the Brattleboro Museum and Art Center.

0:00 (0:34) Depart Brattleboro.

0:30 (0:00) Arrive Bellows Falls.

BELLOWS FALLS, VT - The town derives its "Falls" name from falls in the adjacent Connecticut River, which, in the early 19th century, forced construction of a canal with nine locks to raise or lower river traffic past the cascades.

0:00 (0:25) Depart Bellows Falls, and immediately cross Connecticut River into New Hampshire.

0:25 (0:00) Arrive Claremont Jct., a stop for adjacent Claremont.

CLAREMONT, NH - This community, located on the Sugar River, has the distinction of being Amtrak's only stop in the state of New Hampshire. It is home to New Hampshire Voc Tech College.

0:00 (0:30) Depart Claremont Jct.

0:02 (0:28) Span carries train high over Sugar River.

0:10 (0:20) Cross Connecticut River once again and enter Vermont, then town of Windsor.

This is the birthplace of Vermont. The "Republic's" constitution was signed here July 9, 1777, and the old tavern, where this historic event took place, still stands.

0:30 (0:00) Arrive White River Junction where historic, Colonial-style station serves Amtrak passengers. Restored B&M 4-4-0 steam locomotive stands in square in front of station, while just beyond is Hotel Coolidge, where Calvin once slept. Hotel is named for his father, a friend of hotel's owner.

WHITE RIVER JUNCTION, VT - As you would expect, this is the joinder of the White River with the Connecticut River. Historically a railroad center, this is also the point where the Boston and Maine and Central Vermont meet. While the B&M heads due north, the CV angles northwesterly, the latter being the route of the Montrealer. Hanover, NH, home to Dartmouth College, is less than five miles from here.

0:00 (1:25) Depart White River Junction and follow White River northwestward across very heart of Vermont.

0:10 (1:15) At West Hartford, cross hikers' delight—the Appalachian Trail.

0:25 (1:00) This is South Royalton. Three miles east of here is Sharon, the birthplace of Joseph Smith, founder of the Mormon Church. A 38½-foot polished granite shaft (not visible from tracks) marks spot.

0:30 (0:53) Bethel is northern end of trackage where Vermont's first passenger train made its way from White River

Falls. Town has unique eight-sided library originally constructed as a school.

0:40 (0:42) Montrealer cruises through Randolph. Note unusually wide streets which were designed so that town could become state's capital, being located at geographic center of Vermont. It didn't happen, however. The Morgan horse breed, now Vermont's official state animal, started here.

0:42 (0:40) Having left Third Branch of White River, we now follow beside Dog River.

1:00 (0:15) Just before Northfield, Norwich University, nation's oldest private military institution, is on right.

1:03 (0:12) As we rumble through Northfield Falls, watch for covered bridges. Four of these picturesque structures are located within a quarter of a mile from here.

1:19 (0:00) Arrive Montpelier Junction, suburban stop for Montpelier.

MONTPELIER, VT - Vermont's capital city is home to not only the state's government, but also a large segment of the life insurance industry. Admiral George Dewey, hero of Manila Bay, was a Montpelierite, and his father founded the National Life Insurance Company located here. Rock of Ages Granite Quarry, largest in the world, is just southeast of here near Barre (rhymes with Harry). Barre is also home to the Canadian-owned Bombardier plant which is building Superliner cars for Amtrak.

0:00 (0:15) Depart Montpelier and proceed northwestward through Winooski River Valley.

0:14 (0:00) Arrive Waterbury.

WATERBURY, VT - This is the heart of Vermont's ski country with several slopes nearby. Stowe is only ten miles up the road.

0:00 (0:28) Depart Waterbury, continuing to trace course of Winooski and through very heart of Green Mountains.

0:24 (0:04) July 7, 1984, one of Amtrak's worst accidents occurred on this segment of right-of-way when seven of Montrealer's thirteen cars plunged into a gulley by Winooski River Bridge.

A localized storm had plugged a stone culvert (built around 1850) and washed out the trackbed shortly before the train reached this point. Five people were killed and 133 injured.

0:28 (0:00) Arrive Essex Junction, which serves adjacent Burlington.

BURLINGTON, VT - With over 38,000 population, Burlington is Vermont's largest city. Beautifully situated on the eastern shore of Lake Champlain with the Green Mountains just to the east, it is home to the University of Vermont, the oldest such institution in the state. Ethan Allen, who helped organize The Green Mountain Boys, and led them on a raid that captured Ft. Ticonderoga from the British during the American Revolution, is buried here. John Dewey, the celebrated philosopher, was born here. Ferry service operates between Burlington and Port Kent, New York.

0:00 (0:29) Depart Essex Junction, continuing on Central Vermont, following a course due north through Vermont's dairy and sugar maple country.

0:13 (0:16) Pass through Milton at southern tip of Arrowhead Mountain Lake which is on our left. A pre-Columbian Indian flint quarry is located here.

0:15 (0:14) Cross Lamoille River on Georgia High Bridge built with picturesque granite pilings.

0:17 (0:12) Vermont Whey Company plant, on left, serves regional dairy farmers.

0:29 (0:00) Arrive St. Albans, where two-story brick Amtrak station, on right, is just north of Central Vermont's headquarters, a large three-story brick structure built in 1866 to serve as a passenger station.

ST. ALBANS, VT - Hardly a likely setting for a Civil War skirmish, but on October 19, 1864, the northernmost conflict of that war took place when Confederates raided three of the town's banks. During the War of 1812, smugglers used the area as a base of operations.

Today, the most excitement occurs during the Vermont Sugar Maple Festival, held here in early April with parades, fiddling contests, trips to nearby sugar houses and even rolling pin competitions.

This is also a junction point for the Central Vermont. Southbound passengers will go through U.S. Customs here.

0:00 (0:45) Depart St. Albans past Central Vermont shops, roundhouse and turntable on right.

0:20 (0:25) Just after Stanton, cruise through 4,800-acre Missisquoi National Wildlife Refuge, where most of 400-plus species that inhabit eastern half of the U.S. have been spotted at one time or another.

0:22 (0:23) Negotiate half-mile-long bridge carrying us over neck of Missisquoi Bay. Pivot span in center accommodates occasional boat traffic.

0:32 (0:13) Cross into Canada. During prohibition, this train was nicknamed "The Bootlegger" as it supposedly provided a steady stream of hooch to U.S. customers.

0:40 (0:05) Bridge Richelieu River.

0:45 (0:00) Enter Cantic, Quebec, then back onto siding.

Northbound passengers will go through Canadian Customs at this point. This is not a passenger stop.

0:00 (1:08) Depart Cantic and head across southern Quebec's flat countryside toward Montreal. This is the Richelieu River Valley, where trains on Canada's first railway, the Laprairie and St. Johns, followed the Richelieu as early as 1851. Small agricultural communities with French-speaking citizenry are scattered throughout region.

0:13 (0:55) Small village of Saint-Blaise, off to left, with its silver-steepled white church, is typical of towns encountered throughout province of Quebec. Pristine but plain, they seem as throwbacks to another era.

0:19 (0:48) Enter good-sized town of Saint Jean. On right is College Militaire Royal and then, on right, note rail artistically bent into several-feet-high railroad spike—it's just before red brick station.

0:43 (0:17) Note almost continuous parade of small swimming pools in backyards of homes on left. It's possible to count more than one hundred in an eight-minute stretch.

0:57 (0:11) Slow for St. Lambert, a Montreal suburb immediately across the St. Lawrence from our destination. St. Lambert Lock, a lift station for St. Lawrence Seaway traffic, is here. Then start ascent necessary for crossing St. Lawrence River on Victoria Bridge.

This structure was once known as the Jubilee Bridge when it was opened in 1859, later to be rebuilt in 1898, to handle two sets of rails, an electric interurban line and auto traffic. It is one of the world's longest at 1¼ miles. Those two concrete-lined channels below us are the St. Lawrence Seaway and the St. Lambert Lock which is just one of many locks needed to raise or lower shipping using this waterway. The Seaway is narrow and, unfortunately, cannot handle larger ships of today's maritime fleet. Once over the Seaway, we cross the St. Lawrence itself.

0:59 (0:10) Islands to right were home to Canada's very successful 1967 world's fair—Expo 67. Geodesic dome was the U.S. Pavilion. Skyline of Montreal forms a dramatic scene forward on right. Sloping tower of Olympic Stadium can be seen near horizon at right. Stadium is home to Montreal Expo's baseball team and was site of 1976 Summer Olympics.

1:02 (0:06) Leaving Victoria Bridge, we enter Montreal through Canadian National rail yards.

1:04 (0:04) Slip over nicely landscaped Lachine (pronounced luh-SHEEN) Canal, constructed before seaway to avoid Lachine Rapids.

1:06 (0:02) Sink underground as we near station.

1:08 (0:00) Arrive Montreal's Central Station.

 MONTREAL, QUE. - See page 341.

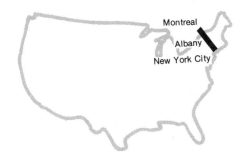

Adirondack

Those who ride this train from New York City to Montreal pass through 200 years of history on nearly 400 miles of track. And for ten hours, those aboard the Adirondack are treated to a changing scene that grows more spectacular as their northbound journey progresses. The old New York Central Route (now Conrail) up the east side of the Hudson River is steeped with riverside beauty, history and New England tradition.

But the thrilling part of this journey takes place farther north as the tracks embrace the western shore of Lake Champlain. Rock cuts, lily ponds, sailboats, Victorian depots, and the Adirondacks of New York and Green Mountains of Vermont line the route. And in the fall, the color is sublime. If you think you can almost hear the salvos from the battles of Lake Champlain and Saratoga, it could be the cannons that are still fired at Ft. Ticonderoga.

Northbound Schedule (Condensed)*
New York, NY - Early Morning Departure
Albany-Rensselaer, NY - Midmorning
Plattsburgh, NY - Midafternoon
Montreal, Que. - Late Afternoon Arrival
*Three hours later, Sundays.

Southbound Schedule (Condensed)
(Four hours later on Sundays)
Montreal, Que. - Midmorning Departure
Plattsburgh, NY - Early Afternoon
Albany-Rensselaer, NY - Late Afternoon
New York, NY - Midevening Arrival

Frequency - Daily.
Seating - Amfleet coaches.
Dining - Sandwiches, snacks and beverages.

Baggage - No checked baggage.
Reservations - Reserved coaches.
Length of Trip - 382 miles in 10 hours.

Route Log

 NEW YORK, NY - See page 21.

0:00 (0:38) Depart New York City's Penn Station through newly constructed tunnel that curls up and over Amtrak's North River Tunnels which bore beneath Hudson to Newark. Then pass beneath city's Jacob Javits Convention Center. Tunnel is part of Amtrak's Empire Connection, a route opened in April, 1991, along Manhattan's west side, that for first time connects Eastern Seaboard cities, such as Washington and Philadelphia, to Albany and rest of Hudson River Valley without having to make a cross-town connection between Penn Station and Grand Central Terminal. This link once carried New York Central freight into Midtown Manhattan.
0:05 (0:31) Through former 60th Street yards of New York Central where Donald Trump once planned 152-story skyscraper —world's tallest.
0:06 (0:30) Submerge beneath Riverside Park.
0:11 (0:25) Emerge near West 125th Street that leads off to right directly into heart of historic Harlem. Glimpses at Hudson River are afforded on left.
0:13 (0:21) Graceful, elegant superstructure of George Washington Bridge now dominates view to left forward. Completed during the Great Depression in 1931,

structure was expanded in 1962 to carry 14 lanes of vehicular traffic. Across Hudson, New Jersey's Palisades Interstate Park extends northward along river's shore. Just before bridge, "Little Red Lighthouse" can be seen on left, now designated a National Historic Landmark.

0:16 (0:20) Pass by 62-acre Ft. Tryon Park, a gift from John D. Rockefeller, Jr. Above to right is The Cloisters, a mix of Gothic and Romanesque architecture built to house Metropolitan Museum of Art's Medieval art collection. Legendary Unicorn tapestries are housed here.

0:17 (0:18) Slip through Inwood Hill Park and then encounter Harlem River Ship Canal, technically Spuyten Duyvil (a Dutch term used to describe junction of Harlem and Hudson rivers) Creek. Spuyten Duyvil Swing Bridge carries tracks over river, while auto traffic of Henry Hudson Parkway is lifted across on right by Henry Hudson Bridge. Before swing bridge could be used, bridge was floated across Hudson to New Jersey for expensive rehabilitation. While crossing Harlem River, leave Manhattan and enter "The Bronx." River was once important barge route, but now mainly accommodates sightseeing tours.

0:21 (0:17) Metro North's commuter lines from Grand Central Terminal, formerly used by Amtrak, now join from right. Tracks now proceed along eastern bank of Hudson River, as barges and freighters traverse waters of this vital inland passage.

0:23 (0:15) At Yonkers large, stately homes nestled along hillsides only preview what will soon become a premier attraction of this Hudson River run. Sign of the times is at right where former Otis Elevator plant is now partially used to house large Kawasaki operation.

0:29 (0:09) On right, fanciful European design highlights station at Ardsley-On-Hudson.

0:31 (0:07) Tappan-Zee Bridge on forward left is first of several dramatic structures that span Hudson River between here and Albany.

0:32 (0:06) Quaint little village of Tarrytown typifies many small communities along route whose resplendent colonial atmosphere reflects a proud historical heritage.

0:35 (0:03) At Ossining, track borders legendary Sing Sing state prison. As previously promised, line from Ossining north borders some of country's most graciously endowed estates. From Roosevelts to Vanderbilts, many of society's elite have chosen to make their homes amidst lush woodlands and verdant hills of this Hudson River Valley.

0:38 (0:00) Arrive Croton-Harmon.

CROTON-HARMON, NY -All trains once paused at this old Dutch community, switching from electric to diesel power. Long-standing regulation still prohibits diesel-powered transport within New York City tunnels.

Croton-Harmon is the site of the historic Van Cortlandt Manor, home of New York's first lieutenant governor. This magnificent estate dates back to the late 1600s, and through time has been host to many American and foreign dignitaries.

0:00 (0:38) Depart Croton-Harmon past further array of magnificent dwellings. Frequently, river inlets intrude on estates and provide picturesque playground for ducks and swans.

0:07 (0:31) Through Peekskill, where nicely restored station is at right.

0:12 (0:26) Train glides beneath soaring Bear Mountain Bridge which carries not only vehicular traffic but hikers following Appalachian Trail.

0:18 (0:20) Across river, scenic Highland Falls tumble down cliffs, while campus of West Point Military Academy presides above. Established in 1802, nation's oldest service academy still resides on site where George Washington once stationed Revolutionary troops to thwart British maneuvers along Hudson River. Grant, Lee, Pershing, MacArthur, Patton, Eisenhower, Westmoreland and Schwarzkopf were some of the Point's more illustrious graduates.

0:20 (0:18) Through Cold Spring, probably best known for its summer theater.

0:21 (0:17) For next few miles, hills bordering route burgeon in size, nearly assuming "mountain" classification.

0:23 (0:15) Pass through double-bore Breakneck Ridge Tunnel.

0:24 (0:14) Ensconced in middle of river, Bannerman's Castle is fascinating recreation of old robber baron's stronghold.

It was used by original owner as a store-house for armaments.

0:31 (0:07) North of Chelsea, cross Wappinger River as it spills into Hudson.

0:38 (0:00) Arrive Poughkeepsie.

POUGHKEEPSIE, NY - Formerly the state's capital during the Revolutionary War, Poughkeepsie has since evolved into a thriving manufacturing center, with a diverse range of products ensuring economic stability. The city at one time became synonymous with the Smith Brothers who made their famous cough drops here.

Located nearby, the Franklin D. Roosevelt National Historic Site and Vanderbilt Mansion are much-frequented historical attractions. Also popular are the many "pick-your-own" farms and orchards surrounding the Poughkeepsie area.

0:00 (0:14) Departing Poughkeepsie, picturesque waterfalls of Fallkill Creek trickle down by trackside on right. Spanning river on left, old cantilever railroad bridge was largest of its type when constructed in 1889. A fire in early 1970s precluded its further use.

0:04 (0:10) Across river, letters "CIA," enscribed on cliffside, face nearby Culinary Institute of America where many of country's renowned chefs honed formative skills.

0:05 (0:09) Shortly after seeing huge, red-roofed house across Hudson (former estate of Father Vine), Franklin Delano Roosevelt's Hyde Park home will be above tracks on right and Vanderbilt Mansion shortly thereafter. Unfortunately, both are set back just far enough so that neither is visible from train.

0:14 (0:00) Arriving Rhinecliff, fine old lighthouse looms in midst of Hudson, while on opposite bank, castle-like mansions embellish scene seemingly plucked from Bavarian landscape.

RHINECLIFF, NY - Rhinecliff is the Amtrak stop for nearby Rhinebeck, a charming community nestled in the hills of the Hudson River Valley. Boasting one of the largest districts of homes on the National Register, Rhinebeck is also the site of Beekman Arms—the

Adirondack - Tappan Zee Bridge
SCOTT HARTLEY

nation's oldest continuously operating hotel. F.D.R. chose to conclude many of his campaigns from this historic inn.

Here, too, is the famed Rhinebeck Aerodrome where, on weekends from July to October, vintage aircraft take to the skies for daredevil excitement. Its museum of World War I aircraft is world renowned.

0:00 (0:21) Depart Rhinecliff.

0:10 (0:11) North of Tarrytown, small peninsulas jutting out in water afford unique setting for many splendid homes, with activity along Hudson River a "front-door" drama for all. Mountains flanking river are part of Catskill chain and will escort train into town of Hudson.

0:15 (0:06) Crossing scenic Roeliff River, docks on right are popular spot for senior fishermen to wile away hours.

0:19 (0:02) On left, exquisite old lighthouse still maintains watchful vigil.

0:21 (0:00) Arrive comely station at Hudson.

HUDSON, NY - Beautiful gardens grace the avenues of this picturesque town, named for Henry Hudson whose "Half Moon" docked here in 1609. Located here, the American Museum of Fire Fighting maintains one of the oldest and most complete collections of firefighting equipment in America. Olana, the elegant estate of acclaimed artist Frederic E. Church, with its Persian-style mansion, is another attraction.

0:00 (0:25) Depart Hudson.

0:25 (0:00) Arriving Albany-Rensselaer (station is actually in Rensselaer, just across river from Albany), downtown Albany skyline stands out on left. Prominent 42-story skyscraper is centerpiece of Empire State Plaza. Left of tower, low-slung Cultural Education Center houses State Museum and Library, while on right, dynamic elliptical structure is Center for Performing Arts. Four smaller towers in background are also part of this ambitious billion-dollar project. Once in station, inspiring domed archways of St. John the Baptist Catholic Church can be seen protruding above treetops on right.

ALBANY-RENSSELAER, NY - A small-town atmosphere with big-city prestige is the claim of Albany, New York's state capital. Replete with cosmopolitan amenities, Albany is likewise a stone's throw from the rural splendor depicted in the paintings of America's beloved Grandma Moses.

The aforementioned Empire State Plaza is the current pride and joy of downtown Albany. Nearly a city unto itself, shops, pubs and restaurants line the interconnecting walkways between the many governmental agencies located here. At the north of the complex stands the State Capitol, its fanciful French Renaissance architecture a dramatic contrast to the sleek, modern lines of the Plaza's other buildings.

As well as a bastion of state government, Albany has remained a vital inland port since the completion of the Erie Canal in 1825. Today, private operators conduct excursions along this historic waterway that recapture the spirit and grace of an earlier era. And then, too, this has long been an important railroading town. Fortunately, an important piece of this past was preserved when Albany's decaying Union Station, where New York Central and Delaware & Hudson trains once arrived on different levels, was saved from the wrecking ball and restored to its original elegance by Norstar, a bank holding company.

In the adjacent town of Rensselaer, one can tour Fort Crailo, the nation's oldest fort built in 1642. Legend has it that a British surgeon wrote the famous "Yankee Doodle" tune while visiting this site.

Amtrak Station, East Street, is located in the city of Rensselaer, just across the Hudson River from downtown Albany. The station has a good coffee shop as well as snack vending machines, a newsstand with a good selection of international newspapers and free luggage carts.

Cab stand at the station; Yankee Doodle **Taxi,** 465-8188 or Red & White, 465-3233. (Always inquire about fare before leaving station in unmetered cabs.) Thrifty **Rental Car,** 465-7315, with downtown Albany location, will pick up and drop off at station during their business hours; courtesy phone in station. Hertz, 434-6911, will allow $5 on cab fare to their downtown location and car can be left at station.

Fort Crailo Motel, 110 Columbia Turnpike, Rensselaer, NY, 12144; (518) 472-1360 or 800-477-3123. Well managed, reasonably priced motel; restaurants within walking distance. Closest to station; a few minutes cab ride for about a $6 fare. $38.

0:00 (0:22) Depart Albany-Rensselaer.
0:04 (0:19) Cross Hudson River. On left, ornate spires and turrets adorn magnificent State University Administration Headquarters. Originally built in 1916 as corporate offices of Delaware and Hudson Railroad, complex is actually three buildings interconnected, with Flemish facades maintaining delightful continuity throughout. Replica of Henry Hudson's "Half Moon" is highlight of weather vane perched atop main tower.
0:05 (0:17) Intriguing amalgam of modern and classical architecture is a most striking feature of Albany's city center on left.
0:06 (0:16) A familiar emblem for many years, large black and white mutt Nipper looms protectively above RCA facility on right.
0:07 (0:15) August 9, 1831, one of North America's earliest steam locomotives made its inaugural run between Albany and Schenectady when Mohawk & Hudson's De Witt Clinton, pulling three stagecoach-appearing cars, chugged up this grade—steepest on Water Level Route. Mohawk & Hudson was first railroad chartered in New York.
0:10 (0:10) On outskirts of town, four lonesome high rises comprise State Office Building campus on left.
0:11 (0:09) Shoreline of Rensselaer Lake adjoins trackside on right.
0:18 (0:04) Approaching Schenectady, attractively landscaped parkways dissect sprawling grounds of General Electric industrial park on left.
0:19 (0:00) Arriving Schenectady, tall, gold-domed City Hall clock tower is prominent fixture on right.

SCHENECTADY, NY - Emerging from the heart of the Industrial Revolution, Schenectady became known as "the city that lights and hauls the world." The American Locomotive Company's Schenectady Works and Thomas Edison's Machine Works were primarily responsible for this designation, the latter eventually evolving into the colossal General Electric Corporation.

Schenectady's "Stockade District" is a premier historical attraction, representing one of the country's best-preserved enclaves of early American architecture and culture. Its name stems from the original 1661 settlement which was surrounded by a stockade to guard against French and Indian attacks.

From here on the best viewing will generally be found on the right (east) side, particularly along Lake Champlain.
0:00 (0:29) Departing Schenectady, city's historic Stockade Area is off to left. Leave Amtrak's Empire Corridor and continue northward toward Montreal.
0:02 (0:27) Gold-domed building off to right is on campus of Union College.
0:04 (0:25) Sprawling, old buildings on left were formerly occupied by American Locomotive Works (Alco), one of America's premier locomotive builders.
0:06 (0:23) Cross Mohawk River.
0:29 (0:00) Arrive Saratoga Springs where modern depot on right will be a disappointment to those anticipating more nostalgia from this historic town.

SARATOGA SPRINGS, NY - At the turn of the century, few spas rivaled Saratoga's popularity with the East's wealthy and socially elite. Stylish Old World bathhouses offered supposedly curative soaks in naturally carbonated mineral water and elegant hotels lined the town's thoroughfares. Fine gardens and even a spouting geyser added to the charm. For those seeking to try their luck, opulent casinos comparable to any in Europe offered gambling while the Saratoga Race Track presented thoroughbred racing. Notables who frequented Saratoga included the likes of Diamond Jim Brady and Lillian Russell, while the Vanderbilts and Whitneys had homes near the track.

Today, society no longer looks upon Saratoga Springs with the same fervor, but the town is still a fascinating summer resort. The fine old hotels, including the famous United States Hotel, have been replaced by newer hostelries, but the thoroughbred race track (the nation's oldest), the bathhouses with their famous mineral water and one of the most beautiful harness racing tracks in the world make for a great summer destination. Culture is also in abundance, headed up by the New York City Ballet and the Philadelphia Symphony, both making this their summer homes.

History buffs will remember that in 1777 the Revolutionary War Battle of Saratoga (actually fought several miles from here at Bemis Heights and Stillwater) brought defeat to 7,000 British troops, Hessian mercenaries and Indians led by Lt. General John Burgoyne and turned the war's momentum in the Patriot's favor. News of this American victory brought about the Franco-American Alliance.

0:00 (0:20) Depart Saratoga Springs.
0:04 (0:16) Under I-87 which links two great cities, Montreal and New York.
0:19 (0:01) Cross back to east side of Hudson River. Scott Paper Company plant, which processes wood pulp into facial and toilet tissue, napkins and wax paper (only Scott facility that makes the latter), is clearly visible upstream, on left.
0:20 (0:00) Arrive Ft. Edward where old relic of a depot still stands at left.

FT. EDWARD, NY - This small upstate town derives its name from the fort constructed on the banks of the Hudson during the French and Indian War. In 1825, locks were constructed here, the highest point on the canal, allowing the Champlain Canal to connect to the Hudson River and creating a continuous trading waterway between the St. Lawrence and the lower Hudson. The canal is still used as part of the New York State Canal System, frequented now by barges with modern-day cargoes such as jet fuel.

This is Amtrak's access to Glens Falls and Lake George.

0:00 (0:23) Depart Ft. Edward and before long pass through pastoral settings which would make most city dwellers envious of their country cousins.
0:11 (0:12) Champlain Canal, on right, is encased by spectacularly beautiful rock cliffs as a prelude to what is yet to come as we near Lake Champlain. From here to Canadian border, scenery is spectacular as Adirondack hugs west shore of 105-mile-long Lake Champlain.
0:15 (0:08) At Comstock, Great Meadows Correctional Facility can be seen on right.
0:23 (0:00) Arriving Whitehall, brick chimney on right once lifted smoke from Champlain Silk Mill prior to Great Depression. Former station, demolished in 1986 in spite of local historical society protestations, has been replaced by simple glass box shelter.

WHITEHALL, NY - This is the northern terminus of the Champlain Canal, complete with locks giving barges access to and from South Bay—Lake Champlain's southernmost extension.

Although the U.S. Navy avoids designating any one place as its official birthplace, Whitehall claims the honor. It was here on May 9, 1775 that Colonists under orders from Benedict Arnold captured Skenesborough (now Whitehall) from a Loyalist, Philip Skene. Two days later, Skene's sailing ship was taken to nearby Crown Point where it was armed for war. The schooner was then used to capture the British naval ship Enterprize. These activities seem to predate other Revolutionary naval beginnings.

0:00 (0:29) Departing Whitehall, note old mansion with clock tower, above town to right on Skene Mountain. Using granite quarried from mountain, structure was built in 1875 by Italian artisans as home for New York State Supreme Court judge. In early 1900s, clock was added to cupola when timepiece was removed from weakened steeple of local Presbyterian Church. Movement is controlled by weights in basement. Building is listed in National Register of Historic Places and, not surprisingly, main floor, in recent years, has served as restaurant.
0:01 (0:28) Hull of U.S.S. Ticonderoga (War of 1812 veteran) has been carefully preserved under protective roof at right.
0:04 (0:25) Here we cross (and get our first view of) Lake Champlain (South Bay). Also, it is here that we enter Adirondack Park, established in 1885—an enormous acreage, much of which is wilderness and largest state park in U.S. Sylvan lily ponds with assorted waterfowl stretch along right side of train.
0:13 (0:16) Navigational buoys are sprin-

kled along channel on right to guide water traffic between Lake Champlain proper and South Bay. Small pleasure craft are often in abundance. Main body of Lake Champlain, discovered by Samuel de Champlain in 1609, now comes into view.
0:20 (0:09) Shoreline on opposite side of Lake Champlain is Vermont.
0:25 (0:04) Fine view of Ft. Ticonderoga, on bluffs ahead and to right, is now afforded.
0:28 (0:01) Train now slips through tunnel immediately under fortification grounds.
0:29 (0:00) Arrive at station serving nearby town of Ft. Ticonderoga.

FT. TICONDEROGA, NY - The nearby restored Colonial fort was originally established in 1755 by the French who sliced off the mountain's top and used the rocks found there for its construction. The fort defended the passage between Lake Champlain and the northern tip of Lake George (which are only about a mile apart) as well as the route between the colonies and Canada, making it one of the most strategic locations of the Revolution. It was first captured by the British, but then continued to change hands.

At the start of the Revolution the fort fell to Ethan Allen, Benedict Arnold and the Green Mountain Boys of Vermont without a shot being fired. They sent its guns to help break the siege of Boston. It was again captured by the British in 1777, a severe blow to the Colonists, only then to be later abandoned and burned after Burgoyne's ultimate defeat at Saratoga.

The fort has been beautifully restored and contains a fine museum with Revolutionary artifacts. During the summer, colorfully uniformed "soldiers" march through the grounds playing traditional fife and drum music, and cannons are periodically fired for added atmosphere.
0:00 (0:20) Depart Fort Ticonderoga.
0:04 (0:16) Enormous International Paper plant is just above tracks on left.
0:14 (0:06) Impressive Blue Ridge rises to an elevation of 2,680 feet off to left. Beyond, but out of sight, are a group of mountains, all rising to over 4,000 feet.
0:17 (0:03) Very fine view of Lake Cham-

plain is afforded on right. Protrusion of land across water is Crown Point State Historic Site, location of ruins of two forts that once secured command of this vital waterway. First fort was built by French in 1734. Later, under British occupation, a three-and-one-half-square-mile stronghold was built—one of Britain's most ambitious military engineering projects in North America.
0:20 (0:00) Arrive at Port Henry's neat but old station, set serenely in Witherbee Park.

PORT HENRY, NY - Several architectural artifacts are worth watching for in this community, Port Henry's train station being but one. On departing, note the two brick buildings sitting above the tracks on the left. The three-story town hall could have easily been used for the movie "Psycho," while the other quaint structure, just to the right of town hall, is a former fire station (now used for a garage).

Not to be outdone by Loch Ness, Lake Champlain boasts its own monster—Champ. Champ's likeness has been captured as a weather vane that adorns the roof of the gazebo in the middle of Witherbee Park on left.
0:00 (0:18) Depart Port Henry. Site of Porter and Lewis Mills, former supplier of lumber to Benedict Arnold's fleet, stood just up draw to left near present brick structure of Niagara Mohawk Power.
0:18 (0:00) Upon arriving Westport, note very attractive geodesic home on right.

WESTPORT, NY - This scenic little shoreline village is perhaps best known for its bass fishing tournaments. But also popular is a summer theater which occupies the freight room of the 1876 train station. This old depot, perched high above the town, is a grand vignette of the past. Still well maintained, its exterior sports a coat of green and ivory paint while the interior shelters some wonderful woodwork of yesteryear.
0:00 (0:42) Depart Westport.
0:09 (0:33) On left, former Delaware & Hudson stone depot once served town of Essex.
0:15 (0:27) Peaks to left reach elevations over 3,600 feet.

0:18 (0:24) Cross high over pretty Bouquet River.

0:19 (0:23) Grey facilities, on both sides of train, refine walstonite ore which is mined nearby. Principal uses of walstonite include the manufacture of ceramics, china and paint.

0:20 (0:22) Through Willsboro, situated in region where lake trout, walleye and salmon are in abundance. New York and Vermont have undertaken a project to stock Lake Champlain with game fish and as a result, Willsboro Dam on nearby Bouquet River provides excellent fishing.

If you have not already been convinced that this is indeed a scenic ride, you might be shortly. Between here and Port Kent, a few miles up line, the route is embellished by spectacular rock cuts, many high above Lake Champlain. Twisting and turning, one view after another is afforded to those on the right side of the train. During one 4½-mile stretch alone, the train must negotiate 128 curves.

0:42 (0:00) Arrive Port Kent.

PORT KENT, NY - This is a flag stop for Amtrak during the summer months. The dock for the summer ferry to Burlington, Vermont (10 miles directly across the lake) can be seen here.

0:00 (0:14) Depart Port Kent.

0:04 (0:10) Cross Ausable River which has its headwaters southwest of here at the base of 5,344-foot Mt. Marcy, highest point in New York.

0:07 (0:07) Leave Adirondack Park. Valcour Island is on right, site of Battle of Lake Champlain, first naval battle between Britain and the Colonies.

0:09 (0:02) Huge Plattsburgh Air Force Base (home of SAC's 380th Bombardment Aerospace Wing) stretches along tracks on left.

0:13 (0:01) Flotillas of pleasure craft occupy marinas on both sides of track, then ruins of four-stall roundhouse are on right.

0:14 (0:00) Arrive Plattsburgh after passing yacht basin on right.

PLATTSBURGH, NY - Military posts have been located in this area continually since colonial times. It was off these shores that the British fought and won the Battle of Lake Champlain in 1777, although the delay inflicted on the British played an important role in America's eventually winning the Revolution. And it was from here that Colonel Zebulon Pike, the discoverer of the peak by the same name, launched an unsuccessful march against what is now Toronto. Later, during the War of 1812, Plattsburgh was the site of two coordinated American victories, one on land and the other in Plattsburgh Bay where American sailors used anchors and winches to pivot their vessels 180 degrees, giving the surprised British two broadsides from each ship.

The SAC base and paper mills now shape the area's economy. A turntable and roundhouse for the old Delaware & Hudson shops is on the left.

0:00 (0:23) Departing Plattsburgh, eagle-crowned obelisk is Macdonough Monument, commemorating naval victory of 1814.

The terrain now becomes more agricultural and flat while the tracks move away from Lake Champlain (that has accompanied us for past two hours) and pass through miles of cornfields. This is the last opportunity to purchase liquor and cigarettes on the train since once into Canada (beyond Rouses Point) they are not available on the Adirondack.

0:15 (0:08) Apples are principal product of Chazy which boasts world's largest McIntosh orchards.

0:23 (0:00) Arrive Rouses Point.

ROUSES POINT, NY - Huddled against the U.S.-Canadian Border, Rouses Point was settled in 1793 by Jacques Rouse, said to have had 26 children. The first pioneer settlement in northern New York now serves as the American Customs checkpoint for southbound passengers. The yellow building on the right is the customs house.

Here, Lake Champlain empties into the Richelieu River which in turn flows into the St. Lawrence. Southbound trains are fueled here to avoid stiff fuel taxes that would have been incurred north of the Border.

0:00 (0:15) Depart Rouses Point and in a minute, Canadian flags identify Canadian-U.S. border.

0:15 (0:00) Arrive Cantic, Quebec.

CANTIC, QUE. - Cantic is where northbound passengers are checked by Canadian Customs. Proof of citizenship is important. Although the ceremonies may sometimes be perfunctory, it is not unusual to be here for an hour while normal inspection procedures are carried out.

0:00 (0:57) Depart Cantic and head across southern Quebec's flat countryside toward Montreal.

This is the Richelieu River Valley, where trains on Canada's first railway, the Laprairie and St. Johns, followed the Richelieu as early as 1851. Richelieu is actually Lake Champlain's drainage course into the St. Lawrence River. Small agricultural communities with French-speaking citizenry are scattered throughout the region.

0:13 (0:44) Small village of Saint-Blaise, off to left, with its silver-steepled white church, is typical of towns encountered throughout province of Quebec. Pristine but plain, they seem as throwbacks to another era.

0:19 (0:38) Enter good-size town of Saint-Jean. On right is College Militaire Royal and then, on right, note rail artistically bent into several-feet-high railroad spike—it's just before red brick station.

0:43 (0:06) Note almost continuous parade of small swimming pools in backyards of homes on left. It's possible to count more than one hundred in an eight-minute stretch.

0:57 (0:00) Arrive St. Lambert.

ST. LAMBERT, QUE. - This is one of Montreal's larger suburbs, located immediately across the river from that city. St. Lambert Lock, a lift station for the St. Lawrence Seaway, is here.

0:00 (0:12) Depart St. Lambert and immediately start ascent necessary for crossing St. Lawrence River on Victoria Bridge.

This structure was once known as the Jubilee Bridge when it was opened in 1859, later to be rebuilt in 1898, to handle two sets of rails, an electric interurban line and auto traffic. It is one of the world's longest at 1¼ miles. Those two concrete-lined channels below us are the St. Lawrence Seaway and the St. Lambert Lock which is just one of many locks

needed to raise or lower shipping using this waterway. The Seaway is narrow and, unfortunately, cannot handle larger ships of today's maritime fleet. Once over the Seaway, we cross the St. Lawrence itself.

0:01 (0:11) Islands to right were home to Canada's very successful 1967 world's fair—Expo 67. Geodesic dome was the U.S. Pavilion. Skyline of Montreal forms a dramatic scene forward on right. Sloping tower of Olympic Stadium can be seen near horizon at right. Stadium is home to Montreal Expo's baseball team and was site of 1976 Summer Olympics.

0:06 (0:06) Leaving Victoria Bridge, we enter Montreal through Canadian National rail yards.

0:08 (0:04) Slip over nicely landscaped Lachine (pronounced luh-SHEEN) Canal, constructed before seaway to avoid Lachine Rapids.

0:10 (0:02) Sink underground as we near station.

0:12 (0:00) Arrive Montreal's Central Station.

 MONTREAL, QUE. - See page 341.

Maple Leaf

The charming Hudson River Valley, an international border crossing at Niagara Falls and the fascinating maritime activities along the western tip of Lake Ontario are just some of the scenes that await those aboard the Maple Leaf. This service, since its inception in 1971, has been the result of a joint U.S.-Canadian endeavor that links New York City with Toronto. The delightful run takes—almost regretfully—only 12 hours to complete.

Northbound Schedule (Condensed)
New York, NY - Early Morning Departure
Albany-Rensselaer, NY - Late Morning
Niagara Falls, NY - Late Afternoon
Toronto, Ont. - Midevening Arrival

Southbound Schedule (Condensed)
Toronto, Ont. - Midmorning Departure
Niagara Falls, NY - Early Afternoon
Albany-Rensselaer, NY - Early Evening
New York, NY - Late Evening Arrival

Frequency - Daily.
Seating - Amcoaches.
Dining - Lounge car, with sandwiches, snacks and beverages.
Baggage - No checked baggage.
Reservations - Reservations required.
Length of trip - 544 miles in 12 hours.

Route Log

For route between New York City and Schenectady, see that portion of Adirondack log, page 51. For route between Schenectady and Buffalo, see that portion of Lake Shore Ltd. log, page 68.

DEPEW, NY - This is a convenient suburban stop for the Buffalo region.
0:00 (0:10) Depart Depew.
0:05 (0:05) Speed slows considerably as train negotiates entangled maze of tracks and switches approaching Buffalo. Downtown skyline looms on forward right, while immediately right, grand clock tower presides atop stately Romanesque archways of old Buffalo Central Terminal.

The terminal, now on the National Register of Historic Places, had as its architect famed station designer Alfred Fellheimer who also created the elegant Cincinnati Union Terminal. After years of political haggling over an appropriate site for a larger New York Central station, it was completed in 1929, shortly before the Crash and the ensuing depression. In spite of such luckless timing, a poor location (two miles from downtown) and the gradual withering of rail service, Central Terminal held on for fifty years before Amtrak delivered a fatal blow with its move to Depew Station farther east.
0:10 (0:00) Arrive Buffalo (Exchange Street Station). City center on right sports interesting blend of architectural styles, though eye seems to gravitate to glistening white tower of Niagara Mohawk's "Electric Building." Modernistic complex on left houses Buffalo Evening News.

BUFFALO, NY - Situated on the eastern shores of Lake Erie, and across the Niagara River from Canada, Buffalo is New York's second largest city with a population approaching 400,000. The metropolitan region represents one of the largest manufacturing centers in the U.S. with steel, chemicals, auto parts and flour production a sampling of its major industries. Railroading is also an important facet of the Buffalo economy, with a large number of separate lines maintaining offices in the city.

Like many cities of this size, Buffalo offers a wide range of cultural opportunities. The Albright-Knox Art Gallery and Buffalo Zoo are consistently rated among the nation's finest. Buffalo, too, is an avid sports mecca, and supports major league franchises in football and hockey.

0:00 (0:34) Depart Buffalo. After traversing short tunnels, Lake Erie appears on left.

0:05 (0:29) Lake waters begin narrowing into Niagara River which flows 35 miles north before spilling into Lake Ontario. Along route, brief interruption of Niagara Falls tends to discourage conventional navigation.

0:06 (0:28) On left, Peace Bridge spans river to Fort Erie, Ontario, a major port of entry into Canada.

Water intake is curious spectacle protruding from water just north of bridge.

0:11 (0:23) Old drawbridge connects Squaw Island with mainland on left.

0:18 (0:16) Passing through Tonawanda, train departs river route temporarily. Clock tower of Tonawanda Middle School is distinctive fixture on left.

0:20 (0:14) Cross New York Barge Canal, offspring of historic Erie Canal, now only a few blocks from its western terminus.

0:27 (0:07) At town of Niagara, International Airport is situated on left, as well as adjacent Niagara Falls Air Force Base.

0:28 (0:06) As train heads westerly towards Canadian border, gravel and cement operation bares another modest crater on right.

0:32 (0:02) Assemblage of towering power stanchions on right readily conjures up images of Martian invasion. Nearby hydroelectric facilities are some of world's largest, tapping mighty resources of Niagara Falls.

0:33 (0:01) Spindly observation towers on forward left are popular vantage points for viewing falls.

0:34 (0:00) Arrive Niagara Falls, New York.

NIAGARA FALLS, NY - The breathtaking falls on the Niagara River continue to be the primary attraction that draws over 12 million tourists to this region annually.

Write **Niagara County Tourism,** 59 Park Ave., Lockport, NY 14094 or call 800-338-7890.

-**Comfort Inn - The Pointe,** One Prospect Pointe, 14303; (716) 284-6835. Excellent location for taking in the American Falls. $98.

0:00 (0:10) Depart Niagara Falls, New York.

0:08 (0:02) Cross into Canada via 1,082-foot bridge spanning Niagara River. From its lofty heights, brief glimpse of falls is afforded on left while torrent of rampaging Whirlpool Rapids is impressive spectacle on right.

0:10 (0:00) Arrive Niagara Falls, Ontario. Journey is delayed here while customs agents board for round of "customary" inquiries. (New York bound passengers are checked by U.S. customs at Niagara Falls, NY.) Amtrak crews are replaced by VIA personnel at this time.

NIAGARA FALLS, ONT. - Like its New York counterpart, the falls are the focal point of this town as well. Observation towers, riverboats, helicopters, cable cars and ground-level catwalks are among the many means available for viewing this natural wonder. Throughout time, less conventional methods have also been pursued. Maria Spelterina once traversed a cable across the falls wearing peach baskets on her feet. The Great Blondin took a more leisurely approach, pausing in the middle of his walk to cook lunch on a miniature stove.

VIA Station is located about five minutes by cab from the Falls and the center of town. There are storage lockers, but no vending machines.

Cabs are available at the station; 5-0 Taxi, 358-3232. During the day, **shuttle buses** to the Falls leave from the transportation center across from the station, 15 minutes before and after each hour, 356-1179. **People Mover buses** run regularly along river, connecting many major attractions; fare good for all day. Intercity **bus terminal,**

357-2133. **Thrifty Rental Car** free pick up and delivery, 356-8529.

Visitor & Convention Bureau, 4673 Ontario Ave., Suite 202, Niagara Falls, Ont., L2E 3R1; (416) 356-6061. Also, closer to the Falls, 5543 Victoria Avenue (at Kitchener).

-Econo Lodge, 5781 Victoria Ave., L2G 3L6; (416) 356-2034. Inexpensive (by Niagara standards) accommodations within a few blocks of the Falls. $65.

-The Oakes Inn, 6546 Nfls.; (416) 356-4514. Next to Minolta Tower. Some rooms with view of Falls. Hotel has its own observation deck. About two blocks from the Canadian Falls. $75 to $178.

-Skyline Brock and Skyline Foxhead (adjacent hotels under common ownership—Brock is the older), 5705 Falls Ave., L2E 6W7; (416) 374-4444. Deluxe rooms, many with excellent view of American Falls. Located at foot of Rainbow Bridge. Dining room at top of the Brock has superb panorama of both falls. $129.

The Falls, of course, are the major attraction. There is also an array of museums (wax, Elvis, French perfume, Ripley's, etc.), fun houses and myriad other rather incongruous attempts at competing with one of nature's most wondrous spectacles.

0:00 (0:20) Depart Niagara Falls through Canadian National rail yards before emerging on rolling farmlands of southern Ontario.

0:06 (0:14) Cross Queenston Chippawa Power Canal.

0:10 (0:10) Winery on right represents a popular enterprise of region. Wire vine supports are also common sights throughout accompanying vineyards.

0:16 (0:04) Cross newest (1932) Welland Canal, an important shipping link connecting Lake Erie and Lake Ontario. Eight separate locks, like set seen on left, allow vessels to negotiate 326-foot elevation differential between two lakes. Entire passage is now completed in less than eight hours, about half the time required to traverse one of older canals seen a few miles downline.

0:20 (0:00) From atop towering bridge, cross original (1842) Welland Canal before arriving St. Catharines.

ST. CATHARINES, ONT. - Situated in the heart of the Niagara fruit belt, bountiful harvests support St. Catharines' claim as the "Garden City." Wine production is important here, too, with tours of these facilities a popular attraction.

Also of interest is the St. Catharines Historical Museum where the significance of the Welland Canal is brought to light. Here, too, is Tivoli Miniature World, a neatly landscaped park bedecked with tiny replicas of the world's most noteworthy landmarks.

0:00 (0:16) Departing St. Catharines, rolling hills become more pronounced with streams meandering picturesquely through their midst. Bountiful orchards embellish landscape and provide a basic economic staple of area.

0:04 (0:12) Approaching Jordan, cross Sixteen Mile Creek. On western edge of town, Lake Ontario can be seen on right while crossing Jordan Harbour.

0:16 (0:00) Arrive "doll-house" station at Grimsby. Railhouse Restaurant is added attraction of this charming facility.

GRIMSBY, ONT. - Another hub of fruit and wine production, Grimsby was the site of Canada's first municipal government, established at a town meeting back in 1790.

0:00 (0:30) Depart Grimsby.

0:08 (0:12) Rural environs are soon displaced by industrial sprawl approaching Hamilton. A most notable feature of city is its seeming lack of centrality with clusters of high rises dispersed through every region. Area that curls around western tip of Lake Ontario is known as The Golden Horseshoe due to its industrial and agricultural productivity.

Hamilton is set atop ledges overlooking scenic Lake Ontario, Hamilton is Canada's third largest port and caters to a flourishing manufacturing trade. Known as the nation's "Steel Capital," tours of these modern foundries are among the city's foremost attractions.

Complementing this progressive industrial climate are a host of cultural offerings. One such diversion is the widely acclaimed Royal Botanical Gardens with over 2,000 acres of exquisite floral dis-

Maple Leaf - Genesee River, Rochester, New York
BRUCE FINGERHOOD

plays. Here, too, is the magnificent Dundurn Castle, its splendid furnishings and appointments reflecting the opulent lifestyle of its mid-19th century inhabitants. Of particular interest to sports fans is the Canadian Football Hall of Fame where over 100 years of gridiron history is brought to life through a variety of electronic exhibits.

0:16 (0:14) Ivor Wynne Stadium on left is home field for Canadian Football League's Hamilton Tigercats.

0:25 (0:05) Emerge on shoreline of Hamilton Harbour, a scenic inlet of Lake Ontario. Countless high rises line harbor's edge, overlooking menagerie of commercial and pleasure boats alike. Train winds about waterfront, eventually settling on northeastern tack towards Toronto.

0:30 (0:00) Arrive Aldershot.

ALDERSHOT, ONT. - This stop serves both the industrial city of Hamilton as well as its lakefront resi-

dential neighbor Burlington.

0:00 (0:12) Depart Aldershot.

0:04 (0:08) Mall at right is in community of Burlington.

0:08 (0:04) Industrial area surrounding Oakville bears profusion of refineries and other petro-related operations.

0:11 (0:01) Cross high over nicely landscaped Sixteen-Mile Creek.

0:12 (0:00) Arrive Oakville.

OAKVILLE, ONT. - In the mid-19th century, a host of city-dwellers chose this scenic locale as the site of their summer homes. Most of these lavish retreats have been immaculately preserved and today are the focal point of a well-documented walking tour. Another interesting attraction is the Gairlock Gardens Gallery, maintained in a 1920s mansion along the lake. Its wild bird sanctuary is a further highlight.

For golfing enthusiasts, the Glen Abbey links, designed by Jack Nicklaus, is of true championship caliber. Its clubhouse was once a monastery and now is home to the Canadian Golf Hall of Fame.

0:00 (0:23) Depart Oakville.

0:02 (0:21) Ford Ontario Truck Plant on left operates private trains for touring this sprawling complex. Automobile carriers by the hundreds line both sides of main line.

0:07 (0:16) At Port Credit, cross Credit River as it flows into Lake Ontario on right.

0:10 (0:13) Cross Etobicoke Creek.

0:11 (0:12) Somewhat faded hippopotamus whimsically adorns facade of Hippo Oil Company on immediate right.

0:13 (0:10) Numerous strings of coaches and other passenger cars stand in VIA rail yard on right.

0:15 (0:08) Approaching Toronto, cross Humber River as it, too, empties into lake. On forward right, downtown skyline boasts a fascinating array of unconventional designs, with dynamic CN Tower a most distinctive landmark.

0:16 (0:07) On right, amphitheater poised on lake's edge is handsome attraction of Ontario Place—a cultural, recreational and entertainment complex built atop three man-made islands.

0:17 (0:06) Elaborate facilities on right are annual home of Canadian National Exhibition, the Canadian equivalent of American state fairs.

0:19 (0:04) Historic Fort York Park on right features restored British garrison from War of 1812.

0:21 (0:02) Bulbous Sky Dome, on right, overshadows all else. Built in 1989 at a cost of $400 million to house baseball's Toronto Blue Jays, it has roof that can be retracted on nicer days.

0:22 (0:01) On right, Canadian National train is appropriate focal point of mural on walls of CN Tower.

0:23 (0:00) Arrive Toronto.

 TORONTO, ONT. - See page 360.

Lake Shore Limited

The historic "Water Level Route" of the old New York Central System is now the path of the Lake Shore Limited, one of Amtrak's three New York-Chicago trains. The trip, which traces through some of this country's very beginnings, might well serve as a refresher course in America's struggle for her political and economic independence.

From New York City, the tracks head northward up the eastern shore of the stately Hudson River until reaching Albany where they veer westward across upper New York State following the Mohawk Valley and the Erie Canal. Upon reaching Buffalo, the route borders the south shore of Lake Erie (hence the name Lake Shore Limited) before slicing across northern Indiana to reach Chicago. Although Boston passengers miss the Hudson River trip, they have the soft, rolling Berkshires of western Massachusetts as a substitute.

The Lake Shore Limited started as an experiment when Congress authorized its tentative start-up in 1975. The train immediately became a permanent and important part of Amtrak's service. Its 18½-hour schedule doesn't equal the 16-hour sprints performed in the late thirties by those 20th Century Limiteds powered by Henry Dreyfuss-streamlined 4-6-4 Hudson steam locomotives, but, on the other hand, those heroic trains of yore didn't have to contend with as many intermediate stops or regulatory-imposed speed limits. Nor does the Lake Shore offer a "Barber,

Fresh Salt Baths, Valet, Ladies' Maid, Manicurist and Stenographer" as advertised by the New York Central for its "Centuries" as early as 1912 on what was then touted as the "fastest train in the world." Today's Lake Shore is no slacker, however, whisking you from a New York City evening to a Chicago lunch in more comfort than that offered by any other mode of transport.

Westbound Schedule (Condensed)
New York, NY - Midevening Departure
Boston, MA* - Late Afternoon Departure
Albany-Rensselaer, NY - Late Evening
Buffalo, NY - Early Morning
Cleveland, OH - Early Morning
Toledo, OH - Late Morning
Chicago, IL - Midafternoon Arrival

Eastbound Schedule (Condensed)
Chicago, IL - Early Evening Departure
Toledo, OH - Middle of the Night
Cleveland, OH - Middle of the Night
Buffalo, NY - Early Morning
Albany-Rensselaer, NY - Midmorning
Boston, MA* - Late Afternoon Arrival
New York, NY - Midafternoon Arrival

*By separate section between Boston and Albany-Rensselaer.

Frequency - Daily.
Seating - Heritage Fleet coaches.
Dining - Complete meal and beverage service between New York and Chicago. Tray meals between Boston and Albany. Lounge between New York and Chicago.
Sleeping - Heritage Fleet with roomettes

and bedrooms. Slumbercoach with economy sleeping rooms between Boston and Chicago.

Baggage - Handled at most stations.

Reservations - Reservations required.

Length of Trip - 959 miles in 19 hours (New York to Chicago)

Route Log

For route between New York City and Albany-Rensselaer, see that portion of Adirondack log, page 51.

 BOSTON, MA - See page 27.

0:00 (0:05) Depart Boston's South Station. Huge central post office facility appears on left.

0:02 (0:03) On left, building signage modestly proclaims "Gillette World Shaving Headquarters."

0:05 (0:00) Slowly slip below grade before arriving Boston's Back Bay Station.

BOSTON (BACK BAY), MA - This station serves Boston's rather elegant Back Bay and surroundings. At one time, much of this area was covered by water from the Charles River, forming vast mud flats. Long thought to be a liability, the land was eventually reclaimed to become a very viable part of the city.

0:00 (0:28) Depart Back Bay Station. Continue below grade for brief time as train continues westward.

0:15 (0:14) Leave last of Boston's sprawling suburbs and enter rural Massachusetts, liberally splotched with pine forests and towns.

0:28 (0:00) Arrive Framingham.

FRAMINGHAM, MA - Long a manufacturing community. A General Motors assembly plant employs a large segment of today's populace.

0:00 (0:28) Depart Framingham.

0:12 (0:16) Under Interstate 495 which skirts western edge of Boston metropolitan area.

0:25 (0:03) Approaching Worcester, glimpse of Quinsigamund Lake is afforded on right.

0:28 (0:00) Arrive downtown Worcester.

WORCESTER, MA - One of the larger manufacturing cities in the Northeast, this city rightfully has considerable community pride in both its past and present. Isaiah Thomas, one of the outstanding printers of the 18th century, lived in Worcester. Old Sturbridge Village, a reconstructed 19th century village, is nearby.

0:00 (1:15) Depart Worcester and cross gentle, rolling countryside of central Massachusetts.

0:47 (0:28) Train accompanies Quaboag River on right for several miles.

0:55 (0:20) Frothy falls in Chicopee River on right add to countryside charm.

1:15 (0:00) Arrive Springfield's grey brick depot, named one of Amtrak's four worst stations in 1972. Fortunately, 1973 remodeling raised it from that lowly classification.

SPRINGFIELD, MA - Another important manufacturing city of the Northeast, Springfield had its start as a mere trading post in the 1630s. In 1794 the United States opened an important armory here, now the Springfield Armory Museum. Today, the Basketball Hall of Fame is located here, and the Strategic Air Command has operations at Westover Air Force Base just northeast of town.

0:00 (1:05) Depart Springfield.

0:01 (1:04) Crossing broad Connecticut River, note grand stone-arched Memorial Bridge paralleling tracks off to left.

0:04 (1:01) Train rattles through Conrail freight yards in West Springfield.

0:39 (0:26) Deciduous trees of Chester Blanford State Forest and Westfield River combine for idyllic western Massachusetts scenery.

0:40 (0:25) Immense, abandoned roundhouse on left is nostalgic glimpse of railroad's former dominant presence in this locale.

0:42 (0:23) "S" curves, rock cuts and abandoned stone bridges continue to embellish scenery.

0:50 (0:15) Cross famous Appalachian Trail as train approaches Pittsfield.

1:05 (0:00) Arrive Pittsfield.

 PITTSFIELD, MA - This is the very heart of New England's ski country. More than 40 ski areas, most with floodlights and ski-making equipment, saturate western Massachusetts. In addition to the attraction of skiing—golf courses, lakes, cultural events and spectacular fall colors make Pittsfield a year-round resort area. Herman Melville wrote his monumental novel "Moby Dick" while living here. The Boston Symphony performs during the summer months at beautiful Tanglewood.

0:00 (0:58) Depart Pittsfield.

0:06 (0:52) Richmond Pond immediately on left is one of many scenic Berkshire lakes in region.

0:16 (0:42) Enter New York and leave Massachusetts as train winds its way through Taconic Range.

0:17 (0:41) Darkness pervades while passing through State Line Tunnel. Now abandoned north bore dates back to 1840, while larger south bore was constructed during line upgrading in 1912. Years ago, watchman was stationed here to keep ice from building up on tracks inside tunnels.

0:27 (0:31) Over attractive Taconic Parkway.

0:34 (0:24) Train now brushes past quaint, old Chatham, on left.

0:58 (0:00) Arriving Albany-Rensselaer (station is actually in Rensselaer across river from Albany), downtown Albany skyline stands out on left. Prominent 42-story skyscraper is centerpiece of Empire State Plaza. Left of tower, low-slung Cultural Education Center houses State Museum and Library, while on right, dynamic elliptical structure is Center for Performing Arts. Four smaller towers in background are also part of this ambitious billion-dollar project. Once in station, inspiring domed archways of St. John the Baptist Catholic Church can be seen protruding above treetops on right.

For route between New York City and Albany, see that portion of Adirondack log, page 51.

 ALBANY, NY - See page 54.

0:00 (0:22) Departing Albany-Rensselaer, reassume westerly tack that will essentially follow route of historic Erie Canal.

0:04 (0:19) Cross Hudson River. On left,

ornate spires and turrets adorn magnificent State University Administration Headquarters. Originally built in 1916 as corporate offices of Delaware & Hudson Railroad, complex is actually three buildings interconnected, with Flemish facades maintaining delightful continuity throughout. Replica of Henry Hudson's "Half Moon" is highlight of weather vane perched atop main tower.

0:05 (0:17) Intriguing amalgam of modern and classical architecture is a most striking feature of Albany's city center on left.

0:06 (0:16) A familiar emblem for many years, large black and white mutt looms protectively above RCA facility on right.

0:07 (0:15) August 9, 1831, one of North America's earliest steam locomotives made its inaugural run between Albany and Schenectady when Mohawk & Hudson's De Witt Clinton, pulling three stagecoach-appearing cars, chugged up this grade—steepest on Water Level Route. Mohawk & Hudson was first railroad chartered in United States.

0:10 (0:10) On outskirts of town, four lonesome high rises comprise State Office Building campus on left.

0:11 (0:09) Shoreline of Rensselaer Lake adjoins trackside on right.

0:18 (0:04) Approaching Schenectady, attractively landscaped parkways dissect sprawling grounds of General Electric industrial park on left. Number of people employed by regional GE operations is about equal to one-third of Schenectady's population.

0:19 (0:00) Arriving Schenectady where tall, gold-domed City Hall clock tower is prominent fixture on right.

SCHENECTADY, NY - Emerging from the heart of the Industrial Revolution, Schenectady became known as "the city that lights and hauls the world." The American Locomotive Company's Schenectady Works and Thomas Edison's Machine Works were primarily responsible for this designation, the latter eventually evolving into the colossal General Electric Corporation.

Schenectady's "Stockade District" is a premier historical attraction, representing one of the country's best-preserved enclaves of early-American architecture and culture. Its name stems from the original 1661 settlement which was surrounded by a stockade to guard against French and Indian attacks.

0:00 (1:11) Departing Schenectady, elevated track bed now affords encompassing view of one of nation's oldest communities.

0:01 (1:10) Cross Mohawk River.

0:08 (1:03) Marker buoys bob conspicuously in midst of Erie Canal which joins on left and follows intermittently to Rochester. In early days, freight and passenger vessels were drawn along this scenic passage by teams of horses, tugging from paths alongside canal.

The Erie Canal was once the major trade passage between the Atlantic Ocean and the Great Lakes, handling a continuous stream of staples such as grain, lumber and coal, and the westward migration of thousands of Americans. Many called it the Eighth Wonder of the World. But like most things, the canal has been changed by time. The railroads, the New York State Throughway and the St. Lawrence Seaway have reduced the canal to more of an historic artifact than a vital trade artery. Today, only an occasional barge load of molasses, asphalt or gasoline can be seen floating through one of the locks, while each year 120,000 pleasure boats take advantage of its no-fee-for-use policy.

New York State spends 115 million dollars a year to keep its present-day barge canal system going, a system made up of the Erie, Oswego, Champlain and Cayuga Seneca canals. Critics contend the canals have outlived their usefulness as instruments of commerce, but so far, preservationists and other supporters have prevailed, arguing that their historic value is worth the expense, not to mention the canals' roles in irrigation, flood control, domestic water supply and tourism.

Even in 1817 when the Erie's construction had just begun, it had its detractors. No less than Thomas Jefferson called it "little short of madness" to start such a project in America's infancy. Jefferson was probably right. America had virtually no workers familiar with canal building, and worse, precious few engineers. If it hadn't been for an American engineer by the name of Canvass White, who walked 2,000 miles of British canals and persuaded an Irish construction engineer named J. J. McShane to come to New York to help, the canal might well have failed.

On October 26, 1825, the impossible project was finished. A 353-mile-long ditch, 40 feet wide at the top, 28 feet wide at the bottom, and four feet deep had been dug from Albany on the Hudson to Buffalo on Lake Erie. Eighty-three locks were necessary to raise traffic from Albany's elevation to Lake Erie, some 571 feet higher. A six-week trip from New York to Buffalo had just been shortened to a ten-day excursion by "fast packet boat." The impact would be immense. A trade route had been created that would make New York the financial center of the world and its port the largest on the East Coast. (And Buffalo would quickly grow from a village to a city of 18,000.)

Amidst great ceremony, Governor Dewitt Clinton, whose dream was now a reality, opened the canal at Buffalo. Cannons had been placed at 10-mile intervals along the entire route between Buffalo and New York City to relay the good news of completion (telegraphy was still a few years away). At 10 a.m. the first salvo was fired and by 11:30 that same morning the last of the cannons was fired, announcing to New Yorkers that the Erie Canal was complete.

Most of what can be seen today, however, is not the original Erie Canal. The original was enlarged in the mid-1800s, widening it to 70 feet and deepening it to 7½ feet, an improvement that allowed for 240-ton-capacity barges—an eight-fold increase. This followed the original route, except at Schoharie Crossing. But the biggest change came between 1905 and 1918 when the canal was modernized as part of the State Barge Canal System. Techniques had been developed to control the currents of the Mohawk River. Its channel was deepened to 12 feet and the river virtually became the canal. This resulted in a near-total abandonment of the first waterway, which generally followed the river's edge. Only remnants of the original Erie can occasionally be spotted from the train.

0:09 (1:02) Pass through Hoffmans where

Mohawk River ferry crossing was established in late 1700s.

0:12 (0:59) On left, shipping locks spanning canal are first of several sets seen along route. Across river, grand window arches highlight old, intriguing Adirondack Power and Light facility.

0:15 (0:55) Passing through Amsterdam, architectural devotees will discover veritable bonanza in variety of classic dwellings, here in another cradle of early Americana.

Amsterdam owes much to the Johnson family who early on cultivated the friendship of the native Indians. This alliance proved most fortuitous in combating attacks during the French and Indian War. Without this support, the Mohawk Valley today might well be a French Canadian province.

On the west edge of town, Guy Park is on the left with a mansion built by Sir William Johnson for his daughter Molly. It was Sir William who organized the Iroquois to fight for the British during the French and Indian War.

0:17 (0:54) Lock Eleven, adjacent to Guy Park and just beyond Johnson Mansion, lifts and lowers vessels a total of 12 feet. Bridge-like structure is used to lift sections of dam to control water level in summer and prevent freeze damage during canal's winter-month closures. To right of tracks, note red Volkswagen precariously perched atop brick chimney, somehow placed there to tout body shop below.

0:18 (0:53) Just beyond stone fence on right is red-shuttered Georgian-style "Fort Johnson," built in 1749 and first home of Sir William. Although no battles were fought here, thick walls contained 18 guns ports—just in case. Besides serving as a military post, it sheltered important Indian council meetings in late 1750s. Sir William's family remained Loyalists, however, and fled to Canada when Revolutionary War threatened their freedom.

Located nearby is the famed Auriesville Shrine which commemorates the martyrdom of three French missionaries who were persecuted, then slain while attempting to convert the Indians in the mid-1600s. A large coliseum was erected here in 1931 to accommodate the many worshippers who gather here.

After Amsterdam, idyllic farms and dairylands are scenically interwoven into a lush, pastoral tapestry with quaint little communities interspersed throughout.

0:19 (0:52) Schoharie Creek, which drains into Mohawk from south, once created slackwater that posed problems for early "canalers." Solution, in 1841, was to build a stone aqueduct which carried boats above creek. Roman aqueduct-appearing ruins can be glimpsed on left.

0:22 (0:49) On right, picturesque creek meanders through splendid dairy farm. Statue of gleaming white steed stands proudly in foreground of adjacent horse farm.

0:39 (0:32) Passing through Nelliston, impressive row of Italianate homes on right has been enshrined in National Register of Historic Places. Immediately thereafter, stone marker across river commemorates stronghold of Fort Plain, once valley headquarters for Revolutionary Army.

0:41 (0:30) On right, charming Old Palatine Church sits amidst fairy-tale setting along banks of Caroga Creek. Built in 1770, church was spared during Revolutionary raids with Tory parishioners purportedly bearing influence on its survival. Today, Palatine remains only pre-Revolutionary church standing west of Schenectady and stands as "the shrine of Lutheranism in the Mohawk Valley."

0:44 (0:27) Just before St. Johnsville, decaying remnants of 18th-century tavern can be spotted on right.

0:52 (0:19) Old mill town of Little Falls is location of Lock 17, highest "single locking" on New York's Barge Canal System—a 40-foot lift.

0:53 (0:18) West of Little Falls, industrial operations begin intruding on landscape. Although many beautiful vistas remain, scenery never quite recaptures sublime enchantment of earlier route.

1:00 (0:11) Just beyond Herkimer, through trees on right, used hearse dealer's sales lot is bizarre scene.

1:07 (0:04) Approaching Utica, cross over Barge Canal and elaborate set of shipping locks.

1:11 (0:00) Arrive Utica through industrial district of which General Electric plant is most prominent member. Half-million-dollar preservation effort was expended at station in 1988 to maintain this once-glorious structure. Marble floors and columns enhance interior of one of America's finest depots.

UTICA, NY - Transcending generations from the original immigrant settlers, Uticans still pride themselves on a strong work ethic that remains the backbone of a vibrant industrial economy. A proud respect for history pervades the community as well, and is reflected in several of Utica's oldest institutions that have been preserved and adapted to modern uses. One such landmark is the Utica Steam Engine and Boiler Works, an 1831 industrial plant that has been converted into a workshop for American and European sculptors. Another example is "The Stanley," a grand old movie palace refurbished to house Utica's Center for the Performing Arts.

0:00 (0:43) Depart Utica.

0:10 (0:33) Obelisk atop hill at left commemorates one of bloodiest Revolutionary War encounters, the Battle of Oriskany. Here, a column of 900 patriots under General Herkimer, trying to reach a besieged Fort Stanwix, engaged General St. Ledger's Army of 1,700 British and Indians. Although Herkimer's forces eventually retreated, arrival of reinforcements and survival of Ft. Stanwix resulted in ultimate withdrawal of St. Ledger to Canada. Two months later, General Burgoyne's forces, surrounded and cut off at Saratoga and failing to receive help from St. Ledger, surrendered to General Horatio Gates.

0:14 (0:29) Entering Rome, sculpture atop Paul Revere brass factory on right portrays "midnight ride" of this famous patriot.

Not only presently noted for its prolific copper production, Rome, too, boasts a fascinating historical heritage. Fort Stanwix, reconstructed on its original site in the downtown district, commemorates the Battle of Oriskany. Legend maintains that the "Stars and Stripes" were first unfurled in battle during this critical engagement. Inspired by these events, the "Pledge of Allegiance" was later penned by local resident Francis Bellamy. On July 4, 1817, Rome was assured further recognition when ground was broken here, commencing construction of the Erie Canal.

After leaving Rome, Canal makes another brief appearance on right.

0:37 (0:06) In downtown Canastota, Canal Town Museum on right has most extensive collection of Erie Canal memorabilia. First motion picture machine was developed in Canastota by Harry Marvin and Herman Casler, inventors of Wurtoscope once seen in every penny arcade in America.

0:38 (0:05) Just a mile or so south of here is Chittenango, birthplace of Lyman Frank Baum, author of "The Wonderful Wizard of Oz." Also, meagre limestone, a cement which hardens under water, was uncovered near here by Erie Canal builder Canvass White. Discovery was important to successful completion of canal.

0:43 (0:00) Arriving Syracuse, nice residential area on left overlooks bustling activity of Conrail yards.

SYRACUSE, NY - Long known as "Salt City," Syracuse traces its industrial roots to one Simon LeMoyne, a French missionary who, in the mid-1600s, noted the peculiar taste in the waters of Onondaga Lake. Although Indians attributed this to evil spirits, it was only a matter of time before the majority of American table salt was produced from this region. Early production techniques are demonstrated at the Salt Museum located here.

Another fascinating attraction is the Canal Museum. Housed in an 1849 "weighlock," the building is equipped with scales that formerly determined tariffs for passage on the Erie Canal.

0:00 (1:24) Depart Syracuse.

0:03 (1:19) Buildings of LeMoyne College are silhouetted atop bluffs on left.

0:06 (1:17) On left, staid neighborhood of older homes surrounds extensive cemetery.

0:08 (1:15) Pass MacArthur Stadium on right, home of minor league baseball's Syracuse Chiefs.

0:09 (1:14) Shores of Onondaga Lake come briefly into view on right.

0:14 (1:09) Race track is most notable feature of New York State Fairgrounds on right.

0:31 (0:52) Just west of Weedsport, canal rejoins on right.

0:33 (0:50) Cross canal, first of several times, as train re-emerges on rolling farmlands. Apple orchards are also seen frequently along this stretch. Area was one of more trying stretches for canal workers who labored in waist-deep, malaria-infested waters of Montezuma Swamp.

0:39 (0:44) Colonial splendor of Clyde is quickly reminiscent of earlier delights. West of town, small cemetery sits tranquilly along banks of canal.

0:58 (0:25) At East Palmyra, dairy farm and small church are poised together in picture-postcard setting atop knoll on left.

1:01 (0:22) Pass through Palmyra. Just four miles south is Hill of Cumorah where, according to Mormon theology, Moroni, last survivor of a great American civilization, buried a set of gold plates recording history of the peoples. As an angel, he delivered these plates to Joseph Smith who, in 1827, translated them into the Book of Mormon. Smith's former farmstead is just southeast of town.

1:12 (0:11) Farmlands quickly give way to industrial climes entering Rochester. Chickering and Sons is famous piano manufacturer on left.

1:18 (0:05) Approaching downtown hub, verdigris-topped clock tower on left is named in honor of Hiram Sibley, founder of Western Union.

1:23 (0:00) Arrive modernistic Rochester station. Tall, distinguished building on right houses international headquarters of Eastman Kodak, world-renowned manufacturer of cameras and film. A multitude of Kodak facilities dispersed throughout city employ over 50,000 people.

ROCHESTER, NY - Set on the banks of the lovely Genesee River, Rochester has come to be known as the "Picture City"—a reference to the illustrious Eastman Kodak Company which was founded here in 1880. Kodak still maintains its international headquarters here, and together with associated operations, comprises the mainstay of the local economy.

One of Rochester's premier attractions is the George Eastman House, home of

Mohawk - below Bear Mountain Bridge
ROBERT A. LAMAY

71

Kodak's founding father. This magnificent Georgian mansion now houses the International Museum of Photography. Here, the evolution of photography is explained through fascinating exhibits of prints and equipment. Specialty collections are also maintained for scrutiny by serious scholars.

Rochester is also home of the National Technical Institute for the Deaf, one of two such colleges in the nation. Its on-campus theater offers many "signed" productions throughout the year.

0:00 (0:54) Depart Rochester across Genesee River. Wing-like protrusions atop Times Square Building on left reflect contemporary trend of recent downtown development.

0:05 (0:49) Endeavors of General Railway Signal Company on left are important facet of safe and timely journeys. Immediately thereafter, cross Erie Canal before skirting atop colossal crater of Limestone Dolomite mining operation on right.

0:24 (0:30) A few miles west of Bergen, woodlands begin thinning and hills dissipate into relatively flat agricultural terrain.

0:37 (0:17) Batavia has two claims to historic fame. One of America's biggest land deals occurred in 1791 when Robert Morris (a signer of the Declaration of Independence) purchased a four-million-acre "farm" (it was most of what is now western New York) from Massachusetts for $333,333.33. Later six Dutch bankers purchased most of that land with an eye to re-selling it to pioneers, a tract that became known as The Holland Purchase. A museum in Batavia now preserves artifacts from that time. Then, along these tracks in May of 1893, a world speed record was set by a steam-powered passenger train which reached 112.5 miles per hour. Never before had humans traveled in excess of 100 miles per hour.

0:45 (0:09) At Lancaster, prison on left and guard shacks on right comprise facilities of Alden Penitentiary.

0:48 (0:06) Airplane sculpted from old garbage cans is amusing attraction of Lancaster Air Park on right.

0:54 (0:00) Arrive Buffalo (Depew Station).

BUFFALO, NY - Situated on the eastern shores of Lake Erie, and across the Niagara River from Canada, Buffalo is New York's second largest city with a population approaching 400,000. The metropolitan region represents one of the largest manufacturing centers in the U.S. with steel, chemicals, auto parts and flour production a sampling of its major industries. Railroading is also an important facet of the Buffalo economy, with a large number of separate lines maintaining offices in the city.

Although frequently the butt of cruel jokes—"There are two seasons in Buffalo, winter and the 4th of July," or to quote from *A Chorus Line,* "Suicide in Buffalo is redundant"—Buffalo offers a wide range of cultural opportunities. The Albright-Knox Art Gallery and Buffalo Zoo are consistently rated among the nation's finest. Buffalo, too, is an avid sports mecca, and supports major-league franchises in football and hockey.

0:00 (1:30) Depart Buffalo.

1:00 (0:30) Rumble through Brocton, birthplace of George Pullman whose name is synonymous with sleeping cars. Having made considerable money moving houses when Erie Canal was first widened, he went on to create an enterprise which became world's foremost producer and operator of sleeping cars.

1:15 (0:15) Enter Pennsylvania and leave New York. Darkness usually prevails during passage through Pennsylvania wine country. Out there somewhere lurk thousands of acres of vineyards. Nearby wineries include Penn Shore Winery, Presque Isle Wine Cellar, Heritage Wine Cellars and Mazza Winery, all located here in Erie County.

1:30 (0:00) Arrive Erie.

ERIE, PA - Located in the narrow neck of northwestern Pennsylvania, Erie is the state's only port on the lake by the same name. Freighters from around the world arrive and depart here daily, providing the city with its most important industry. This port was used by the American Navy as early as the War of 1812. Today, the Flagship Niagara, at the foot of State Street, recalls the stirring victory of Captain Perry over the British in 1813.

0:00 (1:28) Depart Erie.

0:22 (1:06) Enter Ohio and leave Pennsylvania.

0:27 (1:01) Former New York Central depot on left, another structure on National Register of Historic Places, now houses Connaught Historical Railroad Museum. Nickle Plate Road 2-8-4 Steam locomotive, hopper car and caboose repose just east of station.

1:28 (0:00) Arrive Cleveland.

CLEVELAND, OH - It is difficult to envision Cleveland as the capital of "Western Connecticut," but that was the plan in the late 1700s when Moses Cleveland was commissioned to chart the Connecticut Western Reserve, part of a land grant made by King Charles II. Today, Cleveland is the largest city in Ohio (nearly 2,000,000), with a higher concentration of "Fortune 1,000" corporations headquartered here, per capita, than any other U.S. city.

The city has had both the economic ability and the foresight to create a living environment that is to the city's credit. Myriad parks surround the city; the Cleveland Orchestra is one of the finest; and The Cleveland Museum of Art has one of the more outstanding collections of fine art in the world.

Amtrak Lakefront Station, 200 Cleveland Memorial Shoreway, is located on the edge of downtown and next to Cleveland Stadium. There are storage lockers, food and beverage vending machines, luggage carts and free parking adjacent to the station.

Cab stand at the station; Yellow and Zone Cab; 623-1500. **Loop bus** to downtown is one block from the station. **Rapid transit lines** (light rail service) extend from Terminal Tower downtown to: **Cleveland Hopkins Airport,** approximately ten miles from the downtown area; Windemere Station in East Cleveland; and Shaker Heights. **Local buses** also serve Greater Cleveland. For information, call Regional Transit Authority, 621-9500.

Convention and Visitors Bureau of Greater Cleveland, 3100 Terminal Tower, 44113. Call (216) 621-4110 or 800-321-1001.

Holiday Inn Lakeside, 1111 Lakeside Ave., 44114; (216) 241-5100. Three blocks from the station. $79.

Numerous attractions near the station include: **Port of Cleveland,** at the foot of West Third Street, where lake and oceangoing vessels load and unload 30 million tons of cargo each year; **Cleveland Stadium,** immediately behind the station, home of the Cleveland Brown's football team and baseball's Cleveland Indians; and **USS Cod,** a World War II submarine which sank 50 times her own weight in enemy shipping.

Hannah Fountain Mall, between Lakeside and St. Clair avenues across from the station, is Cleveland's major downtown public space; **The Arcade,** 401 Euclid Ave., a multi-storied enclosed mall in a unique architectural surrounding, is Cleveland's first shopping center (built in 1890), offering over 100 individual shops and spectacular views from iron-work balconies.

The **Cleveland Museum of Art,** 11150 East Boulevard, has some of the finest and best endowed art in the world.

0:00 (0:30) Depart Cleveland. Cleveland Stadium looms immediately on right while downtown is on left where pointed, 52-story Terminal Tower is clearly visible.

0:02 (0:28) Cross Cuyahoga River having dubious distinction of catching on fire before America became pollution conscious.

0:13 (0:16) Ford facility, then Goodyear plant are major Cleveland employers, on left. Then Cleveland's busy airport, Hopkins Field, is on right, just before International Exposition Center. Surroundings now become mostly residential before returning to rural Ohio.

0:30 (0:00) Arrive Elyria.

ELYRIA, OH - Named for Herman Ely who founded this city in 1817, Elyria has become one of the many industrially oriented communities of northern Ohio and home to the Easter Seal Society.

0:00 (0:31) Depart Elyria.

0:07 (0:24) Train zips through Amherst, allowing glimpse of two old coaches and caboose on exhibit by station at left.

Lake Shore Limited - near Peekskill, New York
SCOTT HARTLEY

Former New York Central depot is nicely preserved and is also on National Register of Historic Places.

0:13 (0:18) Cross Vermilion River where water tower greets visitors with words "Vermilion Sailors"—the name used by sports teams in this city that still has a commercial fishing fleet. Great Lakes Historical Society Museum is located on lakefront and has fine collection of Great Lakes shipping memorabilia.

0:19 (0:12) Glimpses of Lake Erie are afforded through trees on right.

0:22 (0:09) While in Huron County cross Huron River in town of Huron.

0:31 (0:00) Arrive Sandusky.

SANDUSKY, OH - Because of its fine Sandusky Bay, the city is one of Ohio's most important ports. This, too, is wine country where large quantities of grapes are grown locally. But, for at least three million annual visitors, the draw is venerable, old Cedar Point, an amusement park with more rides than any other park in North America.

0:00 (0:47) Depart Sandusky and pass through industrial area where such familiar names as Chrysler and Litton appear.

0:07 (0:40) Instead of skirting Sandusky Bay, tracks turn north to cross water before returning to a westward tack.

0:14 (0:33) Lake Erie makes its finale in distance on right.

0:18 (0:29) Davis-Bessie Nuclear Power Plant in far distance on right gives off massive steam plume.

0:28 (0:19) On right, enormous mounds of light grey material almost engulf town of Clay Center. These are mountains of screenings from White Rock Quarry that has been in operation since 1880s. Dolomite limestone is unearthed here and shipped throughout U.S. in sizes ranging from four-ton slabs to mere dust particles.

0:39 (0:08) Cross Maumee River as a myriad of industrial plants mark outer reaches of Toledo. Skyline is silhouetted behind bright blue suspension bridge on right.

0:47 (0:00) Arrive Toledo's Central Union

74

Terminal, on right.

 TOLEDO, OH - With a 35-mile-long harbor on Lake Erie, it is easy to understand why Michigan and Ohio both claimed this city in the early 19th century. It took presidential action by Andrew Jackson to finally settle the dispute—in Ohio's favor. (However, Michigan received its Wisconsin-connected Upper Peninsula as recompense.) Today, the city lays easy claim to being the world's leading producer of glass and glass products. A world-renowned collection of ancient and modern glassware is on display at the Toledo Museum of Art.

0:00 (0:53) Depart Toledo.

0:03 (0:50) Steeple-adorned, small brick church on right gives brightness to older residential neighborhoods.

0:13 (0:40) Holland, Ohio marks the end of Toledo's western suburbs. Landscape takes on more definite pastoral flavor as prosperous-appearing farms begin to dot countryside. Curveless stretch of track from here to Bryan is known as the "Air Line."

0:53 (0:00) Arrive Bryan.

 BRYAN, OH - This northwestern Ohio rural distribution center was at one time known as "The Fountain City" because of an abundance of artesian wells, some of which still flow.

0:00 (1:06) Depart Bryan.

0:04 (1:02) Solar panels mounted on ground, through trees on right, identify site of world's first solar-powered radio station, WQTC, which uses 33,600 photovoltaic cells and storage batteries to maintain a constant supply of power to the station's transmitter.

0:09 (0:57) Cross St. Joseph River.

0:13 (0:53) Enter Indiana and leave Ohio. Terrain soon becomes rolling for first time since leaving New York State.

0:15 (0:51) Several wheelless boxcars, perched on elevated rails, serve as ingenious storage sheds for plant on right.

0:43 (0:23) Train crosses, then follows meandering Elkhart River, forming a Currier and Ives setting.

1:06 (0:00) Arrive Elkhart. Note old GG-1 electric and steam locomotives of New York Central, on left, as well as numerous ancient rail cars.

 ELKHART, IN - More band instruments and mobile homes have been produced here than anywhere else in the world. Miles Laboratories (Alka-Seltzer) was founded here and the city remains the headquarters for this pharmaceutical giant. The mobile home industry was born here and still employs a large portion of the populace.

Elkhart County contains a large Amish and Mennonite population, and the Mennonite Historical Library at nearby Goshen boasts the world's largest collection of historical books and reference works pertaining to this Christian denomination. One of the Midwest's outstanding houses is Ruthmere, built circa 1909 by one of the founders of Miles Laboratories.

0:00 (0:20) Depart Elkhart.

0:16 (0:04) Gold dome, far distance right, locates campus of University of Notre Dame.

0:17 (0:03) Stretching for blocks on left is former Studebaker automobile plant where subsequent occupants have manufactured such diverse products as toys, postal vehicles, tools, auto bodies and hand-built Avanti motor cars. On right, watch for former Union Station.

0:20 (0:00) Arrive South Bend.

 SOUTH BEND, IN - Located on one of the southernmost bends of the St. Joseph River (hence the name), South Bend is a major Indiana manufacturing city. But most notably, it is the home of the 1,700-acre campus of the University of Notre Dame. In mid-September, there is a Sweet Sorghum Celebration with folk dancing, turn-of-the-century working implements, music, apple pie, and a Civil War re-enactment of "The Battle of St. Patrick's Landing."

0:00 (1:03) Depart South Bend. On right large Allied-Signal facility is original Bendix plant (now one of many) where this giant manufacturer of auto and air-crafts parts got its start. (Bendix was acquired by Allied-Signal in 1981.)

Gain one hour as train passes from Eastern to Central Time. Set your watch back (forward if eastbound) one hour.

0:40 (0:23) Bethlehem Steel Corporation facility appears on right.

0:45 (0:18) Tracks and catenary of legendary Chicago South Shore and South Bend run parallel to our Conrail right-of-way, off to left.

0:47 (0:16) Where Gary began, enormous U.S. Steel Gary Works stretch along tracks at right beyond rail yards.

0:57 (0:06) Inland Steel plants straddle tracks, plant Number One on left and Plant Number Two on right. Then cross drawbridge spanning Indiana Harbor Canal that links Lake Michigan with Calumet River.

0:59 (0:04) Standard Oil Company of Indiana refinery creates apparatus jungle at left. Lake Michigan is now only 100 feet or so to right.

1:03 (0:00) Arrive Hammond-Whiting.

 HAMMOND-WHITING, IN - Most of Amtrak's trains connecting to points east from Chicago make this their eastern metropolitan Chicago stop. The simple station on the right was built in 1982 at a cost of three million dollars.

0:00 (0:24) Depart Hammond-Whiting.

0:02 (0:22) Cross massive steel lift bridge over Calumet River. To left, Chicago Skyway reaches its peak over river, as around us huge bridges, grain elevators, and ships and boats of all sizes create a rugged industrial landscape.

0:04 (0:20) Roll along a wide right-of-way from which most of tracks have been removed.

0:05 (0:19) Skyway now rises on its steel supports beside us on left.

0:06 (0:18) Pass piggyback yards. Then, on right is foundation of demolished Englewood Station, from which, years ago, Pennsylvania and New York Central engineers raced each other away toward New York in a graphic symbol of their lines' competition.

0:07 (0:17) At right, spectacular view of Chicago skyline is afforded, including Sears Tower, world's tallest building, and John Hancock Building. Now roll across Dan Ryan Expressway (I-90/94) before ducking under Chicago's famous rapid transit—the "El."

0:12 (0:12) To our immediate right is modern replacement for older Comiskey Park, historic home of American Baseball League's Chicago White Sox.

0:14 (0:10) In Conrail piggyback yard at left, it's possible to see large cranes loading semitrailers from almost every major railroad in America onto flatcars.

0:16 (0:08) Cross South Branch of Chicago River before passing under Dan Ryan Expressway.

0:18 (0:06) To left, it's possible to see an entire train gliding slowly through Amtrak's washer building.

0:20 (0:04) Enter clean, modern Amtrak yards.

At right sit examples of nearly every kind of equipment Amtrak owns—coaches and cafes; diners and domes; sleepers, slumbercoaches, and Superliners; P30CH's and F40PH's—all being readied to equip Amtrak trains that roll across America from the Atlantic to the Pacific and from Lake Superior to the Gulf of Mexico. To the left, the Burlington Northern yards are home to a fleet of big green E-9 locomotives, refurbished relics of streamliner days, that now power silver, double-decker Regional Transportation Authority commuter cars between Chicago and the suburb of Aurora.

0:24 (0:00) Leave daylight as we lumber beneath Chicago's huge post office building just before arrival at Union Station.

 CHICAGO, IL - See page 128.

Other New York State Service

Various unreserved turboliner and Amfleet trains run on segments of the route between New York City and Niagara Falls, NY, with tray meals and snacks available. Checked baggage is not handled on these trains, but hand baggage may be carried on board. Several trains offer Custom Class seating.

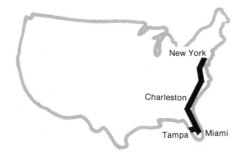

Silver Meteor

The Eastern Seaboard, where much of this country's richest heritage will be found, is visited almost from "top to bottom" by the Silver Meteor. Philadelphia, Washington, Richmond, Charleston, SC, and Savannah are just some of the historic salients of this trip through eastern America.

As early as 1939, the railroads recognized Florida as a strong market for Easterners wanting to enjoy warmer winters. In February of that year, the Silver Meteor was born when Seaboard Air Line commenced its streamliner service between New York and Miami.

And Florida has become one of Amtrak's best markets. There are now three daily trains between New York and Florida—the Silver Star, like the Meteor, also going to both Miami and Tampa, but taking a somewhat different course, and the Palmetto terminating at Jacksonville, Florida. This comparative abundance of service makes it possible to travel the entire distance without having to ride the train overnight, even though it takes more than 24 hours to get from New York to Miami. Unlike other Amtrak long-distance routes, it's possible to stop at, say, Charleston or Savannah in the evening, stay a night or two in one of those delightful cities, then continue on with a morning departure.

The entire trip between New York City and Miami, Amtrak's southernmost point, takes 26 hours. Tampa is served by a separate Meteor section between that city and Jacksonville, Florida.

Southbound Schedule (Condensed)
New York, NY - Early Evening Departure
Washington, DC - Late Evening
Richmond, VA - Middle of the Night
Charleston, SC - Early Morning
Savannah, GA - Midmorning
Jacksonville, FL - Early Afternoon
Tampa, FL - Early Evening Arrival*
Miami, FL - Late Evening Arrival

Northbound Schedule (Condensed)
Miami, FL - Early Morning Departure
Tampa, FL - Late Morning Departure*
Jacksonville, FL - Late Afternoon
Savannah, GA - Midevening
Charleston, SC - Late Evening
Richmond, VA - Middle of the Night
Washington, DC - Early Morning
New York, NY - Late Morning Arrival

*By separate section between Jacksonville and Tampa (through Orlando).

Frequency - Daily.
Seating - Amfleet II coaches.
Dining - Diner with complete meals and cafe or lounge car with sandwiches, snacks and beverages.
Sleeping - Heritage Fleet sleepers with bedrooms, roomettes and Slumbercoach with economy bedrooms between New York and Miami.
Baggage - Checked baggage handled at most stations.
Reservations - All-reserved train.
Length of Trip - 1,391 miles in 26 hours (New York/Miami).

Route Log

For route between New York City and Washington, DC, see that portion of Northeast Corridor log, page 30.

 WASHINGTON, DC - See page 38.

0:00 (0:17) Depart Washington southbound through regions whose roots trace back to earliest periods of American history.
0:02 (0:15) Emerge from tunnel after passing under Mall. Glimpses of Capitol and oldest Smithsonian structure ("The Castle") can be caught through various federal buildings on right.
0:07 (0:10) Perhaps Washington's most charming monument, Monticello-shaped Jefferson Memorial, resides among cherry trees of Tidal Basin, on right.
0:09 (0:08) Cross Potomac River paralleling 14th Street bridge. Washington National Airport is directly downstream to left. Back on right, Washington Monument, world's tallest masonry structure at 555.5 feet, punctuates horizon. Capitol's dome can still be seen toward rear on left.
0:10 (0:07) The Pentagon, headquarters for America's military establishment, is off to right, now mostly hidden by newer buildings.
0:12 (0:05) Glass high rises of Crystal City flaunt their starkness on right. Expansive RF&P rail yards are on left.
0:17 (0:00) Arrive Alexandria.

ALEXANDRIA, VA - This historic Washington suburb sits six miles south of the nation's capital, along the west bank of the Potomac River. Most noted for its outstanding examples of early American architecture, the Alexandria area is also replete with numerous national landmarks. Mount Vernon, beloved home and estate of George Washington from 1754 until his death in 1799, is just a few miles down the Potomac.

0:00 (1:34) Depart Alexandria.
0:01 (1:33) George Washington National Masonic Memorial, with museum of Washington memorabilia, dominates skyline on right.
0:09 (1:25) On right, Amtrak's northern Auto Train terminal handles Florida passengers who want to take their cars along—but not drive them until they get there.
0:10 (1:24) Cross inlet of Potomac River where barges can frequently be seen on right, and various small boats on left. Numerous Potomac inlets and coves can be seen on left for next 20 minutes.
0:26 (1:08) Virginia Electric Power Company's huge Possum Point generating station stands on far shore at left. Enter facilities of Quantico Marine Base (a flag stop for the Palmetto).
0:27 (1:07) Quantico Airfield can be seen on left.
0:29 (1:05) Leave Quantico Marine Base.
0:30 (1:04) Broad expanse of Potomac now stretches into distance to left.
0:31 (1:03) Cross small cove with final look at Potomac before becoming immersed in rolling, wooded interior of Virginia.
0:42 (0:52) Enter Falmouth where industrial and newer residential areas appear on northern outskirts of Fredericksburg.
0:44 (0:50) Cross Rappahannock River (the one George Washington supposedly threw a silver dollar across) and enter historic Fredericksburg (a stop for the Palmetto and the Silver Star).

The history of this city spans the better part of three centuries. John Smith visited here in 1608, George Washington grew up on a nearby farm, Thomas Jefferson and Patrick Henry met here with Washington to plan the nation's future, and three quarters of a million Civil War soldiers battled here. Of particular interest is the James Monroe Museum and Fredericksburg Battlefield.

0:47 (0:47) Twenty-foot-high stone pyramid on left commemorates "The Federal Breakthrough," one of many Civil War battles fought in this region. In December 1862, Union forces commanded by General Meade broke through Confederate lines, only to be repelled. Formerly known as Meade Pyramid, it is now more appropriately called "A Southern Memorial."
0:58 (0:36) Small white frame house on left with U.S. flag and large grassy area in front is Jackson Shrine, where Stonewall Jackson died on May 10, 1863 after being accidentally wounded by his own troops at Chancellorsville, some 27 miles away. His death would be a devastating blow to Lee's forces.

1:08 (0:26) Cross Mattaponi River.

1:21 (0:13) Cross small stream called Pamunkey River.

1:26 (0:08) Enter Ashland and experience charming encounter with an historic Virginia town, originally established by RF&P Railroad as a mineral springs resort. Train seems out of place as it glides past lovely antebellum and Victorian homes, while literally touching doorstep of Randolph-Macon College, on left. College was founded in 1830 in Boydton and moved here in 1868, and is parent of R-M Women's College in Lynchburg. Central business district, rebuilt after 1890s fire (unsuccessfully fought with fire trucks brought in from Richmond on railroad flatcars), contains old Crosses Market on left, while 1922 train station is on right. Just beyond station is reconstructed Henry Clay Inn, original having been built at turn of the century.

1:29 (0:05) Decaying Forest Lodge Hotel, with its four stories of bleached lapboard and ornate balconies, stands on right as forlorn monument to one man's unrealized dream. Constructed after Civil War by John Cussons, English adventurer and Confederate scout, this "luxury hotel" failed to capture imagination of rail travelers. Now largely abandoned and half original size, it once featured lakes, gardens and game preserve on 1,000 acres.

1:34 (0:00) Arrive Richmond, where very attractive modern station greets passengers on northern edge of city.

RICHMOND, VA - Overlooking the James River against a backdrop of rolling countryside, Richmond is truly a cradle of Americana infancy. Setting out from the first English settlement at Jamestown in 1607, Captains John Smith and Christopher Newport traveled up river and claimed the site of Richmond in the name of the Crown. The historical legacy that followed is vast.

In 1775, a convention met to determine delegates to the Second Continental Congress. The state capital was moved to Richmond in 1779 and remains here today. In 1781, Benedict Arnold turned traitor and attacked the town, forcing Governor Thomas Jefferson to flee to safer environs. Chief Justice John Marshall presided over the treason trial of Aaron Burr here in 1807.

In 1861, Richmond was established as the Capital of the Confederacy. Later, after learning of imminent attack, Confederate President Jefferson Davis would evacuate the city and have it burned, lest it fall intact into enemy hands.

Today, Richmond is still dedicated to the preservation of its illustrious heritage. It is said to have more monuments and museums than any other city in the South. Although tobacco has long been the basic economic staple, Richmond boasts a wide variety of industrial and manufacturing operations, producing the likes of chemicals, metals, and pharmaceuticals.

0:00 (0:33) Depart Richmond's station and proceed south through city.

0:08 (0:25) Large Richmond rail yards border main line.

0:14 (0:19) Cross high above James River on venerable Belt Line Bridge, as Interstate 95 spans river on right.

0:18 (0:15) Leave southern suburbs of Richmond.

0:23 (0:10) For next mile or two, acres of brick warehouses and assorted paraphernalia of Defense Central Supply Center line left side of track.

0:33 (0:00) Arrive Petersburg (Ettrick). Note nicely landscaped home made from converted rail car on left.

PETERSBURG, VA - Settled along the banks of the Appomattox River, Petersburg today is a flourishing mecca of tobacco and livestock trade. Yet some 120 years ago, this lush countryside was blighted beneath one of the Civil War's longest and bloodiest sieges.

For ten months, Lee and Grant struggled over this strategic rail hub. When Union forces eventually prevailed, Lee's surrender at Appomattox followed within weeks.

0:00 (1:23) Depart Petersburg (Ettrick).

0:01 (1:22) Virginia State University can be seen perched atop hill in far distance to left.

0:02 (1:21) Cross Appomattox River. Waters originate some 75 miles west of here near Appomattox Courthouse, where one of America's most somber dramas occurred on Palm Sunday in 1865—Lee's surrender to Grant, concluding the Civil

War. Upon crossing river, leave Ettrick which serves as stop for Petersburg, and enter Petersburg itself. Now cross high over line of Norfolk & Western Railroad.

0:06 (1:17) Clatter through CSX rail yards.

0:14 (1:09) Huge Enfield peanut operations are on right.

0:30 (0:53) Through Emporia and cross Meherrin River. It was along this stretch of track that, in December 1864, Warren's Corps attempted to permanently cut rail service to Confederate forces in Petersburg, disassembling miles of track and burning ties.

0:38 (0:45) Leave Virginia and enter North Carolina, America's leading tobacco producer. Plywood plant of Georgia Pacific, on left, marks border.

0:46 (0:37) Cruise high above Roanoke River. Stream has its origin in Blue Ridge Mountains of Virginia and, almost 400 miles later, drains into North Carolina's Albermarle Sound. Then over an intersecting freight line at Weldon (outskirts of Roanoke Rapids) linking Norfolk with Durham. This was at one time an important shipping point, freight being transferred between rail and oceangoing vessels which could navigate inland to this point. Note former station located on line below.

0:52 (0:31) One of South's principal products becomes apparent as cottonfields can be spotted along route.

1:22 (0:01) Cross Tar River. During a particularly fierce Civil War battle, Confederate troops from other states retreated, leaving North Carolinians to go it alone. Later, those that had remained to fight allowed that next time they would put tar on the heels of their faltering comrades so they would "stick better." North Carolinians are now known as Tar Heels.

1:23 (0:00) Rumble along Main Street upon arrival at Rocky Mount where old, picturesque three-story brick depot awaits those detraining on right.

ROCKY MOUNT, NC - Established in 1816, Rocky Mount has developed into one of the world's largest bright-leaf tobacco markets. Cotton and peanuts are also important crops that, together with a broad industrial base, ensure the city's status as a commercial core of the coastal plains.

0:00 (1:25) Depart Rocky Mount.

0:02 (1:23) For next several minutes, pass by sprawling rail yards on left.

0:20 (1:05) Through Wilson, where tobacco warehouses seem to be everywhere. Another bright-leaf tobacco center, its annual auction dubbed "The Greatest Show in Tobaccoland" provides a most unique tourist attraction. This is a stop for Amtrak's Palmetto and Carolinian.

0:35 (0:50) Tall, skinny sheds dotting the landscape, some with little chimneys jutting out from their tops, are tobacco curing barns.

0:44 (0:41) Through Selma. This small agricultural center is another stop for the Palmetto and Carolinian.

1:11 (0:14) One of area's larger cottonfields spreads out along route on left.

1:16 (0:09) Agriculture continues its dominance, as soybean fields now appear on both sides of tracks.

1:25 (0:00) Arrive Fayetteville, where 11-story Wachovia Bank Building on right (city's highest structure) anchors downtown. Region's tobacco barns apparently influenced architecture of depot on left.

FAYETTEVILLE, NC - Established by Highland Scots in 1739, Fayetteville is now a thriving tobacco, cotton and livestock trade center. During the Revolutionary War, Fayetteville served as a headquarters for Tory sympathizers. Fort Bragg military installation is located here.

0:00 (1:21) Depart Fayetteville.

0:05 (1:16) Pigs are major "crop" of agrarian operation on left.

0:23 (0:58) Farming heartland of North Carolina produces cotton, tobacco, soybeans and corn, all in evidence in this region surrounding Buie.

0:36 (0:45) Just after passing through Rowland, leave North Carolina and enter South Carolina, the Palmetto State. (Nickname derives from large number of Palmetto trees growing within state's borders —a palm-like tree looking somewhat like Southern California's joshua trees.) Watch for enormous, gaily decorated Mexican hat perched on tower of motel complex at "South of the Border." Here, impatient North Carolina couples take advantage of South Carolina's less stringent marital laws allowing them to tie the knot without red tape.

0:45 (0:36) Through Dillon, another stop for the Palmetto.

1:06 (0:15) Cross Great Pee Dee River.

1:21 (0:00) Arrive Florence amidst large CSX rail yards.

FLORENCE, SC - Cutting its teeth as a railroad town in the 1850s, Florence developed into a transportation center for goods and troops during the Civil War. It is still an important railroad center, functioning as a division point for the CSX.

And teeth are important to Florence. The town claims to be the denture capital of the world, with three clinics offering one-day service for false teeth, turning out 40,000 sets a year at about half the price found elsewhere.

0:00 (0:32) After departing Florence, watch for preserved steam locomotive on right, a minute or so from station.

0:08 (0:24) Cross Lynches River.

0:13 (0:19) Tobacco barns continue to be centerpieces of many fields that checker region.

0:16 (0:16) Prim little church facing tracks on left is nicely adorned by freestanding bell tower.

0:32 (0:00) Arrive Kingstree where wellpatronized restaurant occupies portion of train station.

KINGSTREE, SC - This agricultural center of 4,500 persons is the hometown of Dr. Joseph Goldstein, winner of the 1987 Nobel Prize for Medicine.

0:00 (0:50) Depart Kingstree, then cross over Black River.

0:14 (0:36) Cross Santee River, which traces northern border of Francis Marion Forest, almost 750 square miles of it. Forest lies on left side of tracks for next 10 or 15 minutes and stretches eastward across coastal plains until reaching Atlantic Ocean. It was named for an American Revolutionary War general whose quickstriking raids from Carolina's marshes earned him nickname of "Swamp Fox."

0:25 (0:25) Monolithic levee on left holds back waters of Lake Moultrie which in turn collects waters of larger Lake Marion.

0:29 (0:21) Cross broad Cooper River, an outlet for Lake Moultrie. Note coal-fired generating plant on right.

0:50 (0:00) Arrive at Charleston's rail station—actually in North Charleston, some distance from downtown.

CHARLESTON, SC - Dating back to the earliest days of Colonial settlement, Charleston has been deeply involved in the preservation of its abundant historical tradition. Set picturesquely at the confluence of the Ashley and Cooper rivers, quaint doll-house neighborhoods and exquisite gardens grace the avenues of this stately Southern seaport. Ironically, its post-Civil-War poverty prevented replacement of the city's old buildings which now bestow Charleston with both charm and elegance.

Founded in 1670 to offset Spanish intrusions further south, and named for King Charles II, Charleston was once regarded as the richest city in the South, combining an extensive Indian trade with a thriving export business of rice and indigo. Today the city remains an important manufacturing center for such diverse goods as fertilizer, paint, and clothing.

In the early 1800s, Charleston stood at the forefront of a pioneering railroad industry. The "Best Friend of Charleston" became the first American steam locomotive in regular service, commencing operations here in 1830.

Fort Sumter, located on the city's waterfront, became an historical landmark when it was fired upon in 1861, thus marking the start of the Civil War. The Citadel (the Military College of South Carolina), one of the last three state-operated military colleges in the nation, is located here. And Charleston's naval base is the third largest in the United States.

The intersection of Broad and Meeting streets brings together a most unlikely combination of City Hall, County Court House, U.S. Courthouse and St. Michaels Church; thus, appropriately dubbed "Four Corners of Law."

0:00 (0:46) Depart Charleston, pass beneath U.S. 52 and 78, then curve sharply to right avoiding spur that leads to downtown Charleston.

0:02 (0:44) Roll through Charleston's expansive rail yards for two or three minutes, then cross Ashley River. Ashley and Cooper (crossed earlier) discharge into Atlantic at Charleston, forming one of East Coast's finest harbors.

0:12 (0:34) Tidal lands of South Carolina's seaboard stretch out on left. For next several miles, numerous rivers and streams cluster together as they approach their final destination.

0:13 (0:33) Through Ravenel, where neat, prim white-painted station on right has served as temporary town hall since fire destroyed city's headquarters in 1990. Station is typical of those once found throughout the South. It had two waiting rooms—one white and one "colored."

0:26 (0:20) Cross Edisto River.

0:27 (0:19) This small hamlet of Jacksonboro once served as provisional capital of South Carolina while Charleston was under siege during American Revolution. The legislature met here in 1782 with sessions held in Masonic Lodge and Tavern.

0:30 (0:16) Then cross Ashepoo River.

0:42 (0:04) And finally, cross Combahee River.

0:46 (0:00) Arrive Yemassee.

 YEMASSEE, SC - This small community is named after the Yemassee Indian tribe that once populated this region. While tilling soil, farmers frequently discover arrowheads and pottery relics.

0:00 (0:45) Depart Yemassee.

0:05 (0:40) Under Interstate 95 which traverses entire East Coast, from Houlton, Maine on Canadian border to Miami.

0:06 (0:39) Cross broad Coosawhatchie River.

0:20 (0:25) Particularly charming Southern scene, with magnificent stand of Spanish moss-draped live oaks on left and palmettos with lovely mansion set back from tracks on right.

0:32 (0:13) Pass across very impressive Savannah River as we near city of same name—and "where Georgia began." We entered that state when we crossed the river.

0:45 (0:00) Arrive Savannah's rail station, located in western suburbs, about a 15-minute cab ride from downtown.

SAVANNAH, GA - Richly steeped in its colonial heritage, Savannah remains a city of grandeur and elegance as envisioned by its founding father, General James Edward Oglethorpe. It was estab-

Silver Meteor - Boynton Beach, Florida
BRIAN BANKS

82

lished in 1733 by the English as a buffer between the northern colonies and the Spanish in Florida.

Early efforts at raising silk proved a disappointment, but cotton and tobacco soon gave Savannah vitality. Oglethorpe tried to forbid "drinkers, slaves, Catholics and lawyers" from his new community, but it didn't matter—he got them all.

Today, ships from all over the world sail out of the Savannah River, many to retrace the route of the S.S. Savannah which departed here in 1819 to become the first steamship to cross any ocean.

Since its fall to General Sherman in 1864, preservation and restoration have been the bywords of this proud city, and the flavor of its colorful past is reflected at every turn.

Savannah's attractively remodeled **Amtrak station** is about six miles from downtown at 2611 Seaboard Coastline Drive. There are no nearby hotels, and cabs are the only way to reach downtown. There is free parking.

For arrival and departure information, call (912) 234-2611. For reservations and other information, call 800-USA-RAIL.

There is a **cab stand** at the station; Yellow Cab, 236-1133. **Travis Field,** Savannah's airport, is about six miles from the station.

Visitors Center, 301 W. Broad Street, is located in what was once a Georgia Central railroad station on the edge of downtown. Write Savannah Convention & Visitors Bureau, 222 W. Oglethorpe Ave., P.O. Box 1628, 31402. Call (912) 944-0456 or 800-444-2427.

Days Inn Downtown, 201 W. Bay St., 31401; (912) 236-4440. Adjacent to the riverfront and historic districts. $74.

-**Best Western Riverfront Inn,** 412 West Bay St., 31401; (912) 233-1011. On the riverfront next to the historic district. $66.

-**Quality Inn Heart of Savannah,** 300 W. Bay St., 31401; (912) 236-6321. Adjacent to the riverfront and historic districts. Continental breakfast. $63.

-**Liberty Inn,** 128 W. Liberty St., 31401; (912) 233-1007 or 800-637-1007. A restored colonial home in the historic district. $95.

-For information and reservations at several historic inns and guest houses, call 800-262-4667.

The **National Historic Landmark District** has more than 1,200 restored buildings, many of which were grand colonial homes, now renovated to provide lodging. This area comprises much of Savannah's downtown and near-downtown.

The **Riverfront Plaza,** composite of restaurants, pubs, and shops imaginatively housed in restored cotton warehouses, is in the heart of downtown. **River Street Train Museum,** 315 W. River St., has collection of antique and operating toy trains on display.

One of the best ways to see Savannah is by **city tour,** offered by various operators. Inquire at your hotel or the Visitors Center.

0:00 (0:50) Depart Savannah southbound into tall, densely wooded forests of southeastern Georgia.

0:06 (0:44) On left, skirt grounds of Hunter Army Airfield.

0:12 (0:38) Cross Ogeechee River, which flows into Atlantic Ocean about ten miles east of here.

0:13 (0:37) Pass through Richmond Hill. Nearby Fort McAllister was key to Savannah's fortifications during Civil War, fending off nine naval assaults before finally succumbing in Sherman's march to the sea. Also located here is Richmond Hill Plantation, a seasonal home built by Henry Ford during 1930s.

0:46 (0:04) Cross Altamaha River.

0:50 (0:00) Arrive Jesup.

JESUP, GA - Founded in 1870, the town was named in honor of Morris K. Jessup, a New York financier who personally subsidized the construction of a local railroad. The route would subsequently be incorporated into the Seaboard Coast Line and now the CSX.

Today, Jesup is an important distribution hub, centrally located among such large industrial meccas as Jacksonville, Savannah and Atlanta. Nearby popular tourist destinations include Brunswick and the Georgia Sea Islands. The Dogwood Festival, an annual springtime celebration, features songfests, concerts and crafts exhibitions.

0:00 (1:14) Departing Jesup, pass Wayne County Court House on left. Built in 1903, spire-topped clock tower crowns this quaint structure. On outskirts of town, logging and milling operations become frequent sights, bordering route into central Florida.

0:15 (0:59) Woodland beauty abounds as train crosses Big Satilla Creek.

0:18 (0:56) Cross Satilla River.

0:42 (0:32) Pass through Folkston, one of three points of access to primeval wilderness area known as Okefenokee Swamp.

0:45 (0:29) Crossing St. Mary's River into Florida, Colonial environs of past 1,000 miles are slowly supplanted by Spanish influence of an even earlier period.

1:14 (0:00) Arrive Jacksonville.

 JACKSONVILLE, FL - Unlike many other Floridian cities, Jacksonville is not a tourist resort. Rather, it has grown to become the state's leading industrial center, with a population nearing 750,000.

Although lying a few miles west of the Atlantic Ocean, Jacksonville is still an important seaport, with an interconnecting passage along the St. Johns River. Three beautiful beaches, directly east of town, provide a weekend haven for city dwellers.

For Tampa section, see Silver Star log starting Jacksonville, page 90.

0:00 (0:59) Depart Jacksonville. As train embarks on sweeping U-turn, tall steel bridges spanning St. Johns River are focal point of city scene on left. Soon, pass through Honeymoon Wye, then encounter CSX's huge Baldwin Yard.

Proceeding south, the diverse landscape of the Florida interior provides an ever-changing spectacle for the sightseer. Dense regions of tall pines and majestic palms stand admist an occasional marsh, but just as quickly give way to the rolling terrain of ranchlands and dairy farms.

0:44 (0:15) On right, Eastern cowpokes show their stuff at Bradford Roping Club Arena.

0:59 (0:00) Arrive Waldo.

 WALDO, FL - This stop affords access to the Gainesville area and University of Florida.

0:00 (0:43) Depart Waldo.

0:20 (0:23) Passing through Lochloosa, Lake Lochloosa can be seen on right.

0:29 (0:14) Thoroughbred horse farm on right features well-kept grounds and "official-size" track.

0:43 (0:00) Arrive Ocala.

OCALA, FL - As well as an agricultural community, the Ocala region boasts some of the nation's top thoroughbred concerns, with many facilities open to the public.

0:00 (0:25) Depart Ocala.

0:25 (0:00) Arrive Wildwood.

WILDWOOD, FL - Throughout much of year, fresh fruit is displayed atop old baggage carts at trackside, available for purchase by passengers.

0:00 (0:34) Depart Wildwood.

0:23 (0:11) Witness more densely wooded terrain over next few miles as train borders fringe of Withlacoochee State Forest.

0:34 (0:00) Arrive Dade City.

DADE CITY, FL - This stop has Amtrak Thruway bus connections to Tampa, Clearwater Beach, St. Petersburg and Sarasota.

0:00 (0:43) Depart Dade City.

0:32 (0:11) Through Lakeland, then note Minute Maid juicing plant on right.

This is the very heart of citrus country. A fifth of all citrus grown in the United States comes from this immediate area—that's a lot of orange juice. Lakeland is also the marketing center for Florida's entire crop. But one other product is as important as oranges and grapefruit. Most of the world's phosphate is mined nearby, almost all of it going into agricultural fertilizers.

Florida Southern College is located here where students study amidst the largest assemblage of buildings designed by Frank Lloyd Wright. The Detroit Tigers have enjoyed spring training here for years. (This is a stop for the Tampa sections of the Silver Star and the Silver Meteor.)

0:43 (0:00) Arrive Winter Haven.

WINTER HAVEN, FL - This is an excellent debarkation point to a multitude of family-oriented attractions, including Cypress Gardens, Walt Disney World and Epcot Center.

0:00 (0:38) Departing Winter Haven, cross canal that feeds Lake Ship on right— part of Chain-of-Lakes system surrounding Winter Haven region. Emerge now into heartland of citrus groves, with trees at times within picking distance of train.

0:08 (0:30) In far distance to left, 205-foot Bok Singing Tower is famous for its 57-bell carillon, ranging in weight from 17 pounds to nearly 12 tons. Tower is set in 128-acre Bok Tower Garden and is highest point on Florida's peninsula.

0:36 (0:02) Beautiful estates come right down to shoreline of Lake Jackson on right.

0:38 (0:00) Arrive Sebring.

 SEBRING, FL - Founded in 1912, Sebring is situated at the geographical center of Florida. The encompassing fertile terrain has nurtured a thriving agricultural economy.

0:00 (0:34) Depart Sebring.

0:15 (0:19) Lake Istokpoga makes brief appearance on right. Sebring auto track, famous for its course of flat curves laid out on a former World War II airfield, is located off to left.

0:26 (0:08) Cross Kissimmee River.

0:34 (0:00) Arrive Okeechobee.

 OKEECHOBEE, FL - This town's name is an Indian word meaning "plenty big water." Lake Okeechobee, largest in southern U.S., lies three miles south and is vital source of fresh water for Miami area.

0:00 (0:51) Depart Okeechobee.

0:23 (0:28) Passing through Indiantown, cross St. Lucie Canal, connecting Lake Okeechobee to Atlantic Ocean.

0:33 (0:19) On right, Pratt and Whitney plant is noted manufacturer of aircraft engines.

With the southeast coastline looming just ahead, the wide-open spaces of the last several hours are quickly displaced by the bustling activity of renowned beachfront resorts.

0:51 (0:00) Arrive West Palm Beach. While sitting in station, note numerous high rises dotting shores of Clear Lake on right.

 WEST PALM BEACH, FL - One of many popular retreats of southern Florida.

0:00 (0:20) Depart West Palm Beach.

0:03 (0:17) Palm Beach airport can be seen on right.

0:07 (0:13) Departure from Palm Beach area is highlighted by scenic canals interweaving throughout attractive residential property.

0:20 (0:00) Arrive Delray Beach.

DELRAY BEACH, FL - Commercial flower growing is a major industry in this tropical resort town.

0:00 (0:12) Depart Delray Beach.

0:05 (0:06) Boca Raton airport borders route on left.

0:12 (0:00) Arrive Deerfield Beach.

DEERFIELD BEACH, FL - Another vacation haven of Florida's southern coast.

0:00 (0:15) Depart Deerfield Beach.

0:07 (0:08) On right, note Pompano Beach Race Track.

0:14 (0:01) Just before arrival Ft. Lauderdale, highway underpass serves as homeless shelter where rows of "beds" can be seen.

0:15 (0:00) Arrive Ft. Lauderdale.

FT. LAUDERDALE, FL - A fort established during the Seminole Wars of 1830s gave its name to this now much-frequented seaside resort.

0:00 (0:09) Depart Ft. Lauderdale.

0:04 (0:05) On left, pass Ft. Lauderdale-Hollywood International Airport.

Cross numerous navigable canals over the next few miles. This area is often called the Venice of America.

0:09 (0:00) Arrive Hollywood.

HOLLYWOOD, FL - Real estate entrepreneur Joseph Young helped this town blossom in the early 1920s by maintaining a fleet of buses to help bring in prospective investors. Nearby is Okalee Village Seminole Indian Reservation.

Since Miami's train station is located in such a poor neighborhood, Hollywood is a reasonable alternative to continuing a few miles farther south to no-man's land. Hotels, car rentals and Tri-Rail are all here.

Rental cars are available from Springer Car Rental with station delivery and pick up; (305) 921-5530 or 800-327-4127. Tri-Rail, into Miami and north to West Palm Beach, stops at the station.

Intown Howard Johnson Lodge, I-95 & Hollywood Blvd., 2900 Polk St., 30020; (305) 923-1516. Small, attractive facility, one block east of the station. $74.

0:00 (0:19) Depart Hollywood.

0:04 (0:15) Tall resort hotels of Miami Beach vicinity jut above horizon on left.

0:18 (0:01) Black brushes of car washing mechanism are poised on siding at right.

0:19 (0:00) Arrive Miami, Amtrak's southernmost destination.

MIAMI, FL - There's always a perceptual reaction at the mere mention of the town's name—cops and cocaine, palms and plush. Miami is a soup that is often brought to a boil, a stew that is often called a modern Casablanca. *Newsweek* described it as "a jazzy, hectic mix of ethnicity, newfangled prosperity and foreign intrigue."

Miami has struggled with its problems and its image. And sometimes it's not always clear just who is winning. But there are still its Miami Beach resorts, particularly the Deco District hotels, its weather and its proximity to the mysterious Everglades and that stretch of tropical islands called The Keys. These endearments make it a place to visit, and tourism is still a dominant force here.

Miami got its start as a citrus-growing area in the 1890s after killing frosts had ruined much of the orange crops in central Florida. However, its start would not have been possible without Henry Flagler extending his railroad from central Florida into the Miami area. Then in the early 1920s, real estate development began to spur the city's growth.

The city is a major international transfer point, having a steady stream of foreign visitors passing through the city each year. Its southern location has contributed to a large Latin population giving the city a strong bilingual character.

Amtrak Station, 8303 NW 37th Ave., is located a considerable distance north of downtown in an industrial area of Hialeah. This is a very modern, attractive facility—incongruous in its environment. There is a large parking lot that is never utilized to any degree, since overnight parking is definitely not recommended. Because of the station's poor location and no rental cars or hotels nearby, rail travelers to Miami may consider the northerly suburb of Hollywood a logical place to detrain.

Even Tri-Rail, the regional commuter rail experiment between Miami and West Palm Beach, doesn't acknowledge the station but breezes past, preferring to stop a few blocks to the south where it intersects with Miami's Metrorail (an elevated, sleek rail system that has yet to live up to expectations).

The station has food and beverage machines, storage lockers, luggage carts and redcap service. The adjacent parking is free. For arrival and departure information only, call 835-1221.

Cab stand is at the station; Metro Taxi, 888-8888. **Local buses** stop at the station, Route L, which runs to Miami Beach via the 79th St. causeway with connections to **Metrorail** and **Tri-Rail** just south of the station at 79th Street. For local bus, Metrorail and Tri-Rail information, call 638-6700. **Rental cars** are at **Miami International Airport,** six miles (about a $10 cab ride) southwest of the station.

Convention and Visitors Bureau, 701 Brickell Ave., Suite 2700, 33131; (305) 539-3000 or 800-283-2707.

There are no hotels or motels very near the station, nor would it be likely anyone would stay there if there were. Logical accommodations for a single overnight are in the airport area where the nearest rental cars will also be found. As mentioned above, the cab ride to the airport is about $10.

-**Ramada Inn Miami Airport,** 5125 NW 36th St., Miami Springs, 33166; (305) 887-2153. Adjacent to airport, continental breakfast included. $69.

-**Days Inn Airport,** 3401 NW Le Jeune Rd., 33142; (305) 871-4221. Restaurant and free airport shuttle. $52.

The **Miami Beach** area, with its white sand beaches and handsomely restored Deco District, is an enjoyable place for a stroll or a week-long stay. For animal, fish and bird fanciers, consider these: **Metrozoo,** 124th Ave. and SW 152nd St., a newer zoo with unusually realistic environments for the various species on exhibit; **Miami Seaquarium,** southeast of downtown on Rickenbacher Causeway, the world's largest tropical oceanarium; and **Parrot Jungle & Gardens,** 11000 S. Red Road (57th Ave.) with exotic birds in a walk-thru tropical setting.

For those interested in 17th-century Italian architecture, there is **Villa Vizcaya,** 3251 South Miami Ave., a spectacular palace re-created by the late James Deering of International Harvester fame at a cost of $20 million, with European antiques, formal gardens, marble fountains and crystal pools. And for those seeking the ocean, Crandon Park offers over two miles of public beach on Key Biscayne.

The **Gold Coast Railroad Museum,** 12450 SW 152nd St., houses a good collection of historic railroad cars, including the Ferdinand Magellan—Franklin D. Roosevelt's private car and later used by presidents Truman, Eisenhower and Reagan—and the observation lounge, Silver Crescent, from the old California Zephyr. Steam train excursions are also available.

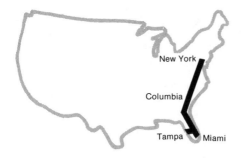

New York
Columbia
Tampa Miami

Silver Star

The Silver Star travels the Eastern Seaboard following a trail somewhat similar to the Silver Meteor, but keeps farther inland through most of the Carolinas. And just as its sister train does, the Star also takes in much of America's most historic environs, in this case locales such as Philadelphia, Washington, Richmond, Raleigh, Columbia, SC and Savannah.

After Kissimmee, Florida, the Star splits, with the Miami section proceeding south, while the Tampa section takes a westward course.

Southbound Schedule (Condensed)
New York, NY - Midmorning Departure
Washington, DC - Early Afternoon
Richmond, VA - Late Afternoon
Raleigh, NC - Midevening
Columbia, SC - Middle of the Night
Savannah, GA - Middle of the Night
Jacksonville, FL - Early Morning
Tampa, FL - Late Morning Arrival*
Miami, FL - Early Afternoon Arrival

Northbound Schedule (Condensed)
Miami, FL - Midafternoon Departure
Tampa, FL - Late Afternoon Departure*
Jacksonville, FL - Late Evening
Savannah, GA - Middle of the Night
Columbia, SC - Middle of the Night
Raleigh, NC - Early Morning
Richmond, VA - Late Morning
Washington, DC - Early Afternoon
New York, NY - Early Evening Arrival

*By separate section between Tampa and Kissimmee.

Frequency - Daily.
Seating - Amfleet II coaches.

Dining - Complete meals offered with buffet-style service between New York and Tampa. (Kissimmee to Tampa, sandwiches and beverages.) Lounge service between New York and Tampa.
Sleeping - Heritage Fleet roomettes and bedrooms. Slumbercoach between New York and Tampa.
Baggage - Checked baggage handled at most stations.
Reservations - All-reserved train.
Length of Trip - 1,424 miles in 27½ hours (New York/Miami).

Route Log

For route between New York and Rocky Mount, see that portion of Silver Meteor log, page 77.

0:00 (1:20) Depart Rocky Mount.
0:02 (1:18) For next several minutes, pass by sprawling CSX rail yards on left.
0:20 (1:00) Through Wilson, another bright-leaf tobacco center, where tobacco warehouses seem to be everywhere. Its annual auction, dubbed "The Greatest Show in Tobaccoland," provides a most unique tourist attraction.
0:35 (0:45) Tall, skinny sheds dotting the landscape, some with little chimneys jutting out from their tops, are tobacco curing barns.
0:44 (0:36) Through Selma, a small agricultural center, and point where our route now swings back toward Raleigh, departing from the southbound CSX tracks followed by the Silver Meteor and the Palmetto.

1:20 (0:00) Arrive at Raleigh's attractive Georgian-style station.

RALEIGH, NC - Capital of North Carolina (named for Sir Walter who never saw the area) and the fastest growing city in North Carolina, Raleigh is a neat-appearing community with over 300 parks, plazas and "green spaces." A heavy emphasis has been placed on education with nine institutions of higher learning located in the metropolitan area, including North Carolina State University with an enrollment in excess of 20,000.

Of particular interest are Andrew Johnson's birthplace (our 17th president), the North Carolina Museum of Art, and the North Carolina Museum of History.

0:00 (1:06) Depart Raleigh.

0:07 (0:59) Brick fortress-appearing buildings on left comprise North Carolina Central Prison.

0:08 (0:58) Attractive campus of North Carolina State University lies immediately on left.

0:13 (0:53) Leaving Raleigh's suburbs, two barn-like brick buildings on right house veterinarian school of North Carolina State.

0:14 (0:52) North Carolina Fair Grounds are visible off to right.

0:29 (0:37) Cross Haw River.

0:31 (0:35) Train now crosses Deep River. Following battle of Guilford Courthouse, General Cornwallis spent several days constructing a bridge over river about 300 yards upstream to right.

1:03 (0:03) On left, handsome horse farm embellishes Carolina scenery.

1:06 (0:00) Trundling down "Main Street," train arrives Southern Pines (Pinehurst).

SOUTHERN PINES, NC - This is the heart of the "Sandhills" of North Carolina where rolling green hills forested with pines (having needles up to 16 inches long) make this one of the most popular recreational areas in the U.S. Within a 15-mile radius there are: 27 golf courses (that's 91.03 miles of golf); 131 tennis courts; 6½ miles of race tracks; and 3,460 acres of lakes and ponds. The World Golf Hall of Fame overlooks the fifth tee of the famed Pinehurst No. 2 Course.

0:00 (0:31) Depart Southern Pines.

0:21 (0:10) On right, North Carolina Speedway, ringed with billboards, looks down at tracks.

0:22 (0:09) Enormous open pit furnishes white and rust colored sands for local construction.

0:26 (0:05) Seaboard shops appear on left in CSX rail yards.

0:31 (0:00) Arrive Hamlet where, at left, colorful painting of red antique steam locomotive adorns wall of building while marvelous old depot serves as Amtrak station and museum on right at foot of "Main Street."

HAMLET, NC - Founded in the late 1800s when John Shortridge established a woolen mill here, the town soon became an important seaboard rail hub. Today, the rail industry still dominates the economy with the Southeast's largest electronic rail yard located here. An old opera house still stands where such notable performers as Caruso once brought culture of the highest level to this small town during its early prosperity. The quasi-Victorian rail station is on the National Register of Historic Places and houses a fine collection of Seaboard Airline Railway memorabilia.

0:00 (1:08) Depart Hamlet.

0:08 (1:00) Leave North Carolina and enter South Carolina.

0:20 (0:48) Cross Great Pee Dee River.

0:34 (0:34) Off to right is Carolina Sandhills National Wildlife Refuge.

0:37 (0:31) On north edge of McBee, impressive-looking plant on left manufactures A. O. Smith water heaters.

0:46 (0:22) Through Bethune, a small agricultural community claiming title of Nation's Egg Capital.

1:08 (0:00) Arrive Camden.

CAMDEN, SC - This is the oldest inland city in South Carolina, having been established in 1732. A major British garrison under General Cornwallis was located here, and the battles of Hobkirk Hill and Camden, as well as 12 other Revolutionary War battles, took place in this vicinity. Today, one can visit Historic Camden, a reconstructed colonial village where the British army spent a demoralizing winter.

The world-famous "Colonial Cup," one

of the nation's richest steeplechase races, is held here each November.

0:00 (0:33) Depart Camden.

0:02 (0:31) Cross broad Wateree River. On right is DuPont's May Plant, producing Orlon, Dacron and nylon.

0:33 (0:00) Arrive Columbia, where capitol building presides over city at left.

 COLUMBIA, SC - One of the first planned cities, it was established in 1786 to be the state's capital and has held that distinction ever since. Some local attractions include: Woodrow Wilson's boyhood home where the nation's 28th president lived as a youth while his father taught at Columbia Theological Seminary; the State House which still shows scars on its outer walls from cannon fire during one of Sherman's campaigns; and State Farmers Market with tempting fresh produce available daily—largest in the Southeast.

0:00 (0:55) Depart Columbia.

0:02 (0:53) Cross over rock-strewn Congaree River.

0:16 (0:39) Gaston Tower, off to left, once served as fire watch tower for South Carolina Forestry Service.

0:55 (0:00) Arrive Denmark.

DENMARK, SC - This community was born out of the intersecting of the Southbound Railroad Company and the South Carolina Railroad which occurred in 1891. At one time cotton was Denmark's most important product, but in 1921 the boll weevil appeared, causing such destruction that cotton is no longer grown here. Today, the soybean is king.

Oddly enough, Denmark has played two important roles in man's war against the mosquito. In 1927, a nearby swampy mill pond was the first ever to be sprayed by air in an effort to kill mosquito larvae. In 1901, a resident of Denmark, James Hanberry, served as one of 14 volunteer "guinea pigs" in Dr. Walter Reed's famous experiment in Havana, Cuba, to find the cause of yellow fever. On February 6th of that year, "Mosquito No. 13" that had sucked blood from fever patients stung Hanberry and proved that the female mosquito carried the dreaded germ.

0:00 (1:19) Depart Denmark.

0:55 (0:24) Leave South Carolina and enter Georgia.

1:19 (0:00) Arrive Savannah.

 SAVANNAH, GA - See page 82.

0:00 (2:04) Depart Savannah southbound into tall, densely wooded forests of southeastern Georgia.

0:06 (1:58) On left, skirt grounds of Hunter Army Airfield.

0:12 (1:52) Cross Ogeechee River, which flows into Atlantic Ocean about ten miles east of here.

0:13 (1:51) Pass through Richmond Hill. Nearby Fort McAllister was key to Savannah's fortifications during Civil War, fending off nine naval assaults before finally succumbing in Sherman's march to the sea. Also located here is Richmond Hill Plantation, a seasonal home built by Henry Ford during 1930s.

0:46 (1:18) Cross Altamaha River.

0:50 (1:14) Through Jesup, an important distribution hub, centrally located among such large industrial meccas as Jacksonville, Savannah and Atlanta. Nearby popular tourist destinations include Brunswick and the Georgia Sea Islands. Dogwood Festival, an annual springtime celebration, features songfests, concerts and crafts exhibitions. Wayne County Court House is on left. Built in 1903, spire-topped clock tower crowns this quaint structure. On outskirts of town, logging and milling operations become frequent sights, bordering route into central Florida.

1:07 (0:57) Woodland beauty abounds as train crosses Big Satilla Creek.

1:10 (0:54) Cross Satilla River.

1:35 (0:29) Pass through Folkston, one of three points of access to primeval wilderness area known as Okefenokee Swamp.

1:37 (0:27) Crossing St. Mary's River into Florida, Colonial environs of past 1,000 miles are slowly supplanted by Spanish influence of an even earlier period.

2:04 (0:00) Arrive Jacksonville.

 JACKSONVILLE, FL - Unlike many other Floridian cities, Jacksonville is not a tourist resort. Rather, it has grown to become the state's leading industrial center, with a population nearing 750,000.

Station at Hamlet, North Carolina
DORIS SWANSON

Although lying a few miles west of the Atlantic Ocean, Jacksonville is still an important seaport, with an interconnecting passage along the St. Johns River. Three beautiful beaches provide a weekend haven for many city dwellers.

Here, at Jacksonville, the Miami and Tampa sections of the Silver Star split with the Miami section going through Ocala and Wildwood and the Tampa section going through DeLand and Orlando. This route log traces the Miami section.

This is a major rail operation for CSX, which has an ultramodern $23 million train dispatching operation controlling its entire 20,000-mile system.

0:00 (1:01) Depart Jacksonville.

0:03 (0:53) For five minutes, train slips through large Jacksonville rail yards. After a sharp curve to right, downtown skyline will be just to left. Steel bridge on left carries auto traffic over St. Johns River.

0:11 (0:50) Under Interstate 10.

0:14 (0:47) On left, expanse of modern red-brick buildings houses Florida Junior College at Jacksonville.

0:18 (0:43) After crossing Ortega River, dramatic view of downtown Jacksonville presents itself on left, just across St. Johns River. Note innumerable fishing and pleasure craft docked on north bank of Ortega River, both sides of train.

0:21 (0:40) U.S. Naval Air Station (Jacksonville), with blue WWII PBY and other aircraft at entrance, is on left.

0:30 (0:31) Through trees on left, glimpses are afforded of very attractive waterfront homes.

0:38 (0:23) St. Johns River appears again, briefly, on left.

0:40 (0:21) One of Florida's larger dairy farms, with hundreds of black and white Holsteins, appears on right.

0:53 (0:08) Twin cooling towers and giant stack dramatize coal-burning Seminole

91

Silver Star - Miami, Florida
HOMER R. HILL

Cooperative Generating Station on left.

0:56 (0:05) Cross tributary of St. Johns River. On right, highway bridge spanning that broad waterway carries U.S. 17 traffic between Jacksonville and Orlando.

1:01 (0:00) Arrive at Palatka's finely restored depot.

PALATKA, FL - The town gets its name from a Seminole Indian word meaning "crossing over" or "cow's crossing." Palatka is one of Florida's older cities, dating back to 1820. During the Civil War its St. Johns River location worked to its disadvantage, permitting federal gunboats to rake the town with cannon fire. Today, that same river is a boon to tourism, providing fishermen an ideal place to catch trophy widemouth bass and other game fish.

An annual Azalea Festival is held in the Ravine Gardens State Park, when more than 100,000 plantings of azaleas burst into springtime splendor the first two weeks in March.

0:00 (0:46) Depart Palatka.

0:06 (0:40) Drawbridge now carries train across a curl of St. Johns River.

0:13 (0:33) Passing through Park Crescent, brief look at 13-mile-long Crescent Lake is caught through trees on right.

0:24 (0:22) Just beyond small lakes on left, but out of view, is Lake George—actually an enormous widening of St. Johns River. Watch for nursery stock (shrouded from direct sunlight by black netting) for next several miles, and, of course—citrus orchards.

0:38 (0:08) Typical citrus packing plant is next to tracks on left.

0:46 (0:00) Arrive DeLand.

DELAND, FL - DeLand has experienced a rather checkered history. First signs of known civilization are the remains of an old sugar mill just north of town, believed to be English or Spanish, and possibly dating back to 1570. Later, in 1587, in the area now known as Daytona Beach, a group of Franciscan missionaries established a settlement but were driven out by the Indians and English. Then, in the late 1700s, the British operated plantations here but left when Florida was ceded to Spain. Permanent settlement finally occurred in 1870 by Mathias Pay of Ohio.

Today, DeLand is the home of Stetson University, named in 1886 in honor of the famous hat-maker. Houseboat tours on the St. Johns River are a popular attraction.

0:00 (0:18) Depart DeLand.

0:12 (0:06) Cross St. Johns River, once again on a drawbridge.

0:18 (0:00) Arrive Sanford, southern terminus of Amtrak's Auto Train. Facilities for loading and unloading autos can be seen on left. Diesel locomotive shops can also be seen.

SANFORD, FL - In 1870, General Henry Sanford, who had been the U.S. minister to Belgium, purchased over 12,000 acres and laid out the town that now bears his name. In 1880, President U. S. Grant was present at ceremonies here, marking the beginning of the construction of the South Florida Railroad which, by 1884, linked Jacksonville with this central Florida community.

Sanford is host to the unique "Golden Age Games" held during the second week of each November. People age 55 and older from throughout the U.S. and foreign countries compete in a broad spectrum of sporting events.

0:00 (0:21) Depart Sanford.

0:20 (0:01) Area becomes more arid, more urbanized as we enter Orlando's metropolitan area. Just one of area's many fine golf courses is on left.

0:21 (0:00) Arrive Winter Park where beautiful downtown park, complete with swaying palms, provides most attractive station setting.

WINTER PARK, FL - The first building was erected in Winter Park in 1881—a depot. In 1885, Rollins College, today a four-year liberal arts college, offered the first courses of higher learning in Florida. The Cornell Fine Arts Center is one of the finest university museums in the state. The Maltbie Museum, displaying shells from around the world, is also on this campus.

Visitors to Winter Park can enjoy Scenic Boat Tours with 12-mile cruises through Chain-of-Lakes and canals, and Genius Drive, a winding road through a private estate with more than 100 peacocks wandering freely on this beautiful acreage. This is one of the prettiest towns in Florida, with lush foliage and winding brick streets, many lined with vine-draped oaks.

0:00 (0:13) Depart Winter Park.

0:05 (0:08) Passengers are now "treated" to an unusual trip through a hospital. Buildings of Florida Hospital line both sides of track with a walkway connection directly overhead.

0:08 (0:05) Note Statue of Liberty presiding over small, attractive flower display in street at right.

0:11 (0:02) Just before reaching Orlando's present train station, old Church Street Station, now a popular shopping area and night spot, is on immediate left. Note 0-6-0 steam engine now on permanent display.

0:13 (0:00) Arrive Orlando.

ORLANDO, FL - Originally a sleepy agricultural town dependent on the citrus industry, Orlando has experienced growth in the last three decades that is now legendary. Tourism, due to the area's mild year-round climate, and particularly the proximity to Disney World and its newer offshoots, largely accounts for its recent surge.

It claims to be the world's number one vacation destination. The fact that a half million rental cars cruise central Florida's highways backs this boast.

It's a city where Disney has set the standard. Other local industries seem to pick up on the young, neat, well-trained and highly organized theme—a theme that Disney has perfected.

Amtrak Station, 1400 Sligh Blvd., an attractive Spanish-style depot, is situated just to the south of Orlando's central business district. There are food and beverage vending machines, luggage carts and redcap service. Ample free parking is adjacent to the station. For arrival and departure information only, 843-7611.

Cab stand is at the station; Yellow Cab, 699-9999, and Gray Line Taxi, 422-5550. Nearest **local bus** stop is at Orange Ave., three blocks east of the station; call 841-8240 for information. Several **rental car** companies service the station: Air Rail Rent-A-Car, (407) 649-9283 or 800-228-8024, has cars at the station; National and Avis both provide shuttle

Orlando

- Amtrak Station
1 - Visitors Information
2 - Disney Attractions
3 - Harley Hotel
4 - TraveLodge

-Harley Hotel of Orlando, 151 E. Washington St. (at Rosalind), 32801; (407) 841-3220 or 800-321-2323. A Helmsley hotel. Downtown, overlooking Lake Eola. Spacious, attractive rooms. Two miles from the station. $55.

-Comfort Inn South, 8421 S. Orange Blossom Trail, 32809; (407) 855-6060. Free shuttle to Disney, 15 miles. Few miles south of station. $40.

Walt Disney World, Epcot Center and **Disney MGM Studio** are several miles from Orlando. These are the major reasons people come to Orlando. Unfortunately, there is no bus service between Orlando and these attractions. A car is about the only practical way to see most of Orlando's offerings. (Several hotels near Disney World, however, offer free shuttle service to Disney.)

Kennedy Space Center, 60 minutes east of Orlando, provides tours of launch pads and other facilities. **Cypress Gardens,** 55 minutes southwest of Orlando, has acres of gardens and cypress trees which can be seen from foot paths and electric boats.

0:00 (0:20) Depart Orlando. Upon leaving metropolitan area, landscape is still dominated by now familiar citrus groves.
0:20 (0:00) Arrive Kissimmee.

KISSIMMEE, FL - Kissimmee is the closest rail station to Disney World and Epcot Center. South of town is Reedy Creek Overlook reached by a boardwalk that winds through Spanish moss and a cypress forest. Merry "D" Wildlife Sanctuary is in the same area.
0:00 (1:08) Departing Kissimmee, Monument of States can be seen on left, a 70-foot-high pyramid comprised of thousands of rocks (and other items) collected from all states and some foreign countries.
0:38 (0:30) This is Auburndale, a major intersection for two routes of the historic Seaboard Coast Line. In rail vernacular, this is known as "The Auburn Diamond." Here, the Silver Star's Miami and Tampa sections split when southbound and join when northbound. Expect at least a 15-minute delay to accommodate this switching, backing and coupling. Although it is not really important to understand what's

service between the station and their downtown locations. **Orlando International Airport** is approximately nine miles south of the station.

Orlando Orange County Visitors Bureau, 7208 Sand Lake Rd., Suite 300, 32819; (407) 363-5871. Or visit the Visitors Center at 8445 International Drive.

The first two hotels listed below are in downtown Orlando, reasonably close to the station. If you plan to spend most of your time at one or more Disney attractions, you might want to consider the Comfort Inn, some distance from the Orlando station but offering free shuttle service to Disney, or the Wynfield Inn Maingate listed under Kissimmee, below.

-Travelodge Orlando Downtown, 409 North Magnolia (at Livingston), 32801; (407) 423-1671. Well-managed downtown bargain. About two miles from the station. $32.

happening, it is important to be in the right section of the train at this point.

For Miami section, see Silver Meteor log, starting Winter Haven, at page 84.

1:08 (0:00) Arrive at Lakeland's immaculate white-brick station.

Tampa

🚂 **Amtrak Station**
1 - Visitors Information
2 - Plant Museum
3 - Harbor Island
4 - Ybor City
5 - Dark Continent - Busch Gardens
6 - Days Inn
7 - Holiday Inn

LAKELAND, FL - This is the very heart of citrus country. A fifth of all citrus grown in the United States comes from this immediate area— that's a lot of orange juice. Lakeland is also the marketing center for Florida's entire crop. But one other product is as important as oranges and grapefruit. Most of the world's phosphate is mined nearby, almost all of it going into agricultural fertilizers.

Florida Southern College is located here where students study amidst the largest assemblage of buildings designed by Frank Lloyd Wright. The Detroit Tigers have enjoyed spring training here for years. This is also Amtrak's closest stop to Cypress Gardens (at Winter Haven).

0:00 (0:32) Depart Lakeland.
0:07 (0:25) Train slows to 35 mph while coursing through heart of Plant City, spring training camp of Cincinnati Reds.
0:20 (0:12) Cross Tampa By-Pass Canal.
0:32 (0:00) Arrive Tampa, where station is backdropped by Tampa's glassy skyscrapers.

TAMPA, FL - The first adventurers to reach Tampa were Panfilo Narvez in 1528 and DeSoto in 1539. The area was soon abandoned by the white man, however, and it was not until 284 years later in 1823 that the first settler gave Tampa some semblance of permanence. The following year Ft. Brooke was established when four companies of the U.S. Army sailed into the bay from Pensacola.

The railroad reached Tampa in 1883 which helped bring about the development of Tampa's large fishing industry. In 1885, V. M. Ybor was persuaded to bring his cigar-making operations from Key West to the Tampa area, and Ybor City was laid out northeast of Tampa to accommodate this new industry. Tampa's

first famous cigars were thus manufactured in 1886.

Teddy Roosevelt set up headquarters in the Tampa Bay Hotel in 1892 with 30,000 soldiers camped nearby for training during the Spanish American War, and Tampa became the major embarkation point for troops headed for Cuba. The first regularly scheduled commercial airline flight ever flown landed here, arriving from nearby St. Petersburg.

Today, Tampa is the industrial center of western Florida, with fishing and citrus processing being mainstays. Its mild climate has made it not only a major tourist area but also a favorite retirement center.

🚉 **Tampa Amtrak Station,** 601 Nebraska Ave. at Twiggs Street, is a modern, efficient, "temporary" structure immediately behind Union Station. The latter was built in 1912 in Italian Renaissance style, and has been boarded up for some time pending possible restoration.

There are snack vending machines, luggage carts and redcap service. There is limited free parking in front of the station. Pay-parking is at the Twiggs Street Parking Garage.

For arrival and departure information only, call 221-7600.

Cab stand at the station; United Cab, 253-2424 and Yellow Cab, 253-0121. **Local bus** information, call 254-HART. Avis, 221-1666, will pick up **rental car** customers at the station and cars can be dropped off at the station. **Tampa International Airport** is approximately six miles west of the station.

Tampa/Hillsborough Visitor Information Center, 111 Madison St., Suite 1010 (corner of Madison and Ashley), 33602; (813) 223-1111 or 800-826-8358.

Days Inn Convention Center, 515 Cass E., 33602; (813) 229-6431. Nicely maintained, spacious rooms, non-smoking floors, covered parking. On the edge of the central business district, seven blocks from the station. $29.

-Holiday Inn Downtown, 111 W. Fortune, 33602; (813) 223-1351. About a mile from the station, on the edge of the central business district. $59.

Tampa's downtown is focused on the **Franklin Street Mall,** a pleasant urban stretch of stores, restaurants and services. The south end of the Mall is anchored by the smartly landscaped City Hall Plaza, surrounded by hotels, offices and popular bistros. And on the southern edge of the Plaza, a people mover transports pedestrians to **Harbor Island,** an array of specialty shops, restaurants and quick-service eateries.

Ybor City, just a few blocks east of the station, bounded roughly by 5th and 11th avenues and 12th and 22nd streets, is Tampa's Latin Quarter. What was the beginning of Tampa's cigar industry is now filled with many historic sites, as well as **Ybor Square** which is a fine collection of shops and restaurants featuring fine Spanish cuisine.

Busch Gardens, north of downtown in the area of Busch Blvd. and 40th St., features seven adventure lands, with wild animals, thrill rides, tropical landscaping, restaurants and other entertainment. The **Henry B. Plant Museum,** 401 West Kennedy Blvd., across the river from downtown, contains art treasures from around the world. It was named after an entrepreneur who brought the railroad to Tampa.

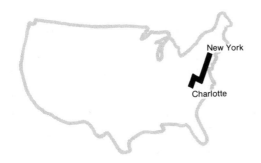

New York

Charlotte

Carolinian

The Carolinian (perhaps better called the North Carolinian) offers the people of North Carolina train service that runs during reasonable hours and, traversing the state in an east/west orientation, provides service to such population centers as Charlotte, Greensboro, Durham and Raleigh. At Raleigh, the train then follows the route of the Silver Star to New York City. Between Greensboro and Charlotte (its southern terminus) the Carolinian follows the route of the Crescent.

Southbound Schedule (Condensed)
New York, NY - Early Morning Departure
Washington, DC - Late Morning
Raleigh, NC - Late Afternoon
Greensboro, NC - Early Evening
Charlotte, NC - Midevening Arrival

Northbound Schedule (Condensed)
Charlotte, NC - Early Morning Departure
Greensboro, NC - Midmorning
Raleigh, NC - Late Morning
Washington, DC - Early Evening
New York, NY - Late Evening

Frequency - Daily.
Seating - Amcoaches.
Dining - Sandwiches, snacks and beverages with table seating.
Baggage - No checked baggage.
Reservations - All-reserved train.
Length of Trip - 702 miles in 14 hours.

Route Log

For route between New York and Rocky Mount, NC, see that portion of the Northeast Corridor log, page 30 and Silver Meteor log, page 77.

0:00 (0:19) Depart Rocky Mount, NC.
0:02 (0:15) For next several minutes, pass Wilson's sprawling CSX rail yards on left.
0:19 (0:00) Arrive Wilson.

WILSON, NC - Another bright-leaf tobacco center; tobacco warehouses seem to be everywhere. Its annual auction, dubbed "The Greatest Show in Tobaccoland," provides a unique tourist attraction. Wilson is also one of the country's leading antique markets. It is also home to Atlantic Christian College.
0:00 (0:21) Depart Wilson.
0:15 (0:06) Tall, skinny sheds dotting the landscape, some with little chimneys jutting out from their roofs, are tobacco curing barns.
0:21 (0:00) Arrive Selma.

SELMA, NC - This small agricultural center is also a major rail junction. From Selma, the Carolinian departs the route of the Palmetto and Silver Meteor and heads west toward Raleigh.
0:00 (0:52) Depart Selma, heading westward through rolling landscape dotted with tobacco farms.
0:52 (0:00) Arrive at Raleigh's attractive Georgian-style station.

RALEIGH, NC - Capital of North Carolina (named for Sir Walter who never saw the area) and the fastest growing city in North Carolina, Raleigh is a neat-appearing community with over 300 parks, plazas and "green spaces." A heavy emphasis has been placed on education with nine institutions of higher learning located in the metropolitan area, including North Carolina State University with an enrollment in excess of 20,000.

Of particular interest are Andrew Johnson's birthplace (our 17th president), the North Carolina Museum of Art, and the North Carolina Museum of History.

0:00 (0:39) Depart Raleigh on Norfolk Southern line.

0:07 (0:32) Brick fortress-appearing buildings, on left, comprise North Carolina Central Prison.

0:08 (0:30) Attractive campus of North Carolina State Univerity lies immediately on left.

0:16 (0:23) Dillard Paper Company facilities are on right.

0:20 (0:18) Through Research Triangle Park, a development started in 1959 for industrial and governmental research. It was placed here due to its proximity to numerous institutions of higher learning in Raleigh, Durham and Chapel Hill. Research Triangle area is regarded as being first nationally in number of PhD scientists and engineers per 100,000 population.

0:39 (0:00) Arrive Durham.

DURHAM, NC - The city got its start when Dr. Bartlett Durham provided a gift of land for a railroad station in the 1840s. The city soon developed an economy based on tobacco and textiles. In more recent years, education and medical research have become the city's focus with thousands employed in health care, education and research. Duke University is Durham's largest employer, and the Duke Medical Center is rated in the nation's top five.

Cultural activities are also found in abundance in Durham. The American Dance Festival, having moved here from New England, lasts for six weeks each year with both major and emerging modern dance companies performing.

0:00 (0:47) Depart Durham and slip past Lucky Strike facility on left.

0:02 (0:45) Liggett and Meyers Tobacco Company operation is on immediate right. East campus of Duke University will also be off to right.

0:04 (0:43) Near this spot is Bennett Place, where generals Johnson and Sherman met to negotiate a surrender that

Carolinian - Mebane, North Carolina
JACK SWANSON

would soon spell Civil War's end.

0:23 (0:24) Historic town of Hillsborough is to right, a focal point of Revolutionary War activity. General Cornwallis pitched camp here for five days in 1781. Although numerous important state conventions were held here in 1700s, efforts failed to make Hillsborough North Carolina's capital.

0:35 (0:12) Through community of Mebane, home of Kingsdown Mattresses and Dixie Fabrics on right. Colonial trading path dating from 17th century, from Petersburg, Virginia to Carolinas, passed nearby.

0:41 (0:06) At Haw River, disparate conglomerate of Cone Fabrics and Cone Granite Finishing is on right.

0:47 (0:00) Arrive Burlington.

BURLINGTON, NC - Textiles have long been a Burlington mainstay. The textile industry in the South was changed dramatically when a local mill produced the first commercially dyed plaids south of the Mason-Dixon line.

An unusual pre-Revolutionary conflict, the Battle of Alamance, occurred a few miles south of Burlington in 1771. Approximately 2,000 "Regulators," frontiersmen who quit paying taxes because they did not trust Easterners to properly represent them, fought and lost to the colonial militia sent to quell the rebels.

0:00 (0:35) Depart Burlington.

0:02 (0:33) Burlington Industries plant is on right, demonstrating city's textile heritage.

0:07 (0:28) Campus of small Elon College, a United Church of Christ institution founded in 1889, is on right.

0:23 (0:12) On right, Lorillard and Newport cigarette facilities are continued evidence of tobacco industry's regional importance.

0:33 (0:02) On right, University of North Carolina at Greensboro, founded in 1891, offers higher education to nearly 12,000 students.

0:35 (0:00) Arrive Greensboro.

For route between Greensboro and Charlotte, see that portion of the Crescent log, page 106.

New York
Richmond
Newport News

Old Dominion

The Old Dominion is Amtrak's access to Newport News, Norfolk, Virginia Beach, and Colonial Williamsburg. Originally, it was thought that this train would carry mostly service personnel to and from the large naval base at Norfolk; however, nearly as many passengers now detrain at Williamsburg as they do at the base. The Old Dominion has its northern terminus at New York and follows the route of the Silver Meteor between New York and Richmond. It then takes CSX tracks between Richmond and Newport News.

Although it follows the course of the James River, it is generally too far north to allow passengers to see the many magnificent plantations that border the shore of this historic stream. But the history of the region can be felt. McClelland used Berkeley on the James River as his headquarters in the summer of 1862. The trip through Williamsburg, passing within view of the historic section of America's colonial capital, is exciting, even if one does not plan to disembark here. Jamestown, the first English settlement in the New World, is just a few minutes away. Then, still further downline, the route passes near Yorktown, where America literally won her independence on the battlefield.

Southbound Schedule (Condensed)
New York, NY - Early Afternoon Departure
Washington, DC - Late Afternoon
Richmond, VA - Early Evening
Newport News, VA - Midevening Arrival

Northbound Schedule (Condensed)
Newport News, VA - Early Morning

Departure
Richmond, VA - Midmorning
Washington, DC - Early Afternoon
New York, NY - Midafternoon Arrival

Frequency - Daily.
Seating - Amcoaches.
Dining - Sandwiches, snacks and beverages.
Baggage - No checked baggage.
Reservations - All-reserved train.
Length of Trip - 412 miles in 8 hours.

Route Log

For route between New York City and Washington, DC, see Northeast Corridor log, page 30, and from Washington to Richmond, the Silver Meteor log, page 77.

0:00 (1:05) Departing Richmond's Staples Mills Road station, head south into older section of downtown Richmond.

0:09 (0:56) Off to right a few blocks, granite building with oxidized copper-looking dome is Science Museum of Virginia. This former Seaboard Coast Line station bears a resemblance to Washington, DC's Jefferson Memorial, perhaps because John Russel Pope designed both structures.

0:16 (0:49) Pass through Brown Street rail yards, then 17th Street rail yards.

0:19 (0:46) Foreboding and vacant Main Street Station has, to date, successfully resisted restoration efforts. Downtown Richmond is immediately beyond.

100

0:20 (0:45) Tobacco is important to Richmond's economy, although not as dominant as in years past. Weathered sign on enormous old brick building at left indicates that Lucky Strikes have been produced here.

0:21 (0:44) Just before crossing old drawbridge across S.R. Canal, James River can be seen briefly on right.

Further downstream (to the southeast) some of the finest plantations and homes ever to grace the South still can be visited along the northern shore between Richmond and Williamsburg. Unfortunately, these great estates cannot be seen from the train since they are about 10 miles south of the tracks. The most famous of these is Berkeley, the ancestral home of two U.S. presidents, William "Tippecanoe" Harrison and Benjamin Harrison, and where General Butterfield composed "Taps" while attached to McClelland's forces headquartered there in 1862. Jamestown, where America was born in 1607, is also along the northern shore of this historic river.

0:23 (0:42) Pass through CSX Fulton Yards located in Richmond's eastern industrial suburbs.

0:28 (0:37) Acres and acres of new railroad ties are stored on immediate left.

0:29 (0:36) Modernistic Nabisco bakery on right churns out $150 million worth of cookies, crackers and pretzels annually. The plant produces "high volume" products, including Ritz Crackers, Oreo Cookies and Premium Saltines. "Almost Home" brand products have also been produced here.

0:31 (0:34) Runways and terminal facilities of Richard Evelyn Byrd International Airport are visible to left. Virginia Army National Guard helicopters are also frequently seen here.

0:37 (0:28) Evidence that we are entering Virginia's low-lying region appears in form of swamplands during next few miles, mostly on right.

0:44 (0:21) Derelict, but picturesque, old Providence Forge station on right is structural clone of beautifully restored depot further downline at Lee Hall.

0:46 (0:19) Symmetrical rows of thousands of pine trees distinguish New Kent Forestry Center on right.

Operated by the Virginia Division of Forestry, this is the second largest producer of forest tree seedlings in the nation. Up to 60 million pine seedlings are started each year and sold primarily to the lumber industry. The loblolly pine is the Center's principal product. Efforts toward producing a genetically superior tree are being made here with assistance from the University of North Carolina. Watch for deer, quail and other wild creatures since this is also a wildlife preserve.

0:50 (0:15) Sailboats and other small craft can often be seen on broad expanse of Chickanominy River (a tributary of the James further south) which curls up to tracks on right.

1:05 (0:00) Arrive at Williamsburg, where station is just three blocks from this colonial capital's historic area.

WILLIAMSBURG, VA - Williamsburg was the capital of colonial Virginia for 81 years—from 1699 to 1780. Like Washington, D.C., it was originally planned and constructed with its governmental role in mind. A carefully planned restoration and preservation effort was started in 1926, and today, Colonial Williamsburg is a marvelous collection of historic structures, crafts, homes, gardens and tree-shaded streets. During the day, artisans work their historic crafts dressed in colonial attire for viewing by the public.

If you come here, plan to spend at least a day to take in the stores, shops, restaurants and perhaps an overnight stay in one of the historic hotels. Although there is no charge to stroll through the Historic Area, an admission ticket is necessary to gain entrance to artisan shops. Your ticket also entitles you to use the buses which make frequent trips between the Historic Area and the Visitors Center about a mile away. Tickets are available at the Visitors Center and the Information Booth on the edge of the Historic Area.

Williamsburg Transportation Center, 468 North Boundary St., is only three blocks from the historic district. There are storage lockers, luggage carts, food and beverage machines and free parking.

Cab stand is at the station; Colonial Cab, 565-1240. There is a **public bus** between the historic area and the

Visitors Center. **Patrick Henry International Airport** is 15 miles from the station.

? **The Colonial Williamsburg Information Center** is on the edge of Williamsburg. Write Colonial Williamsburg Foundation, Box 1776, 23187; (804) 220-7645 or 800-HISTORY. The Information Center should be visited prior to touring Colonial Williamsburg itself.

Governor's Inn, 506 N. Henry St., 23185; (804) 229-1000 or 800-HISTORY. Near the Historic Area and only three blocks from the station. $80.

-**Williamsburg Inn,** Francis St. (on the edge of the Historic Area), Box B, 23187; 800-HISTORY. Rooms in hotel are furnished in regency style. Pricey and unique; 1½ miles from the station. $265.

There are also numerous Holiday Inns, Quality Inns, Best Westerns, etc. in the area. Call 800-446-9244 for reservations.

Colonial Williamsburg is a village full of 18th-century buildings and peopled with actors in attire of that era. Don't miss the Governor's Palace, the Capitol, Burton Parish Church, Raleigh Tavern, the Magazine and Guardhouse, to name but a few. Be sure to obtain an Official Guidebook and map when you purchase your ticket.

0:00 (0:10) Departing Williamsburg, a glimpse can be caught of Palace of Governors (topped by a small tower and flanked by two chimneys) just beyond brick wall on right which is boundary of historic district. This has served as residence of seven royal governors as well as first two governors of Virginia.
0:06 (0:04) Parking for Busch Gardens is on immediate right—a 360-acre "theme" amusement park.
0:10 (0:00) Arrive at Lee Hall's attractively restored depot, a dolled-up twin to one seen at Providence Forge.

LEE HALL, VA - This is a suburban stop for Newport News and serves nearby Fort Eustis on Mulberry Island, headquarters of the U.S. Army Transportation Center.
0:00 (0:10) Depart Lee Hall.
0:02 (0:08) Cross what appears to be a river but is actually an arm of City Reservoir.

0:12 (0:00) Arrive Newport News station, still some distance from downtown area.

NEWPORT NEWS, VA - Here at the mouth of the James River, four cities cluster around the water's edge and make the absolute most of their coastal status. Newport News, Norfolk, Portsmouth and Hampton share one of the finest harbors in the world. The bay is over 14 miles long and 40 feet deep.

Maritime activities run the gamut. Newport News Shipbuilding and Dry Dock Company is the world's largest shipbuilder, with the luxury liner United States and the nuclear aircraft carrier Enterprise both to its credit. It employs 25,000 workers when the yards are in full swing. Nearby Norfolk boasts the world's largest naval base, being the home port for over 100 vessels of the Atlantic and Mediterranean fleets. And maritime commerce is immense. Huge tonnages of coal, tobacco and other goods pass through the harbor facilities each year.

Even though this is an industrial center, there is much to interest visitors. Waterfront restaurants with fine seafood menus; Virginia Beach, a short bus ride away, with resort hotels, boardwalks and arcades; and harbor tours are all quite popular. History buffs will definitely want to visit Yorktown where the most decisive battle of the American Revolution was fought. And if naval warfare is of interest, be sure to take in Fort Monroe. Had you been at this site on March 9, 1862 you would have had a front row seat for that mighty, but inconclusive, battle between the iron clads, Monitor and Merrimack. (The Merrimack was actually called the "Virginia" by the South after they raised this scuttled Union frigate and encased her wooden sides in armor.) And, understandably, the finest collection of ship models to be found anywhere is housed in the Mariner's Museum which is located in Newport News.

Other Mid-Atlantic & Florida Service

The **Palmetto** is a daily reserved train between New York City and Jacksonville,

Florida, following the route of the Silver Meteor but making more stops. Both southbound and northbound trains depart early morning and arrive at their final destinations late that night. The train has Amcoaches and food consists of sandwiches, snacks and beverages. Checked baggage is handled at most stations.

The **Virginian** is daily (except northbound Sundays) direct service between New York City and Richmond, leaving New York midafternoon and arriving Richmond late evening and departing Richmond early morning and arriving New York early afternoon. Reserved train; sandwiches and beverages. The train does not run northbound on Sundays.

Auto Train is Amtrak's unique service for those who want to travel by train between Washington, DC and central Florida—and take their cars along. The train leaves each end point in the midafternoon and arrives at the other in the early morning the next day. Lorton, VA (south of DC) is the northern terminal, while Sanford, FL (one-half hour from Disney World), is the southern end.

The train provides a "sitdown" dinner with china and linens, and a continental breakfast for sleeping car passengers. The train offers dome cars, lounge service, bedrooms and roomettes, and entertainment consisting of feature-length motion pictures. A complimentary buffet-style dinner and continental breakfast are provided to coach passengers. It is an all-reserved train, and although no checked baggage is handled, extra bags can be stored in your car (with no access during the trip). Only passengers with autos are permitted and should arrive two hours early for boarding. No autos will be accepted less than one hour before departure. Autos must have four inches of ground clearance and cannot be higher than 65 inches. There is limited space for vans which should not exceed 85 inches in height, and specific reservations should be made for these. Superliner coaches are slated to be placed on this train.

In addition to passenger fares, one way for an auto can run in the neighborhood of $175 in season.

The **Piedmont** is a daily train between Raleigh, Greensboro and Charlotte, following that segment of the Carolinian's route.

The **Tidewater** offers additional service to Newport News, Thursday through Sunday.

Crescent

The Crescent provides direct, no-change service between New York City and New Orleans. The route follows the Northeast Corridor between New York's Pennsylvania Station and Washington, DC, then takes the tracks of the Southern Railway through Atlanta and Birmingham before finally reaching New Orleans.

This train has a distinct case of dual personalities. The northern facet is the bustling, urbanized Northeast Corridor, predominated by New York City, Philadelphia, Baltimore and Washington, DC, while the southern and longest segment leaves one with the relaxed impressions of the rural Deep South. Darkness covers the Carolinas when the Crescent crosses these two states.

The most unique aspect of the trip occurs during the approach to New Orleans, when the Crescent slowly glides for ten minutes or so just above the surface of Lake Pontchartrain. Here, the feeling is more of an ocean liner than a passenger train.

Southbound Schedule (Condensed)
New York, NY - Early Afternoon Departure
Washington, DC - Early Evening
Charlotte, NC - Middle of the Night
Atlanta, GA - Early Morning
Birmingham, AL - Late Morning
New Orleans, LA - Early Evening Arrival

Northbound Schedule (Condensed)
New Orleans, LA - Early Morning Departure
Birmingham, AL - Early Afternoon
Atlanta, GA - Early Evening

Charlotte, NC - Middle of the Night
Washington, DC - Early Morning
New York, NY - Early Afternoon Arrival

Frequency - Daily.
Seating - Heritage Fleet coaches.
Dining - Complete meal service, sandwiches, snacks and beverages. Lounge service is also available.
Sleeping - Heritage Fleet roomettes and bedrooms. Slumbercoach between New York and Atlanta.
Baggage - Checked baggage at most stops.
Reservations - All-reserved train.
Length of Trip - 1,380 miles in 30 hours.

Route Log

For route between New York City and Washington, DC, see that portion of Northeast Corridor log, page 30.

 WASHINGTON, DC - See page 38.

0:00 (0:17) Depart Washington southbound through regions whose roots trace back to earliest periods of American history.

0:02 (0:15) Emerge from tunnel after passing under Mall. Glimpses of Capitol and oldest Smithsonian structure ("The Castle") can be caught through various federal buildings on right.

0:07 (0:10) Perhaps Washington's most charming monument, Monticello-shaped Jefferson Memorial, resides among cherry trees of Tidal Basin on right.

0:09 (0:08) Cross Potomac River paralleling 14th Street bridge. Washington National Airport is directly downstream to left. Back on right, Washington Monument, world's tallest masonry structure at 555.5 feet, punctuates horizon. Capitol's dome can still be seen toward rear on left.

0:10 (0:07) The Pentagon, headquarters for America's military establishment, is off to right, now mostly hidden by newer buildings.

0:12 (0:05) Glass high rises of Crystal City flaunt their starkness on right. Expansive RF&P rail yards are on left.

0:17 (0:00) Arrive Alexandria.

ALEXANDRIA, VA - This historic Washington suburb sits six miles south of the nation's capital, along the west bank of the Potomac River. Most noted for its outstanding examples of early American architecture, the Alexandria area is also replete with numerous national landmarks. Mount Vernon, beloved home and estate of George Washington from 1754 until his death in 1799, is just a few miles down the Potomac.

0:00 (0:30) Depart Alexandria.

0:01 (0:29) George Washington National Masonic Memorial, with museum of Washington memorabilia, dominates skyline on right. Metro subway station on left provides commuters with quick, easy access to downtown Washington.

0:30 (0:00) Arrive Manassas.

MANASSAS, VA - This was the site of intense fighting during the Civil War. The town was burned several times by both Yankees and Confederates, generally in an effort to cut supply lines to fighting troops. The two Battles of Manassas (Bull Run) were fought in July of 1861 and August of 1862 just northeast of town, and are now commemorated by the 5,000-acre Manassas National Battlefield Park. The quaint rail station was built circa 1915.

0:00 (0:32) Depart Manassas.

0:32 (0:00) Arrive Culpeper, where vast Confederate cemetery is at left.

CULPEPER, VA - The Culpeper Minute Men were the very first to respond in 1775 to Patrick Henry's call-to-arms. Then, during the Civil War, the area saw heavy fighting and the town served as headquarters for both sides.

George Washington described this area as a "high and pleasant situation," when he surveyed the county, and the town still prides itself on its fresh water supply and clean air.

Flour milling, furniture, wire rope and automotive parts are now important products. History buffs should enjoy the Culpeper Cavalry Museum.

0:00 (0:49) Depart Culpeper.

0:16 (0:44) Through town of Orange, home to two U.S. presidents, James Madison and Zachary Taylor. Bloody "Wilderness Campaign" of 1864 was waged just east of here.

0:42 (0:07) Pass through Shadwell, birthplace of Thomas Jefferson.

0:49 (0:00) Arrive Charlottesville.

CHARLOTTESVILLE, VA - "These mountains are the Eden of the United States." Thomas Jefferson wrote these flattering words in describing the area in and around Charlottesville. As the county seat of Albemarle, the town was a veritable treasure trove of talent and wisdom—Jefferson, James Madison and James Monroe were all part of the local scene. In more recent times, William Faulkner, Lady Astor and William McGuffey all called Albemarle County their home during some point in their lives.

Of particular interest to visitors is Jefferson's beautiful and cleverly designed home (Monticello) and the estate of James Monroe (Ash Lawn). These two men were close friends, and Jefferson personally selected the Monroe house site, donating his own gardeners to help start orchards at Ash Lawn. Jefferson also founded the University of Virginia which is located here and designed many of its original structures.

0:00 (1:12) Depart Charlottesville. Campus of University of Virginia will be on right.

0:50 (0:22) Through Sweet Briar, home to Sweet Briar College.

1:12 (0:00) Arrive Lynchburg.

LYNCHBURG, VA - A young Quaker by the name of John Lynch established a ferry here in the 1750s, opening up a trade route to Richmond and beyond. Soon, tobacco warehouses were built which established the town's economic foundation. As a matter of fact, tobacco became so important that, just prior to the Civil War, Lynchburg became the second wealthiest town in the country on a per capita basis. After the war, however, the tobacco industry began to move south and other endeavors gradually took its place.

0:00 (1:09) Depart Lynchburg.
0:52 (0:17) Community of Chatham is location of Hargrave Military Academy. Numerous stately colonial-style homes grace southern section of this community.
1:09 (0:00) Arrive Danville.

DANVILLE, VA - This colorful tobacco auction center was the last capital of The Confederacy. Near the end of the Civil War, Jefferson Davis and his cabinet settled here for about a week after being forced from Richmond, then fled southward again after the surrender at Appomattox.

0:00 (1:00) Depart Danville.
0:05 (0:55) Leave Virginia and enter North Carolina.
0:32 (0:28) American Brands Tobacco plant proclaims "Lucky Strike" and "Tareyton" on chimney and water tower on right upon entering Reidsville. Town was named for David S. Reid, governor of North Carolina from 1851 to 1854. His former home stands two blocks to left near center of town, the two-story frame buff-colored structure with brown shutters.
1:00 (0:00) Arrive Greensboro.

GREENSBORO, NC - This is not just golf country—it is the very heart of golf country. No less than eighteen courses in the immediate area offer stiff challenges to any level of player. One of the top PGA tournaments, The Greater Greensboro Open, draws more than 180,000 spectators annually and has a purse in excess of a quarter million dollars.

Of historical interest is Guilford Courthouse National Military Park, where England's General Cornwallis won a costly victory over America's General Nathaniel Greene in March of 1781. The battle, however, so weakened the English troops that they surrendered at Yorktown later that year.

0:00 (0:18) Depart Greensboro.
0:18 (0:00) Arrive High Point.

HIGH POINT, NC - It was a railroad surveyor, marking this location as the "high point" on the route between Goldsboro and Charlotte, who was responsible for giving the city a name which would stick. High Point can easily lay claim to being the nation's furniture capital with 85 furniture factories, including the 15 largest manufacturers in the world, located near here. In the 1950s it replaced Chicago as the nation's largest wholesale furniture market. But the manufacture of another product is equally as impressive. With 14 mills capable of turning out nearly a million pairs of stockings a day, High Point has the distinction of being the largest hosiery producer in the world.

0:00 (0:38) Depart High Point.
0:38 (0:00) Arrive Salisbury.

SALISBURY, NC - This attractive community is the center for Rowan County, with a widely diversified manufacturing base as well as agriculture consisting mostly of livestock and small grains. Salisbury was hometown to at least two notables, frontiersman Daniel Boone and former Secretary of Transportation Elizabeth Dole.

0:00 (0:47) Depart Salisbury.
0:47 (0:00) Arrive Charlotte.

CHARLOTTE, NC - Located on the North Carolina/South Carolina border, Charlotte is the largest city visited by the Crescent between Washington, DC and Atlanta. This thriving city is a center for commerce, industry, finance and communications. Two of its banks boast assets outranking all others in the Southeast. Charlotte is the home town of evangelist Billy Graham. It also bears the unlikely distinction of being the site of the first authenticated gold discovery in the U.S, and the famous Charlotte Motor Speedway holds stockcar and motorcycle races, drawing thousands each year. Its enormous stockcar stadium incorporates forty luxury condominiums overlooking the first turn.

0:00 (0:28) Depart Charlotte.
0:28 (0:00) Arrive Gastonia.

GASTONIA, NC - The Crescent makes a jog in its southerly course to stop at this textile-oriented city, some

28 miles west of Charlotte, before heading into South Carolina.

0:00 (0:57) Depart Gastonia.

0:07 (0:50) Enter South Carolina and leave North Carolina.

0:57 (0:00) Arrive Spartanburg.

SPARTANBURG, SC - Having experienced two decades of industrial boom, Spartanburg has become a truly "international" city with the influx of persons of various nationalities. The county lays claim to being the most prolific peach producer in South Carolina.

0:00 (0:39) Depart Spartanburg.

0:39 (0:00) Arrive Greenville.

GREENVILLE, SC - The numerous textile manufacturing plants located here give rise to Greenville's title, "Textile Center of the World." Outlet shops of these many factories are favorites of both local and visiting bargain hunters. The city has also been home to some well-known religious figures. Rev. Jesse Jackson was born here, and in 1927 evangelist Dr. Bob Jones chose this location when he founded Bob Jones University.

0:00 (0:35) Depart Greenville.

0:35 (0:00) Arrive Clemson.

CLEMSON, SC - This charming college town was known as Calhoun, named for the political giant John Calhoun. In 1943 the name was changed to that of the university located here. Clemson University, with an enrollment of almost 10,000, allows visitors to tour their unusual greenhouses and gardens, featuring over 2,200 varieties of plants. Also, Clemson's famous ice cream and blue cheese are favorites of dairy product connoisseurs.

0:00 (0:35) Depart Clemson.

0:35 (0:00) Arrive Toccoa.

TOCCOA, GA - Toccoa is the home of Toccoa Falls Bible College which features the spectacular 186-foot Toccoa Falls on its campus.

0:00 (0:41) Depart Toccoa.

0:41 (0:00) Arrive Gainesville.

GAINESVILLE, GA - This agricultural community of northeastern Georgia is situated near the northern end of Georgia's largest body of water, Lake Sydney Lanier, featuring a 1,200-acre family recreation resort on the Lake Lanier Islands.

0:00 (0:55) Depart Gainesville.

0:27 (0:28) Surroundings become more forested as train moves deeper into The South.

0:35 (0:20) Industrial and commercial developments begin to proliferate near Atlanta.

0:45 (0:10) Medieval-appearing buildings of Oglethorpe University are just to right.

0:47 (0:08) Inviting fairways and greens of Standard Golf Club stretch out on left.

0:51 (0:04) Atlanta's modern skyline is forward on left.

0:55 (0:00) Arrive at Atlanta's Peachtree Station.

ATLANTA, GA - Atlanta grew quickly from its founding as a railhead in the early 1800s to become a major manufacturing center of the South. During the Civil War it served as an arms marshalling point and the intersection of four railroads until General Sherman almost totally destroyed the city during his march-to-the-sea campaign.

The city made a quick recovery, however, becoming the center of the Reconstruction process following the war. Later, it became the capital of Georgia.

Today, with a metropolitan population in excess of 2,000,000, it is the financial, industrial and transportation center of the South. Its MARTA urban rail system is one of the finest transit operations in the country. For many, Atlanta is also a vacation destination, offering numerous options for both fun and leisure. Major league sports, a symphony, numerous historic sites and fine shopping are all found here.

Now, the big excitement in Atlanta is about 1996. The city was the successful bidder for the 1996 Summer Olympic Games.

Brookwood (Peachtree) Station, 1688 Peachtree St., N.W., is located approximately four miles north of the center of downtown in a bustling neighborhood. The station actually straddles the main line of the Southern. There are food and beverage vending machines. Parking is across the street at the Masonic Temple. Advance arrangements must be made for long-term parking, (404) 874-

Atlanta

🚂 Amtrak Station
1 - Visitors Information & Peachtree Center
2 - Underground Atlanta
3 - Martin Luther King Historic District
4 - TraveLodge

can be reached by MARTA commuter rail.

? **ACVB Visitor Information Center,** Peachtree Center Mall. Write or call: Atlanta Convention and Visitors Bureau, 233 Peachtree St., N.E., Suite 2000, Atlanta, GA 30303; (404) 521-6688. Information centers are also located at Lennox Square (north) and at Underground Atlanta.

Travelodge Atlanta Peachtree, 1641 Peachtree St., N.E.; (404) 873-5731. Reasonably priced and near restaurants. One block from the station. $39.

-**Bed & Breakfast Atlanta,** 1801 Piedmont Ave., N.E., Suite 208, 30324; (404) 875-0525 or 800-967-3224. A reservation service for B&Bs in homes or inns in the Atlanta area, including close-in locations. All accommodations have private baths. Several locations are convenient to the Amtrak station. $40 to $100.

On the southern edge of the central business district is **Underground Atlanta.** Rather ominous sounding, it's actually a six-block labyrinth of eclectic shops and restaurants, albeit devoid of sunlight. Nearly abandoned when the city built a system of viaducts that covered the area, a $140 million rejuvenation has turned it into one of Atlanta's "in" places. It is served by MARTA's rail system (Five Points station).

In the heart of downtown, **Peachtree Center** is the focal point of downtown shopping, hotels and restaurants, all in an urban indoor environment. The **Martin Luther King, Jr. Historic District,** on the edge of the central business district, includes the birthplace of that civil rights leader, his gravesite and Ebenezer Baptist Church where he preached. Take MARTA rail to King Memorial station.

For the professional consumer, the really power shopper, there's Lennox Square, reached by MARTA rail, located in upscale **Buckhead.** Stores include Saks, Neiman-Marcus, Lord and Taylor, Abercrombie and Fitch, and Macy's.

And on Fridays and Saturdays, **The New Georgia Railroad,** using restored antique passenger cars pulled by a steam locomotive, runs a dinner train to Stone Mountain Village. Call (404) 656-0769 for New Georgia RR schedules and informa-

8514, call weekdays. Redcaps are available.

Cabs are usually at the station at train time; Yellow Cab, 521-0200. **Buses** are one block away at the corner of Peachtree and 26th streets. Take the #10 bus south to the nearest **MARTA** commuter rail station (Arts Center); for MARTA rail and bus information call 848-4711. For **rental cars,** Budget will pick up or pay cab fare from the station to their downtown location; (404) 530-3000. **Hartsfield Atlanta International Airport** is nine miles south of the station and tion.

0:00 (2:20) Depart Atlanta and immediately cross busy Interstate 75.

0:16 (2:04) Cross Chattahoochee River as train proceeds through industrialized area of Atlanta.

0:18 (2:02) Leave Atlanta's suburbs and return to rolling forests of Georgia.

0:40 (1:40) Note old trolley on left, gaily painted and now put to some stationary use.

0:45 (1:35) Large-leafed vines that are so prolific along right-of-way are kudzu. Brought here from Japan many years ago to control erosion, plant is now bane of southern agriculture, enveloping everything it encounters. Ramshackle, abandoned house on left is completely covered by the stuff.

1:27 (0:53) Attractive course on left provides sport for golfers of Tallapoosa.

1:35 (0:45) Cross Tallapoosa River—just one of many streams between Atlanta and New Orleans.

1:36 (0:44) Leave Georgia and enter Alabama.

 Gain one hour as train passes from Eastern to Central Time. Set your watch back (forward if eastbound) one hour.

1:45 (0:35) Train crosses over U.S. Highway 78 and plunges into woods of Talladega National Forest.

2:20 (0:00) Arrive Anniston.

ANNISTON, AL - Anniston is an industrial hub of eastern Alabama. Numerous industries include the enormous Anniston Army Depot just west of the city.

0:00 (1:30) Depart Anniston.

0:07 (1:23) For next four minutes pass sprawling Anniston Army Depot on right, nation's largest military storage depot. Tanks and other miscellaneous vehicles and equipment can be found here.

0:10 (1:20) Numerous tanks and other armored vehicles on display along highway on right seemingly stand guard over depot complex.

0:27 (1:03) Northern tip of beautiful Logan Martin Lake touches tracks on left.

0:42 (0:48) No train trip would be complete without a tunnel. Pass through only one on today's run, Chula Vista Mountain Tunnel.

1:02 (0:28) Two lofty bridges carry us across Gahaba River.

1:19 (0:11) Industrial suburbs of Birmingham commence, contrasting sharply with miles of forest lands just traversed.

1:25 (0:05) One of Birmingham's former iron making facilities, Sloss Furnace, is on right. It is now a National Historic Landmark and a museum devoted to early-day iron and steel technology. Concerts and festivals are also held here.

1:27 (0:03) Vulcan, world's largest cast iron statue, keeps watch over city from atop Red Mountain on left. Vulcan was Roman god of fire and patron of metal workers. In recent times, Birmingham has used it as a safety symbol, displaying a red light when a traffic fatality has occurred and a green light on fatality-free days.

1:30 (0:00) Arrive Birmingham. University of Alabama's sprawling Medical Center, employing 11,000 people, can be seen to left of station.

BIRMINGHAM, AL - Although this is the very heart of Alabama's coal and steel production, the city has experienced an economic rebirth fostered by biomedical and other high-tech industries. An outstanding downtown shopping area, parks, tree-lined streets, theaters, museums and various festivals all greatly enhance Birmingham's lifestyle. This is the hometown of Nat King Cole, Phil Harris and Willie Mays.

0:00 (1:03) Depart Birmingham.

0:05 (0:58) As we leave through southwestern residential suburbs of Birmingham, take a last look at Vulcan, still visible on horizon to left.

0:12 (0:51) Former Pullman-Standard factory, which once produced over 3,000 boxcars a year, now stands in disuse on right.

0:39 (0:24) Road sign on hill on right directs traffic to "Bama Scenic Rock Gardens"—a fine collection of native plants, complete with nature trails.

0:45 (0:18) Through Vance, where Mercedes Benz plans to build their first American automobile plant at a cost of $300 million. Eventually, plant will employ 1,600 workers.

1:00 (0:03) Campus of perennial football powerhouse University of Alabama (The Crimson Tide) can be seen on right as train nears downtown Tuscaloosa.

1:03 (0:00) Arrive at Tuscaloosa's old but nice-appearing station.

TUSCALOOSA, AL - Once the capital of Alabama, the city is now primarily a vibrant university town. Of particular interest is "The Old Tavern," a museum with numerous historical artifacts, originally built as a tavern in 1827.

0:00 (1:35) Depart Tuscaloosa.

0:12 (1:23) Train slips through swamps of southern Tuscaloosa County.

0:15 (1:20) Prehistoric Indian mounds flash by quickly on right as train passes Mound State Monument.

The mounds in this area, several of which are visible from the train, were constructed about 800 years ago by Indians that inhabited this area. Three thousand were estimated to have lived here between 1200 and 1500 A.D. The mounds closest to the tracks originally had homes on them which were used by nobility. The far-distant mounds were ceremonial structures. The tallest mound, back to the right in the trees, now has a reconstructed temple at the top and was thought to have been the central ceremonial area.

0:16 (1:19) Fuzzy white cotton fields appear on both sides of train as "The Deep South" gets deeper.

0:29 (1:06) Cross over muddy, still waters of Black Warrior River.

0:57 (0:38) Cross large Tombigbee River, a link in an ambitious government waterway project (Tenn-Tom) to create an alternative to traditional Mississippi River route between Mississippi's upper tributaries and Gulf of Mexico.

1:12 (0:23) On right, quaint storefronts of York watch train go by from other side of "Main Street."

1:19 (0:16) Enter Mississippi and leave Alabama.

1:29 (0:06) On right, exquisite brick farmhouse, with white colonnades reflecting typical southern architecture, faces charming little pond.

1:35 (0:00) Arrive Meridian.

MERIDIAN, MS - Founded in 1860 at the junction of two railroads, Meridian is now a trade center serving an area with almost 70,000 people. Jimmy Rogers, father of country music and first name to be entered in Nashville's Country Music Hall of Fame, was born here in 1897. The Jimmy Rogers Museum has exhibits including a steam locomotive that pay tribute to this "Singing Brakeman's" life. Also, Merrehope, a twenty-room antebellum mansion of Greek Revival architecture, was one of five Meridian buildings to escape General Sherman's torch during his march to the sea.

0:00 (0:55) Depart Meridian.

0:07 (0:48) Key Field, on right, has interesting mixture of clientele, including sleek private aircraft close to tracks as well as more pugnacious jets of Mississippi Air National Guard parked on apron in distance.

0:19 (0:36) Cross curiously named Chunky Creek.

0:23 (0:32) Large natural gas pumping facility is on left.

0:55 (0:00) Arrive Laurel.

LAUREL, MS - This agricultural and trade center boasts an unusually fine art museum for a community its size. The Lauren Rogers Library and Museum not only has a national reputation for its collection of 19th century American and European art, but also maintains an excellent collection of Georgian silver and Indian baskets. Laurel was the birthplace of Metropolitan opera star Leontyne Price.

0:00 (0:31) Depart Laurel, and literally look right through modern downtown shopping mall on right.

0:30 (0:01) Cross Leaf River which will someday play an important role in a newly planned waterway.

0:31 (0:00) Arrive at Hattiesburg where a steam engine and rail passenger cars stand on display adjacent to station.

HATTIESBURG, MS - Referred to as the "Hub City" and "Gateway to the Gulf South," this progressive community was among the first in the state to qualify for the All Merit Community Award. The 11,000-student University of Southern Mississippi is located here, as well as smaller Carey College, with its well-known School of Music. The city hosts the Magnolia Classic, the only PGA

Crescent - east of Birmingham, Alabama
DORIS SWANSON

tournament in Mississippi. An annual Heritage Tour in March emphasizes the city's railroading and lumbering roots.

0:00 (1:02) Depart Hattiesburg.

0:14 (0:48) Futuristic-looking facility on right, with tall, stack-like tower, is part of R.D. Morrow Generating Plant using the latest in generating technology. Cooling water is obtained from five nearby wells and coal from southeastern Kentucky to produce 400,000 kilowatts of power with minimal environmental impact.

0:26 (0:36) Complex on right is Purvis Refinery of Amerada Hess.

0:40 (0:22) Through Poplarville, the birthplace of Senator Theodore Gilmore Bilbo, a highly controversial U.S. senator (1934-40) who was also the first to serve two terms as governor of Mississippi.

The agricultural research center located here is attempting to find a replacement for tung oil (tung tree farms were destroyed by Hurricane Camille in 1969), and also improve the production of blueberries (often called huckleberries) that are indigenous to the Southeast.

1:02 (0:00) Arrive Picayune.

PICAYUNE, MS - This Mississippi border town of 10,000 is the Crescent's last stop in Mississippi. The terrain now starts to flatten out upon approaching Louisiana.

0:00 (0:17) Depart Picayune.

0:07 (0:10) Enter Louisiana and leave Mississippi as train crosses over Pearl River.

0:15 (0:02) Note Albertson's new 6.2-million-dollar shopping center resembling early-day depot located within easy view of tracks.

0:17 (0:00) Arrive Slidell.

SLIDELL, LA - Slidell is actually a bedroom community for New Orleans, just across the eastern tip of Lake Pontchartrain. Because of its healthful air, this side of the lake is happily called the "Ozone Belt."

0:00 (0:53) Depart Slidell.

0:07 (0:46) Now, start an unusual, watery journey as train appears to paddle its way across eastern end of 610-square-mile Lake Pontchartrain on an incredible 6.2-mile-long wooden rail bridge only a few feet above water's surface. Glorious "ocean" sunsets are afforded when sun and train schedules cooperate.

0:17 (0:36) Pick up speed as train reaches terra firma and race past scores of stilted fishing huts along shore.

0:26 (0:27) Tracks and Lake Pontchartrain now part company.

0:33 (0:20) Skyline of downtown New Orleans, our destination, is now clearly visible on left as train takes a roundabout approach in getting there. University of New Orleans Field House drifts by on right, then buildings of University of Tulane Dental School appear on left.

0:51 (---) Stop, and back final few hundred yards to station.

0:56 (0:04) Massive egg-like Superdome is just to right.

1:01 (0:00) Arrive New Orleans.

 NEW ORLEANS, LA - Thoughts of New Orleans stir a swirl of color in the mind. Images of excellent restaurants, the French Quarter, jazz, Mardi Gras and, for trolley aficionados, the St. Charles Streetcar line are some of the visions conjured up at the mere mention of this unique city. It is quite understandably one of the nation's more popular places to visit.

New Orleans has existed under four different flags since it was founded in 1723 by Jean Baptiste Le Moyne, Sieur Bienville. It was first ruled by the French and was the capital of French Louisiana. The Spanish succeeded the French some 40 years later. New Orleans became an American city in 1803 with the Louisiana Purchase, and during the Civil War was a Confederate City. Today, it is Louisiana's largest metropolis and the world's largest (by tonnage) seaport.

Union Passenger Terminal (also known as the Transit Center), 1001 Loyola Ave., is one of Amtrak's more attractive facilities. Modern and efficient, it not only accommodates Amtrak, but it also serves as the Greyhound bus terminal. There are storage lockers, pay-luggage carts, a restaurant, snack vending machines and a gift shop. Pay-parking is in front of the station.

For arrival and departure information, call (504) 528-1610.

Cab stand is at the station; Yellow Cab, 525-3311. Nearest **local bus** stop is across the street, 569-2700. Convention Loop bus shuttles passengers between the Superdome and the French Quarter for a modest charge. **Greyhound** is at the station. **Rental cars** downtown include Budget, 467-2277 and Enterprise, 522-7900. **Airport shuttle** service, 522-3500. **New Orleans (Moisant) International Airport** is 12 miles west of downtown.

French Quarter Information Center, 916 N. Peters Street. Write or call Greater New Orleans Tourist & Convention Commission, 1520 Sugar Bowl Drive, 70112; (504) 566-5011 or 800-633-6511.

Two hotel choices, about midway between the French Quarter and the station, would be:

-**Le Pavillon Hotel,** 833 Poydras Plaza, 70140; (504) 581-3111 or 800-535-9095. Very nice accommodations. Seven blocks from the station. $99.

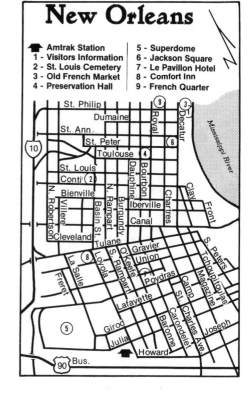

New Orleans

- 🚩 **Amtrak Station**
- 1 - Visitors Information
- 2 - St. Louis Cemetery
- 3 - Old French Market
- 4 - Preservation Hall
- 5 - Superdome
- 6 - Jackson Square
- 7 - Le Pavillon Hotel
- 8 - Comfort Inn
- 9 - French Quarter

-**Downtown Comfort Inn,** 1315 Gravier St., 70112; (504) 586-0100. Well maintained with larger than average rooms. $85.

For French Quarter accommodations, be sure to reserve well in advance. One possibility is:

-**Le Richelieu,** 1234 Chartres St., 70116; (504) 529-2492 or 800-535-9653. Small, charming hotel; one of the city's best. $105.

The **French Quarter** is the core of New Orleans' magnetism; 66 blocks of the old city with restaurants, jazz, shops, small hostelries with ironwork-decorated balconies—and, of course, raucous Bourbon Street. Free tours of the area are offered by the Park Service.

Be sure to take the **St. Charles Street-car** from the central business district through neighborhoods of fine old homes. This is also a good way to reach New Orleans **Audubon Park** and the fine **Zoological Gardens.** The **Riverfront Streetcars,** inaugurated in 1988, now tour 1½ miles of Mississippi waterfront. Also, in the 800 to 1000 block of Decatur Street, is the **Old French Market,** with shops and cafes, and a fascinating farmers market. The **New Orleans Center,** a downtown shopping mall about three blocks from the station, includes Macy's and Lord & Taylor.

Gulf Breeze

In the fall of 1989, Amtrak expanded its Alabama service to include Montgomery and Mobile. The Gulf Breeze, which is combined with the Crescent between Birmingham and New York City, runs as a separate train between Birmingham and Mobile.

The route is through Alabama's pastoral countryside, with scattered forests and cotton fields lining the right-of-way. Highlights include a stop in the heart of Montgomery's restored downtown and a Mobile arrival that slips along that historic city's waterfront.

Southbound Schedule (Condensed)
New York, NY - Early Afternoon Departure
Atlanta, GA - Early Morning
Birmingham, AL - Late Morning
Montgomery, AL - Early Afternoon
Mobile, AL - Late Afternoon Arrival

Northbound Schedule (Condensed)
Mobile, AL - Early Morning Departure
Montgomery, AL - Late Morning
Birmingham, AL - Early Afternoon
Atlanta, GA - Early Evening
New York, NY - Early Afternoon Arrival

Frequency - Daily.
Seating - Amfleet II and Heritage Fleet coaches.
Sleeping - Heritage Fleet sleepers with bedrooms and roomettes. Slumbercoach with economy bedrooms, New York to Atlanta.
Dining - Complete meal service, New York to Birmingham. Lounge car with sandwiches, snacks and beverages.
Baggage - Checked baggage at most stops between New York and Birmingham. Carry-on baggage only south of Birmingham.
Reservations - All-reserved train.
Length of Trip - 1,299 miles in 29 hours.

Route Log

For route from New York to Birmingham, see pages 30 and 104.

 BIRMINGHAM, AL - See page 109.

0:00 (1:50) Depart Birmingham and for next several minutes, wend southward through many of city's more industrial scenes.

0:04 (1:45) One can only speculate how many pancakes could be smothered by contents of Yellow Label Syrup bottle above building on left.

0:26 (1:24) Make first of several crossings of Cahaba River.

0:40 (1:10) Solar panels, on right, are evidence of environmental effort by Alabama Power.

0:46 (1:04) At southern edge of Calera, tan building, assorted cabooses and locomotives comprise Heart of Dixie Railroad Museum, just off to left.

1:01 (0:49) After passing through Thorsby, large plant on right is Union Camp Corporation's veneer board operation. Timber in yard is moved by huge contraption, looking more like a scorpion than a log snatcher.

1:36 (0:14) After Deatsville, Draper Correctional Center is imposing facility off to left.

Former Union Station - Montgomery, Alabama
JACK SWANSON

1:39 (0:11) Natural gas pumping paraphernalia of Southern Gas Company is on left.

1:45 (0:05) Cross Alabama River which flows south into Gulf of Mexico. Its nine-foot channel allows navigation to Great Lakes by way of controversial Tennessee-Tombigbee Waterway. Fort Jackson, when built in 1814 just upstream at junction of Coosa and Tallapoosa rivers, marked end of Creek Indian War.

1:47 (0:03) Pure white dome of State Capitol Building, one of just a few capitols to be designated a National Historic Landmark, can be seen off to left just before arrival Montgomery.

1:50 (0:00) Arrive Montgomery where remodeled old grain elevators, on right, once served as Amtrak station. Historic old Union Station can be seen forward left.

MONTGOMERY, AL - In 1540, Hernando de Soto visited this location and symbolically drove a Spanish flag into the banks of the Alabama River. But it was almost two centuries later before the French created the first permanent white settlements, East Alabama and New Philadelphia, which later merged to become the city of Montgomery.

Montgomery, named for a Revolutionary War hero, became Alabama's fourth capital after the seat of government was moved here from Tuscaloosa in 1846. Jefferson Davis was sworn in as president of the Confederacy on the capitol steps in 1861, and Montgomery served as the first capital of the Confederacy from February 8 to May 21, 1861.

This is the birthplace of the civil rights movement. In 1955, a black seamstress, Rosa Parks, was arrested for refusing to give up her seat on a city bus to a white man, and a year-long bus boycott by blacks ensued. Ten years later, protesting discriminatory voter laws, Martin Luther King led a 50-mile march from Selma to the steps of the State Capitol, only a block from his first ministry, the Dexter Avenue Baptist Church. Today, the Civil Rights Memorial, completed here in 1989, has become one of Montgomery's attractions. The memorial was designed by Maya Lin, the same artist who created the Vietnam

115

Memorial in Washington, DC.

Montgomery has paid considerable attention to its heritage. Commerce Street, an early-day mixture of commercial and residential buildings, and later home to elaborate warehouses, has been the object of a remarkable restoration effort that began in the 1970s. This handsome thoroughfare, just south of the station, can easily be seen from the train. The street goes directly beneath the tracks and served as a passageway for wagon loads of cotton on their way to riverboats that once docked on the shores of the Alabama River, just north of the station. The area is now Riverfront Park. And the nation's first electric trolley system, known as the "Lightning Route," is still remembered in the form of trolley tour buses called "Lightning Trolleys" that carry tourists through the city's historic areas.

0:00 (0:42) Departing Montgomery, Commerce Street is dazzling scene of immaculate storefronts, back to left. On immediate left, Montgomery's wonderful old Union Station now houses a bank, bakery and restaurant. Colorful stained glass panels adorn peaks of 1897 train shed. Over 40 passenger trains a day stopped here at the time of its construction.

0:35 (0:07) Over two centuries ago, naturalist and botanist William Bartram followed Indian trails through this region while studying plants, birds, insects and fish.

0:42 (0:00) Arrive Greenville.

GREENVILLE, AL - This town of 8,000 is the trading center of Butler County and is the halfway point between Birmingham and Mobile.

0:00 (0:38) Depart Greenville.

0:12 (0:26) On left, huge lumber mill of Union Camp Corporation transforms locally grown trees into sheets of plywood.

0:38 (0:00) Arrive Evergreen.

EVERGREEN, AL - Amtrak has utilized the old Louisville & Nashville depot, now on National Register of Historic Places. The long, grey frame structure now houses a small waiting room, a small market and the local chamber of commerce.

0:00 (0:22) Depart Evergreen.

0:07 (0:15) Cotton fields appear from time to time, forming soft, white blankets laid helter skelter throughout countryside.

0:22 (0:00) Arrive Brewton.

BREWTON, AL - This small Alabama community relies heavily on the manufacture of paper products to maintain its economy.

0:00 (0:28) Upon departing Brewton, large Container Corporation of America facility turns out myriad paper container products.

0:07 (0:21) This wide-spot-in-the-tracks is called Pollard. Established at juncture of Alabama & Florida and Mobile & Great Northern railroads, it was named for Charles T. Pollard, builder of Alabama & Florida Railroad. One of Confederacy's largest military training camps and a huge stores depot were here and suffered considerable devastation during Federal raids of December 1864 and March 1865.

0:14 (0:17) At Flomaton, enter CSX yards, where L&N tracks join from left. Tracks carry Sunset Limited and route drops south to Pensacola before turning east toward Jacksonville, Florida.

0:28 (0:00) Arrive Atmore.

ATMORE, AL — The community believes in centralized community services. Beyond the jet trainer in the park adjacent to the tracks is the City Hall, Fire Department, Chamber of Commerce and YMCA, all in a neat-appearing light-brick structure.

0:00 (0:21) Depart Atmore and immediately pass under Burlington Northern Railroad bridge.

0:04 (0:17) Atmore Country Club and golf course are just across highway to left.

0:21 (0:00) Arriving town of Bay Minnette, now closed Reichold Chemical plant is on left. On right, roof with fencing could hold picnic bench, but actually serves as Amtrak "station."

BAY MINNETTE, AL - Town is home to the University of South Alabama Baldwin County. The Reichold Chemical plant had been in operation for nearly 60 years, producing coatings and resins, then 1989 closure dealt economic blow to community.

The Baldwin Area Transit System (BRATS) provides bus service from the station to virtually any area of the county, including beaches.

0:00 (0:32) Depart Bay Minnette.

0:10 (0:32) Cross Tensaw River on first of five drawbridges between here and Mobile.

0:15 (0:17) Rumble over Mobile River on second drawbridge.

Amtrak's worst train wreck occurred just west of here at 2:50 in the morning on September 22, 1993 when the eastbound Sunset Limited plunged off the bridge over Big Bayou Canot. Three locomotives, a baggage car, a baggage dorm and two Superliner coaches went into the murky, 16-foot-deep waters, while a third coach was left jutting out over the end of the bridge and the remainder of the cars were still upright. Apparently, just moments before, two barges had broken loose from their tug and struck the bridge (which was barely seven feet above the water) causing a severe misalignment of the tracks. The tragedy resulted in 47 deaths, most from drowning.

0:18 (0:14) Now cross Bayou Sara on third drawbridge.

0:19 (0:13) On left, Mobile River now accompanies train approaching Mobile. Skyline is forward right.

0:20 (0:12) Fourth drawbridge carries train across Chicasaw Bogue.

0:25 (0:07) Roll beneath swooping Bay Bridge carrying vehicular traffic to and from Blakely Island and beyond.

0:26 (0:06) Trundle over Threemile Creek and last drawbridge, and then through freight yards. Alabama state docks, capable of handling 34 ocean-going vessels at one time, are seen on immediate left. Land on other side of Mobile River is Blakely Island situated in Polecat Bay, a northern extension of Mobile Bay. Freighters and other maritime vessels are usually prominent sights here. Battleship U.S.S. Alabama, permanently moored in harbor, is just beyond structures at left, but not visible from tracks.

0:28 (0:04) Elaborate, grey structure with red roof, off to right, is former GM&O Terminal, closed in 1957. Tallest structure in downtown Mobile, on right, is 34-story First National Building.

0:31 (0:01) Train now burrows right through Mobile's fancifully designed new Convention Center.

0:32 (0:00) Arrive Mobile's CSX-Amtrak station. In middle of Government Street on right, statue of Admiral Raphael Semmes, who was commander of Confederate States Steamer Alabama, seemingly welcomes Amtrak passengers to Mobile.

MOBILE, AL - A handful of modern skyscrapers alongside Mobile Bay marks the downtown of Alabama's only seaport, in sharp contrast to the collection of handsome Old South neighborhoods that make Mobile a city of charm and grace. Mobile is at its best in the spring when the city's 35-mile Azalea Trail, comprised of several streets lined with those showy flowers, is in full bloom.

Mobile has lived under six flags: French, British, Spanish, the State of Alabama, Confederate and U.S. It was the last Southern stronghold to surrender to Union Forces during the Civil War after being completely blockaded by the Union Navy. (It was during this blockade that Admiral Farragut supposedly exclaimed: "Damn the torpedoes! Full steam ahead!") The Bay remains important to Mobile, whose maritime trade and shipbuilding are still vital to the city's economy.

Amtrak Station, Government and Water streets, occupies a portion of the former CSX station, conveniently wedged between the compact central business district and the Mobile River. The station waiting room is small, marginally adequate at best, and parking is very limited. Red caps are available.

Write or call **Mobile Convention & Visitors Bureau,** One St. Louis Centre, Suite 2002, 36602; (205) 433-5100 or 800-666-6282. Visit the Information Center at historic Fort Conde; 434-7304.

Yellow Cab, 476-7711; **local buses,** 344-5656. Budget **rental cars,** 633-0660, offer pick up and delivery in the downtown area. **Mobile Municipal Airport** is on the west edge of the city.

Holiday Inn Express, 255 Church St., 36602; (205) 433-6923. Large motel in attractive setting next to central business district and convenient to visitors center. Complimentary continental breakfast. Five blocks from the station. $42.

-Malaga Inn, 359 Church St., 36602; (205) 438-4701. Former antebellum townhouses with private balconies and patios create front portion of hotel. Pleasant central courtyard. Six blocks from the station. $55.

-Radisson Admiral Semmes Hotel, 251 Government St., 36602; (205) 432-8000. Very attractively maintained older high rise, three blocks from the station. $74.

-Adams Mark Mobile (formerly Stouffer's), 64 Water St., 36602; (205) 438-4000 or 800-444-2326. Modern high rise with large, bright rooms. Second floor dining room overlooks station and new convention center. Immediately across intersection from station. $105.

-Holiday Inn, 301 Government St., 36602; (205) 694-0100. Circular high rise, five blocks from the station. $73.

Grayline of Mobile has **city tours** which provide an excellent way to sample this historic city when time is limited. Two of the area's outstanding examples of early Southern living are: **Bellingrath Gardens and Home,** 26 miles south of the city, with 65 acres of gardens and landscaping where one can enjoy breakfast or lunch in an Old South setting; and **Oakleigh Mansion,** nearer to downtown, a Greek Revival mansion noted for its graceful lines and beautiful gardens.

Two blocks from the station is **Fort Conde Historic French Fort,** a reconstruction of the original built circa 1724-36 and serves as the city's information center.

The **Battleship Alabama Memorial Park** is the permanent anchorage for that World War II battle wagon, the submarine USS Drum and a B-52 bomber. The highlight of the Park is the tour of the Alabama herself.

Gulf Breeze - Mobile, AL
JACK SWANSON

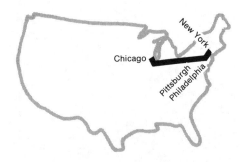

Broadway Limited

From New York City to Chicago, the Broadway Limited traces much of the route traveled by its famed predecessor of the same appellation. That Broadway Limited (named for the formerly wide, multi-tracked roadbeds of the Pennsylvania Railroad—now a part of Conrail) began in 1902 and was the arch rival of the New York Central's 20th Century Limited which started the same year. In the 1920s the trains captured the imagination of the traveling public with their celebrated "speed wars" between New York and Chicago—speeds that approached 130 mph. They were among the world's premier trains. The old Broadway was finally discontinued in 1967, America's last all-Pullman service, after suffering a terminal decline in ridership. Today's Broadway Limited takes a course along the busy Northeast Corridor between New York and Philadelphia before it turns westward. After Philadelphia, the train passes through Pennsylvania's rolling Amish countryside into the Alleghenies where it climbs around the famous Horseshoe Curve, on into Pittsburgh and finally across northern Ohio and Indiana before reaching its western terminus, Chicago.

Westbound Schedule (Condensed)
New York, NY - Early Afternoon Departure
Philadelphia, PA - Midafternoon
Harrisburg, PA - Late Afternoon
Pittsburgh, PA - Late Evening
Akron, OH - Middle of the Night
Chicago, IL - Early Morning Arrival

Eastbound Schedule (Condensed)
Chicago, IL - Midevening Departure

Akron, OH - Middle of the Night
Pittsburgh, PA - Early Morning
Harrisburg, PA - Early Afternoon
Philadelphia, PA - Midafternoon
New York, NY - Late Afternoon Arrival

Frequency - Daily.
Seating - Heritage Fleet coaches.
Dining - Complete meal and beverage service. Lounge service is also available, with sandwiches, snacks and beverages.
Sleeping - Heritage Fleet with bedrooms, roomettes and Slumbercoach with economy bedrooms.
Baggage - Checked baggage at most stops.
Reservations - All-reserved train.
Length of Trip - 915 miles in 20½ hours.

Route Log

For route between New York and Philadelphia, see that portion of the Northeast Corridor log, page 30.

 PHILADELPHIA, PA - See page 32.

0:00 (0:25) Depart Philadelphia's 30th St. Station with city clearly visible back to right.

The course is now due west toward Harrisburg and Pittsburgh. The Philadelphia suburbs dominate for about 30 minutes, on what local commuters have long referred to as the "Main Line," until the train departs Paoli, where the pastoral scenes of central Pennsylvania farmland begin.

This nicely engineered section of trackage between Philadelphia and Harrisburg is Amtrak's Keystone Corridor. Although it has been electrified since 1938, The Broadway Limited retains its diesel units for this run.

0:01 (0:24) To right, City Hall can be seen, topped by enduring statue of William Penn—a long-time informal height restriction for buildings in Philadelphia. Barrier was broken, however, with construction of One Liberty Place, now visible as tallest structure on skyline.

0:15 (0:10) Rosemont College campus is at right.

0:19 (0:06) On left, passing through Strafford, note commuter station which is architectural curiosity. Originally built for Philadelphia's American Centennial Celebration in 1876, it was later moved to this site.

0:22 (0:03) Legend has it that proprietress of local inn once greased tracks along this portion of line to stall commuter trains which would not have otherwise stopped at her hostelry.

0:25 (0:00) Arrive Paoli.

PAOLI, PA - This stop, named after a revolutionary in Corsica, is the western edge of the densely populated Eastern Seaboard. Historic Valley Forge, where General George Washington and his Revolutionary Army suffered through a trying winter, is just two miles to the north of here.

0:00 (0:43) Depart Paoli.

0:12 (0:31) Derelict Downington station welcomes visitors with sign "No Trespassing—Amtrak Police" on left.

0:18 (0:25) Long, black buildings of Lukens Steel plant are sprawled on left at Coatesville.

Route now plunges into the fascinating "Pennsylvania Dutch" country. Beautiful farms, set in these rolling Pennsylvania hills, have been operated by the Amish with little change in lifestyle in the last 300 years. Watch for black-attired farmers in their horse-drawn buggies sharing the roads with more modern conveyances.

0:27 (0:16) Note unusual gingerbread-adorned three-story home above on left.

0:30 (0:13) Millstone standing on edge, below on left, is interesting relic of earlier time.

0:36 (0:07) Handsome Amish barns dot landscape. Horse-drawn buggies are now common sight through very heart of Pennsylvania Dutch country.

0:37 (0:06) Small airport, on left, has unusually charming setting, with homes actually abutting runway.

0:41 (0:02) Cross Conestoga River.

0:43 (0:00) Arrive Lancaster.

LANCASTER, PA - The train halts briefly in this city which produced arms for the American Revolution, and where the first Woolworth store was opened in 1879. The nation's oldest iron mine is but a few miles north at Cornwall and The Pennsylvania Rifle (misnamed The Kentucky Rifle according to Pennsylvanians) was developed here during the 1700s. The city is now the commercial center and heart of Amish farming country.

Several of the country's finest farmers' markets are in this area. The Pennsylvania Farm Museum, north of town on State 272, and the Pennsylvania Railroad Museum at Strasburg are local attractions. Also at Strasburg is the ever-popular Strasburg Railroad, America's oldest short-line railroad.

0:00 (0:35) Depart Lancaster and roll past Amtrak's Communication and Signal Training Center on left.

0:07 (0:28) Through Mt. Joy, where manufacturing plants of familiar names such as National Standard, NCR and AMP are in evidence.

0:13 (0:22) First commercial telegraph lines in U.S. were strung along this railroad right-of-way between Lancaster and Harrisburg. In 1846 first message was transmitted and logically asked, "Why didn't you write, you rascals?"

0:22 (0:12) Four spectre-like cooling towers in distance, to left, each rising 372 feet from its base, belong to infamous Three Mile Island nuclear power plant, which came close to meltdown in March 1979.

0:26 (0:09) Pennsylvania State University's attractive Harrisburg campus lies just beyond highway on right.

0:27 (0:08) On immediate left, runways of Harrisburg International Airport parallel tracks.

0:28 (0:05) Bethlehem Steel's Steelton

plant stretches beside tracks on right.

0:32 (0:03) Large bridge on left carries forerunner of interstate highways across Susquehanna River—the Pennsylvania Turnpike.

0:35 (0:00) Arrive Harrisburg's finely remodeled intermodal Amtrak station. Handsome #4859 GG-1 electric locomotive stands on permanent display between train and depot.

HARRISBURG, PA - This city of 55,000 is now over 200 years old. In 1812 it became the state capital and subsequently one of the finest capitol buildings in the nation was built here—just beyond the station. Built in 1906 at a cost of $10 million, the capitol's interior marble was shipped here from Europe. Its exquisite dome was patterned after St. Peter's Basilica in Rome. The unusual William Penn Memorial Museum, which houses an historic treasure trove, and Archives Building are also particularly noteworthy.

0:00 (1:07) Depart Harrisburg and immediately on left is State Capitol Building just described.

0:04 (1:03) Slip through rail yards of Conrail. Locomotive shops will soon appear at right.

0:11 (0:55) Cross over Susquehanna River on Rockville Bridge, four miles north of Harrisburg. Structure is world's longest and widest stone-arch bridge and contains 48 arches made of Pennsylvania white sandstone. It is 3,820 feet in length, has a 52-foot roadbed and is 42 feet above Susquehanna. First train crossed this bridge in 1902 on Easter Sunday.

0:15 (0:52) Pier for former bridge across Susquehanna now supports mini-Statue of Liberty in midstream on right. Supposedly, some imaginative youngsters sculptured it using old venetian blinds.

0:24 (0:43) Pass through Duncannon, leave Susquehanna River, and enter easternmost hills of Allegheny Mountains. From here to Altoona, tracks accompany Juniata River. Line was originally built to compete with Erie Canal and is still a busy freight road as will be noted from numerous Conrail freight trains.

0:44 (0:23) Two new, rather short chairlifts at right would indicate Pennsylvania has, at least, semblance of ski industry.

0:52 (0:15) Large wooden Indian with uplifted arm welcomes clients of campground

Broadway Limited - Horseshoe Curve, Pennsylvania
HOMER R. HILL

on right.

0:55 (0:12) Across Juniata River, on right, Empire Poultry, largest supplier of poultry to East Coast, is barely visible from train.

1:07 (0:00) Arrive Lewistown.

LEWISTOWN, PA - This industrial town is in the very heart of Pennsylvania. The Frank McCoy House, former home of General Frank Ross McCoy, will 'be of interest to historians.

0:00 (0:39) Depart Lewistown. On right, plant of FMC, producer of industrial chemicals, is substantial contributor to town's economy.

0:23 (0:16) Blue Mountain on left is prominent Allegheny ridge stretching along horizon.

0:31 (0:08) Sand from quarry on right is used in local glass production.

0:39 (0:00) Arrive Huntingdon.

HUNTINGDON, PA - A small industrial town, Huntingdon is attractively situated along the Juniata River. The popular Raystown Lake recreational area lies just to the south. This is home to Juniata College.

0:00 (0:42) Depart Huntingdon. Immediately on right is large Owens-Corning Fiberglass plant which melts small fiberglass marbles into large tanks which are sometimes visible next to plant.

0:13 (0:29) Cross Spruce Creek, a fine trout fishing stream which at one time provided sport for former president Jimmy Carter. Enter Spruce Creek Tunnel for a sudden but brief period of darkness.

0:14 (0:28) Camp Espy farms, on right, fattens cattle for Eastern markets.

0:37 (0:05) Rumble through short tunnel.

0:44 (0:00) Arriving Altoona, Broadway Ltd. slips through enormous Altoona rail yards, and then past Railroaders Memorial Museum, on left, where numerous rail cars and locomotives can be seen, including Raymond Loewy-designed GG-1 electric locomotive. Famous K-4, 234-ton steam locomotive, a design that dates back to 1914, is also here. Engine was formerly on display at nearby Horseshoe Curve. At one time, Pennsylvania Railroad had 400 of these, which served as standard passenger engines on this line until World War II. On opposite (right) side of train, predominant structure is Cathedral of Blessed Sacrament. Station is very efficient intermodal transit center.

ALTOONA, PA - A supply point for building the Pennsylvania Railroad, Altoona now has one of the world's largest assemblages of rail maintenance facilities.

0:00 (1:00) Depart Altoona and commence a steep climb toward Gallitzin Summit. Ascending grades will now range from 1.75% to 1.85%, forcing most westbound freights to add helper engines at Alto, just west of Altoona.

0:10 (0:50) Reservoirs below on left are part of Altoona's domestic water storage system.

0:12 (0:48) Horseshoe Curve (the Pennsylvania Railroad's rulebook spelled horseshoe as two words), a beautiful hairpin turn, nearly a half-mile long, is one of railroading's most notable landmarks.

The Curve permits a tolerable 1.73% grade through this section of mountains which will allow 6 diesels to pull 125 fully loaded freight cars around its perimeter. A shortcut across valley's mouth would have produced a 4.37% grade, but those same diesels would then handle only 43 cars. At one time four sets of track rounded the curve, but one set was removed in 1981 as an economy move. Pennsylvania Railroad GP9 diesel Number 7048 is now displayed on the inside of the Curve. The Curve was designated a National Historic Landmark in 1967. In 1992, the Curve was rededicated with the completion of a new visitors center and funicular that transports visitors from the center to the level of the Curve itself. The two trams were built in the shops of the Durango & Silverton Narrow-Gauge Railroad in Durango, Colorado.

0:24 (0:36) Pass through one of three tunnels, as route handily crests Alleghenies. Allegheny and Gallitzin tunnels, each over a mile in length, usually handle westbound traffic while shorter New Portage Tunnel takes eastbound trains that must descend a 2.27% grade.

At one time, though, it was not so easy. Just three miles to the south, from 1834 to 1855, the Allegheny Portage Railroad, with its system of canals, trains and incline railroads, ingeniously lifted sectionalized canal boats (people, cargo and all) over these mountains on a series of inclined planes and level stretches, allowing continuous transportation between Philadelphia and Pittsburgh. However, construction of the Horseshoe Curve provided a direct rail link and ended operations for one of America's most unique transportation systems.

0:55 (0:05) Cranes using powerful electromagnets can often be seen at work loading scrap onto gondola cars on left.

0:56 (0:01) Johnstown plant of Bethlehem Steel on left. Also, note church on left with three onion domes.

1:00 (0:00) Arrive Johnstown.

JOHNSTOWN, PA - In 1889, the nation's most disastrous flood devastated this city of steel mills. An overly enlarged dam, 14 miles east of here on the Conemaugh River, formed a reservoir some two miles long. The lake was the centerpiece of the South Fork Fishing and Hunting Club, a secretive retreat for many of Pittsburgh's wealthy and socially elite. Two excursion steamers plied the waters in the summer months. On May 31 of that year, after a day of drenching rain, the poorly maintained dam began to give way. Warnings earlier in the day were ignored by the populous—citizens who had heard similar warnings almost every spring. At 3:10 in the afternoon the inhabitants heard a "roar like thunder," then were suddenly engulfed by a 36-foot wall of water. Over 2,200 people died and hundreds more were never accounted for.

Johnstown's history of flooding has continued. In 1936, 25 lives were lost and in 1977, 85 persons died.

Bethlehem Steel is still the principal employer, but the town's economy has been less than vibrant. In 1983, when the steel market hit bottom, Johnstown had the highest unemployment in the U.S.

0:00 (0:54) Depart Johnstown. Incline on slope behind station is a people conveyor providing unusual access to community atop hill. Seventy-one percent grade may make it world's steepest incline. Bethlehem Steel's bar and rod plant is on right.

0:02 (0:52) Sign painted on brick building, "Conemaugh & Black Lick Railroad Company," touts former Bethlehem Steel operated railroad.

0:46 (0:06) Pass through Latrobe, home to past training camps of formidable Pittsburgh Steelers and to Arnold Palmer.

0:52 (0:00) Arrive Greensburg.

GREENSBURG, PA - Near this western Pennsylvania town is Bushy Run Battlefield where Colonel Henry Bouquet defeated hostile Indians in 1763.

0:00 (0:44) Depart Greensburg.

0:20 (0:24) Numerous older brick buildings on right are home to historic Westinghouse Air Brake Division.

0:25 (0:18) Elderly Edgar Thomson Works of USX-US Steel are trackside on left.

0:44 (0:00) Arrive Pittsburgh.

PITTSBURGH, PA - Once known for its steel mills and smoke, Pittsburgh now exemplifies what can be done with urban renewal when the determination (and money) to do so exists. The city now has clean air, shiny skyscrapers and beautiful parks as a result of a massive effort undertaken in recent years.

The downtown is quite compact and more walkable than most cities of comparable size. The city is also unusual in that it still has maintained many ethnic neighborhoods through its years of development and growth. With a metropolitan population in excess of two million and located in the "Golden Triangle," where the Allegheny and the Monongahela rivers join to form the Ohio River, the city is one of the nation's primary industrial centers.

Amtrak Station, Liberty Avenue at Grant Street, is located near the heart of downtown in the remodeled quarters of what was once Penn Central Station. Platforms are at street level, but the station is down one flight by escalator or elevator, beneath exclusive apartments. There are storage lockers and food and beverage vending machines. Pay-parking is in front of the station and also covered parking at the Greyhound terminal across the street.

Yellow Cab, 665-8100, and Peoples Cab, 681-3131. Nearest **local bus** stop, half block from the station. Light-rail stop is behind station, free service within downtown area; 231-5707.

Pittsburgh

Legend:
- ⚓ Amtrak Station
- 1 - Visitors Information
- 2 - Station Square
- 3 - Inclines
- 4 - Point State Park
- 5 - The Priory
- 6 - Westin William Penn

Greyhound is across the street from the station. **Greater Pittsburgh International Airport** is 20 miles west of the city.

❓ **Visitor Information Center,** Gateway Center, Downtown Pittsburgh, (412) 281-9222. Write Pittsburgh Convention and Visitors Bureau, 4 Gateway Center, 15222.

🏨 Hotels in the downtown Golden Triangle area are fairly expensive; two are included since one is close to the station and the other is at Station Square. The other accommodations shown are a few minutes cab ride from downtown and are logical alternatives.

-**Westin William Penn,** 530 William Penn Place, 15230; (412) 281-7100 and 800-228-3000. Four blocks from the station. $120.

-**Station Square Sheraton Motor Inn,** 7 Station Square, 15219; (412) 261-2000. Next to Station Square, a 300-room resort-conference facility with views of river and downtown Pittsburgh. Few-minute cab ride (light-rail station within two blocks) from station. Station transportation available. $122.

-**The Priory,** 614 Pressley St., 15212; (412) 231-3338. European-style hotel on the transitional North Side about a half mile from the station (but not very walkable). Formerly a rectory for a German Catholic Church, it has been made into a

24-room hostelry. Complimentary breakfast and evening wine. Shuttle service in the morning. Prices range from $65 to $135 with most rooms at $88.

-**Hampton Inn Greentree,** 555 Trumbull Dr., 15205; (412) 922-0100. Continental breakfast included. Between downtown and the airport, about three miles from the station. Can be slow going into town in the rush hour. Continental breakfast. $65.

Point State Park is at the confluence of the Allegheny and Monongahela rivers, where one will find the only local remnant of the French and Indian War, the Fort Pitt Blockhouse. Also located here are a large fountain, the Fort Pitt Museum with historic exhibits, and military drills held during the summer months.

Station Square, just across the Smithfield Bridge from downtown, includes shops, restaurants, a marina and the Industrial Transportation Museum with antique railroad cars and trolleys. This area also contains the historic buildings of the P&LE Railroad.

Inclines to the top of Mount Washington can be ridden from their lower stations, either at Station Square or west of the Fort Pitt Bridge, both on West Carson Street. Observation platforms are at the top of each, and a restaurant is at the summit of the westernmost incline.

The **Carnegie Institute,** at 4400 Forbes Ave. in the eastern section of Pittsburgh, contains two fine museums: The **Museum of Art** has an outstanding permanent collection of European paintings and sculpture, as well as American works; the **Museum of Natural History** has various exhibits of plant life, current and prehistoric wildlife, as well as other exhibits.

(Note: Route between Pittsburgh and New Castle may be switched to alternate routing in near future.)

0:00 (2:27) Depart Pittsburgh, traveling east for a few minutes before swinging northward, following a CSX (ex B&O) route to Chicago.

0:25 (2:02) Cruise beneath Pennsylvania Turnpike, America's first superhighway. Features considered commonplace today, four lanes of concrete divided by a median, lengthy merging lanes, limited access, moderate grades and well-banked swooping curves, all were startling innovations when highway opened more than fifty years ago on October 1, 1940. Toll to drive entire length of Pennsylvania was $1.50—an amount many thought would restrict its use to only a handful of drivers. In its first year, Turnpike carried 2.4 million vehicles, nearly double most optimistic forecasts.

0:46 (1:41) To left, B&O caboose now serves as visitor center for small community of Mars.

0:52 (1:35) MSA Research Corp., to right at Evans City, is world leader in developing mine safety appliances and underwater breathing devices. Adjoining sister company Callery Chemical produces boron-related products.

1:12 (1:15) Through unique village of Harmony, but due to lower elevation of roadbed, only a glimpse can be had of some of town's original buildings. To left is one of them, a brick structure known as Neff Haus.

In 1804, Johann George Rapp and his followers left the duchy of Wurtemberg, Germany to escape religious persecution and founded the Harmony Society at this spot in 1805. It soon became one of America's most successful communal groups, constructing 130 buildings and cultivating 2,000 acres. Rapp's 500 followers pledged all of their worldly possessions to Rapp and the society "for the common good." Their ultimate extinction was sealed, however, when, in a mood of religious fervor, they adopted the practice of celibacy. Over 100 members are buried in the local cemetery, where only one headstone exists, that of George Rapp.

For reasons not too clear, the Rappists sold Harmony to a Mennonite in 1815, moved to Indiana and later back to Pennsylvania, where they ultimately faded into history. Today, Mennonites are still living in Harmony.

1:32 (0:55) Cross Slippery Rock Creek, flowing down from Slippery Rock State College, just a few miles north of here.

2:10 (0:17) Through city of New Castle, where much of America's home and hotel pottery is manufactured. Area was once tribal center of Delaware Indians.

2:18 (0:09) Pass through town of Edinburg, birthplace of Ira D. Sankey, famous singing evangelist and fellow worker with Dwight L. Moody in both Europe and America.

2:21 (0:06) Leave Pennsylvania and Ohio.

2:27 (0:00) Arrive Youngstown.

YOUNGSTOWN, OH - This community was first settled in 1797 and named for John Young who purchased the original site from the Connecticut Land Company. The city ultimately grew to one of the world's major steel centers, becoming the fourth largest producer in the U.S. Today, its industries are quite diversified.

0:00 (1:10) Depart Youngstown.

0:46 (0:24) On right is entrance to Ravenna Army Ammunition Depot.

0:47 (0:23) Clatter across intersection with Conrail (ex Pennsylvania Railroad), route of Capitol Limited, in Ravenna. Town was founded in 1799 by Benjamin Tappan, an early glassmaker.

0:54 (0:16) This is Kent, home to Kent State University, where several students were killed during a clash with Ohio National Guard during Vietnam protests.

1:02 (0:08) Trundle through Cuyahoga Falls, a large Akron suburb and summer home of Cleveland Symphony Orchestra.

1:10 (0:00) Arrive Akron, where nearby Quaker Square has shopping, restaurants and night spots in some of original silos and mills of Quaker Oats Company.

AKRON, OH - After B. F. Goodrich established the first rubber factory here in 1870, the city ultimately, with the help of the automobile, grew to become the largest rubber and tire manufacuring center in the world. It is also America's largest producer of lighter-than-air craft. It is also home to the famous Soap Box Derby.

The town's name is derived from the Greek word "akros," meaning high place. Akron was the high point on the Ohio and Erie Canal, 950 feet above sea level.

0:00 (2:00) Depart Akron.

1:04 (0:56) Through small town of Nova, where townsfolk are resisting controversial effort to build "hazardous waste" incinerators.

1:30 (0:30) Pass through Willard, "City of Blossoms," which has small but interesting railroad museum with B&O memorabilia.

1:47 (0:13) Tracks angle through Tiffin where Heidelberg College, established in 1850, can be seen a block to left upon entering town, and then past Tiffin University near center of town, also to left.

2:00 (0:00) Arrive Fostoria.

FOSTORIA, OH - This agricultural and glass manufacturing center of nearly 16,000 people is Amtrak's closest stop to nearby Lima. Several highways intersect here, as well as rail lines of the Baltimore & Ohio, the Chesapeake and Ohio and the Norfolk and Western. A rail intersection (diamond) is just west of the old station.

0:00 (1:30) Depart Fostoria.

0:06 (1:24) Cross South Branch of Portage River.

0:10 (1:20) Approaching Bairdstown, a bit of Americana appears to left. Barn is advertising medium trying to convince consumer to "Chew Mail Pouch Tobacco."

0:25 (1:05) Into Deshler, which is sometimes called "Corn City," sometimes "Crossroads of the B&O." Dekalb hybrid seed plant is on right with vat-like structures, while B&O diamond is in center of town. Then, on right, large green metal building houses Deshler Products Division of Sherwin Williams where paint rollers, trays and other painting accessories are manufactured.

0:31 (0:59) Numerous farmers in this area beat summer heat by building "swimming holes" next to their homes, some with elaborate diving towers. Several such pools can be spotted along tracks.

0:33 (0:57) Through small town of Hamler, where famous actor Joe E. Brown was born and raised. Highway through town, to left of tracks, is named in his honor.

0:50 (0:40) Entering Defiance from east, enormous factory off to right is General Motors Central Foundry which produces engine blocks and other castings for numerous makes of GM cars.

0:52 (0:38) Into Defiance and cross Auglaize River. Town named for fort of same name, built during "Mad Anthony" Wayne's campaign against the Indians.

Wayne said, "I defy the English, the Indians and all the devils from hell to take it." Fort was at confluence of Auglaize and Maumee rivers. Town is off to right, as is The Defiance College founded in 1850. After leaving Defiance, track will soon cross Maumee River.

1:16 (0:14) Leave Ohio and enter Indiana. (Note that Indiana does not observe daylight saving time.)

1:20 (0:10) Cross St. Joseph River.

1:26 (0:04) Roll through historic Auburn.

Here, the town's automobile background is wonderfully preserved in one of the country's finest auto museums—the Auburn-Cord Dusenberg Museum. Over 140 automobiles from all eras are wonderfully displayed in what was once Auburn Automobile Company's administration building and factory show room. Mr. Cord, a company driving force, believed "If you can't be big, you have to be different." Their autos reflected that philosophy. The National Automobile and Truck Museum is also being formed in Auburn, located next to the existing Auburn Museum.

1:30 (0:00) Arrive Garrett where Amtrak shelter, on right, serves as station.

GARRETT, IN - This town is also a stop for nearby Auburn and much larger Ft. Wayne, the latter located just 27 miles to the south. Garrett's railroading heritage is memorialized by painting of locomotive on water tower next to tracks.

0:00 (0:45) Depart Auburn.

0:16 (0:29) At Albion, imposing brick Noble County Court House dominates downtown area, a few blocks to right.

0:44 (0:01) Entering Naponee, grey structures to right of train house Fairmont Homes, large constructor of mobile homes and travel trailers.

0:45 (0:00) Arriving Naponee, note Amish buggy parked on canopy over entrance to downtown store at right.

NAPONEE, IN - This is Amish country, where farmers are blessed with rich, fertile farms. Naponee serves as an agricultural trading center for this simple, unpretentious society.

0:00 (1:20) Depart Naponee. Watch for Amish riding in quaint horse-drawn buggies.

0:02 (1:19) On right, popular tourist attraction, Amish Acres, has buildings and working demonstrations that have preserved Amish way of life. It is now listed on National Register of Historic Places.

0:10 (1:10) Tracks continue to angle across Indiana farmland toward Chicago's industrialized environs. Tracks will more or less follow U.S. Highway 6, named for Grand Army of the Republic.

1:00 (0:20) Intersect combined I-80 and I-90.

Train passes from Eastern to Central Time Zone.

1:07 (0:13) Where Gary began, enormous U.S. Steel Gary Works stretch along tracks at right beyond rail yards.

1:14 (0:06) Inland Steel Plants now line tracks. Then cross drawbridge spanning Indiana Harbor Canal that links Lake Michigan with Calumet River.

1:16 (0:04) Standard Oil Company of Indiana refinery creates apparatus jungle at left. Company's first plant was built here in 1889. Lake Michigan is now only 100 feet or so to right.

1:20 (0:00) Arrive Hammond-Whiting.

For route description from here to Chicago, see that portion of Lake Shore Ltd. log, page 76.

CHICAGO, IL - Rail passengers traveling across the U.S. funnel through Chicago like sands through the neck of an hourglass. A quick look at a map of the United States tells why Chicago has grown up to become the nation's major transportation hub, where much of America's east-west traffic has to converge. Lake Michigan, cutting strategically into the heart of the Midwest, provided early-day shipping access to a developing frontier. With the coming of the railroad, tracks soon radiated from The Windy City in almost every direction, a pattern that is still followed today.

Oddly, in spite of heavy volumes of traffic, trains don't go through Chicago—just their passengers do. All through-passengers must change trains. It's always been this way, and it's unlikely to be otherwise in the foreseeable future. So everyone arriving in Chicago on Amtrak gets off here, at least for a little while. This phenomenon, along with 160-or-so commuter trains a day, makes Chicago Union Station a very busy place.

The 1926 depot was the object of a major remodeling project in the early 1990s, greatly improving the interior's efficiency. Two 24-story office towers were also planned.

Union Station, 210 S. Canal St. (at Adams St.), is in the heart of downtown. Its cavernous, marble-pillared waiting room still contains the original hardwood benches, while a much newer passenger lounge is conveniently located adjacent to the train platform area. There

Chicago

Lake Michigan

- Amtrak Station
1 - Visitors Information
2 - Chicago Board of Trade
3 - Adler Planetarium
4 - Museum of Science and Industry
5 - Sears Tower
6 - Field Museum of Natural History
7 - Art Institute of Chicago
8 - John G. Shedd Aquarium
9 - Bismark Hotel
10 - Quality Inn Downtown
11 - Midland Hotel
12 - Palmer House

are and snack bars and a cafeteria in the station, and several restaurants are within easy walking distance. A posh, bordering on elegance, Metropolitan Lounge is available to first-class ticket holders. Luggage carts are obtained by inserting four quarters into cart dispensers. Luggage lockers are available in southwest corner of the "Great Hall." There is no free parking; parking garages and lots are nearby.

Cab stand at the station and it is usually well supplied; Checker, 421-1300. **Greyhound** is about a mile from the station. **Local buses** are just outside the station; for bus and commuter train information, call 836-7000 (suburbs, 800-972-7000). Train to **O'Hare International Airport,** 19 miles northwest of downtown, is two blocks away at Clinton and Congress. **Midway Airport** is nine miles southwest of downtown.

Visitor Information Center, located in the old pumping station across from the Water Tower, 163 E. Pearson; (312) 280-5740. The State of Illinois also has a center in the Sears Tower with some Chicago information. Or write Chicago Tourism Council, 806 North Michigan Ave., 60611.

Bismark Hotel, 171 W. Randolph St. (at Wells), 60601; (312) 236-0123 or 800-643-1500. Fine old hostelry, well maintained and managed. Seven blocks from the station. $95.

-**Quality Inn Downtown,** One Mid City Plaza (Madison at Halstead); (312) 829-5000. West of downtown, off the Kennedy Expressway. Five blocks from the station, but not a nice walk. $69.

-**Midland Hotel,** 172 W. Adams (at LaSalle), 60603; (312) 332-1200 or 800-621-2360. Excellent hotel, only four blocks from the station. Discount if reserved through Quikbook, 800-221-3531. $139.

-**The Palmer House,** 17 E. Monroe, 60603; (312) 726-7500 or 800-HILTONS. Long-time favorite of visitors. Eight blocks from the station. $134.

"The Loop," bounded by Van Buren, Wells, Lake and Wabash, has some of the best shopping in the city, particularly along State Street. The **Magnificent Mile** on North Michigan Ave. is home to an assemblage of Rodeo-Drive-class stores, including Saks, Bloomingdales, Neiman-Marcus and Marshall Field's. The **Sears Tower,** Wacker Drive and Jackson, is the world's tallest building at 110 stories. It's just two blocks east of the station and has an observation deck for the best view in town. The **Chicago Board of Trade,** 141 West Jackson, is the largest commodities futures market, with several tours during the day, five blocks from the station.

Also downtown, but somewhat farther away: the **Field Museum of Natural History,** Roosevelt Rd. and S. Lake Shore Dr., is one of the nation's finest; the adjacent **Shedd Aquarium** has an outstanding collection of marine life; and just east of these two attractions is the **Adler Planetarium** with daily multimedia shows that display much of the heavens.

Two of Chicago's major attractions are out of the downtown area: the **Museum of Science and Industry,** 57th St. and South Lake Shore Dr., with acres of outstanding technological exhibits, is one of the best such museums in the world; and the **Brookfield Zoo,** 1st Ave. and 31st St., in Brookfield, is one of the largest zoos in the nation.

Other Pennsylvania Service

The **Pennsylvanian** links New York City with Pittsburgh by way of Philadelphia. Daily New York departures are early morning with late afternoon arrivals in Pittsburgh. Pittsburgh departures are midmorning (early afternoon on Sundays) and New York is reached nine hours later.

Numerous other **Keystone Service** trains connect Harrisburg and Philadelphia.

Chicago
Pittsburgh
Washington, DC

Capitol Limited

Between Washington, DC and Pittsburgh, the Capitol Limited runs on the tracks of CSX Transportation. The stretch beginning some 40 miles west of Washington at Point of Rocks and continuing to Cumberland, Maryland is the oldest section of operating railroad in the U.S., with passenger activity dating back to more than 160 years ago. This is the original main line of the Baltimore and Ohio Railroad and follows along the equally-as-historic Chesapeake & Ohio Canal. At Cumberland, the Capitol Limited swings northward through the scenic hills of southwestern Pennsylvania.

West of Pittsburgh the Capitol's route follows Conrail to Cleveland, then continuing on Conrail, takes the same route used by the Lake Shore Limited across northern Ohio and Indiana into Chicago.

Westbound Schedule (Condensed)
Washington, DC - Late Afternoon Departure
Cumberland, MD - Early Evening
Pittsburgh, PA - Late Evening
Cleveland, OH - Middle of the Night
Chicago, IL - Early Morning Arrival

Eastbound Schedule (Condensed)
Chicago, IL - Late Afternoon Departure
Cleveland, OH - Late Night
Pittsburgh, PA - Middle of the Night
Cumberland, MD - Early Morning
Washington, DC - Late Morning Arrival

Frequency - Daily.
Seating - Heritage Fleet coaches and dome car.*
Dining - Complete meal and beverage service with linens and china. Lounge service, with sandwiches, snacks and beverages.
Sleeping - Heritage Fleet with bedrooms and roomettes.*
Baggage - Checked baggage handled at Washington, DC and most stops Pittsburgh to Chicago.
Reservations - All-reserved train.
Length of Trip - 780 miles in 20½ hours.

*This train should have Superliner cars, beginning in 1994 or 1995.

Route Log

 WASHINGTON, DC- See page 38.

0:00 (0:20) Depart Washington.
0:02 (0:18) Familiar obelisk of Washington Monument can be seen back on left.
0:03 (0:17) Streamlined "Metros" of Washington's subway stand in storage yard on immediate left. Route now curls to left away from Northeast Corridor.
0:07 (0:13) Beautiful white building on left with dazzling blue and gold tiled dome is National Shrine of the Immaculate Conception—largest Catholic church in United States and seventh largest church in world. Catholic University of America is located here.
0:13 (0:07) Suburbs momentarily give way to a few wooded hills before modern office parks and shopping centers of Rockville appear.
0:20 (0:00) Arrive Rockville where curi-

ous architecture of church on left resembles hamburger with toothpick stuck in top.

ROCKVILLE, MD - First settled in the early 1700s, it was frequented by travelers on a "great road" between Georgetown and Frederick. Rockville is now one of Washington's larger suburbs.

0:00 (0:42) Depart Rockville.

Leave more populous fringes of Washington and settle back to enjoy Potomac countryside, punctuated by an occasional rural community.

0:04 (0:38) At trackside in Gaithersburg, small, charming depot still serves D.C. commuters on right.

0:11 (0:31) Deep red depot on left at Germantown is special trackside adornment.

0:19 (0:23) Cross high over Monocacy River which empties into Potomac half-mile to left.

0:21 (0:21) Through trees on left, broad Potomac River flows placidly toward Washington. Long-since-abandoned Chesapeake and Ohio Canal, now overgrown with shrubs and trees, is still visible between tracks and river.

Quaint rock bridges spanning this historic canal can be seen from time to time. Opened in 1850 shortly after the completion of the B&O Railroad, this 184-mile waterway connected Cumberland with tidewater at Georgetown following the course of the Potomac. It took about a week for freight-laden canal boats to make the entire trip.

Locks, stone aqueducts and the 3,080-foot Paw Paw Tunnel contributed to its hefty $22 million cost. Operations finally ceased in 1924. Today, canoes in its placid waters and bicycles along its towpath are common sights.

0:26 (0:16) On right at Point of Rocks, MD, church-like station, complete with steeple, is another fascinating elderly depot. Designed by Frances E. Baldwin and standing at spot of original B&O main line from Baltimore, station now serves as commuter stop. Spot received its name from prominent bulge of granite that once jutted out over tracks.

During the Civil War, Stonewall Jackson initiated one of his more brilliant strategies

near here. For a 44-mile stretch west of Point of Rocks, the B&O main line expanded to two sets of tracks. Jackson convinced the Union-oriented B&O to run their eastbound and westbound trains simultaneously on these two lines and then proceeded to cut them off at each end. The engines were quickly taken apart and shipped overland on wagons, mostly to Raleigh, North Carolina, where they were reassembled and placed into Confederate service.

0:27 (0:12) Through short tunnel. Then in 3 minutes, through another.

0:35 (0:07) Quaint old roundhouse still stands in rail yards on left.

0:41 (0:01) Into another tunnel, then cross Potomac into West Virginia where Shenandoah River confluence can be seen just to left, and enter Harpers Ferry.

0:42 (0:00) Arrive Harpers Ferry. Note unusual signal on roof of rather forlorn-looking station on left.

HARPERS FERRY, WV - Originally a ferrying point in 1733, the town gained prominence in the 1790s when a national armory was established here. As early as 1836, a railroad bridge linked Maryland with West Virginia by crossing the Potomac at this point.

The first wooden trestle had an unlikely "Y" junction in the middle—branching off to the Shenandoah Valley on the left. This bridge and its many successors were subsequently destroyed by war or flood, including being dismantled by John Brown who hoped to incite a slave uprising with his infamous raid on the armory. Today, Harpers Ferry is a National Historical Park.

0:00 (0:20) Depart Harpers Ferry.

0:01 (0:19) Small hydroelectric plant of an earlier era is on right.

0:04 (0:16) Low dam, which formerly funneled water from Potomac into aqueduct leading to power plant just described, appears on right.

Twin silos off to left are part of state-operated training farm for youth.

0:20 (0:00) Arrive Martinsburg.

MARTINSBURG, WV - Since 1941, when the B&O Railroad first reached here, Martinsburg has been closely tied to railroading—for better or for worse.

Capitol Limited - Harpers Ferry, West Virginia
JACK SWANSON

In 1849, shops and roundhouses were built with extraordinary workmanship and architectural detail, only to be later destroyed by Confederate troops during Stonewall Jackson's 1862 campaign. The present station was the only survivor and is nation's oldest functioning train station. The outstanding roundhouses and most of the other buildings were rebuilt in the 1860s. Then in 1877, workers of the B&O went on strike, which developed into the largest railroad strike in the nation's history. A plaque commemorating this event is on the left, next to the old five-story brick station.

Unfortunately, two separate fires, both set by vandals, destroyed both roundhouses in recent years.

0:00 (1:25) Depart Martinsburg. West Roundhouse and ruins of East Roundhouse described above are on right.
0:13 (1:12) Fine panorama of distant mountains comes into view on right. These distant scenes start to diminish as terrain gradually becomes more confining.
0:15 (1:10) Potomac is visible once again on right.
0:23 (1:02) On left, flashy iris beds show off during springtime.
0:26 (0:59) Small airstrip accompanies tracks at right. This is Hancock, a town built in three states—Maryland, Pennsylvania and West Virginia.
0:37 (0:48) Passengers now are afforded an excellent look up serene Potomac to right.
0:51 (0:34) Enter very short tunnel.
0:53 (0:32) Enter lengthy Graham Tunnel that blots out daylight for about one minute. Both entrance and exit repose in West Virginia, but most of interior is located in Maryland.
0:54 (0:31) Make a quick trip into Maryland and then back into West Virginia as train crosses Potomac twice in rapid succession. More short tunnels are encountered.
1:16 (0:09) Bid final farewell to West Virginia and Potomac as train crosses that stately river for last time and enters Cumberland, Maryland.
1:20 (0:05) Control tower for expansive CSX rail yards loom on left. Then CSX locomotive shops appear on right.
1:25 (0:00) Arrive Cumberland.

CUMBERLAND, MD - At one time, Cumberland was known as "Washington Town" (George Washington's military career started and ended here) and also "Mills Creek," but it was finally christened "Cumberland" after the fort by the same name. The fort was located here during the French and Indian War (1756-1763). Both Colonel Washington and General Braddock left from here on expeditions against the French.

In June of 1755, Braddock led a force of 2,300 men, 200 wagons and 600 horses from Ft. Cumberland to a point near Ft. Dusquesne, now Pittsburgh, where he and nearly a thousand others were killed in what has been considered by most historians as a series of tactical blunders. It was this engagement that triggered the war with the French and Indians when the British disputed France's attempt to control the Mississippi and Ohio river valleys.

Today, Washington's headquarters, a small log cabin, is all that remains of the fort.

0:00 (2:20) Depart Cumberland. (From here to Pittsburgh, best viewing will be on left.)

0:03 (2:16) Pass through "The Narrows" where Wills Creek cuts through Allegheny Mountains. Originally a trading route, it was later a military wagon road. Some believe General Braddock came through here on his ill-fated march to Ft. Dusquesne. Road finally became first federally financed U.S. highway (The National Pike —now U.S. 40). This was also passage for America's first east-west railroad.

0:04 (2:15) Stone quarries are on immediate right.

0:09 (2:11) Leave Maryland and enter Pennsylvania. Large red barn on left marks the approximate boundary.

0:26 (1:54) Wills Creek begins to narrow, and countryside becomes more mountainous as tracks climb toward summit at Sandpatch.

0:28 (1:52) Brief trip through Falls Cut Tunnel.

0:32 (1:48) Pass through village of Glencoe with its colorful array of quaint frame stores and houses.

0:41 (1:39) Rushing waters of Wills Creek, on left, are favorite of trout fishermen in early spring.

0:45 (1:35) Enter Sandpatch Tunnel,

nearly a mile long and consuming two minutes before emerging at other end; it is longest of trip.

0:47 (1:34) Crest summit of Alleghenies at Sandpatch. Marker on right places elevation at 2,258 feet.

0:50 (1:31) Pass beneath curving bridge of Western Maryland Railroad where trains loaded with bituminous coal from nearby mines cross regularly.

0:55 (1:26) Pass through Meyersdale which is destination of special trains from Pittsburgh carrying syrup lovers to maple syrup festival held here each spring.

1:01 (1:22) At Blue Lick, pass beneath intriguing, abandoned rail bridge of Western Maryland Railroad. Watch for Belgian draft horses cavorting in field in front of barn on left. Ridge forming backdrop is abandoned strip mine.

1:04 (1:19) Those sitting on left should be able to spot two huge stone grain-grinding wheels, long since abandoned in Casselman River next to tracks. Quarry for millstones, with holes in cliff face, is at right.

1:05 (1:18) Serpentine trails etched on hillside across river on left are roads for logging trucks.

1:06 (1:17) Unusual series of "caves," just to right, were once former rock quarry.

1:11 (1:11) At Rockwood, another rail bridge, carrying branch north to Johnstown, crosses over Casselman River.

1:20 (1:01) Quaint log home across Casselman River on left is one of many spots where deer can frequently be spotted from train.

1:24 (0:58) Pass through Pinkerton Tunnel for 20 seconds and emerge on single set of tracks, where traffic is now controlled by operator at nearby Confluence.

1:25 (0:57) Pass through Shoefly Tunnel and return to luxury of two sets of tracks.

1:29 (0:52) Enter darkness for about one minute as train negotiates Brook Tunnel. Train normally saves three miles by taking "highline" at this point, while "lowline" branches off to left following more leisurely river route.

1:36 (0:45) We are rejoined by "lowline" and Youghiogheny (pronounced yawk-a-haney) River on left. Pass through Confluence and cross sleepy Laurel Creek.

1:43 (0:37) High ridge of Sugar Loaf Mountain can be seen on right, while fallen trees near river below show evidence of hard-working beavers. Watch for canoes which frequent this popular river in summertime.

1:49 (0:31) Enter Ohiopyle, where Ohiopyle Falls are located (just out of view and beyond town on left). Laurel Highlands Trail leaves town on right, taking energetic hikers to Johnstown, some 45 miles "as a crow flies."

Between here and Connellsville, watch for fishermen trying their luck for elusive perch, pike, trout, walleye, and bass, all stocked in the Youghiogheny. Kayaks and rafts can frequently be seen in the summer. Maple trees combine to produce a color spectacular in the fall, making this a favorite sightseeing run at that time of year. Evergreens are mostly hemlock.

1:58 (0:21) Road across river on left, zigzagging up through trees, is used to bring rafts up from stream after float trips from Ohiopyle. Derelict boxcar in river below on left is from wreck occurring more than 20 years ago.

2:03 (0:14) Cross Indian Creek spanned by small stone-arch bridge—one of few remaining. Summer youth camp, just across river on left, is located in heart of state game lands. Abandoned rail right-of-way across river is now a popular hiking trail.

2:15 (0:00) Arrive Connellsville.

 CONNELLSVILLE, PA - In the late 1700s, vast coal deposits were discovered in the immediate area, but were thought to have no value because of their soft and crumbly character. However, it was later discovered that by roasting this coal in ordinary "beehive" coke ovens for two or three days, it made outstanding metallurgical fuel and became known as the famous pearl-grey Connellsville Coke. Always a railroad town (it is still a division point with a large classification yard), during World War II the "Connellsville Canteen," consisting of 800 women volunteers, served meals to more than 600,000 servicemen that came through on troop trains in a two-year period!

0:00 (1:26) Depart Connellsville, and in a moment, cross under a towering railroad trestle that also spans river on left.

0:06 (1:20) Forsaken structures just to left are ghostly remains of whiskey distillery.

0:23 (1:03) Enormous black slag heaps are first evidence that Pittsburgh is near.

0:24 (1:02) Pass far beneath another railroad bridge.

0:28 (0:58) Pass under Interstate 70.

0:54 (0:32) Enter heavily populated suburbs of Pittsburgh as train can't make up its mind as to which side of Youghiogheny River it should follow.

0:58 (0:28) Through McKeesport, a heavily industrialized suburb of Pittsburgh, where the Youghiogheny flows into the Monongahela River, then pass series of impressive steel mills, mostly belonging to industrial giant U.S. Steel.

1:11 (0:15) Skyline, featuring many new high rises, is discernible forward to left.

1:13 (0:13) University of Pittsburgh's Cathedral of Learning soars majestically skyward on hill to left. Carnegie Mellon University is on right. Enter Schenley Tunnel as train leaves Oakland and enters Pittsburgh.

1:26 (0:00) Arrive Pittsburgh.

 PITTSBURGH, PA - See page 124.

0:00 (1:45) Depart Pittsburgh on tracks of Conrail.

0:38 (1:07) Through Beaver Falls, birthplace of former football great, Joe Namath.

1:00 (0:45) Leave Pennsylvania and enter Ohio.

1:45 (0:00) Arrive Alliance.

 ALLIANCE, OH - This small Ohio industrial town also serves as an Amtrak stop for nearby Canton. Mount Union College is located here.

0:00 (1:18) Depart Alliance.

0:22 (0:56) Trundle through Ravenna, where Capitol Limited crosses route of Broadway Limited.

1:18 (0:00) Arrive Cleveland, where Lakefront Stadium is imposing feature on right.

CLEVELAND, OH - See page 73.

For route between Cleveland and Chicago, see that portion of Broadway Ltd. log, page 73.

Cardinal

The Cardinal makes a thrice-weekly trek between New York City and Chicago by way of Charleston, WV, Cincinnati and Indianapolis. With stops at several small towns, it is perhaps the last of America's full-service locals.

The route is a particular treat through West Virginia's spectacular New River Gorge. In the fall, the color is superb. Eastbound passengers can also view some of the Ohio River scenes during daylight hours across northern Kentucky. Interpretive guides explain points of interest between Charleston, WV and White Sulphur Springs, eastbound during the summer.

Westbound Schedule (Condensed)
New York, NY - Midmorning Departure
   (Sunday, Wednesday, Friday)
Washington, DC - Early Afternoon
Charleston, WV - Late Evening
Cincinnati, OH - Middle of the Night
Indianapolis, IN - Early Morning
Chicago, IL - Late Morning Arrival (Monday, Thursday, Saturday)

Eastbound Schedule (Condensed)
Chicago, IL - Early Evening Departure
   (Tuesday, Thursday, Saturday)
Indianapolis, IN - Late Evening
Cincinnati, OH - Early Morning
Charleston, WV - Midmorning
Washington, DC - Early Evening
New York, NY - Late Evening Arrival
   (Wednesday, Friday, Sunday)

Frequency - Tri-weekly, see above.
Seating - Amcoaches.*
Dining - Tray meal table service and lounge car with sandwiches, snacks and beverages.
Sleeping - Roomettes and bedrooms and slumbercoach with economy bedrooms.
Baggage - Checked baggage handled at most larger cities.
Reservations - All-reserved train.
Length of Trip - 1,154 miles in 26½ hours.

*It is planned to reequip this train with Superliner cars.

Route Log

For route between New York and Washington, see that portion of the Northeast Corridor log, page 30.

 WASHINGTON, DC - See page 38.

0:00 (0:17) Depart Washington southbound through regions whose roots trace back to earliest periods of American history.

0:02 (0:15) Emerge from tunnel after passing under Mall. Glimpses of Capitol and oldest Smithsonian structure ("The Castle") can be caught through various federal buildings on right.

0:07 (0:10) Perhaps Washington's most charming monument, Monticello-shaped Jefferson Memorial, resides among cherry trees of Tidal Basin on right.

0:09 (0:08) Cross Potomac River paralleling 14th Street bridge. Washington National Airport is directly downstream to left. Back on right, Washington Monument, world's tallest masonry structure at 555.5 feet, punctuates horizon. Capitol's dome can still be seen toward rear on left.

0:10 (0:07) The Pentagon, headquarters for America's military establishment, is off to right, now mostly hidden by newer buildings.

0:12 (0:05) Glass high rises of Crystal City flaunt their starkness on right. Expansive RF&P rail yards are on left.

0:17 (0:00) Arrive Alexandria.

ALEXANDRIA, VA - This historic Washington suburb sits six miles south of the nation's capital, along the west bank of the Potomac River. Most noted for its outstanding examples of early-American architecture, the Alexandria area is also replete with numerous national landmarks. Mount Vernon, beloved home and estate of George Washington from 1754 until his death in 1799, is just a few miles down the Potomac.

0:00 (0:32) Depart Alexandria.

0:01 (0:29) George Washington National Masonic Memorial, with museum of Washington memorabilia, dominates skyline on right. Metro subway station on left provides commuters with quick, easy access to downtown Washington.

0:32 (0:00) Arrive Manassas.

MANASSAS, VA - This was the site of intense fighting during the Civil War. The town was burned several times by both Yankees and Confederates, generally in an effort to cut supply lines to fighting troops. The two Battles of Manassas (Bull Run) were fought in July of 1861 and August of 1862 just northeast of town, and are now commemorated by the 5,000-acre Manassas National Battlefield Park. The quaint rail station was built circa 1915.

0:00 (0:32) Depart Manassas.

0:32 (0:00) Arrive Culpeper where vast Confederate cemetery is on left.

CULPEPER, VA - The Culpeper Minute Men were the very first to respond in 1775 to Patrick Henry's call-to-arms. Then, during the Civil War, the area saw heavy fighting and the town served as headquarters for both sides. George Washington described this area as a "high and pleasant situation" when he surveyed the county, and the town still prides itself on its fresh water supply and clean air.

Flour milling, furniture, wire rope and automotive parts are now important products. History buffs should enjoy the Culpeper Cavalry Museum.

0:00 (1:00) Depart Culpeper.

0:16 (0:44) Through town of Orange, home to two U.S. presidents, James Madison and Zachary Taylor. Bloody "Wilderness Campaign" of 1864 was waged just east of here.

0:53 (0:07) Pass through Shadwell, birthplace of Thomas Jefferson.

1:00 (0:00) Arrive Charlottesville.

CHARLOTTESVILLE, VA - "These mountains are the Eden of the United States." Thomas Jefferson wrote these flattering words in describing the area in and around Charlottesville. As the county seat of Albemarle, the town was a veritable treasure trove of talent and wisdom—Jefferson, James Madison and James Monroe were all part of the local scene. In more recent times, William Faulkner, Lady Astor and William McGuffey all called Albemarle County their home during some point in their lives.

Of particular interest to visitors are Jefferson's beautiful and cleverly designed home (Monticello) and the estate of James Monroe (Ash Lawn). These two men were close friends, and Jefferson personally selected the Monroe house site, donating his own gardeners to help start orchards at Ash Lawn. Jefferson also founded the University of Virginia which is located here and designed many of its original structures.

0:00 (0:58) Depart Charlottesville. Campus of University of Virginia will be on right.

0:05 (0:56) Off to right, ridge of mountains holds beautiful Shenandoah National Park and spectacular Skyline Drive, extending northward from Waynesboro.

0:35 (0:23) Pastoral valley, serene and green, makes great viewing off to left as we ascend renowned Blue Ridge Mountains. Cardinal ducks into tunnel for full minute before regaining daylight.

0:58 (0:00) Arrive Staunton.

STAUNTON, VA - Located in Augusta County which, when formed in 1738, extended as far as the

Mississippi and the Great Lakes, Staunton is distinguished by being the birthplace of both Woodrow Wilson and the McCormick reaper and home to the Statler Brothers. During the Revolutionary War, the town was pressed into serving as Virginia's capital for a few days. The town is also recognized as having the largest remaining collection of 19th-century architecture in Virginia. Scenery is abundant, and just east of here is the junction of two of the nation's more scenic roadways: Skyline Drive and Blue Ridge Parkway.

The unique Museum of American Frontier Culture, opened in 1988, consists of four different farms, each representing major cultures who settled the American frontier.

0:00 (1:10) Depart Staunton.

0:17 (0:53) Elliott Knob rises to elevation of 4,458 feet above sea level, back to right.

0:34 (0:36) Through two short tunnels; there will be many more as we progress westward and into West Virginia mountains.

1:06 (0:04) Extensive CSX rail yards begin on approach to Clifton Forge.

1:10 (0:00) Arrive Clifton Forge, also a stop for nearby Hot Springs, site of historic The Homestead resort.

 CLIFTON FORGE, VA - This is the very heart of western Virginia's vacationland. The surrounding area has such points of interest as: Humpback Bridge, a covered bridge of unusual architecture; Fort Young, built during the French and Indian War; Falling Spring, a 200-foot waterfall; and the Allegheny Central Railroad, Virginia's only "scenic" railroad.

0:00 (0:49) Depart Clifton Forge and continue through CSX yards; locomotive shops are on left.

0:10 (0:39) Pretty Covington, below to right, has idyllic setting beneath mountain backdrop.

0:25 (0:24) Picturesque covered bridge stretches across small stream below on left.

0:38 (0:11) Steep, deep valley to left now provides truly breathtaking view.

0:49 (0:00) Arrive White Sulphur Springs. Four private cars of CSX are permanently moored just to east of station at right,

including "Stonewall Jackson" and "Virginia."

WHITE SULPHUR SPRINGS, WV - This is home to one of the world's renowned spas, Greenbrier Resort. Well-to-do Southerners began building cottages here in the 1800s, drawn to the area by the natural sulphur springs and cool climate. Many of these summer homes still stand and can be rented for somewhat more than a room in the main hotel, which was constructed in 1913. Just three miles east of here, the first organized golf club in the U.S. was formed in 1884 on the Oakhurst Estate. And today, golf is the principal attraction at the Greenbrier with no less than three championship courses to be played. The station is at the very doorstep of this elegant playground; note the entrance just across the road to the right of the train.

0:00 (1:01) Depart White Sulphur Springs.

0:31 (0:30) Through flag stop of Alderson where gaggle of two-story, light-brick buildings, enclosed by barbed wire, to left above, is federal prison for women. Prison stresses vocational rehabilitation and is only federal industrial-oriented prison for women. Both Tokyo Rose and Squeaky Fromme did time here.

0:45 (0:16) Stream that has been following on right is Greenbrier River.

0:49 (0:11) Into Big Bend Tunnel, started in 1870, taking three years to complete.

This mile-long bore now has a twin tunnel for two-way traffic. Tradition makes this the site of the steel driver's ballad "John Henry" and his statue stands above the east entrance. He supposedly died from a race with a steam drill while working on the inside of the tunnels.

0:59 (0:03) At juncture of two streams, join New River and start through what is probably highlight of trip—dramatic New River Gorge. Large dam upstream, about a quarter of a mile to left, retains enormous Bluestone Lake.

1:01 (0:00) Arrive Hinton where rambling, decrepit brick station, on right, greets Cardinal.

HINTON, WV - This small town is in the shadow of Bluestone Lake,

Cardinal - New River Gorge Bridge, West Virginia
SCOTT HARTLEY

a very popular West Virginia recreational area. Historically a railroad town, Hinton now boasts a population of 4,600 and is the county seat.

0:00 (0:30) Depart Hinton.

0:04 (0:26) Bass Lake, a typical early-day mountain resort village, composed mostly of small cabins, is in trees on right.

0:08 (0:22) Small but dazzling Sandstone Falls momentarily interrupt river on left.

0:11 (0:19) New I-64 bridge crosses above.

0:30 (0:00) Arrive Prince.

PRINCE, WV - This small mountain community rests at the east end of the New River Gorge.

0:00 (1:04) As we depart Prince, New River will become increasingly rock-strewn and the scenery more spectacular.

Paradoxically, the New River, formed during the Mesozoic Period, is one of the oldest streams in the world. The gorge it has created has its own ecosystem, supporting over a thousand species of plants and more than 150 species of birds. And during a time now past, as many as 14 passenger trains a day thundered along its tracks.

0:15 (0:50) Through community of Thurmond, another Cardinal flag stop. Coal mining has long dominated town's economy.

0:35 (0:30) Look forward—above and to left.

The magnificent New River Gorge Bridge spans the entire valley carrying auto traffic from one rim to the other, some 876 feet above the river! The main span is 1,700 feet long making it the world's longest steel arch span. It is the nation's second highest bridge (only Colorado's Royal Gorge Bridge is higher), and it weighs a total of 88 million pounds.

On "Bridge Day," the second Saturday in October, hundreds of thrill-seekers gather here to go over the railing and parachute to the gorge floor below. This is the only day jumping from the span is legal. The bridge accounts for most of such BASE jumps in the U.S.

0:46 (0:18) Mouth of three-mile-long Hawk's Nest Tunnel is beyond dam on right. Tunnel, which diverts river water for hydroelectric power, created an awakening for safety in the workplace after several hundred workers died of silicosis.

0:51 (0:13) At Glenn Ferris, on right, beautiful Kanawha Falls interrupt river's smooth flow. Old piers of pre-Civil War bridge can be spotted in Gauley River that flows into New River from north. Bridge was just beyond highway and Conrail bridges and was destroyed by Confederates in 1861. Individual placed three crosses on island in New River "for the glory of God."

1:04 (0:00) Arrive Montgomery.

MONTGOMERY, WV - This stop is home to West Virginia Institute of Technology. School stretches out along left side of tracks, readily visible from station. Salt-making brought early settlers to this valley, where chemical industries now predominate. The town was originally called Coal Valley, but renamed for James C. Montgomery in 1891.

0:00 (0:30) Depart Montgomery.

0:04 (0:26) London hydroelectric plant and dam are on right.

0:05 (0:25) Through community of Pratt,

noted for its residential architecture (ranging from early plantation to Victorian styles) and early labor unrest. Labor organizer "Mother Jones" spent her 84th birthday in prison here.

0:09 (0:21) Another electricity producer, Kanawha Power Plant, is on shores of Kanawha River at right.

0:10 (0:20) Rusty flotilla of ancient barges reposes on far shore of river.

0:28 (0:02) As we enter Charleston, state government office complex, with gold-domed capitol building as centerpiece, is off to right.

0:30 (0:00) Arrive Charleston, with downtown just across river to right. Beautifully landscaped far shore sets off striking skyline.

CHARLESTON, WV - The Kanawha River cuts deeply through the Appalachians at this point, carving out a steep valley setting for Charleston, the state's capital. The capitol building is generally considered to be the most beautiful in the nation, featuring a 300-foot dome supported by Roman porticos and colonnades. Designed by internationally recognized architect Cass Gilbert, the capitol is open for tours enabling visitors to see its ornate rotunda and elegant legislative chambers. Adjacent to the capitol is the newly built Science and Cultural Center. Also of interest is Sunrise, the name given to two grand mansions situated on 16 landscaped acres atop a hill overlooking the city. These mansions now house a children's museum and an art gallery. Several fine glass factories in this area are special attractions.

0:00 (0:58) Depart Charleston, and proceed through a region heavily concentrated with chemical plants and other industrial operations.

0:10 (0:48) This is Institute. Sprawling facility, looking somewhat like a refinery with myriad pipes and towers, is Union Carbide's methyl isocyanate plant—the only location where this chemical is manufactured in the United States. Similar facility in Bhopal, India, in December 1984, created the world's worst industrial accident when a deadly gas leak killed over 2,500 persons.

0:58 (0:00) Arrive Huntington's modern, white-brick station on left.

HUNTINGTON, WV - Situated on the banks of the Ohio River, where West Virginia, Ohio and Kentucky all converge, Huntington has long been an important railroading town. Today, visitors can experience a bit of earlier times by visiting Heritage Village which is in a restored B&O rail yard. Only a few miles north of here, where the Kanawha flows into the Ohio River, is the site of the first battle of the American Revolution—the Battle of Point Pleasant.

0:00 (0:18) Depart Huntington; downtown area is off to right.

0:13 (0:05) Trundle across Big Sandy River Bridge and enter Kentucky.

0:18 (0:00) Arrive Catlettsburg.

 CATLETTSBURG, KY - This stop also serves Kenova, WV and Ashland, KY.

0:00 (1:00) Depart Catlettsburg.

From here to Cincinnati, the Cardinal follows along the scenic Kentucky shoreline of the Ohio River. Today, the Ohio is still heavily utilized as a means of transportation, with tugs and barges continually plying this stretch of the river. It's the numerous dams and locks, easily visible from the train, that make this waterway navigable. Industrial scenes, such as electric power plants, dot the shores; and one can frequently spot stately homes on the Ohio bluffs across the river. All of these combine to make this one of the more enjoyable segments of "training" in the U.S. Unfortunately, westbound passengers normally miss this segment because of darkness.

0:08 (0:52) Twin highway bridges span Ohio on right. On left is Ashland, seventh largest city in Kentucky. Note one home, apparently sitting above all, on forested ridge behind city. Both steel production and oil refining are important industries here. Charcoal furnaces dating back to 1800s can still be found nearby.

0:12 (0:48) Pass by two monstrous, rust-bathed Armco steel mills on immediate right.

0:16 (0:38) Grind to an unadvertised stop for fuel and water in midst of huge CSX rail yards at Russel. This "recharging" takes about eight minutes or so.

0:44 (0:12) Off to right is Greenup Dam and Lock. Portion of lock is visible, just this side of river.

Nineteen navigational locks dot the Ohio River between Pittsburgh, PA and Cairo, IL, with the Greenup Lock being number nine upstream. Built in 1959 by the Army Corps of Engineers, it is 340 miles below Pittsburgh and 641 miles above Cairo. Port of Huntington, which we passed through earlier, generates more tonnage (mostly coal) than any other inland waterport in the nation—18 million tons annually.

0:57 (0:00) Arrive South Portsmouth.

 SOUTH PORTSMOUTH, KY - This is a stop for Portsmouth, Ohio just across the river.

0:00 (0:49) Depart South Portsmouth.

0:42 (0:07) Large conveyor system travels over train and down to river where quarried material is then loaded onto river vessels.

0:47 (0:02) Impressive suspension bridge, on right, carries Highway U.S. 62, one of few bridges that link Kentucky with Ohio.

0:49 (0:00) Arrive at Maysville's very attractive small station.

MAYSVILLE, KY - This charming pioneer river gateway was first settled in 1784. Fifteen French-style houses from the 1800s are nicely maintained in an area called "Little New Orleans," while several other colorful frame houses can be seen on the hillside above on the left. The world's second largest loose-leaf tobacco market features burley auctions December through February. It is also the hometown of Rosemary Clooney.

0:00 (1:19) Depart Maysville. Back on right, excellent view is afforded of coal-fired power plant, sizeable enough to require four stacks. Just to south, between here and Lexington, lies thoroughbred heaven—Kentucky's lush bluegrass country.

0:25 (0:54) Captain Anthony Meldahl Dam with its shipping locks creates brief pause in river's westward flow.

0:29 (0:50) Train literally passes through operating limestone quarry.

0:31 (0:48) Telltale cooling tower of nuclear power plant rises dramatically from opposite shoreline. This is Wm. H. Zimmer Nuclear Power Station which, when and if ever completed, would provide 810 megawatts of power to region. Initially estimated to cost $240 million, actual costs have exceeded $1.6 billion. Total completion cost could be $3 billion.

0:42 (0:37) Train traverses flood plain where houses on right rest on stilts to avoid river's potential overflow.

0:44 (0:35) Magnificent homes line bluffs across river.

0:49 (0:30) Pass beneath Interstate 275 which spans river on right.

1:04 (0:15) Cross Licking River where Cincinnati's skyline is now visible in distance on right. Saucer-like Riverfront Stadium, home of football's Bengals and baseball's Reds, rests imposingly on far shore.

1:06 (0:13) Leave Covington, Kentucky and enter Cincinnati, Ohio as we cross Ohio River. Large bridge to right is aptly named Suspension Bridge, while Brent Spence Bridge, carrying interstates 75 and 71, is off to left. Fine view of stadium and city's skyline, to right, is afforded from center of river. Lesser structure beyond stadium is Coliseum. Delta Queen riverboat is frequently berthed just below Coliseum.

1:19 (0:00) Arrive at Cincinnati's Union Terminal, located about a half-mile from downtown. (Eastbound passengers to Washington, DC, note that best viewing will be on left side of train.)

CINCINNATI, OH - Cincinnati is one of America's most attractively situated midwestern cities. Located in the Ohio River Valley just across from northern Kentucky, its business and industrial areas occupy separate terraces above the river, while these, in turn, are dominated by seven residential-studded hills forming a sweeping arc around the downtown area.

The city's beginning can be traced to its convenient river location, and early days saw a busy river trade carried on by picturesque paddle-wheeler riverboats plying the Ohio. Early-day Cincinnati was marked by a small town appearance with its large population being strung out along the shores of the river; it was, perhaps, this atmosphere that caused many notables to refer to the city as one of the most appealing in America.

Among those attracted by its charm was Alphonso Taft who moved here from Connecticut in 1883. He raised a family which included a son, William Howard Taft, who would become the nation's twenty-seventh president.

Cincinnati Union Terminal, 1301 Western Ave. (Dalton St. and Ezzard Charles Drive) is a truly magnificent Art Deco structure, completed in 1933. After a hiatus of several years, passenger train service returned to this splendid edifice in the summer of 1991. The building also houses the Cincinnati Museum of Natural History, the Cincinnati Historical Society Museum and an OMNIMAX theater.

Cab stand at the station; Yellow Cab, 241-2106. **Local bus** information, 621-4455. **Greater Cincinnati Airport** is approximately 11 miles southwest of the rail station.

Visitor Information Center at 5th and Vine at Fountain Square. Write Cincinnati Convention and Visitors Bureau, 300 W. 6th St. (at Plum Street), 45202. Call (513) 621-2142, or 800-344-3445.

Clarion Hotel, 141 W. 6th St. (at Elm), 45202; (513) 325-2100. Newly renovated, in the heart of downtown. Mile from the station. $59.

-Holiday Inn Queens Gate, 800 West 8th Street (at Linn), 45203; (513) 241-8660. Five blocks from the station. $69.

Downtown attractions include: **Fountain Square,** with an 1871 bronze statue purchased in Munich, Germany; **Fourth Street Art Colony,** at Fourth and Elm, with galleries and shops; **Public Landing,** near the Riverfront Stadium, which is the home port forills, Kroger and Mosier Company.

0:00 (1:05) Depart Cincinnati, retracing our route out over middle of river, then proceed northward through industrial areas of city, including plants of Carthage Mills, Kroger and Mosier Company.

0:39 (0:26) Sign on left welcoming us to Wyoming refers to town—not state.

0:48 (0:17) Under Interstate 275.

1:05 (0:00) Arrive at Hamilton's rather ancient brick station.

HAMILTON, OH - One of southern Ohio's larger cities, Hamilton is located on the northern fringes of Cincinnati.

0:00 (0:55) Depart Hamilton.

0:18 (0:37) Slip through Oxford, home to Miami University which was founded in 1809.

0:23 (0:32) Through College Corner; leave Ohio and enter Indiana, a state that refuses to recognize daylight saving time.

0:36 (0:19) Huge stone Union County Court House dominates center of Liberty. Town is birthplace of Ambrose E. Burnside, Union army commander and inventor of breach-loading rifle.

0:55 (0:00) Arrive Connersville.

CONNERSVILLE, IN - The Whitewater Canal once stretched 101 miles and connected numerous Ohio towns including Connersville and Cincinnati. Just a mile south of here is the Whitewater Valley Rail Road, Indiana's longest scenic railroad. Tour trains run on weekends and holidays, making a 16-mile trek to Metamora with a two-hour sightseeing layover.

0:00 (1:20) Depart Connersville.

0:25 (0:55) Into Rushville, where handsome red-tile-roofed limestone courthouse with central clock tower is centerpiece of town. Wendell L. Wilkie, 1940 Republican nominee for president, was a lawyer and business leader in Rushville. He and other members of his family are buried in East Hill Cemetery at east edge of town off to right of tracks.

1:00 (0:20) Geodesic dome with steeple, on left, is home to Brookville Road Community Church.

1:20 (0:00) Arrive Indianapolis, where Union Station has been made focal point of major downtown development.

INDIANAPOLIS, IN - It was in 1820 that Indianapolis was chosen to be the Indiana capital, principally because of its location as the geographic center of the state. Much like Washington, DC, the layout of the city was made after deciding to make it a governmental home using a wheel-and-spoke design for the streets. At the very hub of the city is Monument Circle with the Soldiers and Sailors Monument serving as an axle.

But Indianapolis' claim to national fame has to be The Indianapolis 500—that dazzling spectacle of color, motion and sound that takes place every Memorial Day. The city is jammed with people for this renowned event, including the two weeks preceding. If you are planning to attend the big race, or any of the other festivities, make reservations and be sure to make them early.

Union Station, 350 South Illinois, P.O. Box 1485, 46225. A beautifully restored Romanesque-Revival structure, America's oldest union railway depot (1888), now has over 100 shops, restaurants, nightspots—and a Holiday Inn (without direct access from the station) where guests can stay in actual Pullmans.

Cabs are usually available at train times; Yellow Cab, 487-7777. **Greyhound and Southeastern Trailways** have a combined terminal a half mile from the station at 127 N. Capitol. **City buses** at the station, 635-3344. **Weir Cook Airport** is approximately five miles from the station.

Indianapolis Convention & Visitors Association, One Hoosier Dome, Suite 100, 46225; (317) 639-4282 or visit 201 S. Capitol; 684-2450 or 800-323-4639.

Holiday Inn Union Station, 123 W. Louisiana; (317) 631-2221. Adjacent to the station (see station information above). $92.

-Courtyard by Marriott, 501 W. Washington (at West), 46204; (317) 635-4443 or 800-321-2211. Seven blocks from the station. $75.

-Omni-Severin, 40 W. Jackson Place, 46225; (317) 634-6664 or 800-843-6664. Gracious accommodations; good weekend rates. One block from the station. $99.

Union Station, with its shops and restaurants, has become an attraction itself. The new **Indianapolis Zoo** is located on the west edge of downtown in White River State Park.

Farther out, the **Speedway,** with its 2½-mile oval and museum, can be visited throughout the year. The very fine **Children's Museum,** at 30th and Meridian streets, is one of best of its kind.

0:00 (0:54) Depart historic Union Station. Immediately, bulbous Hoosier Dome fills our windows to right. Beyond that modern structure, downtown Indianapolis, with attractive capitol as its centerpiece, comes into view.

0:20 (0:35) Pass through Brownsburg, and enter more rural surroundings.

0:24 (0:30) Roll through Pittsboro. A few minutes later, I-74 comes into view on our right, just before Cardinal rolls through Raintown.

0:33 (0:21) I-74 stays visible for several miles as we pass through Lizton, Jamestown and New Ross in midst of typical Indiana flatlands.

0:54 (0:00) Curve sharply to right at Conrail's Ames Tower, now just a modern shack, as train transfers off Conrail onto Seaboard System (former Louisville & Nashville, former Monon Railroad) tracks before we arrive at Crawfordsville.

CRAWFORDSVILLE, IN - A small glass shack serves as the Amtrak station here, next to a red-brick depot bearing the Seaboard System logo. Wabash College, founded in 1832, is located here.

0:00 (0:31) Depart Crawfordsville. Cross high above Cherry Creek as it winds its way prettily through woods; then slide under I-74.

0:10 (0:21) Roll through Cherry Grove; then under U.S. 231 and through village of Linden, where we cross Norfolk & Western (N&W) tracks. To left, large grain elevator sports its own white center-cab switcher locomotive.

0:23 (0:08) Pass along a classically scenic stream, meandering through woods and valleys to our left. Soon, cross stream in one of prettiest areas of journey.

0:31 (0:00) At Lafayette, move slowly under stone bridge and through backyards of homes almost close enough to touch. Tippecanoe County Courthouse, a beautifully ornate-domed building, painted white with brown trim, comes into view as our tracks run down center of Fifth Street (as they have since early Monon days). We pull to a stop squarely in middle of Fifth Street at one of Amtrak's unique stations: the Potpourri Gift Shop. (Plans have been made to re-route trains to avoid this down-the-street course, by moving over west two blocks.)

LAFAYETTE, IN - Purdue University is located here. Each fall more than 4,500 members of 18th-century reenactment groups—military units, traders, crafts people and merchants, as well as voyageurs and most of the midwest's fife and drum corps—gather for two days along the Wabash River southwest of here at Fort Ouiatenon. This is known as the Feast of the Hunters' Moon, commemorating the French and Indian gatherings of the 1700s, when the voyageurs arrived from Canada in their 40-foot canoes filled with goods to trade. More than 50,000 spectators annually witness the event.

0:00 (1:32) Depart the "station," passing on left old depot still bearing its Monon Route insignia.

0:03 (1:29) Stop briefly in Seaboard Yards to change train crews. Famous Lafayette Shops are above us on hill to right.

In the 1888 football game between Wabash College and Purdue University, Wabash, after seeing the immense size of some of their opponents, accused Purdue of adding boilermakers from the Monon Shops to their team. The name stuck. Today, Purdue teams are still called the Boilermakers.

0:07 (1:25) Roll under U.S. 52, then cross broad Wabash River a couple minutes later. Shortly thereafter, pass under I-65, main Indianapolis-Chicago freeway.

0:11 (1:21) Sign, on left, marks Tippecanoe Battlefield State Memorial, where General William Henry Harrison defeated Indians led by Prophet, brother of Tecumseh. Then pass through town of Battle Ground, and leave Wabash River Valley for flat Indiana farmland which we'll trundle across almost entire way to Chicago.

0:17 (1:15) Pass through Brookston, a pretty tree-lined town, then travel due north through Chalmers.

0:26 (1:06) At Reynolds cross tracks of old TP&W—Toledo, Peoria & Western— now merged into the Santa Fe.

0:31 (1:01) Sign, on left, picturing a semi-trailer truck, welcomes us to "Monon, a community built by the transportation industry and Home of the Monon Trailer." It doesn't mention the old Monon Railroad.

0:35 (0:57) Vulcan Materials Company quarry opens rocky ground to left.

Gain one hour as train passes from Eastern to Central Time. Set your watch back (forward if eastbound) one hour.

0:40 (0:52) Soon, light-blue Monon water tower comes into view and train curves sharply left past red-brick Monon depot on our right. Between train and northbound tracks to Michigan City, IN sits an old Monon caboose.

0:52 (0:40) Roll through Pleasant Ridge, then through Rensselaer; a stop for the Hoosier State but not the Cardinal. St. Joseph College is here.

1:02 (0:30) Pass through town of Fair Oaks before ducking again under I-65.

1:12 (0:20) Cross Kankakee River into Shelby. A few minutes later, roll through Lowell and then Creston.

1:22 (0:10) To our left we see Cedar Lake, and then through city of same name.

1:32 (0:00) After passing through St. John and under U.S. 41, enter residential tree-lined outskirts of Dyer, where a child's little treehouse sits in yard before train's arrival at station.

 DYER, IN - Another glass-shack station, functional but without aesthetic value, serves southeastern suburbs here.

0:00 (1:10) Depart Dyer. Amtrak has recently rerouted the Cardinal between Dyer and Chicago from its former Conrail route. New routing is through Maynard, IN, Thornton Junction and Dolton.

1:04 (0:06) To left, it's possible to see an entire train gliding slowly through Amtrak's washer building.

1:06 (0:04) Enter clean, modern Amtrak yards.

At right sit examples of nearly every kind of equipment Amtrak owns—coaches and cafes; diners and domes; sleepers, slumbercoaches, and Superliners; P30CH's and F40PH's—all being readied to equip Amtrak trains that roll across America from the Atlantic to the Pacific and from Lake Superior to the Gulf of Mexico.

1:10 (0:00) Leave daylight as we lumber beneath Chicago's huge post office building just before arrival at Union Station.

CHICAGO, IL - See page 128.

International

As its name implies, the International travels in two countries, providing direct passage between Toronto and Chicago. Amtrak and VIA Rail Canada run this train as a joint venture with personnel changes at the border. The path heads west out of Toronto, gliding across southeastern Ontario's flat farmscapes until it crosses into Michigan at Port Huron. From there, it makes a rainbow descent across Michigan to the southern tip of Lake Michigan before proceeding into Chicago.

The International has been a popular way for citizens of Toronto to conveniently visit Chicago, and for Chicagoans to take in Canada's second largest city. The train is heavily used by Michigan State University students, particularly at school break periods, traveling to and from Lansing.

Westbound Schedule (Condensed)*
Toronto, Ont. - Early Morning Departure
Port Huron, MI - Early Afternoon
East Lansing, MI - Midafternoon
Chicago, IL - Early Evening Arrival

Eastbound Schedule (Condensed)*
Chicago, IL - Early Morning Departure
East Lansing, MI - Early Afternoon
Port Huron, MI - Late Afternoon
Toronto, Ont. - Midevening Arrival

*Departures are three to four hours later on Sundays.

Frequency - Daily.
Seating - LRC-1 coaches.
Dining - Sandwiches, snacks and beverages.
Baggage - No checked baggage.

Reservations - Reservations required to and from Canada.
Length of Trip - 501 miles.

Route Log

For route from Toronto to Sarnia, see Canadian Corridor, page 368.

0:00 (0:10) Depart Sarnia.
0:04 (0:02) We literally sink out of sight for about four minutes as train glides into opening of Grand Trunk's St. Clair Tunnel, built in 1886, passing beneath St. Clair River.

The St. Clair River connects Lake Huron (to the north) with Lake St. Clair (to the south) and is the artery for all shipping out of Lake Superior and Lake Huron heading through the St. Lawrence Seaway for Detroit and other points east. Midway through the tube we leave Canada and enter the United States. We haven't escaped customs, however; that detail takes place at our next stop, Port Huron. Customs forms handed out by the conductor earlier will be collected here. Although the stop can be quite perfunctory, waits up to an hour can occur.
0:10 (0:00) Arrive Port Huron.

PORT HURON, MI - This city of 34,000 has been a significant Great Lakes port and is home to the Fort Gratiot lighthouse, the oldest on the lakes.

This is also the eastern terminus of the Grand Trunk Western, and the boyhood home of Thomas Edison. Edison worked

146

as a "news butcher" on the Grand Trunk, selling sandwiches and candy on the trains. This job was short-lived, however, when phosphorous he was experimenting with in the baggage car burst into flames and ignited the car. He also printed a paper on the train called the *Weekly Herald,* the first printed on a moving train.

0:00 (0:45) Having finished with U.S. customs procedures, depart Port Huron.

0:04 (0:41) Entering Grand Trunk Western's Tunnel Yard, old roundhouse stands on left.

0:30 (0:15) On left, in front of Champion assembly plant, rows of white Ford cabs and chassis await transformation into motor homes.

0:45 (0:00) Arrive Lapeer.

LAPEER, MI - This is a small agricultural community of 6,000.

0:00 (0:20) Depart Lapeer.

0:02 (0:18) Brick buildings behind chain link fence on right belong to Oakdale Center, a mental health institution.

0:11 (0:09) Landing strip, complete with assemblage of small planes, parallels tracks on left.

0:16 (0:04) AC Spark Plug off to right is easily identified by white and orange initials on silver standpipes.

0:30 (0:00) Arrive Flint.

FLINT, MI - Second only to Detroit in U.S. auto production, Flint produces Chevrolets, Buicks and GM car bodies. General Motors supplies 40% of Grand Trunk railroad's business. With a population of 160,000, Flint is the third largest city in Michigan.

0:00 (0:20) Depart Flint.

0:03 (0:17) GM truck plant on left produces Blazers and GM buses.

0:04 (0:16) Further back on left, grey buildings house another GM plant producing parts and truck assemblies, while hundreds of auto transport cars are parked on sidings awaiting new-vehicle shipments.

0:20 (0:00) Arrive at Durand's enormous grey stone 1905 depot, on left. Train stops on a major intersection of Grand Trunk.

DURAND, MI - This is the hub of the Grand Trunk's rail operations. Durand is also served by the Ann Arbor Railroad. Although no longer the railroad center of seventy years ago when residents could count an incredible 42 passenger trains, 22 mail trains and 78 freight trains per day, 75% of the Grand Trunk's carloadings still pass through Durand. A fine Railroad History Museum, three blocks from the depot, focuses on train crews, depots, famous train wrecks, track maintenance and workers.

0:00 (0:26) Depart Durand.

0:25 (0:03) High rises of Michigan State University come into view as we enter East Lansing. Stadium, one of college football's largest, is off to right. Now pass directly through campus.

0:28 (0:00) Arrive East Lansing where unusual bell tower can be observed off to right.

EAST LANSING, MI - Adjacent to the capital city of Lansing, East Lansing is home to Michigan State University which is known for its research capabilities—and 44,000 students. The metropolitan area has a population of 250,000, and has origins dating back to the beginning of the century when R. E. Olds produced and sold one of the first automobiles.

0:00 (0:50) Depart East Lansing.

0:03 (0:43) Cross Grand River and glimpse State Capitol Building at right. Structure has a high rise center with an antenna-like pole on top.

0:06 (0:44) Snake through power plant and then past Oldsmobile plant on right.

0:07 (0:43) The broad Grand River, on left, provides recreational opportunities during the summer months, including water-skiing.

0:11 (0:39) Meijer grocery chain's huge automated facility covers several acres on right.

0:12 (0:38) Past large Delta Power Plant.

0:22 (0:28) Windmill fancier obviously lives in farmstead at right where three miniature wind pumps serve as lawn embellishments.

0:23 (0:27) Green and white piles in front of Owens-Corning plant are made up of glass waiting to be recycled into bottles.

0:28 (0:22) In spring, watch for pails hanging from maple trees to collect syrup throughout this area.

0:35 (0:15) Cross Battle Creek, so named

because of an Indian skirmish that took place on its banks in 1825.

0:37 (0:13) At left, built into hillside by tracks are long-abandoned brick ovens.

0:44 (0:04) Now enter Battle Creek through Grand Trunk Western's rail yards where derelict steam locomotive and two tenders can be spotted at left. Shops are grey buildings across yards to left. Then past five-story, red brick Post cereal plant (next to new windowless addition).

0:50 (0:00) Arrive Battle Creek's ultra-modern, intermodal station, on immediate right. Station features unusual seating and imaginative use of brick and glass. Both Greyhound and city buses share this facility with Amtrak.

This is the end of the Grand Trunk tracks. From here to Niles, we will follow Amtrak rails, then Conrail into Chicago.

BATTLE CREEK, MI - Literally built on the cereal industry, both Kellogg and General Foods have two enormous facilities here, the largest of their type anywhere.

0:00 (0:28) Depart Battle Creek, and pass Ralston Purina plant on left.

0:05 (0:23) Sprawling vacant complex on left was once operated by Clark Equipment Co., builders of materials handling machinery.

0:21 (0:07) Morrow Hydro Dam and Power Plant are situated off to left.

0:27 (0:02) Cross Kalamazoo River as we enter city of same name. Note some streets are still paved with brick.

0:28 (0:00) Arrive Kalamazoo where lengthy red brick and tile-roofed station on left greets passengers with an informative sign that welcomes passengers to Kalamazoo, while announcing Chicago is 138 miles away and Detroit is 142.

KALAMAZOO, MI - The city with the funny name that everyone has heard of gets its name from the river we just crossed. Kalamazoo is an Indian word roughly translated as "where the water boils in the pot." This town of 80,000 has a diverse industry base, and is home to Western Michigan University with an enrollment of 19,000 students.

0:00 (0:44) Departing Kalamazoo, note fine collection of older homes with classic pillared front porches on left.

0:02 (0:41) Slip through campus of afore-mentioned Western Michigan University.

0:13 (0:29) Watch for vineyards on both sides of tracks. This is wine country.

0:17 (0:27) Besides wine, grapes are also made into juice and jellies. Note Welch plant on right which processes grapes grown in this area. Wisps of escaping steam help identify plant.

0:32 (0:12) Through Dowagiac where steel furnaces were at one time produced. One of those factories is on right.

0:43 (0:01) Large factory of venerable Simplicity Pattern Co., world-wide suppliers of sewing patterns, is on left.

0:44 (0:00) Arrive Niles, with old Michigan Central depot and clock tower on right. This classic 1892 Romanesque station was restored in 1988, and has appeared in several movies, including *Continental Divide* and *Midnight Run*.

NILES, MI - This railroad and agricultural town of 13,000 is the last stop before leaving Michigan. The Indiana border is just five miles straight south.

0:00 (1:13) Depart Niles.

0:02 (1:11) Cross St. Joseph River which flows northwest and into Lake Michigan.

0:05 (1:08) Vineyards continue, inter-mixed with fruit orchards.

0:22 (0:51) Lake Michigan's waters come into view. A marina with hundreds of pleasure craft is at right as we near Grand Beach.

0:25 (0:48) Enter Indiana and leave Michigan.

Gain one hour as train passes from Eastern to Central Time. Set your watch back (forward if eastbound) one hour.

0:32 (0:41) Cross a lift bridge at Michigan City, with another marina at right.

0:40 (0:33) Collection of lake-side sand hills, known as Indiana Dunes, is popular destination for weekend recreationalists, at right.

0:44 (0:29) In small town of Porter, join route of Lake Shore Limited into Chicago.

0:50 (0:23) Bethlehem Steel Corporation facility appears on right.

0:55 (0:18) Tracks and catenary of legendary Chicago South Shore and South Bend run parallel to our Conrail right-of-way, off to left.

0:57 (0:13) Where Gary began, enormous

U.S. Steel Gary Works stretch along tracks at right beyond rail yards.

1:07 (0:06) Inland Steel plants straddle tracks, Plant Number One on left and Plant Number Two on right. Then cross drawbridge spanning Indiana Harbor Canal that links Lake Michigan with Calumet River.

1:09 (0:04) Standard Oil Company of Indiana refinery creates apparatus jungle at left. Lake Michigan is now only 100 feet or so to right.

1:13 (0:00) Arrive Hammond-Whiting.

For route description from here to Chicago, see that portion of Lake Shore Ltd. log, page 76.

Detroit
Toledo
Chicago

Lake Cities

The Lake Cities is a 1980 extension of one of Amtrak's Chicago-Detroit trains to Toledo, OH, where it provides connections with the Lake Shore Limited to and from points east, such as Cleveland, Albany, Boston and New York.

The Chicago-Detroit route, Amtrak's "Michigan Corridor," was once the pride of the Michigan Central. Its deterioration began under the New York Central, and became total under the bankrupt Penn Central. The State of Michigan and Amtrak have refurbished old and built new stations, and Conrail and Amtrak have rebuilt the track into a smooth and fast raceway again for the Detroit-Chicago trains.

Westbound Schedule (Condensed)
Toledo, OH - Late Morning Departure
Detroit, MI - Early Afternoon
Battle Creek, MI - Late Afternoon
Chicago, IL - Early Evening Arrival

Eastbound Schedule (Condensed)
Chicago, IL - Midafternoon Departure
Battle Creek, MI - Early Evening
Detroit, MI - Late Evening
Toledo, OH - Late Evening Arrival

Frequency - Daily.
Seating - Unreserved coach seats, usually Amfleet, and reserved Custom Class.
Food Service - Sandwiches, snacks, and beverages.
Baggage - Carry on. No checked baggage service available.
Length of Trip - 335 miles in 7 hours.

Route Log

TOLEDO, OH - With a 35-mile-long harbor on Lake Erie, it is easy to understand why Michigan and Ohio both claimed this city in the early 19th century. It took presidential action by Andrew Jackson to finally settle the dispute—in Ohio's favor. Today, the city lays easy claim to being the world's leading producer of glass and glass products. A world-renowned collection of ancient and modern glassware is on display at the Toledo Museum of Art. Considerable other attractions are in Toledo, including the Port of Toledo Observation Deck and the Waterfront Electric Railway offering old-fashioned trolley trips.

0:00 (1:40) Depart Toledo's yellow brick and glass Central Union Terminal, crossing Swan Creek and passing tower to Airline Junction Yard, where route of The Lake Shore splits away to left.

0:09 (1:31) Curve sharply left, roll across I-75, pass a large American Motors plant on left, then pass under I-75 as it loops back to northeast.

0:20 (1:20) Cross Chessie System tracks at Alexis Tower. Lights of Raceway Park are visible on left upon arrival in Toledo at night. Pass under State Highway 184 and cross Silver Creek less than a mile south of Michigan border.

0:23 (1:17) Now in Michigan, cross Halfway Creek and run parallel to tracks of Grand Trunk Western (GT) Railroad at right.

0:36 (1:04) To left, large open quarry ringed by huge boulders lies just south of Monroe, where we cross River Raisin on its way to Lake Erie. Only battle in Michigan between regular forces occurred near here during War of 1812. Massacre of wounded Americans after their surrender gave rise to battle cry, "Remember the Raisin." General George A. Custer was raised in Monroe, and La-Z-Boy, famous recliner manufacturer, also claims this as its home town.

0:41 (0:59) Cross I-75 on its way to Detroit, then parallel an overgrown, but still visible, abandoned railroad right-of-way on left.

0:55 (0:45) Roll through Newport, then South Rockwood, across Huron River, and then through Rockwood.

1:08 (0:32) In Gibralter pass a large Chrysler plant and slip under Fort Road, State Highway 85.

1:13 (0:27) After FN Tower, where we intersect again with GT, huge McClouth Steel Products Corporation's Trenton Plant occupies several blocks on right.

1:22 (0:18) Between Wyandotte and Ecorse cross South Branch of Ecorse River. Evidence of decline of nation's steel industry looms on left—abandoned facilities of Michigan Steel Works.

1:24 (0:16) Roll through Conrail's River Rouge Yard, then cross river into city of Detroit.

1:37 (0:03) Pass West Detroit Tower, rattle through main plant of General Motors' Cadillac Division, then cross I-75. Ambassador Bridge, a beautiful sight at night, connects Detroit with Windsor, Ontario on right.

Oddly enough, as we look toward Canada out the right side of the train, we are looking almost due south at "our neighbors to the north."

1:40 (0:00) Arrive Detroit.

Twilight Limited - Chicago, Illinois
HOMER R. HILL

DETROIT, MI - In 1701, the French colonist Antoine de la Mothe Cadillac landed on what is today's riverfront area of Detroit and established Fort Pontchartrain, later the site of battles during the French and Indian Wars. After the settlement burned to the ground from an accidental fire in 1805, it was rebuilt following, to some extent, the layout of the streets in Washington, D.C. Detroit ultimately became "Motor City" largely because of the imagination and determination of people like Henry Ford, good transportation facilities and an available work force at the time the auto industry was being born.

In the 1970s, Detroit, led by Henry Ford II, made a heroic effort to put a new shine on the city's rusting image in the form of a massive ($350 million) urban development project called the Renaissance Center—"RenCen" for short. Quadruplet 39-story glass office towers surrounding a nearly twice-as-high core hotel were built on the banks of the Detroit River to revitalize the city's downtown. The result was certainly architecturally striking.

But there is debate over the success of the project. Although RenCen's office space has been virtually 100% occupied, its retail impact has been meager. And there has been another curious problem. People continually get lost in RenCen's legendary maze-like confines—so much so that a $27-million remodeling was undertaken in the late 1980s to make the place more "user friendly."

Amtrak Station. (Amtrak is moving from its former Michigan Central Station location to the New Center area which is about three miles north of downtown and near the GM headquarters and Wayne State University.)

Cab stand at the station; Checker Cab, 963-7000. Hertz **rental cars** are downtown, across from Days Inn, 964-2678. Detroit's major airport is **Metropolitan Airport,** 16 miles southwest of downtown. Closer-in **City Airport** is served by Southwest Airlines. Detroit's **People Mover,** elevated and fully automatic trains, snakes counter-clockwise around the downtown area. Trains are one or two cars in length, arrive at any of the 13 stops every 3 or 4 minutes, and take

approximately 15 minutes to make the entire loop. **Detroit Trolley** is another way to see the downtown, running along Washington Blvd. **Local buses,** 962-5515.

Visitor Information Center, 2 East Jefferson Ave., 48226; (313) 567-1170.

Days Inn Downtown, Washington Blvd. at Michigan Ave., 48226; (313) 965-4646. Located in the heart of downtown, just a block from a People Mover station. $55.

-**Ramada Hotel Downtown,** 400 Bagley; (313) 962-2300. About two blocks from a People Mover station. $74.

While downtown, be sure to ride the **People Mover** mentioned above. The **Renaissance Center,** also mentioned above, has numerous shops and is an adventure to explore. **Greektown,** a small downtown enclave, has some great Greek restaurants and numerous small shops anchored by Trapper's Alley, a fashionably converted five-story warehouse with its own collection of boutiques and cafes. Both the Renaissance Center and Greektown are stops for the People Mover.

Detroit's most popular attraction is out in Dearborn. The **Henry Ford Museum** and adjacent **Greenfield Village** are seen by well over a million visitors each year. The Museum has four acres of floor space devoted to displaying the industrialization of America, including a newly developed Automobile-in-American-Life exhibit, complete with a 1940s Texaco station and a 1946 diner. Greenfield Village has over 100 buildings on 240 acres, with the likes of the Wright Brothers home and cycle shop, Edison's Menlo Park Laboratory and rides on an 18th-century steam train.

0:00 (0:17) Depart Detroit.

0:06 (0:12) Continue backwards deep into yards of Cadillac plant before stopping and pulling forward alongside loading docks holding auto carriers from many different railroads. Pass West Detroit Tower again, where tracks to Toledo curve away to left.

0:12 (0:04) Slip through a large Conrail yard. Off to left, Ford Motor Company's huge River Rouge Plant is an impressive sight. Cross I-94.

1:16 (0:00) Arrive at modernistic Dearborn station, built in 1978 to serve Detroit's western suburbs.

DEARBORN, MI - This is the birthplace of Henry Ford. The 12-acre Henry Ford Museum is here, and adjacent is the 240-acre Greenfield Village, a wonderful collection of historical American buildings and artifacts.

0:00 (0:30) Depart Dearborn with Ford Motor's Central Office Building appearing at right. Cross over Southfield Freeway, then over concrete-lined River Rouge for an excellent view on left of Henry Ford Museum and Greenfield Village complex.

0:10 (0:20) Roll past Wayne Tower and Junction and enter another set of rail yards, then pass under I-275.

0:20 (0:12) Enter Willow Run Yard, and then Ypsilanti, site of Eastern Michigan University. Ancient freight depot on left now holds a farmers' market.

0:23 (0:07) Make first of an incredible 11 crossings of meandering Huron River as it twists and turns through and between "Ypsi" and western edge of Ann Arbor.

0:25 (0:05) Cross Huron River a fifth time, as a dam appears on right. Route then follows river along a beautiful parkway on both sides of tracks.

0:30 (0:00) Run past University of Michigan Hospital high above to left, then follow Huron as it curves right. Pass famous Gandy Dancer Restaurant located in fine Michigan Central depot, on left, as train arrives at new orange brick Ann Arbor station on opposite side of Plymouth Road viaduct.

ANN ARBOR, MI - The University of Michigan is located here, making this a major stop on the corridor. An interesting station feature is the stairway to Plymouth Road with the Amtrak name and logo engraved into the concrete.

0:00 (0:37) Depart Ann Arbor, and immediately resume Huron River crossings.

0:02 (0:35) Dam on immediate right broadens river into attractive lake with numerous small boats on far side.

0:10 (0:27) Final crossing of Huron places river on right as it meanders through a wooded park. Then cruise through Dexter, with interesting mill and dam on left.

0:15 (0:22) This is crossroads community of Four Mile. A bit later, Chelsea is reached, a pretty little town of old homes and tree-lined streets.

0:25 (0:12) At Grass Lake, pass small but beautiful stone depot. A few minutes later rumble through Leoni and then Michigan Center.

0:37 (0:00) After sliding through Conrail's Jackson Yard, arrive at old red brick Jackson station on our right, oldest of the Michigan Corridor's stations, built in 1876 and restored between 1976 and 1978.

JACKSON, MI - Named after Andrew Jackson, the town was founded in 1829 by travelers over the Territorial Road (now roughly paralleled by I-94). It was first called Jacksonopolis and later Jacksonburgh. Several years later, on July 6, 1854, 1,500 Michigan residents assembled here and organized a new political group named the Republican Party. Today, Jackson is home to Michigan's oldest and largest state prison.

0:00 (0:21) Depart Jackson as its downtown rises on left, then past Jackson's airport a few minutes later. Then continue journey through countryside.

0:18 (0:03) After Parma, Kalamazoo River flows serenely through a farm pasture and marshy area immediately to left, just beyond an abandoned railroad bed.

0:21 (0:00) Arrive at Albion.

ALBION, MI - Albion is home to Albion College, which was passed on our right as we rolled into town.

0:00 (0:30) Depart Albion and, a few minutes later, pass Marengo and continue along Kalamazoo River, wending its way through marshes below to left.

0:14 (0:16) After Marshall, cross I-69 a few minutes later, and follow river through Caresco.

0:25 (0:05) After crossing I-94, enter "Cereal City"—Battle Creek—with Kellogg's huge plant and Tony the Tiger (and son) in its front yard on right. A quick succession of Battle Creek sights parade past. Just beyond to left, an old GT steam engine sits on silent display. Then General Foods' Post cereals plant looms up suddenly on left. Old Grand Trunk depot comes into view on right, and GT tracks to Lansing and Port Huron, used by

Amtrak and VIA's International, curve to right behind us.

0:30 (0:00) Arrive at New Battle Creek Transportation Center, built to accommodate all public area transportation systems.

For route between Battle Creek and Chicago, see that portion of International Log, page 148.

Grand Rapids

Chicago

Pere Marquette

The Pere Marquette began service August 5, 1984 between Grand Rapids, MI and Chicago, IL over the tracks of the Chessie System's Chesapeake & Ohio Railroad. The route hadn't had passenger train service since Amtrak took over in 1971 and discontinued the old Pere Marquette, namesake of the railroad incorporated into the C&O in 1947 and a French missionary explorer of the Great Lakes.

The train provides a daily round trip between Grand Rapids and Chicago, leaving the Michigan metropolis early in the morning and returning later that evening.

Westbound Schedule (Condensed)*
Grand Rapids, MI - Early Morning Departure
Chicago, IL - Midmorning Arrival

Eastbound Schedule (Condensed)
Chicago, IL - Late Afternoon Departure
Grand Rapids, MI- Late Evening Arrival

*Two hours later on Sundays.

Frequency - Daily.
Seating - Unreserved coaches.
Food Service - Sandwiches, snacks, and beverages.
Baggage - Carry on. No checked baggage service.
Length of Trip - 177 miles in 4 hours.

Route Log

GRAND RAPIDS, MI - After Detroit, this is Michigan's largest city, with a population of 181,000, famous for its manufacture of home and office furniture since early in its history. The Gerald R. Ford Museum is here in the former president's home town. The newly developed Grand Center features modern convention facilities with the five-star-rated Amway Grand Plaza Hotel, downtown's only major hotel, nearby. Most of the "chain" hotels are several miles south along 28th Street.

0:00 (0:38) Depart Grand Rapids' attractive, new wood-sided depot south of downtown at the corner of Market and Wealthy. (A depot on a more grandiose scale was demolished some years ago to make way for an interstate highway.) Swing sharply right and roll through Chessie's Lamar Yard.

0:12 (0:26) Pass through mixed residential-industrial suburb of Grandville, then under I-196 and finally pick up speed.

0:20 (0:18) Enter Hudsonville, with its fairgrounds and greenhouses, followed by flat, fertile vegetable fields.

0:27 (0:11) Zeeland, where seventy percent of all U.S.-produced grandfather clocks are made, is easily identified by city water tower.

0:38 (0:00) Lake Macatawa lies at right upon arrival at Holland. Depot, surrounded by a tulip-filled park, sits unused as passengers occupy a small adjacent shelter.

HOLLAND, MI - Each May witnesses the famous Tulip Time Festival when this area celebrates its Dutch heritage with parades, dancing and a lavish display of millions of tulips.

0:00 (0:36) Depart Holland past buildings

of Hope College, then re-enter agricultural land while crossing I-196.

0:09 (0:25) Quickly through hamlet of East Saugatuck and curve left across a pleasant little stream. Then ride high above it and surrounding woods in valley to left.

0:13 (0:23) Stream again comes into view at left. Sway through New Richmond and, a couple minutes later, cross Kalamazoo River on its way to Lake Michigan ten miles west.

0:22 (0:14) Breeze through Fennville, where Pere Marquette sometimes makes a special stop in mid-October for town's annual Goose Festival. Now, after scenic areas of rivers, ravines and ridges, terrain flattens out again.

0:26 (0:10) In next several minutes, roll through towns called Pearl, Bravo and Pullman, and finally reach Grand Junction, where several tracks connect with ours. Orchards are in abundance in this region.

0:36 (0:00) Cross Black River and arrive at Bangor.

 BANGOR, MI - The old depot, just outside our window on the right, now houses the "Bangor Train Factory, Manufacturer of the Kalamazoo Toy Train."

0:00 (0:35) Depart Bangor, continuing journey through apple orchards of western Michigan.

0:08 (0:27) Cross Paw Paw River upon reaching Hartford, where Fruit Exchange's wooden skids and boxes lie at left.

0:17 (0:18) After passing grey wooden Watervliet depot, and crossing Paw Paw River again, Pere Marquette rambles through downtown Coloma. A few minutes later, duck under I-196 and then cut through Riverside.

0:25 (0:10) A large electric power station looms at right. At left, Paw Paw appears again as it meanders through trees in search of a marsh beyond.

0:30 (0:05) Curve sharply left approaching a drawbridge over St. Joseph River between Benton Harbor and St. Joseph. Train slows to a mere 15 miles per hour on bridge, giving a longer look at Lake Michigan and lighthouse guarding river's mouth.

0:35 (0:00) Curve left and arrive at an old, grey stucco depot. At left, just north of station, a stairway up bluff begins under a concrete arch engraved "St. Joseph, Michigan."

 ST. JOSEPH-BENTON HARBOR, MI - Michigan's Twin Cities join 28 other southwestern Michigan communities each spring as sponsors of the Blossomtime Festival in anticipation of the coming fruit harvest. The Benton Harbor Fruit Market is said to be the largest of its kind in the nation.

0:00 (0:28) Depart St. Joseph-Benton Harbor as a bluff looms on left and Lake is visible on right. After gradual ascent to top of bluff, Lake Michigan now spreads out on right until view is obliterated by a clutch of factories as Pere Marquette moves farther inland.

0:06 (0:22) Through fields of grapes, then pass under I-94 and cut quickly through downtown Stevensville.

0:11 (0:17) Here, at Bridgman depot on our right, is milepost 100. Cross Galien River.

0:14 (0:14) Paralleling highway on right is I-94. A barn inscribed "Dunes View Farm" is a reminder that distant hills are actually stabilized sand dunes from Lake Michigan and nearby Warren Dunes State Park.

0:19 (0:09) Pass through Sawyer, and again roll under I-94.

0:26 (0:02) Cross another stream and follow it for a moment. Then cross handsome set of tracks of Amtrak's Chicago/Detroit Corridor.

0:28 (0:00) Arrive at a glass bus shelter that serves as New Buffalo's train station.

 NEW BUFFALO, MI - Michigan's largest marina is located here on Lake Michigan.

0:00 (0:48) Depart New Buffalo.

0:08 (0:40) Terrain becomes more urbanized upon approaching Michigan City, IN.

0:24 (0:24) Sign at right proclaims "Indiana Dunes Recreational Area." Pass under I-94 and Chesterton water tower comes into view on left.

0:29 (0:19) Approach white and green Porter Tower, on right, where our Chessie tracks meet Conrail at left and Amtrak's Michigan line at right. Our speed limit is now 79 mph. South Shore Line and its clutter of catenary—overhead wire to power electric locomotives—is on left.

Gain one hour as train passes from Eastern to Central Time. Set your watch back (forward if eastbound) one hour.

0:35 (0:13) Where Gary began, enormous U.S. Steel Gary Works stretch along tracks at right beyond rail yards.

0:42 (0:06) Inland Steel plants straddle tracks, Plant Number One on left and Plant Number Two on right. Then cross drawbridge spanning Indiana Harbor Canal that links Lake Michigan with Calumet River.

0:44 (0:04) Standard Oil Company of Indiana refinery creates apparatus jungle at left. Lake Michigan is now only 100 feet or so to right.

0:48 (0:00) Arrive Hammond-Whiting.

For route description from here to Chicago, see that portion of Lake Shore Ltd. log, page 76.

Other Michigan Service

The **Wolverine** and **Twilight Ltd.** provide both morning and evening service between Detroit and Chicago, in addition to the Lake Cities. There are plans to extend these trains north of Detroit to Royal Oak, Birmingham and Pontiac.

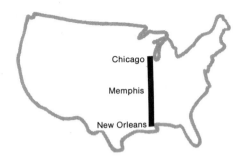

City of New Orleans

Until 1981, this overnight train between Chicago and New Orleans was called the Panama Limited. A curious name until one realizes that Midwesterners once set sail for the Orient from New Orleans rather than make the arduous trip across the Rocky Mountains to reach San Francisco. The train was inaugurated at the time the Panama Canal was built.

There was a City of New Orleans, however, but it made a daylight run between these two great towns, carrying some of America's most colorful travelers —gamblers, migrant workers, jazz musicians, to name but a few. "Don't you know me, I'm your native son?" asked Arlo Guthrie.

But one train between Chicago and New Orleans was all Amtrak could afford, and the Panama Limited survived. It kept that name until a New Orleans mayor persuaded Amtrak to re-name the train for its southern destination—a much more appropriate appellation.

"The City" travels a direct route between Chicago and New Orleans through Memphis and Jackson. The train passes through eastern Illinois, the western edges of Kentucky and Tennessee, and then through the very heart of Mississippi. The Kansas City to New Orleans train, the River Cities, is a section of this train between Centralia and New Orleans.

Southbound Schedule (Condensed)
Chicago, IL - Early Evening Departure
Champaign-Urbana, IL - Late Evening
Carbondale, IL - Late Night
Memphis, TN - Early Morning
Jackson, MS - Midmorning
New Orleans, LA - Early Afternoon Arrival

Northbound Schedule (Condensed)
New Orleans, LA - Midafternoon Departure
Jackson, MS - Early Evening
Memphis, TN - Late Evening
Carbondale, IL - Middle of the Night
Champaign-Urbana, IL - Early Morning
Chicago, IL - Early Morning Arrival

Frequency - Daily.
Seating - Amcoaches and dome car.
Dining - Tray meals, sandwiches and beverage service. Lounge service.
Sleeping - Heritage Fleet roomettes and bedrooms.*
Baggage - Checked baggage at larger cities.
Reservations - All-reserved train.
Length of Trip - 924 miles in 19 hours.

*This train should have Superliner cars beginning sometime in 1994.

Route Log

 CHICAGO, IL - See page 128.

0:00 (0:41) Depart Chicago Union Station, backing southbound from beneath Chicago's main post office terminal.
0:03 (0:39) Still in reverse, slip past Amtrak's coach yards and car-washing facility.
0:04 (0:37) Route of California Zephyr and Southwest Chief swings away to west on tracks of Burlington Northern.
0:05 (0:36) Cross South Chicago River.

0:07 (0:34) Train finally ends its backward ways and starts forward, curling slowly right (east) onto Illinois Central tracks, following historic St. Charles Air Line right-of-way. Illinois Central was nation's first major land grant railroad (two-and-a-half-million acres for 7% of its gross revenues) and boasts the likes of Casey Jones, Abraham Lincoln and Mark Twain as employee alumni.

0:09 (0:32) Chinatown's colorful storefronts are just off to right.

0:12 (0:29) Amtrak's best offering of Chicago's spectacular skyline holds forth at left. Dominant building with twin antenna is famous Sears Tower, nation's tallest skyscraper, while slope-sided John Hancock Building (also with two antennae) is also apparent. Tallest white monolith, closer to Lake Michigan, is marble-faced Standard Oil Building that may receive a $30 million face lift due to problems related to its weighty facade.

0:13 (0:28) No major U.S. city train departure would be complete without a display of artistic graffiti, now below on left.

0:14 (0:27) Curling south, giant Soldier Field, home of NFL's Chicago Bears, is just off to left, while Field Museum can be seen beyond. Shortly, dome of Adler Planetarium can be discerned back left along lakefront.

0:18 (0:23) Pass beneath entrance to McCormick Place and McCormick Hotel. Black, flat Exposition Center is quite visible back to left after returning to daylight.

0:20 (0:21) Now, waters of Lake Michigan lap against Burnham Park paralleling Lake Shore Drive, on left.

0:22 (0:19) Architecturally interesting collection of older buildings faces tracks, on left. Jackson Park with its world renowned Museum of Science and Industry lies beyond. Campus of University of Chicago stretches off to right.

0:24 (0:17) Rumble beneath Chicago Skyway and tracks of Conrail at aptly named Grand Crossing.

0:27 (0:14) Buildings of Chicago State University border tracks on right.

0:34 (0:07) Cross Little Calumet River.

0:38 (0:03) Expansive Markham Yards of Illinois Central now stretch along route on left. Black IC switchers can be spotted

shuffling long consists of freight cars among various tracks.

0:41 (0:00) Arrive at attractive community of Homewood.

HOMEWOOD, IL - Giant oak and pine trees surround this well-to-do Chicago suburb. Homewood's per capita income places it among 200 most affluent American cities.

0:00 (0:30) Depart Homewood.

0:30 (0:00) Arrive Kankakee, where popular eatery is housed in Amtrak station.

KANKAKEE, IL - Set along the banks of the Kankakee River, many vestiges of Kankakee's early French influence still pervade this city. Renowned for its abundant gladiola harvests, unusual rock formations surround the many limestone and sand quarries that are noteworthy here as well. Frank Lloyd Wright once lived here.

0:00 (0:52) Depart Kankakee and cross Kankakee River.

0:26 (0:27) This is Gilman, IL, a stop northbound only. Besides an agrarian focal point for Iroquois County, Gilman has been a modest rail center and division point for the Illinois Central.

0:50 (0:00) Arrive Rantoul.

RANTOUL, IL - The Rantoul stop affords easy access to Chanute Field, one of the largest technical training centers of the U.S. Air Force. Aircraft and missile exhibits are the focus of its on-base museum.

0:00 (0:14) Depart Rantoul.

0:14 (0:00) Arrive Champaign-Urbana.

CHAMPAIGN-URBANA, IL - Defying consolidation since the mid-19th century, Illinois' "Twin Cities" still maintain separate identities. Champaign has evolved into a commercial and industrial center, while Urbana is more collegiate-oriented with the University of Illinois campus lying primarily within its boundaries.

Boasting a one-of-a-kind campus facility, the University's Krannert Center for the Performing Arts is similar in concept to New York's Lincoln Center, where separate theaters have been specifically designed for different types of productions. Also of interest is the Wilber Mansion, a turn-of-the-century Victorian home restored as the Champaign County Historical Museum.

0:00 (0:38) Depart Champaign-Urbana.
0:38 (0:00) Arrive Mattoon.

MATTOON, IL - An industrial community and service center for the surrounding farmlands, Mattoon is a convenient stop for students attending Eastern Illinois University in Charleston. Also nearby is the Lincoln Log Cabin State Park where the modest home of our nation's 16th president has been restored atop its original foundation.

0:00 (0:25) Depart Mattoon.
0:25 (0:00) Arrive Effingham.

EFFINGHAM, IL - As well as a service center for smaller agricultural communities, Effingham supports an active manufacturing industry with products spanning the gamut from church furniture to golf clubs.

0:00 (0:44) Depart Effingham.
0:44 (0:00) Arrive Centralia.

CENTRALIA, IL - Centralia, one of three cities comprising this metropolitan area, is an industrial-oriented community with railroad shops and yards providing major employment for the region. An immense carillon, sixth largest in the world, dominates the town's skyline. This is where the River Cities joins the southbound City of New Orleans.

0:00 (0:54) Depart Centralia.
0:54 (0:00) Arrive Carbondale.

CARBONDALE, IL - As its name implies, Carbondale sits in the midst of extensive coalfields which provide the basic industrial staple of this community. The home of Southern Illinois University, Carbondale is but a short distance from the Crab Orchard National Wildlife Refuge, a haven of outdoor recreation and a popular winter haunt for thousands of Canadian geese. Here, too, is Bald Knob, a high point in the Ozarks overlooking three states. Each Easter, sunrise services are held beneath the cross at its summit.

0:00 (1:48) Depart Carbondale.
0:58 (0:50) Through the town of Cairo.

Situated at the confluence of the mighty Ohio and Mississippi rivers, Cairo was the early Civil War headquarters of General Grant, affording him complete command of operations along these waterways. Today, bridges across three rivers connect the states of Missouri, Kentucky and Illinois. Locals have dubbed this portion of Southern Illinois as "Little Egypt" (not to be confused with the dancer) because of its resemblance to the flat silt banks of the Nile River Valley.

0:59 (0:49) Cross Ohio River and enter Kentucky.

Shortly, the train crosses a geologic feature known as the New Madrid Fault which caused North America's strongest earthquake (probably an incredible 8.7 on the Richter scale) during the winter of 1811-12. Nearby, the Mississippi actually changed direction and as far away as Boston church bells were clanging from the shock. Experts say the fault, more than 500 million years old, is building up pressure and might some day trigger the nation's worst natural disaster.

1:48 (0:00) Arrive Fulton.

FULTON, KY - Until recently, the majority of banana shipments from Latin America stopped in Fulton while refrigerator cars were re-iced, and the fruit was prepared for distribution. Although this practice has since been discontinued, the town's International Banana Festival remains a popular summer event, with Latin American music, crafts and food highlighting the festivities. The town once concocted a two-ton banana pudding (world's largest, of course) to commemorate this tropical fruit.

0:00 (0:51) Depart Fulton.
0:51 (0:00) Arrive Newbern.

NEWBERN, TN - This small town serves as a stop for nearby Dyersburg. Dyersburg was founded in 1821 and was named in honor of Colonel William Henry Dyer who served under General Andrew Jackson during the War of 1812. Today, bountiful crops of cotton and fruit are processed by local industry.

0:00 (1:34) Depart Newbern.
1:32 (0:02) Dawn is usually breaking on approach to Memphis. On right, Hernando-Desoto Bridge, with lights aglow, spans Mississippi River carrying Interstate 40 traffic between Memphis and Little Rock. Great American Pyramid is incongruous

City of New Orleans dome car
JACK SWANSON

sight on right. Festival Island (formerly Mud Island) is home to a park focusing on Mississippi River history and geography and is separated from shore by Wolf River. Once a muddy trap for river vessels, the island's reclamation has turned it into a Memphis showplace. Venerable Peabody Hotel, on left, is easily identified by rooftop neon sign. Then historic Beale Street can be seen off to left.

1:34 (0:00) Arrive Memphis.

MEMPHIS, TN - Memphis was born in 1819 when Andrew Jackson, yet to be elected president, laid out a town on the Chickasaw Bluffs overlooking the Mississippi River. This unusually high location above the Mississippi turned out to be fortuitous, since many towns established along the banks of that great river were ultimately washed away or abandoned due to recurring flooding.

Although severely decimated by several yellow fever epidemics in the 1800s, the city not only came back, it is now the largest city on the Mississippi between St. Louis and New Orleans. Memphis has laid claim to numerous distinctions, including: the "Hardwood Center of the World"; the world's largest mule-trading market; the "Birthplace of Blues"; four times winner of the nation's "cleanest city" award; the home of W. C. Handy and Elvis Presley; and the home of the first Welcome Wagon.

Central Station, 545 South Main St., is a terminally (no pun intended) forlorn structure in one of the worst areas of town, an area where passengers should not walk at night. Fortunately, there are plans to improve Amtrak's situation, probably by redeveloping its current site. The present station has storage lockers and adjacent free parking (no security).

Cab stand at the station; Yellow Cab, 577-7777. **Local buses** stop in front of the station; MATA, 274-6282. A tour shuttle route is designed to loop around major tourist attractions. **Memphis International Airport** is approximately eight miles southeast of the station.

Visitor Information Center, 340 Beale Street. Information may also be obtained from Memphis Convention and Visitors Bureau, Morgan Keegan Tower, 50 N. Front St., Suite 450, 38103; (901) 576-8181.

Ramada Convention Center Hotel, 160 Union Ave., 38103; (901) 525-5491. Attractive downtown hotel, about two miles from the station. $55.

-Wilson World Graceland, 3677 Elvis Presley Blvd., 38116; (901) 332-1000 or

800-333-9457. Excellent value. Across from Graceland. $42.

-**The Peabody,** 149 Union, 38103; (901) 529-4000 or 800-833-2548. Venerable landmark, located downtown, about two miles from the station. $190.

Memphis and the Mississippi River are inseparable. Recognizing this, the City of Memphis has spent over $60 million developing **Mud Island,** just offshore of the downtown area. The Island is a showcase for all aspects of the River—recreational, educational, cultural, historic and scientific, all set along a five-block river walk that is actually a flowing model of the entire Mississippi River Basin.

Memphis' newest attraction is **The Great American Pyramid,** on the edge of downtown. This 32-story "wonder" houses a sports complex and the **American Music Awards Hall of Fame.** An inclinator carries visitors along the outer edge of the pyramid to its glass-enclosed observation area, 32 stories above the city. The **Heritage Trolley** runs along Main Street between the north edge of downtown and the Amtrak station. Stops include the Pyramid and Beale Street.

Some of the city's past can be savored in **Victorian Village,** downtown in the area of 680 Adams Street, where various historic buildings have been restored. Some of these are open to the public.

Nightlife and blues, a Memphis tradition, can be found downtown along **Beale Street** where W. C. Handy lived and wrote much of his beloved music. **Overton Square,** at Madison and Cooper, comprises three blocks of shops, nightclubs and unique restaurants.

The best-known tourist attraction in town is still **Graceland,** the showplace home of Elvis Presley, where visitors can get a firsthand look at "The King's" lifestyle. The estate is south of downtown at 3717 Elvis Presley Blvd.

And the legendary **Peabody ducks** are mandatory for anyone visiting Memphis for the first time. At 11 am each day, the hotel's ducks that reside in a rooftop penthouse are herded into an elevator and brought to the lobby for their ritualistic feeding.

0:00 (1:13) Depart Memphis.
0:48 (0:25) Cross Coldwater River.
0:50 (0:23) Entering town of Coldwater, cotton gin with yellow cotton wagons is on right.
1:08 (0:05) Cross Tallahatchie River.
1:13 (0:00) Arrive Batesville. Because of train's length and platform's brevity, "City" usually makes a second "spot" stop for convenience of passengers.

BATESVILLE, MS - Set admist an array of colorful and fragrant flowers, Batesville is the home of the highly regarded "Art-Mart," a midsummer festival drawing craftsmen and artisans from across the South. Nearby Enid and Sardis lakes are also popular attractions, offering a multitude of recreational possibilities.

0:00 (0:41) Depart Batesville.
0:41 (0:00) Cross Yalobusha River immediately preceding arrival at Grenada.

GRENADA, MS - Originally established as two separate towns, it became one community early on with a celebration that was highlighted by a wedding of a groom who hailed from one township and a bride who resided in the other.

At once a vital mecca of cotton production, Grenada caters as well to a growing tourist trade, lured primarily by the nearby Grenada Lake recreation resort.

0:00 (0:21) Depart Grenada across rolling farmlands and forests of the Deep South. Of many agricultural products, cotton is by far most prevalent. Cotton wagons and ginning plants are as common to this region as tractors and grain elevators to Midwest. Boxcars brimming with fresh-cut hardwood are also a frequent sight, indicative of another flourishing industry.
0:04 (0:17) Railroad is principal customer of lumber mill, on right, where thousands of cross ties await shipment.
0:21 (0:00) Arrive Winona. Across from station, on left, stands time-honored Wisteria Hotel, its rooms now rented as apartments.

 WINONA, MS - On January 31, 1860, a ceremonial spike was driven just south of Winona, linking the Great Lakes region with the Gulf of Mexico. This was a major boon to Winona farmers who previously depended on oxcarts for distribution of their crops. Since completion of the rail line, Winona has maintained an active agricultural and industrial economy.

Still scattered throughout this area are a number of resplendent antebellum homes, several of which are open to the public.

0:00 (0:25) Departing Winona, beautifully preserved white mansion stands distinctively on left.

0:17 (0:08) Flat, swampy wetlands, now most apparent, are commonplace between Memphis and New Orleans.

0:25 (0:00) Arriving Durant, quaint gazebo on right would seem popular spot for officiating town festivities.

DURANT, MS - Another agricultural service community, Durant is surrounded by a number of Indian reservations. These include tribes who originally inhabited the region when it was first explored by DeSoto in 1541. Kosciusko, hometown of Ophra Winfrey, is just 18 miles east of here.

0:00 (0:30) Depart Durant.

0:02 (0:28) Two dozen or so dangling silver gourds serve as birdhouses in yard on right.

0:12 (0:18) Surrounded by extensive cotton fields, pass through appropriately named town of Pickens. A few miles downline, note woodlands on left that have been ravaged by fire.

0:18 (0:12) Pass through small town of Vaughan that was site of famous "Casey Jones" wreck.

Trying to make up lost time, an unsuspecting Casey ran his speeding train into a derailed freight just north of town. He died in the wreck and was supposedly found with one hand on the throttle and the other on the brake. Chronicles of this legendary engineer, as well as other railroad memorabilia, are housed here in a restored depot museum.

0:19 (0:11) Cross Big Black River.

0:30 (0:00) Madison County Court House, on left, immediately precedes arrival at Canton station.

CANTON, MS - Primarily a manufacturing hub of textiles and lumber products, Canton's modest population is swelled by 20,000 each May and October during the nationally acclaimed Canton Flea Markets.

0:00 (0:32) Depart Canton.

0:03 (0:28) Flourishing pecan groves on left represent another agricultural staple of this state.

0:19 (0:15) Intersect Natchez Trace Parkway at Ridgeland.

The Natchez Trace was an early Indian and trappers' trail that extended from Natchez northeastward into Kentucky. Before steam power made it practical to navigate upstream, boatsmen who brought goods and people from the Ohio River Valley down the Mississippi River would often terminate their southward journey at Natchez. Here, having no further use for their boats, they would sell them for lumber, then return home by the cheapest means—on foot along the Natchez Trace. Unfortunately, robbers frequently helped themselves to the rivermen's profits.

0:23 (0:12) Plant of Presto Corporation, well-known cookware manufacturer, can be seen on right approaching Jackson.

0:28 (0:08) On left, Memorial Stadium is scene of fierce gridiron rivalries between "Ole Miss" and Mississippi State University. For rest of season, field is home to Jackson State University and Millsaps College. University of Mississippi Medical Center is situated just south of stadium.

0:34 (0:02) Downtown Jackson skyline appears on forward left, with broad dome of "new" Capitol Building predominant. Built in 1903, golden eagle (flying south, of course) is proudly perched atop this grand structure.

0:36 (0:00) Arrive Jackson. Former Hotel King Edward, once an important Jackson landmark, now stands empty and in utter disrepair, forward on left.

JACKSON, MS - Crossroads of the South, capital of and largest city (over 300,000 population) in Mississippi, Jackson had its humble beginnings as a trading settlement on the banks of the Pearl River. This outpost grew to prominence, only to be burned to the ground by

General Sherman during the Civil War. The city recovered mightily, and is now the trading and transportation center of the state. History buffs will find much to occupy them throughout this region.

0:00 (0:30) Depart Jackson, with "Old" Capitol Building on left. Mississippi Arts Center and Planetarium are housed within white-domed complex, also on left.

0:25 (0:06) Pass through Crystal Springs whose bountiful tomato harvests of early 1900s prompted its designation as "Tomatopolis of the World."

0:30 (0:00) Arrive Hazelhurst past comely residential district on right.

HAZELHURST, MS - Set deep in the heart of farm country, Hazelhurst serves a region devoted primarily to the production of cotton and livestock.

0:00 (0:21) Depart Hazelhurst. On immediate left is Royal Maid Association for the Blind, employing blind workers to manufacture plastic flatware, mops, brooms and other products.

0:14 (0:07) Passing through Wesson, note historic Wesson Hotel on left. During railroad's heyday, a gambling casino was maintained in hotel's attic, and proved a popular diversion for awaiting passengers. Building is presently enshrined in National Register. Adjacent to hotel is campus of Copiah-Lincoln Junior College.

0:20 (0:01) Small Southern mansion on left is appropriate home for Magnolia Manor Antiques.

0:21 (0:00) Arriving Brookhaven, regal magnolia trees line walkways of station. Small monument on right offers brief account of town's historical highlights.

BROOKHAVEN, MS - A recruiting and hospital center during the Civil War, Brookhaven has likewise flourished since completion of the railroad. Today, industrial development is focused around the region's natural resources of petroleum, wood pulp and clay, and provides an attractive balance for Brookhaven's strong agricultural economy.

0:00 (0:21) Departing Brookhaven, fanciful Victorian homes enhance neighborhood on left.

0:03 (0:15) Bogue Chitto River makes first of several brief appearances on left.

0:19 (0:02) Outstanding composition of lake and rural homes, on right, produces one of more attractive scenes along route.

0:21 (0:00) Arrive McComb.

MCCOMB, MS - This southern Mississippi town was named in honor of Colonel H. S. McComb who spearheaded reconstruction of the railroad following its destruction during the Civil War.

McComb is presently renowned as the home of the "Lighted Azalea Trail," an enchanting Easter-time spectacle fashioned by local residents who pin tiny lights around the delicate pink and white blossoms of their azalea bushes.

0:00 (0:53) Depart McComb.

0:10 (0:43) At Magnolia, two outstanding Colonial mansions can be seen on right. Splendid magnolia trees grace yard of larger home.

0:13 (0:40) Cross Tangipahoa River which then follows intermittently on left.

0:19 (0:34) At southern edge of Osyka, cross Mississippi state line into Louisiana.

0:28 (0:26) A few miles south of Kentwood, pass Camp Moore Confederate Cemetery on left. Once a major training camp for Confederate Army, museum of Civil War relics now stands amidst graves of over 500 soldiers.

0:31 (0:22) Wetland homes are often elevated a foot or two above ground for obvious reasons. Builder of house at left was expecting the worst.

0:32 (0:21) Beautiful estates grace landscape on right, just south of Tangipahoa.

0:39 (0:14) Early vestiges of French influence can be detected in curlicues and trelliswork adorning homes of Amite. On left, colossal old bell is enshrined in front of fire station. Standpipe on left proclaims Amite as "The Friendly City—500,000 Gallon Capacity."

0:47 (0:06) On southern outskirts of Independence, note intriguing cemetery on right. Tombs are positioned above ground in deference to saturated soil that would otherwise seep into graves. This is a fairly common spectacle throughout pervading wetlands of southern Louisiana.

0:49 (0:04) Supporting town's claim as one of world's "Strawberry Capitals," copious fields of this delectable fruit line route into Hammond.

164

0:53 (0:00) Arrive Hammond, where station, on right, sports eye-catching brown tile roof.

 HAMMOND, LA - Hammond is considered the state's "Strawberry Capital."

0:00 (1:01) Depart Hammond.

0:09 (0:52) Passing through Ponchatoula, old 2-8-0 narrow-gauge steam locomotive of Louisiana Express can be seen on left.

Now venture forth amidst the haunting beauty of the Louisiana swamplands. From the dark recesses of the encompassing bog, the contorted silhouettes of moss-laden cypress can easily conjure up menacing, untamed images. Yet at once, this primitive wilderness has nurtured the lifeblood and soul around which an entire Acadian culture has evolved.

0:12 (0:50) On right, Interstate 55 sits atop concrete piers, impressively fixed into forbidding landscape below. Grey-green material hanging from trees is Spanish moss, a harmless non-parasite, and one of nature's more attractive embellishments.

0:17 (0:46) Cross Pass-Manchac waterway that connects Lake Maurepas on right with Lake Pontchartrain on left.

0:26 (0:38) Approaching suburbs of New Orleans, train skirts shoreline of Lake Pontchartrain on left. Once inland, delightful sights of this exciting city are unfortunately denied along a rather nondescript route into station.

0:34 (0:31) Duck under I-10 which then follows on left.

0:43 (0:22) On left, Moisant Field is New Orleans International Airport.

0:52 (0:13) Famed Huey P. Long Bridge, carrying both automobile and rail traffic across Mississippi River, is visible on horizon at right.

1:00 (0:05) After crossing beneath major highway interchange, campus of Xavier University can be seen on right.

1:03 (0:03) To forward left, Superdome is an imposing structure in foreground of New Orleans skyline. Sports facility is home of National Football League's Saints. Adjacent to east is modernistic Hyatt Regency Hotel.

1:07 (0:02) Engage in U-turn around publishing headquarters of Picayune States-Item Times. Train then backs into New Orleans station. Elephantine Superdome stands at immediate left.

1:14 (0:00) Arrive New Orleans.

 NEW ORLEANS, LA - See page 112.

Empire Builder

It was James J. Hill, a rugged empire-building tycoon in the finest sense, who constructed his Great Northern Railway around the turn of the century, creating a transcontinental link between St. Paul and the Pacific Northwest. The railroad brought farmers and ranchers to the prairies of North Dakota and Montana, miners to the mineral rich mountains of western Montana and lumberjacks to Washington's forests. And virtually overnight, an international trade with the Orient developed through Seattle's natural harbor, Puget Sound.

In 1929, Hill's Great Northern inaugurated the passenger train called the Empire Builder—a train which became one of the few of that era to have its name live on. Now, the Empire Builder makes this same jaunt across the northern tier of states, but starts in Chicago, following the Milwaukee Road to St. Paul before trekking across the old Great Northern route (now the Burlington Northern) to Seattle. This is America's northernmost passage.

Ken Wescott Jones, a British rail travel authority, described today's "Builder" as "the most comfortable, all-class, non-supplementary-fare train in the world." Add to this proclaimed contentment some of this country's most attractive countryside and the trip becomes an enticement that is hard to refuse. America's fruited plains, her purple mountain majesties, her gleaming shores—they are all on display. The pastoral environs of the upper Mississippi River and the vast expanses of the northern plains contrast sharply with the mountains of Glacier National Park and the Cascades of Washington, a contrast that can only be fully absorbed and enjoyed while traveling on a train.

The Portland section breaks off at Spokane and offers its own attractions with a cruise along the northern shore of the majestic Columbia River, including a memorable trip through the verdant-cliffed Columbia Gorge.

Westbound Schedule (Condensed)
Chicago, IL - Midafternoon Departure
Milwaukee, WI - Late Afternoon
St. Paul/Minneapolis, MN - Late Evening
Fargo, ND - Middle of the Night (2nd Day)
Havre, MT - Midafternoon (2nd Day)
West Glacier, MT - Midevening (2nd Day)
Spokane, WA - Late Night (3rd Day)
Portland, OR* - Midmorning Arrival (3rd Day)
Seattle, WA - Midmorning Arrival (3rd Day)

Eastbound Schedule (Condensed)
Seattle, WA - Late Afternoon Departure
Portland, OR* - Late Afternoon Departure
Spokane, WA - Late Evening
West Glacier, MT - Early Morning (2nd Day)
Havre, MT - Early Afternoon (2nd Day)
Fargo, ND - Late Night (3rd Day)
St. Paul/Minneapolis, MN - Early Morning (3rd Day)
Milwaukee, WI - Early Afternoon (3rd Day)
Chicago, IL - Midafternoon Arrival (3rd Day)

*By separate section between Spokane and Portland.

Frequency - Daily.
Seating - Superliner coaches.
Dining - Complete meal and beverage service, Chicago-Seattle. Lounge service available with sandwiches, snacks, beverages and movies. Cold meal service for sleeping car passengers, Spokane-Portland.
Sleeping - Superliner sleepers with deluxe, family, economy and special bedrooms.
Baggage - Checked baggage handled at most stations.
Reservations - All-reserved train.
Length of Trip - To Seattle: 2,209 miles in 45½ hours. To Portland: 2,261 miles in 45 hours.

Route Log

 CHICAGO, IL - See page 128.

0:00 (0:26) Depart Chicago's Union Station beneath streets of Chicago, emerging amidst some of city's most notable landmarks. On immediate right, Marina City's twin cylindrical towers are an architectural eye-catcher, while on forward right, Merchandise Mart is stoutly entrenched on banks of Chicago River.
0:03 (0:20) Following a quick turn west, smartly tapering design of Hancock Building is readily distinguishable back on right. Multi-tiered Sears Tower, currently world's tallest building at 1,353 feet, dominates skyline back on left.

For the next several miles, elevated trackbed affords encompassing views of Chicago's older north side. Multi-domed and multi-spired churches are impressive fixtures throughout this neighborhood.
0:23 (0:00) Arrive Glenview.

GLENVIEW, IL - Glenview is a convenient suburban stop for the northern Chicago region.
0:00 (1:03) Depart Glenview north through a comely residential district. Between here and Milwaukee, landscape bares an interesting mix of older farms and modern industrial complexes. Underwriter's Laboratories, Fiat, Sara Lee, American Motors and AC are but a few of the corporate strongholds seen throughout this stretch.
0:02 (1:01) On left, skirt grounds of Glenview Naval Air Station where numerous helicopters, fixed-wing craft and a star-spangled water tower can be observed.
0:03 (1:00) Green berm, on right, hides enormous regional landfill, while just beyond, twin towers (circa 1920) mark beautiful complex of Techny, U.S. headquarters for the Chicago Province of the Society of the Divine Word. Once a Catholic religious seminary, it has served as a religious conference and retreat center since 1978.
0:20 (0:43) Passing through Gurnee, Marriott's popular Great American Amusement Park can be seen on left.
0:23 (0:40) At Wadsworth, Des Plaines River follows infrequently on left. A couple miles hence, cross Illinois state line into Wisconsin.
0:30 (0:33) On right, field serves as storage facility for hundreds of new cars awaiting transport to dealers' showrooms.
0:38 (0:25) Old hotel at Sturtevant, on right, is interesting curiosity with its turret-adorned corners.
0:40 (0:23) Looking almost inviting, one of nation's newest prisons, Racine Correctional Institution, is on right.
0:54 (0:09) On right is General Mitchell Field, Milwaukee's airport.
0:58 (0:05) With Milwaukee's skyline coming into full view, note two architecturally outstanding and historical churches to left. St. Josaphat's Basilica, distinguished by its inspiring verdigris dome (modeled after St. Peter's in Rome), was built at turn of the century by poor immigrant parishioners using materials salvaged from Chicago's Federal Building. It was first Polish basilica in North America.

St. Stanislaus Cathedral, readily identified by its twin golden-domed spires, was nation's third Polish church at time of its construction. Colorfully faceted glasswork and sculptured marble bedeck interior of this magnificent structure.
0:59 (0:04) On left, Allen Bradley clock tower is stately landmark in foreground of downtown.
1:03 (0:00) Arrive Milwaukee station, crossing confluence of Menomonee and Milwaukee rivers. Watch for collection of

private, vintage rail cars sometimes parked at left.

MILWAUKEE, WI - Milwaukee, an Indian word meaning "beautiful meeting place by the waters," is the largest city in Wisconsin with a metropolitan population of 1,400,000. It is also one of the nation's leading industrial centers, as well as being an important inland seaport on the Great Lakes.

Of course, a major industry is the brewing of beer—so important that Milwaukee is oft referred to as "beer town." The brewery image should not be misleading. Milwaukee, located on a beautiful bay of Lake Michigan, is one of America's most attractive cities. Nor does the city lack for a healthy dose of culture. It has a fine symphony, a ballet company, theater groups, a top-notch zoo and a well-stocked art museum.

Union Station, 433 W. St. Paul Ave., is on the edge of downtown. The station has a large waiting room, redcaps, a restaurant, a newsstand, a Hertz counter and pay-parking across the street.

Cab stand at the station; Yellow Cab, 271-1800. Hertz **rental cars** are available at the station. **Local bus** stop is at the front door, 344-6711. **Milwaukee Airport** (General Mitchell Field) is six miles south of the station.

Milwaukee Visitors Bureau, 510 W. Kilbourn, 53203; (414) 273-7222 or 800-231-0903.

Ramada Inn Downtown, 633 W. Michigan St., 53203; (414) 272-8410. Attractive and convenient. Three blocks from the station. $66.

-**Marc Plaza Hotel,** 509 W. Wisconsin Ave., 53203; (414) 271-7250 or 800-558-7708. A Milwaukee landmark. Three blocks from the station. $79.

-**Holiday Inn Downtown,** 611 W. Wisconsin Ave.; (414) 273-2950. Four blocks from the station. $86.

Milwaukee is one of several cities that has a **Skywalk** system, permitting weatherproof strolling and shopping. Nearest access is W. Michigan and 4th, three blocks from the station. Spirit of Milwaukee Theatre, on Wisconsin Avenue, between 1st and 2nd streets in the Grand Ave. Mall, has a **multimedia show** giving a Milwaukee overview, four blocks from the station. **First Wisconsin Center,** 11 blocks east of the station, is the state's highest building; the 41st floor has a superb view. **Milwaukee Public Museum,** 800 W. Wells St. and eight blocks from the station, is the nation's fourth largest natural history museum. **Mitchell Park Conservatory,** 524 Layton Blvd., houses horticultural exhibits from around the world in three massive glass domes. **Milwaukee County Zoo** is one of the finest in the world. Both Pabst and Miller offer free **brewery tours.**

0:00 (1:14) Depart Milwaukee.

0:04 (1:10) On left, three unusual glass domes house Mitchell Park Horticultural Conservatory (world's largest curved-glass horticultural structures). Botanical displays representing the world's three climatic conditions—arid, temperate and tropical—are cultivated here in buildings that simulate their native environs.

0:06 (1:08) Milwaukee County Stadium, home of baseball's "Brewers," can be seen on left.

0:07 (1:07) Miller brewery is on right. Immediately thereafter, cross Menomonee River.

0:21 (0:53) Passing through handsome suburb of Elm Grove, campus-like complex on right is Notre Dame Health Care Center, a facility for elderly nuns.

0:30 (0:44) Border edge of Pewaukee Lake on left, with town of same name encircling shoreline.

0:38 (0:36) At Okauchee, Ocono Lake appears on left. Quick glimpse of Okauchee Lake is afforded on right.

With the vestiges of urban influence slowly waning, embark across the open spaces that are America's heartland. Thomas Jefferson once exhorted that we be "a nation of yeoman farmers." To that end, the rustic farmsteads set amidst rolling fields of grain are picturesque reminders that this early American ideal still flourishes.

0:39 (0:36) Still in Okauchee, on right, signage on St. Jerome's Church garage admonishes "Thou Shalt Not Park."

0:46 (0:28) On eastern outskirts of Ixonia, cross Rock River.

0:56 (0:18) Approaching Watertown,

cross Rock River twice again, noting attractive homes lining banks. Proceeding through town, tall spire of St. Bernard's Catholic Church protrudes noticeably above treetops on right. Immediately thereafter, campus and stadium of Maranatha College can also be seen on right.

1:13 (0:01) Cross Crawfish River, then wonderfully crafted tree house is cradled next to tracks on right.

1:14 (0:00) Arrive Columbus where, on right, tidy depot is adorned with city's name in raised relief above front door and unusually sculpted bricks in platforms each side of tracks.

Note interesting design of 125-year-old Zion Evangelical Lutheran Church on left. Large bell mounted beneath its steeple was gift from Emperor of Germany, cast from pieces of French cannon captured during Franco-Prussian War.

Immediately adjacent to church, fanciful clock tower sits atop 1892 Columbus City Hall.

COLUMBUS, WI - Famed for its springtime regalia of redbud blossoms, Columbus is also a convenient stop for students attending the University of Wisconsin in nearby Madison.

0:00 (0:25) Depart Columbus.

0:16 (0:09) While passing through Wyocena, don't miss "Santa's Super Rocket." Looking capable of interplanetary travel, this cosmic contraption was surely the highlight of many Christmases past. Regrettably, it has since been put out to pasture and today ages gracefully in back lots of a Wyocena salvage yard on right.

0:43 (0:00) Arrive Portage.

PORTAGE, WI - Situated on a narrow strip of land between the Fox and Wisconsin rivers, Portage is a prosperous commercial hub of the surrounding farmlands. As its name implies, the town was once a popular stopover for traders and settlers who had to "portage" their gear from one river to the other.

0:00 (0:15) Depart Portage through rail yards that boast a small roundhouse and turntable.

0:07 (0:07) Wisconsin River joins on left. A couple miles downline, American Baptist Indian Church and cemetery are scenically isolated atop bluff on right.

Tree house - near Columbus, Wisconsin
BRUCE LEMAY COLLECTION

0:15 (0:00) Arrive Wisconsin Dells' 1989 station, built to replace former depot destroyed when a coal train derailed here in 1982. Magnificent canyon cut by river can be seen on left. Throughout much of year, boats and rafts traverse its scenic course, providing feature attraction of this popular tourist haven. Area is also highlighted by a host of man-made amusements, several of which surround station site.

WISCONSIN DELLS, WI - From airplane rides to water slides, an amusement-park atmosphere pervades this renowned Midwestern resort. Yet, as previously noted, the natural beauty and drama surrounding "The Dells" is still the mainstay around which the town has flourished.

0:00 (0:42) Depart Wisconsin Dells across Wisconsin River.

0:21 (0:21) Built in 1902, multi-spired St. Patrick's Catholic Church, on right, is prominent feature of "midtown" route through Mauston. On western edge of town, train skirts shoreline of Lake Decorah, on right, formed by dam across Lemonweir River.

0:30 (0:12) Fascinating rock formations are an unexpected delight of Camp Douglas area. Once in town, Camp Douglas Village Hall is a most impressive structure on left.

0:40 (0:00) Arriving Tomah, well-preserved Pullman car of Milwaukee Road houses Chamber of Commerce on left.

TOMAH, WI - In a tribute to its agricultural roots, Tomah is host each July to the Wisconsin Dairyland Grand National Tractor Pull—a grueling test of skill and equipment, attracting hundreds of farmers from across the Midwest and Canada. From "souped up" rigs to stock models, contestants hauling weighted sleds vie for over $100,000 in prize money while an impassioned throng of spectators cheers on its favorites.

Tomah is also noted as the boyhood home of Frank King, creator of the famed comic strip "Gasoline Alley." Many of King's drawings and cartoons are preserved throughout the town. Walt and Skeezix can be seen holding up the sign in front of the Chamber of Commerce office next to the station.

0:00 (0:41) Depart Tomah.

0:01 (0:40) On left, pass Tomah Lake.

0:05 (0:36) Brief intrusion of alpine-like terrain highlights geography surrounding Tunnel City. Quick trip through tunnel appropriately follows.

0:20 (0:31) Entrance to US Army Ft. McCoy is at left.

0:21 (0:22) On right, pass small Sparta airport. At same time, begin following La Crosse River on right to its juncture with Mississippi River twenty miles west.

0:23 (0:18) In Bangor, distinctive Village Hall stands out on right.

0:38 (0:03) Cross La Crosse River.

0:41 (0:00) Two beautiful churches on right preview arrival at La Crosse.

LA CROSSE, WI - An old Indian game that the French dubbed "lacrosse" gave its name to this picturesque community, set at the confluence of the Black, La Crosse and Mississippi rivers. Agricultural, industrial and commercial enterprises all contribute to the town's well-balanced economy.

0:00 (0:33) Departing La Crosse, cross Mississippi River into Minnesota. Islands in middle of this historic waterway divide river into three channels here. Once on western bank, pass through "apple capital" of La Crescent and begin a northerly tack that generally parallels river through Richard J. Dorer Memorial Hardwood State Forest. Oak, birch, maple and walnut are but a sampling of hardwood trees that thrive in these parts.

The ensuing 125 miles is one of the most scenic legs of The Empire Builder route. Quaint little townships, elegant in their simplicity, are splendidly well-preserved along these riverbanks. At their doorstep, barges and riverboats leisurely traverse the waters of the mighty Mississippi. To the west, the lush farmlands and forests of this fertile river valley provide a serene backdrop for a setting that has assuredly inspired many an artist or photographer.

0:01 (0:32) On right, note Number 7 dam and locks.

0:11 (0:22) On right, note Number 6 dam and locks.

0:32 (0:01) Towering 500 feet above the river, Sugar Loaf Mountain is a renowned landmark of Winona on left. According to

Indian legend, silhouette of famous Sioux Chief Wa-Pa-Sha was once prominent feature of mountain prior to quarrying operations of late 1800s.

0:33 (0:00) Another "midtown" route into station avails intriguing insights into this hardy Midwestern community upon arriving Winona. Cozy chalet-style depot greets passengers on left.

WINONA, MN - Since construction of the first sawmills here in the early 1850s, Winona has grown from a one-industry town into a bustling manufacturing center. Essential throughout its development, the influence of the Mississippi riverboat remains an important aspect of the town's present-day charm.

Winona is also a popular connection for passengers traveling to the famed Mayo Clinic in nearby Rochester.

0:00 (1:01) Depart Winona.

0:03 (0:58) Large cluster of grain elevators, on right, evidences major distribution port.

0:14 (0:47) On right, note Number 5 dam and locks.

0:20 (0:41) Numerous fishing camps flourish about Weaver, supporting area's claim as "White Bass Capital of the World." Passing through town, stately structure perched atop bluffs on left was formerly grandiose hotel, recognized in National Register.

0:32 (0:29) Comely Wabasha is home of Anderson House Hotel, Minnesota's oldest operating inn since 1856. As special amenities, complimentary shoeshines are provided, as well as hot bricks to warm the feet in winter. For lonesome travelers, house cats are also available upon request.

0:33 (0:28) Mississippi River widens considerably to accommodate waters of Chippewa River flowing in from east. Waterskiing is said to have originated here in resultant expanse known as Lake Pepin.

0:49 (0:12) Pass through beautiful little town of Frontenac whose roots trace back to original French fort established here in 1723.

0:50 (0:11) On left, T-bar lift ascends slopes of Mt. Frontenac Ski Area.

0:55 (0:06) On right, nostalgic advertisement for Beechnut chewing tobacco weathers picturesquely on side of barn.

0:57 (0:04) Approaching Red Wing, Minnesota State Training School is easily recognized on left by its lofty tower, with Minnesota and U.S. flags fronting property. Internationally acclaimed for success of its "Positive Peer Group" therapy, facility was originally established in 1891, and modeled after castle on Rhine River.

1:01 (0:00) Arrive Red Wing which is situated at upstream end of Lake Pepin. Just south of station, historic St. James Hotel can be seen on left. Its 41 rooms are adorned in Victorian splendor, and each named for a famous riverboat that once plied waters of Mississippi. Built in 1875, Red Wing Shoe Company saved it from decay in late 1970s with an ambitious restoration program. Prior to invention of dining cars, trains stopped here to feed passengers in hotel's well-regarded restaurant.

RED WING, MN - This lovely riverside community takes its name from generations of Sioux Chieftains who chose as their emblem a swan's wing dyed scarlet. Long known for its manufacture of shoes and pottery, tourists are presently discovering a wealth of recreational opportunities in the hills, forests and rivers surrounding Red Wing.

0:00 (1:04) Depart Red Wing. Then scores of boat shelters appear at marina on right.

0:07 (0:57) Prairie Island is home to nuclear power plant, with its reactor domes and banks of cooling units, appearing on right.

0:08 (0:56) On right, note Number 3 dam and locks.

0:16 (0:48) Cross Vermillion River into Hastings. Domed Dakota County Courthouse, built in 1871, can be seen on left.

0:20 (0:44) Cross Mississippi River, its lakes and inlets bordering on left into St. Paul/Minneapolis.

0:28 (0:35) On left, pass large 3-M Plant. Based here in St. Paul/Minneapolis, "Scotch Tape" is one of more well-known products of this diverse corporation.

0:43 (0:21) On left, St. Paul Downtown Airport can be seen across river. At same time, city skyline juts imposingly above horizon in distance.

0:48 (0:18) Central fixtures of downtown hub preside atop palisades on right, over-

Minneapolis

St. Paul

- ▲ Amtrak Station
- 1 - Visitors Information
- 2 - Walker Art Center
- 3 - St. Anthony Falls
- 4 - Orchestra Hall
- 5 - Como-Harriet Street Car
- 6 - State Capitol

looking succession of bridges spanning Mississippi River.

0:49 (0:15) On left, old sternwheelers are frequently moored alongside Harriet Island. From May through September, nostalgic riverboat excursions to nearby Ft. Snelling are popular tourist attraction. St. Paul's former Union Station is expansive brown brick building stretching away from tracks on right.

0:50 (0:14) Modeled after St. Peter's in Rome, magnificent St. Paul Cathedral on right is readily identified by its verdigris domes and outstanding classical architecture.

0:53 (0:11) Whimsical, castle-like facilities on left are home of Landmark Brewery.

1:04 (0:00) Arrive modernistic Minneapolis-St. Paul's Midway Station.

MINNEAPOLIS-ST. PAUL, MN - After Lt. Zebulon M. Pike explored the region, Ft. Snelling was established in 1819 approximately five miles from the current site of St. Paul. Its location as the northernmost navigable portion of the Mississippi River made the region a natural port and trade center. St. Paul received its start as a trading post while Minneapolis was born somewhat

later when flour and lumber mills were started on the other side of the river.

Today, those industries are still important to the area's economy, and the "Twin Cities" are the financial, cultural and industrial focal point of the upper Midwest. Their combined population is well over two million and St. Paul is the capital of Minnesota. Companies like General Mills, Control Data and Dayton Hudson are headquartered here. Clean, modern, young and growing are first impressions, and an elaborate pedestrian "skyway" system throughout downtown Minneapolis makes legendary winters more tolerable.

Midway Station, 730 Transfer Road, St. Paul, is literally "midway" between the two downtown areas of Minneapolis and St. Paul, being approximately four miles from each. Storage lockers, luggage carts and food and beverage machines are available at the station. Free parking is adjacent to the station.

Cab stand at the station; Yellow Cab (direct line in station), 824-0228. Budget **rental cars** are located downtown and Budget, 727-2000, will pick up customers at the station during the daytime. **Local buses** (16A) run along

University Ave. (two blocks south of the station at Transfer Rd.) and provide service to both downtowns; call 827-7733. **Minneapolis-St. Paul International Airport,** seven miles south of station.

Minneapolis Convention and Visitors Assn., has visitors center at City Center on the Skyway level. Write to 4000 MultiFoods Tower, 33 South 6th St., 55402. Call (612) 348-4313 or 800-445-7412.

Although there are motels closer to the station, those listed below are in a more desirable location. These are conveniently situated in the University area near downtown Minneapolis, and the 16A bus line provides service not only to downtown Minneapolis and downtown St. Paul but also to within two blocks of the station. They are about two miles from the station.

-Days Inn University of Minnesota, 2407 University Ave., SE, 55414; (612) 623-3999. Attractive highrise, free continental breakfast, $60.

-Best Western University Inn, 2600 University Ave., SE, 55414; (612) 379-2313. $65.

The nation's longest shopping plaza, **Nicollet Mall,** stretches along Nicollet Ave. in downtown Minneapolis. Saks, Dayton's and Neiman Marcus are just some of the stores that anchor this area. **Loring Park** (and lake) is a great place to relax in the heart of the city. The **Walker Art Center** has one of the finest collections in the country.

The **Como-Harriet Streetcar Line and Minnesota Transportation Museum** can be reached by driving south on Interstate 35W, then west on W. 36th St., then left at Richfield Road. There is a 1908 streetcar transporting riders from Lake Como to Lake Harriet and rail equipment in various phases of reconstruction.

The **Mall of America,** in the suburb of Bloomington, is the largest fully enclosed retail mall and amusement park in the nation. This extravaganza was opened in 1992.

0:00 (1:25) Departing Minneapolis-St. Paul, in distance left, 57-story I.D.S. Tower is prominent landmark of downtown Minneapolis.

1:25 (0:00) Arrive St. Cloud.

ST. CLOUD, MN - Set scenically along the banks of the Mississippi River, St. Cloud is noted for its numerous granite quarries which have supplied stone for many venerable structures throughout the country. In recognition of this vital industry, Anthony Caponi's sculpture of "The Granite Trio" is the centerpiece of St. Cloud's downtown mall.

0:00 (0:59) Depart St. Cloud.
0:59 (0:00) Arrive Staples.

STAPLES, MN - Once a dying railroad town, Staples' fortunes improved dramatically when its Vocational Training Institute was established in 1960. Enrolling hundreds of students, its on-the-job curriculum encompassed many local projects, and at the same time, prepared a work-ready labor force that continues to attract new industry to the region.

0:00 (0:54) Depart Staples.
0:54 (0:00) Arrive Detroit Lakes.

DETROIT LAKES, MN - Surrounded by no fewer than 412 lakes, Detroit Lakes is the hub of a vast recreation haven. Although outdoor adventure is nearly limitless, fishing is still king, with walleye, bass and sunfish the most frequent catches.

Prior to road improvements of the 1930s, steamboats were a popular transport between the immediately surrounding lakes, and also serviced the railroad depot where 14 passenger trains arrived daily.

0:00 (0:56) Depart Detroit Lakes.
0:56 (0:00) Arrive Fargo.

FARGO, ND - Lying in the heart of the fertile Red River Valley, Fargo is North Dakota's largest city, and is a vital commercial and livestock center for a vast region. Ten thousand years earlier, the Fargo townsite was submerged beneath 200 feet of water, dammed by the continental glacier to the north.

Named for the founder of the Wells Fargo Express Company, Fargo is a stop for students attending North Dakota State University located here.

0:00 (1:20) Depart Fargo.
1:20 (0:00) Arrive West Grand Forks, a western suburb of Grand Forks.

GRAND FORKS, ND - As suggested by its name, Grand Forks is situated at the confluence of the Red Lake River and the Red River of the North. Located here, the University of North Dakota lends a collegiate atmosphere to this agriculturally oriented community. A 1980s study named Grand Forks and State College, PA the least stressful cities in America.

Greyhound has daily bus service between Grand Forks and Winnipeg, making this a feasible Amtrak-VIA transfer point.

0:00 (1:23) Depart West Grand Forks.
1:23 (0:00) Arrive Devils Lake.

DEVILS LAKE, ND - Settled along the shores of North Dakota's largest natural lake, Devils Lake is a sportsman's paradise, and acclaimed in particular as the goose- and duck-hunting capital of North America. Not always held in such high esteem, Sioux and Chippewa Indians originally named the lake in deference to the evil spirits that once overturned their canoes in the midst of a fierce inter-tribal battle.

0:00 (1:02) Depart Devils Lake.
1:02 (0:00) Arrive Rugby.

RUGBY, ND - As well as an agricultural stronghold, Rugby is noted as the geographical center of North America. Located a half-mile south of town, a towering stone monument pays tribute to this distinction. Rugby is also less than 50 miles from the U.S.-Canadian border where the beautiful International Peace Garden commemorates the many years of friendship between these two countries.

0:00 (1:06) Depart Rugby.
1:06 (0:00) Arrive Minot.

MINOT, ND - Once a desolate frontier outpost, Minot has blossomed into a flourishing industrial mecca, due in large part to its abundant natural resources of oil and coal. Set along the House River that frequently floods the town, Minot is also host to numerous military installations that further supplement a booming economy.

0:00 (0:50) Depart Minot.
0:50 (0:00) Arrive Stanley.

STANLEY, ND - Grain and livestock production are the foremost concerns of this small agricultural community. A prominent focal point of the town is the resplendent Montrail County Courthouse, located just north of the train station.

0:00 (1:05) Depart Stanley.
1:05 (0:00) Arrive Williston.

WILLISTON, ND - Since completion of the Garrison Dam Project along the adjacent Missouri River, Williston has maintained a dependable agricultural and livestock trade, virtually free from threat of drought that frequently plagued the region. Yet, like Minot, oil discoveries have played an important part in Williston's development.

Just west of Williston are two important historical sites: Fort Union which in its heyday was one of the most active trading posts in the West and Fort Buford where Chief Sitting Bull surrendered following the Battle of Little Bighorn.

0:00 (1:28) Departing Williston, Missouri River joins on left and follows intermittently for next 60 miles.

0:24 (1:04) Cross North Dakota state line into Montana and proceed through one of world's largest grain production belts. Along route, many small communities service needs of this expansive agricultural region. County fairgrounds are a popular adjunct of these remote rural outposts.

Gain one hour as train passes from Central to Mountain Time. Set your watch back (forward if eastbound) one hour.

0:52 (0:36) Just west of Culbertson, enter grounds of Fort Peck Indian Reservation that extends nearly ninety miles west to Nashua.

1:12 (0:16) Cross Poplar River.
1:28 (0:00) Arrive Wolf Point.

WOLF POINT, MT - Once a popular haunt of wolf trappers, Wolf Point is host each July to the "Wild Horse Stampede," acclaimed statewide as the "granddaddy of Montana rodeos."

0:00 (0:45) Depart Wolf Point.
0:40 (0:04) Approaching Glasgow, beautiful farmstead is nestled admist wooded

174

glen on left. Bordering property is Milk River which train follows and crosses periodically to Havre.

0:45 (0:00) Letter "G" inscribed on hillside at right denotes arrival at Glasgow.

GLASGOW, MT - Lying in the heart of the Great Northern Wheat Belt, Glasgow has flourished in earnest since construction of the Fort Peck Dam just south of town. The resultant expanse of Fort Peck Lake continues to generate a healthy tourist trade attracted by its many recreational opportunities.

Glasgow is also renowned as a haven for fossil hunters. Exhibits at the Fort Peck Museum display the many varieties of dinosaur bones that have been found in the region.

0:00 (0:59) Depart Glasgow.

0:10 (0:49) On right, lovely home and outbuildings are attractive highlight of Tampico.

0:37 (0:22) Large bell atop Methodist church on right summons parishioners from many miles around Saco.

0:50 (0:08) Cross arm of Lake Bowdoin. Abundance of waterfowl denotes success of nearby Bowdoin National Wildlife Refuge.

0:59 (0:00) Arrive Malta.

MALTA, MT - Once the center of a great cattle empire, the region surrounding Malta was also the inspirational setting for many works of the famous artist Charles Russell whose paintings so vividly captured the unbridled spirit of the Western frontier.

0:00 (1:13) Depart Malta.

0:09 (1:04) Here in Wagner, at turn of the century, Butch Cassidy and The Sundance Kid carried out one of their many successful train robberies, escaping with nearly $70,000.

0:17 (0:56) Between Dodson and Harlem, traverse northern border of Fort Belknap Indian Reservation. At this time, Bear Paw Mountains can be seen forward on left.

0:30 (0:43) Passing through Savoy, note quaint old country schoolhouse on right. Built in 1916, drought and crop failures of early '70s precipitated a rapid decline in enrollment. School had only four students left when finally closed in 1974.

0:45 (0:28) In Zurich, another venerable schoolhouse stands proudly on right.

A few miles south of town lies historic Chief Joseph Battleground of the Bear's Paw. In 1877, after a 1,700-mile retreat through some of the most rugged country in the West, a disheartened Chief Joseph surrendered proclaiming, "From where the sun now stands, I will fight no more forever."

1:13 (0:00) Finely preserved S-2 steam locomotive of Great Northern Railway previews arrival at Havre station on left.

HAVRE, MT - At once the commercial hub of a sprawling agricultural region, Havre's attention in more recent times has focused on discoveries of natural gas.

Of Havre's many interesting attractions, the H. Earl Clark Museum, with its famous "Buffalo Jump Site," is one of the most popular. Here beneath precipitous cliffs are the skeletal remains of buffalo herds driven to a death plunge by Indian hunters.

0:00 (1:35) Depart Havre.

0:04 (1:31) On right, Milk River departs north for brief tour of Canada before returning to its source amidst Montana's Glacier National Park.

1:35 (0:00) Arrive Shelby. "Hot wire" draped across station roof helps melt snow in winter.

SHELBY, MT - Although oil and farming are the principal concerns here, Shelby is most remembered as the unlikely site of the 1923 world heavyweight championship fight between Jack Dempsey and Tommy Gibbons.

Remembering Dempsey after his death in 1983, a *Time* magazine writer opined that Shelby had a fight "the way Johnstown had a flood." The town of 2,000 constructed a 40,000-seat arena but then had trouble raising the guaranteed purse. While 24,000 attended the Fourth of July bout, only 7,000 bothered to pay; the rest crashed the gates. Dempsey won on points, the promoter skipped town, two banks failed and the town was left insolvent.

0:00 (0:29) Depart Shelby.

0:29 (0:00) Arrive Cut Bank.

CUT BANK, MT - Another bastion of agriculture, livestock and oil production, Cut Bank often has the

Empire Builder - Glacier Park, Montana
JAMES WHITTON

unglorious distinction of recording the nation's coldest midwinter temperatures.
0:00 (0:32) Depart Cut Bank across high trestle spanning Cut Bank Creek. Dramatic panorama of Rocky Mountain peaks begins to jut above the horizon, becoming more and more dynamic as train approaches Glacier National Park. Enroute, pass through territory of Blackfeet Indian Reservation.
0:22 (0:11) On left, small obelisk alongside highway commemorates northernmost explorations of Lewis and Clark when searching for passage through Rocky Mountains.
0:32 (0:00) Arrive Browning.

BROWNING, MT - A seasonal winter stop, Browning lies in the heart of the Blackfeet Indian Reservation, and is a popular shopping haunt for Native American goods. Here, too, is the Museum of the Plains Indian, featuring a permanent exhibit of historic arts from eleven Northern Plains tribes.

0:00 (0:18) Depart Browning.
0:13 (0:05) Dilapidated, yet character-laden fixtures of an early farming settlement are picturesquely poised at base of mountains on outskirts of East Glacier.
0:18 (0:00) Arriving Glacier Park Station, cross Two Medicine River from atop lofty trestle. In early 1900s, Great Northern Railway transported timber in from Washington and Oregon to construct spacious Glacier Park Lodge on right, as well as other hotel facilities within Park. Development not only promoted rail travel along their line, but as well enlightened tourists to a previously untapped vacation haven. Today, lodges are popular "base camps" for multitude of outdoor enthusiasts who flock here each summer.

GLACIER PARK STATION, MT - This seasonal summer stop is the gateway to untold adventure admist the breathtaking beauty of Glacier National Park. Established by Congress in 1910, hundreds of miles of hiking trails

176

now lead to the rich forests, shimmering lakes and flower-blanketed meadows of this Rocky Mountain retreat. As reflected in its name, the Park is also home to 50 "living" glaciers, among the few in the U.S. considered relatively accessible.

Another of Glacier's foremost attractions is the Going-to-the-Sun Highway, a spectacular mid-park route across the Continental Divide. Open from early summer through mid-October, this 50-mile drive is a popular alternative to backcountry exploration.

0:00 (1:43) Departing Glacier Park Station, begin ascent of Marias Pass and Continental Divide just south of Glacier National Park. Within minutes, rolling terrain of last 1,500 miles gives way to jagged intrusions of Rocky Mountains. On western slopes of pass, scenery is even more dramatic as train winds past waterfalls, river gorges and other wondrous spectacles of this diverse alpine geography. Additionally, trackside signposts identify names and altitudes of monumental peaks that encompass these majestic environs.

0:20 (1:23) Arriving 5,213-foot summit of Marias Pass (lowest Rocky Mountain rail crossing in U.S.), tall monument seen on left is commemorative to Theodore Roosevelt for whom adjacent highway is named. Markers proclaiming explorations of John Stevens are stationed on right.

Although reputedly traversed by Indians during inter-tribal raids, abortive and inaccurate attempts at charting this area gave rise to its original designation as "Mystery Pass." It was only when the railroad hired Stevens in 1889 that this elusive passage was at last established as a permanent route through the northern Rockies.

0:53 (0:50) Middle Fork of Flathead River joins on left.

0:56 (0:47) From high atop dramatic trestle, cross Flathead River which then proceeds to follow on right.

1:03 (0:40) Small village of Essex features impressive Izaak Walton Hotel on right. This Tudor-style structure was originally built to house railroad workers. Helper enginers are stationed in Essex to help freights surmount Continental Divide. This is a flag stop for the Builder.

1:43 (0:00) Arrive West Glacier.

 WEST GLACIER, MT - This stop affords access to the western reaches of Glacier National Park.

0:00 (0:31) Depart West Glacier.

0:10 (0:20) Cross Flathead River which is soon joined by South Fork approaching from left.

0:17 (0:13) Large Anaconda aluminum plant on right is one industrial stronghold of Columbia Falls. Once in midst of town, note old steam locomotive preserved on left.

0:31 (0:00) Old Bavarian-style station is a handsome sight on left arriving Whitefish.

WHITEFISH, MT - Set amidst a picturesque valley of the Flathead National Forest, Whitefish is another gateway to outdoor recreation. Besides its proximity to Glacier National Park, Whitefish is only 25 miles from Flathead Lake, the largest natural freshwater lake west of the Mississippi. Closer to home, Whitefish Lake borders the town to the north, and is a noteworthy attraction in its own right.

Activity flourishes here in the wintertime, as well, with vacationers flocking to the slopes of nearby Big Mountain, one of the nation's foremost ski resorts.

0:00 (1:54) Depart Whitefish.

0:44 (1:05) Penetrate seven-mile-long Flathead Tunnel, third longest in North America.

1:45 (0:00) Arrive Libby.

LIBBY, MT - From its formative development as a gold-mining town, Libby is now the center of an active logging industry, with tours of its sawmills and processing plants an interesting attraction. The region is also rich in vermiculite, mined for its use as a horticultural rooting agent.

Situated in the midst of the Kootenai National Forest, Libby is a favorite retreat for sportsmen who cherish the hunting and fishing opportunities of the surrounding wilderness.

0:00 (1:50) Depart Libby.

Gain one hour as train passes from Mountain to Pacific Time. Set your watch back (forward if eastbound) one hour.

1:50 (0:00) Arrive Sandpoint.

SANDPOINT, ID - Set along the shores of beautiful Lake Pend Oreille (a seemingly bottomless lake which produces occasional "sightings" of its own sea monster), Sandpoint is rapidly emerging as one of the most popular vacation resorts of the Northwest. While lakeside activities highlight the summer season, winter's prime attraction is the nearby Schweitzer Ski Area where the view from the summit is equally as enthralling as the powder-laden slopes.

0:00 (1:13) Depart Sandpoint and cross mouth of Pend Oreille River on ultra-long (8,000-foot) deck bridge.

1:13 (0:00) Arrive Spokane.

SPOKANE, WA - From its humble beginnings as a sawmill town, Spokane has emerged as one of the most vibrant cities of the Northwest, set alongside the thundering falls of the Spokane River. Dubbing itself "Monarch of an Inland Empire," Spokane is surrounded by a wealth of natural resources and fertile farmlands that, for more than 100 years, have been the mainstays of its dynamic prosperity. An important rail center as well, the Great Northern Clock Tower (that formerly presided atop one of the nation's finest train stations) remains a cherished landmark of the downtown district.

As a celebration of its good fortunes, Spokane was host to the 1974 World's Fair, its facilities built around the site of the town's original sawmill. Several of the Fair's most prominent attractions are now preserved amidst the beautifully landscaped acreage of Riverfront Park.

Highlighting an impressive list of cultural endowments, Spokane's Museum of Native American Cultures is recognized as one of the most comprehensive collections of Indian art and artifacts in existence. Another interesting diversion is Gonzaga University's Crosby Library where a nostalgic array of Bing Crosby memorabilia pays tribute to one of the school's most distinguished alumni.

Also of interest is Spokane's Old Flour Mill, recently refurbished as a delightful setting for cozy shops and restaurants. Further shopping adventures are also in store along the city's Skywalk, a ten-block enclave of retail merchants, interconnected by glass-enclosed walkways suspended above the downtown streets.

(At Spokane, the Portland and Seattle sections of the Builder divide. Spokane to Seattle route appears first below.)

For route from Spokane to Portland, see page 180.

0:00 (2:05) Depart Spokane.
2:05 (0:00) Arrive Ephrata.

EPHRATA, WA - A town of 5,000, it is in the heart of irrigated farmland with water coming from the Columbia River Basin irrigation project.

0:00 (1:00) Depart Ephrata.
0:40 (0:20) Pass Rock Island Dam, stretching across Columbia River, on left.
0:45 (0:15) Cut sharply to left and cross Columbia, then roll high above its west bank into Wenatchee. If you haven't already done so, wake your friends—a morning of spectacular sightseeing has begun.
1:00 (0:00) Arrive Wenatchee. Note new glass-box depot in place of more traditional one, still standing nearby, that once served ill-fated North Coast Hiawatha which used this route until its discontinuance in October 1979.

WENATCHEE, WA - Another of the world's "Apple Capitals," Wenatchee is nestled in the scenic foothills of the Cascade Mountains that provide the ideal climes for its abundant orchards. Here, too, is the North Central Washington Museum where live demonstrations (butter-churning, bread-making, etc.) enhance one's appreciation of pioneer domestic life. The nearby Ohme Gardens and Mission Ridge Ski Resort are also much-frequented attractions.

0:00 (2:55) Depart Wenatchee, rolling past warehouses surrounded by piles of skids and apple crates with Wenatchee River to left. Evidence of area's two major industries, logging and apples, appear on both sides of train. For first hour westbound from Wenatchee, best scenery occurs on left.
0:20 (2:35) Pass through Cashmere, also with stacks of apple crates and warehouses.

0:22 (2:33) Curving right, squeeze between rocks and Wenatchee River. Train crosses river three times in next five minutes while approaching Cascades, with mountains beginning to appear at left.

0:30 (2:25) Begin gradual climb out of river valley and pass through Bavarian-esque Leavenworth, a 19th-century railroad center that resorted to its alpine-lodging-and-cuckoo-clock appearance in 1962 when town's economy was failing.

0:34 (2:20) Scenic mountains on left offer preview of what is to come.

In the next several minutes, the Builder passes through a beautiful valley dotted with houses, barns and horses, and then enters the first of several tunnels built to establish this incredible route through the Cascades.

0:44 (2:10) Soon after first tunnel, again cross Wenatchee River with beautiful scenery to both sides, then through another tunnel. Soon after emerging, join U.S. Highway 2 at its milepost 82 and railroad milepost 1689 (measured from St. Paul along old Great Northern Railway).

0:59 (1:55) At Merritt, an old wooden water tower is visible to right as train slows for its charge through mountains.

1:01 (1:52) River crossings continue and mountain vistas become more dramatic.

1:05 (1:48) From here, best scenery (westbound) is to right. Roll across trestle over a beautiful canyon, move through another tunnel, and emerge with tumbling river on right which is followed to Cascade Tunnel.

1:14 (1:40) Enter Cascade Tunnel, 2,247 feet above sea level, a 7.8-mile bore beneath forbidding Stevens Pass.

It takes approximately 15 minutes to traverse the tunnel, time enough to check your film for the scenic run through the Cascades and down Puget Sound to Seattle. Completed in 1929, railroad tunnel is the second longest in North America, exceeded only by the 9.1-mile-long Mount MacDonald Tunnel through the Canadian Rockies.

1:29 (1:25) Emerge from Cascade Tunnel, soon passing sign at right indicating that our location is "Scenic" as Builder rolls high above a beautiful valley to right.

1:34 (1:20) Cross roaring South Skykomish River which will be followed to Everett north of Seattle.

1:37 (1:15) Between mileposts 1721 and 1722, a rushing stream and small waterfall appear to left of train. Better scenery from here to Seattle will be to right with tall trees, huge granite rocks, ravines and streams, with our train curving through this landscape and crossing Skykomish on high steel trestles.

1:47 (1:05) Curve to right across a spectacular steel trestle high above fast-moving Foss River on its way to join Skykomish.

1:52 (1:00) Pass Mt. Baker-Snoqualmie National Forest Ranger Station on right.

1:55 (0:57) Roll through village of Skykomish, an old railroad town with several interesting buildings. Skykomish Hotel, across street on right, has been social hub of community since its completion in 1904. Train crews still park their engines in front and go in for hearty lunch. On left, multi-storied concrete structure with broken windows once was power plant that furnished electricity for railroad when 71-mile section from here through Cascade Tunnel was electrified. Diesels, however, ultimately took over in 1956. Old Great Northern depot also still stands.

1:58 (0:54) Pass unusual concrete sculpture on left.

2:09 (0:45) Roll past Sunset Falls, actually more a steep rapids than a true waterfall, on left. Vertical cliffs and spectacular finger-like Mt. Index rise above valley floor beyond river.

2:11 (0:43) Cross river again at village of Index, on right. Large boardinghouse-like building at southwest corner of town, partially hidden by trees, is historic Bush House, a 1904 hostelry which once accommodated such notables as Calvin Coolidge, Teddy Roosevelt, William Howard Taft and William Jennings Bryan.

2:23 (0:31) Two more crossings of river bring us into Gold Bar.

2:33 (0:21) Gradually leave Cascades behind for flatter terrain, and enter Monroe where huge smokestack rises from supermarket parking lot to right. Old depot reposes about 30 yards to right where it appears there are no longer any tracks.

2:55 (0:00) Arrive Everett.

EVERETT, WA - Noted foremost for its lumber production and airplane manufacturing, Everett's location along a natural landlocked harbor is likewise tailor-made for a shipping and fishing industry that continues to flourish. One of the city's most popular attractions is tours of Boeing's 747 assembly plant, located here within the world's largest (by volume) building.

0:00 (0:23) Depart Everett southbound, skirting shoreline of Puget Sound. Whidbey Island can be seen directly right, while peaks of Olympic Range loom majestically in distance.

0:23 (0:00) Arriving Edmonds, state ferries shuttling to and from Olympic Peninsula can be observed on right.

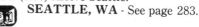 **EDMONDS, WA** - Self-proclaimed as the "Gem of the Puget Sound," Edmonds is a gracious residential suburb, only 15 miles north of Seattle's city center. Here, the Edmonds Museum provides a reflective glance at the town's short but colorful history. Also of interest is the Old Milltown shopping arcade, imaginatively housed in a turn-of-the-century Ford garage.

0:00 (0:31) Depart Edmonds.

0:04 (0:27) Large refinery and dockside facilities are entrenched along waterfront at Point Wells.

0:10 (0:21) Approaching Seattle, colonies of sailboats are a picturesque backyard spectacle for a host of elegant homes, perched atop colorfully foliated sea cliffs on left.

0:14 (0:17) Statue of Leif Ericson maintains vigil over hundreds of boats tethered at Shilshole Bay Moorage on right. Across water lies Bainbridge Island.

0:16 (0:15) Temporarily depart coastline route, crossing Salmon Bay inlet of Puget Sound. In middle of bridge, note elaborate Chittenden Locks on left, affording access to more easterly ports along Lake Washington. To forward left, another throng of sailboats surrounds Salmon Bay Terminal.

0:21 (0:10) Travel through grounds of U.S. Naval Reservation before emerging amidst Seattle's colorful waterfront district.

0:23 (0:08) On right, Pier 70 is largest wooden building to be restored in America. In its heyday, warehouse was chock full of teas and spices arriving from Orient. Today, over 40 imaginative shops and restaurants are tucked within this historic

structure.

On left, Seattle's towering "Space Needle" was architectural centerpiece of 1962 World's Fair. In foreground, delicate arches front grounds of Pacific Science Center.

0:30 (0:01) Enter tunnel, emerging minutes later beneath shadows of two prominent towers on right. White castle-like Smith Tower was tallest building west of Mississippi River when constructed in 1914. Fanciful clock tower to its left rises above King Street Station, the western terminus of Empire Builder route.

0:31 (0:00) Arrive Seattle.

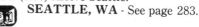 **SEATTLE, WA** - See page 283.

Spokane to Portland Route Log

0:00 (2:36) Depart Spokane.

2:36 (0:00) Arrive Pasco.

PASCO, WA - A city of 18,000, Pasco is heavily involved in agriculture, an industry which has been helped considerably by the Columbia Basin irrigation project. The community also has been closely linked to transportation, with rail lines radiating in all directions, as well as river freight transfers due to its location at the confluence of the Columbia and Snake rivers. This is the Columbia's farthest navigable point for sizeable ships.

0:00 (1:55) Depart Pasco.

1:12 (0:43) Now, Columbia River makes its dramatic appearance at left. This 1,210-mile giant produces more than one-third of America's hydroelectric power! Bluffs on other side are northern edge of Oregon's landscape. River traffic, mostly consisting of tugs pushing barges, will be quite heavy between here and Vancouver.

1:19 (0:36) This is Roosevelt, with grain-loading facilities between tracks and river.

1:25 (0:30) An unusual orchard "oasis," surrounded by slender poplar trees, is above to right.

1:32 (0:23) River begins to look more gorge-like as train moves closer to Pacific Ocean.

1:39 (0:16) Bridge on far side of Columbia carries auto traffic on Interstate 84 across mouth of John Day River.

1:40 (0:15) Impressive John Day Dam backs up Columbia, on left. Navigational lock is on this side of river and handles eight million tons of commercial traffic each year. With 113 feet maximum lift, it is one of world's highest single lift locks. Dam's 16 generating units can produce enough electricity to handle needs of two Seattles. Four more units are planned.

1:45 (0:10) Bridge spanning Columbia is U.S. 97. Maryhill Museum is located here; originally built as a mansion, it was dedicated as a museum by Queen of Romania in 1920s and now houses an extensive collection of rare art. Above tracks is Stonehenge, built as a memorial to World War I dead by railroad entrepreneur Sam Hill and is a replica of its namesake in England.

1:52 (0:03) Through a brief tunnel, one of thirteen between Pasco and Vancouver.

1:55 (0:00) Arrive at rail yards of Wishram.

WISHRAM, WA - This is primarily a stop for railroad workers, with one of the last railroad-operated "beaneries" in the country.

0:00 (0:29) Depart Wishram.

0:01 (0:28) Rail bridge crossing Columbia is Burlington Northern line to Klamath Falls in southern Oregon. The Pioneer, Amtrak's Denver to Seattle section of the California Zephyr, travels the other side of Columbia on Union Pacific tracks.

0:10 (0:19) The Dalles Dam (pronounced dals) staggers across Columbia, making a two-mile-long Z.

The powerhouse, located in the portion of the dam which runs parallel to the tracks, is a half-mile long and contains 22 generators. The dam also has two fish ladders and a navigational lock on the Washington shore. The town of The Dalles, a French word meaning trough and derived from the cut the river makes, can be seen on the Oregon shore. The white building above the shore on a bluff is a unique electric rectifier, changing AC to DC for transmission to Los Angeles.

0:23 (0:06) On clear days, Mount Hood, the highest peak in Oregon at 11,235 feet and continually snow-capped, can be seen rising like a pyramidal spectre in far distance to left.

0:29 (0:00) Arrive Bingen-White Salmon.

BINGEN-WHITE SALMON, WA - This is orchard country.

From here west, foliage will become more abundant as the Columbia Gorge, with its high annual rainfall, is entered.

0:00 (1:13) Depart Bingen-White Salmon.

0:07 (1:06) Venerable Hood River Hotel can be spotted across river, with waterfalls higher up.

0:13 (1:00) More falls cascading down the cliffs can be seen across river. Now enter Columbia Gorge, first explored by Lewis and Clark.

0:16 (0:57) Empire Builder slows to a crawl and now crosses geographic fault that is so active tracks must be realigned almost monthly, with tracks being monitored daily.

0:23 (0:50) Enter a rain forest, having left near-desert country just a few minutes ago.

0:30 (0:43) Bridge of the Gods is forward and to left. This magnificent web of steel crosses Columbia on "exact spot" where legendary natural stone bridge of Indians supposedly fell into river when nearby volcanic peaks argued, causing ground to tremble. Town of Cascade Locks is on far shore.

0:33 (0:40) Bonneville Dam backs up Columbia, forming 48-mile-long Lake Bonneville. Dam utilizes two islands in mid-stream to help close off river's flow. This was earliest of Columbia River dams. Elaborate fish ladders are popular with salmon watchers.

0:38 (0:35) Sheer-walled, 800-foot monolith on right is Beacon Rock, proclaimed to be largest such formation in U.S. and second only to Gibraltar.

0:40 (0:33) Most spectacular of waterfalls on far side is 620-foot Multnomah Falls, second highest in nation. Its downward plunge ends in a beautiful tree-lined pool.

0:46 (0:27) Longest tunnel of day is 2,369 feet in length and penetrates Cape Horn on western edge of Cascades as we exit Columbia Gorge.

1:13 (0:00) Arrive Vancouver where delightful chalet-style depot greets passengers. From here to Portland, Empire Builder follows route of the Coast Starlight.

VANCOUVER, WA - Strategically placed on the Columbia River, where ocean, air, rail and highway transportation converge, Vancouver has become a major shipping hub of the Northwest. Its lengthy history (it is the oldest non-Indian settlement in Washington) saw the likes of a trading outpost of the Hudson's Bay Company, the construction of Fort Vancouver, and the presence of Ulysses S. Grant when he was but a mere lieutenant in the Army. Both Fort Vancouver and the U. S. Grant Museum are open to the public.

0:00 (0:19) Depart Vancouver, crossing Columbia River (and Washington/Oregon state line) into Portland. In midst of river, traverse Hayden Island while vessels and dockside facilities of vast shipping industry abound on both banks.

0:13 (0:06) Cross Willamette River which then follows on left into Portland station. Willamette is another important shipping channel, as evidenced by heavy concentration of maritime-dependent industries along its banks. Dramatic bridges span this waterway, with downtown Portland skyline silhouetted in background.

0:18 (0:01) On left, grand old steamboat now provides nostalgic atmosphere for River Queen Restaurant.

0:19 (0:00) Arrive Portland beneath stately clock tower of Union Station.

 PORTLAND, OR - See page 288.

Empire Builder - West Portal, Cascade Tunnel, Washington
DORIS SWANSON

California Zephyr

Named after a gentle west wind, the California Zephyr breezes along one of Amtrak's most delightful routes. Not so long ago, in the fifties and sixties, its predecessor by the same name was considered the West's premier train. Today's Zephyr unquestionably vies for that same honor, revealing much of America's finest scenery to passengers riding comfortably in state-of-the-art Superliner equipment. The verdant croplands of northern Illinois and southern Iowa, a splendid excursion through the heart of the Colorado Rockies, and finally a trek over magnificent Donner Pass of the Sierra Nevadas are highlights of this two-day adventure.

This trip is also a visit to some very historic moments in U.S. railroading. The first generation of diesel streamliners, the Pioneer Zephyr, made much of its inaugural run along these tracks in 1934, blazing a dawn-to-dusk nonstop dash from Denver to Chicago in just over 13 hours—a stellar accomplishment, even by today's standards. And in the Far West, today's train follows much of the route established when the race was on to build America's first transcontinental railroad—the successful construction of which stands as one of the world's greatest railroading achievements.

This blend of beauty and history makes the California Zephyr a very special train, and riding it a very special event. American poet Joaquin Miller brought things into perspective when he pointed out there is "more poetry in the rush of a single railroad train across the continent" than there is in all of the "story of burning Troy."

Two other trains are joined with the California Zephyr. West of Denver the Pioneer splits off and follows a separate path through Wyoming and beyond to Seattle. West of Salt Lake the Desert Wind leaves the Zephyr and angles southwest through Las Vegas to reach Los Angeles.

Westbound Schedule (Condensed)
Chicago, IL - Midafternoon Departure
Omaha, NE - Late Evening
Denver, CO - Early Morning (2nd Day)
Salt Lake City, UT - Late Evening (2nd Day)
Reno, NV - Early Morning (3rd Day)
Oakland, CA - Late Afternoon (3rd Day)
San Francisco, CA - Late Afternoon Arrival (3rd Day)*

Eastbound Schedule (Condensed)
San Francisco, CA - Early Morning Departure*
Oakland, CA - Midmorning
Reno, NV - Late Afternoon
Salt Lake City, UT - Middle of the Night (2nd Day)
Denver, CO - Early Evening (2nd Day)
Omaha, NE - Early Morning (3rd Day)
Chicago, IL - Midafternoon Arrival (3rd Day)

*Motorcoach transfer between Oakland and San Francisco. Amtrak plans to make nearby Emeryville the stop for San Francisco bus connections, sometime in 1994.

Frequency - Daily.
Seating - Superliner coaches.
Dining - Complete meal and beverage service. Sandwiches, snacks and beverages

in Sightseer Lounge with movies) Chicago-Salt Lake and in cafe car Salt Lake City-Oakland.

Sleeping - Superliner sleepers with deluxe, family, economy and special bedrooms.

Baggage - Checked baggage handled at larger cities.

Reservations - All-reserved train.

Length of Trip - 2,416 miles in 52 hours.

Route Log

 CHICAGO, IL - See page 128.

0:00 (0:35) Depart Chicago.

After emerging from beneath Chicago's huge post office, slowly pull through Amtrak's coach yards, then, picking up speed, take a westward course through lighter industrial areas, with familiar names such as Ryerson Steel, Kroehler, Burlington Northern and Nabisco in evidence. Numerous commuter stops, such as Berwyn, La Grange, Western Springs and Hinsdale, are mere blurs as "Windy City's" majestic skyline, dominated by twin-spiked Sears Tower, slowly narrows on eastern horizon.

0:07 (0:28) Westbound and eastbound Zephyrs meet about now, if each is on time.

0:35 (0:00) Arrive Naperville.

NAPERVILLE, IL - This attractive town has replaced Aurora as Chicago's western suburban stop. Connections are made here to commuter trains serving towns along the Burlington Northern between Chicago's Union Station and Aurora, including Downer's Grove, Hinsdale, La Grange and Cicero, among others.

0:00 (1:06) Depart Naperville.

0:09 (0:57) Upon entering Aurora, note dilapidated stone roundhouse on right. This relic of bygone days is the oldest such structure still standing in U.S. Adjacent buildings are Burlington shops where Vistadome cars and early dining cars were first designed. The Chicago, Burlington and Quincy Railroad got its start here in 1844. Aurora also claims the distinction of being the first city in Illinois to install electric street lights.

0:11 (0:55) Cross Fox River.

0:14 (0:52) Sea of yellow earth-moving equipment on right is produced by adjacent Caterpillar plant.

0:53 (0:13) Two small "mountains" in distance to left are mine tailings which mark spot of one of nation's worst coal mine disasters. In 1909 a fire ignited, resulting in the deaths of over 200 miners.

1:06 (0:00) Upon arriving at Princeton, note quaint community picnic shelter, at left.

PRINCETON, IL - Founded in 1833, this fine old town interestingly claims to be the world's pig capital, while at the same time takes on the motto "where tradition meets progress." Famed abolitionist Owen Lovejoy lived just east of here where he maintained an important station on the Underground Railroad.

0:00 (0:49) Depart Princeton.

0:21 (0:28) On left, Hyster-brand heavy equipment is stored in front of manufacturing facility.

0:23 (0:26) Passing through Kewanee, historic Kewanee Boiler Corporation's old brick buildings face tracks on right.

0:30 (0:19) Hog farming is not limited to the Princeton area, but is prevalent throughout Illinois and Iowa. Small A-frame buildings, on left, are typical shelters for porkers.

0:38 (0:11) When passing through Oneida, be sure to look to left at what must be world's smallest high school—it's about five-foot square and not much higher, with "High School" written over the door.

0:49 (0:00) Arrive at Galesburg's handsome new South Seminary Street Station. (North Broad street station, used by Southwest Chief, is some distance across town from here.) Locomotive 3006, a 4-6-4 Hudson class, donated by Burlington Northern to city of Galesburg, stands next to station, on right, along with a post office car and a way car.

GALESBURG, IL - Reverend George Washington Gale chose this spot for a ministers' college after searching westward on behalf of a fundamentalist Presbyterian group located in Oneida, New York. Famed American poet Carl Sandburg was raised here, and this was the site of a Lincoln-Douglas Debate in

1858. Olmstead Ferris, a "Galesburgite" (and a relative of George Washington Ferris, inventor of the Ferris wheel), was an important experimenter with popcorn—one of the area's important products. This was such a novelty in those days that Ferris gave a corn-popping command performance before England's Queen Victoria and Prince Albert.

0:00 (0:44) Depart Galesburg through Burlington Northern freight yards, then watch on right for Knox College, site of 1858 Lincoln-Douglas debate, and identified by bell-topped building.

0:09 (0:35) Pass beneath main line of Santa Fe. This is route once used by legendary Super Chief between Chicago and Los Angeles, and now traveled by Amtrak's Southwest Chief.

0:18 (0:25) Cruise through Monmouth, birthplace of Wyatt Earp—one of West's most famous lawmen. Event is memorialized on a 15,000-pound block of granite hauled in by former Minneapolis and St. Louis Railroad.

0:41 (0:02) Zephyr now crosses mighty Mississippi River, where splendid views of river and town of Burlington are afforded from a 2,002-foot-long bridge. At midstream, enter Iowa and leave Illinois. From its source to its Gulf-of-Mexico outlet, this great river travels 2,350 miles and drains an area equal to two-fifths of U.S.

0:44 (0:00) Arrive Burlington, where steam engine #3003 is enclosed by fence just beyond station, on left.

BURLINGTON, IA - The Indians considered this neutral territory since it was one of the few locations in the region where important flint could be acquired for tools and weapons. Burlington holds the distinction of having served as a temporary capital of two territories—Wisconsin in 1837 and Iowa from 1838 to 1841—when its river location gave it considerable prominence. Later, the convergence of three railroads made it a major rail hub as the river's dominance waned. Much of the research in developing George Westinghouse's air brake occurred on West Burlington Hill—perhaps one of the most significant advancements in railroading technology. Ripley dubbed one of the town's thoroughfares "crookedest

street in the world." Built with curves to moderate a horse's descent, residents now refer to it as "Snake Alley."

0:00 (0:30) Depart Burlington and slip through older portion of downtown, nearly touching some of buildings that virtually enshroud tracks. Three spires of St. John's Catholic Church are prominent on crest of hill to left.

0:01 (0:29) While passing beneath 6th Avenue Bridge, look up to right for glimpse of Snake Alley (described above), a one-block snake of brick paving.

0:08 (0:22) Burlington shops are on immediate right.

0:12 (0:18) Facility on left is Iowa Army Ammunition Plant—presumably *U.S. Army in Iowa.*

0:30 (0:00) Arrive at attractive little town of Mt. Pleasant with typical Midwest-style frame homes and tree-lined streets.

MT. PLEASANT, IA - Originally accessed by three toll roads which were protected from the elements by plank surfaces, Mt. Pleasant was eventually reached by railroad, putting the expensive toll roads out of business (they charged two cents a mile). Today, the Midwest Old Settlers and Threshers Association holds an annual reunion for five days ending each Labor Day. This event began with a few farmers trying to preserve Midwest frontier heritage, and has grown to become internationally famous—the largest of its kind in the U.S. Each year, more than 200,000 visitors visit this festivity involving antique farm machinery, autos, crafts, "old thresher meals" and much more.

0:00 (0:39) Depart Mt. Pleasant. Historic Iowa Wesleyan College will be on right in just a moment. School was founded in 1842, making it oldest collegiate institution west of Mississippi River.

0:01 (0:38) Acres and acres of yellow school buses and other vehicles are results of Blue Bird Midwest assembly plant on immediate left.

0:05 (0:34) Cross curiously named Skunk River.

0:16 (0:23) Entrance to Fairfield is easily identified by golf course and small lake to right of tracks at east edge of town.

Fairfield has the distinction of being home to Maharishi International University, partially visible off to the right, the only school in the U.S. to make transcendental meditation basic to its curriculum. Started in Santa Barbara in 1973 by Maharishi Mahesh Yogi, the university moved here in 1974 and occupies the 260-acre campus of now-defunct Parson's College. Fully accredited and offering traditional courses ranging from management to physics at both undergraduate and graduate levels, it has 800 students coming from over 50 countries and nearly every state. Two gold domes are twice-daily meditating places for the entire student body.

0:30 (0:09) White stone letters on right, reading "Chief Wapello," commemorate former Fox Indian leader who was buried in this park at his request. It was here in 1842 that a treaty was signed purchasing Iowa from Sac and Fox Indians.

0:39 (0:00) Arriving Ottumwa, John Deere plant and Hormel meat-packing facility on left are typical of industries which have been foundation of community's past.

OTTUMWA, IA - Located on the banks of the Des Moines River, which was one of the many obstacles for westward-bound pioneers, the city is now a major trading center of southeastern Iowa. In the category of fame: "Radar O'Reilly" of TV's M*A*S*H has a pig farm nearby, and the city council proclaimed Ottumwa as the "Video Gaming Capital of the World" when the first American video championships were held here in 1983.

Nearby Blakesburg hosts an unusual antique aircraft convention the week prior to Labor Day when the skies become an apparition of aviation's past. The elegantly stark house which served as a backdrop for Grant Wood's classic painting "American Gothic" is at nearby Eldon.

0:00 (1:15) Depart Ottumwa and for several minutes remain in confines of Des Moines River Valley. Large brick structure on hill to right is Ottumwa High School.

0:05 (1:10) Cross Des Moines River, a serene tributary of Mississippi River.

0:08 (1:07) In Chillicothe, birdhouses fill

"Iron Horse Legacy" mural - Lincoln, Nebraska
DORIS SWANSON

front yard of feathered creatures' friend, on left.

0:10 (1:05) Off to right, smokestack and coal conveyors identify one of newer Iowa Southern power plants.

0:52 (0:23) Through Chariton, long, long complex of buildings is warehouse and corporate headquarters of Hy Vee Food Stores.

1:00 (0:15) Through Lucas where sign in park at right identifies this as birthplace of John L. Lewis, foremost national labor leader of his time, and known for his stern appearance and busy eyebrows. Elected president of the United Mine Workers in 1920 at the age of 26, he and others formed powerful CIO which later merged with AFL. John L. Lewis Mining-Labor Museum is in town beyond park.

1:15 (0:00) Arrive Osceola.

OSCEOLA, IA - The first settlers arrived here in the mid-1800s and named their settlement in honor of a Seminole Indian chief. Supposedly the first Delicious apple tree was discovered 30 miles from here, becoming the ancestor of some eight million fruit trees.

0:00 (0:30) Depart Osceola.

0:02 (0:28) Note large carved bust by Peter Toth of Osceola himself, at shopping center on left.

0:16 (0:14) Cross Thompson River.

0:30 (0:00) Arrive Creston.

CRESTON, IA - Creston has long been a railroad town and at one time sported large rail yards, a roundhouse and shops. One of the early-day engineers gained renown by noisily roasting two ears of corn for lunch each day using his engine's steam whistle. The town's historic three-story depot, with its green trim and tile roof, now houses a museum just to the right of the tracks.

0:00 (1:42) Depart Creston.

0:03 (1:39) Metal grain storage units have replaced many of Midwest's picturesque silos. Papa-, mama- and baby-bear units are seen on left.

0:22 (1:20) Community of Corning, on left, is birthplace of comedian Johnny Carson.

0:39 (1:03) Whimsical water tower, on right, is enormous coffeepot (640,000 cups!) in honor of Mrs. Olsen (Virginia Christine) of TV coffee-commercial fame, who was born here in Stanton. Not surprisingly, town considers itself "Swedish Capital of Iowa." Church with tall granite spire is Mamrelund Lutheran.

0:46 (0:56) In Red Oak, on right, grand old brick Montgomery County Courthouse is centerpiece for town, crowned with a clock tower complete with flagstaff. Completed in 1891, building is now on National Register. Red Oak is home to Murphy Calendar Company, originator of art calendars.

1:00 (0:42) Excellent example of terracing, a conservation practice that both controls erosion and retains moisture, can be seen on hillside at left.

1:08 (0:33) Above, on right, are buildings of Glenwood State Hospital-School. Originally a home for Civil War orphans, today 550 mentally retarded persons are cared for and trained here. This is one of two such hospital-schools in state. Many patients live in residential-type housing resembling a typical middle-income subdivision.

1:12 (0:30) At Pacific Junction, clatter through rail yards of Burlington Northern and cross north-south BN line that follows eastern shore of Missouri River.

1:13 (0:29) Intersect Interstate 29, connecting Omaha and Kansas City.

1:17 (0:25) Enter Nebraska and leave Iowa as Missouri River is crossed. Note large natural gas pipeline also spanning waters at right.

A note about the Missouri. Over 100 years ago steamboats plied these waters between Omaha, just 20 miles north of here, and St. Louis, almost 500 miles downstream. Although often thought of as a river that drains southerly, it actually flows east twice as far as it does to the south. Its headwaters are in the mountainous regions of western Montana where three rivers, the Gallatin, Jefferson and Madison, converge almost simultaneously at Three Forks. The river then starts its long north and east trek through Montana, swings southeastward through North and South Dakota, slips between Iowa and Nebraska, and finally flows eastward across Missouri, joining the Mississippi River at St. Louis.

1:19 (0:23) Red caboose on display at left

in Plattsmouth is just one of what must now be hundreds of these artifacts on display across America.

1:24 (0:18) Zephyr bridges Platte River, once described by a James Michener character as "the sorriest river in America." However, its surface waters and underflow provide vital irrigation to large portions of Nebraska, Colorado and Wyoming. Although too shallow to navigate, its flat valley floor has been an excellent east-west route for trails, highways and railroads crossing Nebraska.

1:29 (0:13) Nearing Omaha, cruise through Bellevue, oldest continuous settlement in Nebraska. Of greater note, however, is Offutt Air Force Base, partially visible off to left, which is headquarters for nation's Strategic Air Command.

1:42 (0:00) Arrive Omaha.

OMAHA, NE - Located on the mighty, muddy Missouri River at the eastern terminus of the Union Pacific Railroad, Omaha has risen from its pioneer beginning on the plains to become both a transportation hub and the major cattle and grain market of the Prairie States.

Amtrak Station, 1003 South 9th Street, is about a mile south of the downtown shopping area. This relatively new and attractive station is almost too small. There are candy bar and beverage vending machines, handcarts and adjacent free parking. (There is only one pay phone inside, often in use, but there is one outside by the tracks that is usually unnoticed.)

Cab stand at the station; Yellow, Happy and Checker have common dispatch, 341-9000. Avis is closest **rental car** agency (about a mile) and will reimburse cab fare to pick up car; returns can be made at the station; (402) 348-0621. Nearest **local bus** stop is at 10th and Pacific, one block away; Metro Area Transit, 341-0800. **Eppley Airfield** is four miles northeast of station.

Greater Omaha Convention & Visitors Bureau, 1819 Farnam St., Suite 1200, 68183; (402) 444-4660.

Red Lion Inn, 1616 Dodge St., 68102; (402) 346-7600 or 800-547-8010. Courtesy shuttle. Ten blocks

from the station. $79.

-Days Inn of Omaha, 3001 Chicago Street, 68131; (402) 345-2222. Complimentary breakfast. Courtesy shuttle to and from the station. Two miles from the station. $47.

Union Pacific Historical Museum, at 12th and Dodge streets, has a large collection of railroad memorabilia, housed in the national headquarters of the Union Pacific. **Omaha History Museum** now occupies the old Union Station, 10th and Marcy streets, three blocks from the present Amtrak station. **Joslyn Art Museum,** 2200 Dodge St., is one of the major fine arts museums in the central U.S. **Boys Town,** on the west edge of Omaha, is the best-known home and school for underprivileged youths; formed by Father Flanagan in 1917. **Strategic Air Command Museum** is south of town in Bellevue, at 2510 Clay Street, with "Red Alert" Theater simulations and several aircraft and missiles on display. A good way to spend an evening waiting for the westbound train is to take in a production at the **Omaha Community Playhouse**—nation's largest with 11,000 members. Henry Fonda made his debut here; 69th and Cass, four miles west of downtown.

0:00 (1:00) Depart Omaha.

Current scheduling takes the Zephyr through Nebraska at night, making most of the state unviewable from the train.

0:30 (0:30) Incongruous "light house," on left, stands next to Platte River, marking location of once-popular summer beach resort area frequented by both Omahans and Lincolnites.

Built in 1939, structure had no real use other than acting as landmark for Linoma Resort. Train now crosses broad waters of Platte River.

0:33 (0:27) Enter Ashland, located on site of old Ox-Bow Trail. Thousands of emigrants and millions of pounds of freight moved along this route from towns such as Plattsmouth and Nebraska City north to Platte River, then westward to settlements, mining camps and military posts. Light brick buildings, a block to left, are treatment plant and pumping station which supplies water to Lincoln some 20 miles from here. Lincoln's water supply comes mainly from wells in Platte Valley.

1:00 (0:00) Arrive Lincoln, where former Burlington steam locomotive and bevy of colorful boxcars are on exhibit as part of restored eight-block Haymarket area.

LINCOLN, NE - Lincoln's rather subdued skyline is dominated by the State Capitol, a 400-foot "Tower of the Plains" which is an early-20th-century architectural masterpiece. Art work and mosaics, both inside and out, depict pioneer life. The only unicameral (one house) legislature in the nation occupies this structure.

Lincoln is also home of the University of Nebraska, a perennial Big Eight football powerhouse. Nebraskans would have you believe the bronze statue atop the capitol dome is of the University's football coach, however, when the building was constructed in 1932, it was supposed to be "The Sower," casting grain upon the plains.

William Jennings Bryan, the "silver-tongued orator from the Platte" and thrice-defeated presidential candidate, once lived in Lincoln.

0:00 (1:24) Depart Lincoln.

0:17 (1:07) Plant on left produces well-known Alpo pet food. Town is Crete, home to Doane College, a Congregational Church-founded liberal arts institution.

0:40 (0:44) Rumble through town of Exeter, named for Exeter, New Hampshire by Burlington and Missouri Railroad which located town in 1871. Railroad preferred to name these newly located towns in alphabetical order. In 1886, Charles C. Smith manufactured his bookkeeping indexing tabs here, which were used worldwide.

0:46 (0:38) In March of 1884, Fairmont Creamery Company was incorporated here in town of Fairmont. It ultimately grew to become one of the nation's largest food processors—Fairmont Foods. Original office still stands on east side of Fairmont Avenue (main street), about two blocks to left of tracks. Original creamery was half-mile east of town.

1:29 (0:00) Arrive Hastings.

HASTINGS, NE - Hastings, together with its nearby rival cities, Grand Island and Kearney, combine to form the major trade and manufacturing hub for this central Nebraska region. Farm machinery and irrigation equipment are just some of the principal products. Of particular interest is "The House of Yesterday," a museum which offers a planetarium and extensive exhibits of both pioneer and natural history.

0:00 (0:51) Depart Hastings.

The rolling-to-flat fertile farmlands that have prevailed since leaving Chicago start to disappear as the more arid plains of the West begin to dominate. If one were to draw a perpendicular line through the United States at this point, this same change would occur no matter where the line is crossed. Irrigated cropland slowly gives way to more arid cattle country, except for the heavily farmed river valleys. And we start to climb—nearly nine feet per mile between here and Denver.

0:15 (0:36) Pass through Kenesaw and cross historic Oregon Trail that was used by hundreds of westward-bound wagon trains.

This was the most used of the various overland routes. The first wagon train traveled this 2,000-mile trail to Oregon in 1841; probably a quarter-million pioneers followed this route during the next 25 years. With completion of the Union Pacific Railroad in 1869, the trail fell into disuse. Its wagon tracks are still visible in several places across the prairies of the West. Sand Hill Station of the famed Pony Express was near here.

0:30 (0:21) Breeze through Minden, where renowned Pioneer Village, re-creating early prairie life, can be glimpsed beyond grain elevators on right. Covered wagon is parked on top of entrance.

0:47 (0:00) Arrive Holdrege.

HOLDREGE, NE - Holdrege is an agricultural trading center for this region, with much of its population being of Swedish extraction. The community was named for George W. Holdrege, a former general manager of the Chicago, Burlington and Quincy—one more instance of a railroad leaving its imprint beyond the tracks that it laid.

0:00 (1:03) Depart Holdrege.

0:07 (1:01) Pass through Atlanta, which

was a detention center during World War II, and located far from more sensitive wartime areas. Facility began with request by local residents for federal conscientious objectors camp to help alleviate severe wartime labor shortage. Instead, town was given a POW camp that held 3,000 German soldiers captured in North African and Italian campaigns. Prisoners were important source of farm labor from 1943 until 1946. Lonely brick chimney and concrete water tower, on right, are all that remain of some 70 buildings and seven miles of paved roads.

0:37 (0:31) Roll through Holbrook, once known as Burton's Bend for Ben Burton who established a trading post here and was one of suppliers of buffalo hunters who eventually killed country's great herds.

0:51 (0:17) Marble monument, just across highway to right, commemorates pioneer women who "drowned in this canyon" enroute to their homestead in May of 1885.

0:59 (0:09) Through Indianola, situated in Republican River Valley, center of major buffalo ranges of Great Plains and favorite hunting grounds of Pawnee, Sioux, Oto and Cheyenne. These tribes, continually at war with one another, spent much time here as late as 1874. In August of 1873, a Pawnee hunting party retreated to this site after suffering tragic losses to Sioux warriors who attacked them west of here at "Massacre Canyon."

1:05 (0:03) Three miles east of McCook, red brick walls just above tracks to right are memorial to Harry D. Strunk, a man instrumental in developing region's rivers.

1:13 (0:00) Arrive McCook.

MCCOOK, NE - Founded as a division point on the railroad in 1882, McCook still enjoys this status. Reclamation projects and oil have added much to the town's economy. Of interest is the Senator Norris Home, a finely restored structure where the father of the Tennessee Valley Authority once lived.

0:00 (2:27) Depart McCook.

0:23 (2:04) Off to left is Massacre Canyon where last battle between Pawnee and Sioux occurred in 1873. Half-mile distant, rough-hewn granite obelisk, with faces of two Indian chiefs facing in opposite directions, memorializes battle. One thousand Sioux warriors surprised and defeated a Pawnee hunting party of 350 men, women and children, killing 69 of them.

0:31 (1:56) Swanson Reservoir on left, resulting from Trenton Dam on Republican River, furnishes important irrigation water and flood control, as well as recreational opportunities. Earthen dam is 144 feet high and was built in 1953 by Bureau of Reclamation as part of Missouri River Basin Project.

Gain one hour as train passes from Central to Mountain Time. Set your watch back (forward if eastbound) one hour.

0:43 (1:44) Benkelman was hometown of Ward Bond of "Wagonmaster" TV series. Near here, during Custer's 1867 campaign against Sioux and Cheyenne Indians, warrior Pawnee Killer led dawn attack against Custer's camp, wounding one sentry. Fateful Battle of Little Big Horn took place in Montana, nine years later.

0:58 (1:29) This area was known as Texas Trail Canyon. Cattle driven through here on Ogallala Trail were subjected to examination for brands and disease at nearby checkpoint. Unknown graves are just to left of tracks.

1:11 (1:16) Enter Colorado and leave Nebraska. Sign on right marks the spot.

1:15 (1:12) Republican River Valley continues to provide a gentle route for tracks. North Fork of Republican is on right.

1:18 (1:09) It was along these tracks that history-making Pioneer Zephyr reached its top speed of 112.5 m.p.h. during its Denver to Chicago sprint in 1934. Today's California Zephyr cruises closer to 80 m.p.h. through here.

1:30 (0:57) Giant irrigation sprinkler on right is typical of those which sweep from a center pivot, creating green circles of crops a quarter-mile across. Water is pumped from enormous but vastly overused Ogallala Aquifer.

1:32 (0:55) Enormous, odoriferous Monfort feedlots are immediately north of tracks. Monfort is world's largest cattle feeder.

1:33 (0:54) In early 1800s, railroad bed was first built through this region. Railroad teamster named Yuma died and was buried at this spot, leaving town just west of here as his namesake.

1:38 (0:49) On left, small, neat brick Yuma train depot is adorned with most unusual chrome canopy.

1:52 (0:35) If dawn has broken, westbound passengers should now see for miles in all directions as train rumbles through eastern Colorado on its way to Mile High City—Denver. This was formerly domain of buffalo, sodbusters and Pony Express riders.

1:56 (0:31) Rocking arms of pumps on right draw oil from one of many isolated "pools" found throughout region.

1:58 (0:29) This is Akron, trading center for an area rich in wheat and ranchland as well as oil production.

2:15 (0:12) Fortunately, train's environment is insulated from aroma of large feedlot on right, where thousands of unsuspecting cattle munch placidly on locally produced crops.

2:18 (0:09) Broad valley off to right has been formed by shallow but wide South Platte River. River originates in central Colorado Rockies and flows northeastward to combine with North Platte River in western Nebraska (where names North and South are dropped).

2:27 (0:00) Arrive Ft. Morgan.

FT. MORGAN, CO - This city was named for a fort built here in 1864 to protect westbound pioneers from Indian attacks. Later an Overland Stage stop was established, which served the route to Denver. Sugar beets, cattle sorghums and oil all make Ft. Morgan one of eastern Colorado's more prosperous cities.

0:00 (1:25) Depart Ft. Morgan.

0:09 (1:16) Off to right a few miles is Orchard, where much of television's "Centennial" was filmed.

0:20 (1:05) Westbound passengers, weather permitting, receive first glimpse of Front Range of Rockies, on right—some eighty miles distant.

0:23 (1:02) Pikes Peak, 14,110 feet high, can be discerned far off to left as a mere bump on horizon—but only on clearest of days.

0:50 (0:35) Another cattle feedlot, a familiar sight throughout eastern Colorado, is on right.

0:52 (0:33) Vast acreage of U.S. Army's Rocky Mountain Arsenal spreads out on left, where controversial nerve gas was manufactured and stored for many years. Massive, expensive cleanup efforts are now underway.

1:05 (0:20) Industrial sights of aptly named Commerce City, a northeast Denver suburb, now prevail.

1:11 (0:14) On right, sign for Riverside Cemetery, founded in 1876, proclaims graveyard as Denver's "pioneer cemetery."

1:13 (0:12) Formerly bustling stockyards area is now largely unused. National Western Stock Show, held here each January, is largest event of its kind, and draws exhibitors from throughout western U.S. and Canada. On left, with its enormous curved roof, Coliseum is focus of those activities. Pass beneath Interstate 70. Denver's newly shaped skyline now dominates on left.

1:22 (---) Front of train is now clearly visible on right as train makes a giant curl northward while Zephyr prepares to back into station. (Train will depart northbound retracing, for a short distance, tracks on which it has just arrived.)

1:31 (0:00) Arrive Denver's Union Station, built in 1881. Generally there is time to get out and stretch here, but verify this with a crew member first.

DENVER, CO - Compared to most cities its size, Denver's history is relatively short, having been founded in 1858 during the gold rush to the mountains. The gold played out, but Denver's climate, its proximity to the mountains and its institutions born of those early years assured Denver's destiny as the trading, financial and tourism center of the Rocky Mountain region.

First-time visitors are often surprised to find a mile-high city not in the mountains, just near them, and a ski-oriented community that gets only 16 inches of moisture per year. Its once modest downtown is now a maze of glassy skyscrapers which sprouted in the 80s—largely the result of an energy boom that later went bust. Denver weathered the resulting recession, and things are happening once more.

Denver was awarded a National League baseball franchise in 1991, and a new stadium is being built just northeast of Union Station. And to the east of the metropolitan area, Denver has built the nation's newest airport.

The town is still a pretty city and a logical point from which to start a Rocky Mountain vacation. Its Civic Center, presided over by the golden-domed state capitol, is a jewel; Denver's parks are some of the finest anywhere; its tree-lined boulevards in east Denver are delights to drive; and its downtown area is easy to shop with free transit up and down the 16th Street Mall.

Union Station, 17th and Wynkoop streets, anchors the revitalized end of downtown. When it was completed in 1881, it was said to be the largest single structure in the West. An 1894 fire destroyed much of the original center section, but the rebuilding produced an even finer appearance. Its classic waiting room still has the old high-back wooden benches, and surrounding this area are a large gift shop, a food counter and "Grandpa's Depot"—the latter selling a large assortment of railroad-related merchandise. The station also has storage lockers, luggage carts and adjacent pay-parking. There are direct phone lines to several hotels and

Denver

- 🚂 Amtrak Station
- 1 - Visitors Information
- 2 - Civic Center
- 3 - Larimer Square
- 4 - Sakura Square
- 5 - U.S. Mint
- 6 - State Capitol
- 7 - Tabor Center
- 8 - Denver Art Museum
- 9 - Tivoli
- 10 - Forney Transportation Museum
- 11 - Oxford Alexis
- 12 - Comfort Inn
- 13 - Queen Anne Inn
- 14 - La Quinta

three rental car companies.

For arrival and departure information only, call (303) 534-2812.

Cab stand at the station; Yellow Cab, 777-7777. Direct phones to Hertz, 297-9400, and Budget, 341-2277, **rental cars** with limited hours pick up and drop off at the station. **Local bus** stop is in front of the station; main terminal is two blocks away; call RTD, 299-6000; schedules and maps available at the station. **Greyhound** bus terminal at 19th and Curtis streets, seven blocks from the station. **Denver's International Airport** is several miles east of downtown.

Denver Metro Convention and Visitors Bureau, 225 W. Colfax, 80202; (303) 892-1112.

Downtown accommodations are still a bargain in Denver, but prices have been firming up a bit as the city's economy recovers.

-**Comfort Inn,** 401-17th St., 80202; (303) 296-0400. Small but luxurious rooms at the uptown end of 17th Street in what was once the "new" annex of Denver's Brown Palace Hotel. Breakfast included. Thirteen "short" blocks from the station. $69.

-**Oxford,** 1600-17th St., 80202; (303) 628-5400 or 800-228-5838. Marvelously restored old hotel with some good weekend packages. Half block from the station. $105.

-**LaQuinta Inn-Denver Center,** 3500 Fox, 80216; (303) 458-1222. At I-25 and West 38th, it is not within walking distance but a good bet for an "overnight." Rail fans might like its near-trackside location. $48.

-**Queen Anne Inn,** 2147/51 Tremont Place, 80205; (303) 296-6666 or 800-432-4667 (except Colorado). A bed and breakfast in historic district on the edge of downtown. Beautifully restored Victorian home. Just what every bed and breakfast should be. Mile and a half from the station. $75-$145.

Downtown attractions include: the **U.S. Mint,** across from the visitors center; **Civic Center,** a handsomely landscaped set of state and city buildings, near Colfax and Broadway; **Denver Museum of Natural History,** in City Park; **Denver Art Museum,** 100 West 14th Parkway; **shopping** at Larimer

Square, Sakura Square, Tabor Center, The Tivoli (all in lower downtown), and the 16th Street Mall with free shuttle buses. If you like antiques, Stuart Buchanan, 1625 Wazee, is probably the largest such store west of the Mississippi, and Wazee Deco, 1819 Wazee, has items bordering on the bizarre. Both stores are handy to the station.

Near downtown is the **Forney Transportation Museum,** 1416 Platte St., and near Golden is the **Colorado Railroad Museum,** 17155 W. 44th Ave. The **Platte Valley Trolley** provides rides from Confluence Park along the South Platte River.

For something different, tour **Coors Brewery** (largest in the world) in Golden and enjoy a meal at **Casa Bonita** (sort of a combination Taco Bell and Disneyland), 6715 West Colfax.

0:00 (1:57) Depart Denver.

We bid farewell to the Burlington and take to the rails of the highly scenic Denver and Rio Grande Western, along route of former Denver and Salt Lake Railroad, exploring the very heart of the Colorado Rockies. The pace is slow. Grinding up laborious grades and negotiating never-ending twists and turns, it takes more than seven hours to reach Grand Junction, 273 rail miles to the west—a less-than-blazing 38 miles per hour.

But this is the Rio Grande. The railroad cut its teeth on narrow-gauge tracks (3 feet between the rails rather than 4 feet, 8¼ inches) which allowed it to snake up canyons and cling to cliffs while reaching almost every remote mining camp in the state. This "baby railroad" could "curve around the brim of a sombrero," so it was said. Mark Twain once wondered why the Rio Grande even bothered to use cowcatchers since their trains couldn't outrun the beasts.

Although the Rio Grande converted to standard gauge long ago, trains on this line still take their time. And that's perfect for seeing the Rockies.

0:01 (1:54) Just to right, Coors Stadium for Denver's new major league baseball team, Colorado Rockies, will soon be built.

0:02 (1:55) Cross usually placid South Platte River. Denver was born just a few hundred yards upstream when gold was

California Zephyr - Flatirons near Denver, Colorado
JACK SWANSON

discovered in 1858.

0:05 (1:52) Slip through extensive freight yards of Rio Grande, as sights of Denver's industrial aspects continue.

0:13 (1:39) Angling through Arvada, a large northwestern Denver suburb, Front Range of Rockies looms directly ahead. Tallest peak in distance to right (north) is 14,255-foot Longs Peak. Immediately to left is 14,264-foot Mt. Evans.

0:22 (1:33) Small complex of buildings and curious tower-like structures, on right, were once used to explore various shale oil extraction techniques.

0:32 (1:19) At Rocky, train reaches formidable foothills, and a giant "S" curve (called "Big Ten" in reference to degrees of curvature) is negotiated while struggling to gain necessary altitude. On inside of upper curve weathered hopper cars filled with sand are permanently anchored to protect trains from fierce west winds which occasionally reach velocities in excess of 100 miles per hour. Grade is a demanding two percent as route steadily ascends across face of foothills before turning westward directly into mountains.

0:40 (1:12) Rumble through first of 28 tunnels between here and six-mile-long Moffat Tunnel.

0:45 (1:10) This area is referred to as Plainview—understandably, as plains of eastern Colorado seem to stretch out forever. Back on right, Denver's entire metropolitan area is now visible. Industrial complex in foreground is Rocky Flats, nation's only processor of plutonium, which is an occasional target of pacifist protests. Plant has a reputation of being one of the "dirtiest" in nuke industry, and faces possible closure. Forward on right is city of Boulder and University of Colorado with its red-tiled roofs.

0:51 (1:06) After having enjoyed sweeping panoramas of plains while train gained altitude along eastern face of Rockies, we now head up South Boulder Canyon into very heart of mountains. This is where eastbound passengers first get one of Amtrak's most breathtaking views—

looking down on evening lights of Denver's metroplex. Lounge car lights are sometimes dimmed for added drama.

0:59 (0:58) Gross Reservoir, one of Denver's many important water storage facilities, is below on right. This collection unit supplies billions of gallons each year to a city which receives only 16 inches of precipitation annually.

1:20 (0:37) Old wooden barn-like structure on left once provided storage for ice cut from adjacent lake in winter. Ice was used in boxcars until modern refrigeration methods made this technique obsolete.

1:35 (0:23) Fine views are afforded of towering Continental Divide directly ahead as train enters Roosevelt National Forest. Watch for deer and elk on slopes above tracks.

1:42 (0:15) At last, plunge into historic Moffat Tunnel where total darkness prevails for nine minutes as train passes beneath Continental Divide.

The construction of the Moffat Tunnel was considered a Colorado need. An efficient east-west railroad directly through the mountains was critical, otherwise the flow of commerce would entirely bypass the state by following routes already established through Wyoming to the north and New Mexico to the south. David Moffat's Denver and Salt Lake Railroad (it never really made it to Salt Lake) had not proven to be the answer. That line's arduous negotiation of Rollins Pass was not only slow, but winters at that elevation turned schedules into shambles. (The original route over the top can still be seen above and to the right before entering the tunnel westbound.) The tunnel was deemed so important that money was raised through a special improvement district which issued bonds and then retired them by levying taxes on virtually all Colorado real estate within earshot of the train's whistle.

When it was finished in 1927, the Moffat Tunnel was 6.2 miles long, the longest rail tunnel in North America. (It was subsequently bettered by the 1929 Cascade Tunnel in Washington and a recently completed Canadian Pacific tunnel.) The feat was of such moment that President Calvin Coolidge pushed a button from the White House triggering the holing-through blast. It took one thousand men digging from both ends, and using 2.5 million pounds of dynamite, nearly four years to complete the task. The main bore is 24 feet by 18 feet, while a smaller 8-foot-diameter bore supplies Denver with West Slope water.

It is now a mere nine-minute trundle through 13,260-foot-high James Peak instead of a five-hour ordeal over the top. Somewhere in the tunnel's innards the rails reach their apex—9,239 feet above sea level, and the highest point anywhere for Amtrak.

1:48 (0:06) We are suddenly awash in brilliant daylight as train pops out of Moffat Tunnel into land where all water now flows westward. Immediately on left is Winter Park ski area.

1:53 (0:00) Arrive Winter Park.

WINTER PARK, CO - This popular ski destination, particularly for Denverites, is in a section of the Rockies composed of mountains and meadowlands called Middle Park, where ranching and tourism are of primary importance. A favorite fishing retreat of former president Dwight Eisenhower was in the mountains off to the left. The depot is actually in the small town of Fraser, adjacent to the Winter Park ski area. For years, Fraser often recorded the coldest wintertime temperatures in the nation, but the situation was finally alleviated when the town's weather station was removed.

0:00 (0:22) Depart Winter Park.

0:10 (0:05) Sparkling trout-filled Fraser River escorts train through remote canyon.

0:25 (0:00) Arrive Granby.

GRANBY, CO - This is a trading center for Middle Park and popular stopping point for travelers. Beautiful Grand Lake and Rocky Mountain National Park are just to the north (right) of here. Incomparable Trail Ridge Road—highest continuous auto road in the world—traverses the Continental Divide through the center of the Park.

0:00 (2:57) Depart Granby.

0:02 (2:53) Here we join Colorado River near its headwaters, and follow its winding course for next 238 miles.

0:13 (2:44) Small mountain community of Hot Sulphur Springs derives its names from local geothermal springs. Indoor swimming pool, on right, capitalizes on this free source of heated water.

0:14 (2:43) Enter Byers Canyon where invincible rocky-spired cliffs tower high above roadbed. Highway on left is U.S. 40.

0:22 (2:35) Emerge from Byers Canyon and for first time since Denver pick up considerable speed as train heads for Kremmling in heart of some of Colorado's best cattle country. Large herds of deer can often be seen along right-of-way, particularly in winter.

0:36 (2:22) Roll through Kremmling. Lofty peaks to left belong to Gore Range and reach elevations in excess of 13,000 feet.

0:41 (2:18) Enter awesome Gore Canyon, where sheer rock sides of this rugged gorge hover menacingly overhead, and where not even an auto road has dared to invade.

0:52 (2:08) Emerge from Gore Canyon. Small meadows and ranches will continue to fleck landscape as we journey westward through middle of Rockies.

0:57 (2:03) Enter Little Gore Canyon; not as exciting as Gore, but still impressive.

1:00 (2:00) Hole in canyon wall at about water level on left was to be intake of ambitious irrigation tunnel, but project was abandoned circa 1913.

1:02 (1:58) Exit Little Gore Canyon.

1:25 (1:36) Remains of historic State Bridge (it preceded railroad) and its modern replacement are just to left.

1:31 (1:21) Curl through old railroad town of Bond, with its handful of rundown buildings. On right, a Rio Grande branch line can be seen angling above, making its way to Steamboat Springs and Craig, Colorado. This was former line of Moffat's Denver & Salt Lake. Zephyr follows Dotsero Cutoff, a 38-mile link completed in 1934 connecting to the Rio Grande's Royal Gorge route. Cutoff and Moffat Tunnel now provide a route that is 176 miles shorter than Rio Grande's first Denver-to-Salt-Lake-City route, which required a southern Colorado excursion through Royal Gorge. (Rail junction just before Bond was Orestod—Dotsero spelled backwards—and eastern end of Dotsero Cutoff.)

1:36 (1:18) Giant waterwheel on left, looking more like an incongruous Ferris wheel, scoops water from river and empties into irrigation ditch.

1:37 (1:17) Enter Red Canyon, where surprisingly red cliffs offer an almost refreshing change from dramatic scenery behind. Eroded rocks play fanciful tricks on imagination—note pilgrims' "Mayflower" resting at anchor just to right.

2:05 (0:52) Spread on right bears pessimistic title, "Rancho Starvo."

2:24 (0:34) Train rolls through Dotsero where Eagle River, from left, now adds to Colorado River's flow. It was from this point that an early Colorado River survey was commenced and marked ".0" or "dot zero." Rails also join Rio Grande's Royal Gorge route which threads its way back through mountains to Pueblo.

2:29 (0:29) Enter Glenwood Canyon where the grandeur of these great cliffs is said to have inspired creation of Vista-domes.

In July of 1944, the general manager of GM's Electro-motive Division was riding through the canyon in the cab of a Rio Grande diesel locomotive when he first visualized glass-canopied rail cars. Five years later they were in service on the California Zephyr. The tracks twist and turn, lazily following the river through this truly beautiful gorge for nearly half an hour.

2:32 (0:26) Across river, construction of controversial Interstate 70 proceeded in spite of early environmental protests. To modify concerns, rock cuts and concrete structures are stained to blend with canyon walls. A paved pathway, designed to withstand occasional flooding, will take hikers and bicyclers along river's edge. Started in 1981, project was not finished until 1993—at a cost of nearly a half billion dollars. Half of road's length through 12.5-mile canyon was elevated. Of America's Interstate Highway System, this is last and most elaborately constructed section.

2:39 (0:19) Dam diverts water into underground penstocks that carry water to power plant farther downstream. At times, Colorado River is nearly dry between here and plant.

2:43 (0:15) On right, Public Service Company of Colorado's Shoshone hydroelectric generating plant is outlet for water diverted upstream. Plant is small, producing a relatively modest 15 megawatts. Below this point, river rafters are frequent sight.

2:52 (0:05) Just before emerging from canyon, handful of houses on right comprise thoughtfully monikered community of "No Name."

2:57 (0:00) Arrive Glenwood Springs at western mouth of Glenwood Canyon. Be sure to note picturesque stone and brick station on left, considered one of most attractive in nation. Its architecture intentionally blends with that of Hot Springs Lodge across Colorado River.

GLENWOOD SPRINGS, CO - Ultra-posh Aspen is just up the Roaring Fork Valley from Glenwood Springs, making this a busy skier stop for the California Zephyr. But many who come to Glenwood are not interested in Aspen—they come here because of the world's largest outdoor hot-water swimming pool. This attraction is just to the right and across the river from the station and is always filled with swimmers—even in the dead of winter. Water is supplied by the adjacent Yampa Hot Springs.

Beyond the pool can be seen the venerable Hotel Colorado, opened in 1893. Built of sandstone and trimmed with Roman brick, it was patterned after the Medici Hotel in Florence, Italy. This hostelry has accommodated numerous well-known personages over the years, including Teddy Roosevelt to name but one. One story has it that when Roosevelt came back empty handed from a bear hunt, the hotel staff made a stuffed bear for him, the first "teddy bear."

That famous gunslinger, Doc Holliday, once lived in Glenwood and is buried in the town's cemetery.

0:00 (1:40) Departing Glenwood Springs, majestic Mt. Sopris dominates Roaring Fork River Valley on left.

0:08 (1:32) Train wends its way through Colorado River Valley encased by red stratified mountains which typify this region of Rockies.

0:18 (1:22) Near New Castle, black slash on left identifies former Wheeler coal mine, long ago abandoned due to persistent fires. Two catastrophic explosions, one in late 1800s and one in early 1900s, resulted in 91 deaths.

0:30 (1:10) This is Rifle. Historically a ranching community, a few years ago it experienced a rather short-lived boom based on prospects of developing vast Colorado shale oil reserves which lie north and west of here. Some of these deposits are visible high up on cliffs, just to right and forward of train.

0:36 (1:03) Anvil Points Oil Shale pilot plant is at base of cliffs on right.

0:42 (0:56) Oil shale town of Parachute received severe economic shock in early 1982 when Exxon withdrew local shale research and development. Community of Battlement Mesa is on higher ground to left. Originally built to house oil shale workers, it is now a retirement settlement.

1:01 (0:37) Enter Debeque Canyon which easily could have been setting for Zane Grey novel.

1:11 (0:26) Colorado River (until 1921, known as "Grand River" east of juncture with Green River in Utah) is momentarily held back by ornate Grand River Diversion Dam, built by U.S. Bureau of Reclamation for irrigation purposes.

1:15 (0:22) Buffalo in field at left are unusual twentieth-century sight.

1:16 (0:21) Coal mine, across river on left, taps some of region's vast coal reserves to fuel power plant on right. Coal is transported via impressive conveyor spanning river.

1:23 (0:14) Emerge from Debeque Canyon and enter famed fruit-growing region of Colorado's Western Slope. Peaches, harvested here at end of summer, are outstanding.

1:28 (0:12) Huge plateau on left is Grand Mesa. Reaching an elevation of more than 10,000 feet, it is reputedly world's largest flat-top mountain.

1:33 (0:07) Unusual variegated palisades on right are known as Book Cliffs.

1:40 (0:00) Arrive Grand Junction's 1905 station on right.

GRAND JUNCTION, CO - This is western Colorado's largest community. Overlooked by white men long after the rest of the state was overrun by fur trappers, it finally saw "civilized" settlement in 1881 when settlers were permitted to stake claims shortly after the Northern Ute Indians were removed to Utah. Five men, including George A. Crawford, a former governor of Kansas who had a reputation of establishing a new town "every decade or so," staked a townsite here. It was first named Ute, then West Denver, and finally Grand Junction because the Colorado (remember it used to be the Grand) and the Gunnison rivers joined here.

Grand Junction's economy was once heavily linked to railroading, but energy-related industries eventually became the dominant force. The fickleness of energy development over the years, however, has now forced the community to work toward broadening the town's economic base beyond coal, oil shale and uranium.

Of particular interest to visitors are nearby Colorado National Monument with its free-standing rock monoliths, Grand Mesa's beautiful forests and lakes, and a unique museum with life-size dinosaurs that growl and snap at visitors.

0:00 (1:18) Departing Grand Junction, broken red cliffs of Colorado National Monument border route on left.

0:12 (1:06) Passing through Fruita, imposing tyrannosaurus rex greets patrons of shops on right. Region was once heavily populated by dinosaurs, and important skeletal remains have been unearthed here.

0:20 (0:58) Refinery on left has processed gilsonite, a hard black asphalt rarely found in usable quantity, but readily available in this region.

0:22 (0:56) Mack was former eastern terminus of narrow-gauge Uintah Railroad which hauled gilsonite from eastern Utah until line was abandoned in 1939.

0:23 (0:55) West of Mack, emerge from short tunnel and follow Colorado River's graceful meanders through spectacular gorges of Ruby Canyon. Twenty-mile stretch is being considered for possible wild and scenic designation.

0:36 (0:41) On right, markings enscribed on canyon wall denote Utah-Colorado boundary.

0:38 (0:39) After a 238-mile joint venture, Colorado River now departs tracks

at Westwater and heads for Arizona. A little farther downstream, river tumbles through Westwater Canyon, a popular run for white-water enthusiasts.

With the departure of the Colorado River, canyonlands are quickly displaced by a vast expanse of desert terrain. Over the next 150 miles, stark mesa tops of the Roan Cliffs stand stoically on the right as the trains weaves through cuts and gullies across this barren landscape. What sometimes appears to be sparkling snow in the heat of the summer is only surface alkalie. Someone once said that horses graze at 40 miles per hour in this country just to stay alive.

0:52 (0:25) On left at Cisco, one of town's many weather-beaten buildings is surprising site of elaborate mural, depicting scenic wonders of Colorado River canyon.

1:15 (0:00) Arriving Thompson, La Sal Mountains are an imposing sight in distance on left. Henry Mountains are prominent lump on horizon left forward.

THOMPSON, UT - Thompson is a stop for nearby Moab, hub of southeastern Utah's vast, scenic wonderlands. Surrounding Moab are such spectacular settings as Canyonlands National Park, Arches National Park, Dead Horse Point and Monument Valley. Since Thompson is a flag stop, Zephyr will pass right on through unless someone is boarding or detraining.

0:00 (1:40) Departing Thompson, note intriguing Desert Moon Hotel on left. Sign touts it as also a retirement home and trailer park.

0:13 (1:27) Rocky debris of eroding mesas is an interesting sight on right, as Roan Cliffs loom closer between Thompson and Green River.

0:25 (1:16) Cross Green River, then through town of same name. At an altitude of 4,080 feet, river crossing lies at lowest point along this section of Rio Grande line. Although dry-farming concerns are foremost here, town is best known for its cantaloupes and watermelons, nurtured by Green's waters.

0:27 (1:12) From tobacco and cigars to candy and ice cream, old billiard hall on right seems to offer something for everyone.

0:54 (0:49) Cross Price River which will

subsequently rejoin in Helper.

1:37 (0:10) Re-emergence of agriculture and ranching spreads around Price signals gradual departure from desert climes.

1:40 (0:00) Arrive Helper.

HELPER, UT - As evidenced by the congestion of this busy rail terminal, Helper is a vital distribution outlet for a region replete with abundant coal resources. So rich are these deposits that they alone could supply the U.S. for 300 years. When founded in 1882, the town was named in deference to "helper" locomotives which were coupled here onto westbound freights for the arduous ascent up Soldier Summit.

0:00 (1:53) Departing Helper, historic Western flavor pervades downtown area on left. Nostalgia buffs should delight in old hand-painted Coca Cola advertisement, weathering gracefully on north side of Main Street apartments.

0:03 (1:50) At Martin, on left, substantial brick building ensconced on hillside houses operating headquarters of Utah Railway Company. Railway is a short-line hauler, collecting coal along 23 miles of company-owned track, then delivering it to Provo using "trackage rights" and "paired trackage agreements" along route of D&RGW.

0:05 (1:46) Balanced Rock perched high above tracks on right has seen numerous attempts to top it with Old Glory. Three valiant efforts in 1929 met with successive defeats. First, a canvas flag was blown from its mast after two months of fluttering, then a silk one lasted but eight days, and finally a 16-gauge steel "flag" snapped off after 48 hours of gusts. Not wanting to see an unfestooned flag pole, citizenry hoisted a 100-pound grease drum as ultimate solution.

As Price River rejoins on left, enter Wasatch Mountains and proceed up 2.4 percent twisting grade to Soldier Summit. Photo possibilities are nearly limitless, as train winds dramatically through scenic environs of Price River Canyon.

0:08 (1:46) On right, pass entangled maze of machinery and apparatus at Castle Gate Preparation Plant. Situated in midst of extensive coal beds, this sprawling operation serves as a "washing" facility

for loads from nearby Price River Coal Company. Sign affixed to main gate proudly proclaims, "The best men in the world work here."

0:10 (1:44) Castle Gate Rock is renowned landmark of this stretch, protruding like prow of ship above trackside on right.

0:40 (1:13) Breaking out onto flat terrain denotes arrival at Soldier Summit—7,440 feet in elevation. Name of pass commemorates Union soldiers buried here in 1860. Train now descends into Spanish Fork River Canyon.

0:49 (0:55) Across next six minutes, Zephyr bends around two giant reversing horseshoe curves to resolve dilemma of steep terrain.

1:25 (0:33) On both sides, recesses carved in sandstone cliffs shelter towering rock spires, poised like chess pieces in their midst.

1:32 (0:24) Enter Thistle Tunnel.

During the heavy spring rains and snow runoff of 1983, the town of Thistle met an untimely end. An enormous mud slide engulfed the bottom of Spanish Fork Canyon on April 14, permanently damming the river and forming what became known as Lake Thistle. The small town was completely submerged under 200 feet of water, as was the highway and the main line of the Rio Grande. Ultimately the Rio Grande tunneled above and to the east of the lake, through Billies Mountain. The tunnel is 3,100 feet long and is laid on a 4-degree curve. The lake was subsequently drained, but the new track and tunnel remain. When we exit the tunnel, the slide area will be quite apparent on the left.

1:49 (0:07) At Springville, attractive two-story Colonial building on right was town's schoolhouse from 1900 until 1967. Recently it was converted into office quarters.

1:52 (0:04) Pacific States Cast Iron Pipe Company on left is predominant fixture of industrial region approaching Provo.

1:56 (0:00) Arrive Provo.

PROVO, UT - Nestled between the Wasatch Mountains to the east, and Utah Lake to the west, Provo has flourished since it was first founded by Mormons in 1849. Of particular importance has been the influx of large industry into the region, attracted in particular by the area's abundant mineral wealth, and a labor force whose strong work ethic is a longstanding tradition of Mormon culture. Provo, too, is the home of Brigham Young University, the largest privately owned college in America. All 50 states and 70 foreign countries are represented among its 27,000-member student body. And Mormons Donnie and Marie Osmond have a recording studio in Provo.

As well as the recreational opportunities afforded by Utah Lake, Provo is also a convenient gateway to the highly acclaimed ski resorts of Sundance and Park City. Both lie a short distance up the magnificent Provo Canyon, which is also the scenic locale of the Bridal Veil Falls aerial tramway and the Heber Creeper steam railroad.

0:00 (0:50) Depart Provo.

0:02 (0:48) Cross Provo River.

0:07 (0:43) Mounds of coal surround furnaces of U.S. Steel Geneva complex on right.

0:10 (0:40) Shoreline of fresh-water Utah Lake borders on left, while Tintic Mountains hover in distance. Mount Timpanagos soars to 11,975 feet on right.

0:16 (0:34) At Lehi, rustic wooden stadium on left bears "Welcome" banner for fans of Lehi Roundup Rodeo.

0:26 (0:24) Across valley on left, cavities of famed Kennecott open-pit copper mine are just beyond lengthy strand of tailings stretched along hilltops.

0:33 (0:17) Highway turnoff on right at Midvale represents only half-hour trek to internationally renowned ski resorts of Alta and Snowbird.

0:45 (0:05) Approaching Salt Lake City, copper-domed Capitol Building and spires of Salt Lake Temple are both readily distinguishable landmarks of downtown skyline on forward right.

0:50 (0:00) Train now glides to stop beside D&RGW's 1910 station, concluding one of railroading's most sublime adventures.

SALT LAKE CITY, UT - Although Jim Bridger first discovered the Great Salt Lake in 1824, it was not until 1847 that a group of Mormons, led by Brigham Young, arrived at the current site of Salt Lake City and decided to settle here. An industrious people, they planted crops on the day of their arrival.

Today, Utah is still predominantly Mormon, the name given to members of The Church of Jesus Christ of Latter-day Saints. The church is well known for its stance against consumption of alcohol, but, interestingly, Brigham Young imbibed and Utah voted to repeal prohibition. The state is not dry and, even more interestingly, owns and operates (near Temple Square) one of the finest wine stores in the U.S.

Two or three years ago, Utah changed their already-puzzling drinking laws to make them nearly incomprehensible. Suffice it to say: It's now possible to have a mixed drink served with a meal at a restaurant, but you need to ask the waitress—she won't ask you; you will have to empty the mini-bottle of booze into the setup yourself; and wine is delivered and uncorked, but you must pour.

The city, which is the capital of Utah and has a metropolitan population (including Ogden) of nearly one million, is laid out in a grid with wide streets, and, to many, has a rather confusing street indexing system with names such as Second South Street and addresses such as 90 South 500 East. Nonetheless, after studying this system, there is a logic to it that is actually quite helpful. The city is clean, modern and architecturally both interesting and attractive.

D&RGW Station, 3rd South & Rio Grande St., is a handsomely remodeled depot of classical architecture, with Amtrak occupying the south wing. A fine Mexican restaurant in the north wing has a unique trackside patio that is a summertime favorite for lunch. There are snack vending machines and a food vending truck at trainside in the mornings. A museum occupies the central portion of the building.

Cab stand at the station; Yellow Cab, 521-2100. **Local buses** are approximately four blocks east of the station on West Temple; 287-4636. All-day bus passes can be purchased at the Salt Palace Visitors Center. **Greyhound** bus terminal, 160 West South Temple, is about a mile from the station. There is no **rental car** service at the station, but cars are available 24 hours at the airport. **Salt**

Lake City International Airport is only six miles west of the station.

? **Salt Lake Valley Convention & Visitors Bureau,** 180 South West Temple (next to the Salt Palace), 84101; (801) 521-2868.

Peery Hotel, 110 West Broadway (Third South), 84101; (801) 521-4300 or 800-331-0073. An elegantly restored small hotel. Free Amtrak shuttle service. Complimentary newspaper and continental breakfast. Four blocks from the station. $89.

-**Hornes Howard Johnson,** 122 West South Temple, 84101; (801) 521-0130. Very sharp hotel in an excellent location. Seven blocks from the station. $77.

-**Anton Boxrud Bed and Breakfast,** 57 South 600 East, 84102; (801) 363-8035 or 800-524-5511. Lovely Victorian on a quiet residential street, close to downtown. Shared and private baths. Well managed. Thirteen blocks from the station. $49-$109.

★★★ In the downtown area, **Temple Square,** South Temple and Main, is the heart of The Church of Jesus Christ of Latter-day Saints. A magnificent six-spired Temple and the near-acoustically perfect Tabernacle are the highlights; beautifully landscaped grounds. Free tours of the Tabernacle and Visitor Center are offered daily. The **Mormon Tabernacle Choir** rehearsals on Thursday evenings are open to the public. Also, their broadcasts on Sunday morning are public. The **Lion House** and **Beehive House,** South Temple and State streets, were residences of Brigham Young. The latter building is open for tours. Downtown **shopping** malls are at 50 South Main (Crossroads) and 45 South Main (ZCMI). Near-downtown Trolley Square is another popular shopping complex. The **Utah State History Museum** is located at the D&RGW depot (Amtrak).

And, of course, the **Great Salt Lake,** with its high salt content, tempts swimmers to try their buoyancy. It lies west of downtown along Interstate 80.

0:00 (4:37) Depart Salt Lake City, skirting southern tip of Great Salt Lake on tracks of Union Pacific, formerly of Western Pacific acquired by UP in 1982.

Since the lake has risen in recent years due to abnormally high rain and snowfalls in the Utah mountains, water now stands to the south of the tracks as well as the north, giving the appearance that the line is built across the lake. Like other lakes in the Great Basin, the Great Salt Lake does not drain, but relies on evaporation to keep from overflowing. Unfortunately, the high levels of precipitation combined with cool, damp summers have produced serious floodings of low-lying properties. In 1979, the situation became so bad that the state legislature, in an effort to get nature's attention, passed a law forbidding the lake from rising any higher. The legislation proved ineffective, however.

The railroad took a more positive approach. In order to put the tracks out of harm's way, it spent several million dollars to raise its roadbed—a roadbed that was thought to be quite safe when it was constructed in 1902. Until late 1983, Amtrak used the Southern Pacific tracks through Ogden which literally crossed the northern portion of the lake, but frequent closures forced today's more southerly routing.

Amtrak's scheduling is such that darkness usually prevails between Salt Lake City and Winnemucca, Nevada—a desert stretch that, in any event, offers little to see during the daytime.

Gain one hour as train passes from Mountain to Pacific Time. Set your watch back (forward if eastbound) one hour.

4:12 (0:00) Arrive Elko, completing Amtrak's longest run without a scheduled stop.

ELKO, NV - Once an important wagon-train stop along the Humboldt River Overland Trail, Elko has emerged as the commercial hub of a vast ranching and mining domain. Its first boom came when the railroad arrived in 1869, but a far more dramatic explosion has occurred in recent years with the development of massive gold-mining equipment that squeezed millions of minute flecks of the precious metal from heretofore unyielding ore located in nearby mines. This technology has generated the nation's biggest gold rush in recent years.

This rather unlikely locale has also seen its share of celebrities throughout the years. Lowell Thomas described it as the West's last cowtown, and Bing Crosby once had a large ranching spread nearby. Crosby was even proclaimed honorary

mayor, and another property owner, Jimmy Stewart, was appointed honorary sheriff.

0:00 (1:50) Depart Elko.
1:50 (0:00) Arrive Winnemucca.

WINNEMUCCA, NV - Winnemucca traces its roots to an 1850s trading post, established at a point where westbound wagons would cross the Humboldt River. Its formative name of French Ford was eventually changed to honor the last great Paiute chief whose people inhabited the region.

Winnemucca was also visited by the notorious Butch Cassidy gang who, in 1900, successfully robbed the First National Bank, despite the efforts of a determined posse who tracked them all the way into central Wyoming.

0:00 (2:48) Depart Winnemucca on Southern Pacific tracks which will carry California Zephyr to its final destination.
0:15 (2:33) Low, soft mountains rise from desert floor everywhere, presenting pleasing surrealistic scene to early-morning risers on westbound Zephyr.
1:55 (0:53) Alkalie-coated dry lake bed on right is typical of region.

Most of Utah and portions of surrounding states lie in what is known as the Great Basin, a large expanse of desert where all lakes and streams stay within the Basin's boundaries. Rivers either disappear beneath the earth's surface or flow into lakes and evaporate. Sinks (depressions that hold water) occur throughout the region, the Great Salt Lake being the largest. The tracks follow the Humboldt River through this portion of Nevada, one of the many streams that are eventually absorbed back into the ground.

2:22 (0:31) At Fernley, Truckee River joins on right. Numerous crossings occur as train traces river to its source atop High Sierras. Hillside scars seen in distance on left are result of limestone mining operations.
2:41 (0:11) Across river on left, what could pass for just another motel is notorious Mustang Ranch, easily identified by its large parking lot, iron fence and guard tower. In past, world's oldest profession has been legally practiced here.
2:53 (0:00) Arrive Sparks.

California Zephyr - Book Cliffs, Thompson, Utah
JACK SWANSON

 SPARKS, NV - Predominantly a railroad town, Sparks is rapidly becoming a major distribution center for western markets, due to Nevada's tax-free warehousing. The Zephyr is also serviced here at this large Southern Pacific division point.

Only 30 miles north of town, the inspiring expanse of Pyramid Lake is a popular recreation haven, and important bird sanctuary as well. The pyramid-like rock formations protruding from its midst comprise a setting of mysterious beauty, used frequently as a backdrop for motion picture productions.

0:00 (0:09) Departing Sparks, elaborate hotels and casinos can be spotted, while industrial ticky-tacky best describes rest of scene.

0:07 (0:02) Approaching Reno, massive MGM Grand Hotel is a prominent fixture on left, set a short distance east of downtown hub.

0:09 (0:00) Arrive Reno. Arched windows and tile roof highlight Spanish design of station.

RENO, NV - In many respects, Reno has never departed from its illustrious frontier heritage—it's just better lighted than it used to be. Although best known as one of the nation's foremost gambling resorts, Reno is also a gateway to the untold beauty and year-round recreation of nearby Lake Tahoe, nestled in the High Sierras only 35 miles southwest of town. It is also a convenient stop for students attending the University of Nevada.

Amtrak Station, 135 E. Commercial Row, is in the heart of downtown.

Cab stand at the station; Yellow Cab, 331-7171. Budget rental cars are about a mile from the station, 444 N. Center, and will pick up and deliver Amtrak passengers during business hours; (702) 785-2880. **Reno Cannon International Airport** is just southeast of town.

Reno-Sparks Convention and Visitors Authority, 4890 South Virginia. Call 800-FOR-RENO or (702) 827-7600; write to P.O. Box 837, 89504.

Numerous hotels are within a few blocks of the station. Those shown below are two of the closest. Weekend rates are higher than those shown. Entertainment packages are usually available.

-**Harrahs,** 210 N Carter St., at 2nd St., 89504; (702) 786-3232 or 800-427-7247. Posh and close. Half block from the station. $75.

-**Eldorado Hotel and Casino,** 4th and Virginia streets, 89505; (702) 786-5700 or 800-648-5966. Two blocks from the station. $59.

As well as the glitzy hotels and **casinos** for which this city is most renowned, a host of additional attractions enhance Reno's stature as one of the nation's foremost gambling resorts. Headlining a long list is **Harrah's Automobile Collection** with its magnificent array of antique and classic cars, a perennial favorite of nostalgia and auto buffs alike. The **gun collection** at Harold's, **antique slot machines** at the Liberty Belle Saloon and **gold exhibit** at Carson City are also popular diversions.

0:00 (0:52) Depart Reno. On left, archway spanning breadth of famous Virginia Street welcomes visitors to "The Biggest Little City in the World." At night, street is ablaze in neon psychedelia, as hotels and casinos vie for attention of potential patrons.

0:03 (0:49) Elegant, multi-domed St. Thomas Aquinas Catholic Church, in distance on left, seems an oasis of temperament admist encompassing hullabaloo and hype.

0:10 (0:42) Attractive ranching spreads surround handsome River Inn Mineral Spa on left.

As train emerges in Tahoe National Forest, proceed across the Sierra Nevadas,

retracing the route of the early "Gold Rush" enthusiasts. Still a marvel of railroad engineering, this magnificent mountain passage remains a lasting tribute to the thousands of Chinese and Irish laborers who miraculously hand-cut much of the current railbed 120 years earlier—the route of America's first transcontinental railroad.

0:18 (0:32) Small hydroelectric plant at Verdi takes water from flume above on left.

0:21 (0:29) Cross Nevada state line into California. On left, wooden flumes clinging to cliffside are nostalgic remnant of mining era. Troughs would originate upstream and transport water to mill sites that were often much higher than adjacent riverbed.

0:28 (0:22) Beautiful yellow mansion stands out on left at small town of Floriston.

0:41 (0:12) Spillway of Boca Reservoir is visible on right.

0:53 (0:00) Arriving Truckee, horses are about only thing missing admist delightfully preserved Main Street of "Old West."

TRUCKEE, CA - Set along the banks of the lovely Truckee River, this rustic Western town has grown from a small logging concern into a bustling vacation retreat. Winter activities are foremost, however, due to Truckee's proximity to a number of California's finest ski resorts.

0:00 (2:09) Depart Truckee past magnificent grouping of Victorian homes before embarking on ascent of Donner Pass. A scenic wonderland, snow-capped peaks still provide an all-too-vivid reminder of ill-fated "Donner Expedition," many of whose members froze or starved to death during unrelenting winter blizzards of 1846.

The route today still remains one of the snowiest in the world. The small town of Norden, elevation 6,963 feet and near the summit, averages over 34 feet of snowfall each winter. Yet sophisticated equipment quickly clears the track for safe and timely travel, with line closures less frequent than those of the adjoining Interstate. It once took 40 miles of snowsheds to protect this right-of-way, but today less than three miles of track are covered by these structures.

0:16 (1:49) Attractive vacation homes and lodges dot shoreline of Donner Lake on right, flanked by picture-postcard backdrop of High Sierra peaks.

0:25 (1:46) Westbound line now passes beneath eastbound, as train enters tunnel that carries westbound traffic under Mt. Judah. Inside, Zephyr reaches highest point in Sierra Nevadas—approximately 7,000 feet.

0:29 (1:42) Exiting tunnel, slopes of Sugar Bowl ski area appear, as chairlift passes directly overhead. Start careful descent of what is known as "The Hill."

0:33 (1:38) With a lot of speed, and a good insurance policy, skiers at Royal Gorge resort on left can practically schuss to cozy confines of Ski Inn Lodge on right.

0:54 (1:17) It was here, near Yuba Gap, that an ill-fated City of San Francisco, with its crew and passengers, became snowbound for four harrowing days in January, 1952.

0:56 (1:15) Interstate 80 passes overhead at Emigrant Gap. Strange-looking green cubicle on stilts, off to right, is fire watchtower.

1:01 (1:09) Unbounded alpine beauty surrounds shimmering blue waters of Spaulding Lake on right.

1:18 (0:52) Pass through quaint old mining community of Blue Canon. Like other small towns seen along western slope, Blue Canon was once a bustling mecca of activity and excitement when "gold fever" ran rampant through its burgeoning population.

1:30 (0:48) Continue tour of this historic region as train winds slowly along cliffs of spectacular American River Canyon.

1:39 (0:29) Natty red fire station stands proudly on right at small town of Alta.

1:47 (0:21) On left, old frame post office is nostalgic fixture at Gold Run.

2:03 (0:05) High steel trestle known as Long Ravine Bridge affords excellent view of encompassing mountainscapes.

2:08 (0:00) Arriving Colfax, clapboard storefronts on right and turn-of-the-century hotel on left are enduring reminders of town's colorful frontier legacy.

COLFAX, CA - Noted today for its bountiful harvests of Bartlett pears, Hungarian prunes and Tokay grapes, Colfax rose to prominence during the Gold Rush era when goods were transferred here to mule train for transport to remote mountain camps.

0:00 (0:45) Departing Colfax, east and westbound lines take separate routes for next 35-mile stretch into Rocklin. Scenery is essentially same for both, except in Auburn where distinctions are made for each train.

Subtle geographic changes can now be detected as train proceeds down western side of Sierra Nevada.

0:33 (0:23) Emerge upon charming little community of Auburn. Founded in days of Gold Rush, town was an important communication and supply link for surrounding mining camps. Today, countless landmarks preserve colorful heritage of this historic boomtown.

For westbound trains, pass steepled Firehouse #1 on right. This 1888 structure houses a hand-pulled hook-and-ladder truck, and boasts oldest volunteer fire department this side of Boston. Fire bell fixed atop adjacent stanchion still bears 1869 San Francisco inscription.

0:35 (0:21) Still in Auburn, westbound passengers can look to right and spot gold-domed Placer County Courthouse standing on grounds that were once site of public hangings.

Eastbound travelers can also view courthouse on right, as well as adjacent structures of Auburn's "Old Town." Red and white bell tower of Firehouse #2 is a distinctive focal point of this historic district. Departing town, note picturesque Auburn Cemetery perched atop hillside on right.

As the descent continues, golden hills slowly displace mountainous terrain. Tucked within their midst are some of the most beautiful ranchlands one is likely to find in any part of the country. A little further downline, abundant orchards and agricultural fields reflect the fertile environs of the Sacramento River Valley.

0:48 (0:18) Royal palms and prickly pear cacti on right are assurances we are approaching warmer climes.

0:53 (0:13) On right, enormous cedar logs are cut, split and resplit until they become mere pieces of firewood.

0:56 (0:10) Approaching Rocklin, intriguing antique store on right is housed in old stone building that assuredly qualifies as an antique in itself.

0:57 (0:09) East and westbound routes rejoin, and together travel through attractive residential neighborhoods of Rocklin. Bohemia Brewery stands next to tracks at left.

1:06 (0:00) Arrive Roseville.

ROSEVILLE, CA - Roseville started as a railroad town and, as will be noted upon departure, the community still relies heavily on this activity. The Coast Starlight, which links Los Angeles to Seattle, joins the route of the California Zephyr at this point and uses the same Southern Pacific tracks between here and Oakland.

0:00 (0:24) Depart Roseville and negotiate miles of switches and tracks through vast Southern Pacific classification yards. Shortly, boxcar rehabilitation shops will appear on right and locomotive shops ("Pride of the Sierras") will be on left.

0:11 (0:14) Approaching Sacramento, pass facilities of McClellan Air Force Base on right, while Haggin Oaks golf course borders on left.

0:16 (0:09) On left, modernistic "Cal Expo" center is September site of lively State Fair. Harness racing is also popular attraction at park throughout summer.

0:18 (0:07) Cross American River.

0:23 (0:02) Travel directly through midst of sprawling Blue Diamond Almond Company. Frequent tours enable visitors to observe procedures involved in processing one of region's most important agricultural products.

0:29 (0:00) Arriving Sacramento, gracious Spanish architecture highlights many buildings of downtown district on left. Ornamental domed tower is City Hall, whose weighty bronze doors require at least two strong men to open for business each morning.

SACRAMENTO, CA - To describe Sacramento as a treasure chest of Western historical lore would still be something of an understatement. Consider first that the famous California "Gold Rush" began here when nuggets were discovered at Sutter's Mill in 1848.

Only 12 years later, the Pony Express was welcomed into town at the completion of its first historic run. And in 1863, a group of Sacramento visionaries began charting a route across the Sierra Nevadas that would eventually become the most ambitious link in the nation's first transcontinental railroad.

Such monumental distinctions would seemingly be hard to surpass, although Sacramento's current role as one of the world's largest food production centers assures it a status of increasingly vital importance. The city, too, maintains statewide prestige as the capital of California.

As might be expected, historical highlights are the emphasis of Sacramento's major attractions, from the reconstructed facilities of Sutter's Fort to the splendid array of Victorian homes preserved throughout the city. Of particular interest to train buffs is the California State Railroad Museum, located only one block from the Amtrak station. Here, sound effects and even simulated motion are used to re-create the romantic atmosphere surrounding the glory years of the railroad.

0:00 (0:20) Departing Sacramento, stately Capitol Building can be seen on left. Built in 1869, gilded globe still remains atop dome, despite protestations of original architect who described it as "simply ridiculous and abominable—a slur on our tastes forever." During 1906 remodeling, "modern" conveniences replaced 45 fireplaces that once heated building. Iron hitching posts surrounding carriage entrance were also lost at that time.

On immediate left is aforementioned California State Railroad Museum, while Sacramento Locomotive Works are on right.

0:02 (0:17) Proceed across Sacramento River, noting on left riverboats along shore and interesting drawbridge a few blocks downstream.

0:10 (0:06) At considerable expense, railroad and highway have been elevated for several miles permitting underlying lands to be flooded for rice farming. On left, over 4,000 columns hold road above muddy croplands.

0:20 (0:00) Arrive Davis. Spanish motif of this handsome station is popular style of depots throughout Southern California.

DAVIS, CA - Long known for its prolific production of agricultural crops, Davis is noted more recently for its pioneering attitude in the field of energy conservation. In 1975, the City Council enacted the nation's first energy conservation building code, setting standards for all new houses and apartments. A city-wide recycling program is also highly successful. Most impressive, however, is Davis' claim that its many miles of scenic bicycle paths account for as much as 25% of the city's total vehicle traffic.

0:00 (0:26) Departing Davis, border University of California at Davis campus on right. Grapevines are part of school's renowned wine research program.

0:08 (0:18) Elongated ancient shed at left sags with age, but still provides shelter for several hundred sheep.

0:24 (0:00) Arriving Suisun-Fairfield, stately, white-pillared Solano County Courthouse stands distinctively on right at terminus of palm-lined Union Avenue.

SUISUN-FAIRFIELD, CA - At once another agricultural stronghold, this "twin-city" stop also affords access to the nearby facilities of Travis Air Force Base.

0:00 (0:20) Depart Suisun-Fairfield, shortly emerging upon waters of Suisun Bay.

0:10 (0:10) On immediate left, hundreds of Merchant Marine vessels are clustered in storage along shoreline, readily conjuring up images of Normandy invasion. Ships are awaiting tow to Sacramento where they will be unceremoniously cut into scrap. Meanwhile, invasion of different sort is evidenced on forward left, where docks are often overflowing with thousands of Japanese auto imports. Unmarked Glomar Explorer, sporting a white heliport platform on its stern, is normally the last ship just before rail bridge. This deep-sea research vessel made headlines some years back when it attempted to retrieve a sunken Russian sub from ocean's floor.

0:16 (0:04) Cross drawbridge spanning Suisun Bay. Prior to its construction in 1930, train was broken down into sections and ferried across water. Once on southern shore, entangled maze of refinery apparatus escorts train into Martinez.

0:22 (0:00) Arrive Martinez. While in station, Martinez Museum can be seen in old frame house on left.

MARTINEZ, CA - This important commercial and military port was also the home of John Muir, one of the nation's earliest and most outspoken conservationists. His house is now preserved as a National Historic Site. Joe Dimaggio Drive is on the right side of the train, honoring the renowned "Yankee Clipper" who was raised here.

0:00 (0:30) Depart Martinez along Carquinez Strait, connecting Suisun and San Pablo bays. Carquinez Bridge looms impressively in foreground right, while on left, famed golden hills are subtly encroaching upon landscape.

0:09 (0:20) With town of Crockett huddled on hillside left, travel directly through midst of C&H sugar refinery. Immediately thereafter, train bears south along shores of San Pablo Bay.

0:29 (0:00) Arrive Richmond.

RICHMOND, CA - Richmond's popularity as a convenient suburban stop is enhanced by its trackside connections with BART, a rapid transit system servicing many outlying regions throughout the Bay Area.

0:00 (0:12) Departure from Richmond affords first view of dramatic San Francisco skyline across bay. Golden Gate Bridge can be seen north of city, while Bay Bridge connects with Oakland to the south. Alcatraz Island is also visible below Golden Gate Bridge.

0:05 (0:03) On right, pass Golden Gate Race Track.

0:12 (0:00) Arrive Emeryville.

EMERYVILLE, CA - A new stop for Amtrak's Coast Starlight and California Zephyr. Sometime in 1994, Amtrak plans to make this the Bay Area stop for those using connecting buses to and from San Francisco.

0:00 (0:06) Depart Emeryville.

0:06 (0:00) Arrive Oakland. Amtrak buses will meet train for passengers enroute to San Francisco. (Plans are to shift this shuttle service to Emeryville sometime in 1994.)

OAKLAND, CA - Oakland, California's fifth largest city, is situated across the bay from San Francisco. The California Zephyr never actually gets to San Francisco, but terminates in Oakland where passengers are then bused across the bay to downtown San Francisco. This is not necessarily a disadvantage, however, since some travelers looking for a San Francisco vacation find Oakland an economic alternative as a base of operations.

Amtrak Station. Amtrak is now planning to relocate from 1701 Wood St. to the Jack London Square area, which move should be completed in 1994, at Alice and Embarcadero.

Cab stand at the station; Bay Area Cab Co., 536-3000. For bus information, call 839-2881; for BART, call 465-BART; Enterprise **Car Rentals,** 3030 Broadway, (510) 893-7000 or 800-325-8007, offers pick up at the station; open weekdays and Saturday mornings. **Ferry Service** between Jack London Square and San Francisco's Pier 39 and Ferry Building. **Oakland International Airport** is ten miles south of the station.

Oakland Convention and Visitors Bureau, 1000 Broadway, Suite 200, 94607; (510) 839-9000.

The following hotels are in the Jack London Square area or nearby:
-**Waterfront Plaza Hotel,** 10 Washington St., 94607; (510) 836-3800 or 800-729-3638. On the wharf at Jack London Square with waterfront views. $120.
-**Best Western Thunderbird Inn,** 233 Broadway, 94607; (510) 452-4565. One block from Jack London Square. $74.
-**Lake Merritt Hotel,** 1800 Madison (at Lakeside Drive), 94612; (510) 832-2300 or 800-933-4683. Wonderfully restored landmark, overlooks lake, adjacent to downtown but in quiet setting. About two miles from Jack London Square. Complimentary local shuttle service. Few blocks from BART. $89.

Lake Merritt, in the heart of downtown, has boat rentals, a sight-seeing launch, parks, a Japanese Garden and a special "Children's Fairyland" (with child-size buildings, animals and puppet show). **Jack London Square,** Broadway and Alice, on the waterfront, has many restaurants, specialty and import shops; Oakland's leading tourist attraction.

 SAN FRANCISCO, CA - See page 293.

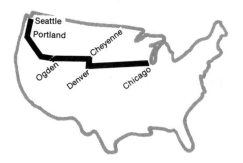

Pioneer

The feature of this excursion is Pioneer's "cruise" along the dramatic Columbia River, following the same route taken by those earlier pioneers that once braved the Oregon Trail. After traversing southern Idaho in darkness, passengers are treated to all the spectacular grandeur of the Columbia Gorge in broad daylight. After Portland, the train courses northward through western Washington to Seattle, its ultimate destination.

Between Chicago and Denver, the Pioneer is combined with the California Zephyr. At Denver, the Pioneer is separated from the Zephyr and heads northward toward Cheyenne, then westward through Wyoming to Ogden, UT where connecting buses provide direct service for Salt Lake City passengers. From Ogden, the train angles northwest through Idaho and on to Portland and Seattle.

Westbound Schedule (Condensed)
Chicago, IL - Midafternoon Departure
Denver, CO - Early Morning (2nd Day)
Ogden, UT - Midevening (2nd Day)
Boise, ID - Middle of the Night (2nd Day)
Portland, OR - Early Afternoon (3rd Day)
Seattle, WA - Early Evening Arrival (3rd Day)

Eastbound Schedule (Condensed)
Seattle, WA - Early Morning Departure
Portland, OR - Late Morning
Boise, ID - Late Evening
Ogden, UT - Early Morning Arrival (2nd Day)
Denver, CO - Late Afternoon Arrival with Midevening Departure (2nd Day)
Chicago, IL - Midafternoon Arrival (3rd Day)

Frequency - Daily, between Chicago and Denver. Three times a week between Denver and Seattle, departing both Denver and Seattle Monday, Wednesday and Saturday.
Seating - Superliner coaches.
Dining - Complete meals, snacks, sandwiches, beverages and lounge service. Movies, Chicago-Denver.
Sleeping - Deluxe, economy, family and special bedrooms.
Baggage - Checked baggage handled at larger cities.
Reservations - All-reserved train, except between Portland and Seattle.
Length of Trip - 2,662 miles in 53½ hours.

Route Log

See the **California Zephyr** for route log from Chicago to Denver, page 185.

 DENVER, CO - See page 192.

0:00 (1:15) Depart on Union Pacific trackage—which will be followed to Ogden. As train heads northward, good views are afforded of Denver's skyline back on right. Just to right, Coors Stadium for Denver's new major league baseball team, Colorado Rockies, is under construction.
0:11 (1:04) On left is home of National Western Stock Show. Event is held here each January and is largest of its kind, drawing exhibitors from throughout western U.S. and Canada. Enormous curved roof of coliseum (focus of those activities) can be seen on left.
0:18 (0:57) Pass through heavily indus-

trialized Commerce City. Arapahoe Power plant of Public Service Company of Colorado belches clouds of steam off to left.

0:39 (0:36) Brighton's former depot now serves as restaurant on right.

0:40 (0:35) Large nondescript building on left once processed sugar beets into Great Western Sugar. Tallest mountain of Rockies' Front Range is directly to left—14,255-foot Longs Peak, which is located amidst other giant peaks of Rocky Mountain National Park.

0:53 (0:22) Ft. Vasquez's walls still stand on left, carefully preserved while divided highway traffic passes nonchalantly on each side.

1:08 (0:07) Cross unimpressive South Platte River.

1:10 (0:05) As train enters Greeley, highrise dorms of University of Northern Colorado are off to left.

1:15 (0:00) Arrive Greeley. Grecian facade of Weld County Courthouse can be seen to left.

GREELEY, CO - Originally a temperance community and named for newspaperman Horace Greeley, the town now is in the heart of an agricultural cornucopia. Weld County, by many measurements, is the most agriculturally productive county in the world! Monfort feedlots east of the city are the world's largest.

0:00 (1:03) Depart Greeley.

0:03 (1:00) On right, one of area's largest cattle auctions, Greeley Producers, can be seen.

0:07 (0:56) Another sugar mill appears on right.

0:36 (0:27) Very unusual rock outcroppings look as though they might have been sculpted from adobe.

0:41 (0:22) Enter Wyoming and leave Colorado. This is a good place to spot pronghorn antelope which populate Wyoming's southern prairies.

1:00 (0:03) Cheyenne can be seen in distance on right. Look now—train does not get much closer.

1:03 (0:00) Arrive Cheyenne's Borie Station. Station is several miles west of Cheyenne—to save cost and time of train making side trip into city. Cheyenne passengers are greeted by bus at trackside.

CHEYENNE, WY - It began in 1867 when the Union Pacific, pushing westward to form part of the first transcontinental railroad, selected this site as a terminal and supply point. Originally called "Shey-an-nah," it was named after the largest family of Indians in North America. Eastern capitalists and foreign nobility began to invest heavily in the area's cattle industry, and by the 1800s, Cheyenne was the wealthiest per capita city in the world. This was when the renowned Cheyenne Club was built, which had splendid cuisine and reputedly the finest liquor in the world. Concerts, theatrical performances and art now mark the city's character rather than the 60 saloons which operated back when the town was first nicknamed "Hell On Wheels." But the West is still alive and well here. In July of each year, Cheyenne holds its rip snorting Frontier Days, the granddaddy of all rodeos.

0:00 (0:52) Depart Cheyenne's Borie Station.

0:06 (0:46) On left are seven very symmetrically organized small concrete footings, which formerly supported a water tank needed when steam locomotives were king. Such towers were placed at approximately 20-mile intervals to supply enough water during arduous climb over Sherman Hill, directly ahead.

0:14 (0:38) Rock fence on right was obviously built when labor was cheap.

0:17 (0:35) Pastoral valley off to left was site of filming of movie *My Friend Flicka.*

0:25 (0:27) It takes sharp eyes to catch it, but several miles off to right, beyond maze of snow fences, is a red pyramidal monument erected to commemorate Ames Brothers, early-day railroad entrepreneurs. Its height belies its great distance from tracks.

0:26 (0:26) Cross 8,018-foot summit of Sherman Hill—highest point on our route. Colorado's mountains are now 60 miles south. Butch Cassidy and his train-robbing Hole-in-the-Wall Gang once greased tracks on western slope of Sherman Hill, stalling eastbound trains and making them easy prey.

0:28 (0:24) Water tower on left was one of many that once served steam locomotives of the Union Pacific.

0:33 (0:19) Pass through quarter-mile-long Hermosa tunnel, first of several between Denver and Ogden.

0:42 (0:10) Fancifully eroded red rocks of Red Buttes area decorate landscape.

0:51 (0:01) Entering Laramie, stadium and fieldhouse of University of Wyoming are clearly visible off to right.

0:52 (0:00) Arrive Laramie where, on right, station's unappealing exterior conceals its very attractive interior.

LARAMIE, WY - Early-day Laramie had a split personality—both wild and civilized. Jack McCall was arrested here for the shooting of Wild Bill Hickok in Deadwood, South Dakota, and Jesse James spent a brief period in the Laramie jail on suspicion of a nearby stagecoach holdup. The University of Wyoming was founded here in 1887, three years before Wyoming's statehood. Women were first called for grand jury duty in Laramie—at that time, a very controversial procedure. And in 1870, Wyoming became the first state to grant women the right to vote, an even more controversial step.

0:00 (1:33) Departing Laramie, town's progressive spirit is evident in newly remodeled older buildings on immediate right. Historic Oregon Trail is off to left. Both Pony Express and Overland Stages used trail, giving rise to Union Pacific's nickname *The Overland Route*.

0:12 (1:21) We're crossing the open Laramie Plains, where small herds of antelope can often be spotted. Snowy Range is off to left.

0:25 (1:08) Snow fences lining nearby hill help reduce drifting across tracks which occur during frequent Wyoming blizzards.

0:39 (0:54) Protrusion on horizon off to right is Como Bluff, one of world's most renowned dinosaur graveyards and fossil beds. It was discovered in 1877.

0:42 (0:51) Bright red buildings, just to right of tracks, is famed "Robbers' Roost" where Butch Cassidy and his gang hid from the law.

0:43 (0:50) On right, three-story beige-colored Virginian Hotel is center of Medicine Bow, where Owen Wister lived for a short time before writing his famous novel "The Virginian." Much of story is based on this locale. Log cabin in foreground was once Wister's home.

0:45 (0:48) Gigantic wind generator stands 26-stories tall on left. At one time, two of these experimental contraptions stood here; the largest was designed to generate four megawatts—enough electricity for a community of 1,500 people.

0:57 (0:36) Pass through Hannah, a coal-mining town since turn of century. Large strip mines with enormous dragline can be seen off to right. Note steam-powered red-nosed rotary snowplow off to right.

1:01 (0:32) Elk Mountain of Medicine Bow Range reaches an elevation of 11,162 feet on left, while on right, two domed concrete slabs mark site of coal mine that exploded in 1930s. Innards still smolder, but smoke cannot be seen from surface.

1:16 (0:16) At Walcott, Hole-in-the-Wall Gang pulled off largest Union Pacific train robbery—close to $5 million by today's values. Train was accosted while stopped for water.

1:20 (0:13) At milepost 666, as train rounds Devil's Curve, vertebra-like formation on right is known as Devil's Backbone.

1:21 (0:12) Stone remains of Ft. Steele stand on west bank of North Platte River on right. Buff building on left side of tracks was gun powder shed. Town was on left.

1:26 (0:07) On immediate right, Sinclair refinery "flares off" undesirable gasses.

1:33 (0:00) Arrive Rawlins.

RAWLINS, WY - A railroad and ranching town, it too had its day with outlaws. In 1878, vigilantes hanged a train robber and at the same time sent notes to 24 other desperados, suggesting they might wish to leave before meeting a similar fate. The next day, 24 one-way train tickets were purchased. Red pigment mined near here was used in paint for the Brooklyn Bridge.

0:00 (1:45) Departing Rawlins, immediately up street to right can be glimpsed old Territorial Prison, now Wyoming State Prison, identified by silver water tower and stone edifice.

0:26 (1:19) About 100 yards west of milepost 705, adjacent to tracks on right, is what Union Pacific calls "Cherokee National Forest" or "Tree of Love on the Range."

The tree was planted by a section gang (it was known as "The Cherokee Gang") worker and his wife after the section hand complained to his spouse of the incessant Wyoming summer heat. She kept it nurtured through the years, taking water from a spring on left side of the tracks, and it grew to the lovely shrub it is today.

0:50 (0:55) Black material that is prominent along the right-of-way is not dust from coal trains, but cinders left from coal burning steam locomotives from early-day railroading.

0:51 (0:54) Here at Tipton, last train robbery in Wyoming was committed. Again, it was the Hole-in-the-Wall Gang, but this time about all that was taken were cavalry horses after dynamited express car produced little of value.

1:14 (0:31) Pass through strip mining operation where two-mile conveyor belt on left takes coal for loading into 100-ton-capacity hopper cars. Coal trains travel continuously at two-tenths mile per hour while receiving their cargoes from overhead bins. Railroad loads two trains per day with most of coal destined for nearby Jim Bridger Power Plant that furnishes electricity to a five-state region. Black Butte Mountain is off to left.

1:22 (0:23) Small one-room log cabin was once homestead of one of Wyoming's more important sheep ranching families.

1:25 (0:20) Well preserved limestone building with adjoining wall at "Point of Rocks," at left, location of remains of historic Rock Point Stage Station which served as relay point in 1862 for Ben Hollady Overland Trail Stages.

1:45 (0:00) Arrive Rock Springs.

ROCK SPRINGS, WY - An early stagecoach stop and outfitting point, Rock Springs has maintained a rugged reputation. The boom and bust of minerals has produced all the problems of erratic growth and a fluctuating population.

0:00 (0:20) Depart Rock Springs.

0:14 (0:06) It takes little imagination to spot rock formation on left known as "Old Man's Face."

0:20 (0:00) Arrive in Green River amidst impressive rail yards of Union Pacific.

GREEN RIVER, WY - Located admist spectacular rock formations on the banks of the Green River, the town was originally an Overland Stage crossing and later an important rail construction point. Before it was torn down, a 32-stall roundhouse provided repairs to the multitude of steam locomotives that once passed through here.

0:00 (1:25) Depart Green River.

0:05 (1:20) Cross over and then climb banks of Green River, whose flow fills rugged Flaming Gorge Reservoir several miles downstream to left.

0:21 (1:04) Albino-looking FMC Chemicals plant, on left, produces soda ash used in soap, glass and other products. World's largest supply is in this area. A typical Wyoming gas field is checkered by green storage tanks and equipment on right.

0:24 (1:01) Mountain Men Rendezvous was held near this spot in 1834.

1:10 (0:15) Darkness pervades while train pierces through a long tunnel.

1:25 (0:00) Arrive Evanston, where turn-of-the-century depot has been beautifully restored. Original baggage scales were constructed then depot built over them. Scales still form portion of station floor. Station was given to city in 1985.

EVANSTON, WY - At first, Evanston was another railroad town, but this activity soon waned in importance. Now, oil, cattle, sheep and tourism make up Evanston's economy. The town boasts the nation's oldest courthouse still in use.

0:00 (1:10) Departing Evanston, watch for 1912 roundhouse, complete with turntable and 27 bays, on left. Tank-car repair firm now uses this wonderful relic. Structure replaced 15-bay roundhouse torn down in 1911.

0:06 (1:04) Enter Utah and leave Wyoming.

0:13 (0:57) Three short tunnels assist crossing increasingly difficult terrain.

0:30 (0:40) Devils Slide power plant on right belches towering columns of steam from its twin stacks.

0:36 (0:34) More tunnels and frequent river crossings are necessary as train descends toward Ogden.

Pioneer - Echo, Utah
DORIS SWANSON

0:46 (0:24) Train courses through lovely pastoral valley, contrasting sharply with earlier scenes in southern Wyoming. Interstate 80 escorts train on right.

0:55 (0:15) Nestled in Weber (pronounced WEE-ber) Canyon, small hydroelectric plant of Utah Power and Light squeezes valuable energy from Weber River on left.

0:56 (0:14) Emerge from mountains and look down to left toward next stop—Ogden.

1:10 (0:00) Arrive Ogden Union Station, a 1924 Spanish Colonial style structure. Antique railway cars and steam locomotives are sometimes parked on adjoining track, some undergoing restoration. Salt Lake passengers will be driven to that city by a connecting bus.

OGDEN, UT - Railroading history was made near Ogden when the Union Pacific and Central Pacific railroads met at Promontory just north of the Great Salt Lake in 1869. This meeting was ceremoniously climaxed on May 10th of that year when a golden spike was driven completing a rail route between both oceans. Immediately after completion of this transcontinental line, Ogden was chosen by the Union Pacific as a major junction point, assuring the city's future growth and prominence.

The Golden Spike National Historic Site, northwest of here, has exact replicas of the engines used in the original ceremonies when the golden spike was driven linking the Atlantic and Pacific. A fine railroad museum in the Ogden Amtrak station has audiovisual displays depicting functions of steam locomotives, historic engines and a rail history relief map. Browning Museum, also in the station, has the definitive gun collection of the world's foremost firearms inventor for whom the museum was named.

0:00 (2:25) Depart Ogden.
2:25 (0:00) Arrive Pocatello.

POCATELLO, ID - It was the Portneuf Valley which provided a transportation corridor to the western

Montana mines in the 1860s that gave birth to Pocatello. Now this city of nearly 50,000 is a vibrant trade center and home of 5,000-student Idaho State University. Enjoying both a mild climate and a proximity to many rivers and lakes, recreational opportunities abound, including several popular geothermal pools.

0:00 (1:30) Depart Pocatello.
1:30 (0:00) Arrive Shoshone.

SHOSHONE, ID - Shoshone is a small southern Idaho trading center situated in one of the more arid regions of the state, receiving 10.3 inches of precipitation annually. Of interest are nearby Shoshone Ice and Mammoth caves.

0:00 (2:05) Depart Shoshone.
2:05 (0:00) Arrive Boise. Situated on a pleasantly landscaped hilltop setting, commanding a fine view of the city, station boasts a handsome clock tower and an unusually attractive waiting room, topped by a high beamed ceiling. Some consider station to be most beautiful in U.S.

BOISE, ID - Although the Oregon Trail passed through here, so did most of those using it—that is, until gold was discovered near here in 1861. Then a fort was established by the federal government to thwart Indian raids along the trail which not only assured Boise protection but also eventual economic success. The railroad brought more activity to the region in 1865—but to the disappointment of the citizenry, bypassed Boise in favor of nearby Nampa when a dispute developed between the Oregon Short Line Railroad and the Boise city fathers. Finally, in 1887 a stub line was completed, giving Boise direct rail access to the rest of the country. Today, Boise boasts capital city status as well as being home to several national corporations, including Morrison Knudsen, Boise Cascade and J R Simplot.

0:00 (0:35) Depart Boise.
0:14 (0:21) Train moves gingerly along "Boise Cutoff" connecting Boise to main line of Union Pacific at Nampa.
0:35 (0:00) Arrive Nampa.

NAMPA, ID - In 1886 several settlers began to build here, naming their new town after a legendary Shoshone Chief—Nampuh (Bigfoot), supposed-

ly being of "huge proportions." The town has had its share of setbacks, most notably in 1903 when an untimely fire burned much of the business district, just when wooden water mains were being replaced that left the town with no water. A "silver-plated" pumper truck was quickly hauled in by special train from Boise, making the harrowing trip in only 20 minutes.

Today, this is the heart of a desert-area-turned-Eden due to the resourceful use of irrigation from deep wells and the Snake River. Of interest is the museum in the restored U.P. Depot and pictographs 20 miles from town, including one of the largest Indian rock drawings on record.

0:00 (0:36) Depart Nampa on main line of Union Pacific.
0:05 (0:31) Mountains on right form a special backdrop for irrigated farmlands.
0:27 (0:09) Enter Oregon and leave Idaho. Metal-superstructured bridge carries us over Snake River on its way toward one of Western Hemisphere's deepest gorges, just 90 miles north of here—Hells Canyon.
0:36 (0:00) Arrive Ontario.

ONTARIO, OR - Located on the beautiful Snake River which divides Oregon and Idaho, Ontario serves as a trade center for eastern Oregon's extensive ranch country.

0:00 (1:50) Depart Ontario and immediately cross twisting course of Snake, as Pioneer pays one last visit to state of Idaho.
0:07 (1:43) Cross Payette River where myriad of bird species can often be spotted along its shores.
0:08 (1:42) Through Payette, birthplace of Minnesota Twins' baseball great, Harmon Killebrew.
0:14 (1:39) Cross waters of Snake River which continue northward flow until eventually reaching Columbia River at Pasco, Washington.
0:31 (1:22) On right, unusual sand dunes stretch lazily for almost half mile.
0:32 (1:21) At Farewell Bend, note campground across river. Here, Oregon Trail made its final contact with Snake River after following it, off and on, for 350 miles. Pioneers camped at this site 100 years ago, including explorer John C. Fremont. Train

now enters one of many canyons of Snake, as bordering mountains rise to almost 1,000 feet above roadbed.

0:36 (1:17) Exit canyon and recross Snake River, as Pioneer enters Oregon and leaves Idaho.

Gain one hour as train passes from Mountain to Pacific Time. Set your watch back (forward if eastbound) one hour.

0:40 (1:13) Through Union Pacific yards at Huntington and enter broadening Burnt River Valley as train slants across northeastern Oregon.

0:48 (1:05) Limestone from mine on right has only short distance to go to reach cement plant, also on right.

0:58 (0:55) Tunnel's darkness interrupts scenery for about half minute.

1:09 (0:44) Another cement plant, on left, takes advantage of area's prevalent limestone.

1:39 (0:14) Having climbed out of Burnt River drainage, crest Encina Pass at 3,998-foot elevation and descend toward Powder River Valley. To left is 5,392-foot Dooley Mountain.

1:53 (0:00) Arrive Baker City.

BAKER CITY, OR - In 1861, Baker experienced its own gold rush when exaggerated stories of fantastic gold-laden streams lured miners here in droves. Now encircled by ghost towns that were once flourishing mining communities, Baker City is the center for wheat farming and ranching. Recreationalists are drawn here by excellent fishing and trips to Snake River country. The dominant white structure in the center of town is the historic Antler Hotel, built in 1912. Of interest is an incredible 80-ounce gold nugget on display in the lobby of a local bank.

0:00 (0:58) Depart Baker City.

0:07 (0:51) Train follows a route bordered by forested Eagle Cap Wilderness Area in Wallowa Mountains on right and Elkhorn Ridge in Wallowa Whitman Forest on left.

0:10 (0:48) After passing through Haines, where steam is rising from a patch of trees, green-roofed building houses town's therapeutic springs.

0:48 (0:10) Hot Lake Resort's overgrown facilities can be seen on left.

0:55 (0:03) Anchoring north end of mountain range on right is 6,725-foot Mt. Prominence.

0:58 (0:00) Arrive LaGrande.

LAGRANDE, OR - Farming and ranching, made possible by the fertile lands of the Grande Ronde River Valley, give LaGrande a rich Western flavor. The scenery and outdoor recreational opportunities of the Wallowa and Blue mountains make this a sportsman's paradise.

0:00 (2:05) Depart LaGrande and start a grinding ascent taking us over ridge of Blue Mountains directly ahead.

0:08 (1:57) Train slips beneath old arched concrete structure which once carried highway traffic prior to Interstate 84.

0:47 (1:18) Train finally crests 4,205-foot summit of lovely forested Blue Mountains at Kamela and starts its downward roll toward Pendleton, a 2.2% grade—steepest of route.

0:58 (1:07) Train follows sweeping reverse curves.

1:47 (0:18) Cross Umatilla River and return to flatter environs of farm and ranch country.

2:04 (0:01) On right, Pioneer slips past one of several world-renowned Pendleton Mills. This particular factory specializes in producing blankets.

2:05 (0:00) Arrive Pendleton.

PENDLETON, OR - This historic Western town (ruts of the Oregon Trail can still be seen at the edge of the city) hosts the renowned Pendleton Round-up during the second full week of each September. The main attraction is one of the nation's most important rodeos, including unusual trick riding and stagecoach races, as well as the standard rodeo fare. Another highlight is the Happy Canyon Pageant when regional Indian tribes compete in age-old ceremonial dances.

0:00 (0:40) Depart Pendleton, following meandering Umatilla River to Pioneer's next stop, Hinkle.

0:02 (0:38) Grandstands for famous Pendleton Round-up appear at right.

0:05 (0:35) Barbed wire and bars do little to enhance Eastern Oregon Psychiatric Center on left.

0:37 (0:03) Enter impressive Hinkle rail yards.
0:40 (0:00) Slip past large Simplot potato processing plant, on left, then arrive Hinkle.

HINKLE, OR - Here, a very small station serves the Hermiston area. If each train is punctual, eastbound and westbound Pioneers will meet here.
0:00 (1:22) Depart Hinkle, and continue to roll through northeastern Oregon's farm and ranch country as route approaches Columbia River.
0:05 (1:17) Hundreds of earthen mounds on right house ammunition of Umatilla Army Ordnance Depot.
0:15 (1:07) Suddenly, broad waters of Columbia River are off to right. This 1,210-mile giant produces more than a third of nation's hydroelectric power! Bluffs on far side are in state of Washington.
0:57 (0:25) Cross 300-mile-long John Day River, named after former Western scout.
0:59 (0:23) On right, John Day Dam momentarily interrupts Columbia's westward flow. Navigational lock is on far side of river and handles eight million tons of commercial traffic annually. With 113 feet maximum lift, it is one of world's highest single-lift locks. Dam's 16 generating units can produce enough electricity to handle needs of two Seattles.
1:01 (0:21) On far side of river, just to right of bridge supporting U.S. 97, are mysterious-looking ruins of Stonehenge, a memorial to World War I dead, built by railroad entrepreneur Sam Hill.
1:05 (0:17) Just to left of that same bridge, set in a small grove of trees on far side, is Maryhill Museum. Originally built as a mansion, it was dedicated as a museum by Queen of Rumania in 1920s and now houses very diverse collections of art.
1:12 (0:10) Deschutes River crosses beneath tracks just before it flows into Columbia.
1:16 (0:06) Mount Hood, like some pyramidal spectre, rises to an elevation of 11,235 feet almost directly ahead, visible now on right.
1:17 (0:05) The Dalles Dam stretches impressively across Columbia on right. Dam's hydroelectric capacity gives it a top-ten ranking in free world. Powerhouse

is located in dam and is half-mile long, containing 22 generators. There are two fish ladders and a navigational lock along Washington shore.
1:22 (0:00) Arrive The Dalles' new transportation center, on left, modeled after former UP depot.

THE DALLES, OR - This was the terminus of the Oregon Trail, and a basalt memorial in a city park marks the spot where it actually ended. Now, The Dalles has become a major shipping point, and, in season, wheat-laden barges and other traffic can be seen headed down-river from here. The Dalles Dam, where visitors can see the powerhouse and a fish-counting station, can be reached by a free passenger train leaving Seufert Park. Also of interest, St. Peter's Catholic Church with 36 stained glass windows donated by pioneer families and an old pipe organ built from rare tigerwood.
0:00 (0:26) Depart The Dalles.
0:01 (0:25) Red spire of "Carpenter Gothic" St. Peter's Catholic Church, tallest structure in town, is at left.
0:04 (0:21) On right, water tower depicts principal industries of area—fishing and cherries.
0:14 (0:12) Small monument on island in river marks burial site of frontier trapper who had expressed a longing to be buried with his "Indian friends." His wish was granted.
0:26 (0:00) Cross Hood River and arrive at town of same name.

HOOD RIVER, OR - This area was probably first visited by white men in 1805 when Lewis and Clark camped in this locale. Hood River is the gateway city to Mt. Hood with its year-round recreational opportunities, including one of the continent's longest ski runs. Sailboarding is popular throughout the Columbia Gorge due to its smooth waters and prevalent winds. Annually, sailboarders from around the world compete in the Gorge Pro-Am. Fruits and berries thrive here, and packing can be observed in October—or perhaps better yet, wine made from these products can be sipped at a local winery.
0:00 (1:13) Depart Hood River and catch glimpse of majestic Mt. Adams on right.

Sadly, Mt. St. Helens is no longer viewable from here since its spectacular 1980 eruption.

0:01 (1:12) Columbia Gorge now begins to take on more dramatic proportions as river cuts through a gap in Cascades while foliage of heavy rain forests blankets southern shore. Farming and ranching of western Oregon are now scenes left behind.

0:05 (1:08) Logging flume on far side of Columbia was last one used in U.S.

0:21 (0:52) At Cascade Locks, Columbia River boat docks and river cruise boats can be seen on right.

This is the site of the historic Cascade Locks built in 1896 to bypass what were then the Cascade Rapids. The town is the beginning of several trails in the gorge as well as the beautiful Pacific Crest Trail.

0:22 (0:51) Bridge on right is "Bridge of the Gods" which now crosses river on "exact spot" where legendary natural stone bridge of Indians supposedly fell into river when nearby volcanic peaks caused ground to tremble by arguing amongst themselves.

0:26 (0:47) Venerable Bonneville Dam, first federal hydroelectric dam on Columbia, is on right. Built in 1933 at a cost of $88 million, it is now but one of nine on entire river. Shipping lock is able to raise or lower vessels 70 feet in 15 minutes, a process that uses 40 million gallons of water. Visitors can watch salmon and steelhead trout find their way up giant fish ladders.

0:29 (0:44) Sheer-walled, 800-foot monolith across river is Beacon Rock, proclaimed to be largest such formation in U.S., and second only to Gibraltar.

0:33 (0:40) Appropriately named Horsetail Falls can be glimpsed at left.

0:36 (0:37) Mostly hidden by trees at left is 620-foot Multnomah Falls. It's high, but still dwarfed by California's 1,430-foot Yosemite and 1,612-foot Ribbon falls.

0:42 (0:31) Rooster Rock, the tall black spire on right, stands watchful guard over river as it makes its way to Pacific Ocean.

0:44 (0:29) Final tunnel before reaching Portland plunges train into momentary darkness for last time.

0:58 (0:10) Interstate 84 (Banfield Freeway) escorts train along a winding course through eastern Portland.

1:10 (0:02) Now in heart of Portland, cross over navigable waters of Willamette River on Steel Bridge. Oceangoing vessels can usually be spotted on either side of train.

1:13 (0:00) Arrive Portland.

 PORTLAND, OR - See page 288.

For route between Portland and Seattle, see the Coast Starlight log, page 283.

Desert Wind

Ample portions of desert landscape are served passengers on board the aptly named Desert Wind as it crosses some of the most arid regions of Utah, Nevada and California. Darkness usually prevails for much of the time between Salt Lake City and Las Vegas, but beyond, travel is during daylight hours allowing for fine desert viewing. The unusual rock formations of Cajon Pass are particularly intriguing.

Between Chicago and Salt Lake, the Wind is combined with the California Zephyr to operate as a single train. A split occurs at Salt Lake City, however, and the Desert Wind strikes out on its own to Los Angeles, tracing the route formerly traveled by The City of Los Angeles, the once-proud flagship of the Union Pacific.

Westbound Schedule (Condensed)
Chicago, IL - Midafternoon Departure
Omaha, NE - Late Evening
Denver, CO - Early Morning (2nd Day)
Salt Lake City, UT - Late Evening (2nd Day)
Las Vegas, NV - Early Morning (3rd Day)
Los Angeles, CA - Early Afternoon Arrival (3rd Day)

Eastbound Schedule (Condensed)
Los Angeles, CA - Late Morning Departure
Las Vegas, NV - Early Evening
Salt Lake City, UT - Middle of the Night (2nd Day)
Denver, CO - Midevening (2nd Day)
Omaha, NE - Early Morning (3rd Day)
Chicago, IL - Midafternoon Arrival (3rd Day)

Frequency - Daily.
Seating - Superliner coaches.
Dining - Complete meal and beverage service Chicago-Salt Lake City. Cold meals for sleeping car passengers Salt Lake-Los Angeles. Movies, except Salt Lake-Los Angeles westbound. Lounge service with sandwiches, snacks and beverages.
Sleeping - Superliner sleepers with deluxe, family, economy and special bedrooms.
Baggage - Checked baggage handled at larger cities.
Reservations - All-reserved train.
Length of Trip - 2,397 miles in 50 hours.

Route Log

See the California Zephyr for route log from Chicago to Salt Lake City, page 185.

 SALT LAKE CITY, UT - See page 201.

0:00 (3:05) Depart Salt Lake City, following Union Pacific rails until we reach Daggett, California.

2:10 (0:55) Pass through Delta, Utah, a farming community of 2,000, situated in Utah's western desert country.

2:57 (0:05) In distance, off to left, cluster of lights pinpoints Milford geothermal power plant of Utah Power and Light Company. Electricity is produced from steam generators which are powered by tapping into underground reservoir of

Cheyenne Ave.

Las Vegas Expwy.

Charleston Blvd.

Sahara Ave.

Spring Mtn. Rd.

Desert Inn Rd.

Sands Rd.

Flamingo Rd.

Tropicana Ave.

Las Vegas

🚂 Amtrak Station
1 - Visitors Center
2 - Union Plaza Hotel, Las Vegas Club, & California Hotel

Glen Canyon. Milford, too, is a paradise for rock hounds, boasting one of the world's most extensive deposits of opalized material. Also found here is the rare snowflake obsidian, once used by the Indians for arrowheads.

0:00 (2:05) Depart Milford.

🕐 Gain one hour as train passes from Mountain to Pacific Time. Set your watch back (forward if eastbound) one hour.

1:53 (0:00) Arrive Caliente. Old Union Pacific depot houses city offices, police department, an art display and Amtrak's waiting room.

📷 **CALIENTE, NV** - As reflected in its name, Caliente (Spanish, for "hot") is blessed with an abundance of geothermal energy. Its hot springs and mud baths were a welcome respite for railroad workers who founded the town at the turn of the century. Today, studies are under way directed at encouraging resort development which could capitalize on this valuable resource.

As well as its geothermal attractions, Caliente offers convenient access to three state parks, including the magnificent Cathedral Gorge 15 miles north of town with dynamic sandstone formations sculpted through time to resemble spires and turrets of a grand cathedral. Also of interest is the nearby ghost town of Delamar, where over 75 million dollars in gold was mined between 1891 and 1909.

0:00 (2:19) Departing Caliente, enter Meadow Valley Wash. Lovely Rainbow Canyon is contained within but unfortunately Desert Wind's schedule calls for traversing this scenic stretch mostly at night—eastbound and westbound. During longest days of year, eastbound passengers might get a view at dusk, and a late-running westbound might offer early morning viewing.

2:19 (0:00) Arrive Las Vegas. Station is located downtown in Union Plaza Hotel. Just beyond Plaza's front door lies dazzling neon maelstrom of world-renowned Fremont Street.

📷 **LAS VEGAS, NV** - From its humble beginning, first as a Mormon settlement and then a railroad town,

500-degree-Fahrenheit water. Although output is a modest 20,000 kilowatts, it is first sizeable facility of its kind outside of California.

3:02 (0:00) Arrive Milford.

📷 **MILFORD, UT** - Predominantly a railroad town for more than a hundred years, a new wave of excitement now surrounds Milford's geothermal developments. Possibilities, such as the nearby geothermal power plant, rouse expectations for new employment and lower energy costs.

Aside from the industrial boon, Milford remains a popular gateway to unlimited outdoor adventure. Within a day's drive and return are six national parks and three national monuments, as well as the recreation resorts of Lake Powell and the city has grown to become famous as a world gambling mecca and "Showtown, U.S.A." Casinos and posh hotels line "The Strip" from one end of town to the other. Even the Amtrak station is located in one of the many high-rise hotels. Nevada's legalized gambling, the city's warm and dry desert climate, and its proximity to populous Southern California combine to account for Las Vegas' uniqueness.

Amtrak Station, 1 Main St., is located in the Union Plaza Hotel. The station itself is quite spartan, with limited seating and some snack and drink vending machines. But down the hall is another world, the Union Plaza's lobby, restaurants and casino.

Cab, 873-2227. **Local buses** in front of the station at Fremont and Main; 228-7433. **McCarran International Airport** is just three miles south of town.

Las Vegas Convention and Visitors Authority, Convention Center, 3150 Paradise Rd., 89109; (702) 892-0711.

Because this is Las Vegas, there is an abundance of reasonably priced hotels throughout the city. Weekend rates are higher than those shown.

-**Union Plaza Hotel and Casino,** 1 Main St., 89101; (702) 386-2110 or 800-634-6575. Amtrak station is in the hotel. $30.

-**California Hotel and Casino,** 12 Ogden Ave., 89101; (702) 385-1222 or 800-634-6255. Within a block from the station. $40.

Gambling, of course, is the chief attraction for millions of visitors each year. Casinos abound and most will be found along "The Strip" (Las Vegas Boulevard). **Shows and Reviews** at the larger hotels are true spectaculars in every sense of the word. Complete listings of these can be obtained from the Chamber of Commerce. Reservations for shows should be made directly with the hotels.

Hoover Dam and the Lake Mead National Recreation Area are located 32 miles southeast on U.S. 93. The dam, built before Las Vegas developed, was an engineering marvel of its time, and still remains so today. Standing 726 feet tall in the Black Canyon of the Colorado River, it is one of the world's tallest.

0:00 (2:54) Depart Las Vegas past lavish hotels and casinos of city's illustrious "Strip" district on left. Train then proceeds southwest across parched landscape of Mojave Desert.

0:25 (2:29) Back on left, Las Vegas now spreads out across valley floor presenting a spectacular sight for eastbound evening passengers.

0:51 (2:03) Whiskey Pete's casino, at right, offering Californians their first chance at Nevada gambling, clearly defines California-Nevada border.

2:39 (0:15) At Yermo, travel through expansive Union Pacific yards.

2:41 (0:13) Calico Ghost Town, snuggled against hillside on right, surrounds site of richest silver strike in California history. Veins were so productive that "nuggets" frequently tipped the scales at a mere half ton or more. Today, flavor of "Old West" is recaptured amidst authentically restored fixtures of this historic boomtown.

Also of interest is nearby Calico Dig. In 1968, a limestone hearth was unearthed, suggesting evidence of prehistoric man over 50,000 years earlier. Area has subsequently become one of North America's most important archaeological sites.

2:42 (0:12) Water-filled tower on left is focus of 1,818 huge mirrors which continually track sun, creating steam for nation's first solar electric facility.

2:43 (0:11) Vast array of military equipment is stockpiled alongside warehouses of Marine Logistics Base Annex on right. Main facilities are located in nearby Barstow.

2:44 (0:10) Passing through Daggett, note two historic structures on right. Venerable 1880s Stone Hotel (and built of stone) was home-away-from-home for Death Valley Scotty, who continuously reserved room #7 (with private entrance) for his personal use. On corner two doors to west is Scott's Market, once a popular spot for miners to convert "high grade" into spendable currency. Destroyed by fire in 1908, reconstructed market became first fireproof building in desert, using cement freighted in from the East. Here, we leave Union Pacific and enter upon tracks of Santa Fe.

2:48 (0:06) Marine Corps Logistics Base on left is largest of two such facilities in country. Operation's main concern is procurement, maintenance and disbursement of all classes of military equipment. It is presently Barstow's largest employer.

2:50 (0:04) On left, McDonald's restaurant and host of shops are imaginatively housed within refurbished railroad cars.

2:54 (0:00) Arrive Barstow.

On the right, "Casa del Desierto" (House of the Desert) is appropriately enscribed across the facade of a grandiose structure next to the station. This old building was originally a Harvey House—just one of a chain of elegant eateries and hotels that once stretched along the Santa Fe. Fred Harvey's restaurants became legendary for good food—many thought it the best in the country—and pretty waitresses, in what was an otherwise wild and woolly West.

Prior to 1876, the year Harvey opened his first restaurant in Florence, Kansas, rail passengers were forced to endure inedible meals foisted on them by the railroad at trackside greasy spoons. (Dining cars were yet to come!) Seeing what he thought was a great opportunity, Harvey sold his idea of fine food in a pleasant atmosphere to the Santa Fe and acquired exclusive rights to establish diners along their entire line. Both parties prospered as passengers soon chose to ride the Santa Fe because of Fred Harvey's restaurants.

BARSTOW, CA - Originally founded as a way station along the old Santa Fe Trail, Barstow has emerged as an important distribution lifeline, strategically located at the crossroads of two major interstates and railroads. Large military installations and a healthy tourist trade further bolster the city's burgeoning economy.

Barstow, too, enjoys a share in technology. Located here is NASA's Goldstone Tracking Station, a vital communications link for orbiting satellites and deep space probes.

An interesting attraction is the Barstow Way Station, with exhibits emphasizing the ecological aspects of the high desert. As well, visitors have an opportunity to sample native plants once used by the Indians for food and medicine.

0:00 (0:33) Depart Barstow through awe-some sprawl of Santa Fe's classification yards. Over next several miles, onset of hillier terrain previews approach into San Bernardino Mountains.

0:21 (0:12) Just beyond peaks of Kramer Range on right lies Edwards Air Force Base, primary landing site of NASA's space shuttle.

0:25 (0:06) Elaborate maze of fences and paddocks is home to fine-looking horses on left.

0:29 (0:04) At Oro Grande, well-preserved steam locomotive is enshrined in town park on left.

0:33 (0:00) Arrive Victorville.

VICTORVILLE, CA - Cement production is an important Victorville industry, as is evidenced by cement plant which crowds tracks just to the left of the train.

0:00 (1:09) Depart Victorville.

0:02 (1:07) Sudden rock outcroppings form scenic little canyon as train crosses Mojave River into Victorville. Once through town, begin ascent of Cajon Pass which will lift us out of the Mojave Desert. Noble joshua tree cactus is a prominent feature of northern climb, while spectacular rock formations line descent into San Bernardino.

0:09 (1:00) Another cement plant borders on right.

0:20 (0:46) Nearing Cajon summit, San Gabriel Mountains are prominent features to right, with San Bernardino Mountains off to left.

0:22 (0:44) Bid farewell to unconfining spaces of West and start dramatic descent of Cajon Pass into Los Angeles Basin.

Since 1885 when Santa Fe's predecessor the California Southern, pushed the first rails over the 3,811-foot top, Cajon Pass has been one of railroading's more fascinating artifacts.

Three sets of tracks now descend Cajon. To the right is the Southern Pacific, the left set is Santa Fe's steeper South Track while in the middle is Santa Fe's gentle but two-mile-longer North Track. Since a third railroad, the Union Pacific, has Cajon trackage rights on the Santa Fe, this can become a very busy place.

Westbound traffic on the Santa Fe will normally descend the three percent grade

Desert Wind - San Bernardino, California
DON R. FLYNN

of the South Track (unless weight dictates the more moderate routing), while eastbound Santa Fe traffic will climb the "casual" 2.2% North Track.

0:29 (0:36) White flatiron-like Mormon Rocks are most prominent geographic feature on right. Infamous San Andreas Fault is nearby.

--- (0:31) Eastbound trains now curl through horseshoe turn known as Sullivan's Curve, named after early-day railroad photographer.

0:41 (0:24) Two Santa Fe routes now become one again. Highway on left is Interstate 15, linking Los Angeles and Las Vegas.

0:48 (0:17) Entanglement of wire and steel bars, looking like a World War II beach defense, serves as breakwater to protect tracks from creek's occasional floodwaters.

0:52 (0:13) Passage beneath I-15 marks finish of Cajon Pass adventure.

1:03 (0:02) Approaching San Bernardino, lush woodlands, colorful shrubbery and majestic palms represent radical departure from environs of last 750 miles.

1:05 (0:00) Arrive San Bernardino. Railroad equipment is maintained within large Santa Fe shops, while nicely landscaped grounds encircle vine-covered station.

SAN BERNARDINO, CA - Lying in the heart of fertile citrus country, San Bernardino was first settled in the mid-19th century by a group of Mormons who modeled the town after their former home of Salt Lake City. Adjoining San Bernardino is the inspiring Rim o' the World Highway, a splendid mountain drive leading to such popular vacation retreats as Lake Arrowhead and Big Bear Lake.

0:00 (1:03) Depart San Bernardino and traverse Riverside/Fullerton branch of Santa Fe.

0:09 (0:54) At Colton, elderly sheds of California Citrus Pulp operation line tracks on right.

0:17 (0:46) Through Riverside, home to March Air Force Base. Boarded up Santa Fe station on right is nostalgic relic of earlier years.

0:42 (0:21) Cross northern end of Santa Ana Mountains, and descend into congestion of southeastern Los Angeles. One last glimpse of San Gabriels is afforded to right where 10,064-foot Mt. San Antonio stands above all.

0:56 (0:07) At Orange Growers Association on left, seedling orange trees await transplantation.

1:00 (0:03) Clusters of attractive industrial parks comingled with residential areas precede arrival at Fullerton.

1:03 (0:00) Arrive Fullerton. Home of well-known Donald Duck citrus juices appears on right next to station. Santa Fe depot is a delight. Its pink stucco facade topped with a dark, red-tile roof is further enhanced by unusually large, arch-shaped windows and fine grill work.

 FULLERTON, CA - As you may have guessed from the citrus juice operation just mentioned, Fullerton has had its roots in the citrus industry. Los Angeles' growth to the south has now made Fullerton virtually indistinguishable from its much larger northern neighbor.

0:00 (0:34) Depart Fullerton.

0:03 (0:31) Perhaps more than one hundred assorted light aircraft at airport serving Fullerton area are in very midst of densely populated area on left.

0:09 (0:23) Pass through refinery operations and active oil wells of Santa Fe Springs. One of area's larger tank farms will soon be seen on right.

0:13 (0:21) Cross San Gabriel River.

0:15 (0:19) Cross Rio Hondo Channel.

0:19 (0:15) Office Building of Santa Fe Railroad on right marks beginning (southern edge) of Santa Fe rail yards.

0:22 (0:12) Acres of truck trailers used on piggyback freight trains are assembled on right at north end of yards.

0:25 (0:09) Train crosses Los Angeles River, then curls sharply right. Diesel shops, roundhouse and its companion turntable are on left where twenty or so Amtrak diesels can generally be counted.

0:27 (0:07) Amtrak coach yard is on immediate left where a gaggle of Superliner cars are stored and await service on trains such as Desert Wind, Sunset Ltd., Southwest Chief and Coast Starlight.

0:29 (0:05) Los Angeles River, encased in concrete on right, has followed our route for several minutes. Take note of old stone bridges that cross over tracks along this section. Their sculpted pilasters are reminiscent of ancient Rome and memorialize

an era of Los Angeles long gone. Excellent view of Los Angeles' cityscape is on left where distinctive white-towered City Hall has center stage.

0:33 (0:01) Curl left off of main line of Santa Fe at Mission Tower.

0:34 (0:00) Arriving Los Angeles Union Station, Dodger Stadium rests atop hill off to right, then Los Angeles County Jail looms on left just before coming to stop at LAUS.

 LOS ANGELES, CA - See page 302.

Southwest Chief

When the Atchison, Topeka and Santa Fe ran its Super Chief between Chicago and Los Angeles, ladies received boutonnieres of fresh flowers, gentlemen were given alligator wallets and it was possible to have your hair cut in the train's barbershop. In the diner, meals were furnished by the Fred Harvey organization. Movie stars and other important personages were commonplace among the train's passengers. It was the first diesel-powered all-sleeper train in the nation.

The Southwest Chief, Amtrak's direct descendant of the Super Chief, still travels those same historic rails, and still provides luxurious accommodations and carries a fascinating clientele. Haircuts are not available and Amtrak doesn't give away wallets, but passengers are treated to the likes of movies in the evening and bingo in the afternoon. There is a Native American guide who travels the segment between Albuquerque and Gallup, describing some of the scenes and historical aspects of that fascinating area.

Originally conceived to intersect northbound cattle drives coming up from Texas and Oklahoma (which it successfully did for 20 years), "The Santa Fe" follows much of the old Santa Fe Trail. This is the shortest and quickest route of the three used by Amtrak between Chicago and Los Angeles. Major stops include Kansas City, Albuquerque and Flagstaff. Ironically, the main line of the Santa Fe does not go through the town by the same name. Passengers destined for Santa Fe, New Mexico detrain at nearby Lamy and complete their trip by van.

Westbound Schedule (Condensed)
Chicago, IL - Late Afternoon Departure
Kansas City, MO - Late Night
LaJunta, CO - Early Morning (2nd Day)
Albuquerque, NM - Late Afternoon (2nd Day)
Flagstaff, AZ (Grand Canyon) - Late Evening (2nd Day)
Los Angeles, CA - Early Morning Arrival (3rd Day)

Eastbound Schedule (Condensed)
Los Angeles, CA - Late Evening Departure
Flagstaff, AZ (Grand Canyon) - Early Morning (2nd Day)
Albuquerque, NM - Early Afternoon (2nd Day)
LaJunta, CO - Midevening (2nd Day)
Kansas City, MO - Early Morning (3rd Day)
Chicago, IL - Late Afternoon Arrival (3rd Day)

Frequency - Daily.
Seating - Superliner coaches.
Dining - Complete meal and beverage service as well as lighter fare, including sandwiches, snacks and beverages. Lounge service with movies.
Sleeping - Superliner sleepers with deluxe, family, economy and special bedrooms.
Baggage - Checked baggage handled at most stations.
Reservations - All-reserved train.
Length of Trip - 2,247 miles in 41 hours.

Route Log

 CHICAGO, IL - See page 128.

225

0:00 (0:55) Depart Chicago's venerable Union Station and emerge from beneath huge Chicago Post Office.

0:04 (0:51) Amtrak coach yards, on right, offer interesting variety of modern-day Amtrak equipment. At Union Tower Junction, continue southward on Santa Fe tracks.

0:10 (0:45) Cross South Chicago River.

For the next 1½ hours, the sights of some of Chicago's more industrial environs will pass by as the Southwest Chief traverses through rail yards, along shipping canals and past power plants, refineries and assorted manufacturing facilities before finally entering rural Illinois.

0:12 (0:38) Chicago's dynamic skyline is now clearly visible back on right. Sears Tower, with its twin antennae, is world's tallest skyscraper with 110 stories.

0:15 (0:29) On left, busy Stevenson Expressway briefly accompanies tracks.

0:38 (0:13) Cross Chicago Sanitary and Ship Canal at Lemont where, on right, former flagstone quarry was accessed through tunnel beneath road.

0:47 (0:03) Somber walls of Illinois State Prison can be seen on left.

0:50 (0:00) Arrive Joliet.

JOLIET, IL - Joliet's economy is dominated by manufacturing and refining, largely developed due to its strategic rail and waterways location. Also, extensive limestone deposits are quarried in this region.

0:00 (0:45) Depart Joliet where industrialization continues with enormous coal-powered generating plants and oil refineries appearing on either side of tracks.

0:14 (0:41) Cross Kankakee River, just one of many tributaries of Illinois River.

0:45 (0:00) Arrive Streator.

STREATOR, IL - Manufacturing of glass containers gives Streator an unusual industrial base. Containers were hand-blown in early days, but mechanization has now supplanted that older art form.

0:00 (0:35) Depart Streator and cross Vermilion River. Typical Illinois farming scenes now prevail throughout this flat, fertile land.

0:34 (0:01) Cross Illinois River whose waters flow 420 miles from Indiana to Mississippi River.

0:35 (0:00) Arrive Chillicothe.

CHILLICOTHE, IL - Just 18 miles upstream from Peoria, this grain-processing community has a delightful setting on the west bank of the Illinois River.

0:00 (0:45) Depart Chillicothe.

0:45 (0:00) Arrive at Galesburg's North Broad Street station. (South Seminary Street Station, used by California Zephyr, is some distance across town from here.)

GALESBURG, IL - Reverend George Washington Gale chose this spot for a ministers' college after searching westward on behalf of a fundamentalist Presbyterian group in Oneida, New York. Famed American poet Carl Sandburg was raised here, and this was the site of a Lincoln-Douglas Debate in 1858. Olstead Ferris, a "Galesburgite" (and a relative of George Washington Ferris, inventor of the Ferris wheel), was an important experimenter with popcorn—one of the area's important products. This was such a novelty in those days that Ferris gave a corn-popping command performance before England's Queen Victoria and Prince Albert.

0:00 (0:54) Depart Galesburg.

0:38 (0:16) After passing through Lomax, Southwest Chief is escorted on right by America's mightiest of rivers—the Mississippi. This 2,350-mile giant drains an area equivalent to two-fifths of U.S.

0:48 (0:06) Just a few miles south of here is historic Nauvoo, a community founded by Latter-day Saints (Mormons) in 1839 after being driven out of Missouri for their religious beliefs.

In 1844, their leader Joseph Smith and his brother were killed by an armed mob at nearby Carthage. This resulted in Brigham Young taking the majority of Nauvoo's residents west to Utah. Today, Nauvoo has been beautifully restored and is open to visitors.

0:49 (0:05) Turn westward and cross Mississippi on bridge with world's largest double-track, double-deck swing span, handling both trains and vehicles. At midpoint, cross Illinois state line and enter Iowa.

0:50 (0:01) Upon reaching west end of bridge, Iowa State Prison is at right. Then on immediate right is factory of well-known pen maker, W. A. Shaeffer, long-time important area employer. Then on left, retired Santa Fe 4-8-4 steam locomotive stands on display while old Santa Fe depot with red caboose now serves as museum of local history.

0:54 (0:00) Arrive Fort Madison, only Iowa stop on route.

FORT MADISON, IA - Built on the site of historic Fort Madison (1808-1813) which protected an early trading post, the city is now a community that is dependent on light manufacturing. The Atchison, Topeka and Santa Fe had planned to take its line through the more southerly Iowa town of Keokuk, but Fort Madison, recognizing the railroad's economic importance, outbid its neighbor, persuading the Santa Fe to build farther north.

0:00 (1:03) Depart Fort Madison, with final view of Mississippi River Valley afforded back on left.

0:12 (0:51) Traverse Des Moines River, and at mid-point, cross Iowa state line and enter Missouri.

1:03 (0:00) Arrive LaPlata.

LAPLATA, MO - This small farming community of 1,400 also serves as a stop for its much larger northern neighbor, Kirksville. America's oldest school of osteopathic medicine was founded there in 1892.

0:00 (0:34) Depart LaPlata.

0:34 (0:00) Arrive Marceline.

MARCELINE, MO - This pleasant little Missouri community was the boyhood home of the now legendary Walt Disney. Walsworth Press, one of the country's largest book printers, is Marceline's major employer.

0:00 (1:39) Depart Marceline.

0:05 (1:34) Swampy environs on right are edge of wetlands comprising Swan Lake Refuge, a way station for hundreds of thousands of migrating waterfowl.

0:11 (1:28) Cross Grand River.

1:39 (0:00) Arrive Kansas City, some 450 miles from Chicago. Santa Fe originally constructed this entire stretch in only nine months.

KANSAS CITY, MO - This second largest city in Missouri has long been one of America's most important rail centers. The city's Union Station, which also served Kansas City, Kansas, was once the third largest rail passenger station in the nation.

Today, everything **is** up-to-date in Kansas City—with the nation's first and perhaps finest shopping center Country Club Plaza (it's much more a neighborhood than a traditional shopping center), a futuristic new airport, and the $500 million Crown Center, about a block from the station, with 85 acres of new office buildings, apartments, and other facilities.

Amtrak Station, 2200 Main St., is located in the downtown area. This is a very modern, new station, constructed adjacent to the much older Union Station. It's somewhat small, but quite functional. There are storage lockers, redcaps, a newsstand, a gift shop and covered pay-parking.

For arrival and departure information only, call (816) 421-3622.

Cab stand at the station; Yellow Cab, 471-5000. Hertz, Avis, National and Budget have downtown **rental-car** locations with station pick up and drop off. **Local buses,** 221-0660. **Kansas City International Airport** is 15 miles north of the station.

Convention and Visitors Bureau, City Center Square, 1100 Main, Suite 2550, 64105. Call (816) 221-5242 or 800-767-7700.

The Westin Crown Center, Kansas City, One Pershing Road, 64108; (816) 474-4400 or 800-228-3000. Luxurious high-rise hotel, 1½ blocks from the station. $150.

-Raphael Hotel, 325 Ward Parkway, 64112; 816-756-3800 or 800-821-5343. Overlooks Country Club Plaza. Small and elegant. Fine location, but considerably south of station. $111.

The following hotels are about 12 blocks from the station and in the heart of downtown:

-Holiday Inn City Center, 1215 Wyandotte, 64105; (816) 471-1333. $69.

-Radisson Suite Hotel, 106 W. 12th, 64105; (816) 221-7000. A pleasant, popular hotel. $79.

Crown Center, near the station at Grande and Pershing, has retail stores, restaurants and theaters. A good place to spend time between trains.

The **Harry S. Truman Library and Museum,** in Independence, has documents, art objects and other memorabilia of the life of this former U.S. president. **Country Club Plaza,** some distance south of downtown, is a highly attractive shopping area, with tile-roofed buildings modeled after Seville, Spain. And the **zoo** in Swope Park is quite nice with special children's exhibits.

0:00 (0:45) Depart Kansas City, Missouri and cross state line into Kansas City, Kansas.

0:45 (0:00) Arrive Lawrence.

LAWRENCE, KS - In 1854, abolitionists established the town of Lawrence only to have it become a focal point of pro-slavery attacks—Quantrill's raid in 1863 being the bloodiest. Lawrence changed, and the University of Kansas was founded here only three years after that infamous incident.

0:00 (0:28) Depart Lawrence.
0:28 (0:00) Arrive Topeka.

TOPEKA, KS - The capital of Kansas is also the location of the world-renowned Menninger Foundation. This institution offers the finest in education, research and treatment of mental illness, and has one of the largest collections of Sigmund Freud's papers in America.

0:00 (1:05) Depart Topeka.
0:32 (0:33) Through Burlingame where in 1863, with most men away fighting with Union forces, womenfolk erected a stone fort from which they successfully defended themselves against Quantrell's raiders.

1:05 (0:00) Arrive Emporia.

EMPORIA, KS - This is where editor and publisher William Allen White wrote and printed his famed *Emporia Gazette.* Turning down opportunities to write for larger newspapers, White chose to stay in Emporia and wrote some of the most important editorials of his time. The paper is still published by members of his family, and a library on the campus of Emporia State University contains many of his mementos.

0:00 (0:12) Depart Emporia.
1:12 (0:00) Arrive Newton.

NEWTON, KS - In 1872, Russian Mennonites immigrated here and brought with them Turkey Red hard winter wheat. Ironically, this Russian wheat import led to Kansas becoming the "Breadbasket of the World." The area is now one of the largest Mennonite settlements in the country.

The Santa Fe intersected the historic Chisholm Trail at this point, a trace that extended as far south as Corpus Christi, Texas.

0:00 (0:34) Depart Newton.
0:34 (0:00) Arrive Hutchinson.

HUTCHINSON, KS - Wheat and salt are Hutchinson's staples. This is the largest prime wheat market in the world, and over 50 elevators handle this commodity, including one structure that holds 18 million bushels and stretches for nearly a half mile! Large salt evaporation plants of Carey, Morton and Barton process rock salt from one of the world's largest salt mines.

0:00 (1:33) Depart Hutchinson.
0:04 (1:29) Forest of white pipes "growing" out of ground on right identifies just one of Kansas' many gas fields.
0:45 (0:48) Profusion of black rocking-arm pumps, on both sides of tracks, pull oil from far beneath ground. These are a common sight throughout oil-productive Kansas.
1:04 (0:29) Passing through Kinsley, note large sign near park on right proclaiming its geographic claim to fame—halfway between New York and San Francisco, 1,561 miles from each. Pioneer sod house and steam locomotive are both restored and on exhibit in park.
1:32 (0:01) Chief glides through Santa Fe rail yards on outskirts of Dodge City.
1:33 (0:00) Arriving Dodge City, note two white sundials made of stones on right and next to station, one representing Central Time, the other Mountain. Today, actual time zone boundary is some 60 miles west of here.

DODGE CITY, KS - Although it had early beginnings as an army outpost and later a fort, it was not really established as a town until 1872 when the Santa Fe Railroad arrived. Then, millions of Texas longhorns were driven for loading and Dodge City became "Cowboy Capital of the World."

The law was slow to arrive, however, and its nickname soon changed to "Wickedest Little City in America." It is said the term "Red Light District" was first used in Dodge. Headlights on locomotives were fair game for a rowdy citizenry, and train crews departing at night would not light them until the trains were safely out of town. Conditions were once so bad that the Army asked the State to spend money protecting its troops from "the meaner element." Both Bat Masterson and Wyatt Earp served as sheriff here, and Boot Hill became famous as the gunfighter's final resting place.

0:00 (0:42) Departing Dodge City, on right, exterior of First National Bank and Trust Co. sports giant mural depicting a stagecoach being drawn by six horses—just in case there's any question about what part of the world you are in. Then, town's rebuilt Front Street is on other side of fence, on right, catering to tourists anxious to sense part of the Old West.

0:06 (0:36) On hill beyond highway to right, tracks of old Santa Fe Trail are still visible.

0:12 (0:30) Here on right, about five miles east of Cimarron, can be seen snake-like mounds of Soule Canal which are all that remain of an early-day attempt at irrigation. A sixty-mile, hand-dug ditch was started to carry water from nearby Arkansas River to Spearville east of Dodge City, but was ultimately abandoned.

0:16 (0:26) Through Cimarron where Santa Fe Trail made its crossing of Arkansas River. Much of our route follows this historic way west.

0:17 (0:25) On right, handsome Warren Ranch raises Herefords, adding to nation's supply of beef. Note large concrete-lined pits beyond highway which store ensilage. Tree-lined Arkansas River is off to left.

0:21 (0:21) More evidence that this is cattle country is seen on right, where huge Ingalls Feed Yard is positioned on slopes that permit important drainage. Several thousand head are fed here each year.

0:42 (0:00) Arrive Garden City.

GARDEN CITY, KS - A lot of "largests" are in this small Kansas community. One of the world's largest natural gas fields and Kansas' largest buffalo herd are near here. An annual Industry, Irrigation and Implement Show in late June and a concrete municipal swimming pool both claim to be the largest of their kinds in the world.

In 1929, before nighttime flying was commonplace, Garden City played an important role in an imaginative coast-to-coast travel option offered by three transportation companies. Passengers could travel by rail between New York and Cleveland on the New York Central's Southwestern Ltd., by plane from Cleveland to Garden City on Universal Air, and by train between Garden City and Los Angeles aboard the Santa Fe's California Ltd. The trip took three nights and two days.

0:00 (1:13) Depart Garden City.

0:06 (1:07) Holcomb is easily identified by city standpipe decorated with horns of longhorn steer, an animal that could endure arid southwestern ranges and was foundation of U.S. cattle industry in 1800s. This is also locale for murders Truman Capote described in his book *In Cold Blood*. Two drifters broke into the H. W. Clutter farmhouse looking for money and wound up killing four family members.

0:31 (0:42) Watch for fields of sunflowers in this part of The Sunflower State. No longer considered a pesky weed, plants are grown for their seeds and also used as cattle feed.

0:50 (0:23) Leave Kansas and enter Colorado.

The State of Kansas had guaranteed the Santa Fe a grant of three million acres, comprised of all odd-numbered sections ten miles either side of its tracks, if Colorado was reached by March 1, 1873. The Santa Fe almost lost this valuable asset when, in December 1872, construction crews mistakenly stopped four miles east of here thinking they had reached the border. When a government surveyor pointed out the mistake, the crews hurriedly pulled up four miles of sidings for the necessary materials and finished the job.

0:56 (0:17) Cross Arkansas River.

This portion of the stream once formed the boundary between Mexico and the United States. Its headwaters are high in the Colorado Rockies near Leadville. From there it flows through the Royal Gorge, out of the mountains at Pueblo, across southeastern Colorado and southwestern Kansas, then through Tulsa, Oklahoma and Little Rock, Arkansas before joining the Mississippi River—a 1,450-mile trip. The river is actually named for a tribe of Indians, rather than the state.

1:13 (0:00) Arrive Lamar where statue known as The Madonna of the Trail commemorates pioneer mothers of the covered wagon days, on left.

In the 1920s, a Daughter of the American Revolution and Harry Truman, then a Missouri county judge, jointly petitioned Congress for an endorsement that would commemorate America's well-known pioneer trails. The National Old Trails Road designation was the outcome, and included such routes as the National Pike and the Santa Fe Trail. Twelve identical statues were commissioned to honor the pioneer women who faced the trails' hardships and were placed at appropriate spots along the Old Trails Road. Lamar was one of those honored places.

The monuments were cast by sculptor August Leimbach of St. Louis, and contain granules of marble, granite and lead ore which give the statues a subdued texture. The mother holds an infant in her left arm, a rifle barrel in her right hand while another child clutches at her skirts.

LAMAR, CO - Ravaged by sand and dust storms in the early thirties, careful conservation efforts have allowed Lamar to become the trading center of southeastern Colorado with cattle and grain important to its economy. Large, shallow lakes nearby make it the "Goose Hunting Capital of America."

The major employer in Lamar is Neo-

Southwest Chief - Garden City, Kansas
JACK SWANSON

plan, a German-owned bus manufacturing firm. The plant can produce up to four buses per day, and is the tallest building in town. It can be seen some distance to the north (right) of the tracks.

0:00 (0:43) Depart Lamar.

0:09 (0:34) John Martin Dam, on right, backs up Arkansas, creating John Martin Reservoir. Dam was constructed during the 1930s as a flood control and irrigation project by Army Corps of Engineers. Firm that contracted for this work was same one that built Panama Canal's locks. Watch for herons, cranes and other waterfowl.

0:21 (0:22) Brick buildings clustered amidst trees, on right, are Fort Lyon Veterans Administration Hospital and National Cemetery. Old Fort Lyon housed a regiment of soldiers whose job was to protect trappers and traders from Indian attacks. Kit Carson died at Fort Lyon in 1868 due to complications from an arrow wound in his shoulder.

0:22 (0:21) Cross Purgatoire River, so-named by French, but earlier called El Rio de las Animas Perdidas (River of Lost Souls) by Spanish. American frontiersmen, however, cared for neither title and called it Picketwire.

0:32 (0:11) If you look sharply, you may be able to spot Bent's Old Fort just across the river, back to right and through trees. It's hard to see though.

The fort controlled the mountain fur trade in the early 1800s, and served wagon traffic along the Santa Fe Trail. As many as 60 persons worked at the fort during its peak.

When the fort's owner William Bent tried to sell it to the Government, the U.S. wouldn't meet his purchase price of $16,000. Piqued over this rebuff, he leveled it with explosives. Later the remains became a stop for Barlow and Sanders stages. Today it is a near-perfect replica of the original fort, having been meticulously restored by the National Park Service.

0:43 (0:00) Arrive LaJunta (pronounced LaHunta).

LAJUNTA, CO - Kit Carson once lived in this southern Colorado town that now serves as divisional headquarters for the Santa Fe Railroad. Situated in the fertile Arkansas River Valley, numerous fruit, melon and vegetable crops are grown in the area—perhaps best-known is the famous Rocky Ford cantaloupe.

Highly regarded Koshare Indian dancers, who are really not Indians but local Explorer Scouts, have preserved Koshare dances throughout the years and have given performances from coast to coast.

0:00 (1:15) Depart LaJunta and leave river valley, swinging southwestward through a patchwork of buttes and prairies called Comanche National Grassland. Santa Fe's Pueblo branch forks off to right, following Arkansas River.

0:02 (1:13) Another preserved steam locomotive is in park-like setting on left, this time Number 1024.

1:00 (0:15) Prominent twin summits of West and East Spanish Peaks of Colorado Rockies can be seen on right. Indians once referred to these two mountains as "Breasts of the World."

1:15 (0:00) Arrive Trinidad.

TRINIDAD, CO - Established in 1859 at the base of the Culebra Range and on the Purgatoire River, Trinidad witnessed a period of unrest between Spanish and non-Hispanic settlers which finally reached a climax in the "Battle of Trinidad" on Christmas Day in 1867. After four days of skirmishing, Federal troops arrived and put an end to the open hostilities. The Old Baca House and Pioneer Museum have fine collections of frontier artifacts and antiques.

Trinidad has distinguished itself as the "Sex Change Capital of the World." Dr. Stanley Biber, a local physician, has performed well over 3,000 of these operations and has a world-wide clientele.

0:00 (1:04) Depart Trinidad and commence a climb of 1,563 feet within next 10 miles as Southwest Chief traverses scenic Raton Pass. Interstate 25 will now accompany train off and on until Albuquerque.

0:15 (0:49) Coal mines on right once furnished coal to both railroad and steel mills in Pueblo.

0:33 (0:31) Wootton Ranch buildings are on right, as well as portion of original Santa Fe Trail.

Richens Lacey "Uncle Dick" Wootton

was a Virginian-turned-Westerner who once hunted buffalo with Kit Carson for provisioning Bent's Fort. However, like Lucien Maxwell, he made part of his fortune by driving several thousand sheep (thought to be descended from a small band brought here by Coronado) to California's hungry Forty Niners in the Sacramento Valley.

He settled here and built a hotel and a 27-mile toll road over Raton Pass as part of the Santa Fe Trail, a venture that did quite well. All had to pay except Indians, Mexicans and posses chasing horse thieves. When the Santa Fe came through, he rejected the railroad's offer of $50,000 for his operation and asked only for a lifetime pass for his family and $25 per month in groceries.

0:38 (0:21) Train crests Raton Pass at an elevation of 7,588 feet—highest point on route between Chicago and Los Angeles. Cross Colorado state line and enter New Mexico by way of one-and-a-half-mile tunnel.

1:04 (0:00) Arrive at Raton at southern base of Raton Pass. On right, Spanish-style station with its pink-and-turquoise color scheme greets detraining passengers.

RATON, NM - Once known as Willow Springs, Raton was founded in the foothills of the Sangre de Cristo (Blood of Christ) Mountains and grew because of coal and the railroad. Livestock is now its economic mainstay.

0:00 (1:53) Depart Raton, then follow southeast boundary of historic Maxwell Land Grant for 62 miles.

The Maxwell Land Grant was huge—roughly three times the size of Rhode Island. To be precise, the grant totaled 1,714,764.94 acres, a holding that stretched from Springer, New Mexico well into southern Colorado.

Mexico originally granted the property to Carloz Beaubien and Guadalupe Miranda, but in 1864, Lucien Benjamin Maxwell, a frontier tycoon of sorts who had accumulated considerable wealth through shrewd and fortuitous dealings, bought the property, only to later lose it when gold was found on his land. Unable to keep the discovery a secret, and tired of fighting off claim jumpers, he sold it all, invested

the proceeds in a railroad and a bank—and lost everything.

0:41 (1:12) At Springer depart from Canadian River and cross Cimarron River. High mountain to right is 12,440-foot Baldy Peak.

1:02 (0:51) Small town of Wagon Mound is named for landmark butte of Santa Fe Trail off to left.

1:31 (0:21) Pass through canyon country where willows and cottonwoods, along with stubby pinon pines, embroider creek bottoms. Just before Watrous, watch for ruins of Fort Union on hillside on left. This historic outpost once guarded old Santa Fe Trail and easier-but-more-Indian-exposed Cimarron cutoff.

1:43 (0:10) Just six miles north of here is Montezuma.

In 1879, Jesse James spent a month there at the Old Adobe House hotel while inquiring about the sheep business and other opportunities. Soon afterwards, The Santa Fe put a spur to the property and erected a luxurious hostelry called Montezuma Hot Springs Hotel and Sanitarium. The 268-room Queen Anne-style castle pampered railroad-traveling tourists for years before finally declining into disuse. In 1982, no less than England's Prince Charles and financier Armand Hammer transformed the former spa into a unique half-high school, half-college with students from around the world. Known as the United World of the American West, it teaches appreciation and tolerance of cultures and political differences of others.

1:47 (0:06) Forward on right, at some distance, are higher peaks of Sangre de Cristos.

1:53 (0:00) Arrive Las Vegas. Note Castaneda Hotel just before station on right. This building, with its tiled roof and arched facade, was part of original Harvey House system of hotels and restaurants along the Santa Fe.

Harvey, himself, was dining here one evening in 1883, when a band of drunken cowhands rode their horses into the dining room and began shooting bottles on display behind the bar, swearing loudly and demanding food. Calmly, Harvey stood up and in a cool but authoritarian voice said, "Gentlemen, ladies are dining here. No swearing or foul language is permitted. You must leave quietly at once." They did just that. Fred Harvey later bought them all lunches, but insisted they wear jackets (which the hotel was always prepared to offer if their guests could not furnish their own).

In 1899, Colonel Theodore Roosevelt arrived by train to rejoin his Rough Riders for their first reunion which was held in this hostelry. This also served as a setting for the movie *Red Dawn* in 1983.

LAS VEGAS, NM - Although in the 1830s a Mexican land grant gave rise to the first permanent settlement of Las Vegas, Coronado probably first visited this region in 1541. The Santa Fe Trail made Las Vegas important regionally, but with the arrival of the railroad in 1879, the town became the major shipping point for the entire Southwest.

0:00 (1:47) Upon departing Las Vegas, an interesting railroad roundhouse appears momentarily on right.

0:02 (1:45) On left, large "H" etched in hillside is for New Mexico Highlands University.

0:29 (1:18) Off to left and forward, Starvation Peak, appearing like a miniature volcano, is site of a supposed tragedy years ago. Supposedly 30 or 40 Spanish settlers, pursued by Navajos, climbed the peak and held off their attackers with rocks. Stories differ whether they then starved to death at the top, or descended because of lack of food, only to be massacred by their Indian foes. Fact or myth? Sign on left identifies its location as 2½ miles away.

0:38 (1:07) Dramatic double-S curve allows marvelous photo opportunities for those hoping to get shots of entire train, fore and aft.

0:50 (0:57) Cross Pecos River where old Spanish mission of San Miguel can be seen on left.

1:16 (0:31) At Rowe, Pecos National Monument is off to right, containing ruins of one of largest pueblos. Known as Cicuye, it had two four-story apartments, with each floor containing 500 rooms. These and other buildings, including a four-towered cathedral built after arrival of Spanish missionaries, supported a population of 20,000. By 1840 only 17 inhabitants were left. Plague and war, including revolt against Spanish, had decimated their people.

1:19 (0:28) Pinon, scrub oak and juniper contrast vividly with red-rock canyons in and around Glorieta. Twisting route through these dry washes offers more opportunities to view entire train.

1:25 (0:22) Glorieta is easily identified by Baptist Assembly's huge retreat building on right. One of West's few Civil War conflicts occurred at Glorieta Pass when Colorado Volunteers defeated Texas Confederates March 28, 1862.

1:42 (0:05) Southwest Chief seems to miss rocks by only foot or so while snaking through spectacular Apache Canyon, one of trip's highlights.

1:47 (0:00) Arriving Lamy, note Legal Tender saloon and restaurant on right, oldest structure (1881) in Lamy.

Restaurant is one of best in Santa Fe area, and has a fine collection of period American paintings and prints, including two works by renowned artist Thomas Moran. Hand-carved cherry wood bar was imported from Germany by first owner who operated premises as a saloon and general store. Building sports National Register of Historic Places plaque—and, supposedly, at least three ghosts.

LAMY, NM (SANTA FE) - Named for the first archbishop of Santa Fe, Lamy serves as Amtrak's stop for Santa Fe, 15 miles to the north. Originally, Santa Fe was supposed to be on the railroad's main line (after all, it was first called the Atchison, Topeka and Santa Fe Rail Road), but by the time the railroad reached New Mexico, Santa Fe had declined in importance as a trade center, and reaching it other than by a spur would pose difficult and expensive construction problems. Coal and timber availability were other reasons for placing the main line farther south. So only a branch was built in 1880 to the town that is the railroad's principal appellation. Sante Fe was the western terminus of the Santa Fe Trail and the railroad's arrival meant the trail would soon fade from scene.

A connecting shuttle van operates between here and Santa Fe, including stops

Southwest Chief - Apache Canyon, New Mexico
DICK WALTZ

at major hotels. This can be booked when train reservations are made.

Santa Fe epitomizes what many search for in the Southwest—charming Spanish architecture, a special sort of relaxed atmosphere, Indians selling beautifully crafted silver and turquoise on the town square, splendid art galleries, wonderful restaurants, and a special sort of relaxed atmosphere.

In about 20 years, Santa Fe will celebrate its 400th birthday. Coronado first explored New Mexico in 1540/42, and in 1610—ten years before the landing of Pilgrims at Plymouth Rock—Spain established Santa Fe as its Colonial Capital. The Palace of the Governors was the original place of government and is still in use today as a public building—the nation's oldest public structure.

Except for a brief period when an Indian uprising forced them to leave, the Spanish were in control until 1824. Santa Fe then came under Mexican jurisdiction until, in 1846, the Army of the West entered Santa Fe and claimed it (and New Mexico) for the United States.

Santa Fe's uniqueness is owed in large part to its architecture that reflects the city's roots. A strict building code was enacted in 1957 to assure its preservation.

It wasn't until the turn of the century that Santa Fe started to grow as an artists' colony. That trend continues even today, and the town is now second only to New York City in art dollars traded. Tourists flock to the galleries that are sequestered in almost every nook along the town's twisting, shaded streets.

 A connecting **Amtrak shuttle van** operates between Santa Fe and Lamy, a stop for the Southwest Chief. Reservations are preferred and can be made when making train reservations, or by calling (505) 982-8829, or writing Lamy Shuttle Service, 1476 Miracerros Loop N., Santa Fe, NM, 87501. The fare is $14 and stops can be provided at Santa Fe hotels. For Capital City **Cab and Village Taxi,** call 438-0000. **Municipal Airport** is nine miles southwest of the city and has limited service. **Albuquerque International Airport,** which serves Santa Fe, is about an hour's drive.

Santa Fe Convention and Visitors Bureau, 201 W. Marcy, Box 909, 87504; (505) 984-6760 or 800-777-CITY.

Most visitors to Santa Fe prefer to stay in a hotel that's near the Plaza. As a result, those accommodations tend to be more expensive than those outlying such as along the very commercial Cerrillos Rd. The Travelodge shown below is within walking distance of the Plaza and a good compromise for those not seeking atmosphere. The other hostelries all exude Santa Fe charm.

-**Travelodge Santa Fe,** 646 Cerrillos Rd., 87501; (505) 982-3551. One of Santa Fe's better motel bargains. Six blocks from the Plaza. $51.

-**Hotel St. Francis,** 210 Don Gaspar, 87501; (505) 983-5700 or 800-666-5700. Comfortably renovated landmark, with antique furnishings. National Register of Historic Places. Afternoon tea in the lobby; excellent dining room. Just 1½ blocks from the Plaza. $90.

-**LaFonda,** 100 E. San Francisco, 87504; (505) 982-5511 or 800-523-5002. Literally "The Inn at the End of the Santa Fe Trail." Historic Santa Fe centerpiece; the only hotel on the Plaza. $130.

-**LaPosada de Santa Fe,** 330 E. Palace Ave., 87501; (505) 986-0000 or 800-727-5276. Individual casitas throughout six acres of landscaping. Many rooms with Spanish fireplaces. Both indoor and outdoor dining. Two long blocks from the Plaza. Some rooms as low as $98.

-**Grant Corner Inn,** 122 Grant Ave., 87501; (505) 983-6678. One of Santa Fe's most popular bed and breakfasts, well-managed and attractively furnished. About three blocks from the Plaza (also, condo units farther out). As low as $60.

Santa Fe is the mecca of **Southwestern art.** Galleries are throughout the city, many clustered in the center of town near the Plaza while the greatest number line nearby Canyon Road. Perhaps the best known art market in Santa Fe takes place under the canopy in front of the Palace of the Governors where Indian artisans spread their silver and turquoise jewelry on the public sidewalk.

Southwestern food is served in a variety of styles, depending on the restaurant you choose—hot, mild, spicy, not-so-spicy—for almost any palate. Ask locally for guidance.

Several fine museums are in Santa Fe. Two of the best are on the Plaza: the **Museum of Fine Arts** with changing exhibits of contemporary and historic art, both Southwest and American; and the **Palace of the Governors,** housing exhibits of New Mexico history.

Three outstanding museums are grouped together in the southeast suburbs: the **Museum of International Folk Art,** boasting the world's largest collection of international folk art; the **Museum of Indian Arts & Culture,** highlighting the traditions and culture of regional Native Americans: and the **Wheelwright Museum of the American Indian Cultures.**

Several old churches and missions are near the center of the city, including: **San Miguel Chapel,** originally constructed in the 1600s, but rebuilt in 1710; **Santuario de Guadalupe,** an 18th-century mission; **Loretto Chapel;** and **St. Francis Cathedral.**

0:00 (1:03) Depart Lamy.

0:06 (0:57) Final look at Sangre de Cristo Mountains is afforded, back on right. Former ranch of folk singer Burl Ives is off to left.

0:07 (0:56) Los Cerrillos, freshly painted in 1988 for Hollywood's film *Young Guns,* passes by.

0:27 (0:36) Note front of Santa Domingo Trading Post, on right, attractively adorned with Indian designs.

0:29 (0:34) Santa Domingo Pueblo, where beehive-shaped ovens are apparent, is at right. Pueblo dates back to 16th century.
0:36 (0:27) Pass by Pueblo of San Filipe Indian Reservation. Here, vivid mural adorning side of church, on right, presents a startling visual contrast with its colorless surroundings.
0:50 (0:13) Sandia Peak, rising to 10,768 feet on left, is eastward buttress of Rio Grande Valley as train approaches Albuquerque.
1:03 (0:00) Arriving Albuquerque, golden globe perched atop tower of Federal Office Building is distinctive feature of downtown skyline on right. Also, University of New Mexico dormitories can be seen on left.

ALBUQUERQUE, NM - Located in the fertile Rio Grande Valley and protected from severe weather by the Sandia Peaks to the east, Albuquerque enjoys a pleasant year-round climate with an ample quantity of sunshine during the winter months.

Albuquerque rightfully claims to be one of America's oldest inland cities. It was in 1706, seventy years before the American Revolution, that a handful of Spanish settled in what is now called "Old Town."

Paradoxically, most of the city's growth has been new. It is the trading and industrial center of New Mexico with industries ranging from nuclear research to the large Santa Fe railroad shops.

Amtrak Station, 314 First St. SW (at First and Lead). January 4, 1993 the former Southwestern style station burned and Amtrak is now considering its replacement.

Native American artisans usually sell jewelry at trainside (but be sure to ask where the jewelry was made).

Cab stand is at the station; Yellow Cab, 247-8888. Budget offers pick-up and drop-off service at the station for **rental car** customers, (505) 768-5900. **Local buses** through downtown, two blocks from the station at Third and Gold; call Sun Tran, 843-9200. **Greyhound/ Trailways** terminal, 300 Second St. SW, is immediately across the street from the former station. **Albuquerque International Airport** is three miles south of the city.

Albuquerque Convention and Visitors Bureau, Box 26866, 121 Tijeras NE, 87125; (505) 243-3696 or 800-284-2282.

La Posada de Albuquerque, 125 2nd St. NW, 87102; (505) 242-9090 or 800-777-5732. Popular, comfortable Southwestern-style hotel. Complimentary full breakfast. Conveniently located on the edge of the central business district, just four blocks from the station. $88.

-Friendship Inn, 717 Central Ave. NW, 87102; (505) 247-1501 or 800-424-4777. On the edge of the central business district. Free shuttle to and from the station, about one mile. $40.

-W. E. Mauger Bed & Breakfast, 701 Roma Ave., 87102; (505) 242-8755. Three-story restored Queen Anne, on the edge of downtown. Eight rooms, each with private bathroom (showers). About a mile from the station. $55-105.

Downtown Albuquerque, with many shops and restaurants, is at the station's doorstep.

An alternative to the standardized stores and restaurants of downtown, **Old Town** is about two miles from the downtown area. This was the first settlement of Albuquerque. Shops and restaurants around a gas-lit plaza offer unique shopping and dining. San Felipe de Neri Church was built in 1793; mass has been held here on an uninterrupted basis since its completion.

The **Museum of Albuquerque** has exhibits of science, history and art; about three blocks northeast of Old Town Plaza, between Mountain Road and Old Town Road. It can be easily reached by walking from the plaza.

Indian Pueblo Cultural Center, 2401 12th NW, is owned and operated by the 19 Indian Pueblos of New Mexico. There are shops with arts and crafts, a museum, a restaurant and dancers. A **visitors center** is also located here.

The **National Atomic Museum,** located on the grounds of Kirtland Air Force Base, has exhibits, movies and tours that focus on the Manhattan Project. This highly secretive development of the first atomic bomb was centered in New Mexico.

Sandia Peak Aerial Tram, the world's

Legend:
- Amtrak Station
- 1 - Visitors Information
- 2 - Indian Pueblo Cultural Center
- 3 - Old Town
- 4 - University of New Mexico
- 5 - Museum of Albuquerque
- 6 - National Atomic Museum
- 7 - La Posada de Albuquerque
- 8 - Friendship Inn & Mauger B&B

Albuquerque

longest at 2.7 miles, takes visitors to the top of 10,378-foot Sandia Peak in 20 minutes, where expansive views of Albuquerque and the Rio Grande Valley are afforded. Restaurants are at both the base and the summit.

In early October, Albuquerque is host to its biggest event, the renowned **International Balloon Fiesta.** Over 500 hot-air balloons from around the world take part for this nine-day extravaganza. If you plan to attend, make hotel reservations early.

0:00 (2:20) Departing Albuquerque, farmlands of Rio Grande Valley soon give way to arid terrain of Southwestern desert.
0:02 (2:18) On left, pass University of New Mexico's sports stadium.
0:04 (2:16) Grounds of Rio Grande Park and Zoo are visible in distance on right.
0:09 (2:11) Manzano Mountains protrude above horizon on left, while Ladron Peak (9,176 feet) is most prominent member of Ladron Mountains on right. New Mexican

ranges represent subclassification of much larger range known as Rocky Mountains.
0:13 (2:07) Cross Rio Grande River.
0:14 (2:06) Handsome mission stands proudly amidst Isleta Indian Reservation on left.
0:26 (1:54) At railroad junction of Dalies, train intersects with "main line," and proceeds westerly across desert landscape, its mystic beauty now further enhanced by a dramatic intrusion of mesas and buttes. An early cradle of Western civilization, area has spawned a vast historical legacy with elements of Indian, Spanish and Frontier cultures all colorfully assimilated into lifestyles and livelihoods of modern-day New Mexicans.
0:28 (1:52) Peak seen in distance on right is Mt. Taylor, named for President Zachary Taylor and nobly presiding at 11,301 feet.
0:34 (1:46) Cross Rio Puerco which flows into Rio Grande a few miles downstream. Also at this time, embark on a gradual 3,000-foot ascent that culminates atop Continental Divide outside Thoreau.

0:48 (1:32) Pass under wooden trestle that supports historic "Route 66."

0:51 (1:29) "Kneeling Nuns," who appear to be praying before a stone altar, is appropriate title of rock formation on right.

0:54 (1:26) Stark gypsum cliffs border on right as train passes through grounds of Mesita Pueblo. Some primitive buildings seen here on left have been inhabited by as many as five generations of same family.

0:55 (1:25) Join small San Jose River on left which train crosses several times over next few miles.

0:58 (1:22) Pass through Laguna Pueblo. As in other pueblos, anthill pilings are frequently spread across rooftops of these adobe structures in deference to their unique watershedding capabilities.

1:02 (1:18) Venerable mission of Acoma Indians is most prominent fixture of Acomita Pueblo, on left.

1:08 (1:12) Picturesquely poised atop bluff on left, resplendent two-centuries-old mission at McCartys Pueblo is reputedly built upon foundation of earlier Franciscan mission. Mission is part of Acoma Indian Reservation.

1:11 (1:09) Exposed lava beds lining trackside on left reflect early volcanic nature of aforementioned Mt. Taylor.

1:20 (1:00) At Grants, importance of uranium mining is evidenced by profusion of gouged hillsides surrounding community.

1:23 (0:57) On right, note large Anaconda uranium smelter.

1:52 (0:28) Imperceptibly, cross Campbell's "Pass" and Continental Divide where waters behind us flow to Atlantic and waters ahead run to Pacific.

2:12 (0:08) Pyramid Rock and spire-crowned Church Rock appear on right.

2:13 (0:07) Structures and storage mounds of Ft. Wingate Army Depot are on right. Fort was originally established near San Rafael in 1862 as a base for Kit Carson's campaign against the Navajos. Garrison was transferred to this site in 1868.

2:14 (0:06) Cliffs on right are part of Red Rock State Park, site of annual Gallup Intertribal Indian Ceremonial where tribes from around the country gather each August for ceremonial dancing and rodeo competition. Then, elaborate workings of El Paso Natural Gas refinery come into view on right.

2:18 (0:01) About ¾ mile east of Gallup's station is venerable El Rancho Hotel, on left. Built in 1937 by brother of movie magnate D. W. Griffith to house actors for Westerns (frequently filmed in region); its guests included John Wayne, Humphrey Bogart, Lucille Ball, Tom Mix and Ronald Reagan. After slipping into bankruptcy in 1987, it was restored and reopened the following year.

2:20 (0:00) Arrive Gallup's inter-modal train station, remodeled in 1988 at a cost of 1.6 million dollars.

GALLUP, NM - Hopi, Navajo and Zuni Indians all live in and around Gallup, and these native Americans comprise more than half of the town's population. Here, visitors can find beautiful silver jewelry, baskets, rugs and pottery in numerous large trading posts, and just east a few miles, the famous Intertribal Ceremonial is held at Red Rock State Park.

Gallup is also a gateway to the Four Corners region (where New Mexico, Arizona, Colorado and Utah make a unique four-state convergence) and Mesa Verde National Park, 150 miles to the north, where ancient Anasazi cliff dwellings can be visited.

0:00 (1:41) Depart Gallup.

0:20 (1:21) Pass beneath I-40, and enter Arizona and southern protrusion of Navajo Indian Reservation.

At Arizona border, enter Pacific Time Zone. Since Arizona does not observe daylight saving time, set your watch back (forward if eastbound) one hour, if rest of country is currently on daylight saving time.

0:32 (1:09) At Sanders, tracks exit Navajo Indian Reservation.

0:56 (0:45) Cross through neck of hour-glass-shaped Petrified Forest National Park. This stark country was heavily wooded 150 million years ago. Now, giant agatized logs and smaller fragments lie scattered throughout area forming world's largest and most colorful concentration of petrified wood. Colorful soils of Painted Desert lend added drama to landscape, particularly when sun is near horizon.

1:14 (0:27) Through Holbrook, one of northern Arizona's larger ranching and trading centers, and former important "gas stop" on legendary Route 66. Little Colorado River follows on left until just before Winslow, when stream swings northwest toward its juncture with Colorado River at eastern end of Grand Canyon.

1:22 (0:19) Electric generating station at right consumes about four carloads of coal each hour to keep much of Southwest supplied with energy.

1:41 (0:00) Arrive Winslow.

WINSLOW, AZ - Another trading center for Navajos and Hopis, Winslow sometimes goes by the nickname "Meteor City." Twenty miles west of town is Meteor Crater, a 4,000-foot-wide, 600-foot-deep hole created when an enormous meteorite, traveling at incredible speed, struck the earth 20,000 years ago.

0:00 (1:02) Depart Winslow.

0:29 (0:33) Cross Canyon Diablo on 560-foot steel bridge, 225 feet above creek's bed. This was one of railroad's major hurdles in its march westward. Original bridge took 15 months to construct and was started on site long before tracks reached this mini-gorge, bridge sections being freighted from railhead using mule power.

0:53 (0:10) San Francisco Peaks, tall mountains right forward, rise to 12,670 feet above sea level and are home to the Hopi Kachinas and Snow Bowl ski area.

1:02 (0:00) Arrive Flagstaff.

FLAGSTAFF, AZ - On the nation's 100th birthday, celebrants stripped a pine tree of its branches so that it could serve as a staff for the country's flag. The site was near a spring and frequently served as a camping spot for California-bound travelers—who soon began to refer to it by its present name. This is the stop for Amtrak passengers visiting the Grand Canyon, with bus connections to and from the station. (Buses leave Flagstaff early in the morning and return late that evening.) Other major attractions include nearby Oak Creek Canyon, Lowell Observatory (responsible for the discovery of the planet Pluto), skiing (Flagstaff's elevation is 6,900 feet) and the fine Museum of Northern Arizona,

with its many Indian artifacts and books about the Southwest.

Amtrak Thruway Bus service is available between Flagstaff and the Grand Canyon as well as Sedona and Phoenix.

0:00 (2:56) Depart Flagstaff.

0:44 (2:12) Rumble across intersection with Grand Canyon Railway, just north of Williams from where seasonal steam train excursion service to Grand Canyon is available.

1:37 (1:39) Through Seligman, established in 1882 at the junction of the Santa Fe's main line and a line to Prescott.

Seligman still gets much of its support from railroad facilities. Tourism is important because of the town's strategic location on Interstate 40 and its Grand Canyon proximity. Cattle ranches provide a wide trading market. Expansion of U.S. Lime Company's mine, 25 miles west, has given the town additional stimulus.

2:56 (0:00) Arrive Kingman.

KINGMAN, AZ - Like Seligman, Kingman was established in 1882 along the Santa Fe's main line. Throughout the sparsely settled West, towns had a propensity to sprout along the tracks, quite unlike the East where railroads were built to serve existing population centers.

0:00 (1:01) Depart Kingman.

Pass from Mountain to Pacific Time as train crosses Colorado River and Arizona state line into California. Since Arizona does not observe daylight saving time, set watch back (forward if eastbound) one hour only if rest of country is not currently on daylight saving time.

1:01 (0:00) Arrive Needles.

NEEDLES, CA - California's easternmost city is located in the arid Mojave Desert, where temperatures frequently are the highest in the nation. Named for a group of nearby rock pinnacles, Needles was first a railroad way station, then a mining town, and finally a city of pipeline companies and tourist industries. Fred Harvey once broke with tradition and used male waiters at Needles Harvey House, since he felt town too bawdy for his prim and proper waitresses.

0:00 (2:31) Depart Needles.

2:19 (0:12) Water-filled tower on right is focus of 1,818 huge mirrors which continually track sun, creating steam for nation's first solar electric facility.

2:20 (0:11) Vast array of military equipment is stockpiled alongside warehouses of Marine Logistics Base Annex on right. Main facilities are located in nearby Barstow.

2:21 (0:10) Passing through Daggett, note two historic structures on right. Venerable 1880s Stone Hotel (also made of stone) was home-away-from-home for Death Valley Scotty, who continuously reserved room #7 (with private entrance) for his personal use. To west on corner, Scott's Market was popular spot for miners to convert "high grade" into spendable currency. Destroyed by fire in 1908, reconstructed market become first fireproof building in desert.

2:31 (0:00) Arrive Barstow.

On the right, "Casa del Desierto" (House of the Desert) is appropriately enscribed across the facade of a grandiose structure next to the station. Extensively damaged by a 1991 earthquake, the structure is undergoing restoration and should house retail shops when completed. This old building was originally a Harvey House—another of those elegant eateries and hotels that once stretched along the Santa Fe. Fred Harvey's restaurants became legendary for good food—many thought it the best in the country—and pretty waitresses, in what was an otherwise wild and wooly West.

Prior to 1876, the year Harvey opened his first restaurant in Florence, Kansas, rail passengers were forced to endure inedible meals foisted on them by the railroad at trackside greasy spoons. (Dining cars were yet to come!) Seeing what he thought was a great opportunity, Harvey sold his idea of fine food in a pleasant atmosphere to the Santa Fe and acquired exclusive rights to establish diners along their entire line. Both parties prospered as passengers soon chose to ride the Santa Fe because of Fred Harvey's restaurants.

BARSTOW, CA - Originally founded as a way station along the old Santa Fe Trail, Barstow has emerged as an important distribution lifeline, strategically located at the crossroads of two major interstates and railroads. Large military installations and a healthy tourist trade further bolster the city's burgeoning economy.

Barstow, too, enjoys a share in technology. Located here is NASA's Goldstone Tracking Station, a vital communications link for orbiting satellites and deep space probes.

An interesting attraction is the Barstow Way Station, with exhibits emphasizing the ecological aspects of the high desert. As well, visitors have an opportunity to sample native plants once used by the Indians for food and medicine.

0:00 (1:42) Depart Barstow through awesome sprawl of Santa Fe's classification yards. Over next several miles onset of hillier terrain previews approach into San Bernardino Mountains.

0:21 (1:21) Just beyond peaks of Kramer Range on right lies Edwards Air Force Base, primary landing site of NASA's space shuttle.

0:25 (1:17) Elaborate maze of fences and paddocks is home to fine-looking horses on left.

0:29 (1:13) At Oro Grande, well-preserved steam locomotive is enshrined in town park on left.

0:33 (1:09) Towering facility crowding tracks on left is Victorville cement plant.

0:35 (1:07) Sudden rock outcroppings form scenic little canyon as train crosses Mojave River into Victorville. Once through town, begin ascent of Cajon Pass which will lift us out of the Mojave Desert. Noble joshua tree cactus is a prominent feature on northern climb, while spectacular rock formations line descent into San Bernardino.

0:42 (1:00) Another cement plant borders on right.

0:56 (0:46) Nearing Cajon summit, San Gabriel Mountains are prominent features to right, with San Bernardino Mountains off to left.

0:58 (0:44) Bid farewell to unconfining spaces of West and start dramatic descent of Cajon Pass into Los Angeles Basin.

Since 1885 when Santa Fe's predecessor, the California Southern, pushed the first rails over the 3,811-foot top, Cajon Pass has been one of railroading's more fascinating artifacts.

Three sets of tracks now descend Cajon. To the right is the Southern Pacific, the middle set is Santa Fe's steeper North Track, while on the left is Santa Fe's gentler but two-mile-longer South Track. Since a third railroad, the Union Pacific, has Cajon trackage rights on the Santa Fe, this can become a very busy place.

Westbound traffic on the Santa Fe will normally descend the three percent grade of the South Track (unless weight dictates the more moderate routing), while eastbound Santa Fe traffic will climb the "casual" 2.2% North Track.

1:05 (0:36) White flatiron-like Mormon Rocks are most prominent geographic feature on right. Infamous San Andreas Fault is nearby.

--- (0:31) Eastbound trains now curl through turn known as Sullivan's Curve, named after early-day railroad photographer.

1:16 (0:24) Two Santa Fe routes now become one again. Highway on left is Interstate 15, linking Los Angeles and Las Vegas.

1:22 (0:17) Entanglement of wire and steel bars, looking like a World War II beach defense, serves as breakwater to protect tracks from creek's occasional floodwaters.

1:26 (1:13) Passage beneath I-15 marks finish of Cajon Pass adventure.

1:37 (0:02) Approaching San Bernardino, lush woodlands, colorful shrubbery and majestic palms represent radical departure from environs of last 750 miles.

1:39 (0:00) Arrive San Bernardino. Railroad equipment is maintained within large Santa Fe shops on right while on left nicely landscaped grounds encircle vine-covered station.

SAN BERNARDINO, CA - Lying in the heart of fertile citrus country, San Bernardino was first settled in the mid-19th century by a group of Mormons who modeled the town after their former home of Salt Lake City. Adjoining San Bernardino is the inspiring Rim o' the World Highway, a splendid mountain drive leading to such popular vacation retreats as Lake Arrowhead and Big Bear Lake.

Big Mac connoisseurs should know that

McDonald's opened its first outlet in San Bernardino.

0:00 (1:03) Depart San Bernardino and traverse Riverside/Fullerton branch of Santa Fe.

0:09 (0:54) At Colton, elderly sheds of California Citrus Pulp operation line tracks on right.

0:17 (0:46) Through Riverside, home to March Air Force Base. Boarded up Santa Fe station on right is nostalgic relic of earlier years.

0:42 (0:21) Cross northern end of Santa Ana Mountains, and descend into congestion of southeastern Los Angeles. One last glimpse of San Gabriels is afforded to right where 10,064-foot Mt. San Antonio stands above all.

0:56 (0:07) At Orange Growers Association on left, seedling orange trees await transplantation.

1:00 (0:03) Clusters of attractive industrial parks comingled with residential areas precede arrival at Fullerton.

1:03 (0:00) Arrive Fullerton. Home of well-known Donald Duck citrus juices appears on right next to station. Santa Fe depot is a delight. Its pink stucco facade topped with a dark, red-tile roof is further enhanced by unusually large, arch-shaped windows and fine grillwork.

FULLERTON, CA - As you may have guessed from the citrus juice operation just mentioned, Fullerton has had its roots in the citrus industry. Los Angeles' growth to the south has now made Fullerton virtually indistinguishable from its much larger northern neighbor.

0:00 (0:34) Depart Fullerton.

0:03 (0:31) Perhaps more than one hundred assorted light aircraft at airport serving Fullerton area are in very midst of densely populated area on left.

0:09 (0:23) Pass through refinery operations and active oil wells of Santa Fe Springs. One of area's larger tank farms will soon be seen on right.

0:13 (0:21) Cross San Gabriel River.

0:15 (0:19) Cross Rio Hondo Channel.

0:19 (0:15) Office Building of Santa Fe Railroad on right marks beginning (southern edge) of Santa Fe rail yards.

0:22 (0:12) Acres of truck trailers used on piggyback freight trains are assembled on right at north end of yards.

0:25 (0:09) Train crosses Los Angeles River, then curls sharply right. Diesel shops, roundhouse and its companion turntable are on left where twenty or so Amtrak diesels can generally be counted.

0:27 (0:07) Amtrak coach yard is on immediate left where a gaggle of Superliner cars are stored and await service on trains such as Desert Wind, Sunset Ltd., Southwest Chief and Coast Starlight.

0:29 (0:05) Los Angeles River, encased in concrete on right, has followed our route for several minutes. Take note of old stone bridges that cross over tracks along this section. Their sculpted pilasters are reminiscent of ancient Rome and memorialize an era of Los Angeles long gone. Excellent view of Los Angeles' cityscape is on left where distinctive white-towered City Hall has center stage.

0:33 (0:01) Curl left off of main line of Santa Fe at Mission Tower.

0:34 (0:00) Arriving Los Angeles Union Station, Dodger Stadium rests atop hill off to right, then Los Angeles County Jail looms on left just before coming to stop at LAUS.

 LOS ANGELES, CA - See page 302.

Chicago
St. Louis
San Antonio
Dallas
Houston

Texas Eagle

From Chicago, the Texas Eagle travels to St. Louis through Abe Lincoln's central Illinois, on through the Ozarks to Little Rock, across eastern Texas to Dallas and Ft. Worth, then a final southward thrust to San Antonio. There is also a separate section that splits off at Dallas to serve Houston. Through coaches and sleepers are available to and from Los Angeles, by way of the Sunset Limited, three days each week.

When traveling from Chicago to Los Angeles, there is a four-hour layover at San Antonio in the middle of the night. Traveling from Los Angeles to Chicago the layover is one hour in the early morning.

Southbound Schedule (Condensed)
Chicago, IL - Late Afternoon Departure
Springfield, IL - Late Evening
St. Louis, MO - Late Evening
Little Rock, AR - Early Morning (2nd Day)
Dallas, TX - Midafternoon (2nd Day)
San Antonio, TX - Late Evening Arrival (2nd Day)
Houston, TX - Late Evening Arrival (2nd Day)*

Northbound Schedule (Condensed)
Houston, TX - Early Morning Departure*
San Antonio, TX - Early Morning Departure
Dallas, TX - Late Afternoon
Little Rock, AR - Late Evening
St. Louis, MO - Early Morning (2nd Day)
Springfield, IL - Midmorning (2nd Day)
Chicago, IL - Early Afternoon Arrival (2nd Day)

*By separate section to and from Dallas.
Frequency - Daily, between Chicago and St. Louis. Three times a week between St. Louis and San Antonio/Houston, departing St. Louis Sunday, Tuesday and Friday and departing San Antonio and Houston Sunday, Tuesday and Thursday.

Seating - Superliner coaches.
Dining - Complete meal and beverage service, Chicago-San Antonio. Lounge service with sandwiches, snacks and beverages, and movies, Chicago-San Antonio. Sandwiches and snacks, Dallas-Houston.
Sleeping - Superliner sleepers with deluxe, family, economy and special bedrooms.
Baggage - Checked baggage handled at larger cities.
Reservations - All-reserved train, except coach travel between Chicago and St. Louis.
Length of Trip - 1,308 miles in 30 hours (Chicago-San Antonio).

Route Log

 CHICAGO, IL - See page 128.

0:00 (0:43) Depart Chicago's venerable Union Station and emerge from beneath huge Chicago Post Office.
0:04 (0:51) Amtrak coach yards on right offer interesting variety of modern-day Amtrak equipment.

For forty minutes the sights of some of Chicago's more industrial environs will pass by as The Texas Eagle traverses through rail yards and past power plants, refineries and assorted manufacturing facilities, before finally entering rural Illinois.
0:06 (0:35) Cross South Branch Chicago River, then turn west following Sanitary

and Ship Canal out of city. Illinois has more active miles of canals than any other state. Stevenson Expressway briefly accompanies tracks on left.

0:15 (0:28) Chicago's dynamic skyline is now clearly visible back on right.

0:21 (0:22) Illinois Central freight yards stretch along route on left.

0:28 (0:15) Rumble over Calumet Sag Canal connecting Chicago Sanitary and Ship Canal with Lake Michigan—an engineering feat that reversed flow of Chicago River so that it now flows out of Lake Michigan.

0:37 (0:06) Note towpath along banks of Illinois and Michigan Canal, on right.

0:40 (0:03) On left are dreary walls of Joliet Correctional Center.

0:43 (0:00) Arrive Joliet.

JOLIET, IL - Joliet's economy is dominated largely by manufacturing and refining, developed largely due to its strategic rail and waterway location.

0:00 (0:50) Depart Joliet.

0:06 (0:44) Size of cavernous limestone quarry on left is brought into perspective by focusing on huge trucks at bottom.

0:13 (0:37) Earthen mounds (in distance through trees) are actually munitions storage bunkers of U.S. Army Arsenal.

0:17 (0:33) Cross Kankakee River.

0:22 (0:28) Large windowless structure with two enormous "silos" is Commonwealth Edison's Briarwood Nuclear Power Station. Golf course on left rests on reclaimed coal strip mine.

0:34 (0:16) As train enters Dwight, small white church with spire-like steeple is Pioneer Gothic Church where Prince of Wales attended services in 1860. Travel down Main Street of Dwight where rambling old depot on right dates back to 1892. Designed by Henry Ives Cobbs, designer of first buildings of University of Illinois, it was considered finest between Chicago and St. Louis. Just beyond, across West Main Street, is one-story brick structure with clock on top. This is one of three banks designed by Frank Lloyd Wright, and only one still standing. Two doors to right of that is a state hospital, originally a fine hotel. Its lights were first turned on by Teddy Roosevelt while making a brief stop here in 1903. Then on

left, magnificent windmill, built in 1896 to supply water to a private estate, is Dwight's pride. Tower houses an 88-barrel cypress tank, while 3,000-pound fan wheel was constructed in Argentina to replace original which was broken by a 1975 storm.

0:50 (0:00) Arrive Pontiac.

PONTIAC, IL - Pontiac is primarily an agriculturally oriented trading and distribution center.

0:00 (0:31) Depart Pontiac. (Northbound Texas Eagle does not stop here.)

0:25 (0:06) Pass under Interstate 55 and enter outskirts of Normal. Archaic, institutional buildings off to right once housed Illinois Soldiers' and Sailors' Children's School, but now stand vacant.

0:27 (0:04) Watterson Towers, impressive twin high rises on right, are dormitories of Illinois State University; campus lies just beyond.

0:31 (0:00) Arrive Bloomington.

BLOOMINGTON, IL - This is the birthplace of former vice president Adlai E. Stevenson and the site of Abraham Lincoln's "Lost Speech" which launched him toward the presidency. Once dependent on coal mining, the Bloomington-Normal area now has a much broader based economy, boasting facilities of several well-known companies, including the corporate headquarters of State Farm Insurance. This is also the home of Illinois State University, with an enrollment of 1,900—the state's first public institution of higher learning. Illinois Wesleyan University also provides courses for 1,650 students. Of interest is the Hudelson Museum of Agriculture and The Original American Passion Play presented each spring.

0:00 (0:30) Depart Bloomington.

0:27 (0:00) Arrive Lincoln.

LINCOLN, IL - First town to be named in honor of Abraham Lincoln, an historical marker in the shape of a watermelon on the grounds of Lincoln's old Chicago & Alton Depot, just to the left, marks the spot where he christened the city "Lincoln" in 1853—with watermelon juice. Amtrak station is glass enclosure just south of depot. Chamber of Commerce

Texas Eagle - Belt Junction, Texas
HOMER R. HILL

occupies north end of depot, utilizing two old cabooses for most unusual entryway. Domed building, a block to the left, is Logan County Courthouse.

0:00 (0:30) Depart Lincoln.

0:32 (0:00) Arrive Springfield where the capitol complex is dominated by the awesome State Capitol Building directly to the right. Ground was broken for construction in 1886 where its massive dome and rotunda now rest on bedrock. Multi-columned building midway between train and Capitol is State Supreme Court Building.

SPRINGFIELD, IL - In 1837, the state capital moved to Springfield, and simultaneously a circuit-riding Abraham Lincoln decided to settle here and opened his law office. Also, the only home he ever owned is about five blocks east of the tracks. The Lincoln Depot, where he delivered his famous "Farewell Address" before departing for Washington in 1861, is also a few blocks east of the present Amtrak route. Also of interest is the Old State Capitol, a painstakingly restored Greek Revival structure where the legislature met when the capital was first moved to Springfield. Lincoln delivered his "House Divided" speech here. The current capitol building is also open to visitors and has regular tours.

0:00 (0:37) Depart Springfield.

0:08 (0:29) Cross tip of beautiful Lake Springfield where attractive homes of Springfield's more affluent suburbanites can be seen nestled in trees on left.

0:21 (0:16) Pretty little Virden golf course adjoins tracks on left.

0:37 (0:00) Arrive Carlinville. Southbound stop only.

CARLINVILLE, IL - At one time this agricultural center had aspirations of becoming the state capital. It was hoped the silver-spired Greek Revival county courthouse (off to the left about three blocks) would house the state's young legislature, but Carlinville was never selected, and extreme cost overruns infuriated the citizenry.

But the town lays claim to something of a more lasting consequence—the largest assemblage of Sears Roebuck mail order homes. Between 1909 and 1937, Sears sold 100,000 precut houses that arrived by train, ready for assembly, even including the fixtures. Segments arrived to coincide with construction schedules with the paint arriving last. These "HonorBilt" homes ranged in price from a mere $595 to $5,000, depending on the degree of simplicity or amount of "elegance."

One hundred fifty-six of these were erected in Carlinsville's Standard Addition, a subdivision built by Indiana Standard for their coal miners. Today, nearly all are occupied and lovingly maintained.

0:00 (0:30) Depart Carlinville.

0:05 (0:25) Terrain becomes momentarily rolling and forested, suggesting the Mississippi River could be near.

0:30 (0:00) Arrive Alton.

ALTON, IL - Located on the mighty Mississippi River, across from St. Louis, this historic area was first visited by white men when, in 1673, Marquette and Joliet recorded a description of a bird-like monster painted on the river's cliffs below the present townsite. Lewis and Clark built their first camp and spent the winter here before making their great Northwest expedition.

In 1858, the seventh and last of the Lincoln-Douglas debates was held in Alton. During the Civil War this was a main supply point for the Union Army. The first Illinois state penitentiary was located here, and the world's tallest man, at eight feet eleven inches, was born, educated and buried in Alton. Two of the nation's corporate giants, Owens-Corning and The Olin Corporation, started here.

0:00 (0:40) Depart Alton.

0:07 (0:33) Cross Cahokia Diversion Canal whose banks have been built up to contain sometimes high waters of Mississippi.

0:10 (0:30) At Lenoe, parallel route of former "Wabash Cannonball," which ran from St. Louis to Detroit.

0:17 (0:23) Factory of renowned candymaker, Nestle, is on left.

0:18 (0:22) Industrialization, including foundries and other heavy industry, becomes more apparent as we near St. Louis.

0:23 (0:17) Train curls slowly to right as it prepares to cross great Mississippi River on Merchants Bridge.

0:24 (0:16) Now high over Mississippi an excellent view of St. Louis is afforded on left. Soaring Gateway Arch is clearly visible. At midstream we enter Missouri and leave Illinois.

0:27 (0:13) As train turns southward again, square brick spire of antique water tower still stands on hill to right.

0:32 (0:08) Gateway Arch and skyline forward on right create exciting approach to city.

0:34 (0:06) Pass under Martin Luther King Memorial Bridge and then Eads Bridge with fascinating steelwork. Bridge was completed in 1874 and designed by a self-educated engineer James Eads. Its spans were largest ever constructed at that time.

0:36 (0:04) Mississippi River sternwheeler can often be seen docked on left.

0:37 (0:03) Imposing Busch Memorial Stadium, home of baseball's Cardinals, is just to right.

0:40 (0:00) Arrive St. Louis, where passengers are greeted by 3-D murals on rose and white Thomas Edison Building, just east of the station.

ST. LOUIS, MO - Founded in 1764 by two French fur traders as a trading post, St. Louis grew rapidly into one of the most important cities in the Frontier West. Due to its location at the confluence of the Mississippi and Missouri rivers, it was readily accessible for river boat travel and farther exploration to the west. Lewis and Clark began their two-year expedition from this point. Railroad construction after the Civil War made St. Louis an even more dominant factor in the nation's development.

Today, the view of this metropolis of 2,400,000 is dramatized by perhaps one of the most striking and imaginative structures to be built in any American city, the Gateway Arch.

Amtrak Station, 550 South 16th Street. A small "temporary" (1978)

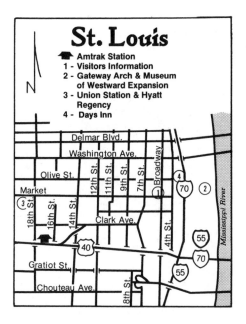

St. Louis

Amtrak Station
1 - Visitors Information
2 - Gateway Arch & Museum
of Westward Expansion
3 - Union Station & Hyatt
Regency
4 - Days Inn

facility located in an industrial area near downtown, between 15th and 16th, two blocks south of Clark (and a few blocks from the old Union Station). There are storage lockers and food and beverage vending machines. Free parking is adjacent to the station. For arrival and departure information, 331-3300.

Cab stand is at the station; Yellow Cab, 361-2345. Both Budget and Hertz have downtown **rental car** locations and will pick up and drop off customers at the station. Nearest **local bus** stop is four blocks from the station on Market Street, 231-2345. **Metrolink** is the city's new electric light rail system connecting downtown with East St. Louis and eventually the International Airport. **Lambert St. Louis International Airport is** 16 miles northwest of the station.

Convention and Visitors Commission, 10 S. Broadway, 63102; (314) 421-1023 or 800-247-9791. Funphone, call 421-2100.

All of the accommodations below are in the downtown or near-downtown area.

-**Hyatt Regency St. Louis,** St. Louis Union Station, 1820 Market; (314) 231-1234. A luxury hotel located in the original

Union Station. Five blocks from the Amtrak station. $119.

-**Drury Inn-Union Station,** 201 S. 20th St., 63103; (314) 231-3900. Nicely restored former railroad hotel on west side of Union Station, about seven blocks from the Amtrak station. $86.

-**Hampton Inn-Downtown,** 2211 Market St., 63103; (314) 241-3200. Two blocks west of Union Station, about eight blocks from the Amtrak station. $86.

-**Days Inn Downtown at the Arch,** 333 Washington Ave., 63102; (314) 621-7900. Directly across from Gateway Arch, in the heart of downtown. About two miles from the station. $69.

Gateway Arch, 11 North 4th Street, a magnificent 630-foot-high monument, the nation's highest. This fourth most attended man-made attraction in the world has trams at each of the two bases to carry passengers to an observation deck with an incredible view of the metropolitan area. Obtain tickets early to avoid being disappointed, since sellouts are frequent.

-**Museum of Westward Expansion,** underground beneath Gateway Arch, portrays early pioneering efforts.

-**St. Louis Union Station,** 1820 Market St., has been beautifully restored to accommodate shops, restaurants, and the Hyatt Regency Hotel. It's five blocks from the station.

-**Forest Park,** seven miles west of downtown, on U.S. 40, has several attractions, including: **St. Louis Zoological Park** with more than 2,500 animals and exhibits; **St. Louis Art Museum,** with 70 galleries containing more than 15,000 art objects, is one of the nation's finest.

The **National Museum of Transport,** 3015 Barret Station Rd., exhibits the history and technology of both transportation and communication. Included are airplanes, autos, locomotives, rail cars, buses and horse-drawn vehicles. The **Missouri Botanical Gardens,** 4334 Shaw Boulevard, is a National Historic Landmark, and considered to be one of the most beautiful botanical displays in the nation. There are 79 acres of gardens in the heart of the city, including the largest Japanese garden in the U.S. Then there is the **Fox Theatre,** completed in 1929 and restored in 1982, virtually a wonder of the world with its overly ornate decor, home to Broadway productions and other entertainment.

0:00 (3:45) Depart St. Louis.

0:35 (3:10) St. Louis Ship Co. shipyards are on left.

0:40 (3:05) Through Jefferson Barracks, site of historic 18th-century military post.

3:45 (0:00) Arrive Poplar Bluff.

POPLAR BLUFF, MO - This winner of an All American City Award has the undulating Ozarks for recreation while the nearby fertile lands of southeast Missouri produce an abundance of cotton, rice, corn, soybeans, beef and hogs. Local manufacturers turn out such varied products as custom kitchen cabinets, Christmas ornaments, shoes and living room furniture. Nearby Wappapello Lake, with its rugged shoreline, offers fine bass fishing and water sports.

0:00 (0:52) Depart Poplar Bluff.

0:18 (0:34) Enter Arkansas and leave Missouri.

0:52 (0:00) Arrive Walnut Ridge.

WALNUT RIDGE, AR - Several points of interest are near this northeastern Arkansas trading center. Old Davidsonville State Park is the site of one of Arkansas' earliest settlements, and Lake Charles State Park has superb camping on the shores of its 645-acre lake.

0:00 (0:34) Depart Walnut Ridge.

0:34 (0:00) Arrive Newport.

NEWPORT, AR - Had it not been for the resistance of steamboat men and townspeople of nearby Jacksonport, the railroad (then the Cairo and Fulton) would have gone through that upstream community instead of Newport. Steamboating on the navigable White River faded around the turn of the century and Newport, with its rail service, prospered. The Old Jacksonport Courthouse has memorabilia from Civil War times when the town was a major mustering point for Confederate troops.

0:00 (1:20) Depart Newport.

1:19 (0:01) Cross Arkansas River separating North Little Rock from Little Rock.

1:20 (0:00) Arrive Little Rock's old multi-storied brick station on left, topped by intriguing clock tower.

LITTLE ROCK, AR - The capital of Arkansas and largest city in the state, Little Rock is attractively situated on tree-covered Ozark bluffs overlooking the Arkansas River. Its history runs the gamut from frontier trading post, to a Union-occupied Confederate city, to today's bustling central Arkansas metropolis.

Union Station, Union Station Square, Markham and Victory streets, two miles west of downtown. Amtrak has moved out of the cavernous, marble-floored waiting room on the upper level of this elderly structure and has opted for a more convenient but smaller space at track level. There is free parking by the station.

For arrival and departure information only, call (501) 372-6841.

Cab stand is at the station; Black and White, 374-0333. Nearest **local bus** stop is one block at 3rd & Victory. **Adams Field Municipal Airport** is three miles east of the city.

Little Rock Convention & Visitors Bureau, Statehouse Convention Center, Markham and Main, Box 3232, 72203; (501) 376-4781.

Camelot Hotel, Markham and Broadway, 72201; (501) 372-4371 or 800-937-2789. A mile from the station. $65.

-**Arkansas Excelsior Hotel,** 3 Statehouse Plaza, 72201; (501) 375-5000 or 800-527-1745. Next to Convention Center. A mile from the station. $92.

The Old State House, 300 W. Markham, is one of three historical capitol buildings that can be found here; free programs. **State Capitol Building,** Woodlawn and Capitol streets, houses the current state legislature. **Arkansas Arts Center,** MacArthur and Park, has many fine exhibits, and **Burns Park** has a scenic covered bridge. **Quapaw Quarter** has several stately Victorian homes open to the public. The very popular **Zoo of Arkansas** attracts visitors from all over the nation.

0:00 (0:45) Departing Little Rock, on left, size of State Capitol Building makes it appear much closer than three city blocks. At night, floodlights on its Batesville granite walls produce surrealistic, white brilliance. Massive dome, reaching 230 feet above ground, is clad in 16-carat gold leaf.

0:09 (0:36) Under Interstate 30 as light industrial scene now changes to residential.

0:16 (0:29) Texas Eagle seems to have left civilization behind as landscape becomes heavily forested with pines and hardwoods.

0:20 (0:25) Small, colorfully eroded hillside has become a "mini-Bryce Canyon" on left.

0:27 (0:18) Through Benton where bauxite is king. Ninety-eight percent of aluminum in U.S. comes from this region. Town even has a home built with this clay-like substance.

0:28 (0:17) Cross Saline River on southern edge of Benton.

0:45 (0:00) Arrive Malvern.

MALVERN, AR - This stop serves the spa city of Hot Springs and Hot Springs National Park, just 23 miles from here. Nestled in the lovely Ouachita Mountains and featuring 47 thermal springs, the resort is the most visited spot in Arkansas. The Park is one of the nation's oldest, and its "Bathhouse Row" displays the finest group of historic bathhouses remaining in the U.S.

0:00 (0:22) Depart Malvern.

0:06 (0:16) Note large ponds with numerous waterfowl on right.

0:21 (0:01) At left, large plant in distance with silver standpipe is Fafnir Bearing, manufacturer of ball bearings.

0:22 (0:00) Arriving Arkadelphia, cross Ouachita River. Large plant on right with green standpipe is Reynolds Metal aluminum plant. Town itself is actually off to right beyond trees.

ARKADELPHIA, AR - Aluminum is important now, but in earlier times, steamboat traffic once reigned supreme, docking here after steaming up the Ouachita River.

0:00 (1:10) Depart Arkadelphia.

0:18 (0:52) Cross Little Missouri River.

0:24 (0:46) Rather neat depot, on right, with red tile roof is distinguishing feature of downtown Prescott as train chugs along "Main Street."

0:28 (0:42) Some Southern-style ranching is carried on in this part of state with typical herds being Brahma crosses. Watch for rodeo variety bulls on right.

0:36 (0:34) On right, fine old smokestack of brick factory helps pinpoint Hope, Arkansas, President Bill Clinton's home town. Watermelon lovers will be interested to know that world's largest grow here—a record 200-pounder having been harvested in 1979.

0:49 (0:21) Cross 1,300-mile-long Red River which originates in northern Texas, creating a portion of Texas-Oklahoma border. Continuing southward (to left), it joins Mississippi River near Alexandria, Louisiana. Sometimes tinted red by its high silt content, this stream drains 90,000 square miles of land. Natural gas pipeline is suspended over water beyond highway bridge to left.

1:02 (0:08) Texarkana Municipal Airport is on immediate left.

1:10 (0:00) Arrive at Texarkana's ugly old station located at the Texas-Arkansas state line, where front of train comes to rest in Texas and rear portion stops in Arkansas.

TEXARKANA, AR/TX - This city lies carefully balanced on the Arkansas-Texas border and even boasts a post office straddling the state line—the only federal building in the U.S. sitting in two states. Of particular interest is the Texarkana Museum with exhibits emphasizing the city's history. The beautifully restored Perot Theatre features shows, ballets, concerts and film festivals. Numerous lakes make this area a fisherman's paradise.

0:00 (1:15) Depart Texarkana on trackage of Texas and Pacific, an affiliate of Missouri Pacific, and enter Texas heading due south along Lone Star State's eastern border.

0:06 (1:09) Enormous rail tie manufacturing and storage operation stretches for almost a mile along right side of tracks.

0:23 (0:52) Through Atlanta, Texas. Nearby, over 25 sites of prehistoric Caddo Indian villages have been found.

1:15 (0:00) Arrive Marshall where rail station, looking more like an old brick mansion, greets train's departees on left.

MARSHALL, TX - This northeastern Texas town is located amidst cypress-fringed bayous and pine

forests. Both its natural beauty and mild climate make it a popular tourist area, while oil, agriculture, lignite processing and manufacturing are economic mainstays. During the Civil War, saddles, harnesses and ammunition were produced here for the Confederacy, and it became the wartime capital of Missouri. This is also the birthplace of Lady Bird Johnson. **0:00** (0:28) Depart Marshall. For some time now, Eagle will slip past one industrial operation after another, most turning out the stuff for which Texas is best known. Oil equipment manufacturers and other petroleum-related industries dominate the flat landscape.
0:28 (0:00) Arrive Longview.

LONGVIEW, TX · This industrialized community is heavily oil oriented with refineries, oil equipment manufacturing and the loading end of the famous "Big Inch" pipeline. Oil isn't the only industry in Longview, however; Schlitz turns out 4½ million barrels of beer a year from Texas' largest brewery. The R. G. LeTourneau Museum with early earthmoving equipment on display and the Caddo Indian Museum with artifacts from that prehistoric culture are both located here.
0:00 (2:18) Depart Longview.
0:15 (2:03) Through Gladwater and the very heart of famed East Texas oilfield, one of nation's biggest producers.

0:23 (1:55) On right, white board fence looks like it belongs on a Kentucky horse farm, but actually encloses Ambassador College, founded by Garner Ted Armstrong and his brother Herbert.

0:29 (1:49) Jarvis Christian College is just to right.

0:37 (1:41) What looks like world's largest collection of antique merchants is at right.

1:39 (0:39) Enter Dallas' fastest growing suburb, Mesquite (pronounced meskeet), named for that scraggly, thorny shrub that thrives in Southwestern U.S. and northern Mexico.

1:54 (0:24) In far distance to right, top of Ferris wheel identifies location of Texas State Fair Grounds, where Texans hold what they claim is biggest fair in nation.

2:00 (0:18) Dallas cityscape is now clearly visible on right.

2:17 (0:01) Flat-roofed Reunion Arena sports complex, home to Dallas Maverick basketball, is on left.

2:18 (0:00) Arrive Dallas. White marbled Union Station is on right while spectacular glass facades of Hyatt Regency Hotel and spherically domed Reunion Tower rise abruptly above us on left. Station and hotel complex are conveniently connected beneath train by an attractive underground concourse.

For Route Log between Dallas and Houston, see page 256.

DALLAS, TX - Dallas began in 1841 as a trading post which was started by a Tennessee lawyer, John Neely Bryan, who named the post after "his friend Dallas." Although no one today knows who that "Dallas" was, the County of Dallas was eventually named after George Mifflin Dallas, Vice President of the United States under James Polk.

As is true with so many western cities, early growth was due to the arrival of the railroad. In the early 1870s, rail lines extended both to the east and to the north making the city an important distribution center. Today, with a metropolitan population (including Ft. Worth) of 3,000,000, Dallas is one of the Southwest's leading financial, industrial and transportation centers, and entertains more than two million tourists annually.

Union Station, 400 South Houston St. This beautifully renovated marble structure, included in the National Register of Historic Places, is located on the edge of downtown. There are a variety of restaurants (on the 2nd floor), a gift shop and a florist in this popular setting. Luggage carts and adjacent pay-parking are available. Luggage can be stored at the baggage counter. A visitors information counter is also located in the station. An underground walkway connects to the Hyatt Regency Hotel and the Reunion Tower (observation deck and restaurant).

For arrival and departure information only, call (214) 653-1101.

Cab stand at the station; Yellow Cab, 426-6262 and Executive Cab, 554-1212. Avis **rental cars** are available on the premises. Nearest **local bus** stop is in front of the station; 979-1111. **Dallas-Ft. Worth Regional Airport** is 17 miles west of the city; call Super Shuttle (817) 329-2000 (local but dial area code) for transportation to and from D/FW. Closer in, but less used, **Love Field** can be reached by bus from downtown.

Visitor Information Center, in Union Station. Write Dallas Convention and Visitors Bureau, 1201 Elm St., Suite 2000, 75202. Call (214) 746-6679.

Hyatt Regency Dallas, 300 Reunion Blvd., 75207; (214) 651-1234. Dazzling architecture. Connected to the station by a block-long concourse. $169.

-Holiday Inn Downtown, 1015 Elm, 75202; (214) 748-9951. Six blocks from the station. $88.

Dealey Plaza and the **Texas Book Depository,** site of President Kennedy's assassination, are but three blocks north of the station on Houston St. **Reunion Tower** has an observation deck and a revolving restaurant with commanding views of the city, across tracks from the station and reached by an underground concourse. **West End MarketPlace,** a former cracker factory, has several floors of unusual shopping and eating, about a mile north of the station at 603 Munger. **Neiman Marcus,** at Ervay and Commerce, seven blocks from the station, is regal king of the nation's department stores. And two miles of **subterranean** and elevated **pedes-**

trian-ways with over 200 shops and restaurants, connect various downtown hotels, retailers and financial institutions.

0:00 (0:57) Depart Dallas and head westward through solid development which has made Dallas and Ft. Worth almost appear as one city.
0:02 (0:55) Look back on left for a fine view of Hyatt Regency Hotel and Reunion Tower. Texas Book Depository (light brick with green-trimmed windows), which played such an important role in President Kennedy's assassination, is off to right.
0:03 (0:54) Newer Dallas jail facility is just to left.
0:12 (0:45) Top of Dallas Cowboys' Texas Stadium is in far distance to right.
0:15 (0:42) Unique in its neatness, auto junk yard at left displays merchandise in prim rows—each car with hood raised.
0:17 (0:40) Hensley Field and Texas National Guard aircraft are on left.
0:18 (0:39) Jets and helicopters of Dallas Naval Air Station are parked on left.
0:19 (0:38) Vaught complex, longtime military aircraft manufacturer, is just to left.
0:20 (0:37) Pass through Grand Prairie. Located here because of railroad, town boomed with defense plants during World War II.
0:25 (0:32) Unusual tower in distance to right belongs to Six Flags Over Texas, a huge entertainment park—one of Texas' most popular attractions. General Motors assembly plant, at left, was once slated for closing but then was granted reprieve by GM's top management.
0:27 (0:30) Enter Arlington. University of Texas at Arlington is on right while Arlington Stadium is about a mile in distance.
0:30 (0:27) Perched on hilltop right is "The Home for Aged Masons."
0:35 (0:22) Off to left, it is possible to catch a glimpse of 2,275-acre Arlington Lake, owned by city of Arlington and popular with boaters and fishermen.
0:52 (0:05) Ft. Worth skyline is now on right. Train stops, then backs into Ft. Worth station.
0:57 (0:00) Arrive Ft. Worth.

 FT. WORTH, TX - This city began as a military camp during the war with Mexico and then became a major shipping point for cattle after the Civil War. Now one of Texas' major cities, it has a wide assortment of industries including aviation plants of General Dynamics and Bell Helicopter. An impressive downtown convention complex covers 14 blocks and features an unusual "Water Garden" of fountains and ponds.

A culturally conscious city, Ft. Worth offers musicals, concerts, ballets, theater performances and numerous outstanding museums to satisfy almost any taste. The Amon G. Carter Museum of Western Art has permanent collections of both Remington and Russell. The Kimbell Art Museum has works that span from prehistoric to Picasso. The domed Casa Mana Theatre is one of the nation's most notable theaters-in-the-round. Pate Museum of Transportation has an antique railroad car, vintage autos, military aircraft and a minesweeper on exhibit.

Ramada Hotel - Ft. Worth Downtown, 1701 Commerce St., 76102; (817) 335-7000. Highrise in center of business district, one block from the station. $76.

0:00 (0:40) Depart Ft. Worth.
0:06 (0:34) Last look at downtown Ft. Worth is afforded back on right.
0:19 (0:21) Numerous small aircraft dot the edge of interestingly named Luck Field.
0:38 (0:02) On left, enormous rail shops of Santa Fe Railroad are largest construction and repair shops in Texas.
0:40 (0:00) Arrive Cleburne.

CLEBURNE, TX - Named in honor of Confederate General Pat Cleburne, the city is the trading center for an area featuring farming, dairying and livestock.

0:00 (1:05) Depart Cleburne.
0:08 (0:57) On edge of Rio Vista at right, three large flags help identify "The Cow Pasture Bank" (actually, First State) which provides airstrip in rear for its fly-in customers.
0:15 (0:50) Train now imperceptibly crosses Balcones Fault where flat prairies quickly turn to more hilly terrain.
0:17 (0:48) Cross legendary Brazos River. Off to left is 15,760-acre Lake Whitney, formed by damming Brazos River. This

45-mile-long reservoir is one of nation's most popular water recreation areas with four million visitors annually.

0:42 (0:23) Cross Bosque River which winds its way along our route for next 30 minutes.

0:52 (0:13) Climb up out of Bosque River Valley and cut through unusually rocky terrain.

1:05 (0:00) Arrive McGregor.

MCGREGOR, TX - This community serves as a stop for its much larger neighbor 19 miles to the west—Waco. At one time, Waco was referred to as "Six Shooter Junction" when cattle drives along the Chisholm Trail frequented the town. Now, the city relies on five "C"s for its support—cattle, cotton, corn, collegians and culture. It is the home of Baylor University as well as several other institutions of higher learning. The Old Suspension Bridge, still used to cross the Brazos, was the largest in the nation when built in 1870 and was used as a pattern for the Brooklyn Bridge.

0:00 (0:25) Depart McGregor.

0:24 (0:01) Santa Fe shops appear at right approaching station in Temple.

0:25 (0:00) Arrive Temple where train is greeted by an attractive brick station whose familiar emblems are a reminder that we have been on Santa Fe tracks since Ft. Worth.

TEMPLE, TX - Since its inception in 1880, Temple has always been closely tied with railroading when it grew along the Gulf, Colorado and Santa Fe Railroad, and the Missouri, Kansas and Texas lines. Railroad shops are still located here. Temple is one of the Southwest's leading medical centers, whose facilities include King's Daughters Hospital, Scott-White Hospital and Clinic, and (quite aptly) the Santa Fe Hospital.

0:00 (0:56) Depart Temple.

0:12 (0:41) Rolling, forested hills provide a most aesthetic backdrop for area's ranches.

0:16 (0:40) Poultry farm on left seems to provide separate, small A-frame home for each rooster.

0:45 (0:11) Cross San Gabriel River.

0:56 (0:00) Arrive Taylor.

TAYLOR, TX - Having been on the Missouri, Kansas, Texas tracks since Temple, we now change to Missouri Pacific trackage, which leads to San Antonio. Taylor is a railroad junction point and retail center for the surrounding farm and ranch country.

0:00 (0:46) Depart Taylor.

0:28 (0:18) Large cement plant on left is just one of many between here and San Antonio.

0:35 (0:11) Enter suburbs of Austin.

0:39 (0:07) Train passes Camp Mabry, on right, where military aircraft and armored vehicles have been put on display along tracks.

0:43 (0:03) Pass under an immense highway interchange as train nears center of Austin.

0:46 (0:00) Arrive at Austin's station, somewhat west of downtown.

AUSTIN, TX - In 1839 a site was chosen on the north shore of the Colorado River (not the one of Grand Canyon fame) to become the capital of the Republic of Texas. The site was well-chosen, as Austin has grown to be a hub city of Texas, with healthy industries, numerous colleges and universities, and is still the seat of government. The University of Texas at Austin, the state's largest university, is located here. Of particular interest: the State Capitol Complex; the Elisabet Ney Museum, with many works of this prominent 19th-century sculptor; the home of O. Henry, where this short-story writer (William Sydney Porter) once lived; and the Lyndon B. Johnson Library and Museum, with artifacts from his presidency.

0:00 (0:40) Depart Austin.

0:04 (0:36) Ornate dome of capitol, constructed of Texas pink marble, is off to left. Train makes a curve to right and crosses Colorado River.

0:07 (0:33) Last view of Austin's skyline and capitol dome back on left.

0:22 (0:18) On right, quaint little storefronts in town of Buda seem to stare at train as it zips past.

0:39 (0:01) On outskirts of San Marcos, train slips through scenic campus of Southwest Texas State University—alma mater of Lyndon B. Johnson, the nation's 36th president.

0:40 (0:00) Arrive San Marcos.

SAN MARCOS, TX - Besides Southwest Texas State University, San Marcos is the site of the Republic of Texas Chilympiad (state chili cooking contest), held each September, with the winner going to the World Chili Cook-off each November at Terlingua, Texas. For eight days in June, the Texas Water Safari is celebrated here—one of the world's toughest canoe races. Entrants must canoe down hundreds of miles of rivers and saltwater bays, traveling from San Marcos to Seadrift.

0:00 (1:43) Depart San Marcos.

0:02 (1:41) Tower, off to right, was once used to train World War II paratroopers.

0:19 (1:23) Cross Guadalupe River.

0:26 (1:16) Enter German community of New Braunfels, famous for sausages, breads and pastries. This small town was once fourth largest city in Texas.

0:29 (1:13) Tracks pass through huge limestone quarry supplying raw material for cement plant at right.

0:34 (1:08) Southbound, swing right while tracks that carry northbound Texas Eagle can be observed branching off to left.

0:55 (Southbound only.) San Antonio International Airport is on right.

0:58 (Southbound only.) Enter outskirts of San Antonio with Alamo Cement Plant on left, then pass directly through Olmos Basin Golf Course.

--- (0:59) (Northbound only.) Multiple soccer fields are at right (northbound), then enormous polo complex amply accommodates this upper-crust diversion.

1:26 (0:11) Lone Star Beer brewery is on immediate right. Skyline is dominated by 750-foot Tower of the Americas, built for HemisFair held in 1968.

1:28 (0:10) Cross San Antonio River. Adjacent to station, huge structure with cable-suspended roof is Alamodome. Completed in 1993, it is city's sports, convention, and concert center.

1:29 (0:00) Arrive San Antonio.

(Note - Trains northbound from San Antonio take a slightly different route on departure, going to Craig Junction where main line is rejoined. This adds 19 miles, but eliminates reversing trains in San Antonio.)

SAN ANTONIO, TX - San Antonio, a city now in excess of one million, was named by Captain Domingo Teran who was exploring the region for Spain in 1691 and arrived in the area on the feast day of Saint Anthony of Padua. However, a permanent settlement was not established until 27 years later when the Mission of San Antonio de Valero was built, later to become known as the Alamo.

San Antonio has the distinction of having been under six different flags since its beginning: French, Spanish, Mexican, Republic of Texas, Confederate and American. It was the scene of one of the most historic and dramatic battles in our nation's history, when 188 Texans defended the Alamo against the Mexican Army led by General Santa Ana, falling on March 6, 1836 after all of its defenders were killed. Later that year, Texas successfully ended Mexican rule and became a Republic.

Today, with its rich past intermixed with the new and modern, San Antonio is clearly one of the more fascinating cities in the United States. The restoration of its charming river-front area is one of the major urban-renewal achievements of our time.

Amtrak Station, 1174 E. Commerce St., is an appealing, Spanish-style structure with an interior that has been restored to its original stateliness. A grand staircase beneath a vivid stained-glass window, and an arched baroque ceiling give the interior a feeling of opulence rarely found in American train stations. The station still has storage lockers, and food and beverage vending machines are curiously located in the entryway to the ladies rest room. Free parking is adjacent to the station.

Cab stand at the station; Yellow Cab, 226-4242. Nearest **local bus** stop is in front of the station, 227-2020. **San Antonio International Airport** is eight miles north of the city center.

Visitors Information Center, 317 Alamo Plaza, immediately across from the Alamo. Write the San Antonio Convention and Visitors Bureau,

San Antonio

Amtrak Station
1 - Visitors Information
2 - La Villita
3 - Market Square
4 - The Alamo
5 - HemisFair Plaza
6 - Paseo del Rio
7 - Menger Hotel
8 - La Quinta Convention Center
9 - Crockett Hotel

P.O. Box 2277, 78298; call (210) 299-8155.

Menger Hotel and Motor Inn, 204 Alamo Plaza, 78205; (210) 223-4361 or 800-345-9285. This venerable landmark is still an excellent place to absorb San Antonio's relaxed Southwest charm. Five blocks from the station. $118.

-La Quinta Convention Center, 1001 E. Commerce, 78205; (210) 222-9181. Closest hotel to the station and convenient to downtown. Three blocks from the station. $82.

-Best Western Crockett, 320 Bonham, 78205; (210) 225-6500 or 800-292-1050. Nicely restored 1909 hotel, next to the Alamo and River Center, six blocks from the station. $95.

The Amtrak station is approximately five blocks from the downtown area reached by traveling west on E. Commerce Street. The heart of San Antonio's appeal is Paseo del Rio, nearly two miles of cobblestone walkways with bridges, tropical foliage, fine shops, restaurants and nightclubs set along the river. Boat rides offer a unique way to see much of this area. **The Alamo,** at Alamo Plaza, is one of the most famous shrines in the country. Tours, a museum, slides and a movie about the battle help re-create the struggle that took the lives of its 188 defenders. **HemisFair Plaza,** which was the site of the 1968 HemisFair, now contains the Convention Center and several attractions including the **Tower of Americas** topped by an observation deck and revolving restaurant. The **San Antonio Streetcar** travels through the downtown area. **Alamodome,** next to station, is San Antonio's ultramodern all-purpose arena for concerts, sporting events and conventions.

Rivercenter is San Antonio's new downtown shopping arcade featuring 125 shops and cafes, an I-MAX theater and a Marriott.

255

La Villita, at Villita and South Alamo, is a restored portion of the city which houses craft shops, art galleries and boutiques. And just west of the central business district is colorful **Market Square** where farmers' produce is sold in the early morning.

Route Log for Dallas to Houston

0:00 (1:25) Depart Dallas, slipping past Reunion Tower and Reunion Arena sports facility on right, then past modernistic home of *Dallas Morning News* on left.

0:05 (1:20) Multi-storied Sears warehousing and distribution facility dwarfs all else on left.

0:07 (1:14) At Tower 19, northbound Texas Eagle swings to east, then stops and backs up into Dallas so cars are in proper position to be joined with San Antonio section before continuing to Chicago.

0:10 (1:11) White refinery-like structure at left is Proctor and Gamble soap factory.

0:15 (1:06) Traverse long bridge spanning Trinity River. This stream that bisects Dallas was once thought to be capable of handling shipping traffic, but waterway plans were ultimately abandoned as impractical.

0:17 (1:04) Through Southern Pacific's Miller Yard where SP locomotives and other rolling stock are in evidence.

0:24 (0:57) Concrete bridges above carry I-20 and I-635 traffic.

0:41 (0:40) Cleverly designed rest stop along I-45 sports miniature lake and other attractive ornamentations, on left.

0:44 (0:37) Round-steepled First Baptist Church in Palmer, on right, was built around turn of century. Before its construction, members were sometimes baptized across street in small pond. Nation's new "Super Collider," world's largest atom smasher was being constructed just west of Palmer, its outer edge to be a mere mile or so from downtown. However, in 1993, Congress, in a rare fit of frugality, axed the project after 14 miles of tunnel had been constructed at a cost of $2 billion.

0:48 (0:33) Rolling fields and cattle-filled pastures of Texas' ranching country continue to afford lovely pastoral scenes. In spring, blankets of bluebonnets (they're blue, of course) and black-eyed Susans (they're yellow) add a feathery softness to the countryside.

0:55 (0:26) Large facility of Ennis Business Forms is on left. Firm is a major manufacturer of business forms, most being customized to customers' specifications, and is headquartered here in Ennis, TX.

1:03 (0:18) Stacks of black plastic pipe on left at Alma conjure up images of huge licorice sticks.

1:21 (0:00) Arrive Corsicana.

CORSICANA, TX - The roots of Corsicana go back to 1849, but it wasn't until 1894, when the city drilled for water and struck oil, that the town began to bloom. Petroleum is still important, with refineries and other oil-related companies located in this city of 22,000.

World-renowned Corsicana Fruit Cakes are produced here, the only such bakery product to receive New York's prestigious Gourmet Society Culinary Merit Award. Several hundred thousand of these "Deluxe" brand delights are sold through the mail each year, utilizing nearly a half million pounds of Texas pecans. The manufacturer, Collin Street Bakery, is about two blocks from the station, but can't be seen from the train.

Navarro College is here with Texas' most outstanding collection of arrowheads. This is also the home town of Country-and-Western singer Lefty Frizzell.

0:00 (2:10) Depart Corsicana.

0:02 (2:08) K mart distribution center occupies huge, windowless building on left.

0:26 (1:44) Through attractive little community of Mexia, named for Mexican general who served under Santa Ana before finally leading an unsuccessful rebellion against the dictator and losing his life. Town was named for him after his family donated townsite.

0:33 (1:37) Cross Navasota River.

1:30 (0:40) Entering rail yards at Hearne, excellent look at railroad turntable is afforded on left.

2:08 (0:02) Clock tower is centerpiece of main entrance to Texas A & M University on right.

2:09 (0:01) Kyle Field, University's football stadium, hugs tracks on left while school's fine baseball stadium is on right of campus bisected by tracks. (Chancellor of University would like to see tracks tunnel beneath campus, but railroad has not been receptive to this rather costly concept.)

2:10 (0:00) Arrive College Station.

 COLLEGE STATION, TX - This is home to Texas' first institution of higher learning, Texas A & M University. The school is renowned for its ROTC and military Cadet Corps programs.

0:00 (1:55) Depart College Station.

0:22 (1:33) Again, cross Navasota River.

0:26 (1:29) Through historic town of Navasota, which in 1822 had Anglo-American settlers, some of first in Texas. Note interesting architecture of some of older limestone buildings on left.

1:00 (0:55) Highway signage at both edges of Waller alerts motorists that Waller is "Not just another Texas small town."

1:23 (0:32) Ranchlands slowly give way to citified outer limits of Houston megalopolis.

1:55 (0:00) With almost futuristic-looking skyline on right, arrive Houston.

HOUSTON, TX - See page 269.

Other Chicago Area Service

The **Illini** provides daily service between Chicago and Carbondale with runs each direction late in the day.

Chicago-Milwaukee has several trains each way, each day, including the Empire Builder.

The **Illinois Zephyr** carries passengers from Quincy, IL to Chicago early in the day and returns in the evening. Daily. Sandwiches, snacks and beverages; no checked baggage.

The route is the same as the California Zephyr between Chicago and Galesburg, but between the latter and Quincy, this train forges its own route through Macomb and Quincy. It is the only Amtrak service to these two communities. Macomb, IL, named in honor of Alexander Macomb, a U.S. General during the War of 1812, is home to Western Illinois University. Quincy is a town of 42,000, and a century ago, was the second largest city in Illinois. Its importance declined along with the steamboat.

The **State House** leaves Chicago mid-afternoon and takes the route of the Texas Eagle to St. Louis, arriving there late evening. St. Louis departures are early morning with late afternoon Chicago arrivals. This daily train is unreserved, has sandwiches and beverages and no checked baggage.

The **Ann Rutledge** links Chicago with Kansas City through St. Louis. Daily unreserved service leaves Chicago late morning, arriving in Kansas City late evening. Northbound trains leave Kansas City early morning and arrive in Chicago midevening. Sandwiches, snacks and beverages, no checked baggage. Custom Class is available.

The **Loop** links Chicago and Springfield with morning service to Springfield and late afternoon service to Chicago, except Sundays. Snacks and beverages.

The **Hoosier State,** in addition to the Cardinal, provides Chicago-Indianapolis service with runs to Chicago in the morning and to Indianapolis in the evening. Custom Class is available.

Kansas City ▬▬ St. Louis

Mules

The Mules cut across the very heart of Missouri, carrying passengers between Kansas City and St. Louis through undulating farmlands and forests along the Missouri River. A Thruway bus between St. Louis and Centralia, IL connects these trains with the City of New Orleans. The westbound train is called the Kansas City Mule, while the eastbound is known as the St. Louis Mule.

Southbound Schedule (Condensed)
Kansas City, MO - Midafternoon Departure
Jefferson City, MO - Early Evening
St. Louis, MO - Late Evening Arrival

Northbound Schedule (Condensed)
St. Louis, MO - Early Morning Departure
Jefferson City, MO - Midmorning
Kansas City, MO - Early Afternoon Arrival

Frequency - Daily.
Seating - Amfleet coaches.
Dining - Sandwiches, snacks and beverages. No food service between St. Louis and Carbondale.
Baggage - No checked baggage.
Reservations - All-reserved train.
Length of Trip - 282 miles in 5½ hours.

Route Log

 KANSAS CITY, MO - See page 227.

0:00 (0:19) Depart Kansas City, heading due east and somewhat below grade. Shortly, pass beneath Interstate 70 which stretches from Baltimore to western Utah, and then under Interstate 435 that carries traffic through eastern suburbs of city.
0:08 (0:11) Cemetery with tombstone forest on hillside left obviously has "no vacancies."
0:19 (0:00) Arrive Independence.

INDEPENDENCE, MO - This large Kansas City suburb was the home of former president Harry S. Truman who came into office when Franklin Roosevelt died April 12, 1945. He served until 1953. Not long after becoming president, he made one of the most difficult decisions ever made—the approval to drop an atomic bomb on Japan.

But Independence's historical importance commenced much sooner when it was an important way station for the Santa Fe, California and Oregon trails. Among those who stopped here were Mormons who left a considerable imprint on the city. Independence is now the world headquarters of the Reorganized Church of Jesus Christ of Latter Day Saints.

Just north of here is Liberty, where Jesse James got his start by robbing his first bank.
0:00 (0:16) Depart Independence.
0:05 (0:11) On left, Truman High School

258

bears name of town's favorite son.

0:16 (0:00) Arrive Lee's Summit where old red-brick depot is no longer used.

LEE'S SUMMIT, MO - This metropolitan suburb was once the domain of the Osage Indians until they were forced off their land in 1825. Lewis and Clark passed through the county shortly before they spotted their first bison in nearby Kansas. It was the Missouri Pacific Railroad that finally assured the town's future, however, when in 1846 the town became one of the largest shipping points between Kansas City and St. Louis.

0:00 (0:40) Depart Lee's Summit.

0:38 (0:02) Rumble across branch of Blackwater River.

0:40 (0:00) Arriving Warrensburg, about three blocks before station, as tracks curve slightly to the right, across street on left was "Warrensburg Brewery Cave" (now boarded up), formerly used to store beer in its cool environs. This use came to a sudden end in 1873, however, when Carrie Nation of Temperance League fame burned it out. Today, only a small house marks the site.

WARRENSBURG, MO - Few towns have had as interesting a past as Warrensburg.

On the south edge of town are Pertle Springs, at one time having its waters shipped to every state in the Union because of their "curative" powers. A renowned resort area surrounded the springs with as many as 10,000 attending camp meetings. The Democratic National Convention was held there in 1895. The land was eventually purchased by Central Missouri State College.

Just a block south of the station was the old Estes Hotel which, in 1899, served as a depot for a small steam train that made eight runs daily to the Pertle Springs Hotel.

The first business area of the town was just a block to the left (north) of here, but an 1866 Christmas Eve fire destroyed most of the buildings. A few of the original facades can still be seen, however. Carrie Nation attended the State Normal School here, now Central Missouri's State University just three blocks south.

The old courthouse was the site of perhaps the most famous of legal trials involving canines. In 1870, Leonidas Hornsby was found guilty of killing his brother-in-law's dog, but it was the eloquent eulogy given the dog Drum by the plaintiff's lawyer that apparently swayed the jury.

Be sure to note the old Missouri Pacific depot with Richardsonian Romanesque architecture, built in 1890 of Warrensburg sandstone.

0:00 (0:30) Depart Warrensburg.

0:24 (0:16) Limestone quarry forms large excavation at left.

0:30 (0:00) Arrive Sedalia's modern brick station on left.

SEDALIA, MO - Founded in 1857, Sedalia owes its beginnings to the railroad, serving as a provisioning point and later a military post during the Civil War. One of America's best-known composers, Scott Joplin, composed the "Maple Leaf Rag" in a local saloon known as the Maple Leaf Club. It was this song that first brought him both fame and success. Now, if you're here in mid-August, all the excitement is about the state fair.

0:00 (1:04) Departing Sedalia, note monument to aforementioned Scott Joplin and Maple Leaf Club.

0:02 (1:02) Through Missouri Pacific rail yards where seemingly thousands of red cabooses stand in storage at left.

1:02 (0:02) Entering Jefferson City, broad Missouri River comes into view on left. Highway bridge spanning this great river carries auto traffic north to Columbia, home of University of Missouri, and to Fulton, home of Westminster College. (It was on campus of latter that Winston Churchill delivered his famous "Iron Curtain" speech in 1946.) Then, perched above and to right, is Missouri's sparkling white state capitol. Built in 1917 of Missouri limestone, its Renaissance dome towers 260 feet above ground.

1:04 (0:00) Arrive Jefferson City where Amtrak now occupies first level of former Union Hotel, circa 1855.

JEFFERSON CITY, MO - Named for Thomas Jefferson, the site of this city was chosen as the state capital in 1821. Its location on the Missouri River,

259

Ann Rutledge - near Hermann, Missouri
JACK SWANSON

halfway between St. Louis and Kansas City, made it a logical choice. Today, "Jeff City" has a population of 35,000.

0:00 (1:41) Depart Jefferson City, following Missouri River until just east of Washington, approximately 80 miles downstream.

0:07 (1:34) Neat-appearing buildings with silver water tank on hillside to left are Missouri Department of Corrections minimum security prison.

0:10 (1:31) Train slows as it carefully crosses Osage River.

0:14 (1:27) Note houses on each side of river perched on stilts to avoid Missouri overflows.

0:29 (1:12) Huge form of electric generating facility (reminiscent of Three Mile Island) dominates horizon on left.

0:37 (1:04) Cross Casconade River.

0:45 (0:56) Pass through historic town of Hermann. Some Bavarian-like architecture can be spotted here and there, looking uphill to right. This small town, with strong German heritage, is home to two wineries, one of which can be seen at right, just east of bridge.

1:13 (0:28) Tracks bid farewell to Missouri River and start a gradual ascent towards St. Louis.

1:15 (0:26) Briefly encounter darkness while passing through tunnel for five seconds.

1:17 (0:24) Turquoise buildings with white roofs comprise Purina Poultry Research Center, which is a reminder that Ralston Purina makes farm feeds as well as breakfast foods.

1:18 (0:23) Through one more short tunnel.

1:36 (0:05) Three venerable steam locomotives, long since retired from duty, stand in forlorn deterioration at left.

1:39 (0:02) Over Interstate 270, then past attractive fairways of Greenbriar Country Club on left.

1:41 (0:00) Arrive downtown Kirkwood. Be sure to take note of quaint Kirkwood depot with its swooping roof lines and circular tower.

KIRKWOOD, MO - This is a western suburb of St. Louis, and the last stop before that city.

0:00 (0:20) Depart Kirkwood.

0:03 (0:16) Two more country clubs pass

by on left, first Westborough, then Algonquin.

0:19 (0:01) On left, restored St. Louis Union Station, with its marvelous old train shed, now houses shops, a beer garden and a luxury hotel. Also, various privately owned rail cars can frequently be seen parked there. In its heyday, Union Station handled as many as 276 trains daily. Unfortunately, Amtrak does not stop here, but rolls on to its "temporary" depot opened in 1978.

0:20 (0:00) Arrive St. Louis.

 ST. LOUIS, MO - See page 246.

Sunset Limited

On April 4, 1993, the route of the New Orleans/Los Angeles Sunset Limited was extended eastward from New Orleans to Jacksonville, Florida and on south to Miami, making the Sunset America's first regularly scheduled transcontinental trail. This extension filled a significant gap that forced rail travelers between the Southeast and the Southwest to go by way of Washington, DC.

The first through trains between New Orleans and the West Coast were started in February 1883 and were known as the Atlantic Express and Pacific Express (depending on the direction they were heading). But in 1894, the Sunset Limited title was bestowed on this service, appropriate enough since passengers from New Orleans to Los Angeles headed into two sunsets before reaching the end of the line.

Today, the run between Miami and Los Angeles takes nearly three full days, reaching an elevation of nearly a mile high at 5,074-foot Paisano Pass, Texas and sinking to 202 feet below sea level near Salton, California.

There are through coaches and sleepers between Chicago and Los Angeles by a connection with the Texas Eagle at San Antonio.

Westbound Schedule (Condensed)
Miami, FL - Early Afternoon Departure
New Orleans, LA - Late Morning Arrival (2nd Day); Early Afternoon Departure (2nd Day)
San Antonio, TX - Middle of the Night (3rd Day)
El Paso, TX - Early Afternoon (3rd Day)
Phoenix, AZ - Late Evening (3rd Day)
Los Angeles, CA - Early Morning Arrival (4th Day)

Eastbound Schedule (Condensed)
Los Angeles, CA - Late Evening Departure
Phoenix, AZ - Early Morning (2nd Day)
El Paso, TX - Late Afternoon (2nd Day)
San Antonio, TX - Early Morning (3rd Day)
New Orleans, LA - Midevening Arrival (3rd Day); Late Evening Departure (3rd Day)
Miami, FL - Late Evening Arrival (4th Day)

Frequency - Tri-weekly. Departs Los Angeles and Miami Sunday, Tuesday and Friday. Arrives Miami and Los Angeles Wednesday, Friday and Monday.
Seating - Superliner coaches.
Dining - Complete meal and beverage service as well as lighter fare. Lounge service is also available with movies. Dinner is not served upon departure from Los Angeles.
Sleeping - Superliner sleepers with deluxe, family, economy and special bedrooms.
Baggage - Checked baggage handled at larger cities.
Reservations - All-reserved train.
Length of Trip - 3,066 miles in approximately three hours short of three days.

Route Log

For route log from Miami to Jacksonville, FL (by way of Orlando) see that portion of Silver Star log, page 91.

 JACKSONVILLE, FL - See page 90.

0:00 (1:01) Depart Jacksonville. Train will back out of station, unless train was switched through wye at Grand Junction just before arrival.

0:03 (0:58) Back into wye in order to turn train for forward travel.

0:12 (0:49) Final maneuver positioning Sunset for its Los Angeles-bound journey occurs at Moncrief Yard where train curls westward.

0:17 (0:44) A gaggle of blue and grey business rail cars of CSX can often be observed parked on siding at left. View of Jacksonville skyline is afforded back to left.

0:35 (0:26) Through Baldwin, where route of Silver Meteor departs to south.

1:01 (0:00) Arrive Lake City.

 LAKE CITY, FL - One of Florida's older towns, today's Lake City has an economy driven by phosphate mining, timber and tobacco.

0:00 (0:53) Depart Lake City.

0:11 (0:42) A sprinkling of blueberry farms now appears along the right-of-way.

0:23 (0:30) Through attractive community of Live Oak, where clock-tower-capped Suwannee County Courthouse is focal point of downtown. Live Oak is home to Florida's oldest and biggest tobacco market.

0:26 (0:27) On left, elaborate entrance leads to a curious collection of small brick buildings. Compound was once a motel but now serves as unusual-appearing apartments.

0:37 (0:16) Cross Suwannee River, made famous by Stephen Foster's *Old Folks at Home*. River drains part of mysterious Okefenokee Swamp into Gulf of Mexico and forms boundary for eight of northern Florida's counties. It is unlikely, however, that Foster ever saw the river.

0:53 (0:00) Arrive Madison.

 MADISON, FL - This community of 3,500 inhabitants serves as the county seat of Madison County on the eastern edge of Florida's panhandle.

0:00 (1:19) Depart Madison and start to traverse virtual length of Florida's panhandle.

0:21 (0:58) One of numerous Amtrak "Main Street" encounters occurs when we trundle through center of elderly Greenville.

0:39 (0:40) At left, older home, with yard containing enormous live oak tree and wicker lawn chairs (and sometimes two dogs), is quintessence of Deep South gentility.

1:07 (0:12) More Deep South atmosphere is encountered when tracks pass through swamp of murky water, cypress trees and Spanish moss.

1:16 (0:03) Look directly up U.S. Highway 27 to right for quick look at Old Capitol. After new capitol was built, this structure was restored and now serves as Florida's State Building.

1:19 (0:00) Arrive Tallahassee's rambling old station at right. Once a freight depot, structure's west end has been remodeled to serve Amtrak customers.

 TALLAHASSEE, FL - This city has served as the capital of Florida since 1824 and was one of two Confederate capitals not captured by Union troops (Austin, Texas being the other). Besides state government, Tallahassee is also the center of higher education in northern Florida. 28,000-student Florida State University is here as well as 6,000-student Florida A&M.

0:00 (1:53) Depart Tallahassee. After departure, some Florida State University facilities can be seen off to right.

0:13 (1:40) Cross Ichlockonee River.

1:08 (0:45) Cross impressive Apalachicola River. River traffic can often be seen on these waters.

 Gain one hour as train passes from Eastern to Central Time. Set your watch back (forward if eastbound) one hour.

1:13 (0:40) Near Sneads, Apalachicola Correctional Facility is off to right.

1:29 (0:24) Cross modest-sized Chipola River on eastern edge of Marianna.
1:53 (0:00) Arrive Chipley.

CHIPLEY, FL - A town of 3,300 people, Chipley serves as the trading center for northern Washington County.

0:00 (1:20) Depart through heart of Chipley, rolling along "Main Street" with its collection of depressing old buildings.
1:00 (0:20) Through De Funiak Springs, which claims one of world's two "perfectly round" lakes. A large, natural clear spring is nearby in state recreational area.
1:20 (0:00) Arrive Crestview's doll-house station, at right.

CRESTVIEW, FL - Crestview is the county seat of Okaloosa County and serves as a stop for nearby Eglin Air Force Base.

0:00 (1:00) Depart Crestview.
0:09 (0:51) Cross good-sized Yellow River.
0:45 (0:15) Train now makes dramatic ascent over Escambia Bay on relatively new two-and-one-half-mile-long CSX trestle, while Interstate 10 is off to left.
0:53 (0:08) Now enjoy a lengthy ride beside Escambia Bay, one of two northerly extensions of Pensacola Bay.
1:00 (0:00) Arrive Pensacola.

PENSACOLA, FL - Pensacola's history is one of changing rule, a city with a five-flag past. Spain fought both the French and British for the city, first losing then regaining possession. Finally in the early 1800s, some two-and-a-half centuries after Spain's first presence, Andrew Jackson claimed victory for America. The fighting for Pensacola was not yet put to rest, however. During the Civil War, Union troops captured the city, giving the North a strategic location for establishing blockades of Confederate ports along the Gulf. Today, Pensacola is Florida's largest deep-water port.

Because of the area's weather, the U.S. Navy has made Pensacola the home of naval aviation. The choice in 1914 to place the U.S. Naval Air Station there (on the site of old naval shipyard) played a significant part in shaping the town's economy and character.

0:00 (1:20) Depart Pensacola, and head due north to circumvent obstacle known as Mobile Bay.
1:03 (0:17) Leave state of Florida and enter Alabama.
1:05 (0:15) At Flomaton, join route of Gulf Breeze, the CSX line linking Birmingham with Montgomery and Mobile.
1:20 (0:00) Arrive Atmore.

ATMORE, AL — The community believes in centralized community services. Beyond the jet trainer in the park adjacent to the tracks is the City Hall, Fire Department, Chamber of Commerce and YMCA, all in a neat-appearing light-brick structure.

0:00 (0:21) Depart Atmore and immediately pass under Burlington Northern Railroad bridge.
0:04 (0:17) Atmore Country Club and golf course are just across highway to left.
0:21 (0:00) Arriving town of Bay Minnette, now closed Reichold Chemical plant is on left. On right, roof with fencing could hold picnic bench, but actually serves as Amtrak "station."

BAY MINNETTE, AL - Town is home to the University of South Alabama Baldwin County. The Reichold Chemical plant had been in operation for nearly 60 years, producing coatings and resins, then 1989 closure dealt economic blow to community.

The Baldwin Area Transit System (BRATS) provides bus service from the station to virtually any area of the county, including beaches.

0:00 (0:32) Depart Bay Minnette.
0:10 (0:32) Cross Tensaw River on first of five drawbridges between here and Mobile.
0:15 (0:17) Rumble over Mobile River on second drawbridge.

Amtrak's worst train wreck occurred just west of here at 2:50 in the morning on September 22, 1993 when the eastbound Sunset Limited plunged off the bridge over Big Bayou Canot. Three locomotives, a baggage car, a baggage dorm and two Superliner coaches went into the murky, 16-foot-deep waters, while a third coach was left jutting out over the end of the bridge and the remainder of the cars were still upright. Apparently, just moments before, two barges had broken loose from their tug and struck the bridge (which was barely seven feet above the water) causing a severe misalignment of the tracks. The tragedy resulted in 47 deaths, most from drowning.

0:18 (0:14) Now cross Bayou Sara on third drawbridge.

0:19 (0:13) On left, Mobile River now accompanies train approaching Mobile. Skyline is forward right.

0:20 (0:12) Fourth drawbridge carries train across Chicasaw Bogue.

0:25 (0:07) Roll beneath swooping Bay Bridge carrying vehicular traffic to and from Blakely Island and beyond.

0:26 (0:06) Trundle over Threemile Creek and last drawbridge, and then through freight yards. Alabama state docks, capable of handling 34 oceangoing vessels at one time, are seen on immediate left. Land on other side of Mobile River is Blakely Island situated in Polecat Bay, a northern extension of Mobile Bay. Freighters and other maritime vessels are usually prominent sights here. Battleship U.S.S. Alabama, permanently moored in harbor, is just beyond structures at left, but not visible from tracks.

0:28 (0:04) Elaborate, grey structure with red roof, off to right, is former GM&O Terminal, closed in 1957. Tallest structure in downtown Mobile, on right, is 34-story First National Building.

0:31 (0:01) Train now burrows right through Mobile's fancifully designed new Convention Center.

0:32 (0:00) Arrive Mobile's CSX-Amtrak station. In middle of Government Street on right, statue of Admiral Raphael Semmes, who was commander of Confederate States Steamer Alabama, seemingly welcomes Amtrak passengers to Mobile.

 MOBILE, AL - See page 117.

0:00 (0:35) Depart Mobile, and for a short while, pass by numerous docks bustling with maritime activity.

0:06 (0:29) Brookley Airport and industrial complex is now at left.

0:07 (0:25) Cross three creeks in next three minutes, Eslava, Montlimar and Halls Mill, while still in confines of Mobile.

0:26 (0:09) Leave state of Alabama and enter Mississippi.

0:35 (0:00) Arrive Pascagoula.

 PASCAGOULA, MS - Situated at the mouth of the Pascagoula River, this port city enjoys a diverse economy based on maritime industries such as shipbuilding and maritime commerce. It is also a favorite vacation destination for those seeking ocean-oriented recreational opportunities.

0:00 (0:22) Depart Pascagoula.

0:01 (0:19) Cross Pascagoula River and then West Pascagoula River. River is famous for its legendary singing sound, which is subject to numerous scientific theories, but none have been proven. Ships at left are being built for Navy by Ingalls Shipyard.

0:16 (0:06) Learning Depot Day Care, at left, has picked up on railroad's proximity for decorative theme.

0:20 (0:02) Cruise directly across mouth of Biloxi Bay, then enter city of Biloxi.

0:22 (0:00) Arrive Biloxi.

 BILOXI, MS - Established in 1717, Biloxi was one of the earliest white settlements in the lower Mississippi Valley. It was in Biloxi that Jefferson Davis, president of the Confederacy, spent his retirement years. His antebellum mansion, Beauvoir, overlooks the Gulf and provided a quiet place for Davis to write his history of the Confederacy. The home still has many of its original furnishings and can be toured year round.

0:00 (0:15) Depart Biloxi. Keesler Air Force Base, electronics training center for U.S. Air Force, will be on right.

0:15 (0:00) Arrive downtown Gulfport, where attractive brick station awaits on left.

GULFPORT, MS - Planned as a rail/sea terminus, Gulfport is the beneficiary of some of the widest streets of any of the towns along the coast. In 1882, the town became the unlikely setting for the world heavyweight boxing championship when John L. Sullivan beat Paddy Ryan.

0:00 (0:18) Depart Gulfport, with glimpses of Gulf afforded at left.

0:15 (0:01) Train now ventures forth onto two-mile trestle that spans mouth of St. Louis Bay. Highway 90 bridge parallels on

Sunset Limited - Convention Center, Mobile, Alabama
JACK SWANSON

right, while waters of Mississippi Sound meet horizon on left.

0:18 (0:00) Arrive Bay Saint Louis dollhouse station.

 BAY SAINT LOUIS, MS - This city is the location of NASA's National Space Technology Laboratory. Guided tours of its space shuttle complex are available.

0:00 (1:17) Depart Bay Saint Louis.

0:10 (1:07) Note smattering of houses on stilts at left, many appearing to have water access only.

0:13 (1:04) Creep across Pearl River and enter Louisiana while departing Mississippi. Watch for alligators that can often be spotted in waters below as train progresses through these wetlands.

0:19 (0:58) Offshore oil rigs are visible in Gulf to left.

0:20 (0:57) Cross The Rigolets—grassy lowlands laced with channels that drain Lake Pontchartrain, to north, into Lake Borgne and Gulf of Mexico at left.

0:24 (0:53) Tugs with barges and other ships can sometimes be seen moving through grasses on left. Craft are actually plying waters of Intracoastal Waterway.

0:30 (0:47) Cross over major waterway known as Chef Menteur Pass, connecting Lake Pontchartrain to Lake Borgne and Gulf.

0:35 (0:42) On left, impressive flocks of white seagulls blanket New Orleans landfill.

0:37 (0:40) Large, multi-storied, blockish building, on left identified by NASA lettering, is NASA's Michoud Space Center.

0:45 (0:32) Now cross Inner Harbor Navigation Channel connecting Lake Pontchartrain to Mississippi River. Boats, cranes, barges, all make interesting maritime scene.

0:47 (0:30) Downtown New Orleans skyline now comes into good view, left forward.

0:49 (0:28) Route ducks beneath Interstate 10.

0:54 (0:23) LSU School of Dentistry makes brief appearance at left.

0:55 (0:22) Just one of several golf courses contained in City Park is on left while Park itself is on both sides of track.

1:00 (0:17) Typical above-ground cemeteries, necessitated by water table that is just below ground's surface, can be seen both sides—Rosedale at left, Metairie across highway at right.

1:08 (0:09) Gigantic golden blister to left is famed Superdome.

1:10 (0:07) Facilities for newspaper publishers *Times Picayune* appear on right.

1:12 (0:05) Cruise beside Amtrak's coach yards and engine shops.

1:17 (0:00) Arrive New Orleans.

 NEW ORLEANS, LA - See page 112.

0:00 (1:25) Departing New Orleans, imposing Superdome structure can be seen directly on right. This multi-purpose sports complex is home of National Football League's Saints. Adjacent to east is modernistic Hyatt Regency Hotel.

0:04 (1:15) On left, train winds around publishing facilities of *Picayune States-Item Times.*

0:08 (1:11) Just prior to major highway interchange, campus of Xavier University can be seen on left.

0:14 (1:05) On forward left, magnificent 4.4-mile-long Huey P. Long Bridge comes into view. Within minutes train will ascend its lofty heights, affording "airliner" view of encompassing sights. On right lie industrial parks of Jefferson Parish while, on left, New Orleans skyline is silhouetted against rolling Louisiana landscape. And below, barges and freighters ply waters of mighty Mississippi River at one of nation's busiest ports. Avondale Shipyards occupy shoreline at right.

0:30 (0:49) Gradually descend from bridge into swamplands of famous "Bayou Country." Here, admist haunting imagery of this forbidding wilderness, lies heartland of Cajun culture.

0:40 (0:39) At Harahan, intriguing "aboveground" cemetery on right is typical of many such cemeteries in southern Louisiana where saturated soil discourages conventional burials.

0:46 (0:33) On right, vast grain loading facilities are entrenched along banks of Mississippi River.

0:48 (0:31) Highway 90 joins on left, and follows for nearly 1,100 miles to El Paso, Texas.

0:50 (0:29) On right, first of many refineries reflects abundant petroleum resources of this area. In distance, another dramatic bridge spans Mississippi River.

0:58 (0:21) Cross Bayou Des Allemands. ("Bayou" is common Southern colloquialism for slow-moving river.)

1:03 (0:16) Sugarcane crop on left represents an important staple of state's agricultural economy.

1:13 (0:06) At town of Lafourche, cross bayou of same name.

1:17 (0:02) In distance, on right, is campus of Nichols State University.

1:19 (0:00) Cross Bayou Blue and arrive Schriever station.

SCHRIEVER, LA - An industrial oriented town of southern Louisiana, Schriever has become home for offshore-drilling related industries.

0:00 (1:23) Depart Schriever.

0:12 (1:11) Slip through watery confines of cypress-imbedded Chacahula Swamp.

0:14 (1:09) Gargantuan equipment of offshore-drilling rigs is assembled at McDermott plant on left.

0:17 (1:06) Pontooned helicopters, seen on left, play an important role in offshore industry. Immediately thereafter, cross Bayou Chene whose banks are clustered with maze of freighting apparatus.

0:22 (1:01) Approaching Morgan City, miles of pipe and drilling rods border tracks on right, soon to tap depths beneath ocean floor.

0:26 (0:57) Intracoastal Waterway on left affords convenient access to miles of inland industries which line its banks.

0:27 (0:56) At eastern edge of Morgan City, cross Atchafalaya River that, too, is a scene of bustling dockside activity. If Mississippi River had its way, it would flow through this 200-foot deep channel, but Army Corps of Engineers has built dams to keep Mississippi flowing through New Orleans instead. Only overflow is permitted to come this way.

0:38 (0:45) Near Patterson, cross large outlet of Grand Lake.

0:43 (0:40) At Garden City, some fine plantation estates can be seen on right.

0:52 (0:31) A few miles east of Franklin, cross outlet of Bayou Teche.

1:06 (0:17) Attractive church, on right, and ornate "above-ground" cemetery, on

left, highlight journey through Jeanerette.

1:22 (0:01) On right, stately colonial mansions accent gracious neighborhood of New Iberia. Immediately adjacent can be seen lofty domed towers of St. Peter's Catholic Church.

1:23 (0:00) Arrive New Iberia.

NEW IBERIA, LA - A blend of France and Spain in a semi-tropical setting gives New Iberia a special sort of charm. Several attractions draw tourists to this modern business community, including: Shadows on the Teche, an antebellum plantation and museum; Mintmere and the Armand Broussard House, two more antebellum plantation homes; and Jungle Gardens on Avery Island, where a bird sanctuary exists on 200 landscaped acres, and Tabasco Sauce is manufactured.

0:00 (0:22) Depart New Iberia.

0:10 (0:12) Sugarcane, one of state's predominant crops, is grown in field on left.

0:19 (0:03) Lafayette Municipal Airport is immediately across U.S. 90 on right. Cross Vermilion River.

0:22 (0:00) Arrive Lafayette.

LAFAYETTE, LA - This fast-growing city is in the very heart of "Cajun" country. Many oil-related firms have located here, and it is home for the University of Southwestern Louisiana. Longfellow described this country as "The Eden of Louisiana" in his poem "Evangeline"—and it is indeed, with soft-flowing bayous, verdant, moss-covered forests and flowers blooming year-round. Each fall, "Festivals Acadiens" is held here, featuring Acadian culture with Cajun food, music and crafts.

0:00 (1:25) Depart Lafayette.

0:22 (1:03) Pool-table-like fields, both sides of train, are often flooded for raising rice, a major regional crop.

0:37 (1:00) Cross Bayou Nezpique which drains into Lake Arthur, Lake Charles and Intracoastal Waterway—the latter being a series of connecting bodies of water that extend from Brownsville, Texas along the Gulf and then up the Atlantic coast until it reaches Boston— the world's longest such waterway. Shipyards are at left and sternwheeler is frequently docked here.

0:43 (0:42) Nostalgic Bull Durham adorns

one of Jennings' buildings at right.
1:25 (0:00) Arrive Lake Charles.

LAKE CHARLES, LA - A deep-water port with access to the Gulf of Mexico has made this the industrial center of southwestern Louisiana. Oil, cement and chemicals are just some of the varied products that are produced or processed here. Of interest is the Imperial Cacasien Museum with a 300-year-old Sallier Oak still offering protective shade.
0:00 (1:25) Depart Lake Charles.
0:04 (1:21) While crossing Calcasien River, look at railing of adjacent highway bridge for crossed-dueling-pistol decor.
0:38 (0:47) As we cross Sabine River, bid farewell to Louisiana and welcome to Texas, largest of the 48 contiguous states. Don't expect to see the open ranges quite yet, as countryside is still heavily agricultural, with rice fields and sorghums more dominant than herefords and angus.
1:18 (0:07) Cross a shipping channel as we near Beaumont; downtown will be off to right. Here, terrain starts to open up a bit, as Texas begins to look a bit more like Texas.
1:25 (0:00) Arrive Beaumont.

BEAUMONT, TX - Although settled much earlier by French and Spanish fur trappers, Beaumont was truly born in 1901 when the world's greatest oil well, the Lucas Gusher of Spindletop fame, blew in and started a new era. Besides being an industrial giant, it is both a major port and an agricultural center. Beaumont has a tradition of producing fine athletes. Numerous professional football players have been produced by local high schools, and Babe Didrikson Zaharias, perhaps the world's greatest woman athlete, called this her home.
0:00 (1:37) Depart Beaumont.
0:14 (1:23) Small Beaumont Municipal Airport on right handles private craft with commercial aircraft using airport southeast of town.
0:25 (1:12) On right, some of area's rice fields, which use flood irrigation during growing season, appear just before Nome, TX.
0:47 (0:50) Cross Trinity River about two miles west of Liberty, TX.
1:08 (0:29) Cross large San Jacinto River

which flows into Galveston Bay just south of here.
1:09 (0:28) Just before Sheldon, St. Regis Paper mill is clearly visible through trees on right.
1:12 (0:25) Far in distance, across enormous pipe storage yard on left, it is possible to pick out 570-foot-high San Jacinto Monument—looking like a small smokestack on the horizon. It was here that Texas finally won its independence from Mexico with Santa Ana's capture by Sam Houston's Texas army in 1836.
1:18 (0:19) Small campus of Southern Bible College is on left as we near Houston.
1:22 (0:15) Sprawling Southern Pacific yards are adjacent on left.
1:26 (0:11) Note considerable rail freight containers awaiting use on left and railroad tie manufacturing operation on right.
1:37 (0:00) Arrive Houston where, to left and beyond station, America's most dramatic skyline of modern architecture should impress any visitor. Although basic structures withstood hurricane of 1983, storm broke thousands of windows and filled streets with six inches of glass.

HOUSTON, TX - Houston, the largest city in Texas with a metropolitan population of nearly three million, grew for two reasons: its excellent port facilities, enhanced by the construction of a ship canal to Galveston, and the discovery of oil in the immediate area.

In the late 1970s and early 1980s, spurred by a then-booming oil industry, Houston's skyline grew into a compacted maze of geometric patterns and reflections. A resurgence in the American skyscraper occurred here, creating a look that is the epitome of modernism.

Amtrak Station, 902 Washington Ave., 77002, is a small, efficient structure located on the edge of the downtown area. There are storage lockers, luggage carts, food and beverage vending machines and ample adjacent free parking.

For arrival and departure information only, call (713) 224-1577.

Cabs are usually available at train times. United Cab, 699-0000. Avis and Budget will pick up **rental car** customers at the station. Nearest **local bus** stop is two blocks from the station, 635-4000. **Houston International Air-**

port (to the north) and **William P. Hobby Airport** (to the south) are both considerable distances from downtown.

? **Greater Houston Convention and Visitors Council,** 3300 Main St., 77002. Call (713) 227-3100 or 800-231-7799.

Heaven on Earth Plaza Hotel, 801 Calhoun St. (at Milam), 77002; (713) 659-2222. Former Days Inn, located in a rather marginal area of downtown (southern fringe). Free shuttle to and from the station, about two miles. $55.

Allen Park Inn, 2121 Allen Parkway, 77019; (713) 521-9321 or 800-231-6310. Large motor hotel with lots of amenities, just out of the immediate downtown area. Will pick up at station, about two miles. $70.

Downtown has a four-mile **underground pedestrian-way,** lined with shops and restaurants, with maps for self help. Inquire at the visitors center or your hotel. Also downtown is **Sam Houston Park,** 1100 Bagby, near the Allen Center, with a collection of historical buildings that can be toured. The **Houston Civic and Cultural Center** covers 16 blocks and contains performing arts facilities.

Houston's biggest attractions, however, are not downtown. NASA's **Johnson Space Center** is 30 minutes southeast of town with two-hour, self-guided tours. The **Port of Houston** has two-hour boat tours of the nation's third largest port. And **San Jacinto Battleground,** where Texas won its independence and current mooring place of Battleship Texas, is east of downtown, off Hwy. 225 and Farm Road.

0:00 (4:08) Depart Houston.
0:26 (3:42) Impressive skyline of Houston's Galleria is off to right.
0:43 (3:25) Plant of Imperial Sugar Company is on right in aptly named Sugar Land, TX.
0:45 (3:23) White and tan buildings, about one-fourth mile distant on right, are facilities of Central State Farm, Department of Corrections.
0:53 (3:15) Cross huge Brazos River just before entering Richmond. Note elegant old frame depot on right.
1:15 (2:53) Cotton and soybeans, growing

on both sides of tracks, are typical crops of southern Texas. Rice fields are also prevalent along this stretch.
1:24 (2:44) Silo-like elevators on right marked "Rice Industries" are for storing and shipping local rice crops.
1:48 (2:20) Cross a Colorado River—not of Grand Canyon fame, but smaller river that drains an enormous section of west-central Texas plains before emptying into Gulf of Mexico.
1:49 (2:19) In Columbus, be sure to note stylish old courthouse on left, complete with clock-embedded dome.
2:03 (2:05) At Weimar, former rail station on left now serves as attractive community library.
3:35 (0:33) Nearing San Antonio, runways of Randolph Air Force Base are off to left.
4:02 (0:06) East Yards of Southern Pacific are on left as Sunset Ltd. nears center of San Antonio.
4:08 (0:00) Arrive San Antonio where nicely renovated station on right is but a stone's throw from heart of downtown. Tower of Americas, constructed for 1968 HemisFair, bolts skyward. Adjacent to station, huge structure with cable-suspended roof is Alamodome. Completed in 1993, it is city's sports, convention and concert center.

 SAN ANTONIO, TX - See page 254.

0:00 (3:04) Depart San Antonio.

As the train now proceeds across the vast expanse of the west Texas prairie, sage, yucca and cactus periodically punctuate this otherwise arid landscape.
2:56 (0:08) Approaching Del Rio, pass grounds of Laughlin Air Force Base on left. Nice collection of older military aircraft enhances entrance.
3:04 (0:00) Cross series of finely landscaped canals arriving Del Rio, where, on left, light brick Southern Pacific Depot will soon serve as fine intermodal transportation center.

DEL RIO, TX - This "Queen City of the Rio Grande" is the largest city between San Antonio and El Paso. Sheep and Angora goat production is the prevalent industry, giving rise to the town's claim of "Wool and Mohair Capital of the World." The Mexican border is just to the south where Ciudad Acuna, a city of 40,000, offers night spots and shops for those wanting a taste of Old Mexico.

0:00 (2:24) Departing Del Rio, Mexican city of Acuna can be seen atop bluffs on left. This is last recognized port of entry until El Paso. Rio Grande, obscured at this time, represents border between U.S. and Mexico.

0:11 (2:13) Rio Grande now joins on left.

0:16 (2:08) Cross waters of Amistad Reservoir, which has 850 miles of shoreline. Constructed just below confluence of Rio Grande and Devil's River, Amistad was joint project of U.S. and Mexico, with Spanish word for "friendship" reflected in its name.

For the next 200 miles, a perceptive eye can detect subtle changes in the desert vegetation, as the train climbs nearly 3,500 feet to the high prairies surrounding Alpine.

0:48 (1:36) Suddenly, train embarks across Pecos High Bridge spanning magnificent canyon cut by Pecos River 321 feet below. This awesome spectacle, certainly one of trip's scenic highlights, was perhaps not so endearing to early pioneers who had to cross by wagon without benefit of bridges. High Bridge was completed in 1892. After original was replaced in 1944, it was cut into numbered sections and shipped to Guatemala where it now serves as a highway bridge.

We are in the western end of the state and it will take The Sunset Limited nearly seven more hours to reach El Paso. This is mercurial, however, compared with those historic Butterfield Stages that took more than two full days to cover the same route.

1:04 (1:20) It was near here, on a trestle high over Deadman's Gulch, that a silver spike was driven in January 1888, completing a New Orleans-San Francisco route—nation's second transcontinental rail line. (Actual section of track was abandoned when Pecos High Bridge went into service.)

1:06 (1:18) Pass by Langtry on left where Judge Roy Bean once enforced his own brand of "law west of the Pecos." Visitors center is replete with memorabilia of this

Alamodome - San Antonio, Texas
DORIS SWANSON

legendary "lawman."

A monumental airlift took place here in 1954 when devastating storms, spawned by Hurricane Alice, left an eastbound Sunset Limited stranded, unable to travel in either direction due to washed out track. Some 200 passengers had to be evacuated by helicopter.

1:26 (0:58) Sunset route was especially vulnerable to outlaws who could easily retreat across nearby Mexican border. In 1912, last attempted train robbery in these parts took place at Baxter's Curve, just west of Val Verde and Terrell county line. Two desperados, one of whom had ridden with Butch Cassidy and The Sundance Kid, boarded a westbound train from their galloping horses, only to have their villainous effort end in failure when they were shot to death during the incident.

2:09 (0:15) Ruins of wall built by U.S. Infantry to defend against Pancho Villa in 1916 still stand near tracks at Dryden on left.

2:24 (0:00) Arrive Sanderson.

SANDERSON, TX - Now a railroad shipping point for this sparsely settled ranching country, Sanderson was once the lair of renegades, outlaws, cattle rustlers and general ne'er-do-wells. Judge Roy Bean operated a saloon here as well as one in Langtry, Texas.

0:00 (1:40) Depart Sanderson. Sheep pens on right are a time-worn testimonial to an industry that, to this day, remains a vital economic mainstay of region.

0:05 (1:35) At right, cave and earthen mound were used by Apaches for shelter and cooking, respectively.

0:32 (1:09) Glass Mountains can now be discerned in distance to right. Throughout Texas and New Mexico, mountain ranges represent subclassifications of much larger range known as Rocky Mountains. Del Norte Mountains are on left.

0:57 (0:44) On forward right and left, Davis Mountains are now interposed upon horizon.

1:06 (0:34) At right, handsome old Gage Hotel in Marathon faces train, while its newer adobe addition is across street to west. Built with the profits from his nearby 500,000-acre ranch, the original structure was opened by Alfred Gage in 1927 to serve as his headquarters whenever he was on one of his many trips to Marathon. He died only a year after its opening. Hotel has been beautifully restored and refurbished with wonderful antiques, making it a popular stop for those visiting nearby Big Bend National Park.

1:38 (0:02) Approaching Alpine, large "SR" enscribed on hillside right identifies campus of Sul Ross State University. Students from over 20 countries attend this school perhaps best known for its rodeo teams.

1:40 (0:00) Handsome Spanish-style station greets passengers arriving Alpine.

ALPINE, TX - This is the trading center and county seat of Brewster County—Texas' biggest county and larger than the state of Connecticut. Its mild winter climate, together with Big Bend National Park 80 miles to the south, have made Alpine a favorite tourist stop.

0:00 (3:33) Small "canyonlands" are a temporary delight departing Alpine.

0:15 (3:18) At Paisano Pass, Sunset Limited reaches 5,074 feet, highest point on route.

0:18 (3:15) On forward left, Chinati Peak (7,730 feet) is most prominent member of Cuesto del Burro Range.

0:22 (3:11) At night (eastbound), be sure to look to right (south) for possible sighting of famous Marfa Ghost Lights. Mysterious glowings were first spotted in 1883 and have been reported off and on ever since. Subject of TV's *Unsolved Mysteries,* many have speculated but no one is certain what really causes these strange shimmerings. Marfa, nine miles to west, throws a party every Labor Day weekend to celebrate this mystery.

0:29 (3:04) Passing through Marfa, watch for sailplanes which frequent updrafts above nearby mesas. Palatial domed building seen on right houses Presidio County Courthouse. Although dome was formerly crowned by "Scales of Justice," ornament was displaced by rifle blast from a disgruntled prisoner who apparently felt that justice had not been served. On west side of "Main Street" is landmark El Paisano Hotel. Over 300 members of cast and crew of movie *Giant* stayed here during film's shooting in 1955, while stars Rock Hudson, James Dean and Elizabeth Taylor were housed in some of Marfa's private homes. Hostelry has been one of best in region, complete with indoor swimming pool.

0:31 (3:02) On western outskirts of town, Mitre Peak (6,100 feet) stands out back on right. White domes of University of Texas' McDonald Observatory are on southern prominence of Davis Mountains in far distance right. At base, Ft. Davis is highest town in Texas at 5,050 feet. Town's courthouse reputedly has turnstiles to keep stray cattle from appearing in court.

0:47 (2:46) On immediate left, $15 million helium-filled "blimp" is one of six such DEA craft floating over Southwest using radar in an effort to stem drug traffic coming up from Mexico. Controversial because of cost and questionable effectiveness, balloons are size of a Boeing 747, are tethered on 10,000-foot cables and can spot planes within 170 miles in any direction.

0:49 (2:44) Antelope herds are a frequent sight throughout this particular region.

0:59 (2:34) Re-emergence of agricultural fields outside Valentine reflects gradual descent off high plains. Sierra Vieja Mountains border on left, while peaks of Van Horns approach on forward right. A scene from movie *Giant* was filmed near old windmill on left.

1:27 (2:06) Highway 90, trackside companion of last 24 hours, now departs north.

Gain one hour as train passes from Central to Mountain Time. Set your watch back (forward if eastbound) one hour.

1:34 (1:59) On left, Sierra Vieja Mountains give way to Quitman Range.

1:57 (1:36) At Sierra Blanca, mountains of same name hover in distance on right, while Quitmans are now dwarfed by Mexican Hueso Range on left. Town has only adobe courthouse still in use in Texas.

2:28 (1:05) Remnants of old fort, which once guarded U.S. mail, can be seen on right at Fort Hancock.

2:40 (0:53) Cotton fields and pecan groves are suddenly popular sights of Rio Grande Valley.

2:48 (0:45) South of Fabens, colorful decorations adorn graves of Hispanic cemetery on right. Stately trees forming row on east side of graveyard are Italian cypress. Once in town, nice mission-style church is notable on left, while large facility on right gins and bundles area's cotton crop.

3:14 (0:19) Approach El Paso through industrial district of which Mobil refinery and Phelps Dodge Copper (note marvelous old brick chimney) operations are predominant. Ahead north, Franklin Mountains encircle city. Supposedly, if light is right (and imagination vivid), silhouette of Ben Franklin can be discerned in their midst.

3:30 (0:03) On left, note publishing facilities of *El Paso Herald Post and Times.*

3:33 (0:00) Arrive El Paso. Station, styled in early mission architecture, with pieces of Mexican pottery displayed atop surrounding walls, was completed in 1905 and designed by firm of Daniel H. Burnham, designers of Washington, D.C.'s Union Station. Back on left, unusual sweeping shell encloses Civic Auditorium and Theatre.

EL PASO, TX - This is the largest U.S. city on the Mexican border, and its southerly neighbor Juarez is likewise the largest Mexican border city. Their combined populations approach one million. Cradled in an ancient mountain pass (hence the name "El Paso"), it is surrounded by mountains over one mile in elevation. Its excellent climate has also made it a popular winter resort. This is Amtrak's gateway to Carlsbad Caverns National Park, 145 miles northeast of here, and is the closest Amtrak comes to connecting with the National Railways of Mexico which can be boarded in Juarez.

0:00 (1:27) Departing El Paso, Mexican sister-city of Juarez can be seen on left atop palisades of Rio Grande. Inscription on mountain above city admonishes "Read the Bible and lead a fuller life."

0:05 (1:22) On right, pass campus of University of Texas at El Paso. Floodlight banks protrude above university's "Sun Bowl" stadium, carved within hillsides on right.

0:06 (1:21) On forward left, massive monument of Christ on cross is ensconced atop Sierra de Cristo Rey. On last Sunday in October, thousands of pilgrims trek four miles to summit to celebrate "Feast of Christ the King." Shrine also represents point where Texas, New Mexico and Mexico all meet.

0:10 (1:17) Sprawling Southwestern Portland Cement Company on right, and Asarco refinery on left, greet train as it crosses Rio Grande from Texas into New Mexico. Proceed along through dramatic outcroppings and rock formations before finally settling back atop parched landscape of Southwestern desert.

0:11 (1:16) Sunland Park Race Track can be seen on right.

0:12 (1:15) White post on immediate left identifies international border, only 30 feet away and Amtrak's closest encounter with Mexico.

0:22 (1:05) Mountains now extending both on right and left are known as the Portillos.

0:23 (1:04) Lee Trevino-designed golf course, lined with homes and condos, is in vivid contrast to surrounding desert in valley off to right.

0:48 (0:39) Ancient lava flows are very visible through this region. Flow now comes within 100 feet of tracks on left.

1:20 (0:07) Florida Peak (7,295 feet) prevails amidst Florida Mountains on left, while Cooke's Peak (8,408 feet) is mainstay of Cooke's Range on right. In Florida Range, mountain with hole through it is Window Peak.

1:21 (0:06) Beyond Floridas, prominent peaks at east end of small range are known as Three Sisters.

1:25 (0:03) On eastern outskirts of Deming, cross Mimbres River.

1:26 (0:01) Note old steam locomotive that now reposes in park off to left.

1:27 (0:00) Arriving Deming, distinctive clock tower of Luna County Courthouse juts prominently above town on left.

DEMING, NM - Situated in a beautiful agricultural area of 70,000 irrigated acres, Deming farmers raise cotton, peanuts, pecans, beans and grain sorghums in abundance. This is a rock hound's delight, and a state park has been established just for their needs—appropriately named "Rock Hound State Park." A warm winter climate, with an average snowfall of only 2.7 inches, makes this a popular spot for retirees.

0:00 (0:48) Depart Deming.

0:15 (0:33) Crest Continental Divide at 4,584 feet, Amtrak's lowest crossing of nation's rooftop.

0:48 (0:00) Arrive Lordsburg.

LORDSBURG, NM - As with so many Western towns, Lordsburg was established with the arrival of the railroad. It is situated near the eastern edge of The Gadsden Purchase, a strip of land acquired by the United States from Mexico in 1854 that permitted the railroad to continue its march westward to the Pacific Ocean.

Nestled between the Burro and Pyramid mountain ranges, this area was once controlled by Cochise, greatest of the Apache chiefs. Now a desert community of 4,250, serving as the trade center for southwestern New Mexico, it enjoys 350 days of sunshine and a typically mild southern New Mexico climate. As was the case in Deming, Lordsburg's weather makes this another appealing retirement area.

Phelps Dodge has recently constructed a large smelter near here to process ore from copper deposits found throughout the region.

0:00 (2:00) Depart Lordsburg.

0:11 (1:49) Large, dry lake bed on right frequently produces deceiving mirage that creates acres of "water" glimmering across its barren sands.

0:19 (1:41) On left, as Sunset crests a ridge, adobe ruins and some live-in shacks mark site of camp where thousands of Chinese laborers were once housed during construction of Southern Pacific.

0:28 (1:32) At left are Chiricahua Mountains which rise to a maximum height of 9,795 feet. Face of Indian warrior Cochise can be clearly distinguished at top of ridge staring skyward as he lies atop "his mountains." Peloncillo Mountains are off to right.

0:30 (1:30) Reddish-brown water tank on right sits in New Mexico while windmill on left is in Arizona as Sunset crosses states' boundary.

1:04 (0:56) Breeze through Willcox, AZ, home of former Western movie star Rex

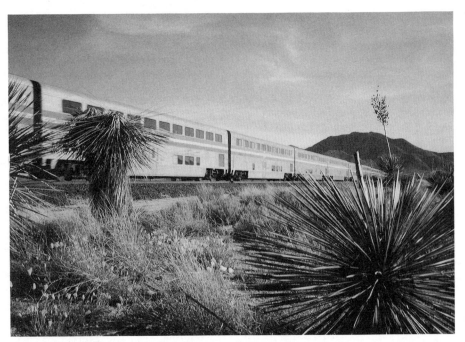

Sunset Limited - Cochise, Arizona
DORIS SWANSON

Allen, whose museum faces tracks at right. Then, to right, just before enormous old depot, bright red rail car houses Sonora Express Restaurant.

Our elevation is now 4,167 feet above sea level, but by the time we reach Phoenix, we will have descended 3,075 feet to an elevation of only 1,092 feet.

1:11 (0:51) Tracks now stretch across broad flats called Willcox Playa. Although much of surface is covered with brown stagnant water, much more is host to clear imaginary water of one of country's more deceiving mirages. Dragoon Mountains, on left, are clearly reflected in this "non lake." Cochise electric power plant is also off to left.

1:18 (0:42) Two aging establishments at left, Cochise Hotel and Cochise General Store, comprise entire business district of Cochise. If guests of hotel plan to eat there, it is necessary to call elderly proprietress in advance and make arrangements.

1:57 (0:03) Small airport on left serves Benson, AZ, our next stop.

1:59 (0:01) Cross San Pedro River whose waters flow north and west into Gila River, and eventually join Colorado River at Yuma, AZ.

It was along this stretch of the San Pedro, in 1540, that Coronado and his expedition, up from Mexico, first entered the present United States in their search for the legendary Seven Cities of Cibola— cities thought to have streets lined with goldsmith shops and doorways studded with emeralds and turquoise. No such cities were ever found, but the horses left behind, and the teachings of Spanish priests, forever changed the lives of the Indians of the Southwest.

1:50 (0:00) Arrive Benson where small shelter on left pretends to be a rail station.

BENSON, AZ - As early as 1860, Benson served as a stop for the old Butterfield Stage. Then in 1880, with the arrival of the railroad, it became a shipping point for the mines around Tombstone. In recent times, ranching and explosives manufacturing have become more important.

0:00 (1:07) Departing Benson, Rincon Mountains form desert horizon on right.

0:07 (1:00) Hillside on left has profusion of yuccas—those plants with clusters of spear-like leaves out of which tall shafts spurt upwards, culminating in tops of clustered whitish blossoms. Resourceful Indians of Southwest made a variety of products from this decorative bush, including sandals, baskets, edible fruit and even soap.

0:11 (0:56) Coal Tower at left (just before Mescal Siding at right) once furnished fuel for steam locomotives from an era past.

0:12 (0:55) Movie set used for TV's *Young Riders* can be glimpsed about a mile off to right. Except during stormy weather, radar surveillance blimp can be seen hovering above Ft. Huachuca in distance to left. Idea is to spot planes bringing in drugs from Mexico.

0:23 (0:45) Precariously perched atop peak on right is "castle" built by one who obviously prefers mountaintop opulence to more mundane flatland setting.

0:25 (0:42) Just ahead lie two overlapping rail bridges, westbound traffic usually taking the higher route and eastbound the lower. Highway bridge also crosses eastbound tracks. Through this stretch, eastbound and westbound tracks are often separated by a half-mile distance or so, with a more curving route on eastbound trackage, permitting an easier uphill grade.

0:27 (0:40) Snaking through several rugged arroyos, excellent views of front of train are frequently offered.

0:35 (0:32) On right, pink Catholic church, with century-plant landscaping, is Shrine of Santa Rita in the Desert.

The church was dedicated in 1935 to the memory of a Japanese scientist, Dr. Jokichi Takamine, who built the first superphosphate works in Tokyo and was the first to isolate the active agent in adrenaline. His widow's second husband, a local rancher by the name of Beach, had a church constructed in honor of Takamine. Built around stained glass windows of a dismantled Methodist church, the interior contains a black marble font designed in Italy and a hand-carved crucifix from Bavaria. The chapel bell came from a Southern Pacific steam locomotive.

0:45 (0:22) Tall tail fins of mothballed military aircraft can be seen on right at Davis Monthan Air Force Base. Up to 5,000 planes have been stored here for salvage.

0:46 (0:21) Numerous World War II aircraft are huddled together at Pima Air Museum, on right, including presidential plane used by Lyndon B. Johnson.

0:49 (0:18) On right, Tucson Electric Power Co. generating facility provides electricity to much of Tucson's metropolitan area.

0:50 (0:17) Parked in yards of Rail Passenger Services, on right, fascinating assortment of vintage rail passenger cars can sometimes be spotted.

0:51 (0:16) Last glimpse of Davis Monthan Air Force Base on right. Olive twin-beamed aircraft are Air Force A-10 attack planes, built with heavy emphasis on survivability. These tank-killing "Warthogs" played prominent role in Gulf War. Their gattling-gun-style 30 mm cannon can spew out two-pound projectiles at rate of 65 per second.

0:52 (0:12) Southern Pacific rail yards extend along route as train enters Tucson. Train sometimes stops at this point to refuel.

1:04 (0:03) University of Arizona campus, distinguished by stadium, is off to right, while Santa Rita Mountains hunker down on horizon to left.

1:07 (0:00) Arrive Tucson where stretched-out mission-style station awaits on left.

TUCSON, AZ - Very possibly the oldest continually inhabited city in North America, Tucson has lived under four flags in the last 300 years: Spanish, Mexican, Confederate, and American. It was first visited by Father Kino, a Jesuit missionary, in the late 17th century. The Spanish Army later chose the site for a frontier fortress, constructing a walled "Presidio" near what is now the center of Tucson. The site of the original Presidio can still be visited, along with many other old structures in the historic area of the city.

A sunny and dry climate contributes to the popularity of Tucson as both a retirement and a tourist community. It has a metropolitan population of 550,000, with a casual, desert style of living predominating. It is also a gateway to Mexico, with the international border just 67 miles to the south at Nogales.

River Rd.
Oracle Rd.
Stone Ave.
Sabino Canyon Rd.
Ft. Lowell Rd.
Grant Rd.
Alvernon Way
Craycroft
6th Ave.
4th Ave.
Campbell Ave.
Speedway
Tanque
5th St.
Kolb Rd.
Toole Ave.
6th St.
Broadway
22nd St.
36th St.
Tucson
2
4
1
3
19
10
N

Amtrak Station
1 - Visitors Information
2 - Historic Area
3 - Park Inn
4 - Holiday Inn

Amtrak Station, 400 E. Toole Ave., 85701. This fine old Spanish-style station is located on the eastern edge of Tucson's small but vital downtown. There are storage lockers and vending machines. There is metered parking in front and a pay-parking lot one block away on Toole Ave.

Cab stand at the station; Yellow Cab, 624-6611. **Local bus** information, 792-9222; Transit Center is one block west of the station; **Greyhound/Trailways,** two blocks from station at 2 South 4th Ave. Budget **rental cars** offer pick up and drop off for Amtrak passengers, 889-8800. **Tucson International Airport** is 11 miles south of the station.

Tucson Convention & Visitors Bureau, 130 S. Scott Ave., 85701; (602) 624-1817.

Holiday Inn Broadway, 181 W. Broadway, 85701; (602) 624-8711. A very popular downtown hotel, five blocks from the station. $65.

-Park Inn Santa Rita, 88 East Broadway, 85701; (602) 622-4000 or 800-437-7275. Former Santa Rita Hotel, a long-time Tucson landmark. Only three blocks from the station. $38.

"Historic" Tucson, the original town, is within walking distance, just west of the station in an area bounded roughly by 6th Ave., Kennedy, Main and Toole. This area includes many old buildings and sites of historic interest including the El Presidio Park which occupies a portion of the original "Presidio" and the Tucson Museum of Art. A brochure describing this entire area with a walking tour map is available from the Visitors Bureau. **Old Pueblo Historic Trolley** runs along 4th Avenue and University.

Not in the downtown area, but a must, is the **Arizona-Sonora Desert Museum,** 16 miles west of Tucson, with a fine collection of desert animals and plants. Drive west and southwest on Speedway, then follow the signs, or west on Ajo and right at Kinney Rd. Also popular, but rather "touristy," is **Old Tucson,** 14 miles southwest of Tucson, which has been used as a set for various Western movies. Shops and gunfights. Near the Desert Museum.

The **Mission San Xavier Del Bac** (the White Dove of the Desert), nine miles south of Tucson, is perhaps the most beautiful mission in the Southwest. Its white structure stands out vividly against the brown desert sand. The **Saguaro National Monument** is in two sections, one east and one west of Tucson. The eastern section is perhaps a bit more impressive and has dense stands of Saguaro cactus. **Kitt Peak National Observatory,** 45 miles west of Tucson, is one of nation's top observatories; tours weekends and holidays. The **Pima Air Museum** has an excellent collection of Air Force planes, dating from the 1940s. The **Sierra Madre Express of Tucson** offers deluxe passenger train tour service to Mexico's Copper Canyon; (602) 747-0346, or 800-666-0346.

0:00 (1:05) Departing Tucson, small but showy downtown skyline appears on immediate left.

0:09 (0:56) Santa Catalina Mountains, off to right, rise to a height of 9,157 feet at summit of Mt. Lemmon and contain Tucson's closest ski area.

0:17 (0:48) Facility of Arizona Portland Cement Company is just beyond Interstate 10 on left.

0:33 (0:32) Pinal Air Park, in distance to left, has world-wide clientele for restoration of aircraft. On right, Arizona Public Service Company plant has enormous oil storage capacity for fuel, while supply tank cars are frequently at siding on right farther downline.

0:34 (0:31) Sprawling pecan orchards provide sudden change of scenery on right. Besides pecans and cotton, truck farming is prevalent between here and Phoenix, raising the likes of cauliflower, broccoli and cabbage.

0:38 (0:17) On left, Picacho Peak juts dramatically from Arizona desert. Westernmost conflict of Civil War was fought 12 miles south of here. Fine stands of saguaro cactus stud hills on both sides and continue on left for several miles, offering finest stands to be viewed on Amtrak.

0:45 (0:20) Bid farewell to Interstate 10 as tracks curve away to right.

0:46 (0:19) On left, warehouses with adjoining storage yard of yellow cubes are Federal Compress, where bales of cotton are received from nearby gins to have them compressed, stored and then sold. Larger yellow blocks are uncompressed bales while smaller ones are sans air. Crops are harvested in March and October but bales are marketed throughout year.

0:55 (0:09) On hill, off to right, low-slung sheds house cows of Goldman Dairy. Dairy is entirely automated, milking 1,200 Holsteins to furnish Phoenix with fresh dairy products.

0:56 (0:08) Facility on left, with enormous piles of scrap metal along tracks, is recycling plant of Proler International Corp., where scrap is shredded and then melted down into ingots of nearly pure tin.

0:57 (0:07) Neatly landscaped single-story brick buildings, across highway to left, are Arizona Training Center for mentally and physically handicapped.

0:58 (0:06) Small community at left of tracks is Randolph, with all streets named after black activists and others who have played important roles in black advancement—names such as Cleaver, Malcolm X, King and Kennedy.

1:05 (0:00) Arrive Coolidge's glass box station.

 COOLIDGE, AZ - This Arizona community of nearly 7,000 is home of Central Arizona College.

0:00 (0:50) Depart Coolidge.

0:02 (0:40) About a mile or so to left is enormous canopy protecting a smaller structure beneath it. This is Casa Grande Ruins National Monument. The protected building was constructed almost 650 years ago out of unreinforced coursed caliche—a desert soil with a high lime content. Main structure was centerpiece of a Hohokam Indian village, but its exact use and purpose is still unknown. Recent studies, however, suggest possible astrological use.

0:15 (0:35) Sprawling H and G Feedlots on left fatten cattle while large shades above pens provide protection from desert sun.

0:17 (0:33) Note grape vineyard on left—just one more crop raised in this fertile area.

0:20 (0:30) Arizona Boys Ranch, where disadvantaged youth are offered a better chance, is immediately adjacent to route on left.

0:23 (0:27) Jets, barracks and aircraft hangers of Williams Air Force Base are off to right.

0:31 (0:19) Agricultural surroundings now give way to industrialized suburbs of Phoenix.

0:46 (0:04) Arizona State University is on right as we enter Tempe. Sports stadium is site of annual Fiesta Bowl football game, while circular building is school's music hall designed by Frank Lloyd Wright.

0:50 (0:00) Arrive Tempe where Amtrak shares depot with Mexican restaurant.

 TEMPE, AZ - A part of the Phoenix metroplex, Tempe is home to Arizona State University with 40,000 students. The school is Arizona's largest and oldest institution of higher learning.

0:00 (0:15) Depart Tempe.

0:02 (0:13) Sunset Limited crosses Salt River which has its sources in Sierra Anchor and White mountains to east, providing water for massive irrigation projects throughout south central Arizona.

0:07 (0:10) Sky Harbor Airport, serving Phoenix, is just to left with major east-west runway paralleling tracks.

0:12 (0:03) Downtown Phoenix stands on right—dominating glass-sided skyscraper houses headquarters of Valley National Bank; brown 24-story structure with disk-like revolving restaurant on top is Hyatt Regency.

0:15 (0:00) Arrive Phoenix.

 PHOENIX, AZ - The capital of Arizona and one of America's fastest growing cities, Phoenix began in 1860 as a small settlement on the banks of the Salt River. As with so many other towns, its first real growth came when the railroad arrived in 1887.

The name "Phoenix" comes from the mythical Phoenix bird which supposedly burns itself on its own funeral pyre every 500 years, and then mysteriously rises from its own ashes. The city was predicted to eventually rise from the ancient Indian ruins found nearby—thus the name.

Although hot in the summer (air conditioning was invented here), its mild winter climate has accounted for its popularity as a winter destination for tourists from colder climes. Its Southwestern architecture in a desert setting lends further appeal. Besides tourism, manufacturing and agriculture (cotton and citrus) are other leading industries.

While the metropolis seems to enjoy(or suffer) a never-ending expansion, downtown Phoenix has remained compact and, by most standards, underdeveloped. A few new high-rise offices and hotels crowd the convention center, while the rest of the inner city tries to fight off urban shabbiness.

But true to its name, downtown Phoenix is now rising from its own ashes. A new Arizona Center, with shops and dining, the Phoenix Mercado, with Mexican boutiques and cafes, a fine collection of early Phoenix residential architecture in Heritage Square, and Symphony Hall, all gathered around the Civic Plaza, have given the downtown a new heart.

Amtrak Station, 401 West Harrison St., 85003; (on 4th Ave. seven blocks south of Van Buren St.) is a recently renovated structure located in a marginal downtown area. There are storage lockers and very limited free parking.

Cab stand at the station; Yellow Cab, 252-5252. **Local buses** are three and four blocks north of the station on Jefferson and Washington streets; 253-5000. Nearby **rental car** availability is Budget at Central and Adams, with station pick-up and drop-off service, 267-1717. **Sky Harbor International Airport** is four miles east of the station.

Phoenix and Valley of the Sun Convention & Visitors Bureau, One Arizona Center, 400 E. Van Buren, 85004; (602) 254-6500.

The following hotels are reasonably convenient to the station and are in good downtown locations:
-**Ramada Hotel,** 401 N. 1st St. (at Polk), 85004; (602) 258-3411. Completely renovated in 1988. Eleven blocks from the station. $69.
-**San Carlos,** 202 N. Central Ave. (at Monroe), 85004; (602) 253-4120 or 800-528-5446. Built in 1927, restored and listed on National Register of Historic Places. Complimentary breakfast. Ten blocks from the station. $79.

Besides the downtown attractions mentioned above, there is the **Arizona Museum of Science & Technology,** 80 N. 2nd Street, which has numerous "hands-on" science exhibits. For an outstanding **view of the city,** enjoy a meal in the revolving restaurant at the top of the Hyatt Regency, 2nd St. and Adams.

Phoenix's major attraction, however, is its winter sun and warmth. To better appreciate this desert environment, the **Desert Botanical Garden** in Papago Park, 1201 N. Galvin Parkway, has pathways through unusual cacti and other desert plants, and the **Phoenix Zoo,** 5810 E. Van Bureau, has over 1,000 animals, many representative of the Arizona-Sonora region.

0:00 (3:20) Depart Phoenix. Darkness usually prevails on stretch between Phoenix and Pomona.

3:20 (0:00) Arrive Yuma.

YUMA, AZ - Yuma does quite well in this southwestern Arizona setting. Irrigation from the Colorado River has turned much of its sand into productive farmland and its climate has made it a popular resort center. Just outside of town is the site of the infamous Yuma Territorial Prison which is now a State Historical Park. Built by convicts, it was nearly escape proof and was considered to be the most secure prison in the West.

0:00 (1:45) Depart Yuma.

Pass from Mountain to Pacific Time as train crosses Arizona state line into California. Since Arizona does not observe daylight saving time, set watch back (forward if eastbound) one hour, only if rest of country is not on daylight saving time.

1:10 (0:35) As Sunset cruises near California's Salton Sea, lowest point on route is touched—202 feet below sea level.

1:45 (0:00) Arrive Indio.

INDIO, CA - Indio had a typical beginning in 1894 when it was a minor stop on the Southern Pacific, and the depot served as the town's social center. Climate and irrigation, however, led to Indio's eventually becoming "The Date Capital of the World," with this tasty fruit being feted each February during the National Date Festival. Just to the south is California's largest inland body of water, the Salton Sea. This recreational lake was formed at the turn of the century when the Colorado River broke through levies and flooded into a depression for two years. Indio also serves as Amtrak's stop for nearby Palm Springs.

0:00 (1:50) Depart Indio.

As the train now emerges upon the Southern California megalopolis, the small farms and dairies which have dotted the landscape since daybreak are suddenly engulfed in the imposing shadows of mammoth industrial operations and the ever-encroaching suburban sprawl.

1:26 (0:24) Coming into Colton, cross concrete-lined Santa Ana River. San Gabriel Mountains now border on right into Los Angeles.

1:42 (0:08) Extensive vineyards surround Brookside Winery on right. Facility is oldest commercial winery in California.

1:43 (0:07) On left, pass Ontario International Airport. (Amtrak plans to make Ontario a scheduled stop in near future.)

1:50 (0:00) Arrive Pomona Commercial Street station. Agricultural theme highlights colorful mural across from station on left. (Amtrak plans to replace this stop with Ontario, mentioned just above.)

 POMONA, CA - In 1875, Solomon Gates was awarded a free lot for naming Pomona after the Roman goddess of fruit. The name remains appropriate to this day, reflecting the city's prominence as a mecca of citrus production. Pomona is also the noted autumn host of the Los Angeles County Fair, boasting the largest attendance of any such fair in the U.S. Nearby, too, is the resort of Mt. Baldy whose ski slopes, trout streams and scenic campgrounds provide a haven of year-round recreation.

0:00 (0:45) Departing Pomona, St. Joseph's Catholic Church is attractive fixture on left. A short distance downline, St. Paul's Episcopal Church is easily recognized on right by its distinctive mission-style architecture.

0:03 (0:42) On right, skirt campus of California Polytechnic University at Pomona.

0:12 (0:33) At La Puente, massive building complex ensconced atop bluffs on right is Indian Hills Convention and Golf Center.

0:16 (0:28) Between La Puente and El Monte, cross oft-dry San Gabriel River.

0:18 (0:26) Pass El Monte airport on right, then proceed across concrete riverbed of Rio Hondo.

0:23 (0:22) Emerging from brief tunnel at Temple City, train travels briskly down median of Interstate 10 past an envious stream of congestion-bound commuters.

0:30 (0:14) Just prior to departing "freeway route," campus of California State University at Los Angeles can be seen on right.

0:36 (0:09) On right, cluster of tall buildings is Los Angeles County Hospital which operates in conjunction with University of Southern California.

0:39 (0:05) Concrete channel, which some-times becomes Los Angeles River, joins and follows on left. Perched atop bluffs on forward left is Dodger Stadium, home of one of baseball's powerhouses.

0:44 (0:01) Engage in U-turn across Los Angeles River and slip past County Jail on left. On forward right, City Hall is predominant tower of downtown Los Angeles skyline, while double-domed building in foreground houses Post Office annex.

0:45 (0:00) Arrive Los Angeles.

 LOS ANGELES, CA - See page 302.

Superliner Economy Bedroom, daytime
JACK SWANSON

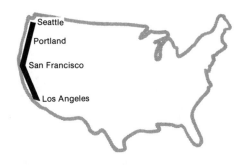

Coast Starlight

Those well populated West Coast megalopolises of Seattle, San Francisco and Los Angeles are all ports of call for Amtrak's Coast Starlight. With numerous intermediate stops that include such popular destinations as Portland, Sacramento, San Luis Obispo and Santa Barbara, the Starlight is now one of America's most patronized trains. Make your reservations early.

A cavalcade of aesthetic delights makes this trip worth taking just for the experience of being there. A grand trek through the Cascades of Oregon, a maritime excursion along San Francisco Bay, a delightful amble over Cuesta Grade and a 113-mile daylight traverse along California's frothy shoreline north of Ventura (much of it only accessible by train) are just some of high points of a trip that offers one fascinating glimpse after another.

Although called the Coast Starlight, fortunately most of the route is traveled during the daylight, leaving only northern California's scenes obscured in darkness.

Amtrak furnishes train-side motorcoach service from Oakland to downtown San Francisco, including a stop at the CalTrain Station at 4th and Townsend.

Southbound Schedule (Condensed)
Seattle, WA - Midmorning Departure
Portland, OR - Early Afternoon
Eugene, OR - Late Afternoon
Oakland, CA - Early Morning (2nd Day)
  (Trainside motor coach service to and from San Francisco.)
San Jose, CA - Midmorning (2nd Day)
Santa Barbara, CA - Late Afternoon (2nd Day)
Los Angeles, CA - Midevening Arrival (2nd Day)

Northbound Schedule (Condensed)
Los Angeles, CA - Midmorning Departure
Santa Barbara, CA - Early Afternoon
San Jose, CA - Early Evening
Oakland, CA - Late Evening (Motor coach service to and from San Francisco.)
Eugene, OR - Early Afternoon (2nd Day)
Portland, OR - Midafternoon (2nd Day)
Seattle, WA - Midevening Arrival (2nd Day)

Frequency - Daily.
Seating - Superliner coaches.
Dining - Complete meal and beverage service. Lounge service also available, with sandwiches, snacks and beverages, and movies.
Sleeping - Superliner sleepers with deluxe, family, economy and special bedrooms.
Baggage - Checked baggage handled at most stations.
Reservations - All-reserved train.
Length of Trip - 1,389 miles in 34 hours.

Route Log

SEATTLE, WA - Seattle lies on the eastern shores of Puget Sound and is flanked by two beautiful ranges of mountains, the Olympics to the west and the Cascades to the east. Although situated relatively far north, its proximity to the Pacific Ocean, warmed by the Japan Current, gives it a very temperate climate

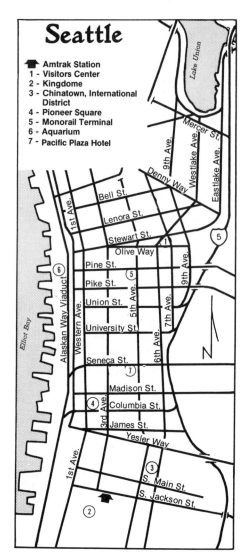

Seattle

🚂 Amtrak Station
1 - Visitors Center
2 - Kingdome
3 - Chinatown, International District
4 - Pioneer Square
5 - Monorail Terminal
6 - Aquarium
7 - Pacific Plaza Hotel

King Street Station, 3rd and South Jackson streets, is located on the south edge of the downtown area next to the Kingdome. The station has vending machines, a snack bar, a newsstand, redcaps, luggage carts, a direct phone for cabs and pay-parking.

Cab stand at the station; Farwest Taxi, 622-1717. **Local buses** are one block from station; free bus rides within the downtown area; call 553-3000. Buses travel through a unique transit tunnel beneath 3rd Ave. in the heart of downtown. To reach **Tunnel Buses** from the station, take stairs up to Jackson St. then one block east. For **rental cars,** Hertz has delivery service at the station, 682-5050. **Monorail** (to the Space Needle) terminal, 5th Ave. and Stewart at Westlake Center. There is a connecting **Amtrak Thruway Bus** between the King Street Station and downtown Vancouver, B.C. **Seattle Tacoma International Airport** is 12 miles south of the station.

The **Waterfront Streetcar** service connects the International District next to King Street Station to Pioneer Square and the waterfront north to Pier 70. Trolley stops close to the station at 5th and Jackson.

For various **marine services:** Alaska Marine Highway System, 676-8445; Washington State Ferries (Coleman Dock), 464-6400; Victoria Clipper (high-speed catamaran, Seattle-Victoria), 448-5000.

Seattle-King County Convention and Visitors Bureau, 8th and Pike, Level One, Galleria, Convention Center, or write them at 520 Pike St., 98101. Call (206) 461-5840.

Pacific Plaza Hotel, 4th Ave. at Spring St., 98104; (206) 623-3900 or 800-426-1165. Popular downtown hotel for economy minded. Attractive, small rooms. $3 cab ride from the station, two blocks from tunnel bus stop. Free continental breakfast. $74.

-Travelodge by the Space Needle, 200 6th Ave. N., 98109; (206) 441-7878. As the name says, it's near the Space Needle at the Seattle Center. $59.

For those interested in touring sports facilities, **the Kingdome,**

year-round.

Founded in the mid-nineteenth century, the city grew to importance largely because of its excellent natural harbor—even though it is more than 100 miles from the open sea. It developed rapidly in the 1870s during the Alaska gold rush and more recently as a leader in aircraft and space technology.

home to three of Seattle's major league teams, is next to the station. **Iron Horse Restaurant** in Pioneer Square, 311 Third Ave. S., has meals delivered to tables by a model train. **Pioneer Square,** in the area of James St. and First Avenue, features shops, restaurants and "underground tours" of an historic downtown area, much of which was covered over after a fire in 1889; includes underground abandoned stores and store fronts. It's approximately five blocks from the station.

Of course, in Seattle **seafood dinners** are a major attraction in and of themselves. Some find seafood restaurants are located along the waterfront between Union and Madison streets. Other sealife, not for eating, can be viewed at the **Seattle Aquarium** at Pier 59. **Tours of the harbor** are available at Pier 57. **Pike Place Market,** from Pike to Virginia on Pike Place, a literal bazaar of fresh fish, produce and other foods.

The **Space Needle** has a great observation deck and a nice restaurant (revolving, of course) at the top. This can be reached from downtown by taking the monorail.

0:00 (0:54) Depart Seattle. Back on right, peaks of Olympic Range hover majestically in distance, while in foreground, castle-like Smith Tower was once tallest building west of Mississippi River. King Street Station's stately clock tower is another impressive fixture of Seattle skyline.

Directly on right is "Kingdome" sports complex, home of baseball's Mariners, basketball's Supersonics and football's Seahawks. Adjacent to Kingdome, small plot enshrines old Northern Pacific caboose.

For the next several miles, pass by the grounds of such recognizable corporations as Westinghouse, Sears, Nabisco, Ford and Zellerbach. Even in the midst of these industrial climes, one is immediately impressed by the general cleanliness pervading this entire Northwestern region.

0:05 (0:49) Silhouettes of steel superstructures on right evidence major dockside activity at Elliott Bay.

0:13 (0:41) On right is King County International Airport. Boeing's original plant was here and the company still uses the airport for flight tests. A museum now occupies the former production facility.

0:14 (0:40) Green River joins on right as it lazily winds through residential district of Tukwila.

0:16 (0:38) Nicely landscaped grounds of Longacres Race Track can be seen on left.

0:22 (0:32) At tidy community of Kent, quaint old depot is noteworthy on left.

0:25 (0:29) Cross Green River.

As the urban congestion begins to thin, small farms and dairy operations become a more frequent sight. These pleasant pastoral environs are enwrapped in an endless blanket of greenery, nurtured by the abundant moisture so common to this part of the country.

0:31 (0:23) Another "modest" Boeing operation can be seen on right.

0:32 (0:22) Cross White River. Soon thereafter, train engages in a broad right turn that eventually settles on a northwesterly tack towards Tacoma.

0:36 (0:18) Cross Puyallup River. Old concrete bridge parallels on right.

0:41 (0:13) Travel directly through downtown streets of Puyallup. Distinguished older buildings now rival for recognition in shadows of more modern intrusions. Wide variety of flowers and shrubs accent attractive neighborhoods on west end of town.

0:43 (0:11) Cross Clark's Creek.

0:47 (0:07) Broad, arching treetops seemingly create tunnel through forest. Splendid covered bridge, crossing overhead, tops off this short but delightful stretch.

0:49 (0:05) Puyallup River joins momentarily on right.

0:51 (0:03) Downtown Tacoma comes into view, perched atop lofty bluff on forward right.

0:52 (0:02) City Waterway joins on right. This inlet of Commencement Bay is central hub of Tacoma's vast shipping industry.

0:54 (0:00) Arrive Tacoma.

TACOMA, WA - The need for lumber in the 1850s gave birth to Tacoma when the first sawmill was established here. Today, two giants of this industry, Weyerhaeuser and St. Regis Paper, produce thousands of wood products. Shipbuilding is also a major industry, and Tacoma has become the second largest seaport on Puget Sound. The world's largest collection of octopi can be seen here, as well as one of the world's tallest totem poles. A week-long Daffodil Festival each spring culminates in the nation's third largest floral parade.

0:00 (0:43) Depart Tacoma, once again traversing banks of City Waterway. Here, shipping, logging and refinery operations share spotlight with bevy of comely shops and restaurants, cleverly housed in renovated wharf facilities.

0:02 (0:41) Tacoma Dome convention facility bulges up on left.

0:05 (0:38) Looming above cliff walls on left is ornate clock tower of Tacoma's Old City Hall. Originally constructed in 1893, building is enshrined in National Register of Historic Places, and now accommodates host of specialty shops, restaurants and office suites. Rounded tower, seen immediately adjacent to Old City Hall, presides atop general offices of Northern Pacific Railroad.

0:14 (0:29) Enter tunnel in midst of which train heads back south before finally emerging on shoreline of Puget Sound inlet. Impressive suspension bridge connects Tacoma with Olympic Peninsula on right. It was here, in 1940, that the original bridge, known as "Galloping Gertie" due to its erractic heavings during high winds, finally galloped once too often in an unusually strong windstorm. An amateur movie photographer captured the rare event and footage is still shown from time to time on TV or in movies.

For the next several miles, clusters of pleasure craft and secluded fishing coves are nicely interwoven along the rocky coastline of the Puget Sound. A magnificent array of gracious homes are ensconced atop the seacliffs, with this picturesque panorama an everyday spectacle.

0:16 (0:27) Fox Island can be seen directly on right, with McNeil Island lying a short distance south.

0:25 (0:18) Continue along seaside route, with Ketron Island now seen in midst of Sound.

0:32 (0:11) Train heads inland now, as farmlands, forests and rolling hills quickly displace nautical environs of last several miles.

0:35 (0:08) Cross Nisqually River.

0:40 (0:03) Cross Lake St. Clair with attractive homes along surrounding shoreline.

0:43 (0:00) Arrive Olympia-Lacy's new intermodal park. On right, Centralia Hotel ad proclaims "Our hack meets all trains," once an enticement for early-day train travelers.

OLYMPIA-LACY, WA - This is as close as the Starlight gets to Washington's capital city, Olympia, just seven miles off to the right and situated at the southern end of Puget Sound.

0:00 (0:20) Depart Olympia-Lacy.

0:03 (0:17) Cross Deschutes River.

0:13 (0:07) Just south of Bucoda, cross Skookumchuck River.

0:20 (0:00) Cobblestone walkways front grounds of handsome brick station as train arrives Centralia. Large white building, situated atop bluffs on left, is Centralia Armory.

CENTRALIA, WA - Founded in 1875 by a slave named George Washington, Centralia has grown to become a major food-processing and supply area. Pioneers constructed an unusual blockhouse along the Chehalis River to defend against Indians, and this interesting structure can still be seen in Fort Borst Park.

0:00 (0:47) Depart Centralia past profusion of logging operations, opportunistically located within easy access of Columbia and Willamette rivers.

0:05 (0:42) Traveling "Main Street" route through Chehalis, another fine old depot stands proudly on left and now serves as Lewis County Historical Museum.

0:12 (0:39) Cross Newaukum River.

0:20 (0:27) Passing through Winlock, note "World's Largest Egg" enshrined in glass monument on right. "Egg Day" festivities, held here each June, likewise recall community's former prominence in poultry industry.

0:30 (0:17) Cross Cowlitz River, which then follows intermittently on right.

0:43 (0:04) After passing through short tunnel, antiquated wooden trestle spans Cowlitz River, on right, which soon empties into Columbia River a few miles downstream.

0:44 (0:03) Approach Kelso-Longview

Coast Starlight - southern Oregon
DORIS SWANSON

with comely neighborhoods clustered along hillsides. A short distance downline, dramatic drawbridge spans Cowlitz River on right.

0:46 (0:01) Early 1900s street scene is subject of colorful building mural on left.

0:47 (0:00) Arriving Kelso-Longview, impressive Cowlitz County Courthouse can be seen across river on right.

KELSO-LONGVIEW, WA - Lumbering has always been the economic mainstay of the Kelso-Longview area. From the time the first sawmill was built in 1848 to the early 1920s, development was slow, but in 1922 Robert A. Long purchased 60,000 acres of timberland and then built the world's largest forest mill, starting the two cities toward becoming a major lumber-processing center. Located at the confluence of the Cowlitz and Columbia rivers, deep water port facilities give direct access to the world's markets.

0:00 (0:42) Weather permitting, departure from Kelso-Longview may afford views of truncated Mt. St. Helens (8,365 ft.) and Mt. Adams (12,307 ft.) on left,

while further north stands imposing Mt. Rainier at 14,410 feet.

0:04 (0:38) On left, pass Kelso-Longview airport.

0:05 (0:37) Cross Coweeman River which too joins Columbia shortly downstream.

0:07 (0:35) Emerge into clearing, affording first view of Columbia River on right. Large stockpiles of timber are corralled out in water awaiting transport. Across river, familiar silhouette of cooling tower readily identifies 460-million-dollar Trojan Nuclear Power Plant.

0:09 (0:33) Cross Kalama River.

0:11 (0:31) While passing through Kalama, note towering totem poles entrenched along river banks on right. Dominant one is world's tallest from a single tree.

0:16 (0:26) On right, private forest of hybrid cottonwood trees is being nurtured for paper production.

0:21 (0:21) Cross Lewis River.

0:25 (0:17) Pass through pleasant little community of Ridgefield. Just south of town, old wooden bridge crosses Lewis River on right. Sudden onset of marshy

287

terrain reflects abundant water resources of area.

0:35 (0:07) On right, train borders shoreline of Vancouver Lake.

0:40 (0:01) United Grain Corp. and Great Western Malting Company dominate industrial sprawl on outskirts of Vancouver.

0:42 (0:00) Delightful chalet-style station greets passengers on left as train arrives Vancouver.

VANCOUVER, WA - Strategically placed on the Columbia River, where ocean, air, rail and highway transportation converge, Vancouver has become a major shipping hub of the Northwest. Its lengthy history (it is the oldest non-Indian settlement in Washington) saw the likes of a trading outpost of the Hudson's Bay Company, the construction of Fort Vancouver, and the presence of Ulysses S. Grant when he was but a mere lieutenant in the U.S. Army. Both Fort Vancouver and the U.S. Grant Museum are open to the public.

0:00 (0:22) Depart Vancouver, crossing Columbia River (and Washington/Oregon state line) into Portland. In midst of river, traverse Hayden Island, while vessels and dockside facilities of vast shipping industry abound on both banks.

0:11 (0:11) On a clear day, magnificent Mt. Hood will loom in distance on right.

0:13 (0:08) Cross Willamette River, which then follows on left into Portland station. Willamette is another important shipping channel, as evidenced by heavy concentration of industry along its banks. Dramatic bridges span this waterway, with downtown Portland skyline silhouetted in background.

Slip beneath Fremont Bridge, Portland's newest, spanning Willamette River. Note fanciful mural on left, advertising "Broadway Deluxe Cab Co."

0:20 (0:02) On left, grand old steamboat now provides nostalgic atmosphere for River Queen Restaurant.

0:22 (0:00) Arrive Portland beneath stately clock tower of Union Station.

PORTLAND, OR - Portland claims to be "a beautiful, clean, green American City," and indeed it is. An attractively restored downtown is the heart of this community set amongst forested hills along the Columbia River. Its mild climate makes it one of the most desirable cities in which to live in the Pacific Northwest, a city with neither a sales tax nor mosquitoes.

And there seems to be energy here. Its seaport ships huge amounts of grain, major electronics firms have located here, there is a snappy new light rail system, and the city is still small enough to enjoy.

Union Station, 800 NW 6th Ave., is in an older section of downtown, but handy to Portland's city center. There are redcaps, a newsstand, vending machines, a snack bar and a very good restaurant. Pay-parking is in front of the station.

Cab stand at the station; Broadway Cab, 227-1234 and Radio Cab, 227-1212. **Local bus** stop is one block south of the station (chart in station). MAX (Metro Area Express) is Portland's new trolley (light rail) system that loops through the downtown core, then crosses Steel Bridge to reach the eastern suburbs, running during the day at 15-minute intervals. Buses and MAX are free within the downtown area; call TriMet, 233-3511, for recorded information. For **rental cars,** Dollar Rent a Car, about five blocks away, will pick up and drop off at the station, 228-3540. **Portland International Airport** is eight miles northeast of the station.

Greater Portland and Visitors Assn., 26 SW Salmon, 97204; (503) 275-9750 or 800-962-3700.

Imperial Hotel, 400 SW Broadway (at Stark), 97205; (503) 228-7221 or 800-452-2323. Simple, comfortable accommodations at reasonable rates; will pay for cab from station if driver goes to desk. Eight blocks from the station. $80.

-Hotel Vintage Plaza, 422 SW Broadway, 77205; (503) 228-1212 or 800-243-0555. For a very deluxe stay in downtown. Eight blocks from the station. $130.

Washington Park, 4001 SW Canyon Road, is one of the nation's nicest, has thousands of roses, a zoo with a train, Japanese gardens, a science museum, and an outstanding Western Forestry Center with exhibits of paper mills, lumbering and other unique aspects of this industry. #63 bus from downtown

Portland

🚂 Amtrak Station
1 - Visitors Information
2 - Washington Park
3 - Imperial Hotel
 & Hotel Vintage Plaza

goes to **Washington Park Zoo.** A miniature train provides transportation between the zoo and the **Japanese Gardens. Gray Line,** 226-6755, with pick up and drop off at hotels, has tours of the city, the northern Oregon coast, the Columbia River and Mt. Hood. The **Annual Rose Festival** is held in early June, with a parade, band and symphonic concerts, sporting events and many other activities throughout the week.

0:00 (1:12) Depart Portland and immediately cross Willamette River. Colorful "butterfly" mural can be seen in midst of commercial district on right. After running on Burlington Northern rails since Seattle, we follow main line of Southern Pacific for remainder of trip to Los Angeles.
0:13 (0:59) On left, pass campus of Reed College.

Proceed for next few miles through attractive suburbs of Milwaukie and Gladstone. On clear days, Mt. Hood may be viewed on left, towering 11,235 feet in midst of Cascade Range. Mountains of Coast Range can be seen on right.
0:27 (0:45) Cross Clackamas River.
0:29 (0:43) Slip through historic Oregon City, end of Oregon Trail and one-time territorial capital. Pioneers believed Willamette Valley to be "The Great Heartland."
0:30 (0:42) Large hydroelectric facility harnesses power from Willamette River which rejoins momentarily on right.

For next several miles, enjoy colorful character of small agricultural communities, as train travels directly through town centers enroute to state capital.
0:40 (0:32) Cross Molalla River.
0:45 (0:27) Cross Pudding River.
0:53 (0:19) Passing through Woodburn, old Southern Pacific steam engine is preserved on left.
1:12 (0:00) Arrive Salem, passing directly adjacent to state government offices on right. Very prominent is gold-colored statue of early pioneer, standing atop marble tower of State Capitol Building. Immediately thereafter, pass campus of Willamette University, oldest such institution in the West.

SALEM, OR - There is some dispute over just who named this capital city of Oregon, but it does seem certain that it was named after Salem, Massachusetts. The capitol, one of the nation's newest, is constructed of beautiful white marble with fine murals and sculptures.
0:00 (0:27) Depart Salem.
0:04 (0:23) On left, pass Salem's Municipal Airport.
0:15 (0:12) Oregon's largest llama herd can be seen on right. These sure-footed camel cousins are becoming popular with hikers, both as pack animals and as wilderness companions.
0:19 (0:08) At south end of Jefferson, cross Santiam River.
0:27 (0:00) Arrive Albany through well-kept residential district. Old stone depot is interesting, yet unobtrusive like rest of town.

ALBANY, OR - The first steamboat reached Albany in 1852, the same year its first industry—a grist mill—was put into production. Finally, in 1870, the railroad reached here, but not until the builder of the then O&C Railroad received a $50,000 "incentive" from the residents so they would not be bypassed by the line. Albany is the home of the World Championship Timber Carnival, featuring tree topping, speed climbing, bucking, log rolling and axe throwing. Also, the largest Veterans' Day celebration in the nation is held here.

0:00 (0:37) Depart Albany.

0:08 (0:30) Cross Calapooia River.

0:25 (0:14) After passing through Harrisburg, cross Willamette River, having narrowed considerably since last observation.

0:36 (0:03) Approach Eugene through large Southern Pacific rail yards, while colorful murals adorn building walls on right.

0:40 (0:00) Lane County Jail borders on right as train arrives Eugene, Amtrak's westernmost stop.

EUGENE, OR - Lumbering remains Eugene's economic mainstay, while the University of Oregon lends a college atmosphere to this west-central Oregon community. Outdoor recreational opportunities are plentiful, most notably on the McKenzie River, which provides excellent fishing and boating.

0:00 (2:58) Departing Eugene, another interesting mural can be seen on right as train heads southeasterly toward Willamette National Forest.

0:02 (2:56) Train skirts University of Oregon campus on right before crossing Willamette River into sister-city of Springfield.

0:11 (2:47) Small home on right, facing tracks, has own red-light rail signal that blinks at train as it passes.

0:19 (2:39) Cross Willamette River, and follow to its source atop Cascade Summit. Numerous crossings occur throughout this stretch.

The ensuing 75-mile ascent is one of the most scenic routes in the country, with the jutting peaks of the Cascade Range providing a dramatic backdrop for the dense and colorful vegetation of the Willamette National Forest.

As the train slowly winds through tunnels and snowsheds, quaint little towns, snuggled within the wilderness, offer fascinating glimpses of a robust, pioneer lifestyle. Majestic waterfalls, tumbling down the mountainsides, further embellish this spectacular scenery.

0:34 (2:22) On left, Lookout Point Reservoir dams Willamette River.

0:56 (1:59) Small town of Westfir is highlighted by beautiful covered bridge, spanning Willamette River on right.

1:00 (1:55) Begin climbing "The Hill" at Oakridge, an ambitious ascent of over 3,600 feet in 44 miles, that culminates atop Cascade Summit.

1:04 (1:51) Cross Salmon Creek.

1:45 (1:10) Arrive 4,840-foot Cascade Summit. Southern descent is much more gradual, proceeding well into California before losing appreciable altitude. Snow-depth gauges can be seen on right between summit and Chemult.

1:53 (0:54) Deep blue waters of Lake Odell border on left. Back on right and left, brief clearings in forest permit inspiring vistas of Cascade peaks.

2:22 (0:25) Cross Little Deschutes River.

2:47 (0:00) Arrive Chemult. Depot is conspicuous because of absence. In its place, a mere wooden gangplank escorts passengers onboard.

CHEMULT, OR - Situated between the Deschutes and the Winema national forests, Chemult is in the very heart of Oregon's mountains and lakes recreational lands. Bend, just 57 miles to the northeast, with year-round sunshine and the likes of swimming, golf, tennis, canoeing, hiking and horseback riding is one of the more popular Oregon vacation spots.

0:00 (1:13) Depart Chemult through dense woodlands of Winema National Forest. Milling and logging concerns are a most frequent sight throughout this stretch.

0:20 (0:56) Famed Crater Lake is perched high in the mountains, just 15 miles to the right.

0:37 (0:36) Cross Williamson River, which follows periodically on right. A few miles downstream, river plunges unexpectedly into colorful, rocky gorge.

0:49 (0:24) Pass through Chiloquin. Nearby Collier Memorial State Park features largest museum of logging equipment in U.S. Just outside town, cross Sprague River, which proceeds to join Williamson River, and flow south into Upper Klamath Lake.

0:59 (0:14) On right, begin skirting shoreline of Upper Klamath Lake, with Mt. McLoughlin (9,495 ft.) towering in distance. Between April and September, large white pelicans are a popular attraction of area.

1:13 (0:00) Arrive Klamath Falls.

KLAMATH FALLS, OR - Klamath Indians once cooked with steam from a vast reservoir of geothermal energy which still lies beneath this area. Thought to be one of the world's largest such stores of energy, it is currently used to heat businesses, schools and homes.

0:00 (2:25) Depart Klamath Falls.

0:21 (2:04) Leave Oregon and enter California as border is crossed just before train rumbles through short tunnel.

0:27 (1:58) Through small town of Dorris, where Mount Shasta now looms majestically ahead, left. At 14,162 feet it is a bit shorter than Mt. Rainier, but because of lower surroundings, Shasta is actually the larger.

0:41 (1:44) Prairies now form Butte Valley National Grasslands.

1:15 (1:10) Cresting 5,202-foot Hebron Pass, train is now nearly a mile high.

1:21 (1:04) Mounds on right, between tracks and highway, were actually built by State of California to provide a nesting environment for Canadian geese.

1:22 (1:03) Beyond highway to right is Grass Lake, a wetlands area that in early 1900s was a lake, complete with 32 room resort hotel. Its fate was sealed, however, when dynamite blast created hole in lake bed allowing water to drain into porous rock below. Area is now home to very rare Grass Lake tiger salamander, not discovered until 1969. Another scarce species, the Greater Sandhill Crane, also can be found here.

2:00 (0:25) Through historic lumbering town of Weed, while scenic Mt. Shasta still dominates scene on left.

2:25 (0:00) Arrive Dunsmuir.

DUNSMUIR, CA - This small recreational community is nestled in the foothills of 14,162-foot Mt. Shasta. Once a major railroad center of the Southern Pacific, it now enjoys an economy dominated by small resorts offering fine fishing in the summer and skiing in the winter.

0:00 (1:49) Depart Dunsmuir. From here scenery becomes increasingly rugged and mountainous and will remain so until Redding.

1:18 (0:26) Lake Shasta is gemstone of Lake Shasta National Recreation Area.

1:44 (0:00) Arrive Redding.

REDDING, CA - Lumbering and salmon fishing are both important to Redding, but its location at the northern terminus of the Sacramento Valley (the most northern point in California where orange and palm trees grow naturally) provides the weather and geography to attract thousands of vacationers to the area. Beautiful Lake Shasta, with its 370 miles of shoreline, offers boating and fishing, while wild and scenic rivers provide white-water canoeing for the more adventuresome. Additional attractions include tours of Shasta Caverns (reached only by boat) and Shasta Dam, three times as high as Niagara Falls and one of the most impressive structures in America. This is also the gateway to Lassen Volcanic National Park.

0:00 (1:12) Depart Redding.

1:14 (0:00) Arrive Chico.

CHICO, CA - Gold attracted the earliest settlers to this area, but it was rich agricultural lands that enticed many to stay. Chico was founded by one of California's most famous citizens, General John Bidwell, when he formed a 28,000-acre farming enterprise named Rancho Del, and which became the most renowned agricultural establishment in the state. Today, ample harvests of rice, almonds, walnuts, peaches, prunes and olives are produced in the area as well as numerous other crops and cattle. Bidwell's elaborate mansion is now a state park. Chico is not only a modern trade center, but is also home of California State University, Chico, where 12,000 students seek degrees in 20 fields, including business, education and nursing. South of here is Oroville Dam—the highest and largest earth-filled dam in the country.

0:00 (0:41) Depart Chico.

0:40 (0:00) Arrive Marysville.

MARYSVILLE, CA - As in the case of Chico, Marysville got its start when early-day prospectors flocked here to work placer claims in the area's streams. Also, as in Chico's case, the permanence of Marysville has been largely due to agriculture. Fruit and other crops are important to this Sacramento Valley town.

0:00 (0:59) Depart Marysville.

0:59 (0:00) Arriving Sacramento, gracious Spanish architecture highlights many buildings of downtown district on left. Ornamental-domed tower is City Hall, whose weighty bronze doors require at least two strong men to open for business each morning.

SACRAMENTO, CA - To describe Sacramento as a treasure chest of Western historical lore would still be something of an understatement. Consider first that the famous California "Gold Rush" began here when nuggets were discovered at Sutter's Mill in 1848. Only 12 years later, the Pony Express was welcomed into town at the completion of its first historic run. And in 1863, a group of Sacramento visionaries began charting a route across the Sierra Nevadas that would eventually become the most ambitious link in the nation's first transcontinental railroad.

Such monumental distinctions would seemingly be hard to surpass, although Sacramento's current role as one of the world's largest food production centers assures it a status of increasingly vital importance. The city, too, maintains statewide prestige as the capital of California.

As might be expected, historical highlights are the emphasis of Sacramento's major attractions, from the reconstructed facilities of Sutter's Fort, to the splendid array of Victorian homes preserved throughout the city. Of particular interest to train buffs is the California State Railroad Museum, located only one block from the Amtrak station. Here, sound

effects and even simulated motion are used to re-create the romantic atmosphere surrounding the glory years of the railroad.

0:00 (0:20) Departing Sacramento, stately Capitol Building can be seen on left. Built in 1869, gilded globe still remains atop dome, despite protestations of original architect who described it as "simply ridiculous and abominable—a slur on our tastes forever."

During 1906 remodeling, "modern" conveniences replaced 45 fireplaces that once heated building. Iron hitching posts surrounding carriage entrance were also lost at that time.

On immediate left is aforementioned California State Railroad Museum. Sacramento Locomotive Works are on right.

0:02 (0:17) Proceed across Sacramento River, noting on left riverboats along shore and interesting drawbridge a few blocks downstream.

0:10 (0:06) At considerable expense, railroad and highway have been elevated for several miles permitting underlying lands to be flooded for rice farming. On left, over 4,000 columns hold road above muddy croplands.

0:20 (0:00) Arrive Davis. Spanish motif of this handsome station is popular style of depots throughout southern California.

DAVIS, CA - Long known for its prolific production of agricultural crops, Davis is noted more recently for its pioneering attitude in the field of energy conservation. In 1975, the City Council enacted the nation's first energy conservation building code, setting standards for all new houses and apartments. A city-wide recycling program is also highly successful. Most impressive, however, is Davis' claim that its many miles of scenic bicycle paths account for as much as 25% of the city's total vehicle traffic.

0:00 (0:44) Departing Davis, border University of California at Davis campus on right. Grapevines are part of school's renowned wine research program.

0:08 (0:36) Elongated antique shed at left sags with age, but still provides shelter for several hundred sheep.

0:24 (0:20) Passing through Suisun-Fairfield, stately while-pillared Solano County Courthouse stands distinctively on right at terminus of palm-lined Union

Avenue. Shortly thereafter, emerge upon waters of Suisun Bay.

0:34 (0:10) On immediate left, hundreds of Merchant Marine vessels are clustered in storage along shoreline, readily conjuring up images of Normandy invasion. Ships are awaiting tow to Sacramento where they will be unceremoniously cut into scrap. Meanwhile, invasion of different sort is evidenced on forward left, where docks are often overflowing with thousands of Japanese auto imports. Last ship before bridge is fabled Glomar Explorer, sporting a white heliport platform on its stern. This deep-sea research vessel made headlines some years back when it attempted to retrieve a sunken Russian sub from ocean's floor.

0:38 (0:06) Cross drawbridge spanning Suisun Bay. Structure is over one mile long and stands 70 feet above water. Prior to its construction in 1930, train was broken down into sections and ferried across bay. Once on southern shore, entangled maze of refinery apparatus escorts train into Martinez.

0:47 (0:00) Arrive Martinez. While in station, Martinez Museum can be seen in old frame house on left.

MARTINEZ, CA - This important commercial and military port was also the home of John Muir, one of the nation's earliest and most outspoken conservationists. His house is now preserved as a National Historic Site. Joe Dimaggio Drive is on the right side of the train, honoring the "Yankee Clipper" who was raised here.

0:00 (0:30) Depart Martinez along Carquinez Strait, connecting Suisun and San Pablo bays. Carquinez Bridge looms impressively in foreground right, while on left, famed golden hills are subtly encroaching upon landscape.

0:09 (0:20) With town of Crockett huddled on hillside left, travel directly through midst of C & H sugar refinery. Immediately thereafter, train bears south along shores of San Pablo Bay.

0:29 (0:00) Arrive Richmond.

RICHMOND, CA - Richmond's popularity as a convenient suburban stop is enhanced by its trackside connections with BART, a rapid transit system servicing many outlying regions throughout the Bay Area.

0:00 (0:12) Departure from Richmond affords first view of dramatic San Francisco skyline across bay. Golden Gate Bridge can be seen north of city, while Bay Bridge connects with Oakland to the south. Alcatraz Island is also visible below Golden Gate Bridge.

0:05 (0:03) On right, pass Golden Gate Race Track.

0:12 (0:00) Arrive Emeryville.

EMERYVILLE, CA - A new stop for Amtrak's Coast Starlight and California Zephyr. Sometime in 1994, Amtrak plans to make this the Bay Area stop for those using connecting buses to and from San Francisco.

0:00 (0:06) Depart Emeryville.

0:06 (0:00) Arrive Oakland. Amtrak buses will meet train for passengers enroute to San Francisco. (Plans are to shift this shuttle service to Emeryville sometime in 1994.)

OAKLAND, CA - See page 209.

SAN FRANCISCO, CA - It was in 1848, when the "city" had approximately 800 residents, that Sam Shannon discovered gold and started San Francisco's first boom. It has never been the same since. It soon became a bustling, thriving supply center and international port, as people and goods streamed into the area. The city has had its setbacks—the most notable being the devastating earthquake that rocked the area April 18, 1906. The entire business district (as well as many other parts of the city) was completely destroyed. But rebuilding was rapid, and expansion continued. The 1989 quake that registered a hefty 6.9 on the Richter Scale severely damaged two areas of the metroplex, but the city has rebounded from that disaster with style.

Two bridges have been key to San Francisco's development. The Bay Bridge linked the peninsula to Oakland in 1936, and then the Golden Gate Bridge was completed in 1937, giving the city an important direct highway to the north. World War II saw further growth as the

San Francisco

San Francisco Bay

Pacific Ocean

- ◀ Transbay Terminal - Amtrak
  Travel Center
- 1 - Visitors Information
- 2 - Fisherman's Wharf
- 3 - Chinatown
- 4 - Union Square
- 5 - Jackson Square
- 6 - Ferry to Sausalito
- 7 - Golden Gate Bridge
  & Fort Point
- 8 - Golden Gate Park
- 9 - Cornell Hotel
- 10 - The Raphael
- 11 - Grant Plaza Hotel

area became an important military region. Today the city has a solid based economy and is the financial hub of the West.

Tourism has also boomed in the City by the Bay—and it's no wonder. Superior restaurants, fashionable stores, a sophisticated blend of cultures, all in a perfect setting. It's America's Paris—but perhaps better.

Amtrak closed its Transbay Terminal facility in 1993 due to security problems. This served as one of two San Francisco locations where passengers departed or arrived by Amtrak buses connecting to trains at the Oakland station. This operation was moved (at least temporarily) to the Ferry Building at Market St. and The Embarcadero. Oakland-connecting Amtrak buses also take passengers to and from the S.P. 4th Street Station at 4th and Townsend, a station that serves CalTrain commuter trains to San Jose.

Amtrak plans to make nearby Emeryville the stop for San Francisco bus connections once Oakland's Jack London Square station is in use.

Cab stand is at the terminal; Yellow Cab, 626-2345; Veterans Cab, 552-1300. BART (subway) runs through lower downtown beneath Market Street, 788-BART. For local bus and cable car information, call 673-6864. Most all major rental cars are located downtown. The airport is 16 miles to the south.

Visitors Information Center is at Powell and Market streets, lower level of Hallidie Plaza, 974-6900. Write or call San Francisco Convention and Visitors Bureau, P.O. Box 6977, San Francisco, CA 94101, (415) 391-2000.

Cornell Hotel, 715 Bush St., 94104; (415) 421-3154 or 800-232-9698. European flavored, small and unpretentious. Fine restaurant in the basement. Breakfast included. Just off Powell. $70.

-The Raphael, 386 Geary St., 94102; (415) 986-2000 or 800-821-5343. One of the nicer affordable boutique hotels. One block from Union Square. $99.

-Grant Plaza, 465 Grant Ave. (at Pine), 94108; (415) 434-3883 or 800-472-6899.

Modest accommodations at a budget price. Excellently located at the gateway to Chinatown. $49.

Sightseeing in San Francisco is relatively easy (except for the hill climbing) due to its unusual compaction and good public transportation.

Fisherman's Wharf, in the area of Jefferson and Taylor streets, is a fine collection of restaurants specializing in seafoods, unusual shops and harbor cruise boats. This is also the location of Ghiradelli Square and The Cannery.

Golden Gate Bridge and Fort Point, at the north end of the city on U.S. 101, is the world's most famous and attractive suspension bridge in a spectacular setting. Golden Gate Park, 1017 acres bounded by Fulton Street, Stanyan St., Lincoln Blvd. and the Pacific Ocean, has many points of interest including: Asian Art Museum, Japanese Tea Garden, Shakespeare's Garden, Golden Gate Golf Course, bridle paths, lakes and beautiful landscaping.

Chinatown, several blocks in the area of Grant and Washington, has many restaurants and shops and the largest Chinese community outside of the Orient.

Union Square, at Geary and Powell streets, is the center of the San Francisco shopping and hotel district. Jackson Square, actually a block bounded by Jackson, Montgomery, Gold and Sansom streets, was once the province of design professionals and home furnishing buyers, but has become a popular spot for sightseers; antique shops, art dealers, and other shops in a 19th-century setting. There are elegant wholesaler window displays. The entrance is on Jackson and Montgomery streets.

Cable Cars provide transportation and great fun. Ferries provide an excellent and inexpensive way to see the Bay and city skyline. Ferries to Sausalito, Larkspur and Tiburon can be boarded at the Ferry Building and Pier 43½ near Fisherman's Wharf. Ferries to Jack London Square leave from Pier 39 and the Ferry Building. Bay cruises are also available at Pier 39 and Pier 43½.

0:00 (1:13) Depart Oakland. Gleaming

295

BART trains contrast sharply with an otherwise uninspiring industrial "Bowery."

0:02 (1:11) On right, impressive Bay Bridge, spanning San Francisco Bay, links cities of Oakland and San Francisco.

0:08 (1:05) Rail fans will be intrigued by cornucopia of older rail passenger cars, both Amtrak and private varnish, reposing in coach yard on right.

0:09 (1:04) Wharfside shops, restaurants and motels of Jack London Square cluster around colony of sailboats and other pleasure craft on right. This may become Oakland stop for Amtrak.

0:19 (0:54) Scene of prim Oakland Hospital, on right, has been gratuitously "enhanced" by lengthy graffiti-laden wall.

0:23 (0:50) Inverted dish, on right, is Alameda County stadium, home of baseball's Athletics and former turf of erstwhile Oakland Raiders.

0:39 (0:34) Flower farm presents a spectrum spectacular on left.

0:46 (0:27) White mountains of pure salt extracted from Bay by Morton and Leslie salt companies loom on right.

0:55 (0:18) Small cove provides shelter for multitude of small sailing craft. Larger structures across Bay are blimp hangers of Moffet Field Naval Air Station, built during thirties and now on National Historic Register.

0:57 (0:16) Tops of roller coasters and several other thrill rides are lofty protrusions above Mariotts Great America amusement park on right.

1:06 (0:07) Scores of tank-like vehicles beside FMC plant on left are armored personnel carriers, both M113s and more sophisticated Bradley Fighting Vehicles. Bradleys played an important role in Gulf War.

1:08 (0:05) View of University of Santa Clara, on right, is dominated by athletic stadium and bubble-enclosed sporting facility.

1:10 (0:03) Ancient brick roundhouse with turntable highlights expansive Southern Pacific rail yards at San Jose.

1:13 (0:00) Arrive San Jose.

SAN JOSE, CA - Spanish conquistadores were the first to set eyes on the lush Santa Clara Valley in 1769. Soon thereafter, in 1777, San Jose was founded, making it the oldest incorporated city in California. Orchards and vineyards abound, and familiar names, such as Paul Masson and Almaden, have wineries here. Education also thrives. Stanford University, Santa Clara and San Jose State College are all situated here, the latter being the state's oldest institutions of higher learning—founded in 1874. Transfer here for peninsula Caltrain service to San Francisco.

0:00 (1:21) Departing San Jose, double-decked Caltrains line tracks on left.

0:16 (1:02) Town of Coyote more or less marks point where industrial and citified environs of Bay Area give way to rich agrarian lands of central California.

0:32 (0:48) Even sealed environment of the Coast Starlight does not always prevent one's nose from verifying that Gilroy is known as "The Garlic Capital of the World."

A great festival is held here each year when cooks and connoisseurs from around the world come to prepare and savor garlic delicacies during the first full weekend in August. Up to ten tons of garlic can be depleted during this gala event. Although the town may occasionally reek a bit, it boasts some nice points of interest which can be observed on the right. First is the attractive St. Mary's Church adorned with its shiny gold bell; a bit further downline is the Old City Hall with its highly unusual clock tower; an interesting zodiac-looking mural enhancing the wall of a track-side building; and then the Spanish-styled depot itself.

0:37 (0:42) Extensive garlic fields now border each side of track.

0:41 (0:34) Starlight now moves one valley westward by traversing through Gabilan Range to reach Salinas River Valley. This pleasant stretch features golden-soft, rolling hills and bare-trunked eucalyptus trees that occasionally line each side of track. Species was originally imported from Australia for use as ties during early railroad construction. Shortly, cross famed San Andreas Fault, milepost 87 at the foot of Chittenden Pass. Tracks must be realigned after quakes that occasionally shake local geography.

0:52 (0:28) Enormous cavern, on left, was

Amtrak station - Santa Barbara, California
DORIS SWANSON

once a dolomite quarry, but after being fairly depleted, aggregate became primary product from this huge hole. Assortment of loading contrivances raise mined material from below and then directly onto rail cars.

0:55 (0:15) Acres and acres of truck farms now spread out across valley.

1:10 (0:12) At Elkhorn Slough, a 2,330-acre wildlife sanctuary, numerous species of waterfowl, including egrets, herons and pelicans, frequent backwater on left.

1:12 (0:10) On right, Moss Landing Power Plant of Pacific Gas and Electric Co. uses natural gas and oil as its power source. Just to south, emitting white clouds of "smoke," is Kaiser Refactories which manufacture firebrick and related products.

1:14 (0:08) Big, bushy "weeds" in field surrounding Castroville are actually tops of artichoke plants. Forget the garlic, we are now in "The Artichoke Capital of the World."

1:19 (0:04) Graves School, a lonely but lovely "one-roomer," makes a nostalgic centerpiece for vegetable field on right.

1:23 (0:00) Arrive Salinas.

SALINAS, CA - Much of the flavor of Salinas' environs has been captured in the writings of Pulitzer Prize winner John Steinbeck, who wrote in glowing prose about his home town's locale. Sometimes referred to as the country's "Salad Bowl," its warm temperatures and abundant sunshine foster an agricultural cornucopia. This is the edge of the Big Sur country, and the Monterey Peninsula is just 12 miles to the west.

0:00 (2:38) Depart Salinas. On right, in downtown Salinas, ancient church-building-turned-restaurant features four skinny towers protruding from its top, bedecked with attractive golden mosaic.

0:05 (2:31) Schilling spice operation is on left.

0:08 (2:29) On right, large Firestone facility appears somewhat out of place amidst surrounding croplands.

0:22 (2:16) Sprawling "confines" of Soledad Correctional Facilities are just to left.

0:29 (2:09) On right, Salinas River now accompanies train along its course through Salinas River Valley.

0:39 (1:59) Just before 1,305-foot tunnel, colorful single-engine planes parked on right are used for dusting crops with pesticides. Tunnel (number 5½) was constructed in 1923 for curve-reducing line change.

0:46 (1:51) Crates of local produce, including lettuce, grapes, tomatoes, onions and carrots, await shipment on docks of packing companies in King City.

0:50 (1:49) An early bit of Americana appears on side of weather-beaten barn, on right, encouraging populace to "Chew Mail Pouch Tobacco."

0:55 (1:44) Swooping S curve of U.S. 101 curls across valley floor in distance to right.

0:56 (1:43) At southern end of San Lucas, small Christ-figure hovers protectively above tiny cemetery, nestled below trackside on right.

1:08 (1:29) Many operating wells can be seen while passing through extensive oil fields of San Ardo.

1:13 (1:24) Train rejoins Salinas River on right, and crosses a few miles downline.

1:26 (1:13) On right, pass Camp Roberts facilities of California National Guard.

1:32 (1:10) Unusual "bell wall" highlights grounds of Mission San Miguel on right. Intriguing adobe structure, built in 1797, boasts best-maintained interior of all California missions.

1:36 (1:06) Endless rows of white fences identify most attractive horse farm on left.

1:40 (1:02) Glide through Paso Robles, historic stage stop and approximate halfway point between San Francisco and Los Angeles.

1:49 (0:54) On right, at Templeton, billboard for Pesenti Winery entices passersby with "tours and tasting room." Although recently rediscovered in region, wine-making was introduced by Franciscans 200 years earlier, cultivating vineyards on mission grounds to supply needs of church.

1:56 (0:47) On outskirts of Atascadero, Santa Lucia foothills border attractive golf course on right.

For the next half hour, the ensuing negotiation of Cuesta Grade can be subtly enthralling. Although not what one might describe as spectacular, this small adventure nevertheless seems to capture much of what is romantic and unique to rail travel itself.

The monolithic rock formations, pro-truding suddenly out of nowhere, seem to typify the many curiosities that are encountered "off the beaten path." The frequent tunnels, engineering marvels unto themselves, at once accentuate the myriad of sounds that are as much a part of the rail experience as the vistas that loom outside.

Winding gracefully around two horseshoe curves into San Luis Obispo, the entire train comes into view. Marvel at its simplicity and the simple pleasures it can provide.

2:32 (0:08) Reversing ten-degree horseshoe curves, Goldtree and Servano, are fitting finale to Cuesta journey—and also herald a return to "civilization" with fortress-like California Men's Colony dominating scene on right.

2:33 (0:07) Cross splendid old trestle, seen moments earlier during descent of Cuesta Grade.

2:36 (0:02) On left, note athletic field and campus of California Polytechnic State University.

2:38 (0:00) Arrive at San Luis Obispo's attractive 1934 depot.

SAN LUIS OBISPO, CA - Originally a mission founded in 1772—Mission San Louis Obispo de Tolosa, named for a 13th-century French saint and bishop (because a nearby volcanic peak was thought to resemble a bishop's cap)—this city is now one of the more popular destinations for those wishing to explore the scenic central coast of California. Morro Bay, Pismo Beach, San Simeon and local wineries are some of the area's highlights. California Polytechnic State University, with an outstanding agricultural program, and smaller Cuesta College are both located here.

0:00 (2:06) Departing San Luis Obispo, note turntable on right, used to reverse direction of locomotives. Proceed thereafter on slow, winding route through more hills of Santa Lucia Range.

0:06 (2:00) If both are on schedule, northbound and southbound Coast Starlights should meet about now.

0:17 (1:49) Passing through Grover City, old Amtrak coaches have been converted into restaurant on right.

0:27 (1:39) Cross Santa Maria River on

outskirts of Guadalupe. Once in town, note beautiful old mission on left.

0:39 (1:27) Another working oilfield abuts trackside at Casmalia.

After Casmalia, the Starlight enters Vandenberg Air Force Base, America's western spaceport. Here, the Strategic Air Command conducts missile crew training and tests both Peacekeeper and Minuteman ICBMs as well as numerous varieties of smaller missiles. It is the only military installation of its kind.

The base is huge. With 154 square miles of real estate and a working population of 12,000, it is the Air Force's third largest. More than 1,600 launches have been conducted here. And although space shots are usually associated with Cape Canaveral, Vandenberg has placed half again as many satellites into orbit as the Cape. Vandenberg's location is ideal for putting objects into polar orbit which allows surveillance of the entire globe.

Various launch complexes can be spotted for the next 25 minutes or so.

0:43 (1:23) Vandenberg's Minuteman Area is off to right.

0:51 (1:15) Three-mile-long Vandenberg Airfield is on left. Strip can accommodate space shuttle landings should base become site for future shuttle launches.

0:52 (1:14) Pacific Ocean now comes into full view. For next 113 miles, spectacular vistas abound as train skirts atop seacliffs, overlooking frothy tumult of pounding surf. Because of Vandenberg and two large ranches, public can see much of this country only by train.

0:56 (1:10) Cross Santa Ynez River. Unusually colorful ground cover is most pronounced over next few miles.

1:00 (1:06) Gantries of SLCs (space launch complexes) Four and Five are spread out for next two miles on left.

1:03 (1:03) Pernales (or Honda) Point, on right, has often been confused for Point Arguello a bit further south, causing more than one maritime calamity after ships have mistakenly turned eastward.

1:04 (1:02) SLC Six, nicknamed "Slick Six," lies huddled in hills on left. This 2.5-billion-dollar spacecraft facility is world's most sophisticated. Designed to be first space shuttle launch facility on West Coast, complex was placed on indefi-

nite hold after 1986 "Challenger" disaster.

1:05 (1:01) Lighthouse on right deters oceangoing vessels from jutting cliffs of Pt. Arguello. Stout rock reef protects tower and keeper's residence from inclement seas.

1:14 (0:52) Exit southern boundary of Vandenberg Air Force Base at Jalama Beach.

1:18 (0:48) Another lighthouse sits prominently atop bluff of Pt. Concepcion. Los Angeles is only about 30 miles south of here, but a much greater distance east, since California's coastline curls sharply inward at this point.

1:41 (0:25) Picnic tables and grassy tracts adorn Refugio State Beach on right. On left, Santa Ynez Mountains loom in background, stretching south past Santa Barbara.

1:48 (0:18) On right, pass El Capitan State Beach.

1:50 (0:16) Small lagoon sits picturesquely below trackside on right. Off-shore drilling rigs and associated facilities at beachside are frequent sights throughout duration of Pacific Coast run.

1:51 (0:15) Late one February evening in 1942, only two months after Pearl Harbor, a Japanese submarine surfaced offshore and lobbed several rounds from its deck cannon into Ellwood oil field off to right. Damage was light, but incident heightened pressures to relocate West Coast Japanese Americans.

1:53 (0:13) Before turning inland toward Santa Barbara station, note San Miguel Island out on right. Three more islands extend south, forming chain that delineates Santa Barbara Channel. Explorer Juan Cabrillo, who discovered islands in 1542, is buried on San Miguel.

1:57 (0:09) In distance on right, lofty bell tower is landmark of University of California at Santa Barbara campus.

2:04 (0:02) Historic Santa Barbara Mission can be seen on left. Dubbed "Queen of the Missions," distinctive structure is only one in California to employ twin-tower design. Lovely fountain fronting building is fed by aqueduct, built by Indians in 1808.

2:06 (0:00) Arrive Santa Barbara. Immediately left of station is 100-year-old Moreton Bay fig tree, its lengthy branches spread majestically across four-lane thoroughfare.

SANTA BARBARA, CA - In 1782, the Santa Barbara Presidio Real, which means "Royal Fortress," was constructed, marking the beginning of the city, but the end of Spain's fortress construction in the New World. Then in 1786, the Santa Barbara Mission was founded which was just one of 21 built by Spanish Franciscans. Although the flags of Mexico, independent California and the U.S. have also flown over Santa Barbara, its Spanish heritage still pervades. Even after a devastating earthquake in 1925 destroyed most of the city, rebuilding made liberal use of white adobe and red-tile roofs, using distinctive Spanish-Moorish architecture. Situated on a sweeping palm-lined beach with mountains for a backdrop, Santa Barbara is one of America's jewels.

0:00 (0:44) Depart Santa Barbara southbound through host of well-endowed residential neighborhoods.

0:02 (0:42) Santa Barbara's palm-lined

beach lies just beyond Cabrillo Boulevard off to right.

0:04 (0:40) Santa Barbara Zoo can be glimpsed at right.

0:05 (0:39) Lagoon, on right, is bird refuge and centerpiece of zoological gardens.

0:07 (0:37) Passing through beautiful little community of Miramar, old station house and passenger cars have been cleverly converted to a restaurant on left.

0:09 (0:35) Overexposed sunbathers are often quite "visible" as train passes by Summerland nude beach on right.

0:22 (0:22) As seacliffs dissipate at Mussel Shoals, remainder of coastline route travels directly along beach into Ventura. Lengthy causeway, seen here on right, extends out to rocky islands where first completely underwater oil well began production in 1964. Tracks follow old stage road that was only open while tide was out.

0:33 (0:11) Cross Matilija Creek as it spills into ocean.

0:34 (0:10) Now heading inland, Ventura County Fairgrounds are conspicuous on right, while resplendent San Buenaven-

Coast Starlight - Santa Barbara, California
DORIS SWANSON

tura Mission stands proudly on left. Since first constructed in 1809, mission has been used continuously, except for four-month period in 1812 when series of violent earthquakes required its temporary closure. San Buenaventura was also only California mission to ever use wooden bells, which have subsequently been removed from belfry and now are preserved in Mission Museum.

0:41 (0:03) Cross Santa Clara River.

0:44 (0:00) Arrive Oxnard's modernistic Transportation Center.

 OXNARD, CA - A fertile plain makes Oxnard a citrus center and food-processing hub. Sugar was once important, but this has given way to lima beans which make up nearly half of the world's supply.

0:00 (0:33) Depart Oxnard through bountiful farmlands and orchards of Simi Valley.

0:09 (0:24) In Camarillo, quaint mission-style church sits atop hillside on left.

0:11 (0:22) On Camarillo's southeastern outskirts, imposing plantation-type estate overlooks fields on left.

0:22 (0:01) Scenic Simi Creek crosses beneath tracks several times as it lazily meanders through area of Moorpark.

0:33 (0:00) Arrive Simi Valley.

 SIMI VALLEY, CA - This is a northern suburb of Los Angeles.

0:00 (0:40) Depart Simi Valley and continue toward Santa Susana.

0:03 (0:30) At Santa Susana, train suddenly embarks on unlikely adventure across "mini-pass" of Santa Susana hills. Imposing rock formations, cactus fields and frequent tunnels (a popular setting for numerous Hollywood Westerns) highlight this delightful, yet seemingly incongruous intrusion. Once at "summit," descend into sprawling expanse of Los Angeles megalopolis.

0:12 (0:28) Passing through Chatsworth, proceed through residential district with swimming pools, an ever-popular adjunct of many homes.

0:19 (0:20) Approaching Van Nuys, scene becomes largely industrial. Sperry, Anheuser Busch, General Motors and Schlitz are but a few of the more renowned corporations whose facilities dot this stretch.

0:20 (0:19) On right, pass Van Nuys airport.

0:27 (0:12) Good view of Santa Monica Mountains is now afforded on right, while San Gabriels border in background on left.

0:30 (0:10) On left, pass Hollywood-Burbank airport.

0:40 (0:00) Arrive Glendale. This tidy Spanish-style depot, replete with ornamental scroll-work, has been used as a backdrop for many motion pictures.

 GLENDALE, CA - Last stop before Los Angeles, and situated on the edge of Hollywood, Glendale is enhanced by many impressive hillside homes.

0:00 (0:14) Departing Glendale, note lush acreage of Forest Lawn Memorial Park on left. Palatial, castle-like building in foreground is "Great Mausoleum." As well as its conventional use, mausoleum boasts a vaunted collection of memorial art, including replicas of Michelangelo's major works, and a glorious stained-glass recreation of da Vinci's "Last Supper."

Also prominent is "Hall of Crucifixion-Resurrection," seen atop Mt. Forest Lawn. Dedicated in 1951, building houses Jan Styka's magnificent painting, "The Crucifixion," which measures 195 feet long and 45 feet high.

0:04 (0:10) A bevy of blue and white, double-decker Metrolink commuter trains are usually parked near their shops at right.

0:05 (0:09) Parallel concrete channel on right that sometimes becomes Los Angeles River.

0:06 (0:08) Perched atop bluff on right is Dodger Stadium, home of Major League Baseball's 1988 champions.

0:09 (0:05) On left, Lawry's California Center is notable manufacturer of spices and food products.

0:10 (0:04) On left, cluster of tall buildings is Los Angeles County Hospital which operates in conjunction with University of Southern California.

0:11 (0:03) Crossing Los Angeles River avails good view of downtown Los Angeles skyline on forward right. Predominant

Los Angeles

Amtrak Station
1 - Visitors Information
2 - Downtown Area (Hotels)
3 - Queen Mary
4 - Disneyland

5 - Six Flags Magic Mountain
6 - Universal Studio Tours
7 - NBC Studio Tours
8 - Knotts Berry Farm

older tower is Los Angeles City Hall, while double-domed building in foreground houses Post Office annex.

0:13 (0:01) On left, pass Los Angeles County Jail.

0:14 (0:00) Arrive Los Angeles.

LOS ANGELES, CA - Los Angeles is big. It has nearly 14 million inhabitants and will someday overtake New York City as the nation's largest metropolitan area. The largest Hispanic population outside of Mexico is here, and the largest assemblage of Japanese outside of Japan call this home. The suburb was

invented here after World War II, and expansion has never stopped.

Los Angeles' reputation is as mixed as its populace—flakey fads and funky fashions; perpetual sunshine and perpetual smog; freeways free of nothing but tolls; Tinsel Town with a lot of tarnish. But obviously, there is a huge attraction here; it is one of the most visited cities in the world.

The first visitor to arrive was Juan Cabrillo, a Portuguese conquistador who landed here in 1542. This was the discovery of California and it was claimed in the name of Spain. Two hundred years later the area was reached by an overland expedition, and in 1781 Governor Felipe de Neve established by proclamation the "City of our Lady Queen of the Angels." In 1822, Spanish rule ended and the city became part of the California Territory.

All southwestern trains wind up in LA, so it is a city that western rail passengers have come to know, even if for only an "overnight" between trains. Whether you're making connections or have come to see Southern California, it's possible to see some of the sights, contrary to conventional wisdom, without owning or renting a car. Amtrak's service between San Diego and Santa Barbara opens up myriad possibilities.

Los Angeles Union Station, 800 North Alameda St., 90012. One of the nation's most attractive stations, built in California Mission/Moorish style, and located in the heart of Los Angeles, has seen extensive renovation to accommodate shops, subway (light rail), commuter trains and a bus terminal. Shuttle buses serve a section of downtown. The station has redcaps, handicap transfer, a restaurant, food and beverage vending machines, newsstand, gift shop, direct phones to some hotels, and adjacent pay-parking.

Call 624-0171 for arrival and departure information as well as reservations and other information.

Cab stand at the station; Independent, 385-8294 and L.A., 627-7000. **Local bus** at the station; 626-4455. Budget **Rental Car** is at the station. Red Line **light rail** service from Union Station to MacArthur Park, where connections are made with Blue Line service to Long Beach can be boarded through subway entrance. Also, Metrolink **commuter trains** to Pomona, Moorpark, Santa Clarita, Riverside and Oceanside can be boarded here. **Los Angeles International Airport** is approximately 18 miles southwest of the station. Amtrak has **connecting bus** service to various Southern California towns, including Bakersfield for San Joaquin trains.

Metropolitan Express Van Shuttle service is provided between the Amtrak station (they meet all trains) and any location throughout the Los Angeles area—door to door. For reservations, call (310) 417-5050 or 800-338-3898. Sample fares: Amtrak station (LAUS) to downtown, $5; LAUS to LAX, $15.

Visitor Information Center, 685 S. Figueroa St., 90071; (213) 689-8822.

Metro Plaza Hotel, 711 N. Main St., 90012; (213) 680-0020 or 800-223-2223. Completed in 1991, it is the most convenient hotel to Amtrak. Sharp, art-deco rooms, in-room safes, pleasant staff. Next to Olvera Street and two blocks from the station. $69.

-**Miyako Inn,** 328 E. First St., 90012; (213) 617-2000. Japanese speaking staff, next to Japanese Village Plaza. About four blocks from the station. $92.

-**Best Western Dragon Gate Inn,** 818 North Hill St., 90012; (213) 617-3077. In Chinatown, about one mile from the station. $60.

It's possible to breathe in much of the city's beginnings just outside the station. **El Pueblo de Los Angeles State Historic Park,** immediately across from station, is the birthplace of Los Angeles. Many rebuilt structures are around the old plaza. **Avila Adobe** is the oldest existing house in Los Angeles. **Olvera Street** has numerous picturesque Mexican shops and restaurants along one of the first streets in the old city. A great place to spend some time while waiting for a train. Two Mexican restaurants, La Golondrina and El Paseo, are popular lunch spots. La Golondrina (the swallow) is in the first brick ediface in LA, built in 1850.

The Museum of Contemporary Art is about a mile from the station, downtown at 250 S. Grand Ave., and **The Music Center of Los Angeles,** at 135 N. Grand, is home of the Los Angeles Philharmonic Orchestra, Joffrey Ballet and other performing arts.

Grayline has various **city tours,** with hotel pick up and drop off.

Of course, **not** within walking distance are some of LA's most popular destinations: Disneyland, The Lakers, The Queen Mary, Universal Studios, goofy Venice, cruises to Catalina and Knott's Berry Farm, to name but a few.

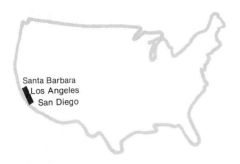

Santa Barbara
Los Angeles
San Diego

San Diegans

Although it's not officially called the Southern California Corridor, that's what it is. It takes several trains daily, scurrying both directions between Los Angeles and San Diego, to handle the demands of this densely peopled strip of Southern California coast. Two San Diegans have extended runs both to and from Santa Barbara. Although speeds can reach 90 mph at times, a clutter of stops holds the running time for most of the trains to 2¾ hours—a time freeway drivers can usually better. However, the train ride hardly compares to the freeway hassle.

Stops along the Santa Fe's "Surf Line" include Anaheim (Disneyland) and San Juan Capistrano (fine beaches and its mission of swallow fame). South of Capistrano the views are particuarly good where the tracks hug the shore for several miles, as sunbathers and surfers speckle the beaches on one side and cliffside houses with ocean views are almost as abundant on the other.

The ultimate southbound destination, of course, is San Diego, where the classic mission-style Santa Fe station is located just a stone's throw from the ever-popular harbor area. The San Diego Trolley (formerly known as the "Tijuana Trolley") departs regularly for the Mexican border.

Train service is handled with Amfleet equipment. Snacks and sandwiches are available on each train while checked baggage is only available on selected trains. Telephones are available in the food service cars and in Custom Class cars. Reserved Custom Class Service, with roomier seating and free coffee, tea, orange juice and newspapers, is available for a slightly higher fare.

Route Log

For route between Santa Barbara and Los Angeles, see page 300.

 LOS ANGELES, CA - See page 302.

0:00 (0:34) Depart Los Angeles Union Station while Los Angeles County Jail looms on right and then Dodger Stadium rests on hill off to left. Curl south at Mission Tower and roll onto main line of Santa Fe.

0:05 (0:29) Excellent view of Los Angeles cityscape on right where distinctive white-towered City Hall has center stage. Take note of old stone bridges that cross over tracks along this section. Their sculpted pilasters are reminiscent of ancient Rome and memorialize an era of Los Angeles long gone. Los Angeles River, encased in concrete on left, parallels our course for several minutes.

0:07 (0:27) Amtrak coach yard is on immediate right where a gaggle of Superliner cars are stored and await service on trains such as Desert Wind, Sunset Ltd., Southwest Chief and Coast Starlight.

0:09 (0:25) Diesel shops, roundhouse and its companion turntable are on right where twenty or so Amtrak diesels can generally be counted. Upon passing this facility, train curves sharply to left and crosses Los Angeles River.

0:12 (0:22) Acres of truck trailers used

San Diegan - San Clemente, California
JACK SWANSON

on piggyback freight trains are assembled on left at north end of Santa Fe rail yards.
0:15 (0:19) Office building of Santa Fe Railroad on left marks southern end of yards.
0:19 (0:15) Cross Rio Hondo Channel.
0:21 (0:13) Cross San Gabriel River.
0:25 (0:09) Pass through refinery operations and active oil wells of Santa Fe Springs. One of area's larger tank farms will soon be seen on left.
0:31 (0:03) Perhaps more than one hundred assorted light aircraft at airport serving Fullerton area are in very midst of densely populated area on right.
0:34 (0:00) Arrive Fullerton. Note home of well-known Donald Duck citrus juice on left just before reaching station. The Santa Fe station, on left, is a delight. Its pink-stucco facade topped with a dark, red-tile roof is further enhanced by unusually large arch-shaped windows and accents of fine grill work. Landscaping with palms furnishes a near-perfect setting for this lovely station.

FULLERTON, CA - As you may have guessed from the citrus juice operation just mentioned, Fullerton has had its roots in the citrus industry. Los

Angeles' growth to the south has now made Fullerton virtually indistinguishable from its much larger northern neighbor.
0:00 (0:07) Depart Fullerton.
0:05 (0:02) Nearing Anaheim, the obvious question is: "Where's Disneyland?" Look off to the right—a sharp eye can spot The Matterhorn, its white top jutting into the California haze.
0:07 (0:00) Arrive Anaheim's $853,000 modernistic station immediately below on right. Imposing edifice immediately behind is Anaheim Stadium, home of California Angels and Los Angeles Rams.

ANAHEIM, CA - Although best-known for Disneyland, that grand-daddy of all theme parks, it should also be thought of as the Valencia orange heart-land of California. Even the county's name is Orange. Its agricultural heritage is more than one hundred years old, having received its start when ex-Fortyniners-turned-farmers moved here from San Francisco and German colonists came here to raise grapes. The name is derived from the nearby Santa Ana River and "heim," the German word for home.
0:00 (0:06) Depart Anaheim.
0:06 (0:00) Arrive Santa Ana, where elaborate, mission-style Transportation

Center is at right.

 SANTA ANA, CA - We are still in Orange County—as a matter of fact, this is the county seat.

0:00 (0:18) Depart Santa Ana.

0:04 (0:14) On right, two enormous hangars which housed World War II blimps are now part of U.S. Marine helicopter operations at El Toro. These two monstrous blisters are actually constructed of wood. Range of Santa Ana Mountains forms a high horizon on left.

0:08 (0:10) Aircraft of Marine Corps Air Station at El Toro can be seen parked on runways at left. Nearby Irvine is a stop for some San Diegans.

0:15 (0:03) Cruise through orange orchards which line either side of tracks.

0:18 (0:00) On arrival at San Juan Capistrano, famous mission with its attendant bell tower can be seen on left adjacent to tracks. Depot itself is also on left, complete with a good restaurant. Boxcars surrounding depot provide unusual retail space.

SAN JUAN CAPISTRANO, CA - The community grew up around the mission which was established in 1776, making the building the oldest in the state. Although this was one of the most beautiful missions built in California, some of its most attractive features were destroyed by an earthquake in 1812. It is world-renowned for its large swallow population that departs about October 23 and returns about March 19 of each year.

0:00 (0:28) Depart San Juan Capistrano.

0:04 (0:24) Suddenly, after having traveled without a hint of ocean, the San Diegan spurts out onto beaches of Capistrano, with Pacific Ocean spreading out before us.

For the next 45 minutes, passengers on the right will be treated with seaside vistas. Those on the left will be able to look up to catch sights of homes perched precipitously on clifftops with stunning ocean views.

0:07 (0:21) Watch on left for evidence of former mud slide which left houses teetering at edge of cliff, some with entire rooms sheered off.

0:10 (0:18) This is San Clemente, identified by a lovely little park rising above the

San Diego Trolley - San Diego, California
DORIS SWANSON

tracks on left and a popular wharf restaurant on pier jutting out over ocean on right. President Nixon's California home was here during his presidency. This is a stop for some San Diegan trains.

0:17 (0:11) Two gigantic concrete beehives contain reactors of San Onofre Nuclear Generating Station sandwiched between tracks and beach on right.

0:23 (0:05) San Diegan now slips through confines of Camp Pendleton Marine base.

0:27 (0:01) Dozens of small sailing vessels clustered in yacht basin on right create a highly appealing maritime scene. Over 800 pleasure craft can be berthed here at any given time.

0:28 (0:00) Arrive at Oceanside where at left is ultra-modern, both in design and function, transit center with structures housing Amtrak and Greyhound terminals, while local transit buses are just to its left. Santa Fe rail yards are on right.

OCEANSIDE, CA - This community, which has a reputation for being "lean and mean," is closely tied to Camp Pendleton U.S. Marine Base that stretches for more than 20 miles northward from the city.

0:00 (0:16) Depart Oceanside.

0:05 (0:11) Monolithic concrete structure on beach at right is San Diego Gas and Electric's first power plant.

0:14 (0:02) Del Mar's horse racing track, one of the finest in Southern California, is just to left.

0:16 (0:00) Arrive Del Mar where one more attractive beach awaits, and luxury apartments are above station on left.

DEL MAR, CA - This pleasant oceanside village has 5,000 mostly upscale residents.

0:00 (0:36) Depart Del Mar.

0:02 (0:34) San Diegan makes a swing inland while last view of ocean is afforded back to right.

0:07 (0:29) While snaking through very rugged terrain, note novel red sculpture in front of nine-story glass building on left—rather like a rocket coming out of an egg beater.

0:22 (0:14) Tropical palm setting of Hilton resort is on right.

0:23 (0:13) Mission-style tower of University of San Diego can be seen atop

bluffs on left.

0:25 (0:06) Convair Division of General Dynamics Corp. is just to right of tracks.

0:31 (0:05) San Diego's Lindbergh Field, unique because of its location near very heart of city it serves, is off to right.

0:36 (0:00) Arrive at San Diego's eye-catching mission-style Santa Fe station. Downtown skyline is just beyond on left and maritime scenes of San Diego Harbor are just a block away on right.

SAN DIEGO, CA - It was in 1769 that Gaspar de Portola, Junipero Serra (a Franciscan priest) and several Spanish soldiers ventured north from Mexico to establish a mission here on Presidio Hill. This first European settlement gave birth to what is now California. However, this was not the first discovery of the area. More than 200 years earlier, Juan Cabrillo sailed into a splendid natural harbor that now serves as home to one of the nation's largest naval bases.

A mild Mediterranean-like climate, together with the Pacific Ocean and the town's proximity to the Mexican border, have combined to make San Diego one of the country's favorite vacation spots. There are 70 miles of beaches and easily as many miles of golf courses. Electronics, aerospace, medical research and tourism fuel its growth—a growth San Diego, so far, has handled quite well.

San Diego Station, 1050 Kettner Blvd., built by the Santa Fe and located on the west edge of the older downtown area, is one of the most attractive depots in use today. Its scale, its Spanish motif, the palm-lined landscape, all blend perfectly in this Southern California setting. There are redcaps, nearby restaurants, a snack cart, espresso bar, food and beverage vending machines and a newsstand. Pay-parking is adjacent to the station.

For arrival and departure information only, call (619) 239-9989.

Cab stand is at the station; USA Cab, 231-1144. USA Courtesy **Auto Rentals** has a counter at the station; there are direct phone lines to Avis, West Coast Rental Car and Get-A-Car. The **"San Diego Trolley,"** the first trolley line built in the United States in 20 years, was completed in 1981 and connects down-

San Diego

🚉 Amtrak Station
1 - Visitors Information
2 - Harbor Excursions
3 - Maritime Museum
4 - San Diego Zoo
5 - San Diego Hotel
6 - Holiday Inn on the Bay
7 - Best Western
8 - Comfort Inn

Horton Plaza, bounded by Broadway, G St., 1st and 4th avenues, one of the most architecturally bizarre shopping malls anywhere, is located in the heart of downtown. It's a delight just to walk through this post-modernism maze of levels and balconies. The **Museum of Contemporary Art** is directly across the street from the station.

Also, next to downtown is the harbor and its **Maritime Museum,** 1306 Harbor Dr., with three ships including the 100-year-old merchant sailing ship, the Star of India. **Cruises of San Diego Harbor** are available at the foot of Broadway. **Tijuana,** 16 miles south, can be reached by the **"San Diego Trolley"** which starts at the station and runs east along "C" Street.

The **San Diego Zoo,** considered by many as the nation's finest, is in **Balboa Park** where there are also numerous museums and lush tropical gardens. **Sea World of San Diego,** at 1720 South Shores Rd., is one of the world's largest marine-life parks.

town San Diego with San Ysidro, CA adjacent to Tijuana, Mexico 16 miles to the south. These trolleys can be boarded next to the station. **International Lindbergh Field** is four miles north of the station.

San Diego Convention and Visitors Bureau Visitor Information Center, 11 Horton Plaza, 1st Ave. and F, 92101; (619) 236-1212.

Hotel San Diego, 339 W. Broadway, 92101; (619) 234-0221; toll free, 800-621-5380. A refurbished older hotel. Four blocks from the station; courtesy shuttle sometimes available. $45.

-Best Western Bayside Inn, 555 West Ash St., 92101: (619) 233-7500. Courtesy Amtrak shuttle. Five blocks from the station. $80.

-Comfort Inn, 719 Ash, 92101; (619) 232-2525. Courtesy Amtrak shuttle. About 15 blocks from the station. $53.

-Holiday Inn on the Bay, 1355 North Harbor Dr., 92101; (619) 232-3861. High rise with balconies, on the bay. Five blocks from the station; courtesy Amtrak shuttle. $110.

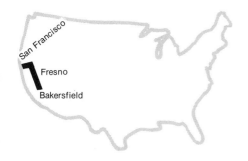

San Joaquins

These trains, combined with connecting bus service at each end, join San Francisco and Los Angeles through California's San Joaquin Valley. With major stops consisting of Oakland (actually Emeryville), Martinez, Fresno and Bakersfield, it would be easy to assume the San Joaquins might someday be renamed the San Ho Hums. Actually, the route has a lot to offer. The traveler who makes the entire run encounters a wide range of both pleasing and interesting scenes. And ridership is high, due in part to the large number of dedicated connecting buses serving other population centers.

In petroleum-rich Kern County the tracks pass through an oil field with more working wells per square mile than will be seen on any other passenger train route in North America. Then the heart of the Valley—one of America's most fertile and productive—has a seemingly unending procession of almond, plum, pistachio and fig groves as well as wine and raisin-grape vineyards, and even occasional cotton fields. These checker the flattened landscape for miles on end but never become monotonous. At the north end of the Valley, there is a dramatic change when the terrain becomes rolling and the Bay Area's maritime scenes suddenly grab one's attention.

San Francisco itself becomes the perfect starting or ending point for this journey. It is only a short connecting bus ride from Emeryville (adjacent to Oakland) to downtown San Francisco.

There are four departures daily from both Emeryville and Bakersfield, with trains leaving each city early in the morning, midday and late in the afternoon. The 300-mile trip takes six hours, with connecting bus service between Bakersfield and Los Angeles Amtrak stations adding 2½ more hours and the bus between Emeryville and San Francisco another half hour—all told, 9 hours. This is somewhat faster than the Coast Starlight following the coast route. Several bus connections to numerous central California towns are offered along the route.

These trains offer tray meal service, sandwiches, snacks and beverages. Checked baggage is handled only on the first train of the day northbound and the southbound train that leaves Oakland midevening, and only at larger cities.

Route Log

BAKERSFIELD, CA - Although agriculture is important (as it has been since the town's humble birth in 1869), oil is king in this community of 100,000. Except for a short bit of excitement in 1885 with the discovery of gold in the area, Bakersfield's real blossoming occurred when oil was discovered at the close of the last century.

Motor coach service connects to Los Angeles and its various suburbs, including Barstow.

0:00 (0:24) Depart Bakersfield's small

trailer-station, and slip through Santa Fe rail yards. Rail fans will want to watch for roundhouse which will be on left shortly after departure.

0:05 (0:19) At end of yards, cross large irrigation canal and swing northward which will be our course until we depart Stockton four hours from now. Here San Joaquins pass through that massive oil field mentioned above, with seemingly hundreds of pumps crowded together making a truly impressive industrial scene. A large refinery is just to right.

0:19 (0:05) Through Shafter, then almond groves line both sides of tracks. In late winter, these trees will be covered with millions of pinkish-white blossoms. Groves will appear off and on until we reach Stockton.

0:21 (0:03) Note staked grapevines, which will also be evident for miles to come. Grapes grown in this region are mostly dried into those "California Raisins," while those north of Fresno will become fine California wine.

0:24 (0:00) Arrive Wasco.

WASCO, CA - This is one of several farming communities that dot the valley.

0:00 (0:27) Depart Wasco and resume ramblings through formal orchards and vineyards.

0:14 (0:13) Sign on left identifies Colonel Allensworth Park named in honor of U.S. Army's first black colonel.

0:22 (0:05) Continue through flat, flat country which almost eliminates the necessity for field-leveling usually essential for ditch irrigation.

0:27 (0:00) Arrive Corcoran.

CORCORAN, CA - Cotton is king in Corcoran. Note huge ginning operation to the left of the tracks.

0:00 (0:17) Depart Corcoran.

0:27 (0:00) Arrive Hanford.

HANFORD, CA - Oddly enough, Hanford boasts one of the best Chinese restaurants in the United States—the Imperial Dynasty. Customers have included presidents, foreign dignitaries and other notables. Motor coach service connects to Visalia—gateway to Kings Canyon and Sequoia national parks.

0:00 (0:32) Depart Hanford.

0:03 (0:29) Dozens and dozens of home-owners on left have obviously been receptive to sales pitch of aggressive redwood fence salesman.

0:10 (0:22) Cross Kings River.

0:18 (0:14) Impressive expanse of grape vineyards spills across thousands of acres, stretching for miles along both sides of tracks.

0:27 (0:05) Cribari Winery is just to right as train slows for Fresno.

0:29 (0:03) Prior to arrival at Fresno, raisin plant is just to left of tracks, with interesting old water tower and faded sign proclaiming "Sunmaid Raisins." Although upper floors are not used, lower portion still is in operation during raisin season. Modest skyline of downtown Fresno is on left.

(Amtrak had plans to shift from Santa Fe and use Southern Pacific tracks between Calwa, four miles south of Fresno, and Stockton. Segment below, however, is log for Santa Fe route still in use at this writing.)

0:32 (0:00) Arrive Fresno.

FRESNO, CA - This is the heart of the San Joaquin Valley and the raisin center of the world. Sunmaid has the world's largest dried fruit packing plant here, and the largest fig orchards are in the immediate area. The county claims to be the most farm-productive in the country. Wineries and winery equipment production are also important.

0:00 (0:29) Depart Fresno's rather bedraggled depot and immediately pass by attractive Santa Fe offices on left. Crossing Fresno Street, note historic water tower in downtown a block to left, looking like an extremely squat rocket. Then on immediate right, wildly painted mural adorns wall in small park next to tracks.

0:08 (0:21) Still in suburbs, campus of Fresno State College is on left.

0:19 (0:10) After appealing golf course on left, cross high over waters of San Joaquin River.

0:28 (0:00) Arrive Madera.

MADERA, CA - This is one of the large agricultural communities in the area.

0:00 (0:30) Depart Madera and cross

Fresno River.

0:06 (0:24) To right and forward of train, Cathedral Range of Sierra Nevada Mountains, rising to over 13,000 feet above sea level, contains spectacularly beautiful Yosemite National Park which Horace Greeley once called "the greatest marvel of the continent."

0:09 (0:21) Grove of pistachio trees stands just to left of tracks.

0:11 (0:19) Visions of Thanksgiving are aroused as we pass by turkey farm on right.

0:24 (0:07) As we slowly swing to left at Planada, large grove of scraggly trees on right, short and stubby, are kadota figs.

0:26 (0:05) Goodyear plant on left turns out large quantities of plastic bags.

0:31 (0:00) Arrive Merced.

MERCED, CA - Here connecting motor coach service carries rail travelers directly to and from lovely Yosemite National Park, some 75 miles to the east.

0:00 (0:21) Depart Merced and note picturesque courthouse two blocks away on left and facing tracks.

0:07 (0:14) Castle Air Force Base is on right at Atwater, where assorted World War II aircraft, tethered next to tracks, are on public display, and include B-29 flown in by General Jimmy Doolittle—his last military flight.

0:11 (0:10) Magnificent stands of almond trees spread out on each side of right-of-way.

0:12 (0:09) Over Merced River, most impressive stream seen on trip so far, which joins San Joaquin River west (left) of here.

0:18 (0:03) Low-lying mountains on distant horizon to left comprise Diablo Range.

0:21 (0:00) Arrive Turlock.

TURLOCK, CA - This is actually Denair, just east of the much larger town of Turlock where locals find diversion by holding a harnessed turkey race each October.

0:00 (0:14) Depart Turlock.

0:03 (0:10) Aircraft hangar in midst of almond grove on left generally has crop-dusting biplanes parked in front, but where is runway? Frequent grade crossings in this area give train's air horn a constant workout.

0:07 (0:06) Cross Tuolumne River.

0:11 (0:02) Pass over concrete-lined Hetch Hetchy Aqueduct cutting cleanly across valley and built to transport water from Sierra Nevadas to Bay Area. A Reagan Administration official once proposed that the Hetch Hetchy Reservoir be permanently drained and its valley turned into another Yosemite. San Franciscans, however, voiced some objections to idea.

0:13 (0:00) Arrive Riverbank where its green-trimmed, white-frame station offers pleasant change for depot-watchers.

RIVERBANK, CA - Riverbank began as a ferrying point on the Stanislaus River during the gold rush of the 1880s. Later the Santa Fe Railroad came through the valley and the settlement soon sprouted into a railroad town. This is Amtrak's stop for nearby Modesto, where Gallo operates the world's largest winery. If Amtrak moves to the Southern Pacific tracks as planned, Modesto itself would become a stop.

0:00 (0:25) Depart Riverbank.

0:01 (0:24) Cross Stanislaus River.

0:12 (0:13) Grape vineyards are virtually everywhere along this portion of route. Franzia Wineries have contracted to buy most of crop grown throughout immediate area.

0:25 (0:00) Arrive Stockton.

STOCKTON, CA - This is California's only inland seaport, with a deep-water channel connecting the city to the Bay Area some 78 miles to the west.

0:00 (0:36) Depart Stockton.

0:26 (0:10) Pacific Gas and Electric power plant is on right.

0:28 (0:08) Enter Antioch, then first evidence of Bay Area's presence will be seen on right where shipping channel of San Joaquin River is just visible. Seagoing vessels are able to navigate into this area via San Francisco Bay. Although hard to spot, San Joaquin and Sacramento rivers join on right as they continue toward San Francisco Bay and Pacific Ocean. Soon, Dow Chemical plant will be on immediate right, where a plethora of blaze-orange windsocks flutter from various positions throughout facility to identify wind direction in case of escaping chlorine gas.

0:36 (0:00) Arrive Antioch-Pittsburg.

ANTIOCH-PITTSBURG, CA - This is one of the Bay Area's most industrialized areas.

0:00 (0:23) Depart Antioch-Pittsburg.

0:07 (0:16) At one time, trains would grind to a halt here, then creep forward, only to repeat process while switching from Santa Fe to Southern Pacific tracks at Port Chicago. This 15-minute line change has been eliminated by new transfer exchange trackage allowing trains to breeze through at 50 miles per hour.

Port Chicago was once a small lumber town called Bay Point. It had a city-owned saloon that was profitable enough to finance the community's water, street lights, sewer and other public services.

0:10 (0:13) Numerous ships across waterway, on right, and anchored side by side have been "mothballed" by U.S. Navy and await salvage operations at Sacramento. Concord Naval Weapons facility is here, with acres and acres of ammunition storage. U.S. Government relocated it a few years back to prevent recurrence of a catastrophe that leveled Port Chicago's buildings when two munitions ships blew up during World War II.

0:11 (0:12) Lift-span rail bridge of Southern Pacific, directly ahead and to right, carries California Zephyr and Coast Starlight across narrows of Carquinez Strait. Second bridge carries Interstate 680 auto traffic, which is major north-south bypass of Bay Area.

0:14 (0:09) Just before reaching bridge, look directly across strait where grey, unmarked Glomar Explorer, sporting a white heliport platform on its stern, is anchored. It's normally the last ship just before rail bridge. This deep-sea research vessel made headlines some years back when it attempted to retrieve a sunken Russian sub from ocean's floor.

0:16 (0:07) At left, expansive Shell refinery and tank farm snuggle against hillside.

0:19 (0:04) Approaching the station at Martinez, note Southern Pacific trackage that crosses bridge on right, making a steep descent alongside us. This is where we join routes of the California Zephyr and the Coast Starlight.

0:23 (0:00) On arrival at Martinez, note semaphore that landscapes station on left.

MARTINEZ, CA - This important commercial and military port was also the home of John Muir, one of the nation's earliest and most outspoken conservationists. His house is now preserved as a National Historic Site. Joe Dimaggio Drive is on the right side of the train, honoring the renowned "Yankee Clipper" who was raised here.

0:00 (0:29) Depart Martinez along Carquinez Strait, connecting Suisun and San Pablo bays. Carquinez Bridge looms impressively in foreground right, while on left, famed golden hills are subtly encroaching upon landscape.

0:09 (0:20) With town of Crockett huddled on hillside left, travel directly through midst of C&H sugar refinery. Immediately thereafter, train bears south along shores of San Pablo Bay and passes beneath Carquinez Bridge.

0:12 (0:17) Dart into momentary darkness while passing through trip's first (and last) tunnel.

0:13 (0:16) Union Oil refinery, on left, truly "graces" hillside with its pastel storage tanks set off by ecologically inspired landscaping.

0:27 (0:02) Huge Standard Oil of California refinery stretches across face of slopes across Bay just before Richmond.

0:29 (0:00) Arrive Richmond.

RICHMOND, CA - Richmond's popularity as a convenient suburban stop is enhanced by its trackside connections with BART, a rapid transit system servicing many outlying regions throughout the Bay Area.

0:00 (0:07) Departure from Richmond affords first view of dramatic San Francisco skyline across bay. Golden Gate Bridge can be seen north of city, while Bay Bridge connects with Oakland to the south.

0:05 (0:02) On right, pass Golden Gate Field Race Track.

0:07 (0:00) Arrive Berkeley.

BERKELEY, CA - This stop provides service for the main campus (there are nine of them) of the University of California. Thirty thousand students study in buildings of striking beauty; most notable architecture is the acclaimed University Art Museum.

0:00 (0:06) Depart Berkeley.

San Joaquin - Stockton, California
DICK WALTZ

0:02 (0:04) Last, grand view of San Francisco can be captured, again off to right, where Alcatraz Island can now be seen directly below Golden Gate Bridge.

0:06 (0:00) Arrive Emeryville.

 EMERYVILLE, CA - This is Amtrak's stop for those using connecting buses to and from San Francisco.

0:00 (0:06) Depart Emeryville.

0:06 (0:00) Arrive Oakland, train's final destination.

 OAKLAND and SAN FRANCISCO, CA - See pages 209 and 293.

Other West Coast Service

The **Mount Rainier** is an unreserved daily train that travels from Seattle to Portland in the evening, and from Portland to Seattle in the morning. Food service consists of sandwiches, snacks and beverages. Checked baggage is not handled, but hand baggage may be carried on board.

Caltrain/SP provides train service between the Southern Pacific station in San Francisco (4th & Townsend) and Amtrak's station in San Jose.

The Capitols provide service along the Bay Area's "Capitol Corridor" between San Jose and Sacramento. (Two of these trains extend beyond Sacramento to Roseville.) There are numerous connecting bus feeders. Sandwiches, snacks and beverages are available on all trains and tray meals on some. No checked baggage.

Alaska Railroad

They say Alaska is different. But, just how different is—well—what really makes the difference. Winters can get so cold that locals sometimes leave their cars running all night; then summers can be so warm that weekends are spent waterskiing. Alaska stretches farther west than Hawaii—and farther east than Maine (since the Aleutians actually cross the International Date Line). Vertically, the state juts from sea level to over 20,000 feet—the highest point in North America. And there is no state income tax; it works the other way around in that Alaska pays its residents an annual allotment out of a fund created from pipeline revenues. Alaskans can continue to tick off such contrasts almost indefinitely.

The principal railroad in Alaska is owned by the state, and one may rightfully conclude that it, too, is a different breed. Passenger trains are immaculately maintained, inside and out. Windows throughout are clear and clean, even in the dome cars; while white linen tablecloths and real china grace the diner, where the bill of fare runs from simple sandwiches to Alaskan Seafood Saute. Almost an overabundance of leg room exists in the coaches. Attractive and enthusiastic tour guides are in each coach to keep passengers informed about interesting points along the route and to answer any questions passengers may have. It is the only U.S. railroad that makes unlimited flag stops; and it's the railroad that was originally constructed to haul gold from the gold fields around Fairbanks, and is now one of the state's top tourist attractions.

For those wanting to go really deluxe, both Gray Line of Alaska (a Holland America-Westours subsidiary) and Princess Tours are operating their own full-length dome cars between Anchorage and Fairbanks. Grayline's operation is called McKinley Explorer, while Princess goes by Midnight Sun Express. These cars are attached to the rear of the regularly scheduled trains and provide upper-level viewing for every passenger. Private dining facilities are on the lower level. Gray Line has four cars, each with surprisingly minimal upper-level sway. Princess runs two cars of equal elegance and offers a large viewing platform on the end-car. To book either tour, see your travel agent, or you may contact Princess directly, 800-835-8907, or Gray Line, 800-544-2206.

Most all passengers on the Anchorage-Fairbanks run stop over at Denali National Park to at least take the wildlife tour (and try, weather permitting, to get some more views of Mt. McKinley). If you plan to spend only one night in the park and travel the entire rail route, consider an Anchorage departure. This allows time to complete the wildlife tour that starts early morning the second day. If you're spending two nights at the Park, you can just as easily depart from Fairbanks. A Fairbanks-to-Denali-to-Fairbanks round trip also works well with a one-night Denali layover.

More and more travelers are discovering the route between Anchorage and Seward. Although the Denali experience on the Anchorage-Fairbanks trip is incomparable, the run down to Seward is one of the most spectacular in the world. Not only are the mountains more Swiss-like, the train passes within one-half mile of three magnificent glaciers.

A one-day, round-trip excursion leaves plenty of time to explore Seward (a delight) or take a half-day cruise on Resurrection Bay.

Schedule for Anchorage-Fairbanks: During the summer season, which is normally from mid-May to mid-September, trains run daily. An "Express" run, from late May through mid-September, making intermediate stops only at Wasilla, Talkeetna, Denali National Park and Nenana, is made seven days per week in each direction. Departure time from both Anchorage and Fairbanks is 8:30 am. A "Local" train, making numerous stops, operates during the summer on a thrice-weekly schedule.

The Express takes approximately twelve hours between the two cities, departing each city early morning. The Local operates only between Anchorage and Hurricane Gulch, making a round trip each of the three days it operates. During the non-summer months there is only one train per week, departing early morning, leaving Anchorage on Saturdays and leaving Fairbanks on Sundays. Viewing in the winter, of course, is minimal due to the limited amount of daylight. The Express trains carry standard coaches and dome cars, and offer complete meal and beverage service. Other trains use rail diesel car equipment and have vending-machine snacks only.

Schedule for Anchorage-Seward: Two attached rail diesel cars make the round trip daily, departing Anchorage early morning and arriving back in Anchorage late evening. The trip takes four hours each way, and trains operate from Memorial Day weekend through Labor Day. Sandwiches and beverages are sometimes available on the train, but not always.

Schedule for Portage-Whittier

Shuttle: From late May to mid-September the railroad provides daily, unreserved shuttle service between Portage (a stop on the Anchorage-Seward line) and Whittier, where there is ferry service to and from Valdez (limited service off-season). This unique transport, offering not only coaches but flat cars carrying motor vehicles with their passengers, is Whittier's only land connection to the rest of Alaska. Call (907) 265-2607 for recorded shuttle train schedule. Call 800-642-0066 for State Ferry reservations; these tickets are sold separately.

Reservations and Fares: Except for the Whittier Shuttle, reservations are required on all trains operated by the Alaska Railroad and should be made as early as possible. Some sample express service fares: Anchorage to Denali Park, $85; Anchorage to Fairbanks with Denali stopover, $130. Anchorage-Seward round-trip fare is $70. For more information, write or call: Passenger Services Department, The Alaska Railroad, P.O. Box 107500, Anchorage, AK 99510; (907) 265-2494, or 800-544-0552 for reservations.

The Railroad also offers several tour packages that offer worthwhile savings.

Route Log

Anchorage-Fairbanks

For **Anchorage-Seward** log, see page 323.

ANCHORAGE, AK - Anchorage is the largest city (geographically) in the U.S., having incorporated huge amounts of real estate within its boundaries. In spite of this, the downtown is fairly easily managed on foot. About a day or two will allow you to take in most things Alaska's largest city has to offer; the town is really more of a base for seeing the southcentral part of the state. (Non-Anchorage residents like to say: When you're in Anchorage, you're only 30 minutes from Alaska.) Most flights from the Lower 48 come into Anchorage, and air fare is usually considerably less than flying to Alaska's second largest city, Fairbanks.

This is the ideal base for riding the Alaska Railroad, being the focal point of the system. The four popular rail destinations are easily reached from here: Fairbanks, that still-frontier city to the north; Denali National Park, with its wildlife tours and Mount McKinley; Seward, a delightful seaport on Resurrection Bay, and reached by one of the most dramatic train rides in North America; and Whittier, the unique marine (ferry boat) access to Valdez through Prince William Sound.

Anchorage is located on Knik Arm of Cook Inlet and shielded from heavy rainfall by the Kenai Mountains to the south. Having a moderate climate, its mild summers are comparable to those of Seattle. Very little evidence is left of the earthquake that registered 8.6 on the Richter Scale and devastated the city in 1964, nor were Anchorage's shores fouled by the 1989 oil spill.

Alaska Railroad Station, 421 W. First Ave., Pouch 107500, 99501, is on the edge of the downtown area.

There is a covered walkway leading up the hill to town, and parking is available in front of the station. Long-term parking needs a permit, available at the ticket window.

If you wish to sit with someone, keep in mind that people line up early for boarding. One day there may be plenty of seating, but the next may be full. Reservations are important. Ticket window hours are 6 am to 11 pm. Call (800) 544-0552, or (907) 265-2494.

Cabs: Yellow Cab, 272-2422. Two blocks to **local buses,** main transit center at 6th Ave. and G St. National, 274-3695, and Avis, 277-4567, have **rental cars** near the station. **Anchorage International Airport** is about four miles southwest of downtown.

Log Cabin Visitor Information Center, W. 4th Ave. and F Street. Call (907) 274-3531, or write Anchorage Convention & Visitors Bureau, 1600 A Street, Ste. 200, 99501. Information on special events, call 276-3200.

Anchorage

- Alaska Railroad Station
1 - Visitors Information
2 - Anchorage Historical & Fine Arts Museum
3 - Alaska Pacific University

Accommodations in Anchorage are expensive, particularly in the downtown area. There are a few Bed and Breakfasts in the downtown area which are somewhat more economical. Anchorage reservations in the summer should be made well in advance.

-Voyager Hotel, 501 K Street, 99501; (907) 277-9501 or 800-247-9070. A small, tastefully decorated hotel in a good location; well managed and one of Anchorage's best hotels. Ten blocks from the station. $135.

-8th Ave. Hotel, 630 W. 8th Ave., 99501; (907) 274-6213, 800-478-4837 (AK only) or 800-825-7287 (lower 48). A converted small apartment building, in a good location, with spacious (suite) accommodations. Nine blocks from the station. $114.

-Holiday Inn, 239 W. 4th Ave., 99501; (907) 279-8671. Popular with tour groups. Downtown, four blocks from the station. $140.

-Anchorage Hotel, 330 E. St., 99501; (907) 272-4553 or 800-544-0988. A beautifully restored small, historic hotel in the heart of downtown. Four blocks from the station. $169.

-Bed and Breakfast-Alaska Private Lodgings, P.O. Box 200047, Anchorage, AK 99520; (907) 258-1717. A bed and breakfast information and reservation service, including downtown B & Bs ranging from $55 to $95.

Be sure to get an **Anchorage Visitors Guide** by writing or stopping at the Visitors Center. It has an elaborate walking tour of downtown, as well as other area attractions. Some highlights of the walking tour include: The **Log Cabin Visitors Center** itself; a walk down 4th Ave., Anchorage's **"Main Street;"** the **Anchorage Historical and Fine Arts Museum,** 121 West 7th Ave., depicting Anchorage and Alaska native cultures; **Resolution Park** at the west end of 3rd Ave., with a view of Knik Arm and Mt. McKinley (on a clear day); and **free films** about the area shown in the Arco Building at 7th and G streets.

If you have a car, or want to take the bus, **The Alaska Zoo** at Mile 7 on O'Malley Road has various species of Alaskan wildlife, including polar bears.

0:00 (1:23) Depart Anchorage with front range of Alaska Mountains looming in distance. A grand spectacle unto themselves, natives regard these mountains as mere "foothills" in respect to monumental peaks that will soon border route a few miles north.

0:04 (1:19) Cross Ship Creek. A mile west, waters widen before flowing into sea, availing several inland docks to ocean-going vessels.

0:08 (1:15) Train skirts fringe of Elmendorf Air Force Base on left, and Fort Richardson Army Installation on right. Elmendorf is Alaska's largest air base.

0:13 (1:10) On left, myriad of military aircraft are poised alongside Elmendorf runways.

0:14 (1:09) Proceed through birch-lined gullies, keeping eyes peeled for great Alaskan moose; 125-mile stretch between here and Curry is favorite haunt of this curious beast.

0:20 (1:03) Brief clearing on forward left provides first breathtaking glimpse of Mt. McKinley. Jutting 20,320 feet skyward, peak is tallest in North America, and actually highest in world if measured from base to crest.

Along the route, "mileposts" are conspicuously tacked on trees and telephone poles, and represent the distance from the line's southern terminus at Seward. Many subsequent entries will be prefaced by milepost designations (MP) as a further aid in identification.

0:29 (0:54) Cross Eagle River, its waters moving swiftly through small canyon.

0:45 (0:38) MP 136. At Birchwood, small airport seen through trees on left is but one of countless such facilities throughout Alaska. Vast distances of forbidding wilderness make airplane most popular and practical means of transportation.

0:48 (0:35) MP 138. On left, begin bordering Knik Arm, an inlet of Pacific Ocean. Tides here can reach 40 feet—third highest in world. In distance, Mt. Foraker (17,400 ft.), Mt. Hunter (14,573 ft.), Mt. Russell (11,670 ft.) and Mt. Dall (8,756 ft.) are a formidable supporting cast surrounding mighty Mt. McKinley.

0:54 (0:29) MP 141. Eklutna Village is home of Russian Orthodox Church established in 1835. Its adjacent cemetery is most unusual, with colorful "spirit houses" built atop gravesites to preserve souls of those buried here.

1:01 (0:22) MP 146. Traverse series of bridges across Knik River. Prior to 1964 earthquake, river was outlet for ice-flows and floodwaters descending from Lake George. Barren trees dot sunken landscape that became tidal flats after quake.

1:08 (0:15) MP 151. At Matanuska, begin travel through scenic agricultural valley, with surrounding peaks an added embellishment. In 1930s, poverty-stricken farmers from Minnesota, Wisconsin and Michigan were allowed to homestead here in a federally sponsored socialistic experiment. Although the effort failed, many stayed, and numerous attractive spreads can still be seen scattered throughout the region.

Despite a brief growing season (100-120 days), long hours of daylight compensate for this shortcoming. A record-size, 76-pound cabbage grown in this region evidences potential of these northern farmlands.

1:12 (0:11) Nearby Pioneer Peak of Alaska Range dominates skyline. To immediate right of Pioneer are East Peak, Middle Peak (with two points) and Goat Mountain (looking somewhat truncated).

1:23 (0:00) MP 159. Recreational lakes border town on arrival Wasilla.

WASILLA, AK — This is a service hub of the Matanuska Valley. On the right, perched on "temporary" cribbing, Teeland's Country Store is the oldest business in Matanuska and Anchorage area. As well as retail merchant, Teeland's was once a veritable museum with old photos, antiques and native artifacts on display. Off to right is a McDonalds with its own caboose. Establishment reportedly had longest line of any McDonalds on opening day.

0:00 (1:29) Departing Wasilla, note towering totem pole fronting property of Kashim Inn.

0:21 (1:08) MP 174. Cross Little Susitna River.

0:30 (0:59) MP 181. On left, clusters of cozy cabins encircle shoreline of Nancy Lake, a popular recreational resort.

0:39 (0:50) MP 185. Pass through Willow, once deemed by voters as future site of state capital. Electorate later nixed move by failing to approve necessary funding. Town's centrality was prime consideration for proposed move from Juneau.

0:55 (0:34) Cross Kashwitna River. For next 45 miles, enjoy spectacular views of Mt. McKinley on left if skies cooperate. (There's a seven-in-ten chance they won't.) Service personnel will generally open vestibule doors to accommodate photographers, while engineer purposefully slows train where vistas are most dynamic. Enthusiasm that pervades crew adds immensely to this delightful adventure.

1:16 (0:13) MP 224. Susitna River joins and follows on left. It will accompany train for next 40 miles.

1:29 (0:00) MP 226. Arrive Talkeetna.

TALKEETNA, AK - A robust frontier atmosphere is well preserved at Talkeetna, a popular staging ground for Mt. McKinley expeditions. The town's name is derived from an Indian word meaning "place where rivers meet" — a reference to the nearby confluence of the Talkeetna, Chulitna and Susitna rivers.

The white building over to the left is Fairview Inn which housed and fed President and Mrs. Warren G. Harding in 1923 when the president was in Alaska to drive the golden spike at Nenana. Harding died about two weeks later in San Francisco, supposedly from food poisoning.

The town has both spirit and a sense of humor. One of its annual celebrations includes a "moose-nugget-throwing" contest.

0:00 (4:25) Depart Talkeetna and cross Talkeetna River.

Over the next immediate stretch, the train begins a gradual ascent of the Continental Divide that culminates 85 miles north at the summit of Broad Pass. Subtle geographic changes can be detected enroute, with the terrain and vegetation reflecting more alpine-like environs. Brilliant pink flowers, growing profusely along right-of-way in July, are fireweed. The large, white flowery plants in moist areas are cow parsnips—sometimes called wild celery.

0:34 (3:51) MP 248. Pass through Curry,

halfway between Seward and Fairbanks. Because of this strategic position, a resort hotel was built here in 1923, off to right. Hostelry sported tennis courts and even an undersized golf course. Years took their toll until, finally, a fire in 1957 ended its colorful career.

0:50 (3:35) MP 258. Sole resident of Sherman has proudly pronounced his home "City Hall," on right.

0:58 (3:27) MP 264. Cross Susitna River as it departs to east.

1:01 (3:24) MP 266. Cross Indian River first of several times as train traces its course through colorful canyon. When train makes its third crossing (in a few minutes) watch for salmon in pool below on left. Just before that, also on left, will be a small cross above river, erected by two mountaineers in remembrance of a friend killed in a climbing accident.

1:19 (3:06) Emergence from canyon affords another fabulous panorama of Mt. McKinley grouping on left. Range is now only 46 miles away—its closest proximity to rail line.

1:42 (2:43) MP 284. A few anxious moments are in store as train crosses Hurricane Gulch from dizzying height of near 300 feet. Chulitna River joins on left and follows route intermittently to its source atop Broad Pass. This 918-foot trestle was most expensive and difficult to build on entire line. View to left is particularly stunning.

1:47 (2:38) MP 287. Footbridge, relic of prospecting times, stretches ladder-like across river on left.

1:51 (2:34) MP 289. Honolulu (without palm trees) is situated halfway between Anchorage and Fairbanks.

1:56 (2:29) MP 292. Cross east fork of Chulitna River.

2:01 (2:24) MP 295. Approaching summit of Broad Pass, journey through midst of wide alpine valley, with jagged peaks flanking this treeless expanse.

2:05 (1:36) MP 297. Frequently, siding called Colorado is where northbound and southbound express trains meet. Tour

Alaska Railroad dining car
JACK SWANSON

guides swap trains here, enabling them to return home (Anchorage or Fairbanks) on same day as departure. (Train may wait here for some time. Log times are adjusted for an approximate 40-minute delay each direction.)

3:00 (1:25) MP 304. On right, imaginative design highlights log house at town of Broad Pass. Adjacent "storage cache," perched atop tower, keeps provisions beyond reach of uninvited guests.

3:09 (1:16) MP 309. Summit Lake borders on right, while imposing peaks of Mt. Deborah (12,399 ft.) and Mt. Hayes (13,832 ft.) hover in background.

3:10 (1:15) MP 310. Marker on right designates summit of Broad Pass. Elevation of 2,363 feet is highest point along Alaska Railroad, yet pass is still lowest crossing of Continental Divide in entire Rocky Mountain chain.

3:25 (1:00) MP 319. Return to hillier terrain as train passes through Cantwell, marked by airstrip on left. On outskirts of town, note overgrown cemetery along hillside on left. Several gravesites are adorned with spirit houses similar to those found in Eklutna.

3:31 (0:54) MP 323. Cross Windy Creek into southeastern region of Denali National Park. Train then climbs atop bluffs overlooking Nenana River Valley on right. River generally parallels route for next 90 miles.

3:57 (0:28) MP 334. At Carlo, handsome log home and another storage cache can be seen on right.

4:18 (0:07) MP 345. Approaching park station, Nenana River Valley is now totally encircled by towering peaks of Alaska Range. Setting is one of most inspiring along entire run.

4:25 (0:00) MP 347. Traverse lofty bridge across Riley Creek as train arrives Denali. Denali is Indian word for "the great one," with obvious reference to nearby Mt. McKinley. Note airpark beside tracks on right.

DENALI NATIONAL PARK, AK - Mt. McKinley is the central fixture of this alpine wonderland, presiding majestically over 3,000 square miles of pristine wilderness. Although a worthy draw in its own right, many other attrac-

tions add to the magic of this enchanting tourist haven.

Abundant wildlife roam freely throughout the park, with caribou, fox, grizzly bear and Dall mountain sheep only a few of the many species to behold. Over 100 varieties of birds have been identified and represent migrations from six different continents. Free shuttle buses take visitors deep into the park, with early-morning departures generally offering the best viewing. Wildlife tours (also by bus) offer guided sojourns along the park's one road. Rangers offer dog sled demonstrations daily, just a short bus ride from the Riley Creek Information Center.

From spring until midsummer, colorful wildflowers spread a regal blanket across the high mountain tundra. Ranger-led nature hikes and campfire chats help visitors further appreciate such spectacles, as well as other aspects of the area's complex ecosystem.

Private operators offer exciting alternatives for backcountry exploration, with flightseeing, rafting and horseback treks quite popular. In wintertime, cross-country ski tours and dog-sled excursions are available for the more adventuresome.

Accommodations at Denali are rather expensive, and tour packages generally offer savings.

The spacious Denali National Park Hotel (907-683-2215) is the "base camp" for many of the park's activities and the only easy walk from the station. Shuttle buses serve most other nearby hostelries. Nearby McKinley Chalets is another logical choice for staying overnight. Denali Crows Nest Log Cabins (907-683-2723) are somewhat less expensive ($120). Perhaps the most economical are McKinley/Denali Bed and Breakfast cabins (907-683-2733) that start around $55. For central reservations information, call (907) 274-5366.

0:00 (1:44) Departing Denali, note cluster of old Pullman cars on left that once provided lodging following fire at McKinley Hotel, and remain as hotel's calling card.

0:10 (1:34) MP 351. Dall sheep are frequently seen between here and milepost 354. On forward right, impressive highway bridge spans Nenana River.

0:17 (1:27) MP 353. Cross northeastern boundary of Denali National Park, passing under previously cited bridge before entering short tunnel. Emerge amidst beautiful Nenana River canyon, winding precariously atop colorful rock ledges while river rages through gorge below.

0:30 (1:14) MP 357. Approaching Healy, note coal seams exposed in rock strata on right. Branch line of railroad extends up valley to east, servicing extensive coal-mining operations.

0:42 (1:02) MP 362. North of Healy, coal crushing and loading occurs here at "Usibelli Tipple," Alaska's only coal mine camp. Coal itself is mined at nearby Suntrana. Watch for coal seams along right-of-way.

0:44 (1:00) MP 363. Beyond Healy, rugged terrain is gradually displaced by more gentle, rolling landscape with birch and aspen groves and scrub brush reminiscent of earlier stretches. On right, old railroad cars are positioned in midst of Nenana River as flood control measure. Such sightings are common over next several miles.

0:53 (0:51) MP 370. Cross Nenana River which then follows on left.

1:20 (0:24) MP 391. Train borders grounds of Clear Military Installation. On left, massive radar apparatus is part of "early warning" defense monitor.

1:43 (0:01) MP 411. Nenana River flows into Tanana River on left approaching community of Nenana. Here, railroad operates barge system that services rural outposts nearly 800 miles to west and over 500 miles to east. On forward right, Mears Memorial Bridge stretches dramatically across Tanana River. Structure is one of longest single-span bridges in world. Turning east into town, note visitors center on right, housed in quaint log cabin with sod roof.

1:44 (0:00) Arrive Nenana's restored station, which now houses Alaska State Railroad Museum.

NENANA, AK - Originally one of Alaska's historic roadhouses was located here; then when the railroad arrived, the town flourished as a construction base. President Warren G. Harding drove a golden spike here in 1923, which concluded the Alaska Railroad's construction. But Nenana has a greater claim to fame—the annual "Ice Classic" lottery. Annually, entrants try to guess the time of the spring ice breakup in the Tanana River, and those with the right time share over $100,000 in prize money.

0:00 (1:50) Depart Nanana, and immediately pass wooden tower on left which is placed on ice to act as a giant trigger to stop official time clock for aforementioned lottery.

On outskirts of town, train heads south into U-turn prior to traversing Mears Bridge. While crossing river, note "Indian fish wheels" positioned along banks. Paddles are propelled by river current and capture salmon swimming upstream to spawn; catch is then deposited into containers on shore. Once across river, monument on left commemorates site where golden spike was driven.

1:27 (0:33) MP 460. Forested hills surrounding Fairbanks provide scenic setting for many outstanding homes secluded in their midst.

1:39 (0:11) MP 465. Picturesque farmstead on left operates in conjunction with University of Alaska, supplying school with fresh produce and meat. Other campus facilities stand immediately to east.

1:43 (0:08) Phillips Field stretches across pasture on right, colorfully bedecked with multitude of small aircraft.

1:46 (0:04) Proceed through industrial district as Chena River joins on right.

1:50 (0:00) Arriving Fairbanks, elegant steeple of Immaculate Conception Catholic Church protrudes above treetops on forward right. Formerly ensconced across river, hierarchy subsequently wanted it moved closer to Catholic hospital. Thus, in 1911, church was jacked up and dragged across ice to its present site.

FAIRBANKS, AK - They count the winters here—not the years. This is the northernmost city in the U.S., only 130 miles south of the Arctic Circle. Temperatures can easily drop to 65 below. It's a hearty lot that live here, but even then, there are limits. It's now policy to close the schools when the thermometer dips to a frigid minus 50.

Alaska Railroad - Princess Tour observation car
JACK SWANSON

In spite of its ice-box image, summers can be spectacularly beautiful, with shorts almost as common as in Los Angeles. Annual average precipitation in Fairbanks is a mere 11 inches, but the area's brief growing season somehow produces unusually lush foliage on the hills that surround the town.

A mixture of old and new, rugged and civilized, Fairbanks got its start in 1902 as a gold-mining settlement when Felix Pedro (pronounced Pee-dro) discovered gold sixteen miles north of here. Fairbanks still maintains a frontier atmosphere, most evident when you walk through downtown. It is Alaska's second largest town and is supported by pipeline-related industries, mining, aviation, government and tourism.

Alaska Railroad Passenger Depot, 280 N. Cushman, Fairbanks, AK 99701. Located on the edge of downtown, just across the Chena River. The station has food and beverage machines and adjacent free parking.

For reservations and other information, call (907) 456-4155.

 Cabs are at the station at train times; North Pole Taxi, 488-7900. Hertz has **rental cars** in the downtown area; 452-4444 or 800-654-3131. **Fairbanks International Airport** is approximately five miles southwest of downtown.

Fairbanks Convention and Visitors Bureau, 550 First Ave., 99701; (907) 456-5774 or 800-327-5774.

During the middle of the summer, Fairbanks' accommodations are under siege and rather expensive. Reservations should be made several months in advance, particularly if you plan to be here during "Golden Days" in the latter part of July. Since many of Fairbanks' attractions are west of downtown, many visitors prefer to stay out along Airport Way, a newer part of town, albeit strip-like.

-**Super 8,** 1909 Airport Way, 99701; (907) 451-8888 or 800-800-8000. Nicely maintained, a short drive from downtown. They will pick up and deliver train passengers. $85.

-**Captain Bartlett Inn,** 1411 Airport Way, 99701; (907) 452-1888 or 800-544-7528. A long-time popular motel, a short drive from downtown. They offer train station pick up and drop off. $120.

-**Fairbanks Downtown Bed & Breakfast,** 1461 Gillam Way, 99701; (907) 452-7700. A nicely run B&B in an older home on the fringe of downtown. Quiet neighborhood. Free shuttle to and from train station. $60 ($70 with private bath).

Downtown Fairbanks is interesting to poke around. Unusual shops without a lot of glitz are in the heart of downtown. Be sure to pick up a walking tour brochure at the visitors center.

-**University of Alaska Museum,** on University of Alaska-Fairbanks campus, has 10,000 feet of display space divided into six sections. Five are devoted to geographic features of the state while the sixth is devoted to traveling shows. A good place to begin a tour of Fairbanks and the surrounding area.

-**Alaskaland** is a 44-acre city "theme

park" which is the site of many attractions providing visitors with a good look at Fairbanks' past and present. Located between downtown and the airport along Airport Way at Peger Rd.

-**Riverboat "Discovery"** provides rides on Alaska's only remaining sternwheeler riverboats and makes a 20-mile trip on the Chena and Tanana rivers each day in the summer. Highlight is a stop at a reconstructed Indian Village, with demonstrations of native lifestyle. (Very popular with large tour groups.)

Anchorage-Seward Route Log

ANCHORAGE, AK - See page 315.

0:00 (3:57) Depart Anchorage, briefly following Knik Arm on right.

0:05 (3:52) If residents of suburbs near tracks are not yet awake, they soon will be, as engineer sounds air horn at several crossings. Jogging trail beside tracks will be quite busy during evening on return.

0:19 (3:34) Alaska's largest shopping mall, Diamond Center, is on left. Suburban mall had typical negative impact on downtown area when it opened a few years ago.

0:21 (3:32) Huge car-squashing operation on right is rather fascinating eyesore.

0:26 (3:26) Airstrip creates common backyard for long row of fine homes and parked aircraft bordering track on right. Some homes have been designed to also act as hangars.

0:29 (3:32) Marsh with viewing boardwalks is Potter State Game Refuge where numerous waterfowl find sanctuary. Water on right is Turnagain Arm—supposedly receiving its name when Captain James Cook explored region, having to continually adjust his vessel's course.

0:38 (3:14) Scenery becomes more dramatic as Hawaii-like mountains with thick vegetation rise steeply from water's edge across bay. Cascading waterfalls enhance this Alaskan setting. Watch for Dall sheep above tracks. Two 1896 gold-mining districts, Sunrise and Hope, lie along far shore, but are no longer active.

0:48 (3:03) Colorful moose mural adorns utility trailer behind mailboxes on left.

1:16 (2:35) At Girdwood, one of five chairlifts of Alyeska Ski Resort is visible on ridge to left. Alyeska is state's largest ski area.

1:31 (2:20) Broken trees, above on left, identify active snowslide area.

1:32 (2:19) Very attractive waterfall displays its plumage to left of tracks.

1:36 (2:15) Twentymile Glacier rests at top of valley to left.

1:39 (2:06) Train pauses for a few moments at Portage. Road to left leads to Portage Glacier viewing. Tracks curling off to left are Whittier Cutoff—Alaska Railroad's connection to Whittier-Valdez ferry service. Motor vehicles can board flatcars to be transported to Whittier and ferry connection. (Whittier has no road link to rest of state.) Note vehicle loading lanes on immediate right. This area was hard hit by 1964 earthquake, sinking nearly 12 feet. High tides covered tracks, and trains could only pass while tides were out. Soon, rails and highway separate and won't meet again until Moose Pass.

1:58 (1:55) Spencer Glacier looms, almost menacingly, on left. Engineer usually stops train here to accommodate photographers.

2:05 (1:50) Enter a tunnel and 30 seconds later emerge, clinging to Placer River

Gorge, where river, full of glacial silt, has carved deeply into earth. Segments of movie *Runaway Train* were filmed along this stretch of track.

2:11 (1:45) Superb waterfall gushes down mountainside across valley to right.

2:16 (1:40) Dirty-faced Bartlett Glacier dominates scene on left. Famous "Loop," a trestle that crossed over itself, once allowed tracks to negotiate rugged terrain. Loop has been replaced by some exceptional hairpin curves—and more powerful locomotion.

2:25 (1:32) Up to left is one more snowy monolith—spectacular Trail Glacier. Over one-half of world's glaciers are in Alaska.

2:52 (1:02) Waters of Upper Trail Lake spread along tracks on right.

2:56 (0:58) Village of Moose Pass is on right, where Seward Highway connects with road to fishing port of Homer. Town was originally construction camp for Alaska Railroad. Middle Trail Lake can be spotted through trees to left.

3:01 (0:53) Lower Trail Lake now accompanies tracks on right.

3:08 (0:51) On right, 24-mile-long Kenai Lake is fed by Snow River to east and is drained by Kenai River at west end.

3:42 (0:12) Nearing Seward, cross Salmon Creek, where fishing for sea-run Dolly Varden is popular.

3:48 (0:06) Seward's airport now appears on left where assorted helicopter and fixed-wing craft can be seen. Resurrection Bay is just beyond. Bay was named by explorer Alexander Baranoff when, in 1791 on Resurrection Sunday, he found shelter from a ferocious storm.

3:49 (0:05) Railroad's Seward yards swing off to left. On return run, train will back into these yards before heading north toward Anchorage.

3:50 (0:04) Huge piles of coal have been brought here from Interior Alaska coal mines, and will soon be loaded by elaborate equipment onto freighters, mostly bound for Korea.

3:51 (0:03) Cruise ships and freighters can often be spotted in harbor on left.

3:54 (0:00) Arrive Seward adjacent to town's colorful Small Boat Harbor at town's northern edge.

SEWARD, AK - Situated on beautiful Resurrection Bay and ringed by snow-capped mountains, Seward is

Alaska Railroad - Seward, Alaska
DEBBIE WORDEN

one of Alaska's more appealing locales. It was further blessed when the 1989 oil spill avoided its shores. Although it rains a lot in Seward, its temperate climate makes it a popular visitor destination.

Named for Lincoln's Secretary of State, William H. Seward, who negotiated Alaska's acquisition from Russia in 1867, the town was established in 1903 by railroad surveyors as an ocean terminal. Tourism and fishing industries are now as important as its shipping activity.

March 27, 1964, Alaska's Good Friday earthquake hit Seward with a vengeance. All of the docks that ring the city were destroyed, and nearly all of the Alaska Railroad yards were lost when a huge wedge of waterfront disappeared into the bay. Tank farms at each end of town burst into flames and created an image of total devastation. But Seward recovered.

Daily **bus** service to Anchorage. **Ferry** service to Valdez and Kodiak. **Rental cars** at Seward Tesoro station, (907) 224-8611.

The **Visitor Information Center** is located in the center of town at 3rd and Jefferson streets, in a vintage rail car. Write Box 749, Seward, AK 99664. Call (907) 224-3094.

-The **Breeze Inn,** at the Small Boat Harbor and near the station, Box 2147, 99664-2147; phone (907) 224-5237; overlooking the bay. $88.

-**Best Western Hotel Seward,** Box 670, 99664; (907) 224-2378. Overlooks Resurrection Bay, Seward's most luxurious hotel. $135.

-**Marina Motel,** near Small Boat Harbor, Box 1134, 99664; phone (907) 224-5518. $85.

The entire town of Seward is within walking distance of the train. Head south and you'll see it all. The **Kenai Fiords Visitor Center** in the Small Boat Harbor has several short films about the Seward area and is worth a stop. Seward has a very fine **museum** located downtown at 3rd and Jefferson, across from the Visitor Center, with earthquake displays, railroad memorabilia and other well-presented historic displays. The **University of Alaska's Marine Education Center,** at the south end of Third Street, has some modest but interesting exhibits on local sea life.

Canadian Rail Service

Whether a traveler is in search of breathtaking mountain scenery, spectacular and rugged coastlines, North America's only walled city, or simply a remote Indian village—it can be found using Canada's rail system. The Canadian, the country's transcontinental train, traces a twisting route of trestles and tunnels through the majestic Rockies, including Jasper National Park, while the Skeena traverses the beautiful wilderness of central British Columbia. The British Columbia Railway snakes along fiord-like Howe Sound, then takes on the direct challenge of the Coastal Range. A northland adventure is offered by the Hudson Bay which makes an excursion to that immense body of water, where Churchill hunkers down on its desolate and polar-bear-populated shoreline. And in the East, the Ocean, after departing Montreal, makes a swing through the Maritime Provinces of New Brunswick and Nova Scotia, before making a triumphant entrance into Halifax along one of the world's most attractive inner harbors—Bedford Basin.

VIA has accomplished a rather spectacular remodeling effort, completely refurbishing their stainless steel transcontinental trains to an elegance not found on any other publicly operated North American trains. Also, modern LRC equipment (Light, Rapid, Comfortable) serves the heavily populated areas in and around Toronto and Montreal, allowing higher speed with unique automatic tilting capability on curves. Domes are included on transcontinental trains affording great roof-top views of the passing scenes.

As in the U.S., Canada has relegated the operation of most of its passenger train service to a government-owned corporation—VIA Rail Canada. Unfortunately, in 1990 the Canadian government severely curtailed VIA's operations. The legendary Canadian no longer runs on CP rail tracks, leaving transcontinental passengers with only one choice of routes, through Edmonton rather than Calgary. Long-distance trains have been relegated to only triweekly service. On the brighter side, most of the former system's routes still see service, albeit less frequently.

In the East, logical access between VIA and Amtrak occurs with direct trains from New York to either Montreal or Toronto. A train connects Chicago and Toronto, crossing the border at Sarnia. VIA can also be found at the border town of Windsor, Ontario across from the Amtrak-served city of Detroit. In the West, connecting bus service is available between VIA in Vancouver and Amtrak in Seattle.

Reservations - Reservations are required for VIA 1 service and sleeping car accommodations. It's a good idea to make reservations as early as possible, although VIA will not confirm reservations earlier than 6 months prior to travel. Coach seats are guaranteed when tickets are purchased. For coach, be sure to specify smoking or non-smoking. Reservations can be made through a travel agent or by calling any of the toll-free numbers in the Appendix.

Tickets - Normally, tickets are purchased through a travel agent or directly from a VIA sales office. It is possible to buy tickets on board, however, and only with cash and only to destinations served by that train. Tickets can also be ordered by mail using a credit card by writing VIA Rail Canada, c/o Ticket Office, Box 989, Moncton, NB, E1C 1E9. Allow about three weeks. VIA will accept American Express, Enroute, MasterCard and Visa credit cards. Personal checks, if drawn on a U.S. bank or Canadian banking institution, may be used with an acceptable form of identification.

VIA 1 Service - In the Quebec City/Windsor corridor, it is possible to ride in first-class seating called VIA 1. Hot meals are included (served at your seat in LRC trains), as well as complimentary beverages. An on-board breakfast might include fruit, juice, muffin or sweet roll, shortbread, cereal, omelette or crepe and coffee, with newspaper and hot towel, while lunch could include an entree selection of steak, Cornish hen or salmon, with shrimp and rice salad along with fruit and cheese. There are special pre-boarding privileges, and in Montreal, Toronto and Ottawa there are handsomely appointed special waiting areas called Panorama Lounge, with complimentary coffee, juice, soft drinks and newspapers. If you want to be pampered, this service is worth the extra fare.

Fares - Fares are generally comparable to those in the U.S. However, several special discounts are available, and it is important to give each consideration in trying to arrive at the lowest fare. These specials can make Canadian rail travel very economical—particularly during off-peak times. For example, VIA has discounted their transcontinental Canadian 25% off between early October and early June, and 40% off early November through mid-December and early January through late April. A travel agent or VIA sales office will be able to help in making these determinations. Seniors, age 60 and older, and students can save 10% off basic transportation, which can be combined with discounted dates for a savings up to 50%. Children ages two through eleven travel at half fare. Those under age two travel free (one child per adult). Children eight through eleven may travel unaccompanied under certain conditions.

And perhaps the greatest bargain, if one plans to travel extensively, is the CANRAILPASS. Here, a travel card is purchased allowing unlimited travel for one fixed price. The price varies, depending on the territory in which travel is permitted, the length of time the pass can be used, and the time of year that travel will take place. A ticket agent (travel agent) can calculate your best price.

Baggage - Up to 100 pounds of baggage may be checked per adult fare. Unusually bulky items, such as canoes, might not travel on the train on which you're riding, however. Bicycles may be checked, but as required on Amtrak, must be boxed (VIA has them) and the handlebars must be turned and the pedals removed. Pets, except seeing-eye dogs, are not allowed in passenger cars and must travel in baggage cars. Cages can be purchased at most stations.

Smoking - Cigarette smoking is permitted only in enclosed sleeping compartments, designated areas of coaches and designated lounge cars. Smoking is not permitted on Corridor (Quebec City-Windsor) trains.

Overnight Travel - VIA will not furnish pillows or blankets to coach passengers, but will in Dayniters. All bedding, of course, is furnished in sleepers.

Flag Stops - Myriad flag stops exist on Canadian routes—so numerous, no effort has been made to include all of them in *Rail Ventures* logs.

Customs - For citizens of the U.S., entry into Canada is relatively simple, with no passports or visas required. Although technically any of three documents will serve as proof of citizenship when entering Canada—a birth certificate, a certificate of naturalization or a passport—if you have a passport, it would be advisable to have it with you. Neither a social security card nor drivers license is necessarily considered proof of citizenship. Persons under 18, not accompanied by an adult, should have a letter from a parent or guardian giving them permission to travel in Canada.

Persons not citizens or legal residents of the U.S. generally will need a passport or some other acceptable travel document. These persons who wish to return to the U.S. should check with a U.S. Immigration Office to make sure they have the necessary papers.

Goods and Services Tax Refunds - Canada has enacted a rather controversial tax in the amount of 7% on goods and services sold ("GST"). Visitors are eligible for a refund when they leave Canada if proof of payment can be shown. Immediate refunds are available at the border, while submissions by mail may take considerable time.

Timetables - To order a VIA timetable, call one of the VIA phone numbers listed in the Appendix.

Schefferville

Labrador City

Sept Îles

Quebec North Shore & Labrador Railway

This is a train reserved for the adventurous. Its amenities are spartan, its destination (Labrador City) is perhaps the coldest city in North America, and just getting to the Quebec North Shore & Labrador Ry. (QNS&L) is a bit of a hassle. But if this doesn't sound discouraging, there is a good chance you will find the trip a rewarding sojourn.

The scenery, particularly the first 100 miles out of Sept Îles, a Quebec city on the north shore of the St. Lawrence River and the train's southern terminus, is a composite of turbulent rivers, imposing mountains, deep gorges and cascading waterfalls. Farther north into Labrador, the country is virtually uninhabited rolling, forested hills. Only occasional railroad settlements and a handful of Indian camps give evidence of civilization—these and the incredibly long iron ore trains rolling south to the port of Sept Îles.

It was to accommodate these immense serpents that the railroad was built in the early 1950s. The enormous iron ore mines that were developed at Labrador City and Schefferville would not have happened without a means of transporting their ore to world markets.

The railroad was built by flying in men and material to a series of airstrips along its path, a project considered to be the largest civilian airlift in history. Topography, logistics problems, severe cold, black flies and

mosquitoes made this one of Canada's most difficult construction projects.

The mines at Schefferville, the northern end of the line, have now been depleted and closed, and the town is not really worth a visit. But the mines are still alive and well at Labrador City, which is at the end of a 37-mile leg of track that veers westward from the line to Schefferville at Ross Bay Jct., milepost 224. Tours of the Iron Ore of Canada Labrador City mine are interesting and can easily be arranged upon arrival during the summer months.

Unfortunately, you can't reach the QNS&L by train. You can fly, drive or be bused to Sept Îles; or you can fly or drive on a new wilderness road to Labrador City. But undoubtedly the most unusual and interesting way to reach Sept Îles is by a combination freight and passenger ship that sails weekly from Rimouski, Quebec, a town with VIA Rail service on the south shore of the St. Lawrence River.

Northbound Schedule (Condensed)
Sept Îles, Que. - Midmorning Monday Departure; Early Morning Thursday Departure
Labrador City, Nfld. - Early Evening Arrival

Southbound Schedule (Condensed)
Labrador City, Nfld. - Midmorning Departure (Tuesday and Friday)
Sept Îles, Que. - Midevening Arrival

Be sure to check scheduling with the railroad

in Sept Îles before finalizing your plans for any trip that includes travel on this train.

Frequency - Twice weekly (see above).
Seating - Reconditioned coaches of various heritages, with reclining seats and footrests. Fuel oil stoves provide heat in colder months. A dome car, once on the Wabash Cannonball, is usually in service during the summer months only.
Dining - Sandwiches, snacks and beverages are available.
Baggage - Checked baggage is handled between Sept Îles and Labrador City.
Reservations - Unreserved train.
Length of Trip - 261 miles in 9 to 10 hours.

Route Log

SEPT ÎLES, QUE. - A surprisingly modern city, it developed from just a small fishing village into a major seaport with the construction of the Quebec North Shore & Labrador Railway in the 1950s. A large natural harbor, attractively accented with seven islands (hence the town's name), Sept Îles is the logical shipping point. The processing and exporting of iron ore is now the community's economic mainstay. And be sure to bring your French/English dictionary.

QNS&L Station, 100 rue Retty, near the edge of the city; (418) 968-7806 (general information) and 968-7805 (tickets). Modest facility, with rather cramped waiting room. Be sure to arrive 30 minutes or so early, since ticket lines can be lengthy. (The train is virtually the only means of transportation for the Montagnais and other Indians that live in the region, most of whom will be traveling between Sept Îles and Schefferville.) Two antique steam locomotives decorate the grounds.

Taxi Carillon, 962-9444. **Rental cars** are available from Budget, 968-9621 and Tilden, 962-3786. Autobus du Littoral, 962-2126, provides **intercity bus** service west to Baie-Comeau, with connections to Quebec City and Montreal. The **airport** is reasonably close to town. For **boat reservations** on the Nordik Express from Rimouski, Quebec, sailing from there Tuesday afternoons, arriving in Sept Îles Wednesday mornings, contact Relais Nordik, 205 Ave. Léonidas, Rimouski, Que. G5L 2T5; (418) 723-8787.

Tourisme Sept Îles, 1401 Boul. Laure, G4R 4K1; (418) 962-1238, provides city **visitor information.**

Hôtel des Gouverneurs, 666 Boul. Laure, G4R 1X9; (418) 962-7071 or 800-463-2820. Sept Îles' nicest hostelry, in a newer shopping area. Excellent dining room. About three miles

QNS&L engines on display, Sept Îles, Quebec
JACK SWANSON

from the station. $59.

-**Hotel/Motel Mingan,** 665 Boul. Laure, G4R 1X8; (418) 968-2121. Attractive facility, across the street from Hôtel des Gouverneurs. $55.

 Museum of Sept Îles, 500 Boul. Laure, one block from the hotels listed above, has both permanent and traveling exhibits (with all explanations in French).

(Note: Best viewing will be on left. Since train schedule varies during any particular trip, milepost references have been included in this log. Certain sidings where stops are generally made are arbitrarily shown as ending and beginning points for times given in the route log.)

0:00 (1:42) MP 0. Depart Sept Îles and trundle past collection of QNS&L passenger cars on right. If dome is not included in today's train consist, it should be with other cars parked here. Dome car was once used on Wabash Cannonball.

0:05 (1:37) Mountains of stockpiled iron ore stand beside tracks at right. Reddish ore is either hematite ore or concentrated pellets, while grey mounds are specular hematite.

0:12 (1:30) Sept Îles' beautiful harbor is off to right. Trees begin to line tracks. Those along route will consist mostly of black spruce, poplar, birch and aspen.

0:28 (1:14) MP 12. Rumble through crudely illuminated (a string of light bulbs tacked to wall) tunnel, 4/10ths of a mile long. Tunnel was difficult to construct, not only due to rock but also mud. Once during construction, tunnel's silty roof gave way, flushing a worker out of tunnel's south portal. Miraculously, he was unharmed.

0:29 (1:13) Out of tunnel and cross high over Moise River, which follows on left. Bridge is most impressive of numerous trestles along route; it's 700 feet long and 155 feet over Moise. Crossing Moise was a political as well as tactical problem, since Moise Salmon Club was here, boasting prestigious American members with names such as Rockefeller and Eisenhower. Scenery now becomes more spectacular.

0:49 (0:53) MP 21. Transmission lines carry electricity generated by renowned Churchill Falls hydroelectric plant. Plant is one of largest underground electric generating facilities in the world.

0:50 (0:52) MP 22. Worst accident during railroad's construction occurred here when runaway work train smashed into a caboose, killing five men who were sleeping inside.

0:57 (0:45) MP 27. Moise River branches to left, while tracks keep a northward tack along Wacouna River.

0:59 (0:43) MP 28. Compound of neat cabins, below on left, once served as fishing retreat for Johnson & Johnson corporate executives and their guests.

1:03 (0:39) Spectacular rapids are created by churning Moise on left.

1:09 (0:33) MP 35. At Nicnam siding, note waterfalls at very top of rock monoliths on left.

1:25 (0:17) More lovely waterfalls above to left. Then radio communication tower of Iron Ore Company of Canada is on right, one of several that appear along route.

1:33 (0:09) MP 53. Above to left, marvelous set of ribbon falls stream down rocky cliff. These falls are most evident during heavy springtime runoffs.

1:42 (0:00) Arrive Tika's collection of small white buildings.

 TIKA, QUE.

0:00 (0:33) MP 57. Depart Tika.

0:15 (0:18) MP 64. Pierce second illuminated tunnel.

0:20 (0:13) MP 68. Many feel this is best sight of trip! Tumultuous Tonkas Falls, on left, is created by spectacular 200-foot plunge of Wacouna River.

0:33 (0:00) Arrive siding at milepost 73.

SIDING MP 73.

0:00 (1:20) Depart siding, MP 73.

0:02 (1:18) MP 74. Colorful Indian camp is nestled next to railroad right-of-way.

0:14 (1:06) MP 82. Terrain has become less mountainous.

0:20 (1:00) MP 84. Gravel pit at left furnished highest quality ballast for railroad.

1:08 (1:12) MP 120. Mountains have long since disappeared, having been replaced by soft, rolling, forested hills. Trees are nearly all black spruce now.

1:20 (0:00) Arrive siding at milepost 129. Collection of white buildings on left belongs to railroad, and crew normally stops here for lunch while southbound ore train passes. These are extremely long trains, sometimes having 260 cars and stretching for nearly two miles. Pelletized ore is hauled in open gondola cars, while concentrate, an extremely fine, sparkling particulate, is transported in special tank cars. Wheels that stick up from top of tank cars aid in automatic unloading at Sept Îles. Loading is also automated, taking about four hours to load a single train.

 SIDING MP 129.

0:00 (0:41) Depart siding, MP 129.
0:31 (0:10) Just before MP 149, cross watershed that is border between Quebec and Labrador (actually, mainland portion of province of Newfoundland). South of here, waters flow into St. Lawrence, while north of here, all streams flow toward Labrador's Atlantic Coast. This was called "the height of the land" at 2,066 feet of elevation.

 Having now entered Labrador, adjust your watch to Atlantic time by setting it forward one hour.
0:41 (0:00) MP 155. Arrive Seahorse, named for nearby lake.

 SEAHORSE, NFLD.

0:00 (0:44) Depart Seahorse.
0:14 (0:30) MP 166. That faded green ground cover is caribou moss. During survey of railroad, one party reported they virtually lived off of this plant, but said stuff "didn't stick to their ribs." Trees have become stunted and muskeg is now prevalent in this northern clime. While great herds of caribou are north of here, moose (many fatefully and unexpainably drawn to the train) are prevalent in this area.
0:36 (0:08) MP 182. Large lake on left is Ashuanipi, and will appear off and on for nearly 35 miles. During construction of the railway, five bulldozers were lost when they fell through the ice on this body of water.
0:44 (0:00) MP 186. Arrive Oreway. Large, modern building on right has served as overnight stop for ore train crews.

Muskeg between here and Ross Bay Jct. caused some of worst railway construction headaches. A unique solution eventually evolved. Dynamite was placed in mud, then covered with fill. When blasted, muskeg could only go outward and was displaced by the new material.

 OREWAY, NFLD.

0:00 (0:49) Depart Oreway.
0:38 (0:11) MP 215. Water on left is Ross Bay, an extension of Lake Ashuanipi.
0:49 (0:00) MP 224. Pull into huge culvert-like train shed upon arrival Ross Bay Jct. Red-roofed, two-story structure to left is railroad bunk house.

 ROSS BAY JCT.
This is the main QNS&L junction, where one set of tracks proceeds straight north to Schefferville, while the line to Labrador City curls west (left). Labrador City cars will be removed from rest of train at this point, or sometimes passengers are transferred to another train awaiting to take them on to Labrador City.
0:00 (0:27) MP 0. Depart Ross Bay Jct.
0:19 (0:08) Road beside tracks is major Labrador highway. Road comes up from Baie-Comeau, Quebec through wilderness to reach Fermont, Que. (across-the-border neighbor to twin cities of Wabush and Labrador City), then on to Ross Bay Jct. Until recently, vehicle traffic wishing to continue on to Goose Bay on Atlantic Coast had to be placed aboard trains at Ross Bay Jct., transported several miles north to Esker, then were unloaded where road continued on to Goose Bay. Road was to be completed by 1992 to make rail link unnecessary and is now called Trans Labrador Highway.
0:27 (0:00) Arrive Menistouc.

 MENISTOUC, NFLD.

0:00 (0:46) Depart Menistouc.
0:20 (0:26) MP 23. Neat little frame house, on left, has fenced walkway across marshes to allow occupants to reach navigable water.
0:21 (0:25) Cross Trans Labrador Highway.
0:37 (0:09) Immense plants of Iron Ore

Company of Canada, known locally as IOC, are off to left. Beyond plant, Smokey Mountain Ski Area is on side of mountain that also contains vast iron ore reserves. **0:39** (0:07) Area's second huge iron ore operation is Wabush Mine. Its plant can now be seen off to left. Town of Wabush is only three miles from Labrador City.

0:46 (0:00) MP 37. Arrive Labrador City.

LABRADOR CITY, NFLD. - Although it was known in the early 1900s that there were commercial deposits of iron ore in this region, because of their inaccessibility, these deposits were left undeveloped until the 1950s when the Iron Ore Company of Canada (IOC) constructed the Quebec North Shore & Labrador Railway to what is now Labrador City and Knob Lake (now Schefferville). The IOC mine is considered to be the world's largest open pit iron ore mine. Labrador City and its neighboring communities of Wabush (only three miles distant) and Fermont (just to the west across the Quebec border) probably produce more iron ore concentrate than any other region in North America. Some 20,000 people live in the tri-city area.

Winters are long and cold here, frequently reaching 60 degrees or more below zero. But winters are mostly sunny and humidity is below that of the Sahara, all of which helps make the weather almost bearable. Summers can be mild, but it rains a lot in this "second" season and black flies are an ever-present curse. Understandably, the people here are the best paid in Canada.

QNS&L Station is on the edge of Labrador City and only a five-minute taxi ride to neighboring Wabush. Station phone, (709) 944-2745.

Labrador West Tourism, P.O. Box 1237, Wabush, Labrador, Nfld., A0R 1B0; (709) 282-3337. Office is located downstairs in the Wabush Hotel.

A-1 Taxi, 944-5169. Avis **rental cars,** (709) 282-6233, offer shuttle service to and from their airport office. **Airport** is conveniently situated between Labrador City and Wabush.

Wabush Hotel, P.O. Box 700, Wabush, A0R 1B0; (709) 282-3221. Large, comfortable hotel with distinctive architecture. Dining rooms and cafe. In Wabush, about an $8 cab ride from the station. $62.

-Two Seasons Inn, Box 572, Labrador City, A2V 2L3; (709) 944-2661. On Avalon Drive in Labrador City. This is the area's newest hotel. Short cab ride from the station. $84.

Both IOC and Wabush offer **mine tours.** You may arrange for a tour by calling Labrador West Tourism, 282-3337 or IOC, 944-8582.

Montreal
Halifax

Atlantic

Linking the Nova Scotian coastal city of Halifax with Montreal, the Atlantic affords its passengers lovely countryside scenes in southern New Brunswick, and, best of all, an outstanding trip around Bedford Basin—that truly spectacular inner harbor at Halifax. Because the Canadian Pacific Railway, some 100 years ago, needed access to an eastern port that was ice free, there is a unique aspect of this trip. Although the Atlantic is a Canadian train running on Canadian-owned tracks, its route short-cuts across United States soil. Stops are made at several towns in northern Maine, ironically providing the only rail passenger service in the state.

Since the US-Canadian border is crossed twice, customs inspections are inevitable. Fortunately, this procedure no longer involves passengers who are neither getting on nor off in Maine.

The stainless steel cars have been beautifully refurbished and provided with electric heat. Unfortunately the Atlantic is in jeopardy of being discontinued since the CP hopes to abandon a major portion of this route.

Westbound Schedule (Condensed)
Halifax, N.S. - Early Afternoon Departure
Moncton, N.B. - Early Evening
Saint John, N.B. - Midevening
Jackman, ME - Middle of the Night (2nd Day)
Montreal, Que. - Early Morning (2nd Day)

Eastbound Schedule (Condensed)
Montreal, Que. - Early Evening Departure
Jackman, ME - Late Night (2nd Day)

Saint John, N.B. - Early Morning (2nd Day)
Moncton, N.B. - Late Morning (2nd Day)
Halifax, N.S. - Midafternoon Arrival (2nd Day)

Frequency - Three times a week, departing both Halifax and Montreal—Monday, Thursday and Saturday.

Seating - Standard coaches and dome car.

Dining - Complete meal and beverage service as well as lighter fare.

Sleeping - Berths, roomettes, and bedrooms. Overnight coach passengers are provided with blankets and pillows. Sleeping cars have a shower in each car.

Baggage - Checked baggage at larger towns.

Reservations - All-reserved train.

Length of Trip - 752 miles in 20½ hours.

Route Log

HALIFAX, N.S. - Halifax was founded by Edward Cornwallis in 1749 as an army and naval base for the English after the French established an imposing fortress at nearby Louisbourg. The deep harbour, protected by both islands and bluffs, made it an ideal naval base, particularly after the Citadel Hill Fortress was constructed as protection. Halifax has remained a military center to this date.

Because of its excellent harbor, Halifax has always been oriented toward ocean industries with ship-repair facilities, containerization docks and various other shipyards still dominating its waterfront. It's a remarkably clean city and attracts thousands of visitors every year, many using this provincial capital as a base for touring the rest of the province. The shores, particularly to the south, are noted for their ruggedness.

In 1917, the largest man-made explosion (prior to the atom bomb) occurred in Halifax Harbor when, on December 6th of that year, the Mont Blanc, a freighter loaded with ammunition, collided with the Imo. The Mont Blanc caught fire and 26 minutes later she blew up, devastating large portions of Halifax and Dartmouth and killing 1,900 persons.

VIA Station, 1161 Hollis St., is a nicely remodeled station on the edge of downtown. There is a snack bar, a newsstand, free luggage carts and redcaps. Thirty-minute free parking is in front of the station. Pay-parking is at the rear of the station.

Call 429-8421 for reservations and other information.

Cab stand and **local buses** at the station; Yellow Cab, 422-1551. Metro Transit, 421-6600. Tilden **rental cars** are a half block from the station, (902) 422-4439. The **airport** is located across the bay and southeast of Dartmouth.

Tourism Halifax, Old City Hall, Duke and Barrington streets; (902) 421-8736. A provincial information office is in The Old Red Store on the wharf at Historic Properties; (902) 424-4247. Write: Box 1749, B3J 3A5.

Halifax Hilton, 1181 Hollis St., B3H 2P6; (902) 423-7231. Comfortable, well-maintained hotel, adjoins the station. $89.

-**Waverly Inn,** 1266 Barrington, B3J 1Y5; (902) 423-9346. An 1876 inn with spacious and comfortable rooms, many furnished with fine antiques. Complimentary breakfast. Two blocks from the station. $55.

-**Halliburton House Inn,** 5184 Morris Street, B3J 1B3; (902) 420-0658. Elegant smaller hotel occupying a Registered Heritage Property. Excellent dining room. Complimentary breakfast. Only two blocks from the station. $85.

Many attractions are within walking distance. A map of Halifax describing a **walking tour** may be obtained from the Visitors Bureau which is about a 15-minute walk north of the VIA station. Points of interest include: the old waterfront where the **"Bluenose II,"** a replica of the famous racing schooner and used for pleasure cruises, is often berthed (the original Bluenose, built in 1921, kept the International Fisherman's Trophy in Canada for 20 years); **Historic Properties,** which is made of nicely restored buildings along the waterfront; and the **Maritime Museum of the Atlantic,** which includes exhibits of such nautical subjects as a "skinned" torpedo and flotsam from the Titanic.

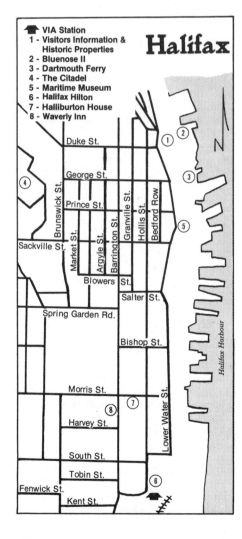

VIA Station
1 - Visitors Information & Historic Properties
2 - Bluenose II
3 - Dartmouth Ferry
4 - The Citadel
5 - Maritime Museum
6 - Halifax Hilton
7 - Halliburton House
8 - Waverly Inn

Halifax

Duke St.
George St.
Prince St.
Sackville St.
Blowers St.
Salter St.
Spring Garden Rd.
Bishop St.
Morris St.
Harvey St.
South St.
Tobin St.
Fenwick St.
Kent St.

Brunswick St.
Market St.
Argyle St.
Barrington St.
Granville St.
Hollis St.
Bedford Row
Lower Water St.

Halifax Harbour

The Citadel, located on a hill overlooking the harbor, with a large star-shaped fortress replacing the earlier wooden one built by Cornwallis. It also has Maritime and Historic Museums.

Musquodoboit Railway Museum, the largest in eastern Canada, is located at Musquodoboit Harbor north of Halifax.

0:00 (1:19) Depart Halifax where lengthy string of retired rail diesel cars lies in storage on right and other VIA passenger cars on left.

0:02 (1:17) Enormous docking facilities are on left, while on right, equally as impressive storage elevators use overhead conveyors to transport grain to loading docks.

0:04 (1:15) Four orange and white gantries handle loading and unloading of oceangoing freighters off to left.

0:12 (1:07) Tracks now make an encompassing arc along westerly shore of beautiful Bedford Basin, on right. Everything from giant oceangoing freighters to smallest pleasure craft speckle harbor, creating a scene that captures very essence of Canada's Maritime Provinces. Two suspension bridges in distance span harbor entrance and connect twin cities of Dartmouth (on left) and Halifax. It was in that general area that munitions ship Mont Blanc exploded in 1917.

0:16 (1:03) Small gazebo-like house on right was built years ago by a British nobleman as solitary retreat.

0:17 (1:02) Wooden hull of half-submerged tug, on right, marks long-ago maritime misadventure.

0:27 (0:50) Eastbound Atlantic pauses briefly at Windsor Junction, where line branches off to left toward Yarmouth.

0:39 (0:38) Elongated waters of Shubenacadie Grand Lake form inviting scene on left as train cuts through rolling Nova Scotian countryside. Many other small lakes can be observed through here.

0:55 (0:24) Cross Shubenacadie River and slip through nice-appearing town with same unusual name (an Indian word meaning "where the potato grows").

1:15 (0:04) Newer brick building on right is home to Nova Scotia Teachers College.

1:19 (0:00) Arrive Truro.

TRURO, N.S. - Located at the tip of Cobequid Bay, actually an extension of the high-tidal-action Bay of Fundy, Truro is one of the largest of the early-Acadian settlements. Here, railroading and manufacturing play important economic roles, while higher education is also prominent. It is the home for Nova Scotia Agricultural College and Nova Scotia Teachers College just mentioned.

0:00 (1:20) Depart Truro and start a twisting trek across upper thumb of Nova Scotia.

0:04 (1:16) Facility off to left with "Stansfield" sign manufactures quality shirts, sweaters and other clothing.

0:16 (0:52) Cross Canada Highway 104 and then travel 87 feet above small, but lovely, Folly River.

0:38 (0:41) Train grinds over summit where Folly Lake lies nestled just to right of tracks, a glacier-formed pond several thousand years old.

0:45 (0:35) Wentworth Valley Ski Area, below on right, provides wintertime sport for skiers from across central Nova Scotia.

1:05 (0:15) Cross River Phillip coursing through pine-laden forests.

1:20 (0:00) Arrive Springhill Jct. where delightfully tiny one-roomer station serves local VIA passengers.

SPRINGHILL JUNCTION, N.S. - This very small town (population 203) was named for springs found in nearby hills. Its once-active coal mines are no longer being operated, and perhaps just as well. Numerous tragic explosions plagued the mines almost from their beginning in the late 19th century.

0:00 (0:22) Depart Springhill Jct.

0:17 (0:05) On immediate right, Sifto Salt plant rests above mine that is source of its product.

0:22 (0:00) Arrive Amherst.

AMHERST, N.S. - Geography buffs will be happy to learn that this is the geographical center of the Maritime Provinces. It is also a manufacturing center, producing such varied products as clothing, structural steel, dairy goods and tanning oils.

0:00 (0:17) Depart Amherst.

0:02 (0:15) Orange-colored rail car on right now serves as Amherst visitor center.

0:07 (0:10) Enter New Brunswick and leave Nova Scotia while crossing Missaguash River.

0:08 (0:09) Historic Fort Beausejour, perched atop knoll on right, stands silent guard over Tantramar Marshes which stretch across 84 square miles on left. These marshes were once tidal flats until French Acadians, more than 200 years ago, resourcefully constructed elaborate dike systems, turning what was once muddy bogs into fertile farmlands. Dikes are still visible today.

0:13 (0:04) Forest of antennae of Radio Canada International (Canada's short-wave radio service) sprout from ground on right.

0:17 (0:00) Arrive Sackville.

SACKVILLE, N.B. - This city of 5,800 persons rejoices in the distinction of possessing the only harness shop in North America still producing horse collars. It is also the location of Mount Allison University, which, in 1875, awarded the first degree given to a woman in the British Empire. Sackville was a seaport until a landslide changed the course of the Tantramar River in 1920.

0:00 (0:51) Depart Sackville.

0:16 (0:35) Perched atop hill on right is Dorchester Penitentiary, maximum security prison holding felons from all of eastern Canada.

0:51 (0:00) Arriving Moncton, needle-like communications tower, which juts above town, is one of tallest such structures in Canada.

MONCTON, N.B. - The present location of the city was first occupied for a short while in the mid-1700s by French Acadians who reclaimed the surrounding marshes by constructing dykes along the river. However, the site was ultimately abandoned when the British forced the Acadians to leave and totally destroyed the settlement. Later, in 1766, several German families from Pennsylvania moved to what is now Moncton, a simplification of the name of Lieutenant General Robert Monckton, who served under Wolfe's command, and captured nearby Fort Beausejour in 1755.

Although shipbuilding was once an important industry in Moncton, it gradually declined and the town with it. Finally, new life came with the railroad, and

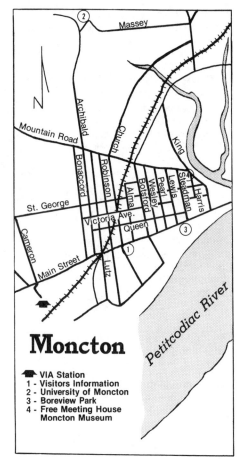

Moncton

- VIA Station
- 1 - Visitors Information
- 2 - University of Moncton
- 3 - Boreview Park
- 4 - Free Meeting House
  Moncton Museum

Moncton became a major rail and trade center for eastern Canada. Several of New Brunswick's attractions are nearby.

VIA Station, 1240 Main St., has snack and beverage vending machines, luggage carts and pay-parking. The Highfield Square shopping mall is adjacent, with shops and restaurants.

For reservations and information, call (506) 857-9830.

Cab stand at the station; Air Cab, 857-2000. Nearest **local bus** stop, two blocks from the station, Main at Highfield Square; Moncton Transit, 857-8517. **SMT bus** terminal, 859-5060, is three blocks from the station. Tilden will pick up and deliver **rental car** customers, 857-0644. Also, Thrifty Rental Car, 858-2277. **Moncton Municipal Airport** is approximately five miles east of the station.

? **Moncton Convention & Visitors Services,** 774 Main St., E1C 1E8; (506) 853-3596.

Keddy's Brunswick Hotel, Highfield and Main St., E1C 8N6; (506) 854-6340 or 800-561-7666. Highrise with top-floor restaurant that provides fine view of the city. Very nice accommodations. Two blocks from the station. $60.
-**Colonial Inn,** 42 Highfield St., E1C 8T6; (506) 382-3395. Complimentary continental breakfast weekdays. Well run by friendly management. Three blocks from the station. $49.

In town, the **Acadian Museum** at the University of Moncton, the only French university in the Atlantic provinces, has displays featuring the Acadian culture of the Moncton area. The **Tidal Bore** can be viewed from Bore Park where the tide comes in. As the tide moves across the vast mud flats, they become a mile-wide river, often 30 feet deep. Timetables for witnessing this event are available at the information center.

Centennial Park has displays including "Old 5270," a Pacific class steam locomotive, a CF-100 jet fighter and a World War II Sherman tank.

Not far from Moncton, **Hopewell Cape** has unusual "flower pot" rocks formed by the enormous tides of the Bay of Fundy.

Fort Beausejour National Historic Park is located just off the Trans-Canada Highway, 35 minutes southeast from Moncton. The fort was built by the French between 1751 and 1755, but was captured by the English before completion. The fort has a commanding view across the expanses of the Tantramar Marsh where the Acadians reclaimed most of the land from the Fundy tides by using extensive systems of dykes.

Nearby, the **Salem & Hillsborough Railroad** offers steam train excursions.

0:00 (0:50) Depart Moncton.

0:07 (0:43) Last look at Shepody Bay is afforded just off to left.

0:10 (0:40) CN diesel shops appear at right. Rail lines curling off to right head toward Campbellton and are route of VIA's Ocean. Upon leaving city, our route courses through countryside of small farms, dairies, homes and splotches of forests. Deer can often be spotted.

0:30 (0:20) Cross Petitcodiac River.

0:44 (0:06) Complex off to left, with two huge, green barn-like structures, is surface portion of mining operation that brings potash from 2,000 feet below. About 50 rail cars can be loaded in a day; material is taken to Saint John for export.

0:50 (0:00) Arrive Sussex.

SUSSEX, N.B. - Recent potash discoveries here have enlivened the town's economy. The only other Canadian potash deposits are in western Saskatchewan. The town has long been an important dairy and craft center.

0:00 (0:52) Depart Sussex.

0:12 (0:40) Through Norton, note many homes with rather interestingly similar architecture—large white structures with black, hippish roofs.

0:15 (0:37) Eye-catching (and tongue-twisting) Kennebecasis River flows along with train, on right.

0:18 (0:34) One of few remaining covered bridges in this region is on right, charm being further enhanced by two churches that form backdrop.

0:34 (0:22) Kennebecasis Bay can now be seen on right with its residential studded shore line. Note fine-looking mansion on hill on far side of water.

0:44 (0:12) Through Rothesay with its numerous summer homes and scattered pleasure craft floating at its docks.

0:52 (0:00) Arrive Saint John. VIA station stands near site of former Union Station demolished in 1971.

SAINT JOHN, N.B. - This is Canada's oldest incorporated city (1785), founded by thousands of Loyalists who landed here in 1783. Benedict Arnold came here to live after having to leave the United States. The city claims some firsts: the first newspaper and the first bank in Canada, and the first police force in North America.

0:00 (0:55) Depart Saint John.

0:08 (0:47) Train crosses high above Saint John River. If tide is out, famous Reversing Falls Rapids can be seen below on right. Twice each day, high Fundy tides cause reversal in water's flow.

0:09 (0:46) Impressive Kimberly Clarke

Atlantic - Rockingham, Nova Scotia
SCOTT HARTLEY

paper mill is on immediate right with its intimidating structures and huge piles of wood chips. On left, one can peer through windows of world headquarters of Moosehead Breweries and see large vats used in brewing process.

0:16 (0:39) Stunning view of St. John River's Grand Bay on right. Numerous cottages can be seen snuggled along shoreline.

0:20 (0:35) Train now bids farewell to river as tracks climb northwesterly toward Fredericton.

0:30 (0:25) New Brunswick's rural charm continues with another covered-bridge scene on left.

0:52 (0:04) Pass by expansive facilities of Gagetown Armed Forces Base, one of largest (geographically) in Commonwealth.

0:57 (0:00) Arrive Fredericton Junction.

FREDERICTON JCT., N.B. - This is the closest the main line comes to Fredericton. Not much here, but it is a stop for connecting buses to the city itself. Fredericton is the cultural center of New Brunswick, as well as the provincial capital.

0:00 (0:50) Depart Fredericton Jct.

0:05 (0:45) Forest lands continue, with birch stands offering their white-barked trunks to lighten this heavily wooded region. Lakes and dairy farms are abundant as we approach the state of Maine.

0:50 (0:00) Arrive McAdam, where gargantuan station, constructed in 1901 from locally quarried granite, is now a national historic site. This three-story dinosaur was originally a combination station and hotel, but hostelry closed in 1959.

MCADAM, N.B. - This was once a major passenger train hub, with branch lines serving various New Brunswick destinations, including St. Andrews where CP once ran and operated the still-famous Algonquin Hotel.

0:00 (0:10) Depart McAdam, and in a few moments enter the state of Maine upon crossing St. Croix River.

Enter Eastern and leave Atlantic time zone. Westbound passengers move clocks back one hour. Eastbound, forward one hour.

0:10 (0:00) Arrive Vanceboro.

VANCEBORO, ME - This is a customs stop for westbound trains. Inspections usually go rather swiftly, but there can be occasional delays. (Through-passengers usually do not have to undergo customs inspections.)

0:00 (4:37) Depart Vanceboro.

The train now traverses the southern edge of the upper wilderness of Maine, still following the Canadian Pacific's track during the dead of night. Occasional stops are made when civilization is contacted at **DANFORTH, MATTAWAMKEAG, BROWNVILLE JUNCTION,** and **GREENVILLE.**

4:37 (0:00) Arrive Jackman.

JACKMAN, ME - This border station is a customs stop for east-bound passenger trains. (Again, through-passengers are usually not checked by customs.)

0:00 (1:10) Depart Jackman.

0:40 (0:30) Leave United States and cross into Quebec.

1:10 (0:00) Arrive Mégantic.

MÉGANTIC, QUE. - Another Canadian town that has largely descended from Loyalist settlers, this community is at the tip of ten-mile-long Lake Mégantic—a fisherman's pristine haven.

0:00 (2:08) Depart Mégantic.

2:08 (0:00) Arrive Sherbrooke.

SHERBROOKE, QUE. - As one might suspect from observing the surrounding forests, the city's economy is heavily dependent on wood products, including lumber, pulp and paper. Winter recreation is also becoming important.

Located at the confluence of the Magog River and the Saint Francois, the city has an attractive setting, spread out across numerous hills with the Magog cutting an impressive chasm through the heart of town. The University of Sherbrooke is here, and boasts a fine art gallery and rather handsome campus.

0:00 (0:43) Depart Sherbrooke, following along banks of impressive Saint Francois River.

0:43 (0:00) Arrive Richmond, where old, rambling brick depot on right still serves as passenger station.

RICHMOND, QUE. - This is a small agrarian-oriented community, and the point where the tracks now diverge from the attractive Saint Francois River Valley. Richmond began with the arrival of the Grand Trunk Railroad in 1853.

0:00 (0:55) Depart Richmond.

0:34 (0:21) At flag stop of Acton Vale, note very ornate, nicely kept station on left.

0:49 (0:06) Slowly ease onto corridor tracks connecting Montreal to Quebec City.

0:53 (0:02) Cross Yamaska River.

0:55 (0:00) Arrive St. Hyacinthe, where cream, blue and rose station awaits on left.

ST. HYACINTHE, QUE. - This town of 40,000 serves as a trade center for local farming activities, and also is home for those who don't mind commuting to Montreal, some 33 miles to the west. The town was not named for lily-like flower but a local landowner.

0:00 (0:33) Depart St. Hyacinthe, then pass town's golf course on outskirts at left.

0:10 (0:23) Royal Hills, those unusual mountains on left, are of volcanic origin dating back millions of years. A quarry can be seen on the slopes of St. Hilaire, two miles away, which is a source of rare minerals, many being found only in this locale. Rougemont Mountain is eight miles distant, while 1,350-foot Yamaska Mountain is 12 miles from here.

0:15 (0:18) Trundle over impressive Richelieu River which drains Lake Champlain, directly south of us in New York State, into the St. Lawrence.

0:33 (0:00) Arrive St. Lambert.

ST. LAMBERT, QUE. - We are now immediately across the St. Lawrence from our destination, Montreal. St. Lambert Lock, a lift station for the St. Lawrence Seaway traffic, is here.

0:00 (0:12) Depart St. Lambert and start ascent necessary for crossing St. Lawrence River on Victoria Bridge.

This structure was once known as the Jubilee Bridge when it was opened in 1859

Montreal

VIA Station
1 - Visitors Information
2 - McGill University
3 - St. Helen's Island
4 - Place D'Armes
5 - Notre Dame Church
6 - Queen Elizabeth Hotel
7 - Hotel Royal Roussillon
8 - Hotel Arcade

St. Lawrence River

Boul. de Maisonneuve
Ste-Catherine
René Lévesque
St. Antoine
St. Hubert
Sanguinet
Ave. Hôtel de Ville
de Bullion
St. Denis
Notre Dame
St. Gabriel
St. Sulpice
St.
St. Dominique
Boul. St. Laurent
St. Urbain
St. François-Xavier
St. Pierre
Sherbrooke
Jeanne Mance
de Bleury
de la Gauchetière
McGill
Wellington
Ave. du Parc
Beaver Hall Hill
Autoroute Bonaventure
Ave. du Prés. Kennedy
University
Peel
Guy
St. Jacques

340

(later to be rebuilt in 1898). It handled two sets of rails, an electric interurban line and auto traffic, and was one of the world's longest bridges at 1¼ miles. Those two concrete-lined channels below us are the St. Lawrence Seaway and the St. Lambert Lock which is just one of many locks needed to raise or lower shipping using this waterway. The Seaway is narrow and unfortunately cannot handle larger ships of today's maritime fleet. The islands to the right were home to Canada's very successful 1967 world's fair—Expo 67. The geodesic dome was the U.S. Pavilion. The skyline of Montreal is a dramatic scene on the right.

0:06 (0:06) Leaving Victoria Bridge, we enter Montreal through Canadian National rail yards.

0:08 (0:04) Slip over nicely landscaped Canal Lachine (pronounced luh-sheen), built years ago to circumvent Lachine Rapids, but discontinued operations when Seaway was opened.

0:10 (0:02) Sink underground as we near end of line.

0:12 (0:00) Arrive Montreal's Central Station.

MONTREAL, QUE. - Montreal is one of North America's oldest cities. In 1535 Jacques Cartier discovered this location which was already inhabited by 4,000 Iroquois Amerindians. However, it wasn't until 1642 that a permanent settlement was established by some devout French laymen.

Although the British captured the town in 1760 during the Battle of the Plains of Abraham (which ultimately led to all of Canada becoming British), Montreal, to this day, remains a city of charming French character. Three-fourths of its populace still speak that language, and the city has a distinct European look and feel.

Located on a collection of islands in the St. Lawrence River, and only 117 feet above sea level, it is dominated by 765-foot Mount Royal from which the city derives its name. Winters here can be hard, but miles of underground shopping and a good subway system make it a town to be visited during any season.

Central Station, 895 la Gauchetiere W. (at University), is located in the very heart of downtown. This is one of VIA's busiest and best stations. Escalators leading down to train platforms stretch across its central plaza while stores and services are ensconced along the perimeter. There are numerous snack bars, restaurants and shops that line the underground arcades leading to other buildings in downtown Montreal. There are redcaps, and pay-parking is adjacent to the station. Panorama Lounge is available to VIA-1 customers.

For reservations and other information, call (514) 871-1331.

Cab stand at the station; Diamond, 273-6331. Budget **rental cars** are at the station. Local buses stop at the station, 288-6287. **Intercity bus** terminal, Voyageur, (514) 842-2281. **Montreal International Airport** is about 15 miles west of downtown.

Visitor Information Center, 1001 Square Dorchester (at Metcalf); (514) 873-2015 or 800-363-7777. Write Greater Montreal Convention & Tourism Bureau, 1010 Sainte-Catherine Street West, Suite 410, H3B 1G2. For central hotel reservation service, located at the Information Center, call (514) 393-9049.

The Queen Elizabeth Hotel, 900 René-Lévesque Blvd. W. (at Mansfield), H3B 4A5; (514) 861-3511 or 800-828-7447. One of Montreal's best. Two floors devoted to "Business Class" with lots of extras, including a complimentary breakfast buffet in a separate dining room. Located above Central Station. $145.

-Hôtel Royal Roussillon, 1610 rue St-Hubert, H2L 3Z3; (514) 849-3214. Attractive accommodations, one of downtown Montreal's best values. Easily reached by subway; get off at Berri-de-Montigny Station (Boul. de Maisonneuve). About a mile north of VIA's Central Station, in a quiet neighborhood. $62.

-Hôtel Arcade, 50 René-Lévesque Blvd. West (formerly Dorchester Blvd.), H2Z 1A2; (514) 874-0906 or 800-363-6535. Small but spiffy rooms. Eight blocks from the station. $59.

Two Bed and Breakfast reservation services include:

-**A Downtown Bed & Breakfast Network,** 3458 Laval Ave. (at Sherbrooke St.), H2X 3C8; (514) 289-9749 or 800-267-5180. A reservation service for numerous B&Bs in the downtown area, including this location.

-**Montreal Bed & Breakfast,** a B&B reservation service, (514) 738-9410.

Much of Montreal is **underground,** with shops, restaurants and services lining miles of walkways underneath portions of the city. A **walking tour** of the old city, roughly defined by McGill, Notre-Dame, Berri streets and the St. Lawrence River, can be taken starting at Place D'Armes (at St. Sulpice and Notre Dame St.). Here one can see Notre Dame Church, Saint-Sulpice Seminary and the Bank of Montreal Museum. From this point, walk east along cobblestone streets to see Place de la Justice and artists exhibiting works. Upon reaching the church and Bonsecours Market, head west and pass by Place Royale, the d'Youville Stables and the Old General Hospital. The old city also has many galleries, charming shops and cafes.

St. Helen's Island has several attractions including: **The Montreal Aquarium** with fine displays of marine life; **St. Helen's Island Museum** at the Old Ford, Montreal's Military and Maritime Museum, with various military and naval artifacts dating from the 15th century; and **LaRonde,** a spectacular amusement park, resulting from the world's fair (Expo '67) held here in 1967.

The **Montreal Museum of Fine Arts,** 1379 rue Sherbrooke W., with excellent permanent art collections as well as traveling exhibits.

Mount Royal Overlook has a great view and a steep climb—206 steps up a stairway with only two landings. Go up Peel Street, through McGill University to Mount Royal Park to the base of the stairs, then climb!

Some distance northeast of downtown, but reached by subway, is the **Botanical Gardens,** 4101 rue Sherbrooke E. Get off the subway at Pie IX Station (the stop for the **Montreal Expos** stadium). There are over 25,000 species and plant varieties, 30 outdoor gardens and nine greenhouses. This is one of the most outstanding botanical gardens in the world.

Montreal Halifax

Ocean

The Ocean is VIA's connection to the Atlantic provinces avoiding the United States. This is an overnight trip between Halifax and Montreal, skirting around the topside of Maine along the St. Lawrence River during the western leg of the journey, with the segment between Lévis, Que. and Campbellton, N.B. normally traveled in darkness.

As in the case of the Atlantic, the Ocean has been given a beautiful facelift. Refurbished stainless steel cars with electric heat provide a most stylish ride.

Westbound Schedule (Condensed)
Halifax, N.S. - Early Afternoon Departure
Moncton, N.B. - Late Afternoon
Campbellton, N.B. - Late Evening
Lévis, Que. - Middle of the Night (Ferry Service to Quebec City) (2nd Day)
Montreal, Que. - Early Morning Arrival (2nd Day)

Eastbound Schedule (Condensed)
Montreal, Que. - Early Evening Departure
Lévis, Que. - Late Evening (Ferry Service to Quebec City)
Campbellton, N.B. - Early Morning (2nd Day)
Moncton, N.B. - Late Morning (2nd Day)
Halifax, N.S. - Midafternoon Arrival (2nd Day)

Frequency - Three times a week, departing both Halifax and Montreal Sunday, Wednesday and Friday.
Seating - Standard coaches and dome car.
Dining - Complete meal and beverage service as well as lighter fare.

Sleeping - Berths, roomettes and bedrooms. Overnight coach passengers are provided with blankets and pillows. Sleeping cars have a shower in each car.
Baggage - Checked baggage at larger towns.
Reservations - All-reserved train.
Length of Trip - 840 miles in 19 hours.

Route Log

For route between Halifax and Moncton, see that portion of the Atlantic route log, page 333.

 MONCTON, N.B. - See page 336.

0:00 (1:00) Depart Moncton.
From Moncton to Rogersville, the Ocean follows eastern margin of interior New Brunswick wilderness, occasionally touching small villages, many of which sprung up when the railroad was completed.
0:26 (0:34) Cross Richibucto River.
0:37 (0:23) Presumably, Bernard's Hog Farm, on left, is local source of delectable "Canadian bacon."
0:54 (0:06) Cross Kouchibouguacis River.
0:58 (0:02) Boat permanently berthed in midst of trees on right is rather ludicrous scene.
1:00 (0:00) Arrive Rogersville.

ROGERSVILLE, N.B. - This small trading center of 1,061 persons is named in honor of James Rogers, former Bishop of Chaltham.

0:00 (0:29) Depart Rogersville.

0:07 (0:19) On left, steps lead up to crude hunting platform in tree. Several such contraptions can be spotted along this portion of route.

0:20 (0:06) First, cross glassy smooth, broad waters of Southwest Miramichi River then, moments later, cross equally as impressive Miramichi River, both burgeoning with waters originating from much of central New Brunswick, and which finally empty into Miramichi Bay in Gulf of St. Lawrence on right (too far to be visible).

0:23 (0:02) Large pulp mill on right is important regional employer. Another such mill will appear on right in four more minutes.

0:29 (0:00) Arrive Newcastle.

NEWCASTLE, N.B. - Situated on the tip of Miramichi Bay, shipping through its fine port facilities generates much of this city's business. Pulp production is also an important economic mainstay. Of interest is McDonald Farm, northeast of here, which is a working farm carefully restored to depict rural life in the early 1800s. Miramichi Folksong Festival is celebrated here each summer.

0:00 (0:50) Depart Newcastle and continue through forested lands of eastern New Brunswick.

0:03 (0:47) For eastbound passengers, having just traveled through miles of forest land, view forward left (back to right westbound) of Newcastle will provide dramatic change of scene.

0:11 (0:39) Home of television fanatic can easily be spotted where three satellite dishes are in one yard at right.

0:44 (0:06) Cross large Nepisiguit River just before it flows into Nepisiguit Bay.

0:50 (0:00) Arrive Bathurst.

BATHURST, N.B. - This city of 16,300 is the urban focal point for mining and other industry in northeastern New Brunswick. Tourists have also found this area with its many scenic waterfalls and beaches. A pretty drive leads to nearby Caraquet where Acadian Historical Village is located—a re-created settlement depicting Acadian lifestyle of the early 1800s.

0:00 (1:20) Depart Bathurst and trace course along Chaleur Bay, on right, until Campbellton. Large brick facility on hill to left is New Brunswick Community College.

0:04 (1:16) Cross Tetagouche River.

0:12 (1:06) To left, church steeple with unusual hole through it identifies Petit Rocher, an Ocean flag stop.

0:34 (0:46) Pass through small coastal community of Jacquet River (flag stop) where good crab and lobster fishing is afforded along shoreline, and then cross Jacquet River.

0:49 (0:31) Apparent narrowness of bay is caused by Heron Island about five miles off shore to right. Across Chaleurs Bay is famed Gaspé Peninsula with Mount Saint Joseph above Carleton, Quebec, its highest visible protrusion.

1:07 (0:13) This is Dalhousie Jct., with newsprint mills and popular public beaches nearby.

1:20 (0:00) Arrival at Campbellton is marked by lovely view of bay. Green steel bridge crosses tip of Chaleurs Bay, connecting Campbellton and Point-à-la-Croix, Quebec.

CAMPBELLTON, N.B. - In 1760, the bay serving this port city provided the setting for the last naval engagement of The Seven Years War. Superb fishing is found throughout this region of New Brunswick, and a well-attended Salmon Festival is held here each July. Nearby Sugarloaf Provincial Park provides not only fishing, but camping and winter sports as well.

Caspian Motel, 26 Duke Street, E3N 3G9; (506) 753-7606. Large downtown motel, just one block from the VIA station. $44.

0:00 (0:24) When departing Campbellton, impressive bridge can be seen on right, spanning tip of Chaleur Bay, fed at this point by salmon-filled Restigouche River.

0:13 (0:11) Through only tunnel on Ocean's route.

0:23 (0:01) Cross Restigouche River and, at midpoint, enter Quebec and leave New Brunswick.

Gain one hour as train passes from Atlantic to Eastern Time. Set your watch back (forward if eastbound) one hour.

0:24 (0:00) Arrive Matapédia.

Ocean observation car
JACK SWANSON

MATAPÉDIA, N.B. - The name Matapédia stems from a similar Indian word meaning "river breaks into branches." Technically speaking, rather than separating, Matapedia and Restigouche rivers join here, just before rushing into bay. This is also where the rail line to Gaspe departs our route. The Chaleur, a direct link between that lovely resort community and Montreal, joins the westbound Ocean (or splits off of the eastbound).

From here to just beyond Amqui, the Ocean stays in the exciting Matapédia River Valley where the swift, sometimes torrential waters of the Matapédia are always a stone's throw from the tracks. The Matapédia, like the Restigouche, is a marvelous salmon fishing stream. Since the Ocean runs along this stretch in darkness, forested hills, spotted with intermittent lakes and harboring considerable wildlife, as well as an occasional picturesque farmstead, are scenes afforded passengers only if the train is considerably off schedule.

0:00 (0:46) Depart Matapédia.
0:28 (0:18) One of region's longer covered bridges (they are sometimes referred to as settlers' bridges) is off to right at Routherville.
0:43 (0:03) Another covered bridge can be seen on left at Heppel.
0:46 (0:00) Arriving Causapscal, sawdust-burning inverted cone (they're called "hells") identifies sawmill on right. Attractive white and grey VIA station awaits passengers.

CAUSAPSCAL, QUE. - The Matapédia River runs directly through this attractive small community, originally settled by Acadians. Farming, logging and, of course, fishing are important to Causapscal's economy.
0:00 (0:18) Depart Causapscal.
0:10 (0:08) At right, large body of water beyond town of Lac-au-Saumon is lake by same name.
0:16 (0:02) Cross Indian Brook.
0:18 (0:00) Arriving Amqui, cross Amqui River just before blue and pinkish cream

VIA station on left.

 AMQUI, QUE. - This small commercial center is situated at the southern tip of 16-mile-long, 5-mile-wide Lake Matapédia.

0:00 (0:18) Depart Amqui.

0:04 (0:14) Note covered bridge off to right, situated between two lakes. Glimpses are afforded on right of Lake Matapédia.

0:10 (0:08) At Val Brillant, "called Queen of the Valley," handsome twin-spired church of "flamboyant Gothic" architecture is on immediate left. Statue of Christ and four old-style street lights grace foreground.

0:18 (0:00) Arrive Sayabec, where another blue and pinkish cream-colored VIA station awaits on right. Church on hill, to right, overlooks Lake Matapédia.

 SAYABEC, QUE. - The only particle board plant in the region is located here at Sayabec (pronounced say-beck), an operation which is fed by abundant local forests.

0:00 (0:38) Depart Sayabec.

0:26 (0:08) Descending toward Mont Joli, St. Lawrence River, once called "road which walks" by Amerindians, comes into view forward right. At this point, waterway has more characteristics of an ocean than a river.

0:34 (0:04) Soar 63 feet above Mitis River on trestle which is more than 400 feet long.

0:38 (0:00) Arrive Mont Joli.

 MONT JOLI, QUE. - Once called Sainte Flavie Station, this industrial center's newer name ("attractive mountain") refers to the beautiful views afforded from the nearby mountain top.

0:00 (0:23) Depart Mont Joli.

0:05 (0:18) Pass through town of Saint-Anaclet. Off to right on banks of St. Lawrence is Pointe-au-Père. It was near here in May of 1914 that ocean liner "Empress of Ireland" sank after colliding with a freighter, losing over 1,000 of her nearly 1,500 passengers. Catastrophe neared proportions of Titanic sinking just two years earlier, when over 1,500 of 2,000-plus passengers lost their lives.

0:20 (0:03) Fine view of Rimouski's large harbor is now afforded on right.

0:23 (0:00) Arrive Rimouski, where downtown is on lower terrace to right.

 RIMOUSKI, QUE. - This is the largest city in the province east of Quebec City. Established in 1696, the city has become important because of its fine harbor that remains open year-round. Although a fire destroyed nearly a fourth of the city in 1950, no evidence of the disaster is visible today.

A regional museum with historic and scientific exhibits is housed downtown in what was once the 3rd Catholic Church of Rimouski, built in 1824. Nearby, a seamen's school trains sailors to become St. Lawrence River pilots who must steer oceangoing ships once such vessels reach the narrower waters of the St. Lawrence. There is also a Museum of the Sea, with exhibits of marine life.

There are weekly **freighter/passenger ship** sailings (Nordik Express) from here to Sept Îles (terminus of the Quebec North Shore & Labrador Railway) each Tuesday, arriving in Sept Îles early the next morning. Contact Relais Nordik, 205 Ave. Léonidas, Rimouski, Que., G5L 2T5, for information and cabin reservations; (418) 723-8787.

Hôtel des Gouverneurs, 155 René Lepage Blvd. E, G5L 1P2; (418) 723-4422 or 800-463-2820. Excellent hotel. Adjacent to bus station and about five blocks from the VIA station. $87.

0:00 (1:07) Depart Rimouski and soon cross Rimouski River on 436-foot-long bridge.

0:18 (0:49) Cross Bic River and enter town of Bic, situated in a particularly attractive region. Supposedly, angel in charge of mountain and island allocation emptied remainder of her basket here at Bic. River is 25 miles wide at this point, narrowing as we continue westward.

0:34 (0:33) Extensive peat bogs through here are commercially "mined" for their soil-conditioning peat moss.

0:35 (0:32) Saint-Fabian has unusual eight-sided barn, only one in region.

1:07 (0:00) Arriving Trois Pistoles, huge three-spired Notre Dame Church, built in 1857, is city centerpiece.

TROIS PISTOLES, QUE. - According to legend, the town's unusual name came about when a sailor's silver cup, valued at three pistoles (a French coin of the day), fell into the river. The town is now a major tourist resort.

Three offshore islands are bird sanctuaries, home to double-crested cormorants (their exclusive diet is fish), eider ducks, blue herons and numerous other marine birds. The largest island, Île-aux-Basques, was supposedly used by Basque fishermen prior to Cartier's local explorations. Their furnaces used to extract whale oil have been restored and can be seen here.

0:00 (0:33) Depart Trois Pistoles.

0:04 (0:29) Cross high over Trois Pistoles River on 541-foot trestle.

0:13 (0:20) Île Verte, that long, narrow island off to right, is only place where salt-meadow lambs are raised. Creatures derive their name since they graze on grass salted by river spray. Island's lighthouse, built in 1809, is oldest on St. Lawrence. This stretch of river is known for its beluga and other species of whales.

0:32 (0:01) Entering Rivière-du-Loup, large lighted cross watches over city from Park of the Luminous Cross on left.

0:33 (0:00) Arriving Rivière-du-Loup, cross river by same name. Largest of eight successive waterfalls that embellish stream can be seen at right. It drops 125 feet.

RIVIÈRE-DU-LOUP, QUE. - In 1680, there was a French trading post located here, a spot where large wolf packs once roamed. Today it is not only a vibrant commercial center but a popular summer resort as well. The town derives its name from the loup seals that live along the shore.

Although the St. Lawrence is considerably narrower here than it is farther east, it is still 14 miles across. There is regular ferry service from Rivière-du-Loup to the north shore.

0:00 (0:39) Depart Rivière-du-Loup.

0:15 (0:24) Through Saint-André, where Saint-André's church, built in 1806, is oldest in region.

0:28 (0:11) Here at Kamouraska, eel trapping is an industry made possible by shallow, flat riverbed. Many homes seen along the lower St. Lawrence River are graced with uniquely curved eaves somewhat resembling a ship's hull. Feature has been given the name "Kamouraska roof."

0:32 (0:07) More peat bogs can be seen in immediate area.

0:39 (0:00) Arrive La Pocatière.

LA POCATIÈRE, QUE. - An important agricultural school is located here, started back in 1859. Bombardier, which is building Superliner rail cars in New England, has a plant in La Pocatière. Attractive modern cathedral is also located here, off to the right of the tracks.

0:00 (0:38) Depart La Pocatière.

0:19 (0:19) Cross Trois Saumons River.

0:33 (0:05) Mont Ste. Anne Ski Area can be spotted in distance across St. Lawrence.

0:38 (0:00) Cross River du Sud on 584-foot bridge upon arrival Montmagny.

MONTMAGNY, QUE. - This community was named after a 17th century governor of New France.

0:00 (0:47) Departing Montmagny, note unusual ten-sided church on right.

0:42 (0:05) Train slowly descends into Lévis, directly across from Quebec City. On right, outstanding views of city, shipyards, river activity and Île d'Orléans (large St. Lawrence centerpiece back to right) are now afforded.

0:47 (0:00) Arrive Lévis, where ferry service to Quebec City is available. Quebec City is immediately across St. Lawrence River on right.

QUEBEC CITY, QUE. - Champlain founded Quebec City in 1608 as a fur-trading post, and in 1620 he established a fort on the higher plateau portion of the city. The city soon developed as a city on two levels with the upper portion, 305 feet above sea level, being a natural defensive fortification, and becoming a military and administrative area. A stone wall was constructed surrounding a portion of this upper city with an entrance through three large gates. The lower city was primarily trade-oriented. Today, an unusual tubular elevator, "Funiculaire," connects these two levels.

Quebec City's strategic location made it

the focal point of two major battles. In 1759 an attack across the Plains of Abraham occurred when the British, led by Wolfe, scaled the cliffs of the city and defeated the French commanded by Montcalm. Then in 1775, American Patriots made an effort to siege Quebec City, and a force led by Richard Montgomery and Benedict Arnold mounted an unsuccessful attempt to capture it. Additional fortifications were built, but were never used as this was the last effort made to take the city by force.

Today, Quebec City is the provincial capital of Quebec. Its strong French-European flavor (over 90% of the population speaks French) and uniquely quaint appearance (it is the only walled city north of Mexico) have made this a popular tourist destination point.

VIA Station, Gare du Palais, 450 rue de la gare du Palais. This grand old station was built by the Canadian Pacific Railway in 1916 and served Quebec City as a rail station until its closure in 1976, forcing downtown passengers to use the suburban Sainte-Foy station. The early 1980s saw a remarkable renovation ($28 million) and service once again restored to the heart of the city starting in late 1985. (The suburban VIA station in Ste-Foy is still operational.)

There are storage lockers, luggage carts, a restaurant, a snack bar, a newsstand and underground pay-parking. There are direct phone lines to taxis and several downtown hotels, including some of those listed below.

For reservations, call 692-3940.

Cab stand is at the station and there is a direct phone line. Taxi Coop, 525-5191. **Bus** terminal on Boulevard Charest, between Dorchester and Caron. Tilden has **rental cars** within walking distance. There is **ferry** service from Quebec City to and from Lévis across the St. Lawrence River for VIA train service to the Atlantic provinces. This ferry service is operated on a 24-hour basis, departing every half hour from 6 am to midnight—less frequently from midnight to 6 am. **Quebec Municipal Airport** is northwest of the city.

Tourisme Quebec, 12 rue Sainte-Anne; (418) 643-2280 or 800-363-7777. Write Tourisme Quebec, C.P. 20000, G1K 7X2.

The following hotels are within the walls of the city:

-LeChâteau Frontenac, 1 rue des Carrières, G1R 4P5; (418) 692-3861 or 800-828-7447. Quebec's most famous landmark. A mile from the station. $154.

-Auberge du Trésor, 20 rue Ste-Anne (at du Fort), G1R 3X2; (418) 694-1876. Small, moderately priced hotel, excellently

St. Anne Street - Quebec City, Quebec
JACK SWANSON

located across from LeChâteau Frontenac, next to the tourism office. Oldest inn in North America. One mile from the station. $85.

-Château de la Terrasse, 6 Place Terrasse-Dufferin, G1R 4N5; (418) 694-9472. 18-room hotel overlooking the St. Lawrence. Two blocks from Le Château Frontenac, one mile from the station. Back rooms, $68; front rooms overlooking the St. Lawrence, $88 (4th floor $82).

-Hôtel Manoir d'Auteuil, 49 rue d'Auteuil, G1R 4C2; (418) 694-1173. Manor-turned-inn, between Kent and Saint-Louis gates. Breakfast included. $75.

A few In-Town Attractions: The Citadel, with its enormous walls overlooking the entire city, is the largest fortification in North America still garrisoned by regular troops. This British-built fortress can best be seen by guided tours.

If you do nothing else, be sure to stroll along Dufferin Terrace, a boardwalk in front of the Chateau Frontenac Hotel that connects to the Promenade des Gouverneurs following the cliffside with sweeping views of the St. Lawrence River

and its maritime activity.

Place Royale, in the lower town along the St. Lawrence River, is the birthplace of Quebec City, and several of the 18th-century houses are open to the public.

The Notre-Dame-des-Victoires Church is one of the oldest in North America. Also, the Quebec Fortifications, 2 rue d'Auteuil, C.P. 2474, built due to the city's strategic location. Covering a large portion of the city, pathways allow easy viewing.

The Cite Parlementaire, which houses Quebec's National Assembly, is located just outside of the walls of the city. **0:00** (0:22) Depart Lévis, and soon begin climb from water level to slightly higher plain for remainder of run into Montreal. Some marvelous views of Quebec City and St. Lawrence River with its ocean-going traffic will be afforded on the right as we make this climb.
0:22 (0:00) Arrive Charney.

CHARNEY, QUE. - At this juncture, trains on the south side of the St. Lawrence traveling from Montreal and Quebec City depart from this line and curl northward to make a spectacular crossing of the river before entering Ste-Foy.

0:00 (1:46) Depart Charney.

0:03 (1:43) Cross a river named Chaudiere, a French translation of an Indian word meaning "boiling kettle."

0:23 (1:23) Through Laurier, a small town of 1,000 named after Wilfred Laurier, an early Prime Minister of Canada.

0:31 (1:15) Cross swift-moving Henri River.

1:02 (0:44) Note rows of rocks in field on right, waste product of a farmer's effort to make his field more productive.

1:07 (0:39) Cross Bécancour River at milepost 66.8.

1:21 (0:25) At St. Léonard, cruise high above Nicolet River.

1:32 (0:14) Under Trans-Canada and Quebec Autoroute 20, stretching from Victoria, British Columbia to St. John's, Newfoundland.

1:38 (0:08) Passing through St. Cyrille where St. Cyrille's Church, with a large silver dome and two lesser domes gracing its grey-stone walls, is centerpiece of town on right.

1:44 (0:02) Note attractive rapids below as Ocean spans St. Francois River.

1:46 (0:00) Arrive at Drummondville's rather tired-looking depot.

DRUMMONDVILLE, QUE. - Le Village Quebecois d'Antan is located here, a fine collection of restored buildings with a costumed staff depicting typical activities in 19th-century Quebec, one of the major historical attractions of the province.

0:00 (0:40) Depart Drummondville.

0:38 (0:02) Cross Yamaska River.

0:40 (0:00) Arrive St. Hyacinthe.

For route between St. Hyacinthe and Montreal, see that portion of the Atlantic route log, page 339.

Chaluer

The Chaluer has literally carried you to "Land's end" when it reaches the town of Gaspé on the tip of Quebec's scenic Gaspé Peninsula. From Montreal, the Chaluer makes an overnight journey down the southern shore of the St. Lawrence River, leaving the excitement of the rocky Gaspé shoreline for daytime passage. The run along the craggy coastal scenery, that many believe to be Eastern Canada's most visually inspiring, is a train ride which in and of itself would justify making the trip. But there are lots of bonuses to be found, such as the towns of Gaspé , with nearby Forillon National Park, and Percé in a delightful seaside setting overlooking monolithic Percé Rock jutting up from the surface of the sea and Bonaventure Island, famous for its large and accessible colonies of gannets.

If you love fall colors, you might consider an early October visit to the peninsula. VIA, recognizing the uniqueness of the Gaspésie, has put some of its finely re-stored cars into service on this route, including a dome car for serious scenery watchers.

Because of train schedules, it is not very practical to make a "pure" rail trip from Montreal to Halifax with a side trip to Gaspé. However, with a bus ride in the mix, you can take the Chaluer from Montreal to Gaspé, where one can rent a car and soak up the area's offering. Then take the bus from Gaspé to Campbellton, New Brunswick (actually, the bus serves Campbellton's suburb of Cross Point, Quebec) for an overnight stay (see that

town for accommodations), then take the Ocean on to Halifax departing Campbell-ton early morning. Schedule carefully, however, since both the Chaluer and Ocean operate only three times a week.

For best viewing, eastbound sleeping car passengers should request accommo-dations on the right side of the train (usually even-numbered) and on the left side (usually odd-numbered) westbound.

Eastbound Schedule (Condensed)
Montreal, Que. - Early Evening Departure
Matapedia, Que. - Middle of the Night (2nd Day)
Carleton, Que. - Early Morning (2nd Day)
Percé, Que. - Midmorning (2nd Day)
Gaspé, Que. - Late Morning Arrival (2nd Day)

Westbound Schedule (Condensed)
Gaspé, Que. - Late Afternoon Departure
Percé, Que. - Late Afternoon
Carleton, Que. - Late Evening
Matapedia, Que. - Late Evening
Montreal, Que. - Early Morning Arrival (2nd Day)

Frequency - Tri-weekly, departing both Montreal and Gaspé on Monday, Thursday and Saturday and arriving Gaspé and Montreal, Tuesday, Friday and Sunday.
Seating - Coaches and dome car.
Dining - Complete meal, snack and bev-erage service.
Sleeping - Sections (berths), roomettes, and bedrooms.
Baggage - Checked baggage handled.
Length of Trip - 840 miles in 16 hours.

Route Log

(Note that this route log is laid out eastbound, rather than the normal westbound format, since most first-time riders on the Chaluer ride toward Gaspé.)

For route between Montreal and Matapedia, see that portion of the Ocean log, page 345.

 MATAPEDIA, QUE. - See page 345.

0:00 (0:57) Depart Matapedia.
0:15 (0:42) Town of Point-â-la-Croix (Cross Point) is passed where green steel bridge crosses narrows of Restigouche River to Campbellton, N.B. off to right. Near here, last naval battle between English and French in North America occurred in July 1760, when a small supply fleet, hoping to salvage New France, was met by the British in what would later be called the Battle of the Restigouche.
0:57 (0:00) Arrive Nouvelle.

 NOUVELLE, QUE. - Just south of this town of 2,000 is Miguasha Park, with its world renowned fossil-imbedded cliffs. The Park is also where the Restigouche River broadens to become Chaluer Bay.

0:00 (0:16) Depart Nouvelle.
0:08 (0:08) Cross Stewart Brook on 175-foot trestle.
0:13 (0:03) Now, tracks hug waters of Chaluer Bay.
0:16 (0:00) Arrive Carleton's neat frame station on right.

CARLETON, QUE. - The proximity to both the ocean and mountains has made Carleton a popular tourist spot. Its beaches are particularly appealing because of the unusually warm waters of Chaluer Bay (a name meaning bay of warmth, so named by Cartier). A drive to the top of nearby Mount Saint-Joseph, which soars to nearly 2,000 feet above Carleton, provides superb panoramas of the town's seaside setting.

Although Carleton received its name from British Loyalists who ultimately forced the Acadian residents to leave, the community is still predominantly French speaking.

0:00 (0:39) Depart Carleton through gorgeous rolling forested hills and idyllic fields. Note shrine to Virgin Mary on side of Mt. Saint-Joseph to left.
0:11 (0:28) Through Maria, which boasts tepee-shaped church. Located on Micmac reservation, village was named for wife of third governor of Canada, Sir Guy Carleton.
0:12 (0:27) Slip past skinny, grass airstrip angling away from tracks.
0:22 (0:17) Make first of two successive crossings of Cascapedia River.
0:24 (0:15) Cross Cascapedia one more time, this time on 604-foot bridge.
0:35 (0:04) Stands of tamarack trees, those lacy-looking "evergreens," line tracks. Needles actually turn yellow in fall before dropping.
0:37 (0:02) Cross Little Cascapedia River.
0:39 (0:00) Arrive New Richmond.

 NEW RICHMOND, QUE. - A year-round port and a thriving forest products industry has allowed this Loyalist-founded community to prosper and grow to its current 4,000 residents. Of note here are its many handsome homes of Anglo-Saxon architecture.

0:00 (0:15) Depart New Richmond.
0:02 (0:13) Large plant, steaming away on left, uses those large piles of woodchips to produce cardboard.
0:04 (0:11) Dramatic view of Chaluer Bay shoreline now comes into view on right forward.
0:15 (0:00) Arrive Caplan.

CAPLAN, QUE. - In 1893, this fishing village was once the eastern end of the rail line on the Gaspé. It wasn't until thirteen years later that it was extended to New Carlisle. Although some say the town gets its name from the large number of small fish known as "capelin" that spawn here every spring, there is also reason to believe it was named for an early settler, Jean Caplan.

0:00 (0:15) Departing Caplan, note woodsheds with roofs but no walls.
0:06 (0:09) Note small boat harbor on right protected by hook-shaped breakwater.
0:15 (0:00) Arrive Bonaventure where typical blue and white station on right has been enhanced by band of mauve.

BONAVENTURE, QUE. - This French-founded community was destroyed by the British during the battle of Restigouche Estuary, but then was resettled by the French Acadians forced from Nova Scotia. It is probably this Acadian heritage that makes this port town as much farming oriented as it is fishing. The town boasts a modest canoe-building industry and a zoo harboring an eclectic assemblage of animals from around the world.

0:00 (0:13) Depart Bonaventure.

0:02 (0:11) Cross Bonaventure River, as train glides through terrain that has been mostly flat for last several miles, interspersed with fields and forests.

0:13 (0:00) Arrive New Carlisle.

NEW CARLISLE, QUE. - Today, many residents of this English-speaking administrative center are descendants of British Loyalists, and several of the town's large, attractive homes are from the Loyalist era. René Lévesque, Premier of Quebec from 1976 to 1985, was born here.

0:00 (0:35) Depart New Carlisle.

0:19 (0:16) Sail high over valley floor on Shigiwake Viaduct.

0:28 (0:07) Off to right, enticing-looking town in distance is our next stop, Port Daniel.

0:34 (0:01) Now cruise across steel frame bridge which spans Little River on Port Daniel's outskirts, with glistening little bay at right.

0:35 (0:00) Arrive at Port Daniel's green and cream station immediately adjacent to harbor.

PORT DANIEL, QUE. - This village of 2,000 was named for Captain Daniel (a contemporary of Champlain) who once visited this area.

0:00 (0:43) Depart Port Daniel.

0:02 (0:41) Church on left seems almost overwhelmed by enormous frame rectory.

0:04 (0:39) Now, at milepost 23.7, curl to left through Cap a L'Enfer Tunnel, 630 feet long and peninsula's only rail tunnel.

0:09 (0:34) Chaluer virtually hangs to side of rocky cliffs. Seals can often be spotted on rocky shore of ocean straight below, as train continues to trace a course above coast.

0:19 (0:24) Train slows as it ventures out over deep draw on Chouinard Gully Viaduct—506 feet long and 106 feet high. It is highest of today's journey.

0:33 (0:10) Through town of Newport which boasts one of world's most modern fish processing plants. Area also produces huge crops of Christmas trees.

0:35 (0:08) Leaving Newport, continue to follow bay's shoreline with occasional excursions inland through forested hills.

0:40 (0:03) Evidence of maritime disaster is quite visible to right, where Peruvian freighter became grounded and split in two in 1983. Derelict still lies on its side not far offshore.

0:42 (0:01) Pulp mill at left dates back to 1915.

0:43 (0:00) Arrive Chandler.

CHANDLER, QUE. - The economic mainstay here is the substantial pulp and paper mill operation by Abitibi-Price. The pulp mill was the first on the peninsula. A good natural harbor facilitates the exporting of newsprint to various parts of the world. Named for a Philadelphian, it should not be too surprising that the town is largely English-speaking.

0:00 (0:18) Depart Chandler.

0:09 (0:09) Slip across brief causeway at milepost 49.

0:16 (0:02) Tracks now make lengthy crossing of Grand River on 686-foot-long trestle.

0:18 (0:00) Arrive Grand Rivière.

GRAND RIVIÈRE, QUE. - Named for the river that flows through it, Grand Rivière is heavily dependent on fishing, particularly crab fishing.

0:00 (0:19) Depart Grand Rivière.

0:13 (0:06) Handsome brick church on right offers relief from region's typical frame architecture.

0:17 (0:02) Suddenly, looming in far distance to right, is Bonaventure Island, home to nearly a quarter-million birds of various species.

0:19 (0:00) Arrive Percé's small station, literally in middle of nowhere. Town is quite distant from here, but tracks go no closer than this.

PERCÉ, QUE. - This renowned resort is the chief tourist destina-

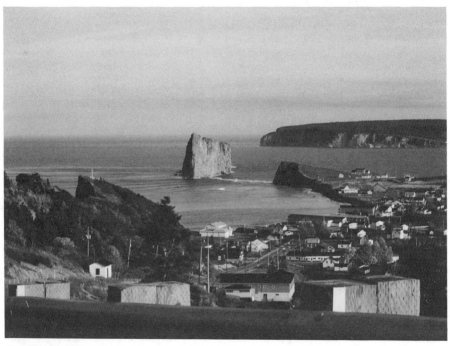

Percé, Quebec
DORIS SWANSON

tion on the Gaspésie. Perched on a spectacular bit of shoreline, with mountains ringing three sides of town, Percé has one of Eastern Canada's most stunning settings. French cuisine, live theater and art galleries give it additional appeal.

Two natural attractions, Percé Rock, a skinny rock mesa rising from the ocean but accessible by foot during low tide, and Bonaventure Island, home to nearly a quarter-million birds, reachable by boat during the warmer months, are coastal jewels. Percé Rock, with its small natural window near one end, gives the town the name Percé—French for pierced. Bonaventure Island is a birder's wonderland, with a gannet colony (one of the world's largest and most accessible gannet rookeries) of 50,000 of these interesting birds. There also are puffins, razor-billed auks, gulls and numerous other species. Boat trips to the island for birding and hiking are available from June until October.

Both the Rock and Island have been designated conservation parks.

On the edge of town, a wildlife interpretation center has exhibits and films which describe not only the area's wildlife, but also its natural features.

There are no car rentals in Percé and the station is a long way from town. Those visiting by train normally ride to the end of the line at Gaspé, about 50 miles further, and rent a car. The drive back to Percé is quite scenic.

There are many motels in Percé. The following are two of them:
-Motel Le Mirage du Rocher Percé, Route 132, G0C 2L0; (418) 782-5151. Overlooks town and the Rock. $92.
-Hotel-Motel Le Bonaventure sur mer. Write RESTourisme Gaspésie, CP 339, G0C 2L0. Call year-round (418) 782-2166. $50.
0:00 (0:25) Depart Percé and head inland away from sea.

0:10 (0:15) Percé Mountains off to left are more rugged than those encountered earlier on route. In fall, colors through here are outstanding.

0:19 (0:06) Slip beneath highway at curiously named town of Coin-du-Banc. Originally settled by Irish, town is still English speaking. Look back for marvelous view of rugged coast and Percé Rock. We have just started across a three-mile-long causeway, where nearby beaches provide excellent agate hunting.

0:24 (0:01) Leaving causeway, one of better views of Percé Rock is now back to right.

0:25 (0:00) Arrive Barachois.

BARACHOIS, QUE. - This coastal village probably derives its name from the East Indian French word for pond.

0:00 (0:44) Depart Barachois.

0:10 (0:34) Body of water at right is Bay of Gaspé while land mass on horizon is Cape Gaspé, location of magnificent Forillon National Park.

0:17 (0:27) At milepost 89, sign announces "Prevel." Here, during World War II, heavy artillery aimed toward sea provided important coastal defense. Now, area has become a popular resort with former army barracks now serving as a fine provincial inn. After Prevel, train will venture across L'Anse-a-Brillant Viaduct.

0:32 (0:12) Encounter one more causeway. Town of Gaspé lies ahead.

0:42 (0:02) Approaching end of line, Gaspé, laid out above its harbor, provides interesting scene straight ahead. Large red brick facility at top of hill overlooking city is former tuberculosis sanatorium, now serving as regional nursing home.

0:44 (0:00) Arrive Gaspé.

Chaluer - Gaspé, Quebec
JACK SWANSON

GASPÉ, QUE. - Gaspé, from the Micmac word "gaspeg" meaning land's end, is a city of 20,000 which serves as the area's administrative center. This is where Jacques Cartier took possession of the country for France. The bay, around which the town is situated, provides a deep water port complimenting Gaspé's rail-head status.

VIA Station is on the edge of town, just a short taxi ride to downtown. Inside is a small waiting room and ticket office. Call 800-361-5390.

Thrifty Car Rental, (418) 368-1610, offers pick-up and drop-off service at the station. **Bus station** is next to Adams Motel.

Adams Motel, 2 Rue Adams, G0C 1R0; (418) 368-2244 or 800-463-4242 (Canada only). Moderately priced accommodations with a good family restaurant. About a mile from the station. $49.

-Auberge des Commandants, 178 Rue de la Reine, G0C 1R0; (418) 368-3355. Best accommodation in Gaspé, if not the entire peninsula. $78.

Gaspé Cathedral, the only wooden cathedral in North America, was built of cedar to help bring it into harmony with its surroundings. Its stained glass windows were a gift from France in 1934 to commemorate the 400th anniversary of the arrival of Cartier. An adjacent, enormous granite cross also honors that historic event. **Pisciculture de Gaspé,** a century-old fish hatchery, where two million salmon and trout are produced annually, is open to visitors. The **Gaspé Museum** reflects the history of the area. Nearby **Forillon National Park** occupies its own small peninsula. This is some of the region's most beautiful wilderness, with seals, bears, moose and other wildlife living in an environment dominated by 500-foot cliffs overlooking the sea. Canada's tallest lighthouse, where visitors can climb to the top, is also here.

Corridor Service

The very heart of VIA's network is the so-called "Corridor," stretching from Quebec City to Windsor, Ontario, with branches to Sarnia, Niagara Falls, Ottawa and Kitchener. And the heaviest used portion is that high-speed track connecting Canada's two largest cities, Montreal and Toronto. LRC trains (light, rapid, comfortable) operate throughout the Corridor.

A multitude of VIA's express trains with VIA 1 service (early boarding privileges, meals served at your seat, complimentary newspapers and magazines), make the trip between Montreal and Toronto on any given weekday. Several more connect Ottawa with Toronto by way of Kingston. Additional trains make runs between Toronto and the border cities of Sarnia, Windsor and Niagara Falls.

Route Log

Montreal-Ottawa-Toronto is at page 365 and Toronto-Kitchener-Sarnia is at page 368. Elsewhere, Niagara Falls-Toronto is at page 61 and Quebec City-Montreal is at page 347.

MONTREAL-TORONTO-WINDSOR

 MONTREAL, QUE. - See page 341.
0:00 (0:18) Depart Montreal's Central Station on CN tracks. In about 60 seconds

emerge from underground, heading southeast, and soon parallel St. Lawrence River.
0:04 (0:14) Cross Lachine (pronounced "luh-sheen") Canal, with its very attractive landscaping. Canal was constructed prior to St. Lawrence Seaway providing bypass around treacherous Lachine Rapids of St. Lawrence River. Nine miles in length, it ceased operations in 1965.

Unfortunately, the Seaway no longer serves as it was originally intended. Many of today's freighters cannot be accommodated by the waterway's rather narrow channel, and the ice blocks traffic west of Montreal three months or more each winter. From time to time, proposals are put forth to modernize the system, but the costs would be enormous.
0:05 (0:13) Several tracks now depart to left to cross Victoria Bridge over St. Lawrence and then on to either Maritime Provinces or New York City.
0:09 (0:09) Re-cross Lachine Canal.
0:10 (0:08) Now slip beneath enormous pile of spaghetti called an interchange, which scrambles and then unscrambles traffic carried by Trans-Canada 20 and Autoroute 15.
0:15 (0:03) Sets of CN and CP tracks branch to right toward huge marshalling yards for both lines.
0:18 (0:00) Arrive Dorval.

DORVAL, QUE. - This is a western suburb of Montreal, home to Montreal International Airport just off to the right.
0:00 (0:23) Depart Dorval.
0:04 (0:19) Note two attractive golf courses lining tracks on right.

0:08 (0:15) Stone buildings and round barn on right are part of Macdonald College's experimental farm.

0:09 (0:14) Cross smaller of two tongues of Ottawa River to reach L'Île de Perrot. River is principal branch of St. Lawrence. Its origin is in central Quebec, some 160 miles above Ottawa, and forms partial boundary between Quebec and Ontario. Rapids and falls make most of it unnavigable, but significant elevation change makes stream ideal for hydroelectric power.

0:12 (0:11) Now cross larger segment of river and upon reaching Quebec's mainland, enter Vandreuil, named for early-day governor of Canada.

0:17 (0:06) A final glimpse can be caught of St. Lawrence off to left.

0:23 (0:00) Arrive Coteau.

COTEAU, QUE. - This is the final stop in the province of Quebec and the outer fringe of Montreal's populous suburbs.

0:00 (0:30) Depart Coteau, where rural countryside and occasional forests begin to prevail over cosmopolitan scenes just reviewed.

0:07 (0:23) Enter Ontario and leave Quebec.

0:30 (0:00) Arrive Cornwall.

CORNWALL, ONT. - Cotton, oddly enough, was once an important product of this most easterly Ontario city, and it was in one of Cornwall's cotton mills that Thomas Edison installed equipment to achieve the first electric illumination of a factory. Today, the city is headquarters for the St. Lawrence Seaway Authority.

0:00 (0:36) Depart Cornwall.

0:34 (0:02) Spanning St. Lawrence, on left, is International Bridge reaching across to Ogdensburg, New York.

0:36 (0:00) Arrive Prescott.

PRESCOTT, ONT. - As the only deep-water port between Montreal and Toronto, shipping has become an important aspect of the city's economy. Of particular interest is Fort Wellington; it occupied a strategic point on the St. Lawrence and saw action during the War of 1812.

0:00 (0:13) Depart Prescott.

0:07 (0:06) Final glimpse of St. Lawrence is afforded on left. Large facility on left is plant of chemicals-producing giant—duPont.

0:13 (0:00) Arriving in Brockville, somber brick structure of Brockville Psychiatric Hospital dominates scene off to left. Also, to left, can be glimpsed a portal of an abandoned rail tunnel that burrowed beneath the town and had doors on each end (a rarity) to prevent ice from forming on its roof.

BROCKVILLE, ONT. - Named after a War of 1812 hero, General Sir Isaac Brock, the city is situated at the eastern end of the popular Thousand Islands resort and vacation area. Oscar of the Waldorf once served as a personal chef for George C. Boldt (who lived in this area) and concocted a salad dressing in honor of these St. Lawrence River jewels.

0:00 (0:23) Depart Brockville.

0:23 (0:00) Arrive Gananoque.

GANANOQUE, ONT. - A popular embarkation point for touring the Thousand Islands area by boat as well as plane. Boat cruises take from one-and-a-half to three hours, some including stopovers at the unfinished castle built by George Boldt.

0:00 (0:18) Depart Gananoque.

0:01 (0:17) Cross Gananoque River.

0:12 (0:06) Cross Cataraqui River and historic Rideau Canal.

0:18 (0:00) Arrive Kingston.

KINGSTON, ONT. - At one point, during its evolution from a fur-trading post to a vibrant industrial center, Kingston was actually the nation's capital. With its location at the point where Lake Ontario empties into the St. Lawrence, this was a logical choice. It is also at the southern terminus of the Rideau Canal which connects the St. Lawrence with Ottawa to the north.

Bellevue House, once the home of Canada's first prime minister, Sir John A. Macdonald, has been restored and furnished for public viewing. Also of interest is Old Fort Henry, now a living museum of military artifacts, with uniformed "soldiers" and booming cannons.

0:00 (0:20) Depart Kingston, as scenery remains that of rolling to flat grasslands punctuated only with occasional groves of trees.

0:05 (0:15) Several small pleasure craft can be spotted at Woods Marina on left.

0:20 (0:00) Arrive Napanee.

NAPANEE, ONT. - During its waterpower heyday, Napanee, now a town of about 5,000, boasted tanneries and mills that produced flour, oatmeal, paper, woolen and leather goods, tools and furniture.

0:00 (0:17) Depart Napanee and span Napanee River on 222-foot viaduct, while falls can be seen to left.

0:12 (0:05) Some interesting aircraft are sometimes parked on apron at Belleville Flying Club at left.

0:17 (0:00) Upon arriving Belleville, note quaint two-story, dormer embellished station on left.

BELLEVILLE, ONT. - This is the gateway to Quinte's Island in the St. Lawrence, where vacationers find long, sandy beaches to be most alluring. The city also offers splendid recreational pursuits with golf, swimming and an excellent yacht harbor.

0:00 (0:12) Depart Belleville.

0:11 (0:01) Cross historic Trent-Severn Canal. Connecting Trenton on Lake Ontario to Georgian Bay (a portion of upper Lake Huron), at 240 miles in length it is longest of province's 540 miles of canals. It contains nearly half of the 100-plus locks found in Ontario.

0:12 (0:00) Arrive Trenton Jct.

TRENTON JCT., ONT. - This stop serves the attractive community of Trenton which has much the same recreational opportunities as does Belleville. Trenton is also the entrance to the elaborate Trent-Severn Canal which provides a 240-mile waterway through some 44 locks, and leads to Georgian Bay on Lake Huron.

0:00 (0:25) Depart Trenton Jct.

0:25 (0:00) Arrive Cobourg's handsome stone and brick station on left.

COBOURG, ONT. - In earlier times, this quaint community of 11,000 persons served as a lake port for steamers and a staging point on the road connecting Toronto, Kingston and Montreal.

0:00 (0:07) Depart Cobourg.

0:05 (0:02) Lake Ontario finally comes into view, about a mile south (left) of us.

0:06 (0:01) Trundle out on 1,232-foot-long Port Hope Viaduct which spans Ganaraska River. To left, harbour basin is filled with pleasure craft during summer months; large facility at right is uranium processing plant. Also to right, beyond parallel Canadian Pacific trestle, is downtown Port Hope.

0:07 (0:00) Arrive Port Hope's restored 1856 gray stone station, on left.

PORT HOPE, ONT. - Once called Toronto, in 1819 the town was renamed in honor of Harry Hope, an 18th-century lieutenant governor of Canada.

0:00 (0:27) Depart Port Hope.

0:18 (0:09) Cement plants are fed raw limestone from cavernous quarry on left.

0:19 (0:08) Numerous sets of transmission lines disappear behind earthen berm shielding Darlington Nuclear Power Plant on left. Plant itself can be glimpsed after passing beneath (west of) power lines.

0:33 (0:00) Arrive Oshawa where auto carriers in rail yards attest to one of town's industries.

OSHAWA, ONT. - Originally a lake port, this city has become a major auto manufacturing center for Canada. Of special interest is the Canadian Automotive Museum with a splendid collection of early automobiles. Parkwood, former home of Canadian auto magnate R. S. McLaughlin, features antiques and gardens.

0:00 (0:17) Depart Oshawa.

0:02 (0:15) Large blue buildings, on left, are Lasco Steel Plant.

0:10 (0:07) Pickering Nuclear Generating Plant is off to left, the origination of several transmission lines.

0:13 (0:04) Frenchman's Bay is on left.

0:17 (0:00) Arrive Guildwood.

GUILDWOOD, ONT. - This is the eastern edge of Metropolitan Toronto, just 13 miles from the heart of the city.

0:00 (0:15) Depart Guildwood.

0:11 (0:04) Distinctive building of Gooderham & Worts ("since 1832") distillery is on right.

0:12 (0:03) Toronto's modernistic skyline now appears ahead of us with tall, spectacular spindle of CN Tower rising 1,821 feet, world's tallest free-standing structure.

0:15 (0:00) Arrive Toronto's Union Station.

TORONTO, ONT. - In the 1600s, the Iroquois Indians had a small village on what is now the site of Toronto. However by the 1700s, the village was gone, and the French had established a mission and fort at this spot. This outpost was short-lived, for in 1759 the occupants burned it to the ground to prevent the British from capturing it. Then in 1793, 30 years after the Treaty of Paris gave Canada to Britain, the town of York was established on this site by John Graves Simcoe, the first governor of Ontario (then known as "Upper Canada"). This modest settlement was the present-day city's forebear.

Situated on the shores of Lake Ontario, Toronto is a commercial and cultural metropolis comprised of 3.6 million people. It lays claim to being Canada's biggest city and the capital of Canada's most populous province, Ontario.

Downtown is robust and sparkling, busy with theaters, fine restaurants, major sporting events and cosmopolitan shopping. People are attracted here, both day and night, in a way that would make any city planner envious. Actor and noted traveler Peter Ustinov once referred to the town as "New York run by the Swiss." That summed it up well.

Getting around Toronto is both relatively easy and inexpensive, making the city all the more appealing. There are trolleys, buses, GO Trains (commuter rail) and perhaps the world's cleanest and safest subway (a reflection of the city itself) that provide Toronto with one of the best urban transit systems found anywhere.

Union Station, Front Street West, between Bay and York streets, is a bustling, attractive station nicely located in the downtown area. Its grand facade is adorned with 22 pillars of Bedford lime-stone. There are storage lockers, restaurants, snack bars, newsstand, miscellaneous shops and redcaps. A Panorama Lounge is provided for VIA 1 passengers.

The station was opened by the Prince of Wales in 1927 and has been changed little throughout the years. Some modern appurtenances include an electronic arrival and departure board and the Panorama Lounge mentioned above. Pay-parking is adjacent to the station. An underground arcade leads to many shops and stores beneath downtown Toronto.

Call 366-8411 for reservations and information.

Cab stand is at the station, but cabs can be scarce during rush hours; call 366-6868. Nearest **local bus** stop is in front of the station; call 393-4636. Tilden, Avis and Budget **rental cars** are available at the station. Both **GO-Trains** and the **subway** serve this station. **Greyhound** and **Voyageur** buses (and others) are at 610 Bay St. at Dundas, about a mile from the station. **Pearson International Airport** is 12 miles northwest of downtown.

Metropolitan Toronto Convention & Visitors Association, Queen's Quay Terminal at Harbourfront, P.O. Box 126, 207 Queen's Quay West, M5J 1A7; (416) 368-9821.

Strathcona Hotel, 60 York St., M5J 1S8; (416) 363-3321. Small accommodations at reasonable rates. Only a block from the station. $70.

-**Bond Place Hotel,** 65 Dundas St., M5J 1E3; (416) 362-6061. Well managed, comfortable hotel; near good shopping (Eaton Center). About a mile and a half from the station, but easily reached by subway (Dundas station is within two blocks). $59.

-**Royal York Hotel,** 100 Front St. W, M5J 1E3; (416) 368-2511 or 800-828-7447. Elderly, dignified Toronto landmark, directly across from the station and can be reached by an underground arcade. $140.

Downtown Toronto is an attraction in and of itself. For shopping there is the stunning **Eaton Centre,** which houses 300 shops and restaurants and 18 movie theaters under a cavernous arched glass arcade, anchored by two of Toronto's department stores. Close to the station,

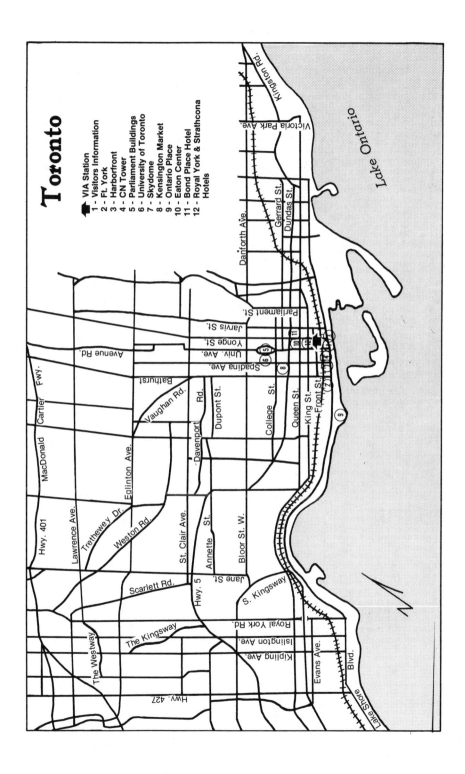

Toronto

- VIA Station
- 1 - Visitors Information
- 2 - Ft. York
- 3 - Harborfront
- 4 - CN Tower
- 5 - Parliament Buildings
- 6 - University of Toronto
- 7 - Skydome
- 8 - Kensington Market
- 9 - Ontario Place
- 10 - Eaton Center
- 11 - Bond Place Hotel
- 12 - Royal York & Strathcona Hotels

Lake Ontario

and visible for miles, is the **CN Tower,** the world's tallest (1,821 feet) freestanding structure. On top, of course, is a revolving restaurant and an observation gal'ery. And vying for "8th Wonder" status is Toronto's new **SkyDome** sports complex, with its retractable roof, North America's largest McDonald's and the Skydome Hotel. It's the house of the Blue Jays (the 1992/3 World Series champs) as well as the Canadian Football League's Toronto Argonauts. The venerable **Kensington Market,** spreading west and north from Dundas and Spadina, is an old market occupying several blocks, and appearing very much like a European bazaar with merchants of Portuguese, West Indian, Korean and other ethnic extractions selling produce, live chickens, bagels and custard tarts. Chinatown is adjacent to the market.

A trip west on **Bloor Street,** easily toured by subway, savors the diversity of Toronto. Downtown Bloor has an assemblage of high fashion stores that fan out to the north. Farther west is the University of Toronto, followed by the Annex, a Ukrainian neighborhood with its European atmosphere. And on the lake is **Harbourfront,** with its marina, shops and ferryboats to the Toronto Islands.

0:00 (0:23) Depart Toronto's Union Station on CN trackage. In about 60 seconds, emerge from beneath terminal's canopy and CN Tower soars skyward directly in front of us on left.

0:02 (0:21) After passing CN Tower, $400-million SkyDome, on left, overshadows all else. This bulbous edifice, completed in 1989, was built to house baseball's Toronto Blue Jays, shops, restaurants and a 350-room hotel. On nicer days, roof can be shifted from a closed to an open position in 30 minutes to put 90% of its spectators in sunshine. While passing this structure, be sure to look up to see whimsical groupings of spectators protruding from building like modern-day gargoyles.

0:04 (0:19) Tops of brick buildings and sign on grassy knoll are all that can be seen of Historic Fort York Park on left. Park features restored British garrison from War of 1812.

0:06 (0:17) Elaborate facilities on left are annual home of Canadian National Exhibition, Canadian equivalent of American state fairs.

0:07 (0:16) Lake Ontario comes into clear view off to left. Amphitheater poised on lake's edge is handsome attraction of Ontario Place—a cultural, recreational and entertainment complex built atop three man-made islands.

0:08 (0:15) Note High Park and lake on right and then cross Humber River and marshes as train traces alongside Highway 2 and curls up and around Humber Bay on left. Fine view of Toronto's skyline is seen back to right.

0:09 (0:14) Cross Mimico Creek which drains into Lake Ontario, as do all other streams of this region.

0:10 (0:13) Through rail yards where, on left, VIA Rail has shops and various equipment standing ready for use. Sleek-looking yellow trains are LRCs (light, rapid, comfortable, with tilting capabilities for rounding curves at high speeds) and newer LRC-1s. "GO Trains" (Government of Ontario) are green and white, double-decked equipment parked on right awaiting call for Toronto commuter service and which can be seen along our route until International's first stop, Oakville.

0:12 (0:11) Cross Etobicoke Creek.

0:15 (0:08) At Port Credit, cross Credit River.

0:20 (0:02) On right, sprawling Ontario Ford truck plant actually operates private trains for touring its facilities.

0:22 (0:01) Observation car of former Florida East Coast Railway has undoubtedly been rescued by rail buff and stands on siding at left.

0:23 (0:00) Arrive Oakville's very attractive, modernistic station.

OAKVILLE, ONT. - In the mid-19th century, a host of city-dwellers chose this scenic locale as the site of their summer homes. Most of these lavish retreats have been immaculately preserved, and today are the focal point of a well-documented walking tour. Another interesting attraction is the Gairlock Gardens Gallery, maintained in a 1920s mansion along the lake. Its wild bird sanctuary is a further highlight.

For golfing enthusiasts, the Glen Abbey links, designed by Jack Nicklaus, is of true championship caliber. Its clubhouse was once a monastery, and now is home to the Canadian Golf Hall of Fame.

0:00 (0:12) Depart Oakville.

0:04 (0:08) Industrial area surrounding Oakville bears profusion of refineries and other petroleum-related operations.

0:05 (0:07) Cross Bronte Creek at Bronte.

0:12 (0:00) Arrive Aldershot.

ALDERSHOT, ONT. - This stop serves the industrial city of Hamilton as well as its lakefront, residential neighbor Burlington.

0:00 (0:11) Depart Aldershot.

0:03 (0:09) On left, brick-domed structure is Halton Ceramics, Ltd.

0:05 (0:07) At Bay View, quick but startling view of Hamilton Harbour is offered with its profusion of both commercial and pleasure boats. Momentarily, note tracks that cut off to left; these carry the Maple Leaf to Niagara Falls and ultimately to New York City.

0:13 (0:00) Arrive Dundas, with town proper lying far below grade on left.

DUNDAS, ONT. - This is a suburb of Hamilton, Canada's steel capital and third largest port. Tours of Hamilton's steel mills are major attractions. Here, too, at Hamilton, is the magnificent Dundurn Castle with splendid furnishings and appointments reflecting the opulent lifestyle of its mid-19th century inhabitants.

0:00 (0:18) Depart Dundas.

0:02 (0:17) Note fairways of Dundas' Golf Course below on left.

0:07 (0:12) Countryside begins to appear increasingly agricultural as fields of corn, wheat and other crops become more in evidence.

0:16 (0:03) Tall, spindly structure off to left is Bell communications tower.

0:17 (0:02) On eastern edge of Brantford, huge building complex, immediately left of tracks, is former Massey Ferguson farm equipment plant which ceased operations in 1980s. Brantford has been considered "Combine Capital of Canada" and factory's closure was severe blow to city.

0:19 (0:00) Arriving Brantford, glimpses of downtown and town hall's tower can be had to left. Fine old station on the left, a brick beauty adorned with a stately square tower, is further enhanced by a semaphore at trackside. Station dates back to 1904.

BRANTFORD, ONT. - The city was named for the Indian chief Joseph Brant who brought his group known as Six Nations Indians from Upper New York State to this site.

This is where Alexander Graham Bell invented the telephone and "placed" the first long distance call which was to Paris, Ontario, a distance of ten miles. Brantford has constructed a museum which displays some of the world's most sophisticated telecommunications equipment, including a NORAD control system.

0:00 (0:24) Depart Brantford.

0:01 (0:23) Fine old three-story brick home sports elegant white gingerbread trim on right. Home and grounds known as Glenhurst Gardens are on left.

0:06 (0:18) Trestle carries International high over Grand River at Paris where three attractive churches predominate cityscape. After crossing river, note wonderful old stone mansion, now converted to retirement facility, on right.

0:24 (0:00) Arrive Woodstock where grey, almost Victorian in style, 1853 station greets us on left.

WOODSTOCK, ONT. - This charming, well-preserved town, with many residences dating to the mid-1800s, was named for Woodstock in Oxfordshire, England in honor of the Duke of Marlborough whose estate was near there.

0:00 (0:10) Depart Woodstock.

0:03 (0:07) At milepost 52, countryside takes on a pastoral ambience as we course through a delightful valley, complete with meandering brook on left and especially attractive homes on hillside at right.

0:07 (0:03) Huge excavation on left is result of extensive quarrying operations. Kilns and other paraphernalia are part of operation.

0:10 (0:00) Arrive Ingersoll.

INGERSOLL, ONT. - This was the birthplace of Canada's cheese industry, with the first factory built in 1864, and still is famous for the manufacture of this dairy product. There is a Cheese Factory Museum where antique cheese-making tools are on display, and a nine-day wine and cheese festival in mid-September.

0:00 (0:18) Depart Ingersoll.

0:02 (0:16) Be sure to note palatial Landfair Stables horse farm, just to right, with its colonial-style home, handsome landscaping and neatly painted fences and outbuildings.

0:07 (0:11) Focal point of Dorchester is ornate single-spired church on left at milepost 68.

0:13 (0:03) Pass through sprawling CN rail yards with shops on left as we enter London's eastern suburbs.

0:18 (0:00) Arrive at London's very busy VIA station, where two major VIA routes intersect and connections can be made for Windsor to the southwest and Stratford to the northeast.

LONDON, ONT. - Located on the River Thames, many of London's streets are named for those of its English namesake. This is one of southeastern Ontario's busier industrial centers. A large air show, featuring aircraft from five countries, is held here the first weekend in June. South of London, the Port Stanley Rail Company runs an excursion train for tourists.

0:00 (0:30) Departing London, many of town's earliest three- and four-story buildings, one block to right, are in vivid contrast with London's newer downtown.

0:02 (0:28) Cross Thames River.

0:03 (0:27) Cross Thames River one more time.

0:05 (0:25) Although hockey is Canada's national sport, soccer is also popular during warmer months. Fields for that latter sport are in park at left.

0:13 (0:17) Tobacco kilns, those skinny barns with multiple doors, dot field on left.

0:30 (0:00) Arrive Glencoe's delapidated 1890s station. Adjacent phone-booth-looking structure now serves VIA customers.

GLENCOE, ONT. - This town of 1,700 is VIA's stop for the agricultural area to the west of London. Glencoe was once the end of the line for the Canada Air Line Railway.

0:00 (0:31) Depart Glencoe.

0:11 (0:19) Seven more tobacco barns appear in fields at left, attesting to hot and lengthy growing season and soil well-suited to that crop.

0:25 (0:06) Asparagus can frequently be seen growing in field on left. Cabbages, tomatoes and soybeans are also grown by area farmers.

0:31 (0:00) Arrive Chatham, where older red-brick station greets arriving passengers.

CHATHAM, ONT. - Just as its namesake in England, Chatham (pronounce it without the h) rests near the mouth of the Thames River. The city has played an important role in shaping American history, acting as a northern terminus for the American Civil War's underground railway (a clandestine routing of slaves to the North and freedom), scene of a major battle during the War of 1812, and where John Brown hatched his plot to attack the federal armory at Harper's Ferry.

0:00 (0:44) Depart Chatham.

0:15 (0:39) Canals with myriad pleasure craft create surprising contrast to agricultural scenes which have dominated trip.

0:16 (0:38) Lake St. Clair now appears on right. Marinescapes continue; boats, lakefront homes, ducks and geese line waters edge for several miles.

0:28 (0:16) Train now cuts directly through very attractive marina.

0:44 (0:00) Arrive Windsor.

WINDSOR, ONT. - Windsor lies just across the Detroit River (one of the busiest shipping channels in the world) from the city of Detroit, making it a major port of entry to Canada. Because of the bend in the Detroit River (and hence in the U.S.-Canada border), Windsor is actually south of its American cousin.

The French first settled the area in the early 1700s with British locating nearby in the late 1700s. Agriculture and distilling were important aspects of Windsor's economy in the late 1800s, which saw the founding of the Hiram Walker distillery in 1858. Today, Windsor is a busy manufacturing city of 250,000 people, with General Motors, Ford and Chrysler having plants and supply industries here.

VIA Station, 298 Walker Rd., just south of Riverside Drive E., is about 1½ miles from downtown, about a four-minute, five-dollar cab ride. There are storage lockers, food and beverage vending machines, a snack bar and pay-parking a block away.

For information, reservations and tickets by mail, call 256-5511. For arrival and departure information, 254-5252.

Cab stand is at the station; Canadian Veteran Cab, 256-2621. **Local bus** service is one block from the station. **Tunnel bus** between Windsor and Detroit stops just east of 500 Ouellette in downtown Windsor and at the Renaissance Center in Detroit. Thrifty **rental cars** are at the station. **Greyhound,** 254-7575. **Windsor Airport** is about 4½ miles south of the station.

Convention and Visitors Bureau, 333 Riverside Dr., W., Suite 103, N9A 5K4; (519) 255-6530.

Travelodge Downtown Windsor, 33 Riverside Dr. E., N9A 2S4; (519) 258-7774. By the river, many rooms with view of river, Detroit skyline and Dieppe Gardens. Two miles from the station. $75.

-**Rose City Inn,** 430 Ouellette Ave., N9A 1B2; (519) 253-7281. Handy to Detroit/Windsor Tunnel Bus (adjacent to tunnel exit), attractive, reasonably priced rooms. Two miles from the station. $45.

-**Ramada Windsor,** 480 Riverside Dr. W., N9A 5K6; (519) 253-4411. On the river, 2½ miles from the station. $65.

Hiram Walker and Sons, Ltd., 2072 Riverside Dr. E., one of the world's leading distilleries, has tours of this Canadian Club producer, adjacent to the VIA station.

Windsor has an outstanding collection of parks and gardens. Some of the best floral displays will be found at **Jackson Park Sunken Garden,** Tecumseh Rd. at Ouellette Ave. There are fountains as well as a World War II Lancaster bomber on display. The **Dieppe Gardens,** located on Riverside Drive at the foot of Ouellette Ave., overlooks the Detroit River, offering an outstanding view of the Detroit skyline. There is also a 1911 Pacific-type steam locomotive on display. **Coventry Gardens and Peace Fountain,** Riverside Dr. E. at Pillette Rd., are a six-acre riverfront park with a 75-foot floating fountain in the Detroit River.

Hiram Walker Historical Museum, located downtown at 254 Pitt St. W., has various artifacts from southern Ontario history and a War of 1812 exhibit.

MONTREAL - OTTAWA - KINGSTON - TORONTO

 MONTREAL, QUE. - See page 341.

0:00 (0:18) Depart Montreal's Central Station on CN tracks. In about 60 seconds emerge from underground, heading southeast, and soon parallel St. Lawrence River.

0:04 (0:14) Cross Lachine (pronounced luh-sheen) Canal, with its very attractive landscaping. Canal was constructed prior to St. Lawrence Seaway providing bypass around treacherous Lachine Rapids of St. Lawrence River. Nine miles in length, it ceased operations in 1965.

Unfortunately, the Seaway no longer serves as it was originally intended. Many of today's freighters cannot be accommodated by the waterway's rather narrow channel, and the ice blocks traffic west of Montreal three months or more each winter. From time to time, proposals are put forth to modernize the system, but the costs would be enormous.

0:05 (0:13) Several tracks now depart to left to cross Victoria Bridge over St. Lawrence and then on to either Maritime Provinces or New York City.

0:09 (0:09) Re-cross Lachine Canal.

0:12 (0:06) Now slip beneath enormous pile of spaghetti called an interchange, which scrambles and then unscrambles traffic carried by Trans-Canada 20 and Autoroute 15.

0:15 (0:03) Sets of CN and CP tracks branch to right toward huge marshalling yards for both lines.

0:18 (0:00) Arrive Dorval.

DORVAL, QUE. - This is a western suburb of Montreal, home to Montreal's Dorval International Airport just off to the right.

0:00 (0:23) Depart Dorval.

0:04 (0:19) Note two attractive golf

Olympic Stadium - Montreal, Quebec
DORIS SWANSON

courses lining tracks on right.

0:08 (0:15) Stone buildings and round barn on right are part of Macdonald College's experimental farm.

0:09 (0:14) Cross smaller of two tongues of Ottawa River to reach L'Île de Perrot. River is principal branch of St. Lawrence. Its origin is in central Quebec, some 160 miles above Ottawa, and forms partial boundary between Quebec and Ontario. Rapids and falls make most of it unnavigable, but significant elevation change makes stream ideal for hydroelectric power.

0:12 (0:11) Now cross larger segment of river and upon reaching Quebec's mainland, enter Vandreuil, named for early-day governor of Canada.

0:17 (0:06) A final glimpse can be caught of St. Lawrence off to left.

0:23 (0:00) Arrive Coteau.

COTEAU, QUE. - Coteau is the last French speaking community along our route to Ottawa.

0:00 (0:24) Depart Coteau.

0:05 (0:19) Note quaint, silver church in St. Polycarpe, to left.

0:15 (0:09) Leave province of Quebec and enter Ontario.

0:20 (0:02) Interesting remains of several stone fences are on right.

0:23 (0:01) Delightful appearing golf course is on right, accented with ponds and pedestrian bridges.

0:24 (0:00) Arrive Alexandria, where neat brick station awaits on left.

ALEXANDRIA, ONT. - This is but one of many small agrarian centers in eastern Ontario.

0:00 (0:11) Depart Alexandria.

0:11 (0:00) Arrive Maxville.

MAXVILLE, ONT. - Maxville is "Home of the Glengary Highland Games," as proclaimed on building to right. This most important Highland gathering in North America takes place here in August (Saturday before first Monday) when pipe bands and dancers show their talents.

0:00 (0:40) Depart Maxville.

0:08 (0:32) Very attractive silver-spired church punctuates Moose Creek's modest skyline on right.

0:14 (0:26) At Casselman, just 29 miles east of Ottawa, note very unusual architecture of church one block to right.

0:15 (0:25) Cross South Nation River.

0:27 (0:13) Carlsbad Springs and Caldonia Springs, both north (right) of here, were once frequented for their supposedly therapeutic waters.

0:39 (0:01) Ottawa's skyline now dominates right forward.

0:40 (0:00) Arrive at Ottawa's very slick and airy station.

OTTAWA, ONT. - As the capital of Canada, Ottawa is a governmental oriented city with very little industry. It is handsomely situated on rounded promontories that are set amongst three rivers and a canal.

Although Champlain used this spot as a base for exploring along the Ottawa River, there was no settlement here until the early 1800s. It was first called Bytown (after Colonel By who constructed the Rideau Canal as a waterway for British gunboats) and was only a small lumbering community when it was designated the capital of Canada by Queen Victoria in 1857. Shortly thereafter, it was renamed Ottawa and subsequently developed into a very carefully planned community.

Today, it is marked by very "British"-looking buildings, six national museums, beautiful parks and abundant flower gardens with showy displays of brilliant colors—particularly the thousands of tulips that bloom in late May.

Ottawa Station, 200 Tremblay Road, is a modernistic steel and glass structure completed in 1966, located about two miles from the downtown area. There are storage lockers, luggage carts, a newsstand, gifts and a coffee shop, and a barbershop. Free parking is adjacent to the station. There is a Panorama Lounge for VIA 1 passengers. And be sure to see the miniature display of steam locomotives in the lobby.

For reservations and information, call (613) 244-8289.

Cab stand at the station; Blue Line Cabs, 238-1111. Frequent **buses** to downtown stop at the station, 741-4390; system maps and schedules are posted at stops. Budget and Hertz have direct phone lines for **rental cars. Ottawa International Airport** is approximately 13 miles southwest of the station.

Visitor Information, National Arts Center (Elgin Street entrance); (613) 237-5158. Write Ottawa Tourism and Convention Authority, 111 Lisgar, K2P 2L7.

Capital Hotel Suites, 88 Albert St., K1P 5E9; (613) 235-1413 or 800-463-7705. Recently renovated small downtown hotel; one of Ottawa's better values with large rooms. Good location, near Parliament Hill. Two miles from the station. $59.

-Lord Elgin Hotel, 100 Elgin St. at Larier, K1P 5K8; (613) 235-3333 or 800-267-4298. Original structure has been remodelled to create larger (but fewer) rooms, all very attractive. Good location, near Parliament Hill, across from National Arts Center. Two miles from the station. $95.

In the downtown area, the **Canadian Parliament Buildings** are set on Parliament Hill overlooking the Ottawa River. Changing of the Guard takes place at 10 am in the summer. Some of the best shopping is at **Rideau Center,** across the canal on Rideau Street and Sparks Street Mall. Various stage productions appear regularly at the **National Arts Center.**

Two of the more outstanding museums are the new **Canadian Museum of Civilization,** in Hull directly across from Parliament Hill, which has 750,000 artifacts on display, History Hall with life-size historic structures, including a prairie depot, an IMAX/OMNIMAX theatre, and much more, and **National Museum of Science and Technology,** 1867 St. Laurent Blvd., about a mile or so southeast of the station, is great for the entire family. Exhibits include such things as autos, buggies and trains. The **National Aviation Museum** is at Rockcliffe Airport.

The **Outaouais & Gatineau Valley steam train** offers 20-mile excursions from Hull to Wakefield. Round trips are five hours with a two-hour stopover in Wakefield. Early May to late October, (819) 778-7246, 199 Montcalm in Hull.

0:00 (0:39) Depart Ottawa.

0:02 (0:37) Large blockish building on left houses Ottawa's postal central distribution operation.

0:05 (0:34) Canada Revenue Center, on right, is some evidence that we are in nation's capital.

0:09 (0:30) Small pleasure craft are docked below on left as we cross Rideau River.

0:20 (0:19) Stream which follows briefly on right is Jack River.

0:36 (0:03) Trees continue to dominate route between Ottawa and Brockville, with spruce and aspen being, perhaps, predominant.

0:39 (0:00) Arrive Smiths Falls.

 SMITHS FALLS, ONT. - This progressive little city has been highly successful in attracting various light industries to the immediate region. Several such enterprises are evident along the route, particularly south of the city.

0:00 (0:26) Depart Smiths Falls.

0:02 (0:24) Planters and Stanley Tools are major local employers, with plants at left.

0:03 (0:23) Cross Rideau River once again.

0:19 (0:07) A gaggle of handsome old-time street light graces farm yard off to right.

0:26 (0:00) Arrive Brockville.

For route from Brockville to Toronto, see Brockville, page 358.

TORONTO - KITCHENER - LONDON - SARNIA

 TORONTO, ONT. - See page 360.

0:00 (0:28) Depart Toronto's Union Station. In a moment, CN Tower will soar skyward on left, then $400 million SkyDome, home to Toronto Blue Jays, will dominate all else on left.

0:15 (0:13) Industrial confines of western Toronto are momentarily interrupted as train crosses high above Humber River and angles through Weston Golf Course.

0:16 (0:12) Labatts Metro Brewery, on right, is producer of one of Canada's popular brews.

0:23 (0:05) Another producer of a popular beverage is at right, Lipton Tea.

0:28 (0:00) Arrive Brampton.

 BRAMPTON, ONT. - A plethora of nurseries and greenhouses give Bramptom the nickname "Flower City." Nearby, the Great War Flying Museum has a fine collection of World War I memorabilia.

0:00 (0:11) Depart Brampton.

0:10 (0:01) Cross over Credit River.

0:11 (0:00) Arrive Georgetown.

 GEORGETOWN, ONT. - This town of 17,000 serves the extreme western edge of the Toronto metropolitan area.

0:00 (0:24) Depart Georgetown.

0:09 (0:15) Gaping excavation on left is result of limestone quarrying operation.

0:23 (0:01) Cross Speed River, then note former CN 4-8-4 steam locomotive on exhibit at right.

0:24 (0:00) Arrive Guelph where an active armory sits off to left, while 1911 station greets passengers on right.

 GUELPH, ONT. - This community has a fine assemblage of architectural styles utilizing locally quarried limestone.

0:00 (0:22) Depart Guelph.

0:01 (0:21) Massive stone edifice above to right with twin towers is Lady of Mercy Church.

0:04 (0:18) At right, faded lettering between windows of sprawling brick structure once advertised everything for barns and stables.

0:16 (0:06) Trundle over Grand River.

0:22 (0:00) Arrive Kitchener's attractive brick station.

 KITCHENER, ONT. - Kitchener and its twin, Waterloo, were originally founded by Pennsylvania Mennonites. Later an influx of German immigrants gave the area an Old Country flavor that persists today.

0:00 (0:27) Depart Kitchener and soon enter some of the most productive dairy country in the world.

Capitol - Smiths Falls, Ontario
BRUCE FINGERHOOD

0:04 (0:23) Large complex of brick buildings on immediate right is Uniroyal Tire plant.

0:15 (0:12) Cross Nith River.

0:27 (0:00) Arrive Stratford.

STRATFORD, ONT. - The Stratford Festival was born here in 1953. From a humble beginning of Shakespearean plays, the event has become world renowned and has expanded to three theaters. The annual celebration now runs from May through October.

0:00 (0:15) Depart Stratford.

0:09 (0:06) Numerous ponies can often be seen galavanting around pony farm on right.

0:15 (0:00) Arrive St. Marys.

ST. MARYS, ONT. - This small agrarian stronghold boasts one of the more attractive small rail stations, which stands on the north side of the tracks.

0:00 (0:27) Depart St. Marys.

0:03 (0:24) Large cement plant is at right.

0:08 (0:19) Appropriately nomenclatured dairy operation, on right, is named "Railroad View Farms."

0:15 (0:12) London's municipal airport is off to left, while attractive golf course embellishes scene.

0:27 (0:00) Arrive London.

LONDON, ONT. - Located on the River Thames, many of London's streets are named for those of its English namesake. This is one of southeastern Ontario's busier industrial centers. A large air show, featuring aircraft from five countries, is here here the first weekend in June.

0:00 (0:30) Departing London, many of town's earliest three- and four-story buildings, one block to right, are in vivid contrast with London's newer downtown.

0:02 (0:28) Cross Thames River.

0:03 (0:27) Cross Thames River one more time.

0:17 (0:02) Tobacco curing kilns, those skinny red barns with multiple doors, dot fields on either side of tracks.

0:19 (0:00) Arrive Strathroy.

STRATHROY, ONT. - This community of 9,000 boasts a lovely Victorian mansion built in 1871, known as "Murray House." The home now houses the Strathroy Middlesex Museum with some rare pioneer artifacts.

0:00 (0:36) Depart Strathroy.

0:20 (0:16) Through small town of Wyoming, not named for the state, but an Indian word meaning "on the great plain.".

0:31 (0:05) Entering Sarnia, industrial sights dominate, with numerous manufacturing and refinery complexes surrounding this seaport at the mouth of Lake Huron

This is the customs checkpoint for the eastbound International heading into Canada.

0:36 (0:00) Arrive Sarnia.

SARNIA, ONT. - As you may have already inferred from the numerous refineries in evidence, this is Ontario's major oil-refining and petrochemical center. It is also a Canadian port-of-entry, where auto traffic is carried over the St. Clair River to and from Port Huron, WI by the Blue Water Bridge. Trains, however, will pass beneath the river.

Jonquière

Montreal

Saguenay

The train is the way to go to Jonquière (although it is possible to make a circle trip using the connection bus between Jonquière and Quebec City). The tracks slice through undulating, forested Laurentians laced with meandering rivers and liberally sprinkled with glossy-surfaced lakes, some of Canada's most attractive wilderness. Sparkling waterfalls, spectacular rock cuts and airy trestles add to the excitement. During the fall, the foliage is exquisite and there is always a chance of spotting some moose or bear. Numerous hunting and fishing clubs, with names such as Jacques Cartier, Iroquois and Orleans, are strung along the route causing the train to make frequent but interesting unscheduled stops.

The service is thrice-weekly, the pace unhurried, and the atmosphere on board is relaxed and friendly. If you can only take the train one way, the return run from Jonquière would be recommended since the more scenic portions will be traversed during full daylight.

The tracks were actually built by four different railroads, the earliest construction occurring a century ago. That first section was only a three-mile stretch between L'Assomption and L'Epiphanie, built by the rather obscure L'Assomption Railway.

Northbound Schedule (Condensed)
Montreal, Que. - Early Afternoon Departure
Hervey, Que. - Late Afternoon
Jonquière, Que. - Late Evening Arrival

Southbound Schedule (Condensed)*
Jonquière, Que. - Late Morning Departure
Hervey, Que. - Late Afternoon
Montreal, Que. - Midevening
*Approximately two hours later on Sun-

day.

Frequency - Tri-weekly. Departs Montreal Monday, Wednesday and Friday. Departs Jonquière Tuesday, Thursday and Sunday.
Seating - Coaches.
Dining - Sandwiches, snacks and beverages.
Baggage - Checked baggage at larger towns.
Reservations - Unreserved train.
Length of Trip - 308 miles in 9 hours.

Route Log

(Note that the route described below, between Montreal and Ahuntsic, is for the southbound train. The northbound train circles around through the Côte de Liesse freight yard west of downtown before arriving in Ahuntsic.)

 MONTREAL, QUE. - See page 341.
0:00 (0:20) Depart Montreal's Central Station in complete darkness for eight minutes while encased by Mount Royal Tunnel. This shaft burrows through Mt. Royal, then emerges three miles northwest of its downtown starting point.
0:09 (0:11) Although you can't tell by looking (the train is below grade here), we are passing through a citified portion of Montreal called Mount Royal.
0:15 (0:05) After curving to right for a northeasterly course out of Montreal, look back to right where beehive-domed Saint Joseph Oratory Museum, known for its beautiful stained glass windows and

mosaics, is at Mount Royal's base; one of the world's most unusual Catholic shrines.
0:20 (0:00) Arrive Ahuntsic.

AHUNTSIC, QUE. - This stop is in a section of Montreal with intermixed modest income housing, newer apartments and industrial operations.
0:00 (0:15) Depart Ahuntsic.
0:04 (0:11) Enormous expanse of stone quarry is just to right of tracks.
0:13 (0:02) Cross multi-laned Route 40, which is major artery between Montreal and Quebec City.
0:15 (0:00) Arrive Pointe-aux-Trembles where waters of St. Lawrence River are visible about three blocks distant on right.

POINTE-AUX-TREMBLES, QUE. - This is the easternmost suburban stop before escaping the metropolitan confines of Montreal and shifting to the pastoral scenes of rural Quebec. From here, the landscape becomes dotted with farmsteads and dairy silos, mild-eyed cattle graze contentedly everywhere and small communities make intermittent appearances, each seeming to have a grey stone church topped with a silver-spired steeple. In spite of its northern location, the area is ideal for tobacco, and fields of this crop, as well as curing barns, can soon be spotted along the route.
0:00 (0:26) Depart Pointe-aux-Trembles.
0:05 (0:21) Cross River des Prairies, actually an offshoot of Ottawa River, just west of its joinder with St. Lawrence. It takes two tries for us to get across. This river and St. Lawrence encircle Montreal, giving it an island status.
0:12 (0:14) Oldest portion of rail line to Jonquière is along this stretch between milepost 117 and 114, originally built by the L'Assomption Railway in 1885-86.
0:18 (0:08) Cross LacOuareau River.
0:26 (0:00) Arrive Joliette.

JOLIETTE, QUE. - This city of 18,000 has long been an important rail head and trade center serving the Lanaudière region of Quebec, the only Quebec region named after a woman. The town was founded in 1832 by her husband, Barthelemy Joliette, a local deputy, notary and businessman. This is tobacco country, with picking occurring in August. Archery

range used during 1976 Olympic Games is still located here.
0:00 (1:04) Depart Joliette and cross L'Assomption River.
0:05 (0:59) Typical tobacco curing barns stand in field on right.
0:07 (0:57) At milepost 97, thick stand of dairy silos in distance gives appearance of small town on horizon. Train is now traveling at a comfortable 60 mph.
0:27 (0:37) Small village of St. Justin, at milepost 78, is demarcation point between plains just visited and wooded, rolling terrain yet to come. Route becomes more and more scenic.
0:29 (0:35) Suddenly, at milepost 76.3, we seem to soar through space as train crosses 175 feet above Maskinonge River, breathtaking because of its abruptness. Don't miss views of surrounding countryside, particularly to right.
0:43 (0:22) Another airy crossing occurs at milepost 65.1, where train traverses 1,071-foot-long bridge over Rivière-du-Loup; again, nice views are afforded.
0:49 (0:16) At milepost 61, cross 165 feet above West Yamachiche River.
0:53 (0:12) Cross East Yamachiche River at milepost 58.
1:00 (0:04) Cross small stream at bottom of Lavern Gully at milepost 52.
1:02 (0:02) Momentary darkness prevails as train chugs through 610-foot tunnel— second of only two tunnels on route, first being Mount Royal Tunnel at beginning of our trip. Upon exiting, cross Shawinigan River at milepost 50.
1:04 (0:00) Arrive Shawinigan.

SHAWINIGAN, QUE. - Located on the St. Maurice River, Shawinigan is the birthplace of Quebec's chemical industry. Cheap hydroelectric power (totalling a whopping 400,000 horsepower) produced at the falls on the river has accounted for aluminum, paper and chemical industries locating here. The town's Indian name means "angular portage."
0:00 (0:30) Depart Shawinigan.
0:03 (0:27) Huge electric transformers on left identify aluminum smelting operation which requires enormous amounts of electric power.
0:06 (0:24) Fine view of Saint Maurice River is afforded on right.

0:10 (0:20) Now, cross high above Saint Maurice River on a 722-foot-long trestle at milepost 43.5.

0:11 (0:19) One of Shawinigan's major industries is on left. Logs are floated down St. Maurice River to damsite where Canadian International Paper's operation turns them into pulp for paper products. Much of pulp is exported south to U.S.

0:15 (0:15) Stop at CN rail yards of Garneau at milepost zero. Milepost numbers, which have been growing smaller, now get progressively larger as we move farther toward Jonquière.

0:20 (0:10) Depart Garneau.

0:24 (0:06) Three-spired church, about one block from tracks on right, identifies village of Herouxville at milepost 3.

0:28 (0:02) Cross small Riviere des Enview at milepost 6.5.

0:30 (0:00) Arriving St. Tite, take note of attractive three-story house on right that has unusual outside spiral staircase between second and third floors.

ST. TITE, QUE. - This small town of 3,000 calls itself "The City of Leather" for the gloves and boots manufactured here.

0:00 (0:20) Depart St. Tite.

0:05 (0:15) Sylvan setting on right features small lake with cottages nestled along its idyllic shoreline.

0:10 (0:10) Twin spires grace unusually attractive church of Ste-Thecle on left.

0:20 (0:00) Arrive Hervey Jct. at milepost 18.7.

HERVEY JCT., QUE. - This rather unimpressive-looking small town is a division point for the railroad. Tracks seen taking off to the left at this junction lead north and then west across a vast lakeland wilderness. The cities of Senneterre and Cochrane, the latter being some 495 rail miles from here, are both reached by this line.

0:00 (0:41) Depart Hervey Jct.

0:13 (0:28) At milepost 23, narrow landing strip on right leads directly into pretty little town of Lac-aux-Sables, testing pilot's skill and townsfolk's nerves.

0:15 (0:26) Expansive waters of very scenic Lac-aux-Sables are on left. Forest now becomes almost continuous while small lakes become more abundant.

0:23 (0:18) Just beyond milepost 30, bridge 323 feet in length carries us over Batiscan River which then follows along left side of train. During autumn, foliage is quite spectacular from here on to Jonquière.

0:40 (0:01) On outskirts of Rivière-à-Pierre, note small hockey rink on right, not only attesting to widespread popularity of Canada's national pastime, but evidence that winters are definitely on the chilly side.

0:44 (0:00) Arrive Rivière-à-Pierre at milepost 40.

RIVIÈRE-À-PIERRE, QUE. - Numerous two-story buildings with a variety of architectural styles pervade Rivière-à-Pierre. From this quaint village, the tracks now turn left 45 degrees and head due north (we've been going northeast) until reaching Chambord, some 120 miles away.

0:00 (1:40) Depart Rivière-à-Pierre. For those traveling during the fall, darkness sets in about now. The return trip, however, offers daylight along the scenic stretches north of here.

From here to Chambord, the undulating, forested countryside is liberally sprinkled with lakes and hunting camps, each with its own particular character.

0:14 (1:26) Lovely Batiscan River, which is flowing south to the St. Lawrence, joins our route again and becomes a familiar scene during the next 50 miles.

0:23 (1:17) White, frothy rapids of Batiscan are particularly appealing for short stretches in either direction from milepost 57.

0:28 (1:12) On left, impressive rocky cliffs of Linton add special flavor to route at milepost 62.

0:30 (1:10) Near milepost 64, on left, three collections of stone piers poking out of river are remains of bridge that carried tracks some fifty years ago.

0:45 (0:55) Note fire lookout tower at tip of mountain on left.

0:59 (0:41) Stadacona, typical of small settlements throughout this region, is at milepost 76.4.

1:35 (0:05) Cross over rapids and bid farewell to Batiscan River which has been our companion since leaving Rivière-à-Pierre.

1:40 (0:00) Arrive Lac Édouard at milepost 95.

🚻 **LAC ÉDOUARD, QUE.** - This remote village is situated on a lake by the same name, one of the region's larger bodies of water. Cottages mark the shoreline and also huddle here and there throughout the nearby woods. Note the old rail station to the left of the tracks.

0:00 (2:02) Depart Lac Édouard. While following lake's edge for a few moments, it is understandable, upon seeing such pristine beauty, why the area has become inhabited.

0:26 (1:36) On right, near milepost 105 and just before reaching Summit Club, watch for pretty Summit Lake with inviting cabins along its shoreline.

0:51 (1:11) From mileposts 115 to 117, excellent views of northern tip of Kiskissink Lake are afforded. Small boats are evidence that lake is popular with fishermen.

1:10 (0:52) One of area's larger lakes, Mirage, is just to left, between mileposts 128 and 130. Pontoon planes can often be spotted here.

1:11 (0:51) Cross Wip River at milepost 129.

1:34 (0:28) Cross Noisy River as it tumbles toward Lake Bouchette to left.

Civilization is found once again upon arrival at Lac Bouchette, one of the larger settlements in the surrounding region, and located on paved Highway 155 leading to Chambord. As a matter of fact, the train straddles the highway as it stops here at milepost 143. On right, rather bizarre colors were selected for house exterior—red, black and green.

1:37 (0:25) On left is Lake Quiatchouan at milepost 144, situated at northern tip of Lake Bouchette.

2:02 (0:00) At milepost 159.5, arrive Chambord (Jct.) where most of remaining passengers usually detrain. Town of Chambord is off to left.

🚻 **CHAMBORD, QUE.** - This charming town on a cove of Lac St. Jean is a popular resort for those seeking recreational opportunities afforded by the lake. Here, fishing for the ouananiche, an aggressive freshwater salmon, is a major attraction, while rivers of the region offer walleye, pike and speckled trout. The lake itself is huge, sometimes being referred to as an inland sea, having a circumference of 140 miles. Note crucifixion scene on the right.

0:00 (0:29) Depart Chambord past CN locomotive shops on left.

0:03 (0:26) Lac Saint Jean now comes into view to left.

0:14 (0:15) At milepost 169, train slips through town of Metabetchouan, where well-known musicians' camp is located. Note outstanding Gothic-style church on right which is constructed of pink granite quarried nearby.

0:25 (0:04) Last view of Lac Saint Jean on left before train twists to east on its final leg.

0:29 (0:00) Arrive Hébertville.

🚻 **HÉBERTVILLE, QUE.** - This small town also serves as a stop for nearby Alma.

0:00 (0:33) Depart Hébertville.

0:03 (0:30) Modest ski hill is visible on horizon off to right.

0:12 (0:21) Church on left, with its modern sweeping lines, is centerpiece of town of Larouche.

0:32 (0:01) Cross Sables River on 231-foot bridge.

0:33 (0:00) Arrive Jonquière.

🚻 **JONQUIÈRE, QUE.** - This city exemplifies what all industrial cities should be. Owing its robustness to the free world's largest aluminum manufacturing complex, Jonquière is modern, clean and attractive. A super-abundance of hydroelectric power has caused Alcan to locate its largest aluminum plant here, even though bauxite (aluminum ore) must be brought in by ship from such faraway places as South America and Africa. One can easily feel the vibrant spirit that has made this city a truly progressive metropolis.

The area was first settled in the early 1800s when Peter McLeod and 21 other men (a collection of Indians and Scotsmen) arrived here to construct and operate a sawmill, its lumber to be sold to Great Britain for her Merchant Marine. Soon, however, interests turned to farming the land that had been cleared, and, in spite of the sometimes bitter winters, the 120-day growing season fostered both vegetable and dairy farming.

Today, paper and aluminum dominate the region's economy, with 75% of the population afforded employment by these two industries. Oceangoing vessels find their way along the St. Lawrence and then up the Saguenay River (meaning "where we set sail") to the port at nearby La Baie. Here, bauxite from South America is offloaded and shipped by rail to aluminum plants in Chicoutimi, Jonquière and Alma. Inexpensive hydroelectric power, critical in aluminum production, is the reason the plants are in this remote locale.

Visitor Information, Bureau of Tourism, 265 boul. du Royaume; (418) 548-4004.

Cab stand at the station. Taxi Jonquière, 542-4569. Budget **rental cars,** 547-7766; will pick up and drop off at station with advance arrangements.

VIA Station, at Pierre and Dominique, is a new, attractive station, about a mile west of the former VIA station. City buses also use this facility as a downtown terminal. There is a small restaurant in the station itself.

Call 800-361-5390 for reservations.

-Hotel Roussillon Saguenay, 2675 boul. du Royaume, G7S 5B8; (418) 548-3124. Large, attractive high-rise hotel, about four miles from the station. $65.

-Hotel Jean Dequen, 2841 boul. du Royaume, G7S 4K6; (418) 548-7173. Small 12-room hotel, about three miles from the station. Ask for a room that does not front on highway. $35.

There is much to do in this remote but fascinating area, although you might consider brushing up on your French. Ninety-eight percent of the populace speak that language, and bilingualism is even less of a trait here than in Quebec City and Montreal (although English is spoken at the hotels listed above). This is part of the region's appeal and adds to the adventure. Highlights include: breathtaking **scenic cruises** on North America's longest fiord; tours of the **Alcan aluminum plant,** the Free World's largest; tours of **Shipshaw,** an Alcan dam and enormous power plant; and, in nearby Chicoutimi, the excellent **Saguenay-Lac**

Route of the Saguenay
JACK SWANSON

St. John Museum with regional artifacts.

Other Quebec Service

The **Abitibi** provides triweekly overnight service from **Montreal to Hervey and Senneterre,** departing Montreal in the evening Monday, Wednesday and Friday, and departing Senneterre late in the day Sunday, Tuesday and Thursday. Service is extended to Taschereau from Senneterre Tuesday and Thursday and to Cochrane on from Senneterre on Saturday. These extended trains return, departing Taschereau Tuesday and Thursday and departing Cochrane on Sunday. There are sleeping cars and snack and beverage service to Senneterre. Coach seats are unreserved.

Cochrane
North Bay
Toronto

Northlander

Heading north (as its name implies) from Toronto, the Northlander's principal destinations are North Bay and Cochrane. The North Bay area is particularly appealing to the outdoorsman, with nearby Lake Nipissing being a major draw. Cochrane, farther to the north, is the southern terminus of the popular Polar Bear Express that takes the adventurous to Moosonee on the lower tip of James Bay. Here, Ontario's oldest permanent English-speaking settlement—Moose Factory—holds forth nearby. To continue on to Moosonee, an overnight stay is required in Cochrane.

Unfortunately, the Northlander is no longer comprised of unique sets of European built, articulated streamliner equipment. These jewels, which once were the reason many rode the Northlander, literally reached the point of no return and became too expensive to maintain. The Ontario Northland Railway, which operates the Northlander, has relaced the streamliner with more mundane equipment.

Northbound Schedule (Condensed)
Toronto, Ont. - Early Afternoon Departure
North Bay, Ont. - Late Afternoon
Cochrane, Ont. - Late Evening Arrival

Southbound Schedule (Condensed)
Cochrane, Ont. - Early Morning Departure
North Bay, Ont. - Early Afternoon
Toronto, Ont. - Early Evening Arrival

Frequency - Daily, except Saturday.
Seating - Standard coaches.
Dining - Full meal service.

Baggage - Carry-on only.
Reservations - Reservation of coach seats on purchase of tickets.
Length of Trip - 482 miles in 9 hours.

Route Log

For route description between Toronto and Washago, see that portion of Canadian log, page 393.

0:00 (0:19) Depart Washago, and terrain immediately begins to shift from rich farming countryside to rugged, forested lakelands called Muskoka. Last ice age carved granite base rock into dramatic shapes making numerous rock cuts necessary along route.

0:04 (0:15) Cross one of region's numerous canals where pleasure craft create colorful scene, on right.

0:19 (0:00) Arrive Gravenhurst.

GRAVENHURST, ONT. - Long popular with the rich and famous, this serene Victorian town is still a tourist center for those wanting to visit the Muskoka Lakes region. The town holds popular summer stock comedies and musicals in the elegantly refurbished Gravenhurst Opera House. And every summer, free Sunday band concerts are performed from a floating stage on Gull Lake.

0:00 (0:33) Depart Gravenhurst.

0:01 (0:32) Aforementioned Gull Lake is just through trees on right.

0:12 (0:21) Pass high over south branch of Muskoka River where falls can be seen at right and boats can occasionally be spotted on left, as train enters Bracebridge. Community of 9,000 is geared to tourism, draw being beautiful Lake Muskoka, just to west of town.

0:29 (0:04) Siding Lake appears at left.
0:33 (0:00) Arrive Huntsville.

 HUNTSVILLE, ONT. - This is another lake-country resort town and offers boat cruises along the Muskoka River to Peninsula Lake. Also, Algonquin Provincial Park, a popular canoeing and fishing area, is just east of here.

0:00 (1:01) Departing Huntsville, Lake Vernon is off to left.
0:01 (1:00) Cross very scenic Hunters Bay.
0:04 (0:57) Lumber mill, a frequent sight throughout Canada's forest lands, is on right.
0:24 (0:37) Golf course, on left, is very inviting scene. North branch of Magnetawan flows nearby, a stream we must cross several times.
0:33 (0:28) Through Burk's Falls where old station once served those boarding popular Magnetawan River steamer.
0:54 (0:07) Through attractive Sundridge, which caters to fishermen hoping to land deep-water trout found in waters of Lake Bernard, on right.
1:01 (0:00) Arrive South River.

SOUTH RIVER, ONT. - Here, canoeists find ready access to Algonquin Provincial Park.

0:00 (0:56) Depart South River.
0:01 (0:55) Cross South River where waterfalls can be seen off to left.
0:07 (0:49) High trestle carries tracks over small Viaduct Creek.
0:15 (0:41) Through town of Trout Creek, where small white church on right seems to wear an ice cream cone for a steeple top.
0:21 (0:35) Outstanding view of charming valley farmlands now presents itself, off to left.
0:51 (0:05) Entering outskirts of North Bay, our CN tracks intersect those of CP Rail.
0:56 (0:00) Arrive North Bay's new ONR Station.

NORTH BAY, ONT. - Rail buffs will recognize North Bay as home base for the Ontario Northland Railway.

Chartered in 1902 as the Timiskaming and Northern Ontario Railway, it started out to serve the farming country north of here, but ultimately found its way to Moosonee, its northern terminus on James Bay, in 1932.

North Bay is a popular destination for fishermen, particularly those wanting to try their luck on adjacent Lake Nipissing. Hunting is also an important North Bay recreational activity.

Boat cruises, leaving from Government Dock near downtown, are quite popular.

ONR Station is a new $3.5 million intermodal terminal, with a short tunnel connecting it to a shopping mall. If your trip originates here, be sure to check with an ONR attendant in the station's lobby for a seat assignment before boarding the Northlander. Call 495-4200.

For **Tilden rental cars,** call 474-3030.

Write **Chamber of Commerce,** 1375 Seymour St., P.O. Box 747, P1B 8J8; (705) 472-8480.

-**The Empire Hotel,** 425 Fraser St., P1B 8K6, (705) 472-8200, is located in the heart of downtown and has quite comfortable rooms. $60.

0:00 (1:29) Depart North Bay.
0:05 (1:24) Numerous small boats are docked at Trout Lake Marina on immediate right.
1:30 (0:02) Arm of Temagami Lake, at left, reaches to edge of town. Note nicely manicured park, boat docks and walkways along shore, a project of Ontario's Development Program.
1:32 (0:00) Arrive Temagami, a Cree Indian word for "deep water."

TEMAGAMI, ONT. - This logging community (mostly harvesting white pine) is also a hunting and fishing center.

0:00 (0:41) Depart Temagami.
0:06 (0:35) Lakes are everywhere; one of area's large bodies of water now appears at right.
0:20 (0:21) Note unusual approach to supporting telephone poles which are propped upright with an abundance of rocks.
0:30 (0:11) Dam on left holds back Montreal River.
0:41 (0:00) Arrive Cobalt.

COBALT, ONT. - Mining was Cobalt's reason for being. It started in 1903 when, legend has it, a blacksmith heaved his hammer at a fox and missed. The heavy tool chipped into a rock and disclosed what turned out to be the world's richest silver vein. The community still bears the imprint of its early helter-skelter construction. Today, Cobalt's Northern Ontario Mining Museum has perhaps the best display anywhere of native silver.

0:00 (0:14) Depart Cobalt.

0:06 (0:08) Looking right, Lake Timiskaming is beautiful setting for Haileybury. Land on far side of lake is province of Quebec.

0:10 (0:04) Plant at right processes some of Ontario's trees into particle board.

0:14 (0:00) Arrive New Liskeard.

NEW LISKEARD, ONT. - This is a farming and dairying center. Northbound passengers may question this, but once the Northlander departs, there can be no doubt. The Little Clay Belt, as it is called, starts just north of town. This fertile farming area can produce many crops grown in more southern climes in spite of a shorter growing season.

0:00 (0:24) Departing New Liskeard, note hundreds of canoes stacked on end in lot of manufacturer on left.

0:02 (0:22) Now, enter upon fertile farmlands of Little Clay Belt, just described. If Iowa were flat, it would look like this.

0:23 (0:01) Cross high over Englehart River.

0:24 (0:00) Arriving Englehart, note 1921 steam locomotive (a 4-6-2, #701), built for the Timiskaming and Northern Ontario Railway and nicely maintained in its green and gold colors, on left.

ENGLEHART, ONT. - This town has its roots in both lumbering and railroading.

0:00 (0:30) Depart Englehart's nicely renovated station. Large pulp mill can be seen off to left.

0:08 (0:22) High trestle carries Northlander above Blanche River.

0:30 (0:00) Arrive Swastika.

SWASTIKA, ONT. - Gold was discovered just south of here after the turn of the century. Swastika was born and soon found itself at the center of one of Canada's richest mineral finds.

0:00 (0:45) Depart Swastika.

0:05 (0:40) Cross arctic divide, beyond which all streams flow north to James Bay. Numerous rivers and creeks are crossed before reaching Matheson.

0:45 (0:00) Arrive Matheson.

MATHESON, ONT. - Matheson, entrenched in Ontario's northern mining region, still maintains itself as an agricultural trade center.

0:00 (0:20) Depart Matheson.

0:12 (0:08) Crossing Driftwood River, look to left to see Monteith Correctional Centre. Just west of here, two famous gold mines, the Dome and the Hollinger, were discovered in the early 1900s.

0:20 (0:00) Arrive Porquis.

PORQUIS, ONT. - At one time, those continuing to Cochrane transferred to an awaiting motorcoach at this community. Now, however, the Northlander continues into Cochrane.

0:00 (0:25) Depart Porquis.

0:25 (0:00) Arrive Cochrane.

COCHRANE, ONT. - Cochrane has all the appearances of a modern-day frontier town, a bustling little city thriving on a blend of tourism, hunting, fishing, mining, lumbering and railroading. This is the southern terminus of the Polar Bear Express, Ontario Northland's popular train to Moosonee on James Bay.

ONR Station is situated on the edge of Cochrane's small downtown area. This is a brand-new facility, completed in 1991, including a hotel occupying space directly above. Call 272-4228.

Write **Cochrane Visitors Center** (June through Labor Day), Cochrane, Ont., P0L 1C0.

Tilden rental cars are one mile from the station, next to the Northern Lites Motel. The inter-city **bus terminal** is at the train station.

Reservations should be made well in advance, particularly during Cochrane's busy summer season.

-First Canada Inns, P.O. Box 1496, P0L 1C0; (705) 272-3500 or 800-267-7899 (Canada only). New in 1991, above the ONR Station, 23 rooms. Reception desk is located in the station lobby. $67.

-The **Northern Lites Motel,** Highway 11, Box 1720, P0L 1C0, (705) 272-4281, is a short cab ride, or a healthy mile walk, from the station and downtown. Rooms are nice and large, and a good restaurant is open throughout the day. $50.

Moosonee
Cochrane

Polar Bear Express

The Polar Bear Express heads north from Cochrane, Ontario into a land of muskegs, wilderness rivers, moose and bears—but, sorry, no polar bears. The end of the line is James Bay, the southernmost extension of Hudson Bay where Moosonee and its sister outpost, island-ensconsed Moose Factory, live an isolated existence. (Sorry again, there is no moose factory at Moose Factory.)

The draw is the uniqueness of the region and the opportunity to visit Ontario's oldest permanent English-speaking settlement—curiously named Moose Factory. That settlement of 1,600 Cree Indians and whites is reached from Moosonee by boat in the summer, by road across the frozen Moosonee River in the winter, and by helicopter during the ice-breakup season. Much of its pioneer past has been maintained, and touring historic buildings and other artifacts gives visitors a strong sense of "the way it was."

A Hudson's Bay Company fort was established on what was then called Hayes Island in 1673, but within 13 years the French captured the installation that had been defended by only 16 men. The English regained it by treaty in 1732. This remote trading post remained virtually unreachable by land until 1923, when the Temis-kaming Northern Ontario Railway, now the Ontario Northland, reached Moosonee. These two largest isolated communities in Ontario still remain relatively unknown.

Schedules and Equipment - The Ontario Northland Railway, owned and operated by the Province of Ontario, runs round-trip excursion trains (The **Polar Bear Express**) daily, except Friday, from late June through early September. Passengers are transported in luxuriously refurbished rail cars that contrast sharply with the surrounding countryside. Departures from Cochrane are early morning and from Moosonee late afternoon. The trip takes just over four hours in each direction.

In addition to these summertime excursions, there is a **local** that runs twice a week in the summer and three times a week the remainder of the year. The local is another experience, carrying Indians and hunters from flag stop to flag stop as well as tourists to Moosonee. The local leaves Cochrane midmorning on Tuesday and Thursday in the summer and Monday, Wednesday and Friday the rest of the year. It leaves Moosonee midafternoon on Friday and early morning on Wednesday in the summer and early morning Tuesday, Thursday and Saturday the rest of the year.

Food service is available on both trains.

Reservations are required for the Polar Bear Express excursion trains. For reservations and information, including tour packages, write Ontario Northland Transportation Commission, 65 Front St.

W., Toronto, Ont., M5J 1E6; or phone (416) 314-3750 (Toronto) or (705) 472-4500 (North Bay).

Route Log

COCHRANE, ONT. - See page 379.

0:00 (4:20) Depart Cochrane as polar bear on town's water tower, on right, watches over all from above.

(Note: Mileposts are quite visible on this line and are included as additional reference points.)

0:10 (4:10) MP 5. Cochrane's airport handles normal variety of wheeled aircraft on runways as well as seaplanes on waters of Lillabelle Lake on right.

0:13 (4:07) MP 7. Farms interspersed with wooded hills will prevail for several miles as train crosses northern rim of Ontario's Clay Belt.

0:19 (4:01) MP 11. Abitibi River is on right. Stream will be followed off and on as it drifts toward James Bay.

0:28 (3:52) MP 18. Large sawmill of Ontario Paper Company is on right at Gardiner.

1:01 (3:19) MP 43. At Island Falls, cabin on right has own little rail conveyance parked on walkway of cross ties on right.

1:02 (3:18) MP 44. One of numerous Ontario Northland communication towers is on right. Company has $20 million invested in system that handles radio, telephone and television transmissions to and from remote Northlands.

1:04 (3:16) MP 45. Cross broad waters of Abitibi River where Abitibi River Island Falls Power Plant and Dam can be glimpsed upriver on right.

1:05 (3:15) MP 46. Slip beneath powerline leading from power station, then pass another lumber operation of Ontario Paper Company.

Little Bear - route of the Polar Bear Express
ONTARIO NORTHLAND RAILWAY

1:09 (3:11) MP 49. Expanse of dead trees was caused by June 1976 forest fire.

1:16 (3:04) MP 55. Green wooden boxes at trackside hold shims of wood used for leveling tracks affected by springtime frost heaves. This phenomenon is typical wherever muskeg or permafrost is prevalent.

1:33 (2:47) MP 69. Fraserdale is the northernmost point for road service in this region.

1:39 (2:41) MP 74. Terrain grows more rugged with aspen and black spruce everywhere.

1:48 (2:32) MP 80. Cross 50th Parallel.

2:06 (2:14) MP 93. Huge Otter Rapids generating facility is on right, one of four highly automated hydroelectric stations in region operated by microwave signals from central location.

2:10 (2:10) MP 96. Note "stuffed folks" standing in yard of Miller's cabin, on right, at Coral Rapids. Diamonds have actually been found in this vicinity. We are now halfway to our destination.

2:47 (1:33) MP 126. Lignite, a very low grade of coal, lies just beneath the surface. Mining these deposits has been considered, but development has yet to occur due to low quality and cost of removal.

3:01 (1:19) MP 131. Cross Onakawana River.

3:09 (1:11) MP 138. Cross first of several "upside-down bridges" on route, designed to permit ice flows and other floating objects to clear structure. Supporting girders are above instead of below bridge, although difficult to see as train passes above.

3:15 (1:05) MP 142. Cross Moose River on 1,800-foot-long trestle, longest on route. Crossing here during ice breakup in spring can be spectacular as tons of ice drift downstream toward James Bay.

3:37 (0:43) MP 158. Cross Otakwahegan River.

3:39 (0:41) MP 159. Cross 51st Parallel.

3:40 (0:40) MP 160. Occasional temporary goose-hunting camps might be spotted through trees. Indians are permitted to hunt year round by aboriginal right.

3:44 (0:36) MP 162. Cross Cheepash River. Extensive gypsum deposits are nearby.

4:02 (0:18) MP 174. Cross Kwataboahegan River on second upside-down bridge.

Others will be at mileposts 176 and 180.

4:20 (0:00) MP 186. Arrive Moosonee, where "Sons of Martha" monument on right commemorates workers who built the Abitibi generating station and extension of railroad to Moosonee. Handsome church, farther to right, is Cathedral of the Oblates Mission.

MOOSONEE, ONT. - This is the northern terminus of the ONR. First impressions are not great, as the town has never fully entered the 20th century. Streets are either muddy, dusty or frozen, depending on the season. But the town has spirit and has been doing a lot to make things more attractive—new sidewalks, boardwalk at the docks, etc. All-terrain vehicles (ATVs) have been banned from the main streets to give tourists better use of the town. (Here, nearly everyone has at least one ATV.) Buildings range from neo-government to early ramshackle, but there is a certain fascination here. Perhaps it's the frontier.

Cree Indians are the major inhabitants, whose lifestyle reflects their long adaptation to living in this remote region. Government and tourism are the major economic mainstays, with the latter holding forth during a very limited season. It is a jumping-off point for hunters and others needing to head farther north toward the Arctic.

In the fall, the town bustles with goose hunters heading to various hunting camps, many such outposts being surprisingly posh and expensive. But Moose Factory Island is where most "tourists" go.

During the winter, the scene changes. This is when the ground (and the river) is frozen, making it possible to travel virtually anywhere by snowmobile. Indian villages north of here, inaccessible by land during the summer months, are reached by "The Winter Road" that consists of packed snow from hundreds of snowmobiles and ATVs. Instead of a time of confinement, it's a time of release.

If you plan to stay overnight, choices are quite limited. Be sure to make reservations well in advance if you plan to be here during the summer. For reservations for both hotels, call (416) 214-1495, or write Polar Bear Lodge, 65

Enterprise Rd., Rexdale, Ont. M9W 1C4.

-Polar Bear Lodge, Box 305, (P0L 1Y0); (705) 336-2345. Comfortable accommodations, with a good restaurant, looks out on the Moosonee River and boat docks, and is about ¾ mile from the station. Open all year. $76.

-Moosonee Lodge, Box 124, (P0L 1Y0); (705) 336-2351. Open mid-June to Labor Day. Also on the river and about 3/4 mile from the station. $76.

⭐⭐⭐ (Before starting out to explore the area, be sure to obtain an ONR guide booklet that describes the area and has a fold-out map.) In Moosonee a visit to the **Museum Car,** which stands across from the station, is easy to work into one's schedule. From there, it's about a half mile straight down First Street (which curves to the left) where the **boats dock.** Just beyond the docks, on the town side of the road, is **Revillon Frères Museum** with artifacts and photos of early Moosonee days.

At the docks, large Rupert House canoes offer an interesting adventure in reaching **Moose Factory,** situated in the Moosonee River. (ONR suggests buying a one-way fare, since there are many boats, and your return, therefore, can be at any time. They also suggest being at the dock for the return at least an hour before train time.) Guided tour boats are also available.

Once on the Moose Factory Island, there are numerous sights to explore. Highlights include: the **Centennial Park Museum,** operated by Ontario Northland Transportation Commission, which has displays explaining how the area was developed from the formation of the Hudson's Bay Company; **St. Thomas Church,** with its unique floor holes to allow floodwaters to enter, thus avoiding a recurrence of an episode when the church floated away; **Anglican Church Parish Hall** where local crafts can be purchased as well as light lunches and refreshments; and the **cemetery** with tombstones dating back to early traders and missionaries.

Hearst

Sault Ste. Marie

Algoma Central

To "ride in the tracks of the black bear," you have to get up early. At the Algoma Central Railway's Sault Ste. Marie ("The Soo") depot, boarding begins at 7:00 am, and it's wise, when you're one of a possible 1,200 planning to ride, to get aboard as soon as possible, especially if you have a family or group that wants to sit together. Usually, by 7:45 only scattered seats remain available.

The ACR's Agawa Canyon Tour train is very popular; some summers have seen more than 100,000 passengers boarding the silver coaches with maroon letter-boards and a black bear and his tracks on their flanks. ACR trains are clean, well-managed, and attractive. The mostly grey locomotives are splashed with a wide, deep-red stripe with yellow trim that is extremely eye-catching.

Incorporated in 1899, the ACR's route wound through dense forests and rugged hills and crossed many rivers and deep ravines. The first 56 miles of rail north of The Soo reached only 42 miles away! Its name at that time, the Algoma Central Hudson Bay Railway, or AC & HB, led some wags to call it the "All Curves and High Bridges."

Besides its most popular Agawa Canyon Tour Train, the ACR operates a Snow Train and its regular Soo-Hearst passenger trains.

Agawa Canyon Tour trains usually arrive back at The Soo on time at 5:00 pm with passengers so enthused about their "ride in the tracks of the black bear" (the former logo for this train) that they crowd shoulder-to-shoulder into the depot's interesting gift shop. Veterans of the trip advise shopping the day before when picking up tickets, preferably before that day's train arrives back at The Soo.

Frequency - Varies by train. Canyon Tours run from early June through mid-October. The Snow Train runs Saturdays and Sundays only from January through mid-March. The Regular Passenger Trains #1 and #2 operate six days a week from mid-May to mid-October, and weekends only the rest of the year (northbound Fri., Sat., Sun.; southbound Sat., Sun., Mon.).

Seating - Coaches only. ACR recommends picking up tickets a day in advance for all trains, even though reservations are available and required only for the Snow Train.

Dining - Varies by train. Dining cars, operated by E. J. Merini Catering, stay with the Canyon Tour and Snow Trains the entire trip, and provide hot breakfasts and lunches, as well as snacks and box lunches. Lunch is available on board Trains #1 and #2 between The Soo and Mile 120, Wednesday through Sunday.

Baggage - No service on Canyon Tour trains. But the regular trains provide baggage cars that carry an unbelievable variety of articles from fishing poles to snowmobiles.

Reservations - Write to: Algoma Central Railway, Passenger Sales, 129 Bay Street, Sault Ste. Marie, Ontario, Canada P6A 1W7. Or phone (705) 946-7300.

Length of Trip - 296 miles in 10 hours (Soo-Hearst).

Route Log

(A more detailed log of the route between Sault Ste. Marie and Canyon is furnished by ACR in its "Guide to Agawa Canyon Tour." Since mileposts are quite visible

Algoma Central Tour Train - Agawa Canyon, Ontario
DEN ADLER

on this route, they are shown below after the passing times. Since Trains #1 and #2 stop almost anywhere and everywhere, no attempt has been made to list all stops and times are approximate.)

SAULT STE. MARIE, ONT. - The ACR is heavily involved in the development of The Soo waterfront. It owns the Station Mall shopping center and the Holiday Inn overlooking the river, both near the depot. Tours of the Soo Locks are available nearby.

Algoma Central Railway Station, 129 Bay Street. An attractive, modern station near the Station Mall shopping center. Call 946-7300.

Get Soo area information from **Algoma Kinniwabi Travel Association,** 616 Queen St. E., Sault Ste. Marie, Ontario, Canada P6A 2A4, Phone (705) 254-4293.

Two good hotels are close to the station: the **Days Inn,** (705) 759-8200, $90, is two blocks; and the **Holiday Inn,** (705) 949-0611, $85, is about four blocks away. Both are near the Station Mall with shopping, restaurants and theaters. Somewhat farther from the station (seven blocks) and with lower rates, the **Northwest Inn,** (705) 942-1970, $38.

0:00 (3:30) Milepost 0. Depart The Soo from ACR's 1973 depot. Some of The Soo's more interesting sights appear in rapid succession on left: Canadian Lock, St. Mary Paper Mill with its Gothic-like structures, mile-long International Bridge and Algoma Steel Corporation.

0:39 (2:51) MP 19. Cross 810-foot-long, 100-foot-high trestle with a sweeping view of Bellevue Valley to left. Lake Superior can be glimpsed in far distance.

1:30 (2:00) MP 57. Idyllic Trout Lake is at right, with cabins and canoes adding woodland charm.

1:38 (1:52) MP 62. On right, boulder-strewn Pine Lake is one of trip's prettiest scenes.

2:20 (1:20) MP 81. Cross Batchewana River.

2:44 (0:46) MP 92. Curve right across Montreal River on ACR's most famous trestle, 130 feet high and 1,550 feet long. Below us to left, ground level drops another 100 feet below base of trestle where one of three dams generating electricity for The Soo is located.

2:52 (0:38) MP 97. Crest highest point on ACR, 1,589 feet above sea level.

3:06 (0:24) MP 102. Begin our descent to canyon floor: 500 feet in 12 miles. Terrific view to left, all the way to Lake Superior. Deep within canyon, Agawa River meanders prettily.

3:20 (0:10) MP 112. At canyon level, cross Agawa. Bridal Veil Falls appears to right, Black Beaver Falls to left.

3:30 (0:00) MP 114. Arrive at Canyon.

CANYON - This is the destination of the Agawa Canyon Tour Train. Here the crew switches the locomotives to the opposite end of that train in preparation for the return trip. The ACR's Guide provides detailed information about, and a map of, the canyon. It suggests planning activities for the two-hour layover before arrival—there's too much to see and do here in just one trip. (Trains #1 and #2 pause here, but not long enough for through passengers to detrain and see any of the sights.)

Things to do here include:

1. Picnic in the developed park near the train or farther away in a more rustic area. Several locations have water pumps.

2. Watch (or join) kids in the play area in the horseshoe pits or on swings, slides or an operating handcar on a set of tracks.

3. If you have the required license, fish the river for speckled trout.

4. View one or both waterfalls.

5. Walk up to the lookout points—the intermediate one is fairly easy to reach; the upper point requires a long climb up wooden stairs. But the view is spectacular, looking over the canyon, the river and the train. The Guide wisely recommends allowing at least 40 minutes for the round trip.

0:00 (1:24) MP 114. Depart Canyon.

0:06 (1:18) MP 117. River's descent is punctuated by series of lovely cascades and waterfalls, on right.

0:11 (1:13) MP 120. Cross notorious "Chinese Bridge," built by a Canadian manufacturer for Nationalist China. Firm had contract nullified by Chairman Mao when he came into power, so bridge was sold at a reduced price to an opportunistic Algoma Central.

0:16 (1:08) MP 123. Sign for Windy Lake Lodge identifies flag stop for fishermen in summertime and skiers in winter. Many backcountry hostelries are sprinkled along this stretch of ACR tracks to accommodate sportsmen who prefer their wilderness liberally laced with comfort.

0:31 (0:53) MP 132. At Millwood, large lumbering operation is on left.

1:00 (0:24) MP 149. Woods present nice stand of birch trees, at right. Similar in appearance to aspens, which are also found along route, birches are distinguished by their whiter-than-snow trunks. Spruce is a prevalent evergreen, while maple is a common hardwood.

1:10 (0:14) MP 157. Train experiences brief encounter with "outside" world as tracks cross Canada's Highway 101.

1:24 (0:00) MP 165. Arrive Hawk Junction.

HAWK JUNCTION, ONT. - There should be enough time to stretch for a few minutes at this Algoma Central division point. The ACR rail yards provide an interesting array of equipment—snowplows, cabooses, diesel locomotives—and long strings of red-painted baggage carts at trackside. If you ordered a hamburger, it will be waiting for you, probably warming on the hood of the cook's car by the station. (These burgers are really better than they sound.)

This is a jumping-off point for the old trappers' canoe route.

0:00 (3:24) MP 165. Depart Hawk Junction and head deeper into wilderness of Canadian Shield. Watch for moose, bear and white-tailed deer.

0:28 (2:56) MP 184. Dubreuilville is scene of bustling lumber operation, with conveyors, cranes, tracks and a wood burner all laboring at left.

0:45 (2:39) MP 195. At Franz, cross main line of CP Rail, route of VIA's Sudbury-White River triweekly rail diesel car service.

0:59 (2:25) MP 206. At Wabatong, note "Petticoat Junction" cottage by Lake Wabatongushi, on right.

1:05 (2:19) MP 210. Finger-like Oba Lake extends along tracks at left. Until now, waters have flowed to south. North of here, streams drain across Arctic Watershed north to Hudson Bay.

1:09 (2:15) MP 212. Cross portion of Lake Oba on quarter-mile-long bridge constructed not on a firm foundation, but on buoyant footings that literally float tracks on lake's surface.

1:14 (2:10) MP 215. Expansive body of water on left is Lake Tatnall.

1:49 (1:35) MP 245. Briefly merge with CN main line and yards at Oba. "The Last Resort" stands at right, presumably final home of retired wag. CN tracks carry VIA's transcontinental trains.

2:10 (1:14) MP 254. Moose rack over door of hunter's cabin, on left, is most appropriate decoration.

2:40 (0:44) MP 275. Mead is first town since Hawk Junction that has luxury of paved highway access.

3:11 (0:13) MP 296. After traveling north all day, train curls east and slows as it enters outskirts of Hearst.

3:23 (0:01) MP 295. Pass one of Hearst's numerous lumber mills, on left. Plywood industry has long been a Hearst mainstay.

3:24 (0:00) MP 296. Arrive Hearst.

HEARST, ONT. - If you visit Hearst in the summer or fall, it's a good idea to have reservations. This is a sportsman's haven with thousands of nearby lakes supplying outstanding fishing as well as excellent goose hunting. Just as important is big game hunting, particularly for moose that abound in this region. Snowmobiling on 130 miles of trails is also popular in the winter months.

Lumbering is the principal industry in this largely French-speaking community. Several large sawmills operate here, some offering tours.

The **station** is a small, efficient facility with CN markings but used by the Algoma Central. It is centrally located, directly behind two of the town's nicer motels and two blocks from George (Main) Street.

The Hearst trains are unreserved, and tickets are not sold until 7:45 am the day of departure. Credit cards are not accepted. (Although MasterCard and VISA are accepted by ACR at Sault Ste. Marie, they cannot be used at the Hearst station.) Call 362-4041.

Bus service is available to and from Kapuskasing, connecting to VIA's Northland.

The Queen's Motel, (705) 362-4361, is directly in front of the station and has large, comfortable rooms, a sauna and whirlpool, and an indoor pool. $52. The adjacent **Companion Motel,** (705) 362-4304, also has nice accommodations. It has a good restaurant and an interesting lounge filled with local color. $56.

White River   Sudbury

Sudbury to White River

White River is still served by VIA, but just barely. The Canadian was removed from the CPR line through White River in January of 1990, but VIA received a mandate to continue service to that town. As a result, rail diesel cars still make triweekly runs between Sudbury and White River. Trains depart Sudbury midmorning, Tuesday, Thursday and Saturday, and depart White River midmorning, Sunday, Wednesday and Friday. The trip takes approximately nine hours. There are numerous flag stops besides the scheduled stops shown.

Route Log

SUDBURY, ONT. - The town was founded in 1823 during the construction of the Canadian Pacific Railway, and it was during this activity that sufficient ore discoveries were made in order to induce serious mining. Today, Sudbury is the largest nickel-producing area in the world. The "Sudbury Basin" is a depression in the earth approximately 17 miles wide and 35 miles in length around which most of the mining activity is carried on by Inco Metals and Falconbridge.

Although geologists are unsure, many believe this basin was formed nearly two billion years ago when an enormous meteorite, several miles across, had a spectacular collision with the earth. The "irruptive" nickel which appears on the edges of the basin gives much of the countryside a lunar-surface appearance.

Geologic formations, including "shatter cones," are so unusually similar to features thought to exist on the moon that U.S. astronauts studied the area prior to their moon landings.

There are two **VIA Stations** in the Sudbury area. The CP station at 233 Elgin Street is a well-maintained facility on the edge of downtown, and now only serves the RDC service to White River. VIA's transcontinental train uses the CN station in nearby Capreol.

For reservations and other information, call 800-361-1235 (from Sudbury).

Cab stand at the CP station; Metro, 673-6000. **Greyhound,** on Falconbridge Highway, is about three miles from downtown. (Greyhound will discharge passengers downtown, about ¾ mile from the CP station.) The **airport** is several miles northeast of town.

The Sudbury Regional Development Corporation, 200 Brady St., P3E 5K3; (705) 673-4161.

Senator Hotel, 390 Elgin St., P3B 1B1; (705) 675-1273. Well-managed hotel with nice rooms and a very good restaurant. Some rooms overlook rail yards and station. Two blocks from the CP station. $60.

One of Sudbury's principal attractions is the **Big Nickel Mine** with half-hour tours. Also, smelter slag pourings each night are both erie and beautiful; call 682-2087 for times. **Science North** is the region's most popular place to visit, containing hands-on science exhibits.

0:00 (0:53) Departing Sudbury, Community Arena stands in forefront of downtown hub on right, while attractive residential district overlooks activity from atop bluffs on left.

0:02 (0:51) On right, many businesses use murals as clever means for advertising goods and services.

0:04 (0:50) Multi-domed St. Volodymyr Ukrainian Greek Orthodox Church on right is a most impressive example of Ukrainian Baroque architecture.

0:06 (0:48) On outskirts of town, train winds through small mini-canyons carved within rocky terrain. Nickel open-pit mines are a frequent observation throughout this stretch. Watch for molten slag being dumped.

0:10 (0:43) Pass through Azilda, named for first white woman settler in this region. Like many other small towns along route, Azilda is a flag stop where passengers may entrain or detrain when prior notice is given.

0:17 (0:35) Typical of most small Ontario communities, elegant church on left at Chelmsford is prominent centerpiece of town.

0:27 (0:27) Cross aptly named Vermilion River.

0:32 (0:23) Beautiful Onaping Falls tumble down by trackside on right.

0:35 (0:20) West of Levack, and continuing nearly to Winnipeg, route wends its way past myriad lakes, so numerous that individual identification would be impractical. At once a scenic wonderland of shimmering beauty, wetlands of Ontario are as well a recreation haven, with hunting and fishing camps nestled picturesquely along many shorelines. Famous Canadian moose is also a frequent visitor to these parts, often seen lumbering through neighboring marshes.

0:39 (0:16) More waterfalls embellish scenery on right.

0:47 (0:09) Beaver colonies, like those entrenched on right, are perhaps most intriguing architectural structures seen throughout lakelands.

0:55 (0:00) Arrive Cartier.

CARTIER, ONT. - A small settlement of about 1,500, named for Sir Etienne Cartier.

0:00 (3:16) Depart Cartier.

0:16 (3:00) Unusually large red weather vane atop shed makes wind-watching a breeze for residents of adjacent home, on left.

0:36 (2:37) Just past Sheahan, cross Spanish River which then follows on right.

0:55 (2:21) Names of many towns along route are derived from Indian geographic descriptions. One such example is found here at Metagama, which, when translated, means "river flows out of lake." Name refers to Spanish River which finds its source a few miles north in Biscotasi Lake.

1:20 (1:56) Ducks and geese are sometimes amusing attraction at Biscotasing, waddling about well-kept grounds of station house on right. Resort community is set atop hillside on left, overlooking arm of Biscotasi Lake. Weathered church is particularly picturesque.

1:44 (1:33) Large timber mill operation, on right at Ramsey, is one of first to be observed in countless succession of such facilities seen throughout Canada. While some enterprises harvest woodlands for lumber, pulping operations are much more prevalent, and represent one of country's most prodigious industries.

2:25 (0:56) On left, follow then cross Wakamagasing River, approaching quaint little town of Sultan.

3:00 (0:21) Cross Nemegosenda River just before passing through Nemegos.

3:14 (0:11) Apparently not designed for sleepwalkers, note island cabin, curiously isolated in midst of Lake Poulin on right.

3:15 (0:10) At Devon, freight chutes on right facilitate loading of wood chips—an important by-product of milling process, used in manufacture of particle board and paper pulp.

3:25 (0:00) Arriving Chapleau, finely preserved CPR steam locomotive, number 5453, is proud fixture of park on left.

CHAPLEAU, ONT. - Although logging is now Chapleau's main thrust, at one time this was the most important railroad town between Sudbury and Lake Superior. Solid bedrock of the Canadian Shield, when not protruding, is frequently only a foot or so below the surface, and construction of the Canadian

Pacific through this area was extremely difficult. Cuts were stubborn and lack of soil for fills was just as troublesome, with soil being shipped in for embankments. Furthermore, there were treacherous sink holes which would sometimes not make themselves known until after several trains had rumbled over them.

Besides logging, Chapleau is a hub of great fishing and hunting with good fly-in services available. Three provincial parks are within 50 miles of this attractive forest community. Next to the steam locomotive is Centennial Museum with natural history and pioneer exhibits, as well as the Rotary International Friendship Table which has wood inlays from around the world. On the station lawn is a monument to Louis Hemon, well known Canadian author, who died near here when struck by a train.

0:00 (3:07) Departing Chapleau, beautiful homes border edge of Kebsquasheshing Lake, both right and left.

0:14 (2:53) Sign at right indicates location of Chapleau Crown Game Preserve. Tracks form southern boundary of this park for several miles.

0:39 (2:28) "Encompassing waterfront vistas" would be appropriate advertisement for structure, half-submerged in Lake Windermere on left.

0:50 (2:17) Small red shack at right was once depot for Bolkow.

1:27 (1:40) Approaching Missanabie, cross arm of Dog Lake, one of region's largest. Once in town, note general store and old hotel huddled scenically along lake shore on left.

2:00 (1:10) Pass through picturesque community of Franz, tucked neatly in cove alongside Hobon Lake. Here, tracks of CP Rail cross those of legendary Algoma Central. Latter is known for spectacular autumn leaf excursions.

2:15 (0:57) Note dam on left as train crosses Magpie River. Structure was one of earlier hydro-power facilities in region.

3:09 (0:06) Join White River on left, then cross several times subsequently. As name might imply, surging falls and foamy rapids are common throughout its course.

3:15 (0:00) Arrive White River.

 WHITE RIVER, ONT. - This small village of 850 is situated at one of the few highway intersections in this region, making it a popular base for hunters and fishermen. Its weather station records some of the coldest temperatures in North America. The mercury once dipped to minus 72 degrees Farenheit— just 6 degrees above the Canadian record.

Continental Motel, Hwy 17; (807) 822-2500. Clean and inexpensive. About one and a half miles from the station. $49.

Canadian

It should be no surprise that a trip spanning the dominion of Canada on board the only transcontinental train in that country is a remarkable visual experience. Nearly every shape and form of Canada's interior beauty sweeps by on one of the longest train rides anywhere. (The longest ride of all shows you a lot of Siberia.) It's almost as though mountains, plains, lakes, rivers and forests were carefully positioned in dramatic sequence just to titillate those cruising on the Canadian.

But it's more than just scenery. VIA has performed a near-miracle in the restoration of the rail cars used on the Canadian. The new Silver & Blue™ class of service and accommodations offer one of the finest railroading experiences in the world.

From start to finish, the Canadian rolls across 3,000 miles of history, although no longer on its original routing. A transcontinental railroad was talked about in Canada as early as 1871, when suggestions of such a project were used to prop up negotiations to bring British Columbia into Confederation. And there was another incentive: Canada could ill-afford to ignore the 1869 golden-spike accomplishment of its neighbor to the south. Not without its detractors, the monumental effort finally began, almost casually at first, but with the appointment of William Cornelius Van Horne in 1881, construction pushed forward with resolve. The tortuous Rockies, the bitter Canadian winters, the locomotive-swallowing muskegs of Ontario, all were formidable adversaries. But on November 7, 1885 the last spike in the last section of track was ceremoniously tapped in at Craigellachie, British Columbia. The following year the railroad was ready, and the first trans-Canadian passenger train puffed out of Montreal on June 28, arriving at its western terminus of Port Moody on July 4. The line was the Canadian Pacific Railway Company, later abbreviated to CP Rail when it reorganized in 1971.

The first train was not called the Canadian, however. Early designations included Trans-Canada Ltd. and Dominion. The name Canadian wasn't bestowed until 1955 when what was then the world's longest dome train pulled out of Montreal, composed of streamlined, stainless steel cars built at Budd Company's Red Lion plant. (By the late 1960's, the train had reached its greatest length—22 cars, including ten sleepers and two diners.)

But another transcontinental line was soon added to compete with the CP. This new route was built by a collection of public and private railroading efforts in the early 1900s, taken over by the Canadian government and operated as the Canadian National Railway, now known as the CN. This more northern and more remote route avoided the muskegs along the top of Lake Superior and the arduous Kicking Horse Pass. The line went through Edmonton and Jasper before crossing Yellowhead Pass and curling southwest to Vancouver. It is this "second" transcontinental route that is now followed by the Canadian. The shift from the CP occurred January 15, 1990 when VIA's operations were severely curtailed and is still bemoaned by many Canadian rail travelers. (The new routing is that of the former Super Continental, many arguing that the Canadian is dead and the Super Continental has simply been renamed.)

Heading westward from Toronto, the Canadian encounters the lake-studded forests of Ontario's Canadian Shield country before a brief pause at Winnipeg. The route then angles across the ultra-flat expanses of Canada's wheatlands before reaching Edmonton, where soon thereafter, passengers get their first look at the Canadian Rockies—dead ahead. The ensuing trip through these giant bastions of western Canada is the crowning touch to a journey still ranked as one of the best of all travel experiences.

Westbound Schedule (Condensed)
Toronto, Ont. - Early Afternoon Departure (Tuesday, Thursday, Saturday)
Capreol (Sudbury), Ont. - Midevening
Winnipeg, Man. - Late Afternoon Arrival and Early Evening Departure (2nd Day)
Edmonton, Alta. - Early Morning (3rd Day)
Jasper, Alta. - Early Afternoon (3rd Day)
Kamloops, B.C. - Late Evening (3rd Day)
Vancouver, B.C. - Early Morning (4th Day) (Friday, Sunday and Tuesday)

Eastbound Schedule (Condensed)
Vancouver, B.C. - Midevening Departure (Thursday, Saturday, Monday)
Kamloops, B.C. - Early Morning (2nd Day)
Jasper, Alta. - Early Afternoon (2nd Day)
Edmonton, Alta. - Midevening (2nd Day)
Winnipeg, Man. - Early Afternoon (3rd Day)
Capreol (Sudbury), Ont. - Early Afternoon (4th Day)
Toronto, Ont. - Midevening (5th Day) (Thursday, Sunday, Tuesday)

Frequency - Three times each week (see above).
Seating - Standard coaches, and Park dome cars.
Dining - Dining car with complete meal and beverage service.
Sleeping - Sleeping cars with berths (sections), roomettes and bedrooms. Sleeping cars have a shower in each car.
Baggage - Checked baggage handled at most stops.
Reservations - All-reserved train.

Length of Trip - 2,765 miles, taking approximately three days.

Route Log

 TORONTO, ONT. - See page 360.
0:00 (0:46) Depart Toronto.

A departure note. The train must leave heading east before curling north and then west into MacMillan Yard. From here, it must back into the Newmarket subdivision at Snyder where it is finally in position to proceed northward to Newmarket, Barrie and Orillia. This process takes about one hour. Arrivals by the Canadian at Toronto are a simple direct approach from the north and west without all the time-consuming maneuvering.

Times shown between here and Newmarket are for eastbound (Toronto-bound) trains only.
--- (0:45) CN Tower, world's tallest free-standing structure at 1,821 feet, soars skyward on right.
--- (0:44) $400-million SkyDome, on right, overshadows lower downtown Toronto. This bulbous edifice, completed in 1989, was built to house baseball's Blue Jays, shops, restaurants and a 350-room hotel. On nicer days, roof can be retracted to an open position in 30 minutes to put 90% of its spectators in sunshine. While passing this stupendous coliseum, be sure to look up to see whimsical groupings of "spectators" protruding from building like modern-day gargoyles.
--- (0:42) Tops of brick buildings and sign on grassy knoll are all that can be seen of Historic Fort York Park, on right. Park features restored British garrison from War of 1812.
--- (0:36) General Electric's Chemical Materials Division Plant #3 is on right.
--- (0:17) Final look at Toronto's skyline is afforded back on right.
1:12 (0:00) Arrive Newmarket.

NEWMARKET, ONT. - Its proximity to Toronto and the rich agricultural lands that surround it make Newmarket an important regional trading center. Of particular interest is the town's historic Quaker Meeting House.
0:00 (0:31) Departing Newmarket, for-

393

mer leather works has been elegantly transformed into The Old Davis Tannery Centre shopping mall, adorned with purple awnings and a wonderful four-faced clock tower, on right.

0:01 (0:30) In early 1900s Canadian Government planned to make Newmarket a Great Lakes port by converting Little Holland River into a canal connecting with Lake Simcoe. Although plan was ultimately aborted, locks on right still survive.

0:31 (0:00) Arrive Barrie with Kempenfelt Bay, an arm of Lake Simcoe, at right.

BARRIE, ONT. - This commercial center of 35,000 is situated on the shores of Kempenfelt Bay, the western arm of giant Lake Simcoe. Barrie is home to the Base Borden Military Museum with its unusually large collection of military memorabilia, and the Simcoe County Museum and Archives devoted to tracing the history of man in this area.

0:00 (0:25) Depart Barrie.

0:01 (0:24) In small park at right, 4-6-0 CN steam locomotive 1531 has been lovingly preserved.

0:02 (0:23) Modernistic work of metal art, on right, appears to be contemplating flight.

0:03 (0:22) Unusual archway spans city street in downtown Barrie, on left.

0:06 (0:19) Numerous small watercraft are docked at marina, on right, creating pleasant maritime scene.

0:22 (0:03) Large complex of brick buildings, attractively ensconced on hillside left, is Huronia Regional Centre, an institution that houses and works with the handicapped.

0:25 (0:00) Arrive Orillia.

ORILLIA, ONT. - This town of 24,000 is situated on the Trent-Severn Canal System, and has an economy maintained by light industrial activities. Stephen Leacock, Canada's foremost humorist, wrote many of his works while living here, and his home, a 19-room lakeshore mansion, can be toured by the public.

0:00 (0:16) Depart Orillia.

0:04 (0:12) Train creeps across swing bridge spanning Trent-Severn Waterway. This 1,006-mile marine system, comprised of rivers, canals and lakes, snakes across Ontario countryside linking Lake Ontario with Georgian Bay. Like Erie Canal, commercial traffic has all but disappeared from its waters while recreational use has blossomed and now dominates.

0:16 (0:00) Slip past old concrete water tower, at right, on arrival Washago.

WASHAGO, ONT. - Nicely situated at the very northern tip of Lake Couchiching, an adjunct to larger Lake Simcoe, Washago comes from a similar Indian word meaning "sparkling waters."

0:00 (1:42) Depart Washago.

0:14 (1:28) Lakeside resort on right often has seaplanes parked in easy view of tracks.

1:00 (0:42) Expansive waters of Lake Joseph are now on right.

1:32 (0:08) Stop momentarily while train switches from CP line to tracks of CN.

1:41 (0:01) Canadian rumbles high above Seguin River on lengthy trestle (1,695 feet). Parry Sound is off to left while town of same name comes into view on right.

1:42 (0:00) Arrive Parry Sound.

PARRY SOUND, ONT. - Excellent fishing, swimming, hunting and boating have made this Georgian Bay community of 5,000 a very popular destination resort area. This is the main access to that area known as 30,000 Islands, the world's largest concentration of islands, which are situated along the shore of the Bay—an eastern satellite of Lake Huron.

0:00 (2:07) Depart Parry Sound on CN tracks.

0:40 (2:30) Cross Shawanaga River.

1:00 (2:10) Cross Magnetawan River.

2:00 (1:10) Cross French River, once a major canoe route between Lake Superior and Montreal.

3:00 (0:10) Black rock outcroppings and white-barked birch trees create bizarre landscape on approach to Sudbury Junction.

Millions of years ago, an enormous meteorite slammed into the earth's crust, forming a gouge some 35 miles in length and exposing rich deposits of nickel and other ores. During the construction of the railroad in the 1800s, these deposits were finally discovered in what is now known as the Sudbury Basin. Sudbury is now the world's largest producer of nickel; the large stack visible in the distance to the left belongs to Inco's smelter and is the world's tallest at 1,250 feet.

Over the years, acid rain from the smoke of Sudbury's mining operations has largely denuded the immediate landscape, but more recent environmental technologies have improved the local scene. As a matter of fact, Sudbury boasts some of the region's finest flower gardens.

3:10 (0:00) Arrive Sudbury Junction.

 SUDBURY JCT., ONT. - This is a brief stop in Sudbury's outskirts. For a description of Sudbury, see page 389.

0:00 (0:32) Depart Sudbury Junction, and skim past eastern edge of greater Sudbury.

0:30 (0:00) Arrive Capreol.

 CAPREOL, ONT. - This is another station used for Sudbury area passengers. Capreol is just a few miles north of downtown Sudbury.

0:00 (0:54) Depart Capreol.

Over the next several miles, the geography becomes increasingly alpine in nature. Rolling hills assume more rugged, angular features, while clusters of evergreens stand tall amidst a thicketed ground cover. Various species of pine, oak and ash, as well as tamarack, balsam, fir, white spruce, birch and hemlock are found in the Great Lakes Forest Region.

Geographic features encountered are characteristic of the Canadian Shield, with extensive lake systems and dense forests nurtured by soil that thinly covers bedrock. This bedrock is 500 million to 5 billion years old and covers one half of Canada as well as portions of the northern U.S. Muskegs (peat bogs) are abundant. Minerals are found throughout the region and mining is still prominent. Many ancient glacial lakes have gradually filled in with clay, creating rich agricultural areas. Approximately one sixth of Ontario (an Iroquois word which could mean "beautiful lake") is covered by fresh water lakes—nearly a half million of them.

0:01 (0:53) Cross very pretty Vermilion River which will accompany route beyond Laforest.

0:54 (0:00) Arrive Laforest.

 LAFOREST, ONT. - This settlement is typical of many found along the railroads through this section of Ontario—small, isolated (no road access) and devoted to a frontier existence. At one time, schooling for children living in these remote reaches was provided by portable "schoolhouses" that consisted of a specially equipped and staffed rail car that would be towed into town by train, left on a siding for a few days, then moved on to the next village.

0:00 (0:55) Depart Laforest.

0:12 (0:43) On right, Key's Camp is just one of many hunting and fishing camps that dot CN's route through this lake country. Colorful canoes add charm to this woodland setting.

0:27 (0:28) Ruel Shoo-Fly Camp is another sportsman's retreat.

0:55 (0:00) Arrive Westree.

WESTREE, ONT. - This is one of the smaller stops, population 10 (more or less).

0:00 (0:30) Depart Westree.

0:18 (0:12) Cross Muskegoma River on 850-foot trestle.

0:19 (0:11) While birch and aspen forests give way to their coniferous relatives, pine and fir; the terrain continues rocky and marshy.

0:29 (0:01) Minisinakwa Lake is on left.

0:30 (0:00) Cross Minisinakwa River and arrive Gogama.

GOGAMA, ONT. - This good-size town (over 600 population) has avoided isolation by situating just off the main highway between Timmins and Sudbury.

0:00 (1:26) Depart Gogama.

0:04 (1:22) Cross Timmins-Sudbury highway.

0:06 (1:20) Cross broad waters of Macaming River.

1:26 (0:00) Arrive Foleyet.

FOLEYET, ONT. - A lumbering community, located on the Timmins-White River highway and the Ivanhoe River, Foleyet is host to numerous moose hunters during the fall. Bear and other game are also found in the region.

0:00 (0:48) Depart Foleyet.

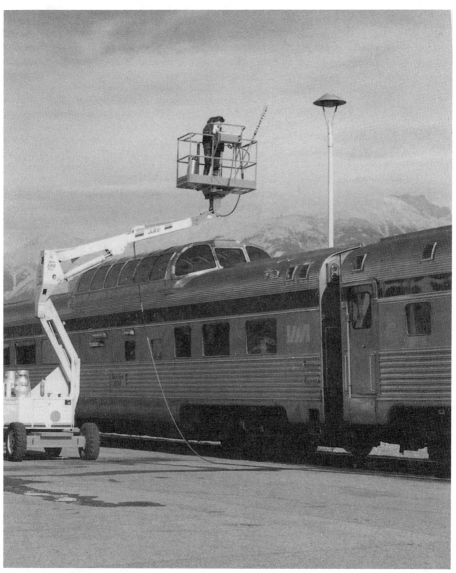

Canadian - Jasper, Alberta
DORIS SWANSON

0:48 (0:00) Arrive Elsas.

ELSAS, ONT. - Elsas is a tiny, remote forest outpost, nicely ensconsed on Kapuskasing (accent the first and third syllables) Lake. It seems half the town meets the baggage car to receive or send some sort of freight—boxes of french fries, furniture, a dog or two, the mail pouch.

0:00 (1:28) Depart Elsas along northern edge of immense Chapleau Game Preserve—one of world's largest.

0:02 (1:26) Nice view of Lake Kapuskasing is afforded on left.

0:50 (0:38) Cross Fire River.

1:00 (0:28) Cross Lower Minnipuka Lake.

1:28 (0:00) Merge with tracks of Algoma Central upon arrival Oba.

OBA, ONT. — Oba's claim to fame is its location on the intersection of the Algoma Central Railway with the CN tracks. The Algoma Central connects Sault Ste. Marie, 245 miles to the south, with Hearst just 51 miles to the north. The line penetrates the spectacular Algoma Canyon, and excursion trains out of Sault Ste. Marie are extremely popular during the height of fall color.

0:00 (0:41) Depart Oba.

0:12 (0:29) Cross Kabinakagami River, another stream whose waters ultimately reach Hudson Bay.

0:27 (0:14) Cross Shekak River.

0:32 (0:09) Sawmill, at left, is one of but many along this stretch of right-of-way.

0:41 (0:00) Arrive Hornepayne.

HORNEPAYNE, ONT. - This is the first town since Capreol that resembles a 20th-century community. Nearly 2,000 people live here, and the city has a city-center building, visible from the train, that houses schools, stores, athletic facilities and various city services.

0:00 (1:00) Depart Hornepayne.

1:00 (0:00) Arrive Hillsport.

HILLSPORT, ONT. - This community of 80 is another town devoted to lumbering.

0:00 (0:45) Depart Hillsport.

0:45 (0:00) Arrive Caramat.

CARAMAT, ONT. - Caramat is nicely situated on a small lake by the same name.

0:00 (0:25) Depart Caramat.

0:24 (0:01) Large pole-producing mill is on immediate left.

0:25 (0:00) Arrive Longlac.

LONGLAC, ONT. - This forest products oriented town anchors the northern tip of 44-mile-long Long Lake, once an important canoe route that was part of a thriving fur trade. Plywood plants are now the community's principal employers.

0:00 (0:39) Depart Longlac.

0:39 (0:00) Arrive Nakina.

NAKINA, ONT. - This is a major outfitting center for sportsmen who hunt and fish the region. Like the other communities along the route, Nakina was nurtured by the building of the railroad. The line from here to Armstrong was constructed by the National Transcontinental Railway and was opened on June 1, 1915. That same enterprise built the line from here to Longlac in 1923.

0:00 (1:34) Depart Nakina, as lakes grow more sparse.

1:15 (0:19) Note fire lookout tower off to left.

1:28 (0:06) Crossing Jackfish Creek on 798-foot-long, 74-foot-high trestle, look to left for view of northernmost waters of Lake Nipigon.

1:34 (0:00) Arrive Ferland.

FERLAND, ONT. - Just to the south of this lumbering hamlet is aforementioned Lake Nipigon, Ontario's largest body of water. It stretches 60 miles from north to south and bulges to 40 miles across at its widest point.

0:00 (0:46) Arrive Ferland.

0:07 (0:39) Cross Mud River on 60-foot-high trestle.

0:46 (0:00) Arrive Armstrong.

ARMSTRONG, ONT. - This forest outpost of 600 is yet another community closely tied to both the railroad and the timber industry. However, unlike so many towns along the CN route, it is not reached solely by rail. It's possible to drive 150 miles straight south and reach the Great Lakes port city of Thunder Bay.

0:00 (10:00) Depart Armstrong.

Both westbound and eastbound trains are scheduled to cross the stretch of tracks between here and Minaki, Ontario during darkness. Stops are made at **SAVANT LAKE, SIOUX LOOKOUT, RED LAKE ROAD** and **REDDITT** as well as numerous flag stops.

Gain one hour as train passes from Eastern to Central Time. Set your watch back (forward if eastbound) one hour.

10:00 (0:00) Cross Winnipeg River and note fine old lodge in distance. Arrive Minaki.

MINAKI, ONT. - Scenic Gun Lake is just to the south of Minaki, where the Minaki Lodge, the structure visible off to the left when entering town from the east, once hosted weekenders that arrived here from Winnipeg by special excursion trains. Originally a CN hostelry, the lodge still operates, having been remodeled by the province of Ontario.

0:00 (2:15) Depart Minaki.

0:05 (2:10) Lakes abound and scenery becomes more attractive than ever.

0:21 (1:54) Through hamlet of Malachi as Lake Malachi, on left, routinely treats villagers to a stunning view.

0:30 (1:45) Note waterfall to right.

0:33 (1:42) Cross into Manitoba, boundary being readily identified by marker on right. We have just entered Whiteshell Provincial Park, a dreamland for canoe paddlers.

1:10 (1:05) Cross main line of CP Rail and former route of the Canadian. Route now runs straight as an arrow directly west toward Winnipeg.

1:25 (0:50) Through Elma, as countryside turns more pastoral. Farms through here were originally 160-acre homesteads granted by government.

2:00 (0:15) Country is now all farming and flat as a pancake, as prairies take over.

2:15 (0:00) Cross Red River Floodway on 903-foot viaduct as train arrives at Transcona.

 TRANSCONA, MAN. - This is an eastern Winnipeg suburban stop.

0:00 (0:17) Depart Transcona; Winnipeg's downtown skyline is directly ahead.

0:13 (0:04) Cross 55 feet above Seine River.

0:15 (0:02) Cross Red River.

0:17 (0:00) Arrive Winnipeg's CN Station.

 WINNIPEG, MAN. - In 1738 the French explorer Gaultier built Fort Route on the present site of Winnipeg. It wasn't until 1812, however, that a permanent settlement was established when Selkirk Settlors (led by Lord Selkirk) arrived and settled along the banks of the Red River, land which was granted to them by the Hudson's Bay Company.

In 1835, the Hudson's Bay Company, whose home offices are now in Winnipeg, built Fort Garry to further protect its fur-trading activities. Then in 1881, with the arrival of the Canadian Pacific Railway, Winnipeg became a major center of rail-road activity.

Agricultural lands attracted various immigrant nationalities in the early 1900s, which gave the town its first real growth and assured its permanence. Today, it is not only the oldest city in the prairie provinces of Manitoba and Saskatchewan, it is also the largest with 600,000 residents. It is the capital of Manitoba.

VIA Station, 123 Main Street, on the edge of downtown, is a handsome structure designed by Warren and Wetmore, architects of New York's Grand Central Terminal. It has a sizeable waiting room, snack bar, snack and beverage vending machines, gift shop, barbershop and storage lockers. A new, attractive ticketing area has been installed and an interesting model railroad display by the Winnipeg Model Railway Club is just off the main lobby. There is pay-parking.

For reservations and information call 800-561-8630. Call 944-8780 for arrivals and departures.

Both **cabs** and **local buses** are at the front of the station. Unicity Taxi, 947-6611; Duffy's Taxi, 775-0101. There is a **cab phone** just inside the station entrance. For **rental car** pick up and deliver at station, call Avis, 989-7521. **Winnipeg International Airport** is approximately four miles west of downtown.

Tourism Winnipeg, 232-375 York Ave., R3C 3J3; (204) 943-1970.

Gordon Downtowner Motor Hotel, 330 Kennedy St., R3B 2M6; (204) 943-5581. Extra large, bright and attractive rooms on the northwest edge of downtown. Thirteen blocks from the station. $49.

-**Quality Inn Downtown,** 367 Ellice Ave., R3B 1Y1; (204) 956-0100. Recently remodeled, located on edge of downtown across from Portage Place. 12 blocks from the station. $63.

-**Charter House Hotel,** 330 York Ave., R3C 0N9; (204) 942-0101. Handsome rooms in a central location. Six blocks from the station. $53.

-**Hotel Fort Garry,** 222 Broadway, R3C 0R3; (204) 942-8251 or 800-665-8088. Historic hostelry, recently restored to its original luxurious state. Formal casino gambling. One block from the station. $79.

Winnipeg

Some of Winnipeg's downtown points of interest, all walkable by the energetic, include: **Dalnavert,** 61 Carlton St., a restored Victorian home of the son of Canada's first prime minister; **The Forks Market,** behind the station at the junction of the Assiniboine and Red rivers, a delightful river park setting for food, shops and galleries; the **Legislative Building,** Broadway and Kennedy, one of North America's more beautiful public buildings with colorful flower gardens; the **Manitoba Museum of Man and Nature (and Planetarium),** 190 Rupert Ave., has excellent sub-Arctic exhibits, including polar bears, northern lights, the railroad to Churchill and Churchill itself (a must before visiting that remote town). The **planetarium** has programs year-round; and **Portage Place,** on N. Portage Ave., spans three blocks and contains 150 shops, restaurants, offices and movie theaters, including an IMAX large-screen movie system. Its centerpiece is a restored clock from the Old City Hall, and contains a 20-bell carillon.

Railfans (and others as well) will enjoy the **Prairie Dog Central** steam train that offers a 36-mile (two-hour) trip to Grosse-Isle from the CNR St. James Station, 1661 Portage Ave., just west of St. James St., Sundays, June through September; (204) 832-5259.

0:00 (0:57) Depart Winnipeg.
0:01 (0:56) Forks Market area and Forks National Historic Park come into view, below left.
0:03 (0:54) Cross Assiniboine River near its juncture with Red River. Waters will ultimately flow north into Lake Winnipeg.
0:06 (0:51) On right, ornate dome is distinctive feature of Winnipeg's Legislative Building.
0:34 (0:23) An interesting two-story depot on right and an old church on left are highlights through Elie. On western edge of town, cross Milk River, with neighborhoods of gracious homes lining its banks.
0:51 (0:06) At Nattress, cross Assiniboine River.
0:57 (0:00) Arrive Portage la Prairie.

PORTAGE LA PRAIRIE, MAN. - Literally translated as "prairie portage," the city is situated at the narrowest point between the Assiniboine River and Lake Manitoba. This spot once served as a resting point for both Indians and early settlers transporting their canoes between these two important waterways.

A fort was established at this strategic site in 1738, and from 1867 to 1868, the town held the distinction of being capital of the "Republic of Manitobah." Today, it remains a transportation hub of the prairies, with the CN and CP rail lines making a unique prairie intersection, while the Trans-Canada and Yellowhead highways join here.

0:00 (1:04) Depart Portage la Prairie where our CN tracks gradually swing to right away from CP main line that continues on to Calgary.
0:07 (0:57) Glide across large depression which carries excess waters of Assiniboine River during those unusual moments when it is in flood stage.
0:12 (0:52) Landscape cannot get any flatter as CN tracks now reach across floor of ancient lake bed.
1:04 (0:00) Arrive Brandon North, where what has to be VIA's smallest station awaits on left. Not much larger than a playhouse, depot is actually complete with benches.

BRANDON NORTH, MAN. - This northern "suburb" stop serves the town of Brandon, a few miles off to left.

0:00 (0:14) Departing Brandon, someone has used old wagon on right to wish passengers a nice day.
0:04 (0:10) Indeed, you can ski Manitoba! On ridge in distance to left is winter sports area known as Glenorky Ski Resort.
0:13 (0:01) A 684-foot trestle carries us 90 feet over waters of Little Saskatchewan River. Look back to right to see spillway of dam momentarily delaying river's journey southward to its juncture with Assiniboine.
0:14 (0:00) Arrive Rivers.

RIVERS, MAN. - Named for the president of the Grand Trunk Railway, this town is but one of many wheat-oriented communities of Manitoba.

0:00 (2:12) Departing Rivers, watch for hangar-like buildings in several communities along this route which house both hockey and curling rinks.
0:35 (1:37) Train is now cruising along a mesa top, with nice view of Assiniboine River twisting and turning through valley below.
0:39 (1:33) Cross Minnewashtack Creek on trestle over 1,500 feet in length.
0:43 (1:29) Trestle carries us high over Birdtail Creek.
1:11 (1:01) After milepost 213, watch for signs on both sides of track which pinpoint Manitoba-Saskatchewan border. From here on, landscape will begin to flatten more and more as we move westward.
1:14 (0:58) Large potash mine can be seen on left across valley. Mineral is used for manufacture of fertilizer.
1:29 (0:43) Rumble across trestle high above Cutarm River.
1:30 (0:42) Two more potash plants come into view, attesting to region's wealth of this mineral, one on left and another in distance right.
1:37 (0:35) Yet another potash plant can be seen off to right.

2:11 (0:01) Passing through extensive rail yards of Melville, note quaint onion-domed church to right.
2:12 (0:00) Arrive Melville.

 MELVILLE, SASK. - One of the larger towns along the route, Melville is a rail division point. Notice enclosed hockey rink just behind town's rather attractive, chalet-style depot.
0:00 (2:19) Depart Melville.
0:23 (1:56) Two churches in Goodeve are particularly eye-catching, one single-domed and one with two domes.
0:31 (1:48) Ukrainian influence is apparent in this part of Saskatchewan. Note Mosque-appearing church in Hubbard on right.
0:47 (1:32) Here is another church with Ukrainian flavor as we pass through town of Jasmine.
1:04 (1:15) Seemingly in middle of nowhere, a horse track and arena suddenly appear.
1:17 (1:02) Hills on either side of us are Touchwood Hills, named after dead poplar trees which make excellent firewood.
1:59 (0:20) Cross over Peter Lake at milepost 101.
2:10 (0:09) Now pass over much larger Boulder Lake.
2:19 (0:00) Arrive Watrous.

WATROUS, SASK. - This town actually has motels, the first we've seen for some time. This is a resort community with hot mineral springs four miles north of here and which the Indians believed had unusual curing properties.
0:00 (0:59) Depart Watrous.
0:11 (0:48) Lake Manitou fills depression on right.
0:19 (0:40) Through Zelma where potash mine is visible on horizon right.
0:26 (0:33) At Alan, huge potash mine and what must be world's largest Quonset hut create impressive industrial scene off to right.
0:33 (0:26) Silver domed and shed-like buildings, on left, are distribution center for Engrow agricultural fertilizer.
0:50 (0:09) Crossing South Saskatchewan River, skyline of Saskatoon is prominent on horizon right, while three-stacked Queen Elizabeth Power Station is at left.

0:59 (0:00) Just before arriving Saskatoon, cross the South Saskatchewan River.

SASKATOON, SASK. - Located on the prairies of Saskatchewan, it is the second largest city in the province with a metropolitan population of nearly a quarter-million. Founded in 1882 as a temperance colony, it has grown to prominence not only as a center of one of the richest agricultural regions of Canada, but more recently as a vital, fast growing center of "clean" industry. Numerous national and international organizations are locating operations here, including Hitachi which selected Saskatoon for its first plant outside of Japan. It is sometimes referred to as the "City of Bridges" due to the large number that cross the South Saskatchewan River here.

VIA Station, Chappell Dr., is located four miles west of downtown. An attractive facility with terrazo floors, spacious. There are storage lockers and some vending machines. Free parking is adjacent to the station.

For reservations and other information, call 800-665-8630.

Cab stand is at the station; United Cabs, 652-2222. United Cabs also has **limo service to and from downtown. Tilden car rentals** are downtown, 652-3355. Nearest **local bus** stop is four blocks from the station (bus trip into town involves a transfer). **Saskatoon Airport** is approximately eight miles north of the station.

Saskatoon Visitor and Convention Bureau, 102 310 Idylwyld Dr. N., Box 369, S7K 3L3, (306) 242-1206.

Park Town Hotel, 924 Spandia Cr. E., S7K 3H5; (306) 244-5564. Renovated in 1990. Large, near-elegant rooms with river and university views available. Three or four blocks from downtown. Five miles from the station. $60.

-**Sheraton Cavalier,** 612 Spandia Cres. E., S7K 3G9; (306) 652-6770. Very tasteful rooms in a downtown location, two blocks from shopping. Five miles from the station. $88.

-**Senator Hotel,** 243-21st St. E., S7K 0B7; (306) 244-6141. Built in early 1890s, but rooms very serviceable. Near the center of town. For the economy minded. $37.

The Mendel Art Gallery and Civic Conservatory is located at 950 Spandia Crescent East, on the west bank of the South Saskatchewan River, just a short walk from the business district. The gallery has permanent Canadian paintings and sculpture, as well as local, national and international shows.

Midtown Plaza is a delightfully executed downtown shopping mall, much of which is located in the old CNR station.

The **Ukrainian Museum of Canada,** 910 Spandia Cres. E., is one of Canada's finest ethnographic museums. Outstanding exhibits include ceramics, costumed dolls, Easter eggs (pysanky), a history of Ukrainian settlement in Canada and one of the finest textile collections in North America.

0:00 (1:10) Depart Saskatoon.
0:13 (0:57) On right, former station at Gandora now serves as a private home.
1:10 (0:00) Arrive Biggar, where sign at station platform proclaims "New York is big, but this is Biggar."

BIGGAR, SASK. - Biggar is smaller than most towns with three museums. Biggar Museum and Gallery tells the story of the area's settlement. The Homestead Museum features a pioneer home, rural schoolhouse, general store and sod home, while five miles east Kisser's Western Relics Museum indeed displays Western relics.
0:00 (1:14) Depart Biggar.
1:14 (0:00) Arrive Unity.

UNITY, SASK. - This small prairie community has its own salt plant that offers tours allowing visitors to see how a variety of salt products are manufactured.
0:00 (1:15) Depart Unity.
0:30 (0:45) Large Manitou Lake off to right is notable for its good-sized island in its middle.
0:40 (0:35) Leave Alberta and enter Saskatchewan. Provincial border is marked by sign at right.

Leave Central Standard Time and enter Mountain Time.
0:50 (0:09) Cross Ribstone Creek (three times).
1:15 (0:00) Arrive Wainwright.

WAINWRIGHT, ALTA. - Wainwright Canadian Forces base is just southwest of this Alberta community. Petroleum production has also been an economic mainstay.
0:00 (0:50) Depart Wainwright.
0:10 (0:40) Train now makes an airy crossing of impressive Battle River which lies some 200 feet below. Steel trestle is nearly 3,000 feet in length.
0:40 (0:10) Numerous sink holes throughout this area provide good habitat for migrating waterfowl, including Canadian geese. These small ponds now dot landscape on both sides of tracks.
0:50 (0:00) Arrive Viking.

VIKING, ALTA. - The name of this Alberta farming community reflects its Scandanavian heritage. Nearby quartzite rocks, carved by Cree Indians, are thought to relate to buffalo fertility rites.
0:00 (1:20) Depart Viking.
0:13 (1:07) Russian Orthodox Church, with its silver and white onion-shaped dome, is architectural jewel of Holden, across small lake on right.
0:25 (0:55) Small red grain elevator on left serves as statement of sorts. Instead of "Alberta Pool," west side has been enscribed "Dirty Shorts."
0:32 (0:48) Huge Beaver Lake can be spotted in distance to right.
0:43 (0:37) Now, large Cooking Lake is on left.
1:06 (0:14) After passing through yards at Clover Bar, cross Saskatchewan River where refineries are most evident on fringe of Edmonton.
1:14 (0:06) Sizeable coliseum on left is home to National Hockey League's Edmonton Oilers. Just to west of coliseum, with numerous flagpoles, is Edmonton Northland where numerous public events are held, including Klondike Days, trade shows, Farm Fair, etc. Even weddings are occasionally booked here.
1:16 (0:04) Edmonton's professional football team, the Eskimos, uses larger stadium on immediate right.
1:20 (0:00) Arrive Edmonton.

EDMONTON, ALTA. - Edmonton has a shopping mall like Crocodile Dundee has a knife. Totally intimidating any would-be competitors, it's the largest in the world. It has twice the stores, half-again as many employees, nearly triple the number of parking spaces and it cost twice as much as the newer Mall of America in Minneapolis/St. Paul. A super-extravaganza that has to be seen to be believed, with stores and more stores (there are over 40 shoe stores alone), it has its own amusement-park attractions that include three roller coasters, a floating replica of the Mayflower (complete with submarine rides around its perimeter), a nifty theme hotel and a beach with surf—all under one immense roof. And some people even go to the Mall just to shop.

With such a dynamo on the west edge of town, it would seem Edmonton's downtown area might wither, even though the town is the provincial capital. This has not happened. The downtown has its own delightful shopping malls, a modern subway and enclosed pedestrian walkways that keep the city vibrant—both day and night, summer and winter.

VIA Station, 1004-104 Ave. in the CN Tower at 100 Street, constructed in the 1960s as part of an urban development project, has an unusual circular interior design with a gift shop, snack stand, storage lockers and pay-parking. (There are free luggage carts, but they have limited usefulness since they can't be taken up the escalators to the train platforms.)

For reservations and information, call 800-561-8630.

Cab stand and **local buses** are at the station. Yellow Cab, 462-3456; Checker Cabs, 455-2211. For **LRT (Subway)** and other transit information, call 421-4636. **Subway** is free within the downtown area and runs along Jasper Avenue and 99 Street. Nearest subway stop is Churchill Station, two blocks away on 99 Street. For **rental cars,** Thrifty has free city pick up and delivery, 428-8555. The **airport** is 17 miles southwest of the city.

Visitor Information Center, Edmonton Convention & Tourism Authority, 9797 Jasper Ave., No. 104, T5J 1N9; (403) 422-5505.

 Quality Inn Downtown, 10209 -100 Ave., T5J 0A1; (403) 428-6442. Small motel in good location. Seven blocks from the station. $59.

-Edmonton House, 10205-100 Ave., T5J 4B5; (403) 424-5555. An all-suite hotel with spacious rooms and lots of extras: pool, exercise room, ping pong, sauna and covered parking. Courtesy shuttle to and from West Edmonton Mall. Six blocks from the station. $72.

-Hotel Macdonald, 10065 - 100 Street, T5J 0N6; (403) 424-5181 or 800-828-7447 (U.S.). A city landmark since 1915, this chateau-style structure was completely renovated by the Canadian Pacific Hotels at a cost of $20 million and reopened in 1991. Five blocks from the station. $129.

-Fantasyland Hotel & Resort, at West Edmonton Mall, 17700-87 Ave., T5T 4V4; (403) 444-3000 or 800-661-6454. For a real splurge, ask for the Canadian Rail Room (there are five) complete with railroad berths, jacuzzi, operational signal crossing, domed ceiling, clocks displaying time zones, and more—all in utter elegance. Or ask about other theme rooms. $190 for Canadian Rail Room. $118 for standard rooms.

Within walking distance, shopping is available at the **Eaton Center,** including miniature golf and movies, just three blocks from the station, at 101 St. and 102 Ave. Across 101 St. is the **Edmonton Center** with still more shops and restaurants. The **Provincial Museum of Alberta,** 12845-102 Ave., has worthwhile nature and cultural exhibits. If you should be in Edmonton on a Saturday during the warmer months, a real treat is the city **market** at 102 Ave. and 97 St., with farmers' produce, flowers, fish and crafts.

The **Alberta Railroad Museum,** 24215 - 34 St., is western Canada's largest railroad museum. And, of course, for more shopping and sheer fun, there's the **West Edmonton Mall** described in the introduction above. Take a Number 10 bus westbound on Jasper Ave. from downtown.

0:00 (1:33) Depart Edmonton retracing tracks eastbound for several minutes before curling north, then west through industrial scenes of Edmonton.

1:00 (0:34) "Onion-domed" church on right at Carvel is fine example of Byzantine architecture. This most distinctive design commonly characterizes churches of Russian, Greek and Ukrainian denominations.

1:01 (0:33) Series of small lakes provide convenient weekend retreats for work-weary urbanites. Mink Lake, on left, and Johnny's Lake, just downline on right, are two of these.

1:09 (0:25) Cross into Wabamun via bridge spanning arm of Wabamun Lake. Town's name is derived from Indian word for "mirror," a reference to adjacent lake.

1:21 (0:12) Golf course on left is additional draw for Gainford area.

1:31 (0:02) With highway bridge paralleling on left, cross beautiful Pembina River approaching Evansburg.

1:33 (0:00) Arrive Evansburg.

EVANSBURG, ALTA. - This stop serves the western fringe of Edmonton's widespread area. The town derives its name from a former mayor of this city.

0:00 (1:03) Depart Evansburg amidst rolling farmlands of western Alberta.

0:09 (0:54) Another onion-domed church is prominent fixture on left at Wildwood.

Edmonton

- VIA Station
1 - Visitors Information
2 - Eaton Center & Edmonton Center
3 - Provincial Museum
4 - City Market
5 - Legislative Buildings

West of town, proceed along fringe of Chip Lake on left.

0:34 (0:29) Old tractor tires make unusual fence, encircling house on right at Peers.

0:46 (0:16) High trestles across Wolf Creek and McLeod River provide sudden drama to this stretch.

1:03 (0:00) Arrive Edson.

EDSON, ALTA. - Located approximately halfway between Edmonton and Jasper, Edson serves as a trading hub for its immediate area. It was named in honor of a vice-president of the Grand Trunk Pacific Railway, Edson Chamberlain.

0:00 (0:54) Depart Edson, passing large cemetery on right.

0:16 (0:38) Cross Sundance Creek atop another lofty bridge.

0:19 (0:35) At Bickerdike, charming chalet-style depot sits on right, with lush farmlands a picturesque backdrop. Ominously named Octopus Lake can be seen on left.

0:29 (0:25) With McLeod River bordering on left, peaks of Rocky Mountains can now be discerned, jutting above horizon in distance. Stands of tamarack trees are interspersed with spruce. Needles of this unique tree (also known as the larch) turn gold in fall and then drop off in preparation for winter.

0:31 (0:23) On right, grounds of Medicine Lodge Detention Center are adorned by colorful array of miniature totem poles.

0:33 (0:21) Train skirts shoreline of Obed Lake on right. Hills now encroaching on landscape preview arrival into Rocky Mountains.

0:52 (0:02) Approaching Hinton, huge St. Regis pulp plant on right is one of Canada's largest.

0:54 (0:00) Arrive Hinton. Depot's A-frame design lends appropriate atmosphere to this recreation gateway.

HINTON, ALTA. - This is the eastern gateway city to Jasper National Park. One of Alberta's two major pulp-processing plants, a St. Regis Pulp and Paper Mill, is located here with tours offered to the public. Also, the Alberta Forestry Museum has interesting exhibits of work of Canada's early forest rangers.

0:00 (1:01) Depart Hinton.

0:05 (0:57) Climb atop bluffs overlooking Athabasca River Valley on right. Within several miles, train emerges in heart of Jasper National Park, with towering peaks and shimmering lakes an encompassing spectacle to behold.

0:13 (0:48) Cross Athabasca River.

0:50 (0:11) Watch for bighorn sheep, elk and other wildlife that sometime graze rail right-of-way along this stretch of track.

0:59 (0:01) Large CN rail yards mark entrance to Jasper.

1:01 (0:00) Arrive Jasper where a steam locomotive, a totem pole and a "bear" all greet passengers.

JASPER, ALTA. - Jasper National Park, named after Jasper Hawes, a fur trapper in this area in the early 1800s, is located in the midst of majestic mountain scenery. Like Banff, it is understandably one of the more popular vacation areas in the Canadian Rockies. Although crowded in the summer, it is not as frantic as Banff. September can be an ideal month to visit here.

VIA Station, 607 Connaught Drive, has a snack bar, a gift shop, storage lockers, luggage carts, a newsstand and redcaps. Free parking is adjacent to the station.

For reservations and information, call 800-561-8630.

Cab stand is at the station; Jasper Taxi, 852-3146. **Greyhound/Brewster** bus terminal and **tour buses,** including icefield tours, are adjacent to the station. Tilden **rental cars** are located in the VIA station, 852-4972. Budget is two blocks from the station at 638 Connaught Drive, 852-3222.

Information Center, 632 Connaught Drive (at Hazel). Write **Jasper Park Chamber of Commerce,** P.O. Box 98, Jasper, Alberta T0E 1E0. Call (403) 852-3858.

Whistler's Motor Hotel, Box 250, T0E 1E0; (403) 852-3361. Attractive rooms and nice restaurant. Across the street from the station. $109.
-**Astoria Hotel,** 404 Connaught Dr., T0E 1E0; (403) 852-3351. Very attractive, smaller hotel, three long blocks from the

Canadian - Canadian Rockies
HOMER R. HILL

station. $89.

-Numerous homes offer furnished **rooms** and moderate rates. Call **Central Reservations,** (403) 852-4242, for availability of these units as well as motels.

⚁ **Pyramid and Patricia lakes,** located about five miles from town on Pyramid Lake Road, are fine examples of glacial lakes in an alpine setting. **Maligne Canyon, Medicine Lake and Maligne Lake** are located east of Jasper in the Maligne Valley. A spectacular gorge leads to the two lakes; Maligne Lake is in a breathtaking mountain setting. **Punchbowl Falls and Miette Hot Springs** are both east of Jasper, the furthest being Miette Hot Springs about 38 miles from town. The falls can be seen about 8 miles before reaching the hot springs, the latter being the hottest spring in the Canadian Rockies.

Jasper Tramway carries passengers to an elevation of 7,380 feet on the Whistlers. A hike on to the summit provides an outstanding view of Mt. Robson. **Athabasca Falls** are 20 miles south of Jasper, with various viewpoints offering excellent views of these magnificent cascades.

0:00 (1:53) Depart Jasper and head toward Yellowhead Pass and some of North America's most magnificent scenery! Trident Range will be on our left and Victoria Cross Range on our right as we make this ascent. Waterfalls, streams, snowfields and tunnels make this a railroading spectacular.

0:24 (1:29) Those small wire fences that occasionally appear on uphill side of right-of-way are slide detectors which activate a red signal should there be a rockslide or snowslide blocking tracks.

🕐 Gain one hour as train passes from Mountain to Pacific Time. Set your watch back (forward if eastbound) one

Jasper

VIA Station
1 - Visitors Information
2 - Park Information
3 - Post Office
4 - RCMP
5 - Whistler Motor Lodge
6 - Astoria Hotel

hour.

0:37 (1:16) Crest Yellowhead Pass at milepost 17.5. This is border between Alberta, just behind, and British Columbia, just entered. Tracks are only 3,718 feet above sea level; however, many of surrounding peaks soar to more than 11,000 feet. Yellowhead is one of lowest passes along entire North American Continental Divide. At this northerly point, waters flowing to east actually, sooner or later, find their way into Arctic Ocean.

0:42 (1:11) Beautiful Yellowhead Lake stretches serenely beside tracks on left. Yellowhead Mountain is highest peak directly across lake.

1:03 (0:50) And now, Moose Lake is alongside of us at left, even larger than Yellowhead.

1:14 (0:39) Red Pass Junction, at milepost 43.9, is a flag stop.

This is where the rail lines divide, with our CN line heading to the left (south) toward Kamloops and Vancouver, while the other (route of the Skeena) continues west to the end of the line at Prince Rupert.

1:19 (0:34) Through short tunnel.

1:30 (0:24) This is avalanche country, apparent as train drifts through another snowshed.

1:35 (0:20) Looking back, view is superb. One of dominant peaks is Mt. Robson at 3,954 meters—that's 12,972 feet—Canadian Rockies' highest.

1:44 (0:09) Rugged peaks to left comprise Selwyn Range.

1:53 (0:00) Arrive Valemount.

VALEMOUNT, B.C. - This is a popular recreation area, particularly for fishermen. The town is situated at the very northern end of the Canoe Reach of skinny Kinbasket Lake.

0:00 (1:40) Depart Valemount.

0:05 (1:35) Excellent views are afforded in all directions; Premier Range is forward to right.

0:12 (1:24) To right, spectacular snowfields of Albreda Glacier create a perpetual blanket of white. Train is now paralleling course of Thompson River which will be followed into Kamloops.

1:15 (0:25) Note spectacular falls off to

left.

1:40 (0:00) Arrive Blue River.

 BLUE RIVER, B.C. - This small way-stop is in a truly idyllic setting, also popular with fishermen, as was Valemount.

0:00 (1:50) Depart Blue River.

0:24 (1:26) Enormous rapids below, on left, make it clear we are headed downhill, as train traverses canyon sometimes referred to as Little Hell's Gate. Tunnel creates momentary darkness.

0:25 (1:25) River now squeezes through Little Hells Gate Gorge.

1:37 (0:13) Two large sawmills, on left, consume huge amount of local timber stands.

1:50 (0:00) Arrive Clearwater.

 CLEARWATER, B.C. - This is a lumbering and farming community. Countryside will evidence more agricultural qualities as we approach Kamloops.

0:00 (1:45) Depart Clearwater, where Clearwater River, on right, adds to already burgeoning North Thompson River.

0:24 (1:21) Note small aerial tram, to left, that offers forest rangers unique ride to fire lookout on Baldy Mountain.

1:10 (0:35) "Current Ferry," on right at McLure, uses force of stream to propel it across North Thompson.

1:45 (0:00) Arrive Kamloops CN station, situated on northern edge of city.

 KAMLOOPS, B.C. - The city is located at the confluence of the North and South Thompson rivers. The first white men to reach the area were fur traders representing the Pacific Fur Trade Company. They arrived here in 1811 and found the Kamloops Indians (of the Shuswap Tribe) eager to trade. This led to the construction of outposts which were eventually taken over by the Hudson's Bay Company in 1821.

Gold was discovered near here in the early 1850s spurring further development. British Columbia became a province of Canada in 1871, permitting the Canadian Pacific Railway to be extended to Kamloops three years later.

Even though this is Canada, Kamloops has a semi-arid climate with tempera-

tures frequently soaring into the 90s during the summer months. Locals take to the beaches of the Thompson River in droves on warmer weekends. It is so warm that Kamloops has a surprising five-month, frost-free growing season.

CN Station, north of town and just off to the west of Hwy. 5, is open one hour before train time and closes on departure. There are soft drink and snack vending machines.

For VIA reservations and information, call 800-561-8630.

Cabs include Yellow Cab, 374-3333 and Kami, 374-5151. Budget **rental cars,** 374-1456, with local pick up and drop off. For **local bus** information, call 376-1216.

Kamloops Travel InfoCentre, 10-10th Ave., V2C 6J7, located off 10th Avenue on the south bank of the South Thompson River, (604) 374-3377.

Kamloops Travelodge, 430 Columbia, V2C 2T5; (604) 372-8202. A few blocks from downtown. $79.

-Coast Canadian Inn, 339 St. Paul St., V2C 2J7; (604) 372-5201. Deluxe accommodations, bordering on elegance. On the edge of downtown. $138.

Kamloops Museum and Art Gallery is located downtown at 207 Seymore Street, about three blocks from the CP Station. Exhibits depict life going back to the fur trade era. Kids should enjoy the **Kamloops Wildlife Park** and the **Waterslides** located 10 miles east of Kamloops on the Trans-Canada Highway. There's even a miniature railway.

0:00 (3:45) Depart Kamloops.

0:01 (3:44) Make first of many river crossings between here and Vancouver, as North Thompson is crossed with view of Kamloops to left. Soon cruise beside Kamloops Lake on left. After lake, route will first follow Thompson River and then Fraser River into Vancouver—no more passes to surmount.

CN and CP tracks parallel each other on opposite riverbanks, frequently exchanging sides. The Canadian uses the CN tracks.

0:55 (2:50) To right is Walhachin, now a

mere grove of cottonwoods. In early 1900s, prior to WWI, settlers irrigated this arid land, hoping to create their own "Garden of Eden." However, men were called to arms leaving their beloved land to the elements. A devastating flood washed out their aqueduct, and Walhachin ultimately met its demise.

1:22 (2:23) Through arid flag stop of Ashcroft, and now swing southward, still following river. Ashcroft is one of driest spots in Canada, receiving less than ten inches of moisture per year.

1:23 (2:22) At milepost 50.3, watch for enormous osprey nest atop abandoned power pole on right (an old wood burner is just beyond). These large birds can sometimes be spotted gliding above Fraser in search of fish, their favorite food.

1:31 (2:14) Here, at milepost 57, the last spike of what is now the CN was driven on January 23, 1915. At that time, it was the Canadian Northern Pacific Railway, and event marked completion of Canada's third transcontinental rail link.

2:02 (1:43) At Spencer's Bridge it is still apparent, on slope to right, where landslide occurred August 13, 1905, when lower portion of mountain came rumbling across valley in matter of seconds, damming waters of Thompson River. Five Indians were buried alive and thirteen more were drowned when waters backed over nearby village. Above to right, waterfall from Murray Creek literally shoots out from mountainside during springtime.

2:33 (1:10) Train enters "Jaws of Death," a particularly treacherous section of river, as canyon becomes narrow gorge. "Suicide Rapids" is term bestowed on frothy waters by intrepid white-water rafters who occasionally test their skills (and luck) along this stretch of river.

2:41 (1:04) Cross Fraser River, just across from Lytton, where muddy waters of Thompson merge into much clearer Fraser, on left. Simon Fraser, fur trader and explorer of British Columbia, put ashore at this point on June 18, 1808. Lytton, with its significant Indian population, lays claim to being longest continually occupied spot in North America.

2:55 (0:50) At Cisco Flats, both railroads now decide to exchange river banks in dramatic style. Original Canadian Pacific

bridge was fabricated in Britain more than 100 years ago, arriving at Port Moody by ship, moved in sections by rail (of course) to present-day site, then erected by San Francisco Bridge Company. Bridge was eventually replaced.

3:42 (0:03) Beside new bridge, former auto aerial tram now rests on far side of river. Tram is one discussed at Boston Bar below.

3:45 (0:00) Arrive Boston Bar.

BOSTON BAR, B.C. - This village was originally a gold-mining center. At one time, before highway bridge was installed, a unique cable tram, only large enough to hold one automobile, serves as an aerial ferry between North Bend, immediately across the Fraser, and the Trans-Canada Highway here at Boston Bar.

0:00 (1:43) Depart Boston Bar.

0:10 (1:33) Across river, on right, creek cascades beneath CP's Skuzzy Creek rail bridge into Fraser River.

0:16 (1:27) Canyon narrows to mere 110 feet forming "Hells Gate," where 200 million gallons of water per minute drain from 84,000 square miles of British Columbia. Each year, 2 million sockeye salmon swim upstream against this torrent to reach their spawning grounds. Simon Fraser reported it as "an awesome gorge."

The Pacific salmon industry was nearly ruined when rockslides in 1914, triggered by construction in the canyon, made passage so narrow that salmon spawning was cut by 90 percent. Subsequently, Canadian/U.S.-built fishways slowed the stream flow enough to bring the salmon population back to normalcy. Now, a Swiss-built tramway swoops bright red gondolas to the bottom carrying 28 passengers per load for impressive view of the canyon. White-water rafters can often be seen challenging the rapids and a treacherous whirlpool called "Devil's Wash Basin."

0:27 (1:16) Glimpse graceful structure of Alexandra Bridge spanning Fraser below on right.

The original Alexandra Bridge was built by Joseph Trutch in 1863 as part of the famed Cariboo Road. It was the first suspension bridge in British Columbia, and actually looked quite similar to its replacement (except the original sported wooden towers). It was destroyed by a flood in 1894, twenty years after its construction.

0:39 (1:05) Waterfall cascades directly overhead while train passes through tunnel.

0:50 (0:53) Obstruction at mouth of Fraser River Canyon is monolithic Lady Franklin Rock, named for widow of Sir John Franklin, Arctic explorer who died in 1847 searching for Northwest Passage. Lady Franklin's efforts to find her husband led her here but she could not probe farther upriver because of this formidable barrier. Her courage, however, inspired numerous expeditions to search for Sir John, ultimately producing thorough exploration of Canadian Arctic region.

0:51 (0:52) Town of Yale is immediately across river.

In its day, Yale was one of the most important and exciting towns in the West. Founded in 1848 as a fur collection point for the Hudson's Bay Company, Yale's place in history was furthered when local gold discoveries occurred in 1858. Then with greater finds 400 miles farther north at Cariboo and Barkersville, construction of the legendary Cariboo Wagon Road started here in 1862.

In 1880, railroad construction was commenced with the blasting of the oldest train tunnel in western Canada, on the CP line just north of here. Andrew Onderdonk was the man chosen to construct various segments of western track, extending from Port Moody to Kamloops Lake. Like his American counterparts farther south, Onderdonk employed thousands of Chinese willing to work hard and often for only about half of that received by white men. The Chinese may have been the real heroes of the Canadian Pacific. Omer Lavellee, in his classic book *Van Horne's Road,* points out that when construction was completed and all the workers were summarily discharged, a local newspaper observed that a thousand white men rushed into the saloons and soon began to wreak havoc on the town. The Chinese merely went into the woods and ate their rice. The paper then chuckled over this difference between "pagans and Christians."

Yale claims the first railway station west of the Rockies, the first town council in British Columbia and the first girls' finishing school on the B.C. mainland (once visited by the Duke and Duchess of York).

0:52 (0:51) Watch for Indian fish drying racks, frequently draped with blue or orange plastic.

0:53 (0:50) Just after crossing Emory Creek, pass location where Onderdonk's first Yale construction locomotive was unloaded from ship to shore in 1880.

1:01 (0:42) Through flag stop of Hope.

1:29 (0:14) Up valley, to right across river, is Harrison Hot Springs, a fine resort in the mountains. As you might suspect, resort's hot springs are a major attraction. Beautiful Harrison Lake, as well as historic Harrison Hotel, add to area's appeal.

1:43 (0:00) Arrive Chilliwack.

CHILLIWACK, B.C. - This agricultural center is located in a broad, fertile valley, actually the delta of the Fraser River. The delta has taken several million years to form, and now covers bedrock with soil one mile deep. Steamboats once made port here during the gold rush days.

0:00 (0:24) Depart Chilliwack.

0:21 (0:03) On hill, in distance right, red tiled roof and tower of Westminster Abbey are visible. This Benedictine Monastery was founded in 1954.

0:24 (0:00) Arrive Matsqui.

MATSQUI, B.C. - This is one more agrarian community, and the last stop before reaching Vancouver's densely populated suburbs.

0:00 (1:02) Depart Matsqui.

0:02 (1:00) Now, cross to north banks of Fraser at Page.

0:22 (0:40) Through Mission, a small community named for an Indian school established here in the 19th century, first and largest of its kind in the province. Attractive station at left was proclaimed in 1909 by a local tabloid as "one of the swellest" along the line.

0:32 (0:30) Cross Stave River. It was near here that Billy Miner pulled off Canada's first train robbery in September, 1904— two years before his $15 holdup east of Kamloops. Miner was glamorized in the

Near Boston Bar, B.C.
HOMER R. HILL

movie *The Grey Fox.*

0:33 (0:27) Literally pass through large lumber mill and yards.

0:39 (0:21) Fort Langley National Historic Park is immediately across river from ferry dock. Built in 1827 by Hudson's Bay Company, fort functioned as provisioning and administrative center for company and was to end American competition in Northwest. It was here that James Douglas declared British Columbia a crown colony in 1858 and fort became first capital.

0:54 (0:06) Cross Pitt River on 1,749-foot bridge with another center-pivot span.

1:00 (0:00) CP Rail repair shops and yards herald arrival at Port Coquitlam.

PORT COQUITLAM, B.C. - Development of this area, including nearby Port Moody, began with the 1858 gold rush. But the first major boom occurred 27 years later when the western terminus of the Canadian Pacific was planned for nearby Port Moody. Real estate skyrocketed in value, with some lots jumping from $15 to $1,000 each. The first shipment of rails arrived from England at Port Moody in May of 1883, and by August, 1885, the Marquis of Langsdowne, Governor General of Canada, was able to cross Canada for the first time without entering the United States (although not entirely by train since the track was not yet finished above Yale). In November, 1885, the trans-Canada route was complete, and the first transcontinental passenger train ceremoniously pulled into Port Moody at noon on July 4, 1886. The boom soon turned to bust, however, when the railroad was extended to a new Pacific terminal at Vancouver the very next year.

0:00 (0:55) Departing Port Coquitlam, cross river by same name before heading first south then west into megalopolis of Vancouver.

0:47 (0:08) At CN Junction, duck beneath elevated tracks of Skytrain, Vancouver's modernistic, computer-operated commuter rail.

0:53 (0:02) Slip past VIA coach barn on left.

Vancouver

🚂 VIA Station
1 - Visitors Information
2 - Gastown
3 - Robonstrasse
4 - Chinatown
5 - Sylvia Hotel
6 - Barclay Hotel

0:55 (0:00) Arrive at Vancouver's stately CN station.

🏛 **VANCOUVER, B.C.** - British explorer Captain George Vancouver discovered this area in 1792. It was a natural for becoming a seaport with its sheltered harbor and nearby forests as an important source of lumber. The arrival of the Canadian Pacific Railroad in 1884 and the development of the fishing industry spurred Vancouver to becoming one of Canada's great cities.

In a sparkling bay and mountain setting, offering relatively temperate weather year-round, the city has become a favorite western vacation spot.

🚪 **VIA Station,** 1150 Station St., is a handsome facility built along classic lines. A huge four-faced clock (fashioned after a railroader's pocket watch) is the focal point of the lobby. The station has storage lockers, luggage carts, vending machines and a hotel phone board showing numerous accommodations. Sta-

tion restaurant has been closed during renovation, but fast food restaurants are within a block. The station is about a mile from the downtown business district.

For reservations and other information, call 800-561-8630.

🚌 Yellow **Cab,** 681-3311, and Black Top, 731-1111. **Local buses** and **Skytrain** (Vancouver's computer-run "elevated") stop in front of the station, 261-5100. Skytrain runs from downtown to New Westminster. Bus service to Seattle's King Street Station connecting to and from the Coast Starlight and Mount Rainier is available from downtown Vancouver. **Vancouver International Airport** is a few miles south of the downtown area.

❓ **Greater Vancouver Convention & Visitors Bureau,** 1055 Dunsmuir St., V7X 1L3; (604) 683-2000 (across from the Burrard Skytrain station).

🏨 **Barclay Hotel,** 1348 Robson St., V6E 1C5; (604) 688-8850. A small, nicely run hotel in the West End, between the downtown business district and Stanley Park. About two miles from the station. $65.

-**Sylvia Hotel,** 1154 Gilford St., V6G 2P6; (604) 681-9321. Overlooks beach on English Bay, next to Stanley Park. Popular small vine-covered West-End hotel. Fine coffee shop and restaurant, both looking out at the Bay. About three miles from the station. $62.

⭐⭐⭐ **Trolley Tours,** much like Washington, DC's Tour Trains, are the slickest way to get around Vancouver's downtown area. A nicely planned route, complete with regularly scheduled stops, permits all-day sightseeing with unlimited boarding and reboarding for one round trip. Stops are made at Vancouver's major attractions. Maps and schedules are available at most hotels; 255-2444. **Stanley Park,** at the foot of Georgia St., is considered to be one of the finest parks in the world. On a beautiful peninsula, forming a bridged link to North Vancouver, the park contains a zoo featuring polar bears, penguins, gardens, trails, picnic sites and tennis courts. An aquarium, with 9,000 specimens of sealife, features killer and beluga whales.

Gastown, Water and Carroll streets, is where Vancouver began. Now an historic site which permits shops to remain open on Sunday (a rarity in Canada), this restored area has fine restaurants, shops and nightclubs. Its zany, steam-spurting clock has become Gastown's trademark. Another downtown lure is a section of **Robson Street** between Hornby and Bute. It's a shopping area with a charming European atmosphere.

Immediately across from the station is **Science World** where visitors experience hands-on science demonstrations. An **IMAX** theatre is also here.

There are two unique attractions in the North Vancouver area. The **Capilano Suspension Bridge** is the world's longest suspension footbridge. It is 70 meters above the Capilano River and is 137 meters from shore to shore. (Not for those who are bothered by heights.) **Grouse Mountain** has shops and a restaurant on the summit, and is reached by Canada's largest aerial tramway. This not only serves skiers, but those wishing to obtain a spectacular panorama of Vancouver.

And rail buffs will want to ride one of the area's biggest attractions, the **Royal Hudson Steam Train.** As its name implies, this is an excursion train pulled by one of the famous Royal Hudson engines, number 2860. The route begins at the British Columbia Railway Station in North Vancouver and makes a six-hour round-trip to Squamish in the summer. The scenery is spectacular. (See British Columbia Railway for route log and station information.)

Hudson Bay

Two strands of silvery steel seem to stretch endlessly toward the horizons both fore and aft of the Hudson Bay on its trip to Churchill. Indian village whistle stops help break the tedium, but soon these become redundant. However monotonous (and certainly never hurried), this 1,055-mile trek from Winnipeg to Churchill is always an adventure and truly one of today's unique travel experiences.

Conceived in the 1870s, the line had a checkered history of starts and stops until finally, beginning in the mid-1920s, 3,000 hard-working emigrants, struggling against frost, blizzards and insects, constructed the final 300 miles of iron, reaching Churchill on Hudson Bay in March 1929.

Its purpose was to provide a shorter route to the world's grain markets, as well as direct access to Canada's interior for inbound goods and new emigrants. Although it has never become the epic transport that was once envisioned, it has indeed provided a means of exporting a portion of Canada's wealth of wheat and has had a profound influence on the development of the North's enormous resources.

After leaving Winnipeg in the evening, the Hudson Bay reaches its northern goal of Churchill in the early morning of the third day. Two nights are spent on the train while making numerous stops to board and detrain local residents traveling from one flag stop to another. Sleeping car accommodations are definitely recommended.

Once there, the day can be spent seeing the sights and still start the return trip that evening. Of course, it's possible to stay longer, but the next return train will not depart for two or three days, depending on the day of the week. The major attraction is polar bear viewing which is best in late October and early November. It is worth noting that during the summer and fall, reservations should be made well in advance. Package tours are also offered by VIA Rail.

Before going, you might consider a visit to the Manitoba Museum of Man & Nature in Winnipeg. There are excellent exhibits of the sub-Arctic, including: polar bears, northern lights (Churchill is one of the best places in the world to see this phenomenon), building the railroad to Churchill, and Churchill itself.

However, the future of this train is in doubt. The CN, owner of the tracks, has openly stated its desire to abandon the line. It would probably be prudent for anyone planning to take this trip to do so sooner rather than later.

Northbound Schedule (Condensed)
Winnipeg, Man. - Late Evening Departure
The Pas, Man. - Midmorning (2nd Day)
Thompson, Man. - Early Evening (2nd Day)
Gillam, Man. - Middle of the Night (3rd Day)
Churchill, Man. - Early Morning Arrival (3rd Day)

Southbound Schedule (Condensed)
Churchill, Man. - Midevening Departure

Gillam, Man. - Middle of the Night (2nd Day)

Thompson, Man. - Late Morning (2nd Day)

The Pas, Man. - Early Evening (2nd Day)

Winnipeg, Man. - Early Morning Arrival (3rd Day)

Frequency - Departs Winnipeg Sunday, Tuesday and Thursday. Arrives in Churchill Tuesday, Thursday and Saturday. Departs Churchill same day of its arrival (Tuesday, Thursday and Saturday) and arrives in Winnipeg Thursday, Saturday and Monday.

Seating - Standard coaches.

Dining - Complete meal and beverage service.

Sleeping - Berths, roomettes and bedrooms.

Baggage - Checked baggage handled between major stops.

Reservations - Required for sleeping cars. Coach seats reserved when tickets are purchased.

Length of Trip - 1,055 miles in 35 hours.

Route Log

 WINNIPEG, MAN. - See page 398.

0:00 (0:57) Depart Winnipeg.

0:01 (0:56) Forks Market area and Forks National Historic Park come into view, below left.

0:03 (0:54) Cross Assiniboine River near its juncture with Red River. Waters will ultimately flow north into Lake Winnipeg.

0:06 (0:51) On right, ornate dome is distinctive feature of Winnipeg's Legislative Building.

0:34 (0:23) An interesting two-story depot on right and an old church on left are highlights through Elie. On western edge of town, cross Milk River, with neighborhoods of gracious homes lining its banks.

0:51 (0:06) At Nattress, cross Assiniboine River.

0:57 (0:00) Arrive Portage la Prairie.

PORTAGE LA PRAIRIE, MAN. - Literally translated as "prairie portage," the city is situated at the narrowest point between the Assiniboine River and Lake Manitoba. This spot served

as a resting point for both Indians and early settlers transporting their canoes between these two important waterways.

A fort was established at this strategic site in 1738, and from 1867 to 1868 the town held the distinction of being capital of the "Republic of Manitobah." Today, it remains a transportation hub of the prairies, with the CN and CP rail lines making a unique prairie crossing, while the Trans-Canada and Yellowhead highways join here.

0:00 (2:40) Depart Portage la Prairie.

For the remainder of the evening, the Hudson Bay travels through southern Manitoba farming country that could easily pass for central Nebraska, flat and fertile lands interspersed only with patches of trees.

1:36 (1:04) One should not laugh at bumper stickers proclaiming "Ski Manitoba." A few miles west (left) is Mt. Agassiz Ski Resort in Riding Mountain National Park.

2:40 (0:00) Arrive Dauphin, where elegant three-story 1912 depot attests to town's former prominence as a CN division point.

DAUPHIN, MAN. - A fort was constructed here as early as 1742 to help establish fur trading in the region, but it wasn't until the railroad arrived in 1896 that European settlers arrived, creating the community that now is a regional trade center. Fort Dauphin Museum has a wide variety of exhibits on display. Canada's National Ukrainian Festival is held here the end of July and the beginning of August.

0:00 (1:36) Depart Dauphin.

1:36 (0:00) Arrive Roblin.

ROBLIN, MAN. - Another farming center. Keystone Pioneer Museum offers displays of agricultural machinery and other rural artifacts.

0:00 (3:55) Depart Roblin.

0:22 (3:33) Enter Saskatchewan and leave Manitoba.

Between here and the town of Hudson Bay, Sask., the train stops at four small communities of east-central Saskatchewan: **KAMSAK, CANORA, STURGIS** and **ENDEAVOUR**.

4:04 (0:00) Arrive Hudson Bay.

HUDSON BAY, SASK. - This eastern Saskatchewan trading center is the last stop on the Hudson Bay's brief westward arc through this province.

0:00 (1:55) Depart Hudson Bay.

0:20 (1:35) Dense forest consists mainly of black spruce, jack pine, aspen (white poplar), tamarack (they lose their needles in the winter) and some birch (similar in appearance to aspen but trunks often have bark peeling away).

1:05 (0:50) Re-enter Manitoba and leave Saskatchewan.

1:55 (0:00) Arrive The Pas.

THE PAS, MAN. - Gateway to the North, it has become a center for lumbering, pulp, fishing and furs, and all traffic to and from the Manitoba north country passes through this rugged community. Moose, deer and caribou along with walleye, trout, pickerel and pike make this a sportsman's paradise. It is also headquarters for various branches of the provincial government in northern Manitoba.

In February, a renowned Trappers Festival is held for three days, when trappers, miners, lumbermen and Indian chiefs indulge in such competitive frolics as woodchopping, dog sledding, singing and dancing.

0:00 (1:12) Depart The Pas and immediately cross icy flow of Saskatchewan River which empties into nearby Cedar Lake—one of Lake Winnipeg's many adjuncts.

0:09 (1:03) Principal employer (along with government) of The Pas is off to right—a large paper mill.

0:11 (1:01) Flin Flon Jct. is where line divides, with a branch on left driving straight north to Lynn Lake.

0:32 (0:40) Clearwater Provincial Park, on left, is summer recreational area for residents of The Pas. Clearwater Lake is centerpiece of Park.

0:59 (0:13) Cormorant Lake sprawls in distance to left where myriad species of waterfowl take refuge. Locals claim lake is warm enough to swim in during "balmy" summer months.

1:09 (0:03) Little Cormorant Lake is on right.

1:12 (0:00) Arrive Cormorant at milepost 41.

CORMORANT, MAN. - This little community gets its appellation from the bird with the same name—an aquatic raven. Located on a narrow neck of land between portions of Cormorant Lake, it was the first large village on the Hudson Bay Railway. The early population was largely French and Scottish, many of whom intermarried with area natives.

0:00 (2:30) Depart Cormorant.

0:44 (1:47) Note outcroppings of pink marble. This area has provided such building material for many of Canada's edifices.

1:03 (1:27) Flag stop of Wekusko (Cree for Herb Lake) where road leads to gold-mining activities at Snow Lake.

1:12 (1:18) Hargrave Lake is on right.

1:20 (1:10) Dense forests of spruce, tamarack and jack pine continue to border tracks, while tripod phone poles solve problem of unstable muskeg.

1:47 (0:43) At milepost 109, make rare highway crossing between The Pas and Churchill. This road leads from Winnipeg to Thompson.

2:30 (0:00) Arrive Wabowden at milepost 136.

WABOWDEN, MAN. - Perhaps the prettiest community along today's route, Wabowden acts as a transfer point for goods destined for more remote regions. The Brandon Experimental Farm is here and has had successful results with vegetables and small grains. Some small farms are operating nearby.

0:00 (1:12) Depart Wabowden, noting long wooden elevated sidewalk along left side of track to avoid musket. Immediately Bowden Lake appears on left. About two miles beyond (and out of view) is Setting Lake—an elongated body of water which serves as part of extensive Grass River canoe route, connecting Flin Flon with Nelson River.

0:07 (1:05) If both are punctual, northbound and southbound Hudson Bay trains should meet about now at Medard (Wednesdays and Fridays only). Unless it's summertime, don't be surprised to see snow plastered to front of southbound.

1:12 (0:00) Native dogs anxiously await train at Thicket Portage (milepost 184) where train's cook usually drops off food

Route of the Hudson Bay - northern Manitoba
JACK SWANSON

scraps which are instantly snapped up by these voracious canines.

 THICKET PORTAGE, MAN. - This is one of the oldest inhabited villages in the area. Besides its native Indian population, a number of Scandinavian and Icelandic settlers have migrated here because of fishing opportunities. Sturgeon, as well as other commercial fish, are shipped from here to the U.S. A veritable maze of regional waterways focuses on Thicket Portage.

0:00 (1:40) Depart Thicket Portage and look left to see neat little yellow and blue church, complete with bell in belfry and white cross on top.

0:24 (1:16) Permafrost, that thawing ground just below the surface, is engineering nightmare. It should be avoided first, kept frozen if it can't be avoided, or (the least practical) removed. It is particularly troublesome along this stretch of tracks and railroad has implanted thermo-probes which can now be seen on either side of track. Freon is used inside these probes to radiate heat from ground to help keep permafrost frozen.

0:30 (1:10) At milepost 199.5, Hudson Bay begins a slow-grinding curl to left and away from main line starting a 30-mile side trip to mining city of Thompson. Terrain becomes increasingly rolling with numerous rock outcroppings and small lakes.

1:07 (0:38) Cross Grass River.

1:28 (---) Hudson Bay slowly backs into wye, pulls out toward main line, and then slowly backs a mile into dead end at Thompson.

1:45 (0:00) Arrive Thompson's VIA station which is about a mile from downtown. A large Inco smelter, visible in distance, is working evidence of city's mining economy.

 THOMPSON, MAN. - Like Sudbury, Thompson's reason for existing is nickel. Huge ore deposits are mined and processed by Inco Metals Company, which has created a surprisingly large and modern city in Manitoba's Northland (714 rail miles from Winnipeg). Tours of Inco's operations (it's the world's most fully integrated nickel production facility) are available in the summer but unfortunately require more time than the Hudson Bay permits. Train is normally here long enough to permit a quick trip into town, but first, be sure to verify train's departure time. The station is about a mile from town.

0:00 (1:33) Depart Thompson, retracing 30-mile route back to main line.

1:23 (0:00) Arrive Pikwitonei at milepost 213.

 PIKWITONEI, MAN. - A Cree word meaning "broken mouth,"

417

Pikwitonei was once a major construction terminal for the railroad, with a roundhouse and other shop facilities. One of the more substantial-appearing villages along the route, it now survives largely on trapping activities. Canoe access to the region's waterways is also found here.

0:00 (3:10) Depart Pikwitonei, and work still deeper into very heart of Indian country where lifestyles have shown little change across time. Watch for mothers carrying papooses in moss bags and occasional Indian camps along right-of-way.

0:21 (2:49) Train crosses one of region's multitudinous lakes at milepost 225.

0:45 (2:25) At milepost 241, powerful Nelson River is crossed at Manitou Rapids. This 612-foot cantilevered span stretches a lofty 110 feet above river below. Waters of Assiniboine, Winnipeg, Red, English and Saskatchewan rivers, after passing through Lake Winnipeg, all course through this impressive gorge, headed toward Hudson Bay. Whirlpools make these narrows particularly dangerous for canoers. Only significant rock cuts on rail line appear here on each side of chasm.

1:56 (1:14) Train usually stops at Ilford (milepost 285). As populous gathers to pick up mail it is obvious that train's arrival is the social event of the day.

2:18 (0:52) Cross under one of world's longest transmission lines carrying power to southern Manitoba from giant hydroelectric plants near Gillam.

2:58 (0:12) Pass through Luke, a flag stop named for mail carrier and trapper Luke Clemens. Some accounts relate that he was a brother of American author Mark Twain (Samuel Clemens), while others indicate he was a nephew.

3:10 (0:00) Arrive Gillam at milepost 326.

GILLAM, MAN. - Before construction was started on the nearby Kettle Generating Station in February 1966, Gillam was a village of only 356 people. With the construction and completion of this great hydroelectric facility (1,272,000-kilowatt capacity), Gillam became a thriving community with a population of more than 3,000. The power plant is situated about five miles from here on the Nelson River. Other hydroelectric projects are also located on the

Churchill

★ VIA Station
1 - Visitors Information
2 - Town Complex Centre
3 - Eskimo Museum
4 - Churchill Motel
5 - Tundra Inn

Nelson, just downstream from the Kettle plant. Heavily dependent on the railroad, Gillam has no highway link to the rest of Canada.

0:00 (6:55) Depart Gillam.

0:07 (6:48) At milepost 331, cross Nelson River at Kettle Rapids where lights of massive Kettle Generating Station can be seen two miles upstream, to left, while Long Spruce Generating Station is downstream.

Before long, the Hudson Bay begins to traverse lowland coastal plains which are covered with frozen muskeg. Spruce and tamarack become sparse and stunted. This will be most apparent when dawn breaks, sometime before our arrival at Churchill in its bleak and barren setting. Additional nighttime stops are scheduled for villages of **WEIR RIVER** and **HERCHMER** at mileposts 373 and 412.

5:27 (1:28) At milepost 445, landscape becomes barren for some miles until "one-sided" trees reappear near Churchill River. Blowing ice crystals with prevailing northeast winds literally burn all growth off that side of trees.

6:43 (0:12) At milepost 503, first sight of Churchill is afforded on right where enormous grain elevator protrudes above horizon.

6:55 (0:00) Arrive Churchill at milepost 509.

CHURCHILL, MAN. - Churchill is situated almost 600 miles (approximately 1,100 rail miles) north of Winnipeg on the shores of Hudson Bay, an outpost where the modern world meets the Inuit frontier. It is an unusually barren but fascinating country where one gets first-hand taste in the North.

The area was first visited as early as 1612 by Europeans looking for a Northwest Passage to the Orient. Then the Hudson's Bay Company, in 1688, established a trading post near the current townsite, commencing trade with shipment of eight casks of whale oil to England.

In 1732, construction of Fort Prince of Wales was commenced by the British across Churchill Harbor from the present townsite and finally completed several years later. It was one of the most imposing fortresses in North America. Not only was the fort protected by its own forty cannon, there were other guns outside the fort, the largest being at Cape Merry battery on the shore of the harbor entrance. In 1782 a French naval force sailed into the harbor and the fort, manned by less than 40 troops, surrendered without firing a shot. Today it is a National Historic Park which can be reached by boat in the summer when the park is open to visitors.

As western Canada developed its agricultural lands, demand increased for means of exporting grain, bringing about the eventual construction of the Hudson Bay Railroad (now part of the Canadian National system) in 1929, and the Port of Churchill in 1931 whose five-million-bushel grain elevators dominate the Churchill scene.

During World War II, the United States established Fort Churchill just east of town when the population was about 500. Later, the population grew to almost 10,000 when a Canadian Forces Base was established here, but eventually shrunk to its present-day size of 1,500 after the closing of the base.

Perhaps the most unique feature of Churchill is the annual migration of polar bears through the town in the fall, a bizarre event that has been featured in a National Geographic TV documentary.

VIA Station, 74092 Churchill, is on the western edge of this compact community. There are no storage lockers, but the baggage room will hold your luggage if you wish. The station is not open the entire day, but is open at train times.

Call 800-561-8630 for reservations and information.

Churchill can be reached only by train or air (and oceangoing freighters in the summer). **Churchill Taxi,** 675-2345. **Rental cars** available at hotels. The **Airport** is near town, with less-than-daily scheduled air service.

Parks Canada has an information center at Bayport Plaza; (204) 675-8863. Write Parks Canada, P.O. Box 127, R0B 0E0.

There are several motels in Churchill in case you plan to stay overnight. Two of them are:

-**Tundra Inn,** 34 Franklin, P.O. Box 999, R0B 0E0; (204) 675-8831 or 800-265-8563, weekdays only. Ask for their remodeled rooms. Four blocks from the station. $83.

-**Churchill Motel,** Box 218, R0B 0E0; (204) 675-8853. Good restaurant. Free shuttle services, three blocks from the station. $70.

All of the town is within easy walking distance of the station. The **Town Centre Complex** houses numerous facilities used by the residents and visitors alike. Under one gigantic roof are a health center, library, school, swimming pool, curling rink, cafeteria, theater, gymnasium, and other game rooms. Inuit and Indian art work are displayed throughout the complex. The **Eskimo Museum** has one of the finest exhibits of Eskimo art found anywhere. **Parks Canada Interpretive Center,** located at Bayport Plaza, has regular slide shows in the months of July and August, on request at other times. Ask to see their movie about building the railroad to Churchill.

Other points of interest in the Churchill area include **Fort Prince of Wales** (see text above) and **Cape Tatnam Wildlife Management Areas,** with 160 species of waterfowl and other birds. In the fall, polar bear viewing expeditions are available. VIA has package tours that are quite popular.

Tundra Buggy Tours, (204) 675-2121, has guided polar bear expeditions that last most of the day for approximately $130, including lunch. They will also arrange helicopter tours which will virtually guarantee seeing bears in season. **North Star Tours,** (204) 675-2629, has shorter, less expensive polar bear tours and also tours to Ft. Prince of Wales and beluga whale watching.

For **dining,** the Trader's Table is popular and has the best atmosphere. There is also a good cafe at the Churchill Motel.

Other Manitoba Service

The Pas-Lynn Lake train makes a ten-hour trip from The Pas, departing late morning on Monday, Wednesday and Friday. The return departs Lynn Lake early morning on Tuesday, Thursday and Saturday. The train has no food service.

Wabowden-Churchill has once-a-week service with the trip being interrupted by an extended layover of a day or more in Gillam. The train has no food service. Only for the masochistic train buff.

Rocky Mountaineer

Although the 1990 VIA cutbacks substantially reduced the opportunities to view Canada's Rockies by train, a very popular train, the Rocky Mountaineer, is offered by the Great Canadian Railtour Co. This trip follows the former Canadian route along the CP through the heart of the Canadian Rockies as well as a leg that follows the CN route north of Kamloops to Jasper and from Kamloops to Vancouver. The trip is designed as a sightseeing excursion and is scheduled so that travel occurs during daylight hours. At night, passengers enroute stay in hotels at Kamloops.

The routes cover Fraser and Thompson canyons between Vancouver and Kamloops. At Kamloops, the train divides into separate sections. One section goes over Yellowhead Pass and past Mt. Robson, the Canadian Rockies' tallest peak, to Jasper, while the other takes a route to Banff/Calgary over Kicking Horse Pass and through the Spiral Tunnels.

Passengers can elect to take one-way trips to either Jasper or Banff/Calgary, or make a round trip. Accommodations at those destinations are not included in the fare, although Kamloops accommodations are included. Light lunches are served at your seat on board and are also included in the fare.

Equipment consists of nicely refurbished Dayniter coaches. Unfortunately, no dome cars are being used.

Excursions are seasonal only and run from late May through early October. Reservations should be made early: 800-665-7245 or (604) 984-3315.

Route Log

For route from Vancouver to Kamloops and from Kamloops to Jasper, see log of the Canadian, page 408.

Banff/Calgary to Kamloops is shown below. (The log runs from east to west in keeping with the format used throughout this book. Although the train runs non-stop (except for crew changes) between Banff and Kamloops, certain cities are shown as stops to give an easy reference point for the times shown in the log.

CALGARY, ALTA. - Calgary is both the oil and cattle capitals of Canada. Even with its half-million-plus population, there is a cowtown image that Calgary has never really shaken off, an image that lends more than it detracts. This is Canada's Fort Worth.

Fort Calgary was originally established in 1875. Built between the Bow and Elbow rivers by the Northwest Mounted Police, the fort was to assist in fur trading and prevent "whiskey travelers" from adversely influencing local Indians. The Canadian Pacific Railway arrived in 1883 at what is now Palliser Square, putting down sidings and, of course, a station. Initially, the town did not even merit division-point status.

The magnificent Canadian Rockies are but a stone's throw west of here, where Banff and Lake Louise attract summer throngs and winter skiers. This proximity resulted in Calgary's selection as host city

Calgary

VIA Station &
Calgary Tower
1 - Visitors Information
2 - Devonian Gardens &
   Toronto Dominion Square
3 - Glenbow Museum
4 - Lord Nelson Inn

for the 1988 Winter Olympics. And Calgary has its own annual summer event that draws thousands each July—the famed Calgary Stampede. This world-famous rodeo is the biggest production of its kind.

Station, 9th Ave. at Centre Street, is beneath the Calgary Tower in the heart of downtown. There is an elevator to the Palliser Mall where there are restaurants, newsstands and the Palliser Hotel. Pay parking is available.

Both a **cab** stand and a **local bus** stop are at the station. Yellow Cab, 250-8311. Tilden has **rental car** pick up and drop off at the station, 237-5063. **C-Train,** Calgary's streetcar LRT system which runs through downtown (free along 7th Avenue), is two blocks north. **Calgary International Airport** is a 25-minute ride from downtown.

Visitor Information Center, 237-8th Ave., SE, T2G 0K8, is three blocks from the station; (403) 262-2766 for information.

-Lord Nelson Inn, 1020-8th Ave. SW, T2P 1J3; (403) 269-8262. About a mile from the station on the west edge of town, has large, attractive rooms with refrigerators, non-smoking floors, free underground parking, and, for rail fans, a view of the CP main line. Three blocks to C-Train. $65.

-Stampeder Inn, 3828 Macleod Trail, S, T2G 2R2; (403) 243-5531 or 800-361-3422. Those looking for a ride on Calgary's C-Train system might consider this motel, since a stop is a block and a half away. $69.

Several worthwhile attractions are within walking distance: the indoor **Devonian Gardens** and **Toronto Dominion Square,** 7th Ave. and 2nd St., with three levels of shopping; the **Glenbow Museum,** 1st St. and 9th Ave., housing beautifully exhibited displays of Western Canadian history and culture, one block from the station; the **Calgary Tower,** directly above the station, offering a spectacular view of the city and a revolving restaurant; and **Energeum,** 640-5th Ave. SW, a huge science hall devoted to energy resources displays.

The **Calgary Exhibition and Stampede** is a rodeo spectacular held each July at Stampede Park, and can be easily reached from downtown by the C-Train.

0:00 (2:10) Depart Calgary.

0:34 (1:36) Bow River joins us on right, and will now escort Canadian to Lake Louise.

0:45 (1:25) Bearspaw Lake, on right, results from damming of Bow.

1:08 (1:02) View up river, on right, affords stunning panorama of Rockies.

1:10 (1:00) On right, stacks of yellow are product of sulphur plant across river.

1:13 (0:57) Ghost Lake, denying its appellation, is quite visible on right.

1:31 (0:39) Surprisingly glacial-green waters of Kananaskis River flow beneath us and into Bow. Some of Rockies' most awesome monarchs create formidable-looking barrier on left—but in moments, train will meet their challenge, starting a journey marked by spectacular scenery and some incredible feats of railroad engineering.

1:56 (0:14) Enter Banff National Park, one of most popular recreational areas in Canadian Rockies. Awesome Goat Range dominates scene on left. Keep sharp lookout for mountain goats and sheep, as well as elk, deer and other wildlife.

2:10 (0:00) Arrive Banff.

BANFF, ALTA. - Banff National Park, named after Banff, Scotland, has long been one of the most popular resort areas in North America. Truly spectacular mountain scenery and heavy winter snows combine to attract thousands year-round to enjoy hiking, camping, auto touring, skiing and just plain relaxing. The townsite has a permanent population of about 4,000, but in the summer it burgeons, making it advisable to have hotel reservations well in advance.

Station, corner of Elk and Lynx streets, is on the edge of Banff townsite and serves Rocky Mountain Railtours.

Cabs and **local buses** are at the station. Banff Taxi, 762-4444. **Avis and Tilden** are about four blocks

from the station. The **Greyhound** and **Brewster Tours** bus terminal is a block from the station.

Visitor Information Center is at Wolf and Banff Ave., 762-8421. Write **Banff/Lake Louise Chamber of Commerce,** Box 1298, Banff, Alberta, T0L 0C0. Call (403) 762-0270 for mailings.

Bow View Motor Lodge, 228 Bow Ave., Box 339, T0L, 0C0; (403) 762-2261. Very spacious, bright rooms. Three blocks from the station. $90.

-**Homestead Inn,** 217 Lynx St., T0L 0C0; (403) 762-4471. Attractive rooms, all with VCRs. Three blocks from the station. $89.

Outdoor activities are Banff's major attractions. These include hiking, camping, fishing, boating and mountain climbing. Horseback riding,

VIA Station
1 - **Visitors Information**
2 - **Bow Falls**
3 - **Natural History Museum**
4 - **Bow View Motor Lodge**
5 - **Homestead Inn**

bicycling, golfing and tennis are other activities readily available. Worthwhile museums include the **Natural History Museum,** 112 Banff Ave., the **Banff Park Museum,** 93 Banff Ave., and the **Whyte Museum of the Canadian Rockies,** 111 Bear St.

Lake Louise, a few miles from town, is without a doubt one of the prettiest spots in North America. The Chateau Lake Louise overlooks this lovely lake with the magnificent Victoria Glacier as a backdrop.

Moraine Lake and Valley of the Ten Peaks is a few miles east of the Lake Louise access road. A beautiful lake surrounded by ten glaciated mountain peaks.

The **Banff Springs Hotel,** historic and expensive, is one of the most renowned resorts in the Canadian Rockies and is worth a visit just to see.

0:00 (0:42) Depart Banff.

0:05 (0:37) Looking back to left, whale-shaped mountain looming above Banff is Mt. Rundle.

0:19 (0:23) Massive shape of 9,393-foot Mt. Eisenhower slips by on right.

0:27 (0:15) Castle Mountain is dominant peak at right, just one of an array of spectacular summits that line each side of valley between Banff and Lake Louise.

0:35 (0:07) Famous Valley of Ten Peaks is now visible to left.

0:37 (0:05) At milepost 112, one of highest peaks to be seen on VIA's system is on horizon to left—11,640-foot Mount Temple.

0:41 (0:01) Approaching station for Lake Louise, beautiful Victoria Glacier which hangs directly above lake can be spotted to left.

0:42 (0:00) Arrive Lake Louise.

LAKE LOUISE, ALTA. - This is the gem of the Rockies. The lake, together with its majestic Victoria Glacier, are overlooked by the famous Chateau Lake Louise, but cannot be seen from the tracks.

0:00 (0:47) Depart Lake Louise and commence climb toward Kicking Horse Pass, first of four mountain passes that line route through Rockies. (Rogers Pass, Eagle Pass and Notch Hill will follow in succession.)

0:10 (0:37) Train conquers summit of

5,403-foot Kicking Horse Pass, crest of Continental Divide, as we enter British Columbia and leave Alberta. Also, enter Yoho National Park and exit Banff National Park. Brown sign on left marks Great Divide.

0:16 (0:31) Beautiful Wapta Lake lies nestled on right. Patrons of lodge across lake have fine view of passing train as it glides along lake shore.

0:22 (0:25) Breathtaking view is afforded down valley of Kicking Horse River. Lower Spiral Tunnel can be seen down to right as we descend "The Big Hill."

0:24 (0:21) Enter Upper Spiral Tunnel which makes 188-degree curl to left under Cathedral Mountain. After traveling 3,255 feet in darkness, train will exit and be headed in opposite direction!

This tunnel, along with its near-twin, Lower Spiral Tunnel, were constructed in 1908 and reduced the grade of the track bed from a beleaguering 4.4% to an acceptable 2.2%. The Trans-Canada Highway now claims the former right-of-way. Before the tunnels were constructed, trains had to come to a complete stop at three "safety switches" that directed runaways to turnouts—like modern-day escape ramps for "eighteen wheelers."

0:29 (0:18) Make one of several crossings of tumultuous Kicking Horse River.

0:30 (0:15) Enter 2,922-foot-long Lower Spiral Tunnel beneath Mount Ogden, while making astonishing 226-degree curve to right—coming almost two thirds of full circle.

0:41 (0:04) Pass through mixture of three tunnels and snowsheds.

0:47 (0:00) Arrive Field.

FIELD, B.C. - Railroading is the reason for Field's mountainside existence. Although the original survey would have placed the railroad above Field, this route was the final outcome. The Roundhouse for helper engines no longer stands, but the turntable can still be seen off to the left. Field was named after Cyrus W. Field who promoted the first trans-Atlantic telegraph cable.

0:00 (1:05) Depart Field and continue gradual descent into valley of Kicking Horse River.

0:20 (0:40) Mount Vaux, 10,892 feet, rules over valley on left.

Rocky Mountaineer - Canadian Rockies
JACK SWANSON

0:28 (0:39) Jagged peak of Mt. Chancellor can be seen to rear on right.

0:32 (0:33) Although train now exits Yoho National Park, glorious mountain vistas continue.

0:38 (0:27) Momentary darkness prevails as Canadian pierces first of several tunnels before arriving at Golden.

0:59 (0:05) Curl through former Corey Brothers Tunnel, which once had to be abandoned due to continual cave-ins. Although tunnel was eventually lined with concrete and put back into service, mountain above it had to be removed in 1950's as final solution.

1:03 (0:02) Narrow path of Kicking Horse merges into broad Columbia River Valley, nicely backdropped by Dogtooth Mountain Range on left.

1:05 (0:00) Arrive Golden.

 GOLDEN, B.C. - Although the forest industry provides Golden its primary source of income, tourism, for obvious reasons, is also a mainstay. Its central location between the peaks of Yoho and of the Selkirks affords easy access to innumerable hiking trails, fishing streams and lakes. River rafting and mountaineering are also popular.

0:00 (2:54) Depart Golden and trace a course northward through gentle Columbia River Valley.

0:45 (2:09) Columbia River parts company as train swings southward along pretty Beaver River, green with glacial silt.

Gain one hour as train passes from Mountain to Pacific Time. Set your watch back (forward if eastbound) one hour.

1:00 (1:54) Enter Canada's Glacier National Park—one of western Canada's more rugged regions, dominated by Selkirk Range and perpetual ice.

1:06 (1:48) Crossing over Suprise Creek,

long, straight cascade will be on right. Trestle is 416 feet across.

1:11 (1:44) Our train performs a "death-defying" crossing, 325 feet above Stoney Creek—Canadian Pacific's highest bridge! When completed in 1885, it was highest such structure in the world. Nice waterfall can be glimpsed up chasm to right, as train edges across bridge's 484-foot-long deck.

1:20 (1:27) Rather than struggle over Rogers Pass, trains go underground, traversing one of two tunnels.

Eastbound freight trains use the five-mile-long Connaught Tunnel through Sir Donald Range of Selkirks—second longest rail tunnel in Canada. Construction of Connaught was started in 1913 after more than 200 persons met death in avalanche tragedies on the route over the top between 1885 and 1911. The tunnel was completed in 1916.

Westbound freights use the recently constructed Mount Macdonald Tunnel, which is 9.1 miles long and surpasses the Burlington Northern's Cascade Tunnel (see route of the Empire Builder through Washington state) as the longest in North America. It is the seventh longest in the world and cost a whopping $24 million per mile to build, the world's most expensive nine miles of railroad track. This new tunnel reduces the 2.4% westbound grade to less than 1%, allowing CP Rail to avoid using up to 24 helper engines on their westbound freights. The tunnel is lined with concrete, not for structural reasons but to minimize resistance to the elaborate ventilation system's air flow.

The Mountaineer uses the shorter Connaught Tunnel both directions so passengers can cross the spectacular Stoney Creek Bridge.

1:27 (1:27) At west portal of Connaught Tunnel, note Illecillewaet Glacier clinging to mountainside, high above to left.

1:29 (1:25) Illecillewaet River escorts train in a steady descent from Rogers Pass.

1:34 (1:20) West portal of Mount Macdonald Tunnel is on immediate right.

1:53 (0:59) Three massive snowsheds protect tracks from devastating winter avalanches. At one time there were 31 such sheds protecting descent through Selkirks, totaling five miles in length. Since mountain scenery was important in wooing passenger traffic, original builders installed "summer tracks" outside confining sheds.

2:20 (0:34) Exit Glacier National Park.

2:35 (0:19) Revelstoke National Park borders train on right.

2:44 (0:10) Cross impressive Illecillewaet River that has followed tracks for some time.

2:54 (0:00) Arrive Revelstoke.

REVELSTOKE, B.C. - In a postcard setting of lush forests, streams teeming with fish, towering mountain peaks on all sides, a ski hill and geothermal swimming, Revelstoke offers something for virtually every taste. The Revelstoke Hydroelectric Project, with its immense dam (Canada's highest concrete dam at 575 feet) and power plant just north of here, has been a prime source of revenue for the city. Also, typical of so many mountain towns, mining and forest products are economic mainstays.

0:00 (1:49) Depart Revelstoke, with fine view of Mount Begbie and Mt. Macpherson on left. Columbia River, which takes a northerly course around Selkirks rather than through them, is crossed one final time. Route now follows along Tonkawatla River toward Eagle Pass.

0:12 (1:37) Idyllic Wetask Lake on Eagle Pass rests beside tracks on left. CP line now accompanies Eagle River until Sicamous. Supposedly, in 1865, surveyor Walter Moberly discovered pass after sighting eagles flying through this small opening in Monashee Mountains.

0:24 (1:25) View of inviting Clanwilliam Lake is periodically interrupted as three short tunnels are encountered.

0:31 (1:18) Two sturdy snowsheds protect tracks from avalanches as Canadian slips past beautiful Three Valley Lake cradled in Three Valley Gap.

0:32 (1:17) Cross Eagle River. In fall, watch for spawning salmon.

0:33 (1:16) Griffin (or Green) Lake is just to right of tracks.

0:38 (1:11) Castle facade of "Enchanted Forest" tourist stop, on left, makes rather bizarre scene in heart of Canadian Rockies.

0:41 (1:08) Very pretty Kay Falls can be

seen cascading down valley side on left.

0:53 (0:56) Here, at Craigellachie, named after a valley in Scotland, final spike was driven into place for last section of trans-Canada railroad. Railroad financier Donald Smith performed honors at modest ceremony (last spike was iron, not gold) on November 7, 1885. Line had taken four and a half years to complete. Monument off to right commemorates event at milepost 28.3.

1:09 (0:40) Valley widens in preparation of entering land of Shuswap Lake.

1:14 (0:35) Enter Sicamous where splendid views of Shuswap Lake are first afforded. Here, a swinging span bridge permits boat passage through Sicamous Narrows connecting Shuswap and Mara lakes. Shuswap has 750 miles of shoreline and is home to both Dolley Varden and Kamloops trout, attracting largest aggregation of houseboats anywhere in Canada (many of which are just to left).

1:16 (0:33) Tracks continue to border serene Salmon Arm of Shuswap Lake.

1:49 (0:00) Arrive town of Salmon Arm.

SALMON ARM, B.C. - This is the commercial hub of the Shuswap areas, as well as being an agricultural center featuring dairy cows, fruit (apples, strawberries and cherries), vegetables, sheep and poultry. An abundance of tourists in pursuit of water-oriented pastimes will be found during the summer months.

0:00 (1:45) Depart Salmon Arm.

0:02 (1:43) Cross 100 feet above Salmon River, as it nears journey's end at Shuswap Lake.

0:10 (1:35) Brief look is afforded down length of Salmon Arm.

0:38 (1:07) Water on right is western-most reaches of Shuswap Lake.

0:40 (1:00) Lake briefly narrows into South Thompson River before opening into Little Shuswap Lake, on right. At this point, Adams River drains into South Thompson from north. Adams is known for its enormous sockeye salmon runs every four eyes.

1:00 (0:45) Valley continues to widen as farm and ranch lands now blanket valley floor. Watch for occasional canoes plying through broad, still waters of South Thompson on right.

1:09 (0:36) Huge cluster of twigs and branches atop power pole on right is an osprey nest.

1:16 (0:29) Fields with awning-like shading across valley to left are ginseng farms. Ginseng is a medicinal herb, and the name comes from Chinese words meaning "likeness of a man" because of the roots' appearance.

1:24 (0:21) At milepost 114, notorious American robber, Billy Miner, held up Canadian Pacific in 1906 and galloped off with only $15 of loot.

1:33 (0:12) Entering outskirts of Kamloops, site of prehistoric Indian dwellings is off to right.

1:45 (0:00) Arrive Kamloops' Lorne Street Station, situated on lower edge of downtown.

For route log from Kamloops to Vancouver, see route of Canadian, page 408.

Skeena

The superlative lakes and mountains of Jasper National Park (during the longer days) and the pristine Coastal Range of British Columbia bedazzle Skeena travelers on a wilderness trip between Jasper and Prince Rupert. The ramble along the Skeena River Gorge into Prince Rupert is one of the best excursions on the continent.

At Prince Rupert, still further adventure awaits, where ferry service is available north to Alaska through the spectacular "Inside Passage," or south to Seattle along British Columbia's scenic and rugged Pacific coastline.

Westbound Schedule (Condensed)
Jasper, Alta. - Midevening Departure
Prince George, B.C. - Middle of the Night (2nd Day)
Smithers, B.C. - Early Morning (2nd Day)
Prince Rupert, B.C. - Midafternoon Arrival (2nd Day)

Eastbound Schedule (Condensed)
Prince Rupert, B.C. - Late Morning Departure
Smithers, B.C. - Late Afternoon
Prince George, B.C. - Late Night (2nd Day)
Jasper, Alta. - Early Morning Arrival (2nd Day)

Frequency - Three times a week, departing Jasper Sunday, Wednesday and Friday and departing Prince Rupert Sunday, Tuesday and Friday.

Seating - Standard coach.
Dining - Complete meal and beverage service as well as lighter fare.
Sleeping - Berths, roomettes and bedrooms.
Baggage - No checked baggage.
Reservations - Reserved coach seats upon purchase of tickets.
Length of Trip - 721 miles in 20½ hours.

Route Log

 JASPER, ALTA. - See page 405.

0:00 (3:40) Depart Jasper and head toward Yellowhead Pass.

Some of North America's most magnificent scenery will soon appear! The Trident Range will be on our left and the Victoria Cross Range on our right as we make this ascent. Waterfalls, streams, snowfields and tunnels make this a railroading spectacular.

0:27 (3:13) Those small wire fences, seen here on uphill side of right-of-way, are slide detectors which activate a red signal should there be a rockslide or snowslide.

Gain one hour as train passes from Mountain to Pacific Time. Set your watch back (forward if eastbound) one hour.

0:42 (2:59) Crest of Yellowhead Pass is reached at milepost 17.5. Enter province of British Columbia and leave Alberta. We are only 3,718 feet above sea level, however, many of surrounding peaks soar to more than 11,000 feet. Yellowhead is one of lowest passes along entire North American Continental Divide. Waters flowing to east ultimately find their way to Arctic Ocean.

0:47 (2:53) Yellowhead Lake stretches serenely beside tracks on left. Yellowhead Mountain is highest peak directly across lake.

1:11 (2:29) Moose Lake now appears alongside at left, even larger than Yellowhead.

1:24 (2:16) Red Pass Junction at milepost 43.9 is flag stop where two rail lines divide. One CN line heads to left (south) down Blue River toward Kamloops and Vancouver, while Skeena will continue on due west, following route of Fraser River as far as Prince George. After that, Skeena River will be traced to train's final destination, Prince Rupert.

1:42 (1:58) Along this stretch, if sky is clear, passengers are treated to a fine view of Mt. Robson which bolts up at end of a valley on right. A dramatic scene indeed, with snowfields clinging to its red, stratified face. It's unmistakably Canadian Rockies' highest at 12,972 feet. Have your camera ready.

2:02 (1:38) Rearguard Falls in Fraser River are formidable obstacle for salmon that come all this way from Pacific Ocean. Falls, however, present a final and insurmountable barrier to salmons' journey. Mountains now start to become less rugged and somewhat softer as train continues westward.

3:21 (0:19) Pass high above Shuswap River.

3:34 (0:06) Dairy cattle grazing in pastures tucked away amongst rolling forests create delicate pastoral scenes.

3:40 (0:00) Arrive McBride.

MCBRIDE, B.C. - This is the first "city" (pop. 800) west of Jasper, having been established during the construction of the Grand Trunk Pacific in 1912. A sportsman's delight, the area offers about any kind of quarry, from Dolly Varden trout to grizzly bear.

0:00 (4:45) Depart McBride.

0:05 (4:40) Below, on right, Oscar's Wild-

life Museum makes a bizarre sight with various colored tractor tires for a fence, and a bear and a moose painted on building's side.

0:29 (4:16) Into a tunnel.

Darkness usually prevails (except longest of days when westbound) between here and Prince George.

4:45 (0:00) Arrive Prince George.

PRINCE GEORGE, B.C. - Although many rail travelers stop here only to change trains (VIA to British Columbia Railway or vice versa), there is reason to spend a little extra time in Prince George—especially for railfans. A growing rail museum, nurtured by an energetic group of local rail enthusiasts, has an excellent collection of rail cars and equipment; and there's even a small passenger train operation in the city's Fort George Park.

Prince George was little more than a spot on the map until the Grand Trunk

Pacific reached this site in 1910. Lumbering and mining contributed to steady growth, and today, Prince George is a city of 70,000, still largely dependent on those two industries.

There are two stations in Prince George: The VIA Station, which is on the edge of downtown; and the British Columbia Railway (BCR) Station located on the outskirts of the city, about four miles south of the VIA Station. Pay shuttle service is available between these two stations, also serving downtown hotels.

-VIA Station, First Ave. and Quebec, serves VIA's east-west route through central British Columbia. There are storage lockers, luggage carts and beverage vending machines.

For reservations, call 800-561-8630.

-BCR Station, 1108 Industrial Way. This is a small but very neat station in an industrial area of the city. For information, call 564-9081. There is very limited long-term free parking. The station also has a small gift counter. Write BC Rail Ltd., Passenger Sales & Service, Box 8770, Vancouver, B.C. V6B 4X6.

Cabs have a direct line at the VIA Station. Prince George Taxi, 564-4444. Budget, 564-8395 and Tilden, 564-4847. Local bus information, 563-0011.

Prince George Visitors and Convention Bureau, 1198 Victoria St., V2L 2L2; (604) 562-3700.

The Coast Inn of the North, 770 Brunswick Street, V2L 2C2; (604) 563-0121 or 800-663-1144. Very nice high-rise hotel. Eight blocks from the VIA Station. $100.

-Simon Fraser Inn, 600 Quebec St., V2L 1W7; (604) 562-3181. Very attractive rooms. Six blocks from the VIA Station. $60.

-Downtown Motel, 650 Dominion, V2L 1T8; (604) 563-9241. Small economy motel, six blocks from the station. $47.

-The Prince George Railway Museum, off of River Road and close to downtown, has a very fine assortment of rail cars, artifacts and other equipment, as well as a gift shop. The jewel is the Nechaco, a 1913 Pullman that was beautifully restored for EXPO 86.

The **Fraser-Fort George Regional Museum,** located in Fort George Park, has a good number of well-displayed artifacts from the region's past. Also in Ft. George Park is the **Ft. George Railway,** offering rides in coaches pulled along a half-mile of track by a Grand Trunk Pacific six-ton work "dinkey," which has unusually small drive wheels that allowed it to operate on very steep grades.

0:00 (1:55) Departing Prince George, follow Nechaco River as it journeys westward toward Vanderhoof and British Columbia lakelands. Country is known for its timber and minerals.

0:55 (1:00) At Isle Pierre, "current ferry" (using stream's force as only source of power) transports vehicles across river.

1:55 (0:00) Arrive Vanderhoof.

VANDERHOOF, B.C. - This is the geographical center of British Columbia. It is also home to 50,000 Canadian geese that find refuge in the adjacent Nechaco Bird Sanctuary.

But each year, the third weekend in July, birds of an entirely different kind gather here when Vanderhoof holds Canada's largest "camp-in" air show. Canadian and U.S. military jets, aerobatics teams, antique fighters and numerous WWII aircraft entertain 20,000 spectators for two exciting days. If you're an airplane fanatic, you'll want to contact: Vanderhoof International Airshow, Box 1248, Vanderhoof, B.C., V0J 3A0, or phone 604-567-3144.

0:00 (1:11) Depart Vanderhoof.

0:02 (1:09) Lumbering operations become more evident; Nechaco sawmills are on left.

0:05 (1:06) Huge Westar Timber Plateau operations sawmill is on left.

0:36 (0:35) Just north of Fort Fraser, "last spike" was driven on April 7, 1914 to complete Grand Trunk Pacific line. After financial problems, railroad was absorbed into Canadian Pacific.

0:37 (0:34) Passing through Fort Fraser, note large depot-like building on right, recently built to house "Last Spike Pub."

0:38 (0:33) Cross broad waters of Nechaco River.

0:45 (0:26) Skeena now skirts border of Fraser Lake on right. In July, fireweed along right-of-way and in nearby fields produces brilliant splashes of reddish purple.

0:53 (0:18) Lumbering industry remains quite evident as Skeena passes Fraser Lake Sawmills.

1:01 (0:10) Cross Stellako River. Its five-mile length reputedly makes it shortest river in province.

1:09 (0:02) Just before Endako, road to left leads to Endako Mine, world's largest open-pit molybdenum mine.

1:11 (0:00) Arrive Endako.

ENDAKO, B.C. - This is a service center, largely dependent on rail-roading (it's a division point) and, of course, the aforementioned Endako Mine.

0:00 (0:49) Depart Endako and follow Endako River.

0:31 (0:18) Yet another sawmill, this time Babine Forest Products sawmill on right.

0:37 (0:12) Tintagel Cairn, visible on right (through bushes), contains stone core which was once part of Tintagel Castle in Cornwall, England. Castle was reputed birthplace of King Arthur (of Round Table fame), and stone was brought here during Canada's centennial in 1967 to help preserve community's heritage. Cairn also contains time capsule to be opened in 2067.

0:42 (0:07) Body of water, on left, is Burns Lake.

0:49 (0:00) Arrive Burns Lake.

BURNS LAKE, B.C. - Originally, Burns Lake was a mere telegraph relay cabin along the Collins Overland Telegraph Line. But when the railroad arrived in 1908, it gained civilized substance.

One of the town's earliest pioneers was quite successful in the hotel business. No longer needing his small cabin, he converted it into a gambling hall. This venerable establishment, known as "The Bucket of Blood," has been restored and now reposes next to the local museum.

The main street has a distinct curve, created when the town's surveyor ran the road around a settler's barn and corral. The landowner, however, claimed the surveyor was drunk and had merely followed a cow path through town.

British Columbia's largest provincial park, Tweedsmuir (and B.C.'s smallest,

Deadman's Island) is near here, and today Burns Lake is an important recreational outpost. Rockhounding is also popular, with large opal and agate deposits located nearby.

0:00 (1:07) Depart Burns Lake.

0:11 (0:56) Decker Lake now extends along tracks on left. Babine Lake, longest natural body of water in province, is just north of here, but too distant to see from train. Naturally, with such a proliferation of lakes, moose are common to the area and can often be spotted along right-of-way.

0:17 (0:50) Skeena slips past one more large sawmill, an operation of Decker Lake Forest Products.

1:07 (0:00) Arriving Houston, "World's Largest Flyrod," on left, just east of visitors center, is an obvious statement about region's most popular sport. Also, note sawmill display on west side of visitors center.

HOUSTON, B.C. - This community of 3,000 persons is the home of two giant lumbering companies, one of which, Northwood Pulp and Timber, has the largest enclosed sawmill in the world. Tours are available. Mining and tourism round out Houston's economy, with rockhounding, snowmobiling and cross-country skiing being popular outdoor activities.

0:00 (1:02) Depart Houston through farm- and ranchlands, set scenically amidst Bulkley River Valley. Peaks of Coastal Range loom in distance, soon to escort Skeena on final leg into Prince Rupert.

0:01 (1:01) Stark, white-frame Christian Reformed Church faces tracks on left.

0:03 (0:59) Just west of Houston, tracks that veer off to left serve those two huge sawmills, mentioned just above. Steam from those operations is visible above trees. Here, Morice River flows into Bulkley.

0:45 (0:17) Pastoral splendor of Bulkley River Valley is epitomized by area surrounding Telkwa where dairy cows, green pastures and hay meadows are backdropped by towering Hazelton Mountains.

0:48 (0:14) Through Telkwa, one of oldest communities in valley, where Telkwa and Bulkley rivers meet. Salmon and steelhead fishing and canoeing are favored activities.

Church at Kitwanga, British Columbia
JACK SWANSON

Novice and intermediate paddlers are particularly attracted to waters.

1:02 (0:00) Arriving Smithers, Hudson's Bay Mountain on left is regally graced with Kathlyn Glacier.

SMITHERS, B.C. - Established in 1913 as a division point on the Grand Trunk Pacific, Smithers was the first village to be incorporated in British Columbia. It now has a population of 4,500, making it the Valley's trading center. In 1979, most Main Street businesses were given a facelift and now bear a resemblance to a Bavarian village—blending nicely with the town's alpine setting.

Smithers' visitor center occupies what was once a buffet club car on the CN line between Toronto and Montreal.

0:00 (1:14) Departing Smithers, challenging golf course on right annually hosts prestigious Labor Day tournament.

0:08 (1:06) Handsome homes dot shore-line of Lake Kathlyn on right, with reflection of Skeena Mountains cast majestically across water. Skeenas are subclassification of Coastal Range. To left is impressive Kathlyn Glacier, cradled in Hudson Bay Mountains.

0:20 (0:54) High Bridge across frothy Trout Creek is first of several dramatic spans soon traversed.

0:30 (0:43) Pass through Moricetown, largest Indian village in Valley. East of here, although not visible from train, Bulkley River squeezes through narrow gorge called Moricetown Canyon, where Carrier Indians still "subsistence fish" for salmon traveling to spawn in Babine Lake. Carriers once used fish traps (no longer legal); now, they fish with long gaffing poles, spearing these large fish with utmost skill.

0:40 (0:33) On right, Bulkley River descends into gorge—a preview of exciting canyons awaiting downstream.

0:42 (0:31) Rail buffs should seize opportunity to photograph train as it winds gracefully (to right) across towering Boulder Creek trestle. A short distance downline, bridge across Porphyry Creek affords similar possibilities.

0:59 (0:15) From high atop rocky ledges, train now embarks on inspiring four-mile adventure through cuts and tunnels of magnificent Bulkley Canyon. Below, cliffs compress Bulkley River into a surging torrent of white water. On opposite bank, waterfalls tumble down into river, further enhancing this spectacular stretch.

1:14 (0:00) Arrive New Hazelton.

NEW HAZELTON, B.C. - Three towns are clustered together here (New Town, Old Town and South Town) as well as myriad nearby Indian villages—all of which make up the area called "The Hazeltons." Indian lore pervades the region, and a reconstructed Indian village from the early 1900s can be explored. Numerous totem poles—one said to be the world's oldest—are found throughout the area. Also, one of the largest collections of Indian carvings outside of a museum is located here. The area is famous for its stylized West Coast Indian art, sought after by international collectors.

0:00 (2:16) Depart New Hazelton. On left, imposing peaks are some of region's tallest, extending 8,000 feet above sea level. Mount Rocher Déboulé, with its 3,000-foot cliffs, dominates.

0:08 (2:08) Trestle across Sealy Gulch is not for faint-of-heart, perched nearly 200 feet above deep gorge.

0:10 (2:06) On right, Bulkley River has emerged from canyon, and now carves swath through verdant pasturelands. In distance, Hazelton Mountains frame this most picturesque setting.

Shortly downstream, Bulkley River flows into Skeena River, descending from north.

0:35 (1:41) Cross Skeena River which then borders route on left into Prince Rupert. On opposite bank, quaint little town of Nash makes enchanting centerpiece of scene seemingly plucked from travel poster.

0:48 (1:28) Kitwanga, a Skeena flag stop, is starting point for Stewart-Cassiar Highway 37 which winds through wilderness

north of here and traverses some of most spectacular scenery in British Columbia. Kitwanga is Indian for "people of the place where there are rabbits." One of region's many totem poles is on left, immediately after passing burned-out rail station. In winter (when trees are defoliated), St. Pauls Anglican Episcopal Church can sometimes be glimpsed off to left, together with free-standing ornate bell tower. Also, street lined with totem poles (called "Tour of Totems") might be seen to left. Then Skeena passes through Indian cemetery with many graves individually fenced in a profusion of styles.

0:58 (1:18) Beautiful farmhouse adorns landscape on right at Woodcock. Jagged, dramatic Seven Sisters Range is at left, with seven very pronounced peaks.

1:06 (1:10) Old post office and general store are venerable structures seen on left at Cedarvale. An independent mission was established here in 1888. Its effectiveness earned town nickname "The Holy City," and for many years absolutely no work was performed on the Sabbath.

Descending gradually toward sea level, proceed along the scenic Skeena River Valley, with awesome glaciers stretched atop nearby peaks. At trackside, colorful mosses and ferns soften the terrain—a remarkable contrast to the rugged alpine climes looming just above.

1:41 (0:34) Old hotel is nostalgic relic on right at Pacific, now struggling to support its own weight.

1:59 (0:17) At Usk, note another "current ferry" that shuttles between homes on riverbanks. Flow of stream forces cable-guided craft from one side to other, while sign on far side instructs motorists to call for service by either ringing gong on pole or honking horn.

2:16 (0:00) Arrive Terrace.

TERRACE, B.C. - The largest community between Prince George and Prince Rupert, with a metropolitan population of 18,000, is the center of large lumbering operations as well as government, transportation and service industries. Visitors will find much of interest in the region, including lava beds, fossils, hot springs—and as always throughout the province—fishing. A 92½-pound salmon was taken by a rod and reel from the Skeena near here, a world's record.

Kitimat, a planned community built in the 1950s, just 50 miles south, has several industries that can be toured. Most renowned is Alcan's aluminum smelter, one of the world's largest. (Call first for Alcan reservations, 604-639-8259).

0:00 (2:10) Depart Terrace through industrial district, with logging operations again most abundant. Two more totem poles will appear at right.

0:04 (2:06) Cross Kitsumkaylus River, first of countless tributaries swelling Skeena River enroute to Pacific Ocean. Mountains of Kitimat Range now border route on both sides.

0:48 (1:22) Stretch between mileposts 39 and 50 features several sets of spectacular waterfalls, cascading down near trackside. (Mileposts are conspicuously tacked on adjacent poles.)

1:01 (1:09) All that remains of Kwinitsa are two small sheds. Lovely little station that once stood at trackside was moved to Prince Rupert where it now serves as railroad museum near Prince Rupert's VIA station.

1:16 (0:54) Highway and tracks once shared narrow shelf along river, making vehicular traffic uncomfortable partner of trains through here. At one point, highway actually went beneath power-line tower. Thousands of tons of rock have recently widened base for more roomy arrangement.

1:27 (0:43) Rustic fishing piers on left are entrenched in general area where freshwater and saltwater begin to mix. At this point, river has widened to near half-mile breadth. Watch for harbor seals that sometimes frequent this segment of river.

1:37 (0:33) Fishing industry quickly takes center stage approaching Prince Rupert. Villages at Cassiar, Sunnyside and North Pacific are surrounded by colorful assemblage of boats, with daily harvests proudly displayed across docks.

Waters now broaden into Chatham Sound, encircling Smith, Lelu and Ridley islands. Ridley is an aspiring seaport, with coal and grain facilities built to cultivate Asian markets.

1:47 (0:23) Cross bridge onto Kaien Island, home of Prince Rupert. Continue along docks, past terminals for Alaska and British Columbia ferries.

2:10 (0:00) Arrive Prince Rupert, its depot tucked neatly within rocky cove.

PRINCE RUPERT, B.C. - When you come to Prince Rupert, bring your raincoat. Its location on Kaien Island, where the Skeena River dumps into the Pacific, accounts for many misty days—some more misty than others. Even the Chamber of Commerce does not deny that the city gets more than its share of rainfall; they simply call it the "City of Rainbows."

But it's part of the atmosphere that makes Prince Rupert a bit like a miniature San Francisco. Dazzling floral displays in the town parks, neat clapboard homes shelved on the hillsides, an interesting waterfront, complete with fishing fleets and seafood eateries, and some gorgeous harbor sunsets. Yet most people are here to catch ferryboats—ferries to Vancouver and Vancouver Island to the south; ferries up Alaska's Inside Passage to the north; ferries to the Queen Charlotte Islands to the west.

And, of course, more than a few travelers arrive or leave by train. Prince Rupert's history began with the arrival of the Grand Trunk Pacific (now the CN) in 1914, built to compete with the Canadian Pacific's transcontinental route. Soon, fishing and fish processing rose to prominence, then the timber industry. Today, tourism has been added as an economic bulwark.

VIA Station is situated on the harbor, directly below downtown. The station is open several hours each day except Sunday. The station has storage lockers, a literature rack, including city maps, and complimentary coffee. There is limited short-term parking; long-term parking is two blocks from the station. For reservations and other information, call 800-561-8630.

Skeena **Taxi,** 624-2185. **Local buses** are four blocks from station. Tilden and Budget **rental cars** are available. **Alaska State Ferries** sail northward up the scenic Inside Passage to Ketchikan, Wrangell, Petersburg, Juneau, Haines, Sitka and Skagway, and southward to Seattle. **British Columbia Ferries** offer service south to Port Harvey on Vancouver Island, as well as the Queen Charlotte Islands.

? Prince Rupert Visitors Bureau is located at 1st Avenue and McBride St. in the Museum Building, P.O. Box 669, V8J 3S1. Call (604) 624-5637.

Prince Rupert has numerous good accommodations, and pricing seems to fairly reflect the degree of quality and location. Those shown below are in the downtown area. If you plan to walk to any of these accommodations from the station, be prepared to climb. A cab is recommended.

-Crest Motor Hotel, 222 West 1st Ave., Box 277, V8J 3P6; (604) 624-6771 or 800-663-8150. An outstanding hostelry, complete with an elegant dining room, on a bluff overlooking the harbor. $95 to $105 (seaside).

-Inn on the Harbour, 1st Ave. and 6th St., Box 700, V8J 3P9; (604) 624-9107. Excellent downtown location, overlooking the harbor with a nice restaurant. $60.

-Aleeda Motel, 900 3rd Ave. West, V8J 1M8; (604) 627-1367. Small, quiet, nicely maintained motel with large rooms, all with balconies. $58.

The following are in the downtown area. Be sure to visit the city's **Sunken Gardens,** small but immaculate; and **Service Park,** again small but colorful. **Sunsets** on the harbor, weather permitting, can be spectacular. Have a good seafood dinner at **Smiles** on the waterfront; be sure to ask for a table with a view of the marina. **Shopping,** of course, is in the downtown area, including two malls. The very fine **Museum of Northern British Columbia,** with exhibits of Indian and regional culture, is at the visitors center. And next to the VIA station is a small but wonderful **Railroad Museum** in the former Kwinitsa depot, depicting how life used to be for those who worked and lived in those remote outposts. It contains an excellent telegraph exhibit.

For a commanding view of the town and the harbor, ride the **gondola** to the top of Mt. Hays, a few minutes by car from downtown. A bit farther is Port Edward, where the century-old **North Pacific Cannery** has been restored as a museum for the fishing industry.

Prince Rupert

- VIA Station
- 1 - Visitors Information & Museum of Northern BC
- 2 - Kwinitsa Ry Museum
- 3 - Sunken Gardens
- 4 - Gondola
- 5 - Crest Motor Hotel
- 6 - Inn on the Harbour
- 7 - Aleeda Motel

British Columbia Railway

Somehow, Norway's rugged and spectacular fiords have been magically transported to Canada. Self-propelled Dayliners (rail diesel cars) of the incredible British Columbia Railway brush along the water's edge as lofty peaks soar dramatically overhead. Traveling 461 miles from North Vancouver to Prince George, the railroad wends through ever-changing but always marvelous scenery, ranging from that just described to the more arid interior mountains of British Columbia.

"Cariboo Class" accommodations are available on through trains, with more roomy seating, complimentary meals, and bar service.

Note that this train uses the BCR stations in North Vancouver and Prince George—not the VIA stations. See North Vancouver (below) for ticket information.

Northbound Schedule (Condensed)
North Vancouver, B.C. - Early Morning Departure
Squamish, B.C. - Early Morning
Pemberton, B.C. - Late Morning
Lillooet, B.C. - Early Afternoon
Exeter, B.C. - Midafternoon
Williams Lake, B.C. - Late Afternoon
Prince George, B.C. - Late Evening Arrival

Southbound Schedule (Condensed)
Prince George, B.C. - Early Morning Departure
Williams Lake, B.C. - Late Morning
Exeter, B.C. - Early Afternoon
Lillooet, B.C. - Midafternoon
Pemberton, B.C. - Late Afternoon
Squamish, B.C. - Early Evening
North Vancouver, B.C. - Late Evening Arrival

Frequency - Summer: Daily each direction between North Vancouver and Prince George. Remainder of year: Daily, each direction between Vancouver and Lillooet; Sunday, Wednesday and Friday, northbound continues on from Lillooet to Prince George; Monday, Thursday and Saturday, southbound from Prince George to Vancouver.

Seating - Dayliner coaches. Cariboo Class has more luxurious seating, but is often more heavily used.

Dining - Food service available on through trains. Cariboo Class includes meals at no extra charge. Coach passengers can purchase light snacks.

Baggage - Checked baggage handled only on through trains to and from Prince George. Baggage for flag stops where agents are not on duty must be claimed from train baggageman before arrival.

Reservations - Reserved seats are required on all trains operating north of Lillooet.

Length of Trip - 461 miles in 13½ hours.

Route Log

NORTH VANCOUVER, B.C. - North Vancouver, just across Burrard Inlet from Vancouver, is the southern terminus of the BCR. It is also the home of the legendary Royal Hudson steam trains that make excursion runs along beautiful Howe Sound to Squamish during the summer months.

BCR Station, 1311 W. 1st Ave., in North Vancouver. Both British Columbia Railway trains to Prince George and Royal Hudson steam trains use this station. A Whistler Ski Train runs on weekends in the winter. The station has a beverage vending machine and storage lockers.

Call (604) 631-3500 for reservations and information. No checked baggage is permitted after ten minutes prior to train departure. Write BC Rail, Passenger Sales Service, Box 8770, V6B 4X6.

Early morning bus service is furnished to the BCR Station from the Vancouver bus terminal, making stops along Georgia Street at regular transit stops until the Stanley Park entrance. In the evening, buses meet the trains to return passengers by the same route. A fare is charged.

0:00 (1:16) Depart North Vancouver.

0:01 (1:15) On left is graceful Lions Gate Bridge. Look back on right where Royal Hudson Steam Train can often be seen poking out from BCR shops.

0:04 (1:12) Under Lions Gate Bridge.

0:06 (1:10) Cross Capilano River at confluence with English Bay on left.

0:10 (1:06) In late summer, bay frequently has dozen or more freighters waiting for berths to load Canadian grain for export. Ships must pay $1000 per day to anchor in harbor.

0:12 (1:04) Dense, lush foliage contrasts nicely with modernistic high rises and beautiful homes of affluent West Vancouver. This is considered to be most expensive real estate in Canada.

0:23 (0:53) A long tunnel (1,700 feet) precedes first view of magnificent Howe Sound on left. Immediate waters are Horseshoe Bay. Area is renowned for its salmon fishing. Dock for ferries to Vancouver Island is below.

0:33 (0:43) Dome of 5,330-foot Mt. Wrottesley dominates opposite shore.

1:02 (0:14) Britannia Beach, at milepost 30, is where mining and smelting operations once stood at base of 6,645-foot Mt. Sheen. Barren top of 6,815-foot Mt. Sedgewick is forward on left, across bay.

1:08 (0:08) Forward on left is sharply defined Mt. Garibaldi, looming 8,787 feet above Squamish.

1:13 (0:03) On right, at milepost 39, is Stawamus Chief—reputed to be second largest rock in world. Monolith is a favorite with rock climbers who pit their skills (and luck) against its massive granite face, which rises 2,138 feet above the bay. Facility across bay is wood fiber plant.

1:16 (0:00) Arrive Squamish at milepost 40.

SQUAMISH, B.C. - Situated at the northern tip of Howe Sound, near Garibaldi Provincial Park and the northern terminus of the Royal Hudson steam train, it is understandable why tourism is big business in Squamish. BCR locomotive shops are located here.

0:00 (1:05) Depart Squamish where rails follow route of Squamish River. Peak bolting up on right is Mt. Garibaldi, reaching 8,786 feet above sea level.

0:09 (0:56) Commence through beautiful Cheakamus Canyon at milepost 47.

0:25 (0:40) Blue-green color of Cheakamus River on right is typical of mountain glacial streams. Cheakamus Canyon now becomes even more dramatic.

0:30 (0:35) Scenery is absolutely stunning, with Cheakamus Range sporting beautiful glaciers, back to left, and falls gracing canyon at right.

0:50 (0:15) Train will sometimes slow down at this point for better view over top of Brandywine Falls which plummet 280 feet to valley floor, below right.

1:05 (0:00) Arrive Whistler.

WHISTLER, B.C. - Quaint chalet architecture pervades this year-round resort, where skiing is the major attraction. The name Whistler comes from the marmot, a woodchuck which lives in the mountains and gives off a loud, shrill noise resembling a whistle.

0:00 (0:40) Depart Whistler.

0:02 (0:38) At Alta Lake, train crests summit of Coastal Range at 2,199-foot elevation (milepost 74). From here a gradual descent leads to fertile Pemberton Valley where root crops, such as potatoes and turnips, thrive.

0:04 (0:36) Blackcomb ski runs cut swaths down Blackcomb Mountain on right.

0:09 (0:31) At milepost 79, long and narrow Green Lake on left has 7,000-foot Rainbow Mountain for fine backdrop.

0:35 (0:03) Cascades of Green River rapids and then Nairn Falls add to charm of grand entrance to Pemberton.

0:40 (0:00) Arrive Pemberton at milepost 95.

PEMBERTON, B.C. - This is the major trading center for the lush Pemberton Valley. It was near here, along the Lillooet River, that early-day prospectors streamed by, seeking their fortunes during the gold-rush days. Massive Mount Currie towers above valley on right, at 8,364 feet.

0:00 (2:05) Depart Pemberton and cross Lillooet River.

0:06 (1:59) At milepost 99, pass through flag stop of Mt. Currie, serving one of British Columbia's largest Indian reservations.

0:10 (1:43) Train is now escorted by Birkenhead River until its arrival at Birken at top of Cascade Range.

0:24 (1:41) At milepost 109, Number Ten Downing Street is curious location (and quarters) for British prime minister. House was built by war veteran who settled here and then worked as a mountain guide. Names of various battles he fought in now serve as exterior decor.

0:33 (1:32) At Birken, Birkenhead Provincial Park is in mountains just to left.

0:48 (1:17) At milepost 123, train begins journey along 15 miles of Anderson Lake shoreline, on right.

0:52 (1:11) Views are momentarily taken away as Dayliner cuts through a short tunnel.

0:58 (1:07) At milepost 129, McGillivray Falls can be glimpsed behind homes on left.

1:18 (0:47) Seton Portage, at milepost 139, lies between Anderson and Seton lakes, and was site of first railway in province. Wooden rails were used to portage boats between lakes!

1:24 (0:40) Into darkness again, this time traveling through tunnel for 2,940 feet—a tunnel built to avoid landslides that once plagued this stretch of trackage. Emerge along banks of lovely Seton Lake, nestled between Mt. McLean on left and Cayoosh Range across lake. Penstocks, those giant tubes on left, bring water from higher environs to power hydroelectric plant of B.C. Hydro and Power Authority. Seton Lake is darker than Anderson, due to glacial silt introduced through penstocks.

1:28 (0:35) At milepost 142, Shalalth was gateway to placer gold mining of Bridge River more than 100 years ago. (This type of mining obtained gold from gravel deposits and is pronounced "plass-er.")

During school months, children board train here to be transported to Lillooet. Note colorful Indian murals on each end of shelter.

1:58 (0:07) At north end of Seton Lake, 9,200-foot Mt. Brew towers above valley on right.

1:59 (0:06) Dam, on right, has fish ladder for convenience of salmon that head upstream to spawn.

2:02 (0:03) Entry into Lillooet affords excellent view of BCR hopper cars being filled with woodchips from adjacent sawmill on right.

2:05 (0:00) Arrive Lillooet.

LILLOOET, B.C. - Located at the confluence of the Fraser River and Cayoosh Creek, placer mining during the last century made Lillooet, pronounced "Lil-loo-ETT," a boom town of the gold-rush era. It was also an important provisioning point on the Cariboo Highway that led to the north. In spite of its mountain setting, temperatures frequently soar above 100 degrees during the summer, which partially accounts for the fine crops of watermelon, vegetables and fruit that are grown here.

0:00 (2:44) Depart Lillooet.

0:04 (2:38) Suspension bridge below right, built in 1903, is one of oldest of its kind in western Canada.

0:05 (2:37) Cross Fraser River, spanned by attractive silvery-steel bridge, and commence steep climb out of canyon for next 30 miles, gaining 3,000 feet in elevation before emerging on Cariboo Plateau at Kelly Lake.

0:11 (2:33) Below left, two fish ladders have been constructed in Fraser. Fish drying racks of natives are usually quite apparent through this area of canyon.

0:29 (2:11) Irrigated fields across valley are used to grow ginseng, a medicinal herb. Ginseng comes from Chinese words meaning "likeness of a man" because of the roots' appearance. It takes four years to produce a crop.

0:36 (2:04) After basic depot at Pavilion, a steady ascent is made, some of the most difficult and spectacular railroading in

North America.

0:48 (1:42) At milepost 183, after passing through Moran, Fraser River snakes through canyon, a dizzying 2,678 feet below.

1:02 (1:32) Kelly Lake, at milepost 193, rests in a glorious setting, with Marble Range forming a most scenic backdrop on left. This is edge of great cattle country of the Cariboo.

1:20 (1:12) Through flag stop of Clinton, center of ranching, where renowned Clinton Ball is held each May during town's annual rodeo.

1:32 (1:00) At milepost 215, flag stop of Chasm is aptly named for a deep canyon on right, formed at close of ice age when a stream from melting ice cut through lava-formed Fraser Plateau. Both rims of chasm will be visible in a moment on right.

2:07 (0:25) At milepost 243, Horse Lake is heart of guest ranch country and is highest point on British Columbia Railway, 3,864 feet above sea level. From here, Dayliner begins a gradual descent into cattle country of Williams Lake through forested, rolling countryside interspersed with open fields and meadows.

2:11 (0:21) Pride of Lone Butte is nicely restored railroad water tower, on right, at north edge of community.

2:22 (0:08) Exeter, our next stop, is below right.

2:28 (0:00) Arrive Exeter.

EXETER (100 Mile House), B.C. - This pretty little village is a trading and distribution hub for local ranching and lumbering activities.

0:00 (1:27) Depart Exeter.

0:16 (1:10) Herd of buffalo can sometimes be seen grazing on right.

0:20 (1:00) Peaceful waters of Lake LaHache stretch along tracks on right from milepost 274 to 281.

1:04 (0:12) Waters of Williams Lake are on right.

1:16 (0:00) Arrive Williams Lake at milepost 314.

WILLIAMS LAKE, B.C. - This is the "Cattle Capital of British Columbia," with thousands of critters being shipped, not only to Canada but also to the U.S. Lumber is also important, with large mills in and around this city of 13,000.

BCR Excursion Train - Lillooet Bridge, British Columbia
HOMER R. HILL

0:00 (1:28) Depart Williams Lake.

0:23 (1:05) An airy crossing of Deep Creek takes place at milepost 331 on one of world's highest railway bridges—a 1,200-foot span, 312 feet above water.

0:30 (1:00) Soda Creek, at milepost 541, marks the point from which venerable river steamers plyed Fraser River to Prince George and back—a 260-mile round trip.

1:29 (0:04) On outskirts of Quesnel, Western Plywood plant processes lumber into multi-layered wooden sheets of construction plywood.

1:33 (0:00) Cross Quesnel River on arrival Quesnel.

 QUESNEL, B.C. - This city, pronounced kwah-NELL, of 8,000 serves as a regional trade center, and is home for several lumber-oriented industries.

0:00 (1:53) Depart Quesnel.

0:02 (1:49) String of lumber mills and pulp plant attest to Quesnel's claim to be one of largest lumber producing cities in world.

0:06 (1:47) Enormous gold pan, pick and shovel greet highway travelers, on left, to Quesnel.

0:27 (1:33) At milepost 400, cross Cottonwood River Bridge which carries train a lofty 234 feet above that river. In 1921, Pacific Great Eastern Railroad (BCR's predecessor) hoped to cross further downstream and form a link between Quesnel and Prince George. That attempt was thwarted by unstable soil, and it wasn't until 1952 that this spot was crossed at a cost exceeding one million dollars.

0:31 (1:22) At milepost 406, cross Ahbau Creek where silver spike ceremony at north end of bridge celebrated completion of Quesnel-Prince George section.

1:00 (0:53) Canyon Creek Bridge, at milepost 426, was once scene of feverish placer mining activities.

1:33 (0:20) From milepost 451 into Prince George, train is escorted by impressive Fraser River.

1:40 (0:13) Pull past lumber mills of Prince George on approach to that city. Then BC Rail yards appear at left.

1:53 (0:00) Arrive Prince George.

 PRINCE GEORGE, B.C. - See page 429.

Vancouver Island Service

The **Malahat Dayliner** runs four days each week northbound and five days each week southbound between Victoria and Courtenay. Service is provided by rail diesel cars. Sandwiches and beverages can be purchased at Nanaimo and Courtenay during station stops. Be sure to purchase tickets early; summer weekends are particularly busy.

Mexico

This section on Mexican train travel is included for those who want to see Mexico and are prepared to withstand the rigors of some service deprivation. It is not for those who are anxious to get to the beaches of Mazatlan or Manzanillo and have little interest in absorbing Mexican culture. It is, however, for those who want to come in contact with the people and places of this intriguing country. It is for those who want to savor the countryside that slips past their window, producing scenes ranging from quaint to spectacular, many of which can only be seen from the railroad. And most definitely it is for those who wish to see Mexico's renowned Copper Canyon.

There are some trains in Mexico which can best be described as "not too bad." There are many, however, that fit in a range somewhere between disappointing and deplorable. The trick, of course, is to try to avoid this latter group. Although there are no guarantees, there are some rules of thumb that should greatly increase your chances. First of all, never travel anything less than first class. Second, the trains that radiate out of and into Mexico City seem to receive better maintenance, inside and out. And third, avoid those trains that travel along Mexico's western coast.

IN GENERAL

Economically, the trains south of the border are a real bargain. First-class coach tickets will cost about 5 cents per mile, while a bedroom occupied by two would be approximately twice that amount per person. The equipment used by the railroads in Mexico is sometimes clean (particularly the sleepers) and sometimes not. On older equipment, it is not unusual for the air conditioning to fail, or for various other mechanical aspects of coaches and sleepers to refuse to function.

The service on board is not dazzling, but is often provided with warmth and sincerity. Although crew members seldom speak more than a few words of English, somehow communication never seems that difficult. Knowing at least some Spanish will come in handy, however. Although dining cars are still carried on some trains, food is now a cold box lunch rather than a cooked hot meal on board. The diner, when there is one, merely serves as a place for sleeping car passengers to eat, while first-class coach passengers are served at their seats. The cost of these boxed meals is extra (no longer included in the first-class ticket price).

Trains usually leave their origination points quite punctually but, as almost anywhere else in North America, don't count on making tight connections. Mexican trains can be particularly tardy, sometimes arriving three or four hours late.

Stations are often situated in the heart of the downtown area, which can be a real help when trying to keep cab fares to a minimum. These buildings are frequently modern, large, busy and rather earthy. The platform areas are often immaculate, but it's best to avoid the station rest rooms. If you enjoy "people watching," stations, such as the one in Guadalajara, offer excellent opportunities.

Making reservations from outside of Mexico is still difficult if made directly with the railroad. Fortunately, however, there is at least one U.S. travel agent who will make Mexican train reservations (see "Reservations" below). Mexico's railroads offer reserved first-class and second-class coach service on their trains. The difference in cost is not great, but the difference in accommodations is generally significant. First-class coaches ("Primera Clase") are sometimes rather attractively refurbished, offering comfortable seats with reclining backs and have air conditioning. (Air can work too well, very well, just barely, not at all, or any combination of these during any given trip.)

Second class ("Segunda Clase"), on the other hand, has thinly padded bench seats, no air conditioning and frequently has a "congested" appearance with various types of baggage ("equipaje") temporarily stored in the aisles. The windows open in lieu of air conditioning, but this feature also permits dust to fog up the cars in more arid climes. For the slight additional cost, first class would normally be the choice.

Sleeping cars are also available on a few trains and, depending on the exact type of accommodation, may cost up to approximately twice that of a first class coach ticket per person. This is still a bargain, and it is certainly the way to go if the trip is overnight. Crisp, white linens and Pullman virgin wool blankets are the rule. Most sleeping cars are old U.S.-built Pullmans, many similar to Amtrak's Heritage sleepers. It is always advisable to have a flashlight with you, just in case of a lighting circuit failure. Sleeping accommodations include sections (upper and lower berths), roomettes and bedrooms. Roomettes and bedrooms contain their own toilet facilities.

FOOD

As mentioned above, box lunches (perhaps a ham and cheese sandwich and a carrot salad) are sold on board to first-class passengers. In addition, on trains without first-class coach service, train personnel sometimes go throughout the train selling sandwiches; however, don't count on it. Also, some stops are long enough to allow passengers to eat outside the train, if they want to be that venturesome. It would be a good idea to take along some sort of survival rations such as granola bars, hard-shelled fruit, cheese and nuts, or even a box lunch such as those available at some hotels.

Purified water is frequently not available, but soft drinks and beer are almost always available on the better trains. It's not a bad idea to take some fresh drinking water along, since you may begin to yearn for something to drink that is bubble free ("sin gas").

CUSTOMS AND CURRENCY

Although crossing the border into Mexico can be done without red tape, to go more than 75 miles beyond the border requires two documents for U.S. and Canadian citizens:
1. Proof of citizenship, such as a passport, voter registration, birth certificate, military identification card or naturalization certificate.
2. An entry permit, commonly called a tourist card, which can be obtained from travel agents, airlines serving Mexico, embassies, Mexican consulates or at entry points. All that is needed to obtain this permit is proof of citizenship.

The Mexican emigration inspector will examine these documents on entry at the border railway station. One copy of the permit will be collected on entry and the remaining copy will be collected upon leaving the country. These permits are free of charge.

Children under 15 may be included on their parents' or guardians' tourist cards.

Many fruits, vegetables and nuts are not allowed into the U.S. from Mexico, and a current listing can be obtained from the U.S. Department of Agriculture.

It is important to accurately declare what you acquired while in Mexico, since failure to do so can subject you to fines and criminal prosecution as well as seizure of the articles involved.

The Mexican peso is a floating currency, which means that the exchange rate can change on a daily basis, and the safest way to get a fair conversion rate is to do so at a bank.

Unlike many Mexican resort areas, the railroads may not accept U.S. currency, so obtaining some pesos before boarding is advisable.

RESERVATIONS

Reservations are necessary for first-class coach and sleeper accommodations. Reservations can be made through the railroad, but by far the easiest (and certainly the quickest) way is to obtain them through a **U.S. based travel agent** in San Antonio, Texas. Write or call: Mexico Air & Rail Vacations, 8607 Wurzbach Rd., Suite V, San Antonio, TX 78240; 800-322-4888 or 800-228-3225. As their name implies, they specialize in Mexican air and rail transportation and offer package plans as well as train tickets without package amenities. Since the National Railroads of Mexico does not pay commissions, a fee has to be tacked on to the ticket price by the travel agent (20%). This additional charge, however, is an assurance that you have a ticket when you arrive, as well as confirmation.

If for some reason you decide to try to make reservations directly with the railroad, it is best to do so in writing and well in advance of travel dates. A three-month head start would not be excessive. Reservations should be confirmed in writing before you arrive to pick up your tickets.

When reservations are confirmed, instructions will be given as to where to send the required fare. The railroad's remittance instructions will state that the funds should be sent by bank cashier's check or money order and in Mexican funds. Tickets will then be held at the ticket window and can be picked up prior to train departure time. Confirmation notices should be presented at the ticket office window when picking up tickets to help expedite the process. If funds are not received by the time specified, your reservations will be cancelled. At least this is the way it's supposed to work. Service can vary a lot from agent to agent.

When writing the railroad for reservations, include the exact dates of travel, number of passengers, ages of any children and accommodations desired. The National Railways of Mexico requires that such requests should be addressed to the representative at the border gateway where entry is planned, or to the "corresponding officer," depending on the point from where you plan your trip as follows:

-For trips **from Mexico City to any point** in Mexico, or for trips **from Monterrey, Veracruz, Chihuahua, Uruapan and Guadalajara to Mexico City,** send requests to Chief Commercial Passenger Department, National Railways of Mexico, Buenavista Grand Central Station, 06358 Mexico, D.F. (Mexico), Tel. 011-525-547-5240 or 011-525-547-9060, extensions 6373 or 6374.

-**From Nuevo Laredo to any point** in Mexico, send requests to Commercial Agent, National Railways of Mexico, Passenger Station, P.O. Box 595, Laredo, TX 78042, Tel. 280 97.

-**From Ciudad Juarez to any point** in Mexico, send requests to Commercial Agent, National Railways of Mexico, P.O. Box 2200, El Paso, Tex. 79951, Tel. 011-521-614-9717.

-**From Nogales, Son. to Sufragio, Culiacán, Mazatlán, Tepic, Guadalajara and Mexico City,** send requests to Mr. Luis Mejia Wagner, Commercial Agent, Calle International No. 10, Nogales, Son. (Mexico), Tel. 011-526-312-0024.

-**From Guadalajara to Tepic, Mazatlán, Culiacán, Sufragio, Nogales and Mexicali,** send requests to Jefe Oficina Comercial de Pasajeros, Estacion de Pasajeros, Washington Esquina Gobernador Curiel, Guadalajara, Jal. (Mexico), Tel. 011-523-650-0570.

-**From Mexicali to Sufragio, Culiacán, Mazatlán, Tepic, Guadalajara and Mexico City,** send requests to Commercial Agent, P.O. Box 231, Calexico, CA 92231, Tel. 011-526-557-2386.

-**Between Chihuahua and Los Mochis** (Copper Canyon, LaJunta, Creel, Divisadero, Sufragio), send requests to Traffic Superintendent, P.O. Box 46, 31020 Chihuahua, Chih. (Mexico), Tel. 011-521-412-2284.

TIMETABLES
The railroad does not furnish current, complete timetables.

BUENAVISTA GRAND CENTRAL STATION
Buenavista Grand Central Station in Mexico City is the largest in Mexico. This is a busy station since many trains fan out from the city, so it is always a good idea to arrive

early to pick up tickets. Lines can be long at times. Located just a little more than a mile north of the "Pink Zone," it is on Av. Insurgentes Norte at F.C. Mosqueta. This is really a split-level station with a front (or middle) level, a lower level and an upper level.

Entering the front level, one encounters an enormous, marble-floored expanse, broken only by an island of landscaping in the center. There are ticket windows, arrival and departure boards, a snack food store, a very helpful bilingual information clerk, and precious little seating. First-class ticket holders proceed through this level to the upper level where there is a waiting area for thru passengers (again with precious little seating), the gates to first-class trains, sleeping-car (dormitorio) check-in counters, a newsstand, a restaurant and pay phones. The lower level has second-class ticket windows, waiting area and boarding gates. The baggage counter, a baggage check room and a lunch counter are also in this area.

Outside there are parking, cabs, and local buses. Although the station is not in a particularly attractive area of the city, a very nice hotel, the Ponte Vedra, is just across Insurgentes Ave. where rooms are available for about $30 per day. From the station's west entrance (lower level), just take the yellow catwalk over the street.

COPPER CANYON

The Copper Canyon train (Chihuahua to Los Mochis) offers what is often cited as the most scenic train trip in North America (and occasionally called the most scenic in the world). The passage should stir the emotions of even the most galvanized traveler. Numerous waterfalls, multi-colored cliffs and canyons, tropical fruit trees, 36 major bridges and 87 tunnels highlight this journey that follows a tortuous 300-mile route from mile-high Chihuahua, crossing the Sierra Madre Occidental Mountains to an altitude of 8,071 feet, and finally descending to Los Mochis at sea level. The highlight is the canyon itself, which is four times the size of the Grand Canyon.

The route was originally conceived in the late nineteenth century by private interests in the United States as a rail line linking the Mexican town of Topolobampo on the Pacific Coast of Mexico with Midwestern U.S. markets. However, it was not until November 1961 that the final link was made between Creel and San Pedro in the heart of the remote mountains of northwestern Mexico. This culminated a 50-year effort on this section alone, and was completed only after the Mexican government, with the expenditure of millions of dollars, took over the project. Although it has never become the major freight line envisioned (linking Kansas City with the Pacific), it does provide important access to a canyon that is four times the size of the Grand Canyon where nearly 50,000 Tarahumara Indians live, a people who are recognized for their unusual running abilities.

The train departs Chihuahua early morning and arrives in Los Mochis early evening. The return leaves Los Mochis early morning, arriving in Chihuahua early evening. The train carries reserved coaches, and is one of Mexico's more popular trains. Box lunches are available on board.

The best viewing of the most spectacular portion of this route will generally occur eastbound (from Los Mochis to Chihuahua), since the westbound train, if late, could pass through this segment during darkness. Since the altitude is quite high for long segments of these trips, it is a good idea to take along a warm sweater or jacket just in case. If possible, sit on the right side eastbound and the left westbound.

Tunnel numbers are high on the left side (westbound) as you enter each tunnel, and anyone wishing to keep track could do so easier on that side. Kilometer signs are low on the right side and impossible to see unless you sit against the right hand side and watch very carefully. Also, keep in mind during the winter, if the train should be late, there is more spectacular scenery in daylight hours eastbound than westbound, which may be important to those not wanting to miss a single cliffside or waterfall.

Leaving Chihuahua, the trip starts out on a serene note, passing through farmland, much of which was settled in the early part of this century by Mennonites from Canada. Scenes are quintessential Mexico, with antiquated farm machinery pulled by oxen or burros here and there. But later, the character of the land changes, with lumbering activities in evidence and tropical orchards and wildflowers enhancing the countryside.

Soon the terrain is quite mountainous, and shortly before reaching Divisadero Barrancas, the journey's midpoint, the tracks actually cross over themselves while making a complete loop to gain elevation.

The stop at Divisadero allows passengers to get out to view the Barranca del Cobre—the Copper Canyon. (It obtained its name from the copper mines that operated in the canyon, not from its color.) Forested, sloping sides descend to more tropical areas near the bottom where one can make out the Urique River. If you look carefully, you may be able to see some of the cliff dwellings of the Tarahumara. Baskets, drums, violins and other hand-made objects are sold by the Tarahumara at trackside. Be prompt on reboarding; it's easy to be left behind.

Later in the day, the deepest part of the canyon can be seen from the train, making one's thoughts turn to track maintenance (fortunately, it's well-maintained). Then, a bit later, the train passes next to a spectacular waterfall at Temoris. Although there are many falls along the route, this is clearly the largest. Tunnels and trestles abound along this stretch as the final descent is made to Sufragio, the intersection with the Pacific Railroad and just 40 minutes from the end of the line at Los Mochis.

Rather than set out on their own, many people prefer to sample Mexican rail travel by way of a tour package. One company that operates Copper Canyon tours is:

-**Sierra Madre Express of Tucson** (800-666-0346) offers deluxe eight-day tours from Tucson. These tours are by private train using sleeping cars and specially designed "patio cars" as well as a dome car.

SOME TRAINS WITH "FIRST CLASS" SERVICE

Besides the Copper Canyon train, several other routes offer First-Class coach service. These are overnight trains and sleepers are only available when indicated:

Laredo - Mexico City (via San Miguel Allende)
Monterrey - Mexico City (sleeper service available)
Guadalajara - Mexico City (sleeper service available)
Piedras Negras - Mexico City (sleeper service available)
Mexico City - Oaxaca
Mexico City - Vera Cruz (sleeper service available)
Mexicali - Guadalajara (not recommended)
Nogales - Guadalajara (not recommended)

Equipment

Much of Amtrak's equipment has been freshly designed and built within the last few years, while all of the older equipment still in service has been refurbished and converted from steam to electric heat—vastly increasing reliability and comfort. Amtrak's long-haul trains west of the Mississippi are now using bilevel Superliner cars giving passengers the ultimate in roominess, comfort and unobstructed high-level viewing of the landscape. It is their height, however, that prevents this equipment from being used in the East where clearances pose a problem. The East is served by both Amfleet rolling stock as well as the older and more traditional cars which Amtrak calls their "Heritage Fleet." Soon, Superliner equipment will begin appearing on selected Eastern routes.

Canada's long-haul equipment, which is the conventional variety similar to Amtrak's Heritage Fleet, has been refurbished. And the elegantly rebuilt trans-continental trains no longer rely on steam generator cars to supply heat. In the heavily traveled "Corridor" between Quebec City and Windsor, LRC (Light, Rapid, Comfortable) trains are in service to augment other trains that serve there.

Mexico has mostly a mixture of older, conventional equipment on long hauls and makes some use of rail diesel cars (self-propelled) on many shorter runs. Maintenance of equipment is also a mixture.

The following is a brief review of the most utilized rolling stock in North America:

Heritage Fleet and Other Traditional Cars - Coaches are equipped with reclining seats which have leg and footrests. Luggage can be stored overhead and often at one end of the car. Rest rooms are also located at one end of the car, generally with ample room for changing clothes. Their heavy construction gives them an extremely smooth ride.

Sleepers in the U.S. offer bedrooms and roomettes. Canada and Mexico not only offer bedrooms and roomettes but also "sections," each with an upper and lower berth. Bedrooms sleep two adults (an upper and lower berth) and can be used as a four-person room by opening a common wall between two bedrooms. Each has a wash basin and an enclosed toilet. Roomettes accommodate one person and have rest room facilities which, unfortunately, cannot be used once the bed is lowered. Sections during the daytime are two facing couches open on the aisle side and make into upper and lower berths at night with heavy curtains between the berths and the aisle. Rest rooms are at the end of the car. Some sleepers have larger bedrooms accommodating three persons called "drawing rooms."

Slumber coaches are offered on a few trains in the East. They have small compartments providing economical sleeping accommodations for either one or two adults. These compartments include bathroom facilities.

Diners offer complete meal service while lounge cars offer more casual seating for cocktails and snacks.

Dome cars are specially equipped coaches or observation cars with "vista domes" mounted in their roofs, permitting 360-degree viewing. Amtrak operates these cars on The Capitol Ltd., Auto Train and The City of New Orleans. The Alaska Railroad and Canada's "transcontinental" trains also have these cars.

Amfleet - This was the first new equipment to go into service in the Amtrak era. Built in the U.S. by Budd, these cars use a strong tubular-shell body and produce a

Viewliner Cars - Maintenance Facility, Washington, DC
HOMER R. HILL

reasonably smooth and quiet ride—with a sleek, almost futuristic appearance. Designed for shorter and medium distance trips, Amtrak has, on occasion, also had to press them into service for longer hauls on some eastern routes. A newer Amfleet II design has larger windows and more spacious seating for those longer runs. Amfleet includes coaches, diners and cafe cars but no sleepers. Heritage sleepers are used in conjunction with Amfleet cars for overnight runs.

Standard Amfleet coaches have reclining seats but no legrests on the shorter hauls. Overhead luggage storage, reading lights, attractive appointments, and rather small windows create an airliner atmosphere. Longer haul Amfleet cars use reclining seats with legrests and allow more leg room by installing fewer seats per coach.

Club seating has only three seats to a row; two on one side of the aisle and one on the other, giving a special luxurious effect. Attendants furnish food and beverage service at your seat with more elaborate menus than those available at the cafe counter. Of course, club fares are higher than coach.

Amdinettes have a cafe counter and tables for light, hot meals and snacks. Trays can be taken to the tables or to coach seats, and some trains offer food service at the tables. Amcafes are coaches with a food and beverage counter in the middle, also offering light meals, sandwiches and other snacks.

Superliners - Coaches are roomy and attractively designed with tasteful appointments. Reclining seats are wide, offer plenty of leg room and have both leg and footrests. Large windows provide excellent viewing and individual overhead reading lights add to the luxury. Folding trays, ala the airlines, are also provided. Luggage can be stored overhead as well as beneath the seats, and extra luggage storage compartments are on the lower level just as you enter. Besides upper-level seating, several seats are on the lower level and are available to handicapped travelers who would find the circular climb to the upper level an obstacle. Rest rooms and a ladies' lounge are also on the lower level.

Most sleeping cars have five deluxe bedrooms, 14 economy bedrooms, a family bedroom and a special handicapped bedroom. Deluxe bedrooms extend almost the entire width of the car, are on the upper level, have two beds for sleeping two to three people, and include an enclosed bathroom that even has a shower. During the daytime there is a sofa and swivel chair for seating. Economy bedrooms sleep two and are fairly compact, but aisle windows give them a more roomy appearance. These have two berths sleeping a total of two and having facing couches during the day. There is also a very thin closet, a fold-down table and individual comfort controls. Luggage storage is virtually nil. There are no in-room toilet facilities, but there is one bathroom upstairs and several downstairs.

The family bedroom is quite spacious, is on the lower level and has room for up to three adults and two children but no toilet facilities. The handicapped "special" bedroom is on the lower level, can accommodate a wheelchair, will sleep two adults and has a specially equipped rest room. Meals will be delivered to these special rooms to avoid going to the diner which is accessed through the upper levels of the train.

Economy bedrooms one through ten are on the upper level with the lower numbers toward the center of the car while 11 through 14 are downstairs, again with the lower numbers toward the center. You may wish to keep these locations in mind when making reservations since the center of the car gives a smoother ride. Deluxe bedrooms are lettered A through E, with A at the end and E near the middle.

Amtrak has converted a lower level dressing-bathroom to a public shower on all Superliner sleepers. Also some former Superliner coach-baggage cars have been converted to all economy bedroom sleepers.

Superliner Diner
JACK SWANSON

Lounge/Cafe cars offer splendid viewing from swivel, upper-level chairs through windows that extend from almost floor level upward and wrap into the ceiling overhead. Downstairs there are tables and a snack bar. The viewing from the upper level of these cars is superb.

Diners have seating for 72 persons at 18 tables, all on the upper level. The kitchen is on the lower level with an elevator arrangement for delivering food to the dining area.

Metroliners - Metroliner Service, Amtrak's high-speed Northeast Corridor service, is provided by specially equipped Amfleet cars pulled by Swedish-designed (but U.S. built) electric locomotives. Older Metroliner trains that were once used for this service are now utilized on short runs in and out of Philadelphia.

Turboliners - Certain service in New York state is supplied by racy Turboliners. These sleek beauties provide streamlined service between New York City and upper New York State. Designed to run in a five-car consist, power is supplied by diesel-electric "power coaches" at both the front and rear of the train. The center car offers food service and the last car usually has a 2-1 seating configuration, draped windows and Custom Class service. This section is reserved seating and, although more expensive, would be the best choice during the busier holiday seasons. Regular coaches are unreserved and are in standard rows of four.

Rail Diesel Cars - These short-distance standbys are in limited use in Canada and Mexico, however they are slowly disappearing in both countries. As their name implies, they are self-propelled, diesel-powered coaches, each having the capability of traveling in either direction. Seats are reclining, but no legrests, and there are folding trays similar to the airlines. Food service is generally not available, although snacks or even sandwiches are sometimes offered where these cars make lengthy runs.

Horizonliners - These are new coaches and diners, initially being put into service on the busy shorter routes out of Chicago (including to Detroit) and San Joaquin service in California. The windows are small, like Amfleet I, but instead of Amfleet's confining tubular construction, the sides are flat with a brushed aluminum exterior. Bombardier, a Canadian company who now owns the rights to both Budd and Pullman-Standard passenger-car technologies, is constructing these new cars at its Barre, Vermont plant.

Viewliners - A long testing and development phase is ending for Amtrak's newest rail cars, a period which saw prototype sleepers that combined the best of Superliner technology and comfort. These are single-level cars (to allow for Eastern clearances) with two rows of windows that give upper berth occupants their own viewing portals. Prototype sleepers have 14 compartments (double or single), two deluxe bedrooms (with showers) and a handicapped bedroom. Every room has a sink and a toilet as well as luggage storage space under the seats and over the aisles. Aisle-side windows give both the room and aisles a more spacious feeling. This new Viewliner equipment (there will also be coaches and diners) is meant to replace Amtrak's well maintained but aging Heritage Fleet.

LRC Trains - Canada is using these trains in their "Corridor" service. Built by Bombardier, LRC's (Light, Rapid, Comfortable) are designed for high-speed service in heavily populated areas, and have an innovative "power-banking" system that allows a higher speed on curves as the train automatically tilts to the inside. Besides their speed, extreme smoothness of ride is a characteristic.

Appendix

Telephone Numbers for Reservations and Information*

AMTRAK

Boston, MA .... (617) 482-3660	From Canada 1-800-872-7245
Chicago, IL .... (312) 558-1075	For Metroliner Service only 1-800-523-8720
Los Angeles, CA.................. (213) 624-0171	
New York City, NY	
(all 5 boroughs) .... (212) 582-6875	
Philadelphia, PA.................. (215) 824-1600	Deaf persons with access to a teletypewriter
Washington, DC.................. (202) 484-7540	can call 1-800-523-6590
All other U.S. locations 1-800-USA-RAIL	
1-800-872-7245	

VIA RAIL CANADA

Newfoundland:
St. John's, Gander, Grand Falls, Corner Brook, Stephenville, Bishops Falls. Call your Travel Agent or nearest CN Roadcruiser office.
All Other Locations 1-800-561-3926

Prince Edward Island:
All Locations 1-800-561-3952

Nova Scotia:
Halifax 429-8421
All Other Locations 1-800-561-3952

New Brunswick:
Moncton............................ 857-9830
Saint John 642-2916
All Other Locations 1-800-561-3952

Quebec:
Montreal............................ 871-1331
Quebec City 692-3940
James Bay - Call your Travel Agent
or VIA Rail Canada .... (514) 871-1331
All Other Locations 1-800-361-5390

Ontario:
Hamilton 522-7533
Kingston............................ 544-5600
London............................. 672-5722
Ottawa 238-8289
Toronto 366-8411
Windsor 256-5511
Other Area 416, 519 and 613 Calls ... 1-800-361-1235
All Area 705 Calls................. 1-800-361-1235
All Area 807 Calls................. 1-800-561-8630

Manitoba, Saskatchewan, Alberta, British Columbia, Yukon and Northwest Territories: 1-800-561-8630

People with speech or hearing problems may communicate through telecommunication devices for the deaf (TDD).
The access numbers are: Toronto Area ... 368-6405
All Other Locations 1-800-268-9503

USA: For VIA train information or reservations in the USA, contact your Travel Agent or call 1-800-561-3949.

*Use the telephone number appearing opposite the city, state or province from which you are calling.

Index

451

452

Your Input is Important to Us:

Rail Ventures is completely revised every two years. Although considerable effort goes into each revision, some mistakes are inevitable. We are always anxious to hear from you regarding corrections, possible improvements or any other suggestions you might have. Also, we are always interested in new photos for each subsequent edition. If you have photos you would like us to consider for future publication, let us know and we will send you our photo policy. Write us any time: Rail Ventures Publishing, P.O. Box 1877, Ouray, CO 81427.